AN INTRODUCTION TO ENVIRONMENTAL LAW AND POLICY IN CANADA
Second Edition

Paul Muldoon
Alastair Lucas
Robert B. Gibson
Peter Pickfield
Julie Williams

emond

Toronto, Canada
2015

Emond Montgomery Publications Limited
60 Shaftesbury Avenue
Toronto ON M4T 1A3
http://www.emp.ca/highered

Printed in Canada on FSC-certified paper.

We acknowledge the financial support of the Government of Canada through the Canada Book Fund for our publishing activities.

Emond Montgomery Publications has no responsibility for the persistence or accuracy of URLs for external or third-party Internet websites referred to in this publication, and does not guarantee that any content on such websites is, or will remain, accurate or appropriate.

Publisher: Mike Thompson
Director, editorial and production: Jim Lyons
Developmental editor: Elke Price
Copy editor: Claudia Forgas
Production editor: Laura Bast
Proofreader: Nancy Ennis
Editorial assistant: Katy Littlejohn
Indexer: Paula Pike
Text designer: Tara Wells
Cover designers: Stephen Cribbin and Simon Evers
Cover image: Alamy (top); Tina Verma (bottom)

Library and Archives Canada Cataloguing in Publication

Muldoon, Paul R. (Paul Robert), 1956-, author
    An introduction to environmental law and policy in Canada / Paul Muldoon, Alastair Lucas, Robert B. Gibson, Peter Pickford, Julie Williams. — Second edition.

Revision of: An introduction to environmental law and policy in Canada / Paul
    Muldoon ... [et al.] Toronto: Emond Montgomery Publications, [2008], ©2009.
Includes bibliographical references and index.
ISBN 978-1-55239-620-9 (pbk.)

    1. Environmental law—Canada—Textbooks.   2. Environmental policy—Canada—Textbooks.   I. Title.

KE3619.M84 2015   344.7104'6   C2014-904539-5
KF3775.ZA2M84 2015

Brief Contents

WB McGill

Detailed Contents

WB McGill

PART I

Introduction: The Evolution, Framework, and Challenges of Environmental Law

CHAPTER 1

CHAPTER 2

CHAPTER 3

PART II

Aspects of Environmental Law

CHAPTER 4

CHAPTER 5

CHAPTER 6

The Relationship Between Canadian and International Law

PART III

Regulatory Regimes

CHAPTER 7

The Basic Structure of Environmental Protection Regimes

CHAPTER 8

Environmental Protection Regimes: Command and Control

CHAPTER 9

Sectoral Regulatory Regimes

PART IV

Integrated Approaches to Environmental Law

CHAPTER 10

CHAPTER 11

CHAPTER 12

PART V

Protecting Environmental Rights

CHAPTER 13

CHAPTER 14

Using Administrative Decision-Making Processes to Protect the Environment

CHAPTER 15

Environmental Bill of Rights and Access to Information

Preface

The second edition of *An Introduction to Environmental Law and Policy in Canada* arrives following an important phase in the evolution of this field. Since the first edition's publication in 2008, significant changes have occurred, both in the realm of political debate and within legal and policy circles. Canada has seen substantial revisions to its environmental laws that reflect, many observers would argue, a profound shift in the philosophy that has been the foundation of these laws for decades. As Chapter 1 points out, the global perception of Canada as a leader in environmental policy has been substantially diminished. One of the goals of this text is to explain and assess this new regulatory landscape.

In the public arena, the overarching issue of "the environment" remains stubbornly low on the list of citizens' concerns. Intense debates continue over how to balance jobs or energy needs with environmental priorities. Conversely, attitudes have indeed shifted on the dramatic consequences of humans' influence on climate systems, the reality of which is no longer a matter of serious debate. New policies to deal with this crucial global problem that many considered radical when the first edition was published no longer seem so.

Scientific and public consensus around climate systems is just one example of how our understanding of the physical world is evolving, and how environmental laws and policies must face up to—and keep pace with—such advances. Similarly, we must not only accept the limits of our biosphere's capacity to sustain the complex industrial society we have created but also consider how our civilization is intertwined with the health of the countless species and ecosystems affected by our intrusions.

But the same human ingenuity that has so reshaped the earth can also produce effective solutions. Alternatives such as renewable energy, more sustainable food systems, more intensive and transit-friendly cities, and national and international policy instruments to ensure a sustainable future will also be explored in the following pages.

This text contains two new chapters, one devoted to the significance of Aboriginal rights and title for environmental law (Chapter 5) and another that uses a broad lens to examine questions at the heart of environmental policy-making, and what makes it such a challenging exercise (Chapter 3). Also new to this edition are case studies on key legal decisions or public policy issues from across Canada. These case studies offer useful examples of environmental laws and policies in action, examining their nuances and relevance, and exploring regional concerns.

In response to feedback from reviewers and colleagues, the text now emphasizes pedagogical features such as maps and discussion questions, and offers a regularly updated companion website that helps instructors and their students keep abreast of the ever-changing policy and legislative landscape at both the federal and provincial levels.

A Note from the Publisher

The publisher wishes to thank the following people for providing their feedback and suggestions during the development of this text: Ian Attridge (Trent University), Scott Brodie (Douglas College), Neil Craik (University of Waterloo), Gary Kay (University of Guelph), Richard D. Lindgren (Trent University), Lydia Miljan (University of Windsor), and Mark Winfield (York University). Thanks also to Laurel Besco, PhD candidate at the University of Ottawa.

For Instructors and Students

For more information on this text, please visit the accompanying website at **www .emp.ca/enviro2e**. Click on the "Updates" tab to find regularly updated links to new federal and provincial legislation and policies, and relevant news items, cases, and reports. A concise and helpful *Guide to Research in Environmental Law*, intended for first-time students in this field, also accompanies this text.

Supplemental teaching resources, including PowerPoint slides, are available for instructors who have chosen this text for their courses. Instructors should contact their Emond representative for more information, or contact us via the website.

Acknowledgments

The authors wish to thank Elke Price and Claudia Forgas, who provided excellent editorial skills, maintained deadline discipline, coordinated content, and brought overall consistency to this enterprise. At Emond, our thanks go to Laura Bast for her attention to detail in the final stages and Mike Thompson for his overall steady hand on the tiller.

The publisher and the authors would also like to acknowledge the contributions of the following people, who provided their expertise in updating and revising various sections of Chapters 9 and 11:

Maureen Carter-Whitney
Joseph Castrilli
Jerry DeMarco
Stephen Hazell
David G. Henley
Theresa McClenaghan
Éric Montpetit

About the Authors

Paul Muldoon teaches environmental law at the School of the Environment, University of Toronto. He is currently a vice-chair of the Ontario Environmental Review Tribunal and associate chair of the Assessment Review Board.

Alastair Lucas, QC is a professor of law and the former dean of law at the University of Calgary. He has also served as the executive director of the Canadian Institute of Resources Law and as a policy adviser at Environment Canada.

Robert B. Gibson is a professor in environment and resource studies at the University of Waterloo, specializing in sustainability and governance.

Peter Pickfield has worked as an environmental lawyer in Ontario for almost 30 years and is an adjunct professor teaching environmental law and policy at both the University of Waterloo and the University of Guelph.

Julie Williams teaches environmental law and policy at the University of Victoria and Royal Roads University. She is also legal counsel at the British Columbia Ministry of Justice.

PART I

Introduction: The Evolution, Framework, and Challenges of Environmental Law

CHAPTER 1

Environmental Law and Its Evolution in Canada

LEARNING OBJECTIVES

After reading this chapter, students will be able to:

- Discuss environmental law and how it can be used to protect and improve the environment.
- Evaluate the scope and importance of environmental regulatory and assessment laws.
- Describe the ideas underlying modern environmental law.
- Compare general application and sectoral laws and how they relate to environmental law.
- Discuss the four evolutionary phases in the development of Canadian environmental law and the implications of these phases.
- Describe the five trends that have affected the core concerns, design, application, and effects of environmental laws in different jurisdictions in Canada.

CHAPTER OUTLINE

Introduction: What Is Environmental Law?

Environmental law is the body of statutes and common law that is and will continue to be used to protect and improve environmental conditions. Some of it deals with pollution control, waste management, endangered species preservation, and other issues that clearly involve the natural environment. The term *environment* is often defined broadly to cover land, water, air, and living organisms, including humans and their built environment, and the interaction of these elements. The scope of this definition is sensible because many aspects of the biophysical environment and the human social and economic environment are deeply intertwined.

---

environmental law the body of legislated statute and common law that can be used to protect and improve environmental conditions

CASE STUDY

Who Is Responsible for Environmental Law in Canada? R v. Hydro-Québec

In the 1980s and 1990s, the courts were increasingly called on to determine whether the federal or provincial government has jurisdiction to address particular environmental issues. Consider, for example, the case *R v. Hydro-Québec*. In 1990, Hydro-Québec was charged with dumping polychlorinated biphenyl (PCB) contrary to regulations under the *Canadian Environmental Protection Act, 1999* (CEPA 1999). Hydro-Québec challenged the authority of the government to charge it with an offence under CEPA on the grounds that the toxic substance provisions of the legislation fell outside federal powers. A majority of the Supreme Court of Canada ultimately held that the provisions were within the jurisdiction of the federal government under its criminal law power. As part of its decision, the court made the following statement about the importance of the environment and the need to address environmental concerns:

> LA FOREST J: This Court has in recent years been increasingly called upon to consider the interplay between federal and provincial legislative powers as they relate to environmental protection. Whether viewed positively as strategies for maintaining a clean environment, or negatively as measures to combat the evils of pollution, there can be no doubt that these measures relate to a public purpose of superordinate importance, and one in which all levels of government and numerous organs of the international community have become increasingly engaged.*

Questions

Canada's Constitution does not refer specifically to environmental jurisdiction. How can the matter of environmental jurisdiction be addressed? What are the appropriate roles of each level of government?

---

* *R v. Hydro-Québec*, [1997] 3 SCR 213, at para. 85.

Although a number of environmental laws exist, many laws of more general application can be used to advance environmental objectives. Examples include the body of **common law** that focuses on property and **tort** law (centred on private legal actions concerning harm to person or property), both of which may be used to prevent environmental harm or compensate those harmed.

---

common law   A system of law based on the English legal tradition, which relies on precedent rather than on codified rules; may also refer to (1) decisions by courts exercising their "common law" jurisdiction as opposed to their "equitable" jurisdiction based on broad principles of fairness, or (2) case law generally as opposed to legislation

tort   civil wrong other than a breach of contract, for which damages may be sought to compensate for any harm or injury sustained

Some environmental laws focus on the prevention of damage. Others are intended to require, or at least to facilitate and encourage, the rehabilitation of degraded environments or the correction of environmentally damaging or dangerous behaviour. All of these laws have a positive environmental agenda. They aim to make things better or, at least, less bad. In this respect, environmental law is unlike the neutral rules of, for example, contract law, which is used to resolve disputes involving individuals or corporations. Environmental law is highly and openly value-laden.

Most of this positive agenda centres on human purposes, including immediate economic interests as well as long-term health and well-being and the democratic benefits of participation in decisions that affect our lives. At least to some degree, environmental law also seeks to benefit the environment itself and the ecosystems that sustain it. But this agenda too serves human interests ultimately, since we are permanently dependent on our environment for the basic prerequisites of survival and for the foundations of most of what enriches our lives.

Another way to understand environmental law is this: environmental law is the process whereby the common resources of society—the air we breathe, the water we drink, the minerals in the ground, the trees, and the lakes—are allocated to those public and private interests that use those resources to provide goods and services for the public at large. Hence, licences are granted to extract aggregate from the ground for highway construction; permits to take water are granted to industry for manufacturing bottling water; and discharge approvals are granted to steel-making facilities to emit pollutants into the air. Environmental law addresses whether such

---

BOX 1.1 » Environmental Protection: "One of the Major Challenges of Our Time"

As part of its decision in *Friends of the Oldman River Society v. Canada (Minister of Transport)*, La Forest J stated:

> The protection of the environment has become one of the major challenges of our time. To respond to this challenge, governments and international organizations have been engaged in the creation of a wide variety of legislative schemes and administrative structures. In Canada, both the federal and provincial governments have established Departments of the Environment, which have been in place for about twenty years. More recently, however, it was realized that a department of the environment was one among many other departments, many of which pursued policies that came into conflict with its goals. Accordingly at the federal level steps were taken to give a central role to that department, and to expand the role of other government departments and agencies so as to ensure that they took account of environmental concerns in taking decisions that could have an environmental impact.*

---

* *Friends of the Oldman River Society v. Canada (Minister of Transport)*, [1992] 1 SCR 3, at 16-17.

allocations should be made, how much is appropriate, and who should participate in such decisions.

Environmental law aims to protect and restore or improve the environment. It does not do so simply because some legislator or court had an idea. Rather, it reflects the values of many Canadians. Opinion polls have confirmed again and again that Canadians value their environment and support action to protect it. Environmental law supports these fundamental values.

The Scope of Environmental Law

Many laws affect efforts to protect or improve the environment. Some of them do so directly, for example, by requiring pollution abatement. Others address environmental matters indirectly or as part of a related agenda, such as protecting health or property. As a result, the boundaries of environmental law are inexact.

The core of environmental law clearly includes **environmental regulatory law**, which governs discharges of harmful substances into the air and water and onto land. **Environmental assessment law**, which requires the study of and attention to environmental considerations in the planning and approval of new undertakings, is also at the core of environmental law. So too is legislation that confers environmental rights on citizens—especially rights to receive environmental information, to participate in environmental regulatory decisions, and to demand that legally required standards be applied. Laws that protect endangered species and natural areas, and the environmental provisions in laws concerning agriculture, forestry, energy, and other major sectors of the economy are also important components of environmental law. Finally, we must include international laws, conventions, and treaties that are focused on environmental concerns such as persistent organic pollutants, substances that deplete the ozone layer, transboundary movement of hazardous wastes, and greenhouse gases. All of these subjects are discussed in later chapters.

Beyond this core, how far does environmental law properly extend? Does it include national and provincial park legislation, a major part of which provides for public recreation? What about wildlife legislation concerned with "managing" wildlife mainly for hunting? Does environmental law include community and regional planning law, a subject that affects virtually all urban and regional economic activity through regulation of the built environment and its infrastructure? Human health

---

environmental regulatory law   law governing the discharge of harmful substances into the air and water and onto land

environmental assessment law   law requiring careful attention to environmental considerations in the planning and approval of new undertakings is included in most statutory definitions of environment. But are the myriad of statutes, regulations, and bylaws that establish and regulate health and related social programs part of environmental law? Don't some tax and economic benefit laws concern or include environmental protection activities? What about the common law elements of property and tort law that have sometimes been used to halt property or natural resource development? And then there is international law, some of which deals with environmental issues. Which of all these areas of law deserve to be called "environmental"? Is there a logical end or a reasonable set of boundaries? Should we just accept that all law is in some sense environmental law? No neat answer exists to any of these questions.

One reason for the difficulty in defining the scope of environmental law (beyond the fact that much of it is recent) is that it draws from a wide range of traditional legal concepts and subjects. For example, environmental regulatory law uses instruments (such as authorizations, prohibitions, and regulatory offences) and institutions (such as decision-making tribunals) that have counterparts in other regulatory areas such as health and safety and telecommunications. It is then relevant to consider at least some decisions in these other areas in analyzing environmental regulatory decisions.

Another reason for the impression of few boundaries is that the environment underlies and supports everything. That is why environmental law overlaps other legal fields and why areas such as health law, planning law, and even tax law are, in a sense, part of environmental law. Laws in all of these areas can be used or adapted for the protection and enhancement of the environment. Recognizing these overlaps, we have included in this text sections on environmental laws in a variety of important sectors, as well as sections on common law tort, property rights, environmental offences, constitutional law, and the arcane administrative law concerning judicial review of environmental regulatory decisions.

All environmental law sources are important. In the practice of environmental law, we may look first to the core environmental rights and regulations or to specific environmental provisions in other laws. But we should remember that sometimes the environment can be protected most effectively by a court ruling that a threatening proposal is unconstitutional, that granting approval for an undesirable project is outside the legal powers of a government board or official, or that the relevant decisions were made in a procedurally unfair way.

Ideas Underlying Modern Environmental Law

Formal environmental law can be traced back centuries, if not millennia, and customary rules about human–environment relations likely go back to our earliest ancestors. Most of what we now call environmental law, however, was introduced within the last few decades. It reflects rising environmental concerns and increased environmental understanding and has also been influenced by ideas about public welfare, citizen participation, philosophy, and ethics that have occupied recent debate on important public issues.

Public Welfare and Citizen Participation

Modern environmental laws are as much about how we govern ourselves as about how we treat the environment. Many of the environmental laws in place today in Canada and other developed countries originated in a burst of environmental law-making in the late 1960s and early 1970s. These new laws focused on preventing as well as reducing pollution and signified a new understanding that environmental damage was a serious problem, that easy technical fixes were not always available, and that prevention is often wiser and cheaper than repair. The new laws responded to a wave of public concern about environmental abuses. Concerned citizens, often led by public interest advocates and assisted by media attention, drove the process.

This pattern has continued throughout the evolution of environmental law in Canada. Few innovations in environmental legislation and few major advances before the courts have been the product of government zeal. Virtually all progressive steps in environmental law have required public initiative, public ingenuity, and persistent public pressure.

Not surprisingly, then, Canadian environmental law rests as much on ideas about democracy as on understandings about how to deal with the environment. Two linked aspects of democracy have been particularly important. These are the public welfare role of governments and the importance of citizen participation in policy deliberations. The public welfare idea is that governments in democracies have a responsibility to defend and advance public well-being. Long-recognized priority areas for government action for public welfare include national security, public safety, education, and transportation. Environmental protection became an important item on the list more recently, largely because of public concern and pressure. Environmental law is a response to the emergence of a public consensus that governments need to act on this important but previously neglected area of public interest.

Getting governments to act on environmental concerns has been only part of the story, however. The development of environmental law in Canada also reflects an unwillingness merely to trust government officials to do what is necessary. From the late 1960s to the present, Canadian campaigns for stronger environmental laws have also consistently included demands for participative rights—that is, legal requirements for the interested and concerned public to be notified about important findings and initiatives, to have timely and convenient access to information, to have opportunities for effective involvement in deliberations before irrevocable decisions are made, and to be able to enforce environmental laws when governments fail to act. Environmental lawyers acting in the public interest have often used common law principles, as well as available statutory provisions, to assert the legal rights of citizens to participate in environmental regulatory decisions and to stop or delay proposed projects likely to harm the environment. They have also pushed, often successfully, for environmental bills of rights centred on opportunities for effective participation.

Efforts to strengthen environmental protection through regulatory laws—by raising standards, extending the reach of government requirements, and expanding the narrow array of public environmental rights—continue today. But these approaches are recognized as having limits and may never be sufficient by themselves. As a result, the public welfare and citizen rights foundations of environmental law are now increasingly being supplemented by efforts to mobilize other players and motivators, including direct communication with policy-makers and legislators, petitions, and the strategic use of social media.

Much of the recent focus of law reform and related environmental initiatives has been on economic tools. While many governments have simply tried to encourage corporations "voluntarily" to exceed regulatory requirements, some have begun to make greater use of law-based economic instruments that give polluters an economic incentive to reduce pollution and waste.[1]

Philosophy and Ethics

The second set of big ideas underlying modern environmental law centres on philosophy and ethics. As we noted above, environmental law is not neutral. It has a positive agenda to improve well-being. That is not to say that environmental law-makers and practitioners always agree on what is required for well-being, or what the priority objectives should be, or even who and what should be included as the intended beneficiaries. But there are some common themes.

Most environmental laws emerged from concerns about threats to human health or other material interests. The initial assumption was that any problems that were serious enough to merit legal attention could be dealt with satisfactorily, one by one, usually through some technological repair. The role of the law was to force attention on the matter where problems were not solved through technological solutions. That assumption fit well with the prevailing belief that we could and should dominate nature through applied science, technology, and other servants of economic progress.

But the real world turned out to be inconveniently complicated. The technical fixes did not always work, or they had unsavoury side effects, or they were far too expensive, or the problems came too thick and fast to be manageable. Years of experience gradually taught that prevention was preferable to repair, that considering overall effects was better than dealing with problems one by one, and that we should adopt precautionary approaches because we will never know enough to be able to predict, much less fix, all of the problems we might cause.

Development through economic growth and technological innovation has brought major gains. But it has also begun to eat away at the world's ecological foundations and is digging a dangerously expanding gulf between rich and poor. In

---

BOX 1.2 » The Tragedy of the Commons

One of the most profoundly difficult moral dilemmas relating to the environment is **the tragedy of the commons**. It refers to situations in which many rational individuals, acting in their own self-interest (for instance, to feed their families), consume a commonly available resource, until doing so eventually becomes detrimental to all, and potentially even ecologically catastrophic. Consider, for instance, fishing boats that continue to fish stocks whose numbers are declining faster than they can reproduce. It is a centuries-old concept, but was widely popularized by ecologist Garrett Hardin in 1968. Hardin uses the example of a pasture for grazing livestock that is "open to all":

> Therein is the tragedy. Each man is locked into a system that compels him to increase his herd without limit—in a world that is limited. Ruin is the destination toward which all men rush, each pursuing his own best interest in a society that believes in the freedom of the commons.*

---

* Garrett Hardin, "The Tragedy of the Commons" (1968) 162:3859 *Science* 1243-48, at 1244.

1987, the World Commission on Environment and Development, convened by the United Nations and chaired by then Norwegian Prime Minister Gro Harlem Brundtland, officially declared that the current path was not sustainable and that a substantial shift in agenda was necessary.[2]

Many of the most recent environmental laws have therefore begun to reflect a new understanding of the world and our place in it. That understanding is as follows:

- We are permanently dependent on a natural environment made of highly complex and interrelated systems at every level, from global climate chemistry to the soil bacteria affecting growth of individual plants.
- We will never control nature in any complete and fully competent way.
- We must find better ways to live in and with the rest of nature by establishing better integrated socio-ecological systems that are farsighted, careful, and adaptable enough to serve present needs without sacrificing the prospects of future generations.

In addition, we now face plenty of evidence that human activities are producing significant adverse effects well beyond the national and provincial reach of most environmental laws. To deal with greenhouse gas emissions that contribute to global climate change and a host of other transboundary pollution, resource depletion, and ecological damage, we will also need to develop better means of designing and applying international controls.

---

tragedy of the commons an ethical problem in which the consumption of a shared resource by rational individuals pursuing their own needs leads to the depletion or loss of that resource for the community as a whole

This new understanding is far from fully accepted or adopted. Its implications are much debated. As well, there is (and perhaps should be) a great diversity of views about how best to express, order, and apply the main principles in corrective action, including correction through environmental law. Some focus on economic tools, while others stress links between social justice and ecological protection or between women and nature. Yet others advocate a less or non-anthropocentric (human-centred) approach that recognizes the intrinsic value of nature and assigns legal rights of some sort to the environment. Emerging versions of sustainability ethics attempt to pull all of these together in an integrated package.

As we will see in the chapters that follow, little of this non-anthropocentric perspective is entirely unprecedented. Many old laws include components that anticipate the new understanding. For example, some environmental assessment laws define the *environment* as encompassing humans and their communities and cultures along with biophysical and ecological systems.[3] The objectives of many other environmental statutes extend beyond benefits for humans and recognize interactions between human beings and natural systems.[4] Humans are sometimes included as merely one category of "living organism."

Many long-standing proposals for the law also anticipate recent ideas. For example, in 1948, Aldo Leopold proposed a "land ethic" that would extend ethical or moral considerations to reflect the interconnections of ecosystems so that soil, plants, and animals, along with humans, would merit moral consideration as important parts of the land on which all live.[5] In a 1972 law journal article,[6] Christopher Stone argued in favour of giving trees standing (capacity) to sue, with the help of human "next friends" (substitute litigants), to protect themselves and their habitat. And in 1973, Laurence Tribe published a paper entitled "Ways Not to Think About Plastic Trees,"[7] in which he proposed moving beyond transcendence (human domination over natural objects) to immanence (respect for natural objects and systems).

Proposals for sustainability ethics also predate the Brundtland commission's introduction of the phrase "sustainable development" into household use. Indeed, the idea that we should integrate moral commitment to environmental protection with advocacy for basic livelihood security, race and gender equality, participative political rights, and other aspects of human justice has a long and distinguished pedigree. Implementation is, however, just beginning. And because of the ambitiousness of the agenda and the extent to which it challenges well-entrenched practices, change in this direction has been and is likely to continue to be slow.

This is the general nature of the relationship between the law and society, or between environmental law and the world of concerns about human–nature relations. Both the big ideas and their application in law continue to evolve. Law is one field, among many, in which the big ideas of the day are introduced, tested, and adjusted or supplanted by new ideas, ideally better ones that have been built on the lessons learned from past failures as well as past successes.

The Role and Place of Environmental Law

Law carries the weight of societal consent and authority. It is composed of the rules and prohibitions that society prescribes through its recognized law-making institutions: the legislatures and the courts. It is not just a set of guidelines, suggestions, or practices that we can choose to follow or not. It lays down requirements that can be enforced through regulatory agencies or the courts.

It is important to keep this mandatory feature of environmental law in mind because so much human activity, including building structures and extracting natural resources, seems to happen under guidelines, codes of practice, and simple convention (or "the way we do this"). But guidelines, codes, and customary practices are only convenient recipes for complying with the basic expectations that underlie or are embedded in environmental (and other) legal requirements.

For example, practitioners of environmental assessment have developed extensive guides and handbooks for doing assessment work. But environmental assessment law and the regulations and formal decisions made under the law set the requirements concerning which proposed undertakings must be assessed, what the scope of an assessment must be, what factors must be considered, how public involvement must be facilitated, what standards must be met, and what follow-up and monitoring must be carried out.

Environmental law is not just about prohibitions and penalties. Many environmental laws are principally devoted to providing legal frameworks for processes that may involve information dissemination, review and research, consultation, planning, actual environmental protection, and remediation actions. Environmental assessment and land use planning laws, for example, centre on establishing structured approaches to decision-making that consider specified factors and provide opportunities for participation by interested and affected parties.[8]

We can put environmental laws into two main categories: environmental **laws of general application** and **sectoral laws** (laws dealing with a resource sector such as water or forests, or an industrial sector such as fisheries or waste management).

Laws of General Application and Sectoral Laws

Environmental laws of general application are typically devoted to conventional environmental issues such as pollution control and natural resource protection, and they apply to everyone and all activities. Laws focused on the activities of particular industrial sectors may be less obviously environmental but can be just as important. They include the many broadly environmental laws that deal with the allocation and

laws of general application   laws that apply to everyone and to all activities

sectoral laws   laws dealing with a resource sector such as water or forests, or an industrial sector such as fisheries or waste management

---

BOX 1.3 » **Acts Administered by Environment Canada**

Environment Canada administers a number of acts of Parliament, either in whole or in part, and is responsible for meeting several obligations in these acts. The acts administered by Environment Canada appear below.

Environmental Protection

- *Department of the Environment Act*
- *International Rivers Improvement Act* (IRIA)
- *Canada Water Act*
- *The Lake of the Woods Control Board Act, 1921*
- *Weather Modification Information Act*

Pollution Prevention

- *Canadian Environmental Protection Act, 1999* (CEPA 1999)
- *Fisheries Act*
- *Antarctic Environmental Protection Act* (AEPA)
- *Arctic Waters Pollution Prevention Act*

Biodiversity and Conservation

- *Species at Risk Act* (SARA)
- *Migratory Birds Convention Act, 1994* (MBCA)
- *Wild Animal and Plant Protection and Regulation of International and Interprovincial Trade Act* (WAPPRIITA)
- *Canada Wildlife Act*

Sustainable Development

- *Federal Sustainable Development Act* (FSDA)
- *Canada Foundation for Sustainable Development Technology Act*

Other Significant Acts

- *Canadian Environmental Assessment Act, 2012*
- *Environmental Enforcement Act* (EEA)
- *Canadian Environment Week Act*
- *National Wildlife Week Act*

Source: Environment Canada, "Acts," accessed October 21, 2014, http://ec.gc.ca/default.asp?lang=En&n=E826924C-1.

---

use of natural resources (such as land, water, forests, agriculture, and fisheries) and have significant effects on environmental systems.[9]

Sectoral laws (such as those governing mining, oil and gas extraction, and nuclear power) may cover a wide range of considerations but include important provisions addressing environmental concerns—for example, concerns about air or water contamination, wildlife habitat damage, human health threats, and maintenance of resources for future generations. For an overview of a variety of sectoral laws, see Chapter 9.

Laws governing activities in particular industrial sectors sometimes appear to overlap or conflict with environmental laws of general application. For example, energy projects are subject to both federal general environmental assessment requirements and evaluations under federal energy sector law. To deal with some of these situations, the laws may provide for harmonization through joint or substitute procedures. An example is the joint board procedure under Ontario's environmental, water, and municipal planning legislation that allows for a single hearing on matters involving two or more different laws.[10] If conflict exists, disputes are resolved by negotiation or, if necessary, by the courts, which apply general principles of statutory interpretation to decide which law prevails. In such cases, the courts carefully assess the language of each law and the objectives that can be understood by reading each law as a whole. Courts ask themselves whether the legislature intended that the general environmental law—that is, the "law of general application"—should apply, or whether the special sectoral law should apply as an exception to the general requirements.

Both environmental laws of general application and special sectoral laws set out enforceable requirements. These requirements can take various forms, of which the most important are the statutory provisions and regulations discussed in Chapter 9. They can also be supplemented by influential guidance documents issued by regulators, covering such matters as desirable and best practices, standard administrative procedures, testing protocols, and enforcement priorities.

Finally, many other powerful laws and law-related influences that do not qualify as environmental law can have significant effects on environmental concerns, including the following:

- liability rules, tax laws, spending powers, and other financial tools that provide the basis for imposing and adjusting incentives for better environmental practices and disincentives for undesirable behaviour;
- general laws ensuring public access to information and other opportunities for effective scrutiny of and participation in important decisions, including environmentally significant ones; and
- the broad law-making power itself, which gives governments the ability to use the plausible threat of new legal obligations to encourage "voluntary" efforts to improve environmental performance.

While we tend to think of particular environmental laws and even categories of environmental laws as individually important, the key consideration is how well the whole suite of laws and related instruments works as an overall regime.

Four Evolutionary Phases in Canadian Environmental Law

The development of Canadian environmental law can be categorized into four evolutionary phases. These four phases show Canadian environmental laws addressing a rough succession of increasingly difficult subjects.[11] Although the phases are reasonably easy to discern in the overall history of federal and provincial environmental law, they certainly did not evolve in a tidy sequential arrangement; nor did they evolve at the same time everywhere.

Phase 1: Common Law Rights and Early Statutes

The 1960s were characterized not just by the Beatles, bell-bottoms, and rebellions against authority. They are also remembered as the decade when legislators began to give serious attention to the environment. Still, a contemporary environmental lawyer transported back to the 1960s would quickly discover that almost her entire kit of environmental law tools was missing. She would find no regulatory statutes with contaminant discharge limits, no approvals based on these limits, and no civil and criminal penalties for failure to comply.

A bit of legal research (the old-fashioned library kind) would show our environmental lawyer the tools available to her. The federal *Fisheries Act* would be there, as it has been since the 1860s, but it would be limited to blanket prohibitions against the discharge of "deleterious substances" in "waters frequented by fish."[12] She would also find public health statutes, a public nuisance offence in the *Criminal Code*, and a scattering of anti-pollution provisions in natural resource development statutes. Courts would not recognize the right of citizens to challenge government statutory decisions (or non-decisions) that resulted in environmental harm, unless the citizens could show direct harm to their persons or property.

The main tools available to an environmentally conscious lawyer in the 1960s were the **causes of action** under the tort and property law components of the common law (or the **civil law** in Quebec). The most promising of these would likely involve lawsuits in **nuisance** and **negligence**. While effective in some circumstances, nuisance and negligence lawsuits were designed to resolve disputes between private parties and compensate persons harmed. As legal tools, they fall well short of providing comprehensive and systematic environmental protection. Private civil actions against polluters that were also important employers and revenue producers, such as natural resource development operations or industrial plants, often ran squarely into unsympathetic judges. But as the 1960s progressed, citizen awareness of environmental problems increased and prompted demands for more effective ways of combatting them.

This is not to say that civil actions are less important today. In addition, in attempting to recover damages or to halt some action that is harmful or may harm the environment, many "test" cases exist where lawsuits are brought in hope of a decision that breaks new ground in terms of introducing or reinterpreting a principle or interpreting a statute. Sometimes, even if a particular legal action is unsuccessful, it may lay the foundation for a more protective legal regime in the future.

Phase 2: Waste Control and Cleanup Laws
In the late 1960s, citizens and governments awakened to the recognition that concerted and comprehensive environmental protection action was needed. Basic air,

---

causes of action   legal grounds for a civil lawsuit

civil law   in Quebec, a system based on the Custom of Paris and later codified using French civil law and Code Napoléon, which applies to private disputes between citizens; the term can also be used to refer to the law between citizens, even in a common law jurisdiction (as opposed to public law, or the law between state and citizens)

nuisance   tort in which the defendant interferes with the use and enjoyment of the plaintiff's property

negligence   failure to act reasonably, with the result being harm to someone else

water, and land pollution statutes were enacted by the provinces in the late 1960s and 1970s. The federal government broadened its *Fisheries Act*. The objective of these changes was the control of harmful substances that were being deposited on land or discharged into air and water.[13]

BOX 1.4 » The Purpose of the Fisheries Act, 2007

2. The purpose of this Act is to provide for the sustainable development of Canada's seacoast and inland fisheries, through the conservation and protection of fish and fish habitat and the proper management and control of fisheries.

Source: Canada, Bill C-32, *An Act Respecting the Sustainable Development of Canada's Seacoast and Inland Fisheries*, 2nd Sess., 39th Parl., 2007.

Governments established regulatory systems to identify waste sources and require permits to control the quantity and quality of substances discharged. The terms and conditions of permits were often the result of closed negotiations between the industrial applicants and the regulators. Failure to comply with these requirements was an offence punishable on summary conviction (a minor offence) and resulted in modest fines for those found guilty.

The discharge of waste that was likely to harm the environment or human life or health was often established as a general offence. In this context, the *environment* was generally defined as air, water, and land upon which human life depends. Governments only gradually issued regulations specifying requirements for control of particular contaminants.

The new statutes were **cleanup laws**, designed to regulate the discharge of human and industrial waste into the environment. Among them were comprehensive statutes dealing with air, water, and land pollution. Examples of these statutes include the Ontario *Environmental Protection Act*, the Quebec *Environment Quality Act*, and the BC *Pollution Control Act*.[14] There were also single-element statutes, such as Alberta's *Clean Water Act*, *Clean Air Act*, and *Land Surface Conservation and Reclamation Act* (these acts were consolidated in the 1990s into the *Environmental Protection and Enhancement Act*).

The underlying assumption was that the natural environment could be used to dispose of, dilute, and cleanse the waste produced by human activity, as long as sufficiently careful management prevented too much contamination at any one time and place.[15] Legislation was a matter of fairly allocating nature's assimilative capacity. Although these laws have changed significantly, this waste control function still remains at their core.

---

cleanup laws laws designed to minimize discharge of human and industrial waste into the environment

Waste control laws were administered by environmental departments that were largely technical agencies, staffed by scientific and engineering experts who administered the permit or approval schemes. These departments developed guidelines, rather than enforceable regulations, for "safe" waste discharge. Initially, much effort was required simply to bring all waste sources under permit.

Phase 3: Toxics Control Laws

When people think of environmentally harmful chemicals or substances, they may expect that the government can step in and quickly deal with the issue. However, the regulation of toxic chemicals is far more complicated.

Emerging evidence in the 1970s and 1980s indicated that waste control laws aimed at allocating **assimilative capacity** did not address the accumulation in the environment of persistent toxic substances. This realization led to new legislative action. Both levels of government, at least in part, have the authority to regulate toxic substances. In *R v. Hydro-Québec*,[16] the Supreme Court of Canada recognized the federal government's authority to regulate toxic substances under the criminal law constitutional power (see the case study at the beginning of this chapter).

The major **toxics control laws** in Canada are the 1975 federal *Environmental Contaminants Act* and its successor, the *Canadian Environmental Protection Act* (CEPA).[17] CEPA is the primary vehicle for the regulation of both existing and new substances in Canada. It provides a number of processes for assessing substances with respect to their risks to environmental or human health, and imposes information requirements on manufacturers and importers introducing new chemicals to Canada. Prior to the enactment of CEPA, over 23,000 substances that were made, imported, or used in Canada on a commercial basis had not undergone a full risk assessment.

The re-enactment of CEPA in 1999 sought to expedite the assessment process by requiring Health and Environment Canada to categorize or identify certain substances that pose a significant risk,[18] namely, those that

- are inherently toxic (cause toxic effects) and persistent (take a long time to break down);
- are bioaccumulative (collect in living organisms and move up the food chain); or
- have the greatest potential for exposure to individuals.

---

waste control laws laws designed to control discharge of waste using permits and approvals

assimilative capacity the ability of air, water, or soil to receive contaminants and cleanse itself without deleterious effects

toxics control laws laws designed to control the manufacture, use, sale, transport, storage, and disposal of toxic substances

CEPA established substance inventories or lists to distinguish new from existing substances, to determine reporting requirements for new substances, and to identify which substances may be subject to risk management provisions:

1. *Domestic Substances List.* Under the general scheme of the Act, all existing substances are placed on the Domestic Substances List (DSL).
2. *Priority Substances List.* Substances can be placed on the Priority Substances List (PSL) and undergo a rigorous assessment of their risks to the environment and human health. Of the 69 or so substances assessed to date, over 40 have been found to be toxic as defined under CEPA.
3. *Toxic Substances List.* If a substance is found to be toxic as defined under CEPA, it may be placed on the Toxic Substances List (TSL). Once a substance is on the TSL, the federal government has very broad authority to regulate the substance. Dioxins, polychlorinated biphenyls (PCBs), and mercury, to name but a few, are regulated under these provisions.

More about the categorization process of existing and new substances can be found at www.ec.gc.ca/CEPARegistry/the_act/guide04/toc.cfm. If a substance meets certain criteria, a screening-level risk assessment is undertaken to determine whether the substance is toxic as defined under CEPA. The assessment of substances may also be based on a review of the assessments undertaken in other countries.

A number of other federal statutes deal with potentially harmful substances. These statutes include the *Pest Control Products Act* (PCPA), the *Transportation of Dangerous Goods Act* (and its provincial clones), and the *Hazardous Products Act*. The PCPA regulates products that are used to control pests, insects, and so on (see Chapter 9). The *Transportation of Dangerous Goods Act*, as its name suggests, imposes restrictions and safeguards on the transportation of materials and goods that could be dangerous to the public in the event of an accident. The *Hazardous Products Act* regulates products that may contain toxic or dangerous substances.

On April 8, 2008, the federal government introduced the *Canada Consumer Product Safety Act*, which was intended to replace and update substantial portions of the *Hazardous Products Act* and to respond to growing fears of toxic contamination of consumer products, such as children's toys. This legislation endows the government with testing powers and the authority to issue mandatory recall orders for unsafe consumer products and to require manufacturers, sellers, and importers to take corrective measures.

Provincial statutes have been tightened with the addition of requirements for the reporting and cleanup of toxic substance spills. As well, liability for spills and contaminated sites rests with landowners and former landowners, and even manufacturers, sellers, and users of toxic substances.[19]

These laws recognize that environmental protection is a long-term process that must address potential intergenerational effects of environmental damage. Because scientific knowledge about the toxicity of particular substances is continually developing, these laws include protocols and processes for identification and effective control of contaminants. The approach is preventive and anticipatory, not merely reactive.

Also reflected in these statutes is the fact that toxic substances respect neither ecosystem nor political boundaries. Consequently, the laws are outward-looking in their development, implementation, and administration. The federal statutes took into account toxics research and international standards. Both federal and provincial laws began to reflect interprovincial and federal–provincial undertakings and commitments more clearly than before. They were also made more consistent with international conditions and Canada's international obligations. For example, in the 1980s, Ontario made it clear that it wanted its water quality program to reflect the zero-discharge objectives for control of persistent toxics under the 1978 Great Lakes Water Quality Agreement between Canada and the United States.[20]

Phase 4: Comprehensive Approaches to Environmental Assessment and Planning and Management Regimes

During the early period when new waste control and cleanup laws were being introduced, many governments in Canada and elsewhere began to consider more anticipatory and preventive approaches to pollution and other environmental problems. Chief among the anticipatory and preventive tools were **environmental assessment** requirements and **planning and management regimes**. Environmental assessment requirements forced proponents of environmentally significant new projects, such as hydro power stations, airports, mines, roads, and landfills, to predict and evaluate the potential effects of these proposed undertakings. Sometimes comparison with reasonable alternatives was required before approvals were granted.

Environmental assessment requirements were imposed hesitantly in most jurisdictions. The federal government relied on a more or less discretionary policy-based assessment process for two decades before it finally passed legislated requirements.[21] Ontario, which applied a strong assessment law to public sector undertakings beginning in 1975, left the private sector largely free of obligations. But eventually, the federal government, every province and territory, many land claim agreement areas,

---

environmental assessment   the identification and evaluation of actual or potential effects (positive and adverse) of an undertaking on the environment; "undertakings" may include policies, plans, and programs as well as projects, and "environment" may include social, economic, and cultural as well as biophysical effects, and the interactions among these effects; environmental assessments may also involve a critical review of purposes, comparative evaluation of alternatives, and a follow-up examination of effects

planning and management regimes   legislative schemes that govern a sector, such as forests, fisheries, farmlands, and watersheds, with the purpose of maximizing the long-term benefits obtainable from the resource while minimizing the detrimental effects of its exploitation

and a substantial number of municipalities had law-based environmental assessment processes.

Although some Canadian assessment processes remain limited in application and ambition, most now go beyond mere evaluation of direct project effects to consider at least some of the following matters:

- cumulative effects (of the project plus other existing and expected activities);
- combinations of ecological, socioeconomic, and cultural effects;
- implications of uncertainties; and
- effects of strategic undertakings (plans, programs, and policies).

Some legal authorities argue that environmental assessment constitutes the only area of environmental law that is unique, and not merely an application of established legal approaches and instruments to environmental issues.

Legislated planning and management regimes have a longer history than environmental assessment. Some law-based processes for decision-making, concerning the management of fisheries, forestry operations, protected areas, and other Crown land uses, for example, go back 100 years or more. But most have been strengthened considerably in recent years in response to a variety of concerns, including the following:

- rising pressures on limited resources, such as old-growth forests;
- conflicts among competing uses, such as those that arise between sprawling suburbs and wildlife habitat; and
- evidence of serious management failures, such as that revealed by the destruction of the north Atlantic cod fishery.

Today many and various legislated planning and management regimes exist. They deal with many types of resources—for example, forests, fisheries, endangered species, farmlands, and watersheds—and many types of sectors—for example, electric power, solid waste, urban growth, and transportation. Not surprisingly, even within the same resource or sector, different provinces have adopted different requirements and procedures. This is evident in the field of forest management, for example.

Despite jurisdictional variations, the general trend is toward more comprehensive approaches that recognize numerous influences and complex implications, consider more response options, give greater respect to uncertainty, and include a wider range of interests.

Many of these regimes no longer focus solely on particular resources or environments, but rather on the interrelations and potential conflicts among many objectives and activities. As a result, environmental law as well as broader land use and other planning laws are beginning to be combined in more comprehensive responses to pressing problems. This change is evident, for example, in the regional growth management initiatives in the rapidly urbanizing areas of southern British Columbia and southern Ontario.[22]

Five Associated Trends in Environmental Law

Several trends have affected the design and application of the environmental statutes, regulations, and administrative practices introduced since the 1960s. While these trends have had different effects in different jurisdictions, each has been or promises to be significant everywhere in Canada.

Regional, Continental, and Global Effects

In the early days, environmental protection efforts focused on the local effects of particular sources and contaminants. The popular view was that "dilution is the solution to pollution." Accordingly, when industrial air emissions were causing undeniable damage in the neighbourhood in which a plant was situated, the accepted response was to require construction of a taller emission stack.

This technique was most famously used in Sudbury, Ontario, where acidifying emissions and other contaminants from the nickel smelters had killed much of the local vegetation and left a moonscape suitable for astronaut training. Construction of a 380-metre (1,250-foot) superstack at the Inco smelter in the early 1970s helped reduce local pollution loads and allowed vegetation recovery.[23] But it also spread the acidifying contaminants much farther. By the early 1980s, the long-range atmospheric transport of acidifying pollutants from Sudbury and a host of other major and minor sources was clearly having serious effects on the overall acidity of precipitation across huge areas of North America and Europe.[24]

The building of Inco's massive "superstack" (visible in the photo above) in the early 1970s helped the decimated vegetation around Sudbury to recover, but it also spread pollution over a vast area.

Source: James Hackland/Alamy.

The **dilution solution** had led to environmental damage on a regional and continental scale. Eventually, environmental authorities in Ontario and other jurisdictions in North America and Europe were moved to rewrite their environmental laws and facility-specific requirements to deal with effects well beyond the local scale.

Today the best-publicized environmental concern is global climate change, which has also resulted from emissions from a multitude of local sources. While responses

---

dilution solution the idea that air or water pollutants do not pose a problem if they are spread out widely enough, such as by the wind or ocean currents

to this problem are still far from adequate, the planetary scale of the challenge and the need for similarly inclusive action is well recognized.[25]

Transparency and Citizen Participation

In Canada, as in many countries, the initial inclination of government authorities was to deny or minimize environmental problems, and to resist imposing the full costs of environmental protection on corporate or individual taxpayers. In the late 1960s and early 1970s, a wave of public interest environmental groups emerged to challenge government authorities. Through effective collaboration with the news media, environmental groups raised public awareness of environmental problems and pushed governments toward stronger and more comprehensive environmental protection laws.

Unfortunately, the failure of governments to take initiative in acknowledging and addressing environmental problems contributed to public distrust of government authorities on issues of environmental protection. This distrust was deepened by the frequent weakness of government efforts to enforce the new laws and by the common practice of developing pollution abatement requirements through secret negotiations between regulatory authorities and polluting industries.

As a reaction to these frustrations, environmental groups began to push for greater transparency in the decision-making process, including the following:

- timely and convenient access to information,
- opportunities for direct involvement in deliberations leading to new policies,
- regulatory requirements and case-specific decisions, and
- rights to demand action and to participate in or pursue public interest litigation.

While not all of these efforts have been successful, most Canadian jurisdictions now make decisions related to environmental law in a much more transparent and participatory way than they did 30 years ago. The Supreme Court of Canada improved access to justice by removing doctrinal barriers to bringing legal challenges. The court substituted relatively flexible criteria for discretionary public interest standing. (The concept of **standing** in courts is discussed further in Chapter 13.) Simply put, the issue is about whether members of the public can challenge the legality of a provision of legislation or a government decision when they may be directly affected by that decision in cases where their property or health may be harmed. The courts have stated that the public can at times bring such lawsuits if certain criteria are met and, most important, if the person bringing the action has a genuine interest in the matter and there is no other way to bring the issues before the court.[26] Many of

---

standing   the right to sue

the more recent environmental laws, such as CEPA 1999[27] and Ontario's *Environmental Bill of Rights, 1993*, encourage public consultation and participation. Citizens may even become decision-makers under provisions for mediated negotiation among stakeholders.[28] It is no longer a two-party government–industry negotiation process.

International Influence on Precaution

Modern environmental law in Canada and other nations is increasingly influenced by international law principles and agreements. Below are examples of international agreements explicitly implemented by Canadian environmental laws:

- The Convention on Biological Diversity[29] was implemented by the *Species at Risk Act* to protect endangered species.
- The London Dumping Convention[30] was implemented by CEPA 1999[31] to reduce marine pollution.
- The Montreal Protocol on Substances That Deplete the Ozone Layer[32] was implemented by CEPA 1999[33] to protect against ozone-depleting substances.

The rising influence of international law results in part from the need for responses to international-scale environmental problems. These problems include climate change, stratospheric ozone depletion, acidic precipitation, biodiversity loss, and trade in toxic substances. Perhaps because of the evident perils involved, international environmental law has also been a forum for significant innovation.

One such innovation that is particularly important is the legal adoption of the precautionary principle, which holds the following:

> When an activity raises threats of harm to human health or the environment, precautionary measures should be taken even if some cause and effect relationships are not fully established scientifically. In this context the proponent of an activity, rather than the public, should bear the burden of proof.[34]

Essentially, the precautionary principle recognizes that the world of environmental interrelations is extremely complex and that our ability to describe it, much less predict the effects of new interventions, is extremely limited. Uncertainty is therefore always present and often important.

In international law, including multilateral environmental agreements, the precautionary principle is now widely accepted and increasingly applied as customary law. Application in Europe is also extensive. In Canada, precaution is frequently advocated in policy statements, sometimes incorporated in statutory objectives and purposes,[35] and often seen in some areas of implementation. Attention to uncertainties, anticipation of worst-case possibilities, and planning for adaptation are now commonly expected in major environmental assessments.

So far, the influence of the precautionary principle on the character of Canadian environmental law and practice has been limited. Little evidence exists that the principle is applied rigorously in permit and approval decisions or in enforcement actions. However, in *114957 Canada Ltée (Spraytech, Société d'arrosage) v. Hudson (Town)*,[36] a notable decision in 2001, the Supreme Court of Canada used the precautionary principle in its interpretation of a municipal government statute to decide whether it authorized a municipal bylaw regulating and restricting pesticide use. Justice L'Heureux-Dubé's use of the precautionary principle was based on her assessment that it was, at least arguably, a principle of customary international law. The Supreme Court also noted this emerging principle in *Castonguay Blasting Ltd. v. Ontario (Environment)*.[37]

Effective and Efficient Application of the Law

Especially since the 1990s, the introduction, design, and application of environmental law in Canada have been affected by increased scrutiny of government initiatives by the public and non-governmental organizations. The main factors driving this trend are the following:

- ideological predispositions and corporate interests,
- concerns about the costs of government programs, and
- doubts about effectiveness.

Environmental laws have not been alone in coming under public scrutiny. But they have received particular attention because industrial interests have associated environmental laws with increased costs. Industry has also suffered long-term frustration as a result of the great diversity of general approaches and specific environmental requirements imposed by different jurisdictions. In response to concerns about costs and regulatory burdens, some governments have repealed or weakened environmental laws. Consider, for example, the virtual elimination of environmental assessment law in British Columbia[38] and the *Canadian Environmental Assessment Act, 2012*.[39] Some governments have also put more emphasis on **voluntary compliance** initiatives.

At the same time, public interest advocates have consistently underlined the continuing failure of current environmental laws and their application to resolve problems in most areas of environmental concern. More positive initiatives include a new generation of environmental statutes with sophisticated enforcement provisions. Environmental laws are now being drafted as broader packages that include legal, economic, educational, and other means to encourage and enforce environmental improvements.

---

voluntary compliance   an approach that relies on industry and individuals to do the right thing, motivated by conscience, public relations, or a desire to avoid regulation

These new approaches give regulators greater flexibility to choose from a broad range of enforcement tools, depending on what is most appropriate in the circumstances. Some such tools include the following:

- tickets for minor offences,
- criminal indictments for endangering life or health,
- mandatory administrative orders,
- administrative penalties, and
- lawsuits.

The broader packages use regulation and the threat of additional regulation along with more general liability provisions, incentives, multi-stakeholder negotiations, and sector-specific "voluntary" programs to push for compliance and performance beyond legal requirements.

To catch the attention of the corporate sector, some jurisdictions have accompanied these more flexible approaches with provisions for large fines and potential imprisonment for serious environmental offences as well as with provisions for corporate officer and director liability. These provisions have given corporations a strong incentive to review and audit their compliance with environmental requirements, take necessary action, and prepare and implement environmental management policies and plans.

Not all of these flexible approaches are well integrated or consistently applied. Moreover, great variation remains from one jurisdiction to the next. When something goes wrong, the various environmental agencies may point the finger of responsibility elsewhere. For example, provincial agencies may blame federal agencies, and vice versa. However, most agencies also guard their mandate, authority, and independence tenaciously.

The resulting differences in environmental requirements across jurisdictions have frustrated not only many corporate interests that are subject to environmental laws but also environmental advocates who would like to push all environmental laws along a little faster. In response, federal, provincial, and territorial governments, especially through the Canadian Council of Ministers of the Environment, began to take some steps toward harmonizing environmental law requirements. This too remains a work in progress.

Beginning in about 2010, there has been a marked retreat federally and in some provinces[40] on procedural and substantive environmental protection requirements for major projects—particularly energy development and facilities. For example, the re-enactment of the *Canadian Environmental Assessment Act* in 2012 limited the application and scope of federal environmental assessment in several ways.[41] Application has been restricted by introducing considerable agency discretion as to when assessment is required. Moreover, the scope of assessment has been restricted, and public participation has been restricted to "interested parties."

For energy facilities, *Canadian Environmental Assessment Act, 2012* along with amendments to the *National Energy Board Act*[42] and the *Nuclear Safety and Control Act*[43] changed environmental assessment and project approval requirements in four major ways:

1. The National Energy Board and the Canadian Nuclear Safety Commission have become the sole decision-makers for projects in their areas. No more joint panels with involvement from the Canadian Environmental Assessment Agency will take place.
2. Time limits for decision (and public review) process have been established.
3. Public participation in some regulatory approval proceedings has been limited.
4. Final project approval powers have been removed from tribunals such as the National Energy Board and vested in the Cabinet.

The time limits and participatory restrictions raise procedural fairness questions. Taken together, the changes suggest a distinct economic development priority and an intention to remove independent public fora from decision-making processes. (Box 1.5 examines the larger context of these policy trends.)

Sustainability Objectives

The final general trend is the continuing spread of official commitments to sustainability or **sustainable development**. The concept of sustainability, popularized by the 1987 report of the World Commission on Environment and Development (the Brundtland commission),[44] has been much debated and often misused. But sustainability's essential role is threefold:

1. to underline the unsustainable character of present inequities and environmental degradation;
2. to recognize the interdependence of social, economic, and ecological well-being; and
3. to encourage attention to the interests of future generations.

In Canada, sustainability has been included as a core purpose of most recent federal, provincial, and territorial environmental statutes. Federal departments and agencies are required to have sustainable development strategies that are regularly reviewed and updated every three years. Manitoba has a *Sustainable Development*

---

sustainable development   "development that meets the needs of the present without compromising the ability of future generations to meet their own needs" (World Commission on Environment and Development, 1987); it involves improving the quality of human life and enhancing equity in the distribution of well-being while living within the carrying capacity of the planet's biophysical systems over the long term

BOX 1.5 » Canada's Waning Commitment to Environmental Protection

In decades past, Canada enjoyed a reputation as an international leader in environmental law reform and progressive environmental policies. But a 2013 report from Washington-based Center for Global Development paints a very different picture of Canada's environmental commitment in the 21st century. The Commitment to Development Index compares the environmental policies of the world's richest countries, measuring rising or falling greenhouse gas emissions, gasoline taxes, and other indicators. Canada's ranking has plummeted, and the country now sits last on the list. In their examination of Canada's lagging legal and environmental performance, Stepan Wood, Georgia Tanner, and Benjamin J. Richardson have noted:

> Trail-blazing accomplishments such as the Berger Inquiry into the Mackenzie Valley Pipeline, the Ontario Environmental Assessment Board, "round tables" on environment and economy, and comprehensive land claims agreements with Aboriginal peoples impressed policy makers and scholars worldwide. Indeed, Canada was known as an environmental law "exporter," setting precedents for other countries and taking a leadership role in international environmental diplomacy. Reinforcing this reputation was Canada's image as a largely unspoiled wilderness. ... But Canada's reputation has waned in recent decades. It is now a laggard in both policy innovation and environmental performance, known for inaction and obstruction on such issues as climate change. Scholarship on Canadian environmental law in international journals has become much more critical. Environmental law courses in non-Canadian universities now typically study Canada, if at all, only as an historical example.*

Figure 1.1   Index Comparing Environmental Policies Among Rich Countries

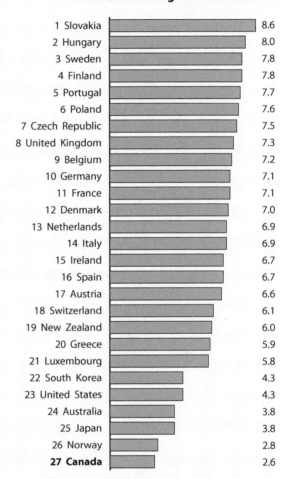

1 Slovakia	8.6
2 Hungary	8.0
3 Sweden	7.8
4 Finland	7.8
5 Portugal	7.7
6 Poland	7.6
7 Czech Republic	7.5
8 United Kingdom	7.3
9 Belgium	7.2
10 Germany	7.1
11 France	7.1
12 Denmark	7.0
13 Netherlands	6.9
14 Italy	6.9
15 Ireland	6.7
16 Spain	6.7
17 Austria	6.6
18 Switzerland	6.1
19 New Zealand	6.0
20 Greece	5.9
21 Luxembourg	5.8
22 South Korea	4.3
23 United States	4.3
24 Australia	3.8
25 Japan	3.8
26 Norway	2.8
27 Canada	2.6

Source: Center for Global Development, Washington, DC, 2013, "The Commitment to Development Index." Reprinted by permission. http://www.cgdev.org/initiative/commitment-development-index/index.

---

* Stepan Wood, Georgia Tanner, and Benjamin J. Richardson, "What Ever Happened to Canadian Environmental Law?" (2010) 37 *Ecology Law Quarterly* 981, at 982.

Act, which is, among other things, meant to encourage and guide government decision-makers to integrate the broad range of interrelated sustainability considerations into their decision-making under existing and future laws, even when these laws have a specific, narrow focus. Several other provinces (e.g., Nova Scotia, Quebec, and British Columbia) have sustainability-centred statutes, plans, ministries, and reporting requirements.

As with the closely associated precautionary principle, the adoption of sustainability objectives is still much stronger in expressed intention than in rigorous application. But important practical applications have been made under environmental law. The *Alberta Land Stewardship Act*, which authorizes province-wide basic-scope land and resource use planning, incorporates sustainable development objectives.[45] Several review panels established under the *Canadian Environmental Assessment Act*[46] have used the law's sustainability purposes as justification for requiring project proponents to show that their proposed undertakings would make a positive contribution to sustainability rather than merely avoid causing significant negative effects.

All of these trends are continuing, and we will return to them at the end of the text, where we consider what may lie ahead for environmental law in Canada. But now, with this brief historical review in hand, we are ready to take a more comprehensive look at the environmental law system.

SUMMARY OF KEY POINTS

- Environmental law is highly normative—encompassing the statutory and common law that can be used to protect the environment.
- Environmental law is aimed at protection of the natural as well as the dependent human environment, including use of environmental resources, prevention of damage, compensation, and public governance and processes.
- First-stage waste control laws of the 1970s led to toxics control laws and eventually to environmental assessment, planning, and management as well as modern laws that incorporate ideas of sustainability and, to a degree, precaution against environmental threats even where the likelihood of harm is not fully known.
- Law is composed of the rules and prohibitions that society prescribes through legislatures and courts and lays down requirements that can be enforced through regulatory agencies or the courts. This mandatory feature of environmental law is important because so much human activity, including building structures and extracting natural resources, happens under guidelines, codes of practice, and simple convention.
- The four evolutionary phases in the development of Canadian environmental law are (1) common law rights and early statutes, (2) waste control and cleanup

laws, (3) toxics control laws, and (4) comprehensive approaches to environmental assessment and planning management regimes. These four phases are not sequential nor have they taken place at the same time in all jurisdictions.

- Many continuing and emerging trends (such as transparency and citizen participation) have affected the core concerns, design, application, and effects of environmental laws across Canada.

KEY TERMS

assimilative capacity

causes of action

civil law

cleanup laws

common law

dilution solution

environmental assessment

environmental assessment law

environmental law

environmental regulatory law

laws of general application

negligence

nuisance

planning and management regimes

sectoral laws

standing

sustainable development

tort

toxics control laws

tragedy of the commons

voluntary compliance

waste control laws

DISCUSSION QUESTIONS

1. The courts' role in the development of Canadian environmental law appears to be relatively minor. Is this correct? Explain.
2. What accounts for the exceptionally broad scope of Canadian environmental law?
3. How can the apparent weakening in the late 2000s of environmental legislation by the federal government and some provinces be explained? Was this already happening as a result of market approaches to environmental regulation and voluntary initiatives?
4. From your reading of the chapter, would you conclude that Canadian environmental law has been successful in protecting and improving the environment?

SUGGESTED READINGS

Gunningham, Neil, and Darren Sinclair. *Leaders and Laggards: Next Generation Environmental Regulation*. Sheffield, UK: Greenleaf, 2002.

Lucas, Alastair R., and Chidinma Thompson. *Canadian Environmental Law*, "Continuing Service," "Federal Regulatory Controls," "Introduction," and "Development of Federal Environmental Legislation." Toronto: Lexis/Nexis, 2009.

M'Gonigle, R. Michael, T. Lynne Jamieson, Murdoch K. McAllister, and Randall M. Peterman. "Taking Uncertainty Seriously: From Permissive Regulation to Preventive Design in Environmental Decision Making." (1994) 32 *Osgoode Hall Law Journal* 53-69.

Webb, Kernaghan. *Pollution Control in Canada: The Regulatory Approach in the 1980s.* Ottawa: Law Reform Commission of Canada, 1988.

Wood, Stepan, Georgia Tanner, and Benjamin Richardson. "Whatever Happened to Canadian Environmental Law?" (2010) 37 *Ecology Law Quarterly* 981.

NOTES

1. Kathryn Harrison, "Talking with the Donkey: Cooperative Approaches to Environmental Protection" (1999) 2 *Journal of Industrial Ecology* 51; Neil Gunningham and Darren Sinclair, *Leaders and Laggards: Next Generation Environmental Regulation* (Sheffield, UK: Greenleaf, 2002).

2. UN World Commission on Environment and Development, *Our Common Future* (Oxford: Oxford University Press, 1987).

3. See, e.g., Ontario *Environmental Assessment Act*, RSO 1990, c. E.18, s. 1, "environment."

4. See, e.g., *Canadian Environmental Protection Act, 1999*, SC 1999, s. 3(1), "environment," and s. 64.

5. Aldo Leopold, *A Sand County Almanac* (New York: Ballantine Books, 1970), at 237-64.

6. Christopher Stone, "Should Trees Have Standing? Toward Legal Rights for Natural Objects" (1972) 45 *Southern California Law Review* 450-87.

7. Laurence Tribe, "Ways Not to Think About Plastic Trees" (1974) 83 *Yale Law Journal* 1315.

8. Steven Kennett, "New Directions for Public Land Law" (1998) 8 *Journal of Environmental Law and Practice* 1.

9. Ibid.

10. See Ontario *Environmental Review Tribunal Act, 2000*, SO 2000, c. 26, sched. F.

11. D. Paul Emond, "The Greening of Environmental Law" (1991) 36 *McGill Law Journal* 742; Alastair Lucas, "The New Environmental Law," in R. Watts and D. Brown, eds., *Canada: The State of the Federation, 1989* (Kingston, ON: Institute of Intergovernmental Affairs, Queen's University, 1989), 167-92.

12. John McLaren, "The Tribulations of Antoine Ratte: A Case Study of the Environmental Regulation of the Canadian Lumbering Industry in the Nineteenth Century" (1984) 33 *University of New Brunswick Law Journal* 203.

13. *Fisheries Act*, RSC 1970, c. 17 (1st Supp.), ss. 2-3, adding what are now ss. 34-42 of RSC 1985, c. F-14.

14. BC's *Pollution Control Act* was replaced by the *Waste Management Act*, RSBC 1996, c. 118, and then the *Environmental Management Act*, SBC 2003, c. 53.

15. Alastair Lucas, "Legal Techniques for Pollution Control: The Role of the Public" (1971) 6 *UBC Law Review* 167; Kernaghan Webb, *Pollution Control Canada: The Regulatory Approach of the 1980s* (Study Paper) (Ottawa: Law Reform Commission of Canada, 1988).

16. *R v. Hydro-Québec*, [1997] 3 SCR 213.

17. The *Environmental Contaminants Act*, SC 1974-75-76, c. 72, later the *Environmental Contaminants Act*, RSC 1985, c. E-12, was repealed and replaced by the *Canadian Environmental Protection Act*, RSC 1985, c. 16 (4th Supp.), and is now the *Canadian Environmental Protection Act, 1999*, SC 1999, c. 33.

18. CEPA, s. 64 specifies toxicity criteria.

19. See, e.g., Ontario *Environmental Protection Act*, RSO 1990, c. E.19, Part X, "Spills," Part XV.1, "Records of Site Condition," and Part XV.2, "Special Provisions Applicable to Municipalities, Secured Creditors, Receivers, Trustees in Bankruptcy, Fiduciaries and Property Investigators"; Quebec *Environmental Quality Act*, CQLR c. Q-2, s. 31.52; Alberta *Environmental Protection and Enhancement Act*, RSA 2000, c. E-12, Part 5, "Release of Substances," and "Contaminated Sites."

20. The agreement was signed on November 22, 1978 and amended by the protocol signed November 18, 1987.

21. See *Friends of the Oldman River Society v. Canada (Minister of Transport)*, [1992] 1 SCR 3.

22. See, e.g., the *Places to Grow Act, 2005* and the *Greenbelt Act, 2005*.

23. See *Smith v. Inco Limited*, 2010 ONSC 3790, rev'd. 2011 ONCA 628.

24. Alastair Lucas, "Acid Rain: The Canadian Position" (1983) 32 *University of Kansas Law Review* 165.

25. United Nations, United Nations Framework Convention on Climate Change: Rio Declaration on Environment and Development (1992), 31 ILM 874. The declaration entered into force on March 21, 1994.

26. See *Minister of Justice (Can.) v. Borowski*, [1981] 2 SCR 575; *Canadian Council of Churches v. Canada (Minister of Employment and Immigration)*, [1992] 1 SCR 236; and *Finlay v. Canada (Minister of Finance)*, [1986] 2 SCR 607.

27. See CEPA 1999, s. 6, "National Advisory Committee"; "Part 2—Public Participation," including "Environmental Registry," "Application for Investigation by Minister," and "Environmental Protection Action."

28. See BC *Environment and Land Use Act*, RSBC 1996, c. 117.

29. The convention entered into force in December 1993.

30. The convention was signed in 1972 and entered into force in August 1975.

31. See CEPA 1999, Part 7, Division 3, "Disposal at Sea."

32. The protocol was signed in 1987 and entered into force in January 1989.

33. See CEPA 1999, Part 7, Division 6, "International Air Pollution." Also see *Ozone-Depleting Substances Regulations, 1998.*

34. Owen McIntyre and Thomas Mosedale, "The Precautionary Principle as a Norm of Customary International Law" (1997) 9 *Journal of Environmental Law* 221.

35. See, e.g., CEPA, 1999, s. 76; *Species at Risk Act*; and Ontario *Endangered Species Act.*

36. *114957 Canada Ltée (Spraytech, Société d'arrosage) v. Hudson (Town)*, 2001 SCC 40, [2001] 2 SCR 241; Chris Tollefson, *A Precautionary Tale: Trials and Tribulations of the Precautionary Principle* (Calgary: Canadian Institute of Resources Law, 2012).

37. *Castonguay Blasting Ltd. v. Ontario (Environment)*, 2013 SCC 52, [2013] 3 SCR 323, at para. 20.

38. Compare the BC *Environmental Assessment Act*, RSBC 1996, c. 119, and the BC *Environmental Assessment Act*, SBC 2002, c. 43, particularly ss. 10-17.

39. See *Canadian Environmental Assessment Act*, s. 83, "Administration."

40. Including Alberta's *Responsible Energy Development Act*; see Nickie Vlavianos, "An Overview of Bill 2," *ABlawg* (blog), November 15, 2012.

41. Meinhard Doelle, "CEAA 2012: The End of Federal EA as We Know It" (2013) *Journal of Environmental Law and Practice* 1.

42. *National Energy Board Act*, RSC 1985, c. N-7, as amended by SC 2012, c. 19, s. 83.

43. *Nuclear Safety and Control Act*, SC 1997, c. 9, as amended by SC 2012, c. 19, s. 122.

44. UN World Commission on Environment and Development, supra note 2.

45. See *Alberta Land Stewardship Act*, s. 1(2), "Purposes of Act."

46. See *Canadian Environmental Assessment Act*, s. 83, "Administration."

CHAPTER 2

The Canadian Legal Framework

LEARNING OBJECTIVES

After reading this chapter, students will be able to:

- Discuss the role of environmental law in Canadian society and what makes it legitimate.
- Understand the significance of reasonableness and fairness.
- Explain the role of the Constitution.
- Describe the constitutional division of powers between the federal and provincial governments.
- Explain how municipalities obtain their jurisdiction.
- Describe the difference between constitutions, statutes, subordinate legislation, and policies.
- Explain how laws are made.
- Explain the concepts of jurisdiction, discretionary decisions, and liability.

CHAPTER OUTLINE

Introduction: Law in Our Society

The law, of which environmental law in its various forms constitutes a part, is a body of rules that governs the behaviour of whatever, or whomever, is subject to it. The laws of physics apply to all things—bungee jumpers as well as billiard balls. The laws of society apply mostly to people, and a particular set of laws applies only in the jurisdiction (the nation or other governing organization) that puts the laws in place. But all laws are authoritative, and this authority is their central quality. While the laws of society are generally more flexible than the laws of physics, all laws worthy of the name are binding.

CASE STUDY

The Strait of Georgia and Halifax Harbour: Water Protection and Overlapping Jurisdictions

In Victoria, British Columbia, a debate has seethed for decades over the dumping of raw sewage into the Strait of Georgia. Some say that the natural currents of the strait disperse the sewage sufficiently to make a treatment facility, which would be expensive, unnecessary and foolhardy. Others—including those just south, in Washington State—say that to continue to dump raw sewage into the ocean is irresponsible.* On the other side of the country, similar concerns have been raised about the dumping of raw sewage into Halifax Harbour.† In addition, harbours in both cities receive cruise ships, freight, and a high volume of other boat traffic. Further, both Victoria and Halifax are moderately large cities that produce a fair amount of pollution through runoff into the ocean. Both cities are incorporated municipalities, with responsibilities for waste, water, and public health and safety. The federal government is responsible for shipping and fisheries. The provincial government is responsible for environmental protection and regulating runoff arising from sources such as agricultural facilities.

The ongoing water protection issues in Victoria and Halifax are a demonstration of Canadian federalism at work. Although confusion and disputes over jurisdiction do arise in such instances, there is a rationale for the division of powers in Canada, and there is a means for sorting out areas of jurisdictional overlap.

Questions

What is the basis for multi-level and overlapping jurisdictions? How can environmental issues covered by more than one jurisdiction, such as sewage and water protection, be addressed in Canada?

---

*   Rob Shaw, "Greater Victoria Politicians Debate Sewage Project Deadline Extension," *Times Colonist*, January 8, 2014, http://www.timescolonist.com/greater-victoria -politicians-debate-sewage-project-deadline -extension-1.783170.

†   "Raw Sewage Flows into Halifax Harbour," *CBC News*, May 12, 2011, http://www.cbc.ca/news/canada/ nova-scotia/raw-sewage-flows-into-halifax-harbour -1.1059448.

The authority behind a human law may come from a long record of accepted customary practice that is enforced informally by the members of a community. More commonly today, the law's authority comes from formally established law-making bodies that are empowered constitutionally to ensure that the laws are accepted and enforced.

To understand environmental law, it is important to begin with some basics. In Canada, the primary law-making bodies are the legislatures and the courts. Canadian legislatures (the federal Parliament and the provincial and territorial legislative assemblies) make law by enacting **statutes** and creating **regulations** under these statutes. Courts make laws in two ways: (1) through decisions that interpret statutes and determine their constitutionality and (2) through decisions that establish or

---

statutes   codified laws passed by legislatures

regulations   legally enforceable rules created by the governor in council (federal) or lieutenant governor in council (provincial) providing practical details of how a statute is to be implemented

adjust the principles of **common law** (judge-made decisions about similar cases stretching back in time).

A third category of law-making bodies are administrative tribunals, boards, and officials. These bodies implement statutory law. Because of the complexity of environmental statutes, discretionary rule making and decision-making powers are often vested in these regulatory bodies. The importance of these bodies is underlined by the fact that Part III of this text is wholly devoted to environmental regulatory regimes.

We accept these categories of law-making bodies as legitimate, and we accept their authority to make, within the limits of the Constitution, laws that are binding. We must comply with their laws or risk enforcement action against us.

Legitimacy is important because the law works best if it is widely accepted. A military dictatorship may be able to impose oppressive laws through the use of brute force, but any regime whose legitimacy is not broadly recognized is difficult to maintain. And any law that is not generally accepted by those expected to obey it is difficult to apply. Enforcement action works best if it is not needed very often.

Law gains legitimacy by being made by legitimate authorities—duly elected legislative bodies, courts, and tribunals that operate with evident consistency and impartiality. But legitimacy is also closely tied to reasonableness. Indeed, a useful way to think about law is to imagine it as the work of a reasonable person. This includes environmental protection decisions by both adjudicative bodies and government officials, but significantly, in both cases, core decisions involving the scope of specific legal powers must be legally correct and not merely reasonable in the particular regulatory context.[1]

In any community, the **reasonable person** is unlikely to be the most attractive or adventurous individual. More likely this person would be called "solid" and "responsible" and would be recognized as having characteristics and ideas common to most people in the community. This hypothetical reasonable person is the basis (though in different ways) for judgments about both civil and criminal liability under specific laws. This person also provides the standard for legal decisions about environmental protection and management, including what should be anticipated or foreseen, how susceptibility to harm should be measured, and how care or precaution should be gauged.

---

common law   a system of law based on the English legal tradition, which relies on precedent rather than on codified rules; may also refer to (1) decisions by courts exercising their "common law" jurisdiction as opposed to their "equitable" jurisdiction based on broad principles of fairness, or (2) case law generally as opposed to legislation

reasonable person   a hypothetical person recognized as having a level of maturity and responsibility common to most people in the community and used as an objective standard for determining liability

Legitimacy and reasonableness are also tied to fairness, particularly in two fundamental principles of good law:

- the law must apply equally to all citizens, including public officials; and
- disputes between citizens and the government must be decided by properly authorized and impartial judicial bodies according to the law.[2]

The first principle recognizes fundamental human equality before the law. The second emphasizes consistency and impartiality in the process of applying the law.

Finally, good law balances consistency and adaptability. Consistency is crucial because the law is a guide for behaviour. If the law and its enforcement are erratic, constantly shifting, or arbitrary, the law cannot be an effective guide. To be useful, the law must apply predictably to everyone, and it must be stable enough that people know what to expect. At the same time, the law must deal reasonably with a variety of different circumstances, and it must maintain its relevance in a world that is changing. In some areas, including environmental law, where improved behaviour is clearly needed, the law has the added challenge of encouraging change.

Formal law is not the only tool that society has for guiding and governing behaviour. Customary practice still applies. Education and economic incentives are also powerful. Nevertheless, the law figures prominently among our means of acting together to protect what we value, to correct what is dangerous, to foster greater understanding, and to ensure more effective and just steps to make our world happier and more sustainable.

Law has grappled with ideas that are central to the development of modern societies. Three of these ideas are particularly important: the economic idea that it is acceptable, even desirable, for people to be self-interested profit seekers; the scientific idea that nature can be broken down into parts, understood, and manipulated for human benefit; and the combination of these two ideas that societies and individuals should pursue economic and scientific progress built on increasingly efficient and innovative exploitation of nature's resources.

Modern societies' adoption of the idea of progress brought many new opportunities and many new challenges. For the law, it introduced a basic tension. On the one hand, societies still needed to maintain order, support honest and peaceable behaviour, and preserve valued public goods. On the other hand, increasing numbers of individuals and powerful interests expect the law to promote economic and scientific advances that inevitably would be disruptive. While the overall results might be largely beneficial, they would undermine the old ways. Embracing progress has meant facing new situations, new possibilities, and new problems.[3]

Environmental law is a response to these fundamental social tensions. It is devoted both to preservation and to change. It is expected to protect resources and maintain biophysical and ecological systems that provide crucial services—for example, clean air and water, viable soil, productive forests, and reliable climate conditions. At the same time, it must facilitate advances that will minimize waste and enhance efficiency in resource use. And it must fit into the larger scheme of law and other tools and activities that aim to enhance social and economic as well as ecological well-being over time. The quote from the Supreme Court of Canada in Box 2.1 reflects the important role of environmental law.

BOX 2.1 » A Conceptual Trap

The Supreme Court of Canada has recognized the danger of falling into the "conceptual trap of thinking of the environment as an extraneous matter in making legislative choices or administrative decisions." As Justice La Forest remarked, "Quite simply, the environment is comprised of all that is around us and as such must be part of what actuates many decisions at any moment."

Source: *Friends of the Oldman River Society v. Canada (Minister of Transport)*, [1992] 1 SCR 3, at 70.

Like many other areas of law today, environmental law must be dynamic as well as conservative, ambitious as well as careful, and a broad contributor to society as well as an effective tool in its own realm.

Legal Systems

Canada's basic environmental legal framework consists of statute law and law established through judicial decisions. But Canada does not have just one legal framework. The country is unique in that it has two legal systems and two corresponding sets of legal traditions. Quebec has a system of **civil law** that dates from the *Quebec Act, 1774*, which was enacted following the British conquest. The rest of Canada is governed by English common law that was applied in the colonial period and has since been advanced by Canadian courts.

In fact, as professors Lorne Giroux and Paule Halley have pointed out, Quebec has a dual legal system, which is reflected in Quebec environmental law.[4] The civil law, originally based on the Custom of Paris and later codified using French civil law and the Code Napoléon, applies to private disputes between citizens. But Quebec public law, which governs relations between citizens and government, is based on English law.

---

civil law in Quebec, a system based on the Custom of Paris and later codified using French civil law and Code Napoléon, which applies to private disputes between citizens; the term can also be used to refer to the law between citizens, even in a common law jurisdiction (as opposed to public law, or the law between state and citizens)

So for Quebec environmental law, the civil law concepts *abus de droit* (abuse of right) and *troubles de voisinage* (neighbourhood annoyances) create rights to protect private citizens against personal or property damage that are very similar to, but not the same as, the common law tort (private wrong) of nuisance. Administrative law and regulatory criminal offence concepts, which are based on English law, are relevant to issues that arise under environmental statutes and apply equally in Quebec and the rest of Canada.

The Role of the Constitution

Canada's **Constitution** occupies the highest level in our hierarchy of laws. It is the "supreme law" with which all other laws must conform.

The constitutions of many countries include provisions concerning environmental protection and improvement. For example, the *Constitution of India* states the following:

> Protection and improvement of environment and safeguarding of forests and wild life.
>   48A. The State shall endeavour to protect and improve the environment and to safeguard the forests and wild life of the country.

> Fundamental duties.
>   51A. It shall be the duty of every citizen of India ...
>   (g) to protect and improve the natural environment including forests, lakes, rivers and wild life, and to have compassion for living creatures.[5]

Most constitutions established since the United Nations Conference on the Human Environment held in 1972 in Stockholm contain some environmental protection principles. Many older constitutions have been amended to add environmental provisions.

Canada's *Constitution Act, 1867* refers to fisheries and public lands but does not expressly allocate environmental management powers. These powers remain absent in the Constitution despite determined lobbying by environmental groups and legal professional organizations in the early 1980s, when constitutional changes were discussed before the passage of the *Constitution Act, 1982*, and in 1987, when the proposed Meech Lake Accord on the allocation of federal and provincial powers was being debated. When the Charlottetown Accord was drafted in 1992, the issue of how to deal with the environment was discussed, but none of the proposals fundamentally affected the division of legislative powers.

---

constitution   a document that establishes the basic framework under which all other laws are created and the basic principles to which all laws must conform

The Constitutional Division of Powers

Constitutional power to make laws is divided between the federal Parliament and the provincial legislatures. The *Constitution Act, 1867* establishes this division and lists federal and provincial subjects (areas of authority). Certain subjects, such as "seacoast and inland fisheries" on the federal list[6] and "management and sale of public lands" and "property and civil rights"[7] on the provincial list, have obvious environmental significance. The *Constitution Act, 1867* does not address other governments that have since taken on more significance in Canada, including territorial, municipal, regional, and First Nations governments.

The provinces' constitutional jurisdiction over property and civil rights, local works and undertakings, and the management and sale of public lands in the province meant that it was the provinces that staked out the environmental regulatory field. The federal government's jurisdiction over fisheries supported its *Fisheries Act*, while other specific federal powers—for example, navigation and shipping, criminal law, federal works and undertakings, and interconnecting undertakings such as railways and pipelines—supported federal environmental legislation over these other subjects. The federal and provincial division of powers are listed in Box 2.2.

BOX 2.2 » Environmental Law and Policy and the Division of Powers

The powers in the *Constitution Act, 1867* that are relevant to environmental law and policy are divided as indicated below.

Provincial Powers: Sections 92 and 109

- Specific areas where the provinces can make laws:
  - s. 92(5)—management and sale of public lands
  - s. 92(8)—municipal institutions
  - s. 92(13)—property and civil rights
  - s. 92(16)—matters of a local or private nature
- Natural resources:
  - s. 92A—the "1982 resources amendment" captures changes in powers to manage and to capture revenues from non-renewable and forestry resources and the generation of electrical energy
- Proprietary interests:
  - s. 109—vests public lands, minerals, etc., with the provincial government (unless interests are federally owned or the federal government has authority over them, as in national parks)

Federal Powers: Section 91

- Specific areas where the federal government can make laws:
  - s. 91(2)—trade and commerce
  - s. 91(3)—taxation power
  - s. 91(10)—navigation
  - s. 91(12)—seacoast and fisheries
  - s. 91(24)—First Nations and Aboriginal interests
  - s. 91(27)—criminal law
- General power—The federal government can also make laws for the "Peace, Order and good Government" of Canada
- Treaty-making power—The federal government can also negotiate internationally, although it cannot implement international agreements without constitutional authority or provincial agreement.

Judicial decisions have reaffirmed existing constitutional provisions or allocated some specific subjects of environmental importance to the federal or provincial governments. Pollution "deleterious" to fish,[8] marine pollution,[9] regulation of highly toxic substances such as polychlorinated biphenyls (PCBs),[10] and environmental assessment of actions related to subjects on the federal list[11] have all been held to be within federal constitutional powers. The control of water pollution (even where fish are present) that results from debris from logging operations in provinces,[12] and the environmental regulation of (otherwise federally regulated) railways in provinces were ruled to lie within the exclusive powers of the provinces.[13]

The Supreme Court of Canada considers environmental protection not to be a distinct subject for constitutional purposes, but rather to be an aggregate matter, made up of many separate elements.[14] Everything from the licensing of toxic substance discharge and criminal offences (federal subjects) to the regulation of local businesses and provincial property (provincial subjects) falls within the sphere of environmental protection. This being the case, environmental protection cannot be allocated exclusively to the federal government as a matter of "national concern" under the residual "peace, order and good government" power that the courts have identified. The result is that the environment is a shared constitutional subject. Most of its various elements can be the subject of either federal or provincial legislation, or both.

If a conflict exists in the operation of federal and provincial environmental laws dealing in different ways with the same matter, so that complying with one government's statute involves breaching another's, then under the doctrine of **paramountcy**, the federal statute prevails. But the scope of this potential operational conflict is narrow, and governments are likely to have the skill to craft laws that are capable of operating without conflict. Although there is no explicit judicial decision on the matter, it is not likely that different federal and provincial environmental standards applying to a particular person or facility will trigger federal paramountcy. Affected persons do not face a compliance dilemma. They can comply with both laws simply by meeting the higher standard.

The Supreme Court of Canada's 1997 decision in *R v. Hydro-Québec* suggests that the federal criminal law power may potentially apply to a wide range of federal environmental laws. But this application may not be as important as it sounds. It is not clear whether criminal law, with prohibitions and offences at its core, is capable of supporting sophisticated regulatory techniques, including frameworks for market mechanisms such as emission-trading systems.

The result is that federal–provincial agreements and other harmonization techniques have proven very useful in clarifying the respective roles of the two orders of

---

paramountcy   overriding, chief in importance, supreme; in Canada, the doctrine of paramountcy holds that where there is a conflict, federal laws prevail over provincial laws

government. Examples include intergovernmental agreements under the federal *Canadian Environmental Protection Act, 1999* to accept provincial regulations as equivalent and withdraw federal regulations, agreements for joint federal–provincial environmental assessment processes, and the Canada-Wide Accord on Environmental Harmonization.[15] The objective of the Accord is national harmonization of environmental standards for greater consistency and efficiency. The Accord received considerable criticism from some members of the public, with certain fearing that standards and other environmental measures would lead to the lowest common denominator among the provinces and the federal government. An environmental organization unsuccessfully attempted to challenge the legality of the Accord: see *Canadian Environmental Law v. Canada (Minister of the Environment).*[16]

Municipal Jurisdiction

Strictly speaking, municipalities draw their powers to pass **bylaws** on environmental matters from the provincial municipal acts that create them and specify their powers to legislate. But these legislative powers, in many ways, mirror the division of federal and provincial legislative powers under the *Constitution Act, 1867.*

Until recently, municipalities were considered to be legally obligated to remain strictly within their listed bylaw powers. Where it was not clear what a particular power to make bylaws covered, judicial interpretation was formal, with more attention given to the text than the problem it addressed. But the Supreme Court of Canada has now made it clear (in the 2001 *Spraytech* case[17]) that it will use a purposive interpretive approach, analogous to that used for constitutional interpretation. This approach is designed to ensure that municipalities can deal effectively with emergent environmental problems such as regulating pesticide use within their boundaries. It must also be remembered that, in addition to municipalities potentially exceeding their powers under provincial municipal acts, their bylaws may also be outside provincial legislative powers under the *Constitution Act, 1867.* In short, municipalities must act within their powers under municipal acts and under the Constitution. For example, a municipality cannot set rules affecting navigation within a harbour because navigation is a federal constitutional responsibility.

Municipalities also deal increasingly with environmental issues in carrying out their traditional functions of land use planning and development control. In addition to being regulators, municipalities are also "corporations" in their functions of developing and managing municipal institutions, facilities, and infrastructure such as roads, bridges, and public transport systems. In this role, they are subject to provincial and federal environmental laws and must behave like good corporate citizens.

---

bylaws legally enforceable rules created by municipalities according to the powers given to them by municipal statutes

Aboriginal Jurisdiction

Self-government institutions that have been established under land claim agreements with First Nations and Inuit peoples represent another group of emerging jurisdictions. These regional jurisdictions are based on the inherent right of self-government that Canada recognizes as an Aboriginal right under section 35 of the *Constitution Act, 1982*. Many land claim agreements are the result of decades of negotiations. They are complex and contain major environmental parts, including entire regimes for wildlife management and environmental impact assessment. When the negotiations are successful, the resulting agreements are ratified by federal statutes and have constitutional authority beyond that of ordinary federal laws.

Land claim agreements typically establish an array of land and renewable resource agencies that regulate and manage water use, wildlife, and land use planning in the different settlement areas. Most such agencies are co-management arrangements with representatives from the Aboriginal organizations and from government departments sharing the responsibilities. The most ambitious creation of a new decision-making regime was the establishment of the territory of Nunavut in 1999, which resulted from the government's 1992 agreement with the Inuit people of the eastern Arctic. Aboriginal jurisdiction is discussed in greater detail in Chapter 5.

Statutes and Subordinate Legislation

There is a hierarchy of environmental legislation, beginning with the Constitution of Canada (see Figure 2.1).

Figure 2.1   Hierarchy of Environmental Legislation

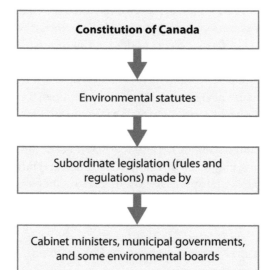

The federal and provincial environmental statutes include powers to make subordinate legislation in the form of regulations and rules. These powers are usually vested in the **governor in council** or the **lieutenant governor in council** (the federal or a provincial Cabinet, respectively), but sometimes they are assigned to ministers or boards. The statutes provide the legislative framework. They specify their objectives and purposes and the general scheme by which they are to be accomplished; specify or create the officials or agencies that are responsible for administering and enforcing them; and enable the making of regulations and rules. The regulations and rules make environmental regulatory systems work. They set out the operational details, including particular limits and obligations, and requirements for providing information, applying for approvals, and paying fees.

How Laws Are Made

Statutes

The creation of a statute begins with a government's development of a policy. The processes for enacting statutes by Parliament and by provincial and territorial legislatures are broadly similar. Initial policy development may include the preparation of public discussion documents, including green papers, which outline the main options that the government is considering, and white papers, which set out the government's preferred approach. Often, as in the case of the *Canadian Environmental Assessment Act* (CEAA), enacted in the early 1990s, and the *Canadian Environmental Protection Act, 1999*, a re-enactment of earlier legislation, the government organizes public consultation in the form of public information, hearings, and workshops. On the other hand, consultation may be limited and perfunctory. This was the case for amendment of the CEAA in 2010 and the re-enactment of CEAA in 2012. In both instances, legislative changes were buried in a large budget implementation act that included a wide range of non-environmental parts. A previously mandated public review of CEAA was limited to a Parliamentary committee hearing evidence by a few invited witnesses.[18]

If implementation of the policy is not merely a matter of spending money or issuing public information, it may require legislation. In cases involving environmental matters, a proposal for legislation is developed by the Department of the Environment or its equivalent. A legal review takes place at this stage, including an assessment of the constitutionality of the proposed legislation and its consistency with statutes of general application, such as the *Freedom of Information and Protection*

---

governor in council   a federal member of Cabinet vested with power to create regulations and rules pursuant to a statute

lieutenant governor in council   a provincial member of Cabinet vested with power to create regulations and rules pursuant to a statute

of Privacy Act. At the federal level, the *Cabinet Directive on the Environmental Assessment of Policy, Plan and Program Proposals*[19] provides for some consideration of the possible environmental effects of proposed legislation. The environment minister then sends the proposal, with the necessary supporting information, to Cabinet, through the provincial Cabinet Secretariat or the federal Privy Council Office.

If, after review, the relevant Cabinet committee approves the proposal, it is sent to the legislative drafters for preparation of a **bill**. Even at this stage of the process, policy development is not necessarily over. Sometimes, a draft bill is used as the basis for public consultation, with the Cabinet committee endorsing this initiative. This was the case in the early 1990s when Alberta's *Environmental Protection and Enhancement Act* was proposed. A committee, which included non-government members, held a series of public hearings and meetings on a draft bill, then prepared a report for the government and the public. Subsequently, a new bill was drafted, taking into account public feedback and new information. The final version of the draft bill is reviewed by the Cabinet committee on legislation and, when approved, it is ready for introduction in the legislature.

The following outline of the federal legislative process also applies, with some modification, to the provincial legislative process:

- *First reading.* The bill is introduced in the House of Commons by the environment minister and given first reading. No debate takes place. The bill is printed and circulated. Sometimes a bill is referred directly to a legislative committee at this stage.
- *Second reading.* The bill is debated, then approved in principle and referred to an all-party parliamentary committee. Usually this is the Standing Committee on Environment and Sustainable Development, but a special committee may be created or the committee may be a committee of the whole House.
- *Committee stage.* If the bill is referred to a committee, the committee studies the bill clause by clause and may hold hearings, at which witnesses may include the environment minister, departmental officials, experts, and citizens. The committee may draft proposed amendments to the bill.
- *Report stage.* The committee adopts any amendments that receive approval from a majority of the committee members, and submits a report to the House with its findings, including recommended amendments.
- *Third reading.* If the environment minister and the government accept the committee amendments, they are adopted and the bill is given a third and final reading. But not all committee amendments are accepted. When the bill to establish the *Canadian Environmental Assessment Act, 1999* was being passed in the early 1990s, the relevant House committee was highly influential,

---

bill a draft statute, subject to change and not yet passed into law

recommending important amendments that were accepted and greatly strengthened the law. In 2003, when Bill C-9, an act to amend the *Canadian Environmental Assessment Act*, was being debated, a legislative committee held lengthy hearings and only some of its amendments were accepted by the environment minister.

- *Senate.* Federal bills require a second legislative step. They must clear three readings and committee review in the Senate. The senators may propose amendments, to which the House may agree. If not, a conference process involving representatives of both bodies may be used to try to resolve differences.

- *Royal assent.* With the third reading, the bill has passed the House of Commons. But it does not become law until it has received royal assent by the governor general (or, in a province, the lieutenant governor). This is usually just a formality.

- *Coming into force.* An additional step is often required to bring the Act into force, thereby making it legally enforceable. The Act comes into force when its "coming into force" section says it does. That may be on royal assent, on a specified date, or upon proclamation (published in the *Canada Gazette*) by the governor in council (or provincial lieutenant governor in council). Parts of the Act may be proclaimed in force at different times. Often this delay exists to permit implementing regulations to be made and administering institutions to be established and staffed. Sometimes the delay is measured in years. Because of regulatory difficulties and other problems, nearly three years passed between the enactment of the *Canadian Environmental Assessment Act, 1999* and the Alberta *Environmental Protection and Enhancement Act* and the date they were finally proclaimed in force.

It is not unusual for parliamentary or legislative sessions to end before a bill makes it to third reading. If this happens, the bill "dies." It may be reintroduced in the next session as a new bill, in the same or revised form, or it may never be reintroduced. You would not be wrong to think that timing of legislative sessions may be used strategically by legislatures and their members. As legislative sessions unfold, legislators are likely to face pressure from various interests, as well as changing political, economic, and social conditions, to act more quickly on some matters and to delay or avoid acting on others. It took over six years and three separate bills before the federal *Species at Risk Act* was finally passed in 2002.

Regulations

The process for making regulations is broadly similar at the federal and provincial levels. In the federal system, a policy is initially developed by government departments or agencies. Formal or informal public information and consultation sessions may take place at this stage, but they are not legally required. Federal departments and agencies must prepare one-year reports on policy plans and priorities, table these in Parliament, and post them on their websites. The federal approach to developing regulations emphasizes consultation, consideration of risks and benefits, the minimization of impacts such as "regulatory burdens" on citizens, and the efficient use of regulatory resources.

During the next stage, legal drafting specialists draft regulations. Draft federal regulations must be accompanied by a regulatory impact analysis statement. This statement comprises six parts: description, alternatives, benefits and costs, consultation, compliance and enforcement, and contact.[20] Some parts of the regulatory impact analysis statement may be approached in less formal ways for provincial regulations.

Federal and provincial regulations have four fundamental requirements, which are outlined in Box 2.3.

You can see that making regulations is a less open process than enacting statutes. Although there is public notice and the opportunity for written comment and, sometimes, public involvement at the early stage of regulation making, what is missing is the open public debate and often extensive media attention that characterizes the legislative process. The lack of open debate is significant for environmental law because environmental statutes are usually framework statutes with critical details, including standards and specific requirements left to regulations.

BOX 2.3 » **Requirements for Federal and Provincial Regulations**

1. *Legal examination*. Proposed regulations must be reviewed to ensure that they are within the legal authority of the enabling statute, are not unusual or unexpected uses of this statutory authority, are consistent with the *Canadian Charter of Rights and Freedoms*, and are drafted according to established standards.
2. *Order-in-council approval*. The federal governor in council or provincial lieutenant governor in council makes a regulation by issuing an order in council. Sometimes a statute says that regulations can be made by ministers or tribunals. For federal regulations, Cabinet approval occurs after approval by the responsible minister and review by Privy Council Office legal specialists and Treasury Board financial officers.
3. *Publication*. The formal announcement of regulatory intent is published in the *Canada Gazette* (or in a provincial gazette). Interested persons are given a time period (usually 30 days, but longer for technical regulations) to express their views. Publication of the final regulation after order-in-council approval constitutes notice to the public of the regulation's contents. Citizens are legally bound by a regulation only after final publication and registration.
4. *Registration*. The federal *Statutory Instruments Act* and the provincial regulations acts require registration to ensure that regulations are accessible to the public. Registration also specifies the date on which the regulation comes into force.

At the federal level, the scrutiny of regulations is undertaken by Parliament's Joint Committee on Statutory Instruments (as required by the *Statutory Instruments Act*). There are also regular reports to Parliament. The objective is to identify, publicize, and make recommendations concerning regulations that are overly intrusive or inconsistent with federal legislation or policies.

The Concept of Jurisdiction

As we discussed earlier, statutes must lie within the **jurisdiction** (power to legislate) of the enacting federal or provincial government under the *Constitution Act, 1867*. Subordinate legislation such as regulations must similarly lie within the legal authority in the empowering statute. Otherwise, the legislation is outside the jurisdiction of the Cabinet, minister, or tribunal that attempted to make it. The same concept applies to municipal councils. Their bylaws must be within their jurisdiction under the authorizing provisions in the provincial government statutes that establish and empower municipal governments.

Determining whether a legislative authority has jurisdiction is not just a technical exercise in reading a statute. Rather, it is an exercise that requires a purposive approach. It involves examining the language of a statutory power within the context of the whole statute and within the external social economic and policy context in which it was enacted. For example, in *114957 Canada Ltée (Spraytech, Société d'arrosage) v. Hudson (Town)*,[21] the town passed a bylaw that restricted application of pesticides within its boundaries. It acted under statutory powers to pass bylaws to regulate for the "peace, order, good government, health and welfare of its citizens." When the bylaw was challenged by a pesticide applicator company, the Supreme Court of Canada refused to follow its own earlier decisions that had taken a narrow technical approach to interpreting municipal enabling powers. Instead, it said that it had to look at the bigger picture of what municipal governments of community representatives should be entitled to do to protect the environment in which their citizens live. It considered the even bigger picture of environmental law, including the idea of "precaution," which is emerging as an international law principle. In this light, the authorizing provision must be given a "benevolent construction." The court found the bylaw to be a valid exercise of the town's jurisdiction.

We have seen that the idea of jurisdiction also applies to the powers of cabinets to make regulations. In this context, particularly where the authorizing provision is more specific than in the *Spraytech* case, the courts take a narrower approach when determining the scope of legislative power. For example, in *Heppner v. Alberta (Environment, Minister)*,[22] the Alberta legislature, acting under its regulation-making powers set out in the *Department of the Environment Act*, established a restricted development area

---

jurisdiction the power to legislate or make a decision

on the edge of Edmonton for the purpose of an energy transmission and utility corridor. The Alberta Court of Appeal ruled that the legislature lacked the jurisdiction to do so because the purposes for restricted development areas in the authorizing statute listed conservation and pollution control; the purposes did not include transportation and utility corridors.

Discretionary Decisions and Policies

The concept of jurisdiction also applies to **discretionary decisions** made by authorized tribunals and government officials under powers conferred by environmental statutes. A discretionary decision-making power offers the decision-maker considerable latitude concerning the basis for a particular decision and the factors that can be taken into account in reaching the decision. In such cases, the clauses in the statute describing the official's decision-making power do not place any specific limitations on the scope of the decision or the relevant factors. Rather, they often state, for example, that the decision must be in the "public interest," or may simply state that the decision-maker "may" decide the issue. With a discretionary decision-making power, no single decision is legally the right one.

Discretionary decisions include key regulatory decisions under environmental statutes, such as whether contaminant discharges should be approved or licensed, or whether forestry, mining, or other public natural resource rights should be granted to private developers. Even if the statutory power includes matters that must be considered in making the decision, these matters may be very broad. As an example, consider how wide a discretion is left to a decision-maker empowered to have regard for economic, social, and environmental effects.

As we will see in Chapter 14, even these discretionary decisions may be challenged through judicial review. Courts assess a decision-maker's jurisdiction using a deferential approach. They consider the relevance and purpose of the factors and (sometimes) the specific information that the decision-maker looked at, and the consistency of the decision-maker's reasoning.

Policy decisions cannot usually be challenged on jurisdictional grounds because they do not involve the exercise of a specific statutory decision-making power. They are exercises in setting objectives and planning, under general powers given to ministers by statutes that establish and define the subjects of their government departments. They are decisions about what actions to take and how to take them. It is putting these policies into operation that requires either legislation or decisions under existing statutory powers. For example, a government policy decision to establish a greenhouse gas emission trading system, expressed in a ministerial statement or a government

---

discretionary decisions   decisions whereby the decision-maker has considerable latitude concerning the basis for a particular decision and the factors that can be taken into account in reaching the decision

policy paper, cannot be challenged for lack of jurisdiction. But a statute to establish this kind of system can be challenged for lack of constitutional jurisdiction. For example, if the trading system requires specific emission limits for a facility, the federal government would have to establish a constitutional basis to impose such limits. If the trading system is established by means of new regulations under an existing statutory power, it can be challenged for lack of jurisdiction under the existing statute. In this instance, the statute has to give clear authority for Cabinet to pass such regulations. The challenge is not a constitutional one; rather, the challenge would be that the provincial legislation did not contemplate this type of initiative being undertaken under the statute. The question in all cases is one that lawyers ask governments with numbing regularity: What is your authority for that? In other words, where is your jurisdiction?

The Concept of Liability

Liability is a legal term that is surprisingly difficult to define with precision, yet it is fundamental to environmental law. It is essentially about obligation. *Black's Law Dictionary* defines **liability** as "every kind of legal obligation, responsibility, or duty."[23] Legal obligations and responsibilities are enforced through the decisions and orders of courts and regulatory tribunals.

Environmental liability arises from obligations imposed by either

- the general law (codes or common law), or
- specific environmental legislation.

A common example is legislation that establishes liability for personal injury or property damage resulting from breach of a requirement of an environmental statute.[24] Of particular importance is statutory liability for damage caused by contaminant spills and liability for damage, remediation, and sometimes restoration of contaminated sites.[25]

Liability can be civil, criminal, or administrative. Civil liability produces obligations to take or cease certain actions and to pay compensation to persons who have suffered harm. Criminal liability is penal, involving public sanction for breach of environmental legislation. Administrative liability is enforced through regulatory bodies and officials; it can impose specific abatement requirements, including compensation obligations in some cases.

Major issues concerning environmental liability include:

- the kinds of environmental damage that result in liability,
- the classes of persons who can be held responsible,

---

liability legal obligations and responsibilities

- the ability to establish through evidence the causal connection between the activity undertaken by one party and the harm endured by another,
- the threshold at which environmental damage entails liability, and
- the standard of care applicable to the obligation to prevent environmental damage.

Liability operates in international as well as in domestic law and, indeed, the major issues with respect to establishing liability under domestic law also apply to the international realm.

SUMMARY OF KEY POINTS

- Like any law, environmental law gains legitimacy through its creation by authoritative bodies—legislatures, courts, and administrative bodies. The basic qualities of good environmental law are rationality and fairness, including procedural fairness. Environmental law must navigate the fundamental tension between development and protection in an ever-changing context.
- Quebec has a system of civil law, and the rest of Canada has a system of common law inherited from Britain.
- Canada's Constitution occupies the highest level in our hierarchy of laws. It is the "supreme law" with which all other laws must conform.
- Canada's Constitution does not expressly provide for "environmental" jurisdiction, but the *Constitution Act, 1867* establishes a division of powers between the federal and provincial governments that have been interpreted to define environmental jurisdiction. Judicial decisions have also clarified the constitutional allocation of authority over environmental matters between the federal or provincial governments.
- If a conflict exists in the operation of federal and provincial environmental laws dealing in different ways with the same matter, under the doctrine of paramountcy, the federal statute prevails.
- Laws are made by bills being introduced to the legislature, then reviewed through three "readings." Once approved, a bill becomes an act. At the federal level, laws must also be approved by the Senate.
- Regulations are a type of subordinate legislation that are authorized by an enabling statute. Regulations are used to provide details, such as technical standards, required forms, and procedures under the enabling statute.
- Liability is a legal obligation, responsibility, or duty, and may be imposed by statute or the courts. Legal obligations and responsibilities are enforced through the decisions and orders of courts and regulatory tribunals.

KEY TERMS

bill	jurisdiction
bylaws	liability
civil law	lieutenant governor in council
common law	paramountcy
constitution	reasonable person
discretionary decisions	regulations
governor in council	statutes

DISCUSSION QUESTIONS

1. Is environmental law a set of organic customary principles that have developed in Canadian society? Explain.
2. In what ways might environmental laws be unfair? How can unfairness be prevented?
3. At this stage, what are your ideas for priority environmental law improvements?
4. What is the role of the Constitution?
5. Provide examples of federal jurisdiction over environmental matters. Provide examples of provincial jurisdiction over environmental matters.
6. What are the key steps taken by legislatures in Canada when passing legislation?
7. You believe someone is liable for an incident of environmental damage. Discuss some of the key issues that may arise around determining whether anyone is liable, who might be liable, what types of penalties may be incurred, and what legal sources you could look to address these questions.
8. You are working on a project that appears to fall under both provincial and federal jurisdiction. How would you go about determining which government had jurisdiction? Could it be both? What happens if a conflict exists between the applicable federal and provincial laws?

SUGGESTED READINGS

Constitution Act, 1867, 30 & 31 Vict., c. 3.

Forsey, Eugene. *How Canadians Govern Themselves*, 8th ed. Ottawa: Library of Parliament, 2012, http://www.parl.gc.ca/About/Parliament/SenatorEugeneForsey/book/assets/pdf/How_Canadians_Govern_Themselves8.pdf.

McKenzie, Judith. *Environmental Politics in Canada*. Oxford: Oxford University Press, 2002.

Parliament of Canada. "The Senate Today: Making Canada's Laws," accessed July 13, 2014, http://www.parl.gc.ca/About/Senate/Today/laws-e.html.

"Raw Sewage Flows into Halifax Harbour." *CBC News*, May 12, 2011, http://www.cbc.ca/
news/canada/nova-scotia/raw-sewage-flows-into-halifax-harbour-1.1059448.

Reich, Charles. *The Greening of America*. New York: Random House, 1970.

Shaw, Rob. "Greater Victoria Politicians Debate Sewage Project Deadline Extension."
Times Colonist, January 8, 2014, http://www.timescolonist.com/greater-victoria
-politicians-debate-sewage-project-deadline-extension-1.783170.

Webb, Kernaghan. *Pollution Control in Canada: The Regulatory Approach in the 1980s*.
Ottawa: Law Reform Commission of Canada, 1988.

NOTES

1. *Canada (Fisheries and Oceans) v. David Suzuki Foundation*, 2012 FCA 40.

2. *Roncarelli v. Duplessis*, [1959] SCR 121.

3. See Stepan Wood, Georgia Tanner, and Benjamin Richardson, "Whatever Happened to Canadian Environmental Law?" (2010) 37 *Ecology Law Quarterly* 981-1040, at 981, 985-87.

4. Lorne Giroux and Paule Halley, "Environmental Law in Quebec," in Elaine Hughes, Alastair Lucas, and William Tilleman, eds. *Environmental Law and Policy*, 3rd ed. (Toronto: Emond Montgomery, 2003), 133-62, at 133.

5. *The Constitution of India*, 2011.

6. *Constitution Act, 1867*, 30 & 31 Vict., c. 3, s. 91(12).

7. Ibid., s. 92(13).

8. *Northwest Falling Contractors Ltd. v. The Queen*, [1980] 2 SCR 292.

9. *R v. Crown Zellerbach Canada Ltd.*, [1988] 1 SCR 401.

10. *R v. Hydro-Québec*, [1997] 3 SCR 213.

11. *Friends of the Oldman River Society v. Canada (Minister of Transport)*, [1992] 1 SCR 3.

12. *Fowler v. The Queen*, [1980] 2 SCR 213.

13. *Ontario v. Canadian Pacific Ltd.*, [1995] 2 SCR 1031.

14. *R v. Crown Zellerbach Canada Ltd.*, supra note 9.

15. Canadian Council of Ministers of the Environment, A Canada-Wide Accord on Environmental Harmonization, 1998, http://www.ccme.ca/files/Resources/harmonization/accord_harmonization_e.pdf.

16. *Canadian Environmental Law Association v. Canada (Minister of the Environment)* (1999), 30 CELR (NS) 59 (FCTD); aff'd. 2000 CanLII 15579 (FCA) and 2001 FCA 233.

17. *114957 Canada Ltée (Spraytech, Société d'arrosage) v. Hudson (Town)*, 2001 SCC 40, [2001] 2 SCR 241.

18. See Meinhard Doelle, "CEAA 2012: The End of Federal EIA as We Know It?" (2013) 24 *Journal of Environmental Law and Practice* 1-17, at 2.

19. Canada, "Strategic Environmental Assessment: The Cabinet Directive on the Environmental Assessment of Policy, Plan and Program Proposals," Privy Council Office and the Canadian Environmental Assessment Agency, 2010, http://www.ceaa-acee.gc.ca/default.asp?lang=En&n=B3186435-1.

20. See, e.g., Canadian Environmental Assessment Agency, "Regulatory Impact Analysis Statement," April 2013, http://www.gazette.gc.ca/rp-pr/p1/2013/2013-04-20/html/reg1-eng.html.

21. *114957 Canada Ltée (Spraytech, Société d'arrosage) v. Hudson (Town)*, supra note 17.

22. *Heppner v. Alberta (Environment, Minister)*, 1977 ALTASCAD 206.

23. "Liability," *Black's Law Dictionary*, 6th ed.

24. See, e.g., s. 42(3) of the federal *Fisheries Act*, which provides that persons who violate s. 36 of the Act are liable to fishermen for their losses.

25. See, e.g., s. 45 of the BC *Environmental Management Act*, SBC 2003, c. 53.

CHAPTER 3

The Context and Challenges for Environmental Law and Policy

Introduction

Law is necessarily a field and occupation for generalists. It is true that law has layers of specialties. Environmental law, for example, is a subfield with multiple further divisions. It has common and civil law versions. It can be delivered through administration or litigation, at all levels from the municipal to global, and in service to corporations, civil society, and governments. And it can demand particular expertise in matters ranging from planning to pollution abatement, the use of regulatory or other tools, applications in particular economic sectors, and so on. In all of these areas of focus, however, the law and lawyers must deal with adjacent subjects, overlapping issues, and a mix of interacting factors. Moreover, in every application facts entwine with values, generic considerations are accompanied by peculiarities unique to the case, and all of these elements participate in the messy drama of the larger human and ecological context.

CASE STUDY

Smarter Growth: Density Versus Urban Sprawl

The Ontario legislature recently passed two extraordinary laws. The *Places to Grow Act, 2005* and the *Greenbelt Act, 2005* were meant to force a major transition in urban and suburban form in one of North America's largest and fastest-growing regions. The target area was the Greater Golden Horseshoe, a stretch of expanding and gradually merging towns and cities, including Toronto and other centres, around the west end of Lake Ontario. In 2011, 8.76 million people lived there—over a quarter of the Canadian population. By 2031, the area's projected population is expected to be 11.5 million.

For 50 years or more, much of the population and economic expansion in the Greater Golden Horseshoe/Greenbelt area had been accommodated in sprawling suburbs served by highways for private vehicles. But by the beginning of 2000, many experts and residents could see that the established approach was not working. Commuting times were rising. The semi-rural quality of life sought by new migrants to the urban fringe was being compromised by constant suburban expansion. High quality foodlands were being overrun. Crucial ecosystem services were imperiled. And servicing the low-density residential and commercial/industrial developments was proving to be too expensive. There were too few paying customers for viable public transit and too few taxpayers for each kilometre of decaying asphalt and pipe or for affordable delivery of timely fire,

Entering The *Greenbelt*
GREEN BELT
Ontario

ambulance, police, and garbage-collection services. The growth was unsustainable. A future of more of the same would be worse.

The response was a major shift in approach to the management of growth and the design of cities. The *Places to Grow Act, 2005* and the *Greenbelt Act, 2005* would direct new residential and employment activities to established nodes and corridors, require greater density in residual greenfield developments, and establish a greenbelt barrier to further sprawl. If all went as planned, the eventually resulting urban form would be more transit friendly, less threatening to foodlands and ecosystems, and less costly to service.

Just how successful this transition will be is yet to be determined. The built environment evolves slowly, even when pushed by ambitious legislation. Also, the context for change in the Greater Golden Horseshoe/Greenbelt area is dauntingly complex. The area is covered by multiple layers of provincial and municipal jurisdiction, and has diverse cultures as well as deeply intertwined economic, ecological, cultural, and social influences, some of which are beyond regional or provincial control. Endless opportunities exist for disagreement, debate, and delay on key issues, such as determining the most appropriate forms for denser communities or the best modes and locations for transit services.

Moreover, the new approach to growth management is only a first step in the direction of regional sustainability. While the two Acts are laudable moves toward a more economically, socially, and ecologically viable urban form, they retain the old devotion to accommodating endlessly continued growth in human numbers and economic activities. So far, no serious attention has been given to the finite capacity of the biosphere to satisfy growing human demands or to the limited ability of more efficient urban design to deliver desirable community life to more and more people. Eventually, these realities will need to be addressed. In the meantime, the *Places to Grow Act, 2005* and the *Greenbelt Act, 2005* show that governments can recognize the perils of increasingly unsustainable behaviour and pursue a better path.

Questions

What are the strengths and limitations of the *Places to Grow Act, 2005* and the *Greenbelt Act, 2005* as tools for enhancing prospects for sustainability in the Greater Golden Horseshoe/Greenbelt area? What local to global interests and circumstances are likely to help or hinder successful application of the *Places to Grow Act, 2005* and the *Greenbelt Act, 2005*? What kinds of legislated initiatives might be used to address other complex areas—such as mining, biodiversity protection and recovery, youth employment, and electric power systems—where transitions to more sustainable practices are needed?

Figure 3.1   Map of the Southern Ontario Greenbelt

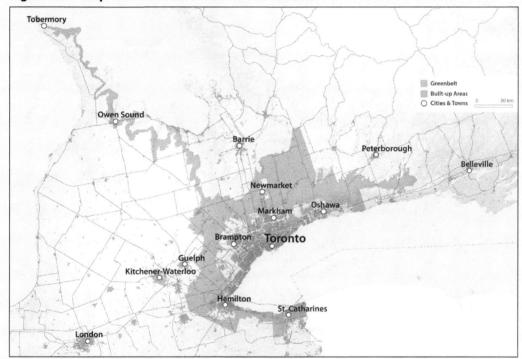

Source: Friends of the Greenbelt /As the Crow Flies cARTography.

This complexity is the source of endless complaints. Why can't the law be a tidy field of objective evaluation and impartial ruling? Why must "environment" be tainted by political, economic, or social influence? Why can't each environmental issue be the responsibility of one clearly identified authority? Why can't environmental requirements be spelled out precisely, with well-defined lines between significant and insignificant, acceptable and unacceptable? Why can't science deliver confidence beyond reasonable doubt in response to every important question? Why can't decisions be reliably quick and predictable? Why can't the world be efficiently simple and well-ordered so that we can get on with the important work of enhancing prosperity and quick-marching progress?

Unfortunately for the complainants, the hopes underlying these questions fit poorly with the essential character of life on earth and with the pace of change in recent decades. Countless everyday frustrations result from wholly unnecessary obfuscation, confusion, or intransigence on somebody's part. But the world is not simple. It is not divisible into independent parts. It is inconveniently, richly, and irremediably complex to a degree that seems always to have been well beyond our capacities for comprehension. Over the millennia, we have learned much. The last few centuries and decades especially have brought world-changing advances in understanding how things work, and how they can be manipulated to give us everything from antibiotics to instant global communications. At the same time, however, we have expanded our apparent confidence and extended the scale, speed, and ambition of our activities. The result is a continuing escalation of human numbers and resource demands, technological ambitions and applications, and resulting opportunities and stresses that have multiplied the phenomena we need to understand and address. It is an example of the Red Queen effect, where "it takes all the running you can do, to keep in the same place."[1]

We face another difficulty. Staying in the same place is not a viable option anymore. Our current place is dynamic, unstable, and characterized by trends toward deeper unsustainability. While the main features of unsustainability are predictably complex, three interconnected global factors are especially significant:

- Human pressures on life-supporting biophysical systems are probably already well over the planet's sustainable carrying capacity. The World Wildlife Fund (WWF) has estimated that human impacts, including those of greenhouse gas emissions, passed the sustainability threshold in the 1970s and by 2008 were 50 percent above what might be sustainable, despite improvements in technologies, regulatory efforts, and awareness.[2] (See Figure 3.2.)
- Many people nonetheless do not have enough for basic well-being. Data from 2011 to 2013 indicate that about one person in eight (842 million people) suffers from material deficiencies serious enough to leave them malnourished.[3]
- Almost all of the gains from economic expansion go to those who are already advantaged. A UNICEF study using two different methods of income comparison found that the richest 20 percent of the global population received 70 to 83 percent of global income in 2007, while the poorest 20 percent received 1 to 2 percent.[4]

In such a world, some of the fundamental premises of prevailing economic and political practice clash with evident reality. In a world of increasingly overshot limits, continuing desperate needs, and profound inequity, economic growth based on even more resource exploitation cannot improve overall well-being, at least not for

Figure 3.2 Our Growing Ecological Footprint

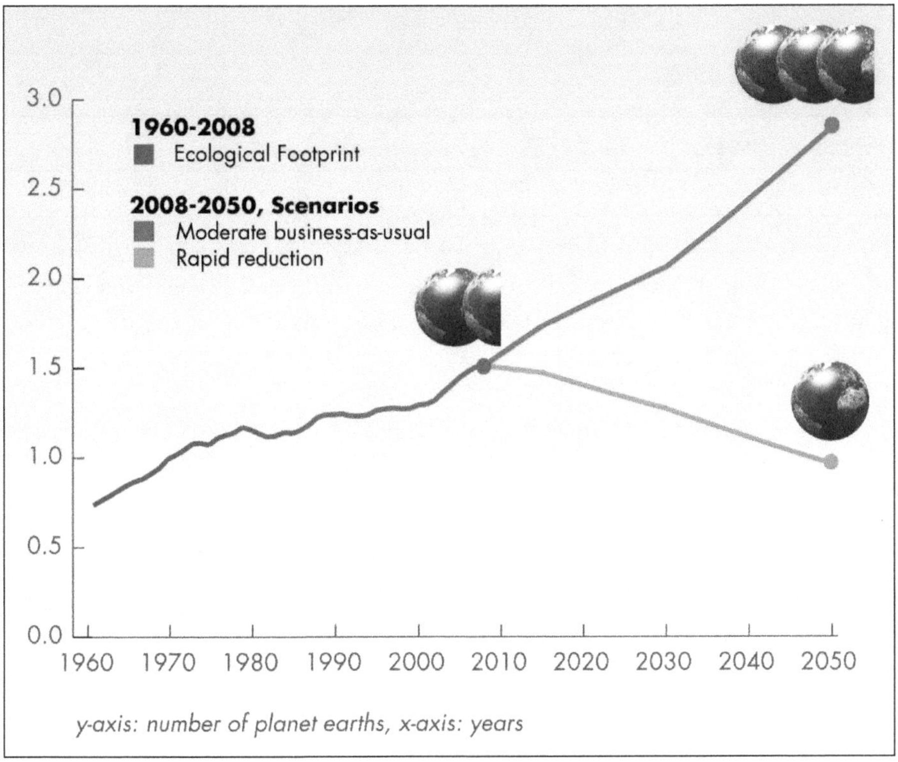

3.0
2.5
2.0
1.5
1.0
0.5
0.0
1960-2008
Ecological Footprint
2008-2050, Scenarios
Moderate business-as-usual
Rapid reduction
1960 1970 1980 1990 2000 2010 2020 2030 2040 2050
y-axis: number of planet earths, x-axis: years

It is estimated that we are now using 150 percent of the earth's sustainable biocapacity. Based on current trends—including an estimated global population of 9 billion in 2050—humans' ecological footprint will be at 230 percent by mid-century.

Source: FootprintNetwork.org.

long and not without worsening the prospects for future generations. Merely ensuring that new activities are less damaging than current ones cannot protect the biosphere. A trickling-down of expanding material wealth cannot be counted on to deal with poverty. And while conventional economic incentives and technological innovation can do much, they evidently cannot always replace what we exhaust and fix what we break. Faith in growth, mitigation of damage, trickle-down wealth distribution, and automatic economic and technical fixes is no longer viable. Instead of merely running faster, we need to move to a different path. And most of the responsibility and capacity for making that move lies with the rich countries, including ours.

For environmental law, these are the two central aspects of the big picture context and challenge: the practical need to accept and embrace complexity, and the moral imperative to make a transition to more sustainable foundations for livelihoods and well-being. This chapter explores these central aspects and considers their implications for environmental law.

Complexity Basics

Probably since the origins of our species, humans have tried to understand the workings of the world. Usually we have recognized that much of it is beyond us. Most cultures accepted trickster spirits or unpredictable divinities. Briefly in the 19th century, the rise of modern science provided expectations of certainty. The core idea was that essentially simple laws of nature acted on individual components of the universe—from atoms to galaxies and viruses to human beings—and that by identifying these laws and applying properly rigorous methods, we could figure out everything, dominate nature, organize ourselves rationally, and progress steadily upwards.[5] Then came the 20th century, with its subatomic physics, systems ecology, and brutal wars among the most advanced nations. Today, the foundations of certainty have become wobbly again.

At least, that is what has happened in the realms of philosophy, advanced science, and cultural criticism. On the ground, for example in the design and application of environmental law, the idea of simple laws and consequent certainty persisted long after its best-before date. Most of the environmental regulatory regimes initially established in the 1970s assumed that the world was a very simple place. They addressed particular contaminants one by one as if they did not interact and as if controlled laboratory studies of individual substances would tell us all we needed to know about the effects of the chemical soups we breathe and ingest. The old regimes considered impacts in the traditional silos of air, land, and water without accounting for the many interrelated pathways for pollution. Often, they also seemed to assume that contaminants and other environmental abuses do not cross political and administrative boundaries and do not require integrated interjurisdictional responses.

Much the same is true of the old approaches to planning and management. Forest management regimes, for example, were typically based on the assumption that forests existed chiefly to supply us with lumber and pulp fibre and that other roles and purposes—such as traditional harvesting, ecological services, recreational opportunities, wildlife habitat, and carbon sink provision—could be safely ignored.

While the old thinking still underpins a significant portion of environmental law and practice today, we now know better. The best of the new environmental laws recognize that the most important threats to nature and our health and well-being come from combinations of contaminants, development projects, and planning decisions. They act across the lines of municipal, provincial, and national jurisdictions, and through a host of mechanisms—from watershed-based planning and landform protection to global environmental agreements. And they recognize that even with the best scientists and unlimited resources, we will never know all we need to know to make fully competent decisions. The world is too complex for that.

What we have been learning in environmental law parallels and is informed by developments in other fields where the study of component parts and the search for firm rules of behaviour have given way to greater appreciation of complex interactions and interdependencies, system dynamics, uncertainty, and surprise. Ecosystem studies may be the most visible field of **complex systems** application. But similar ideas inform advanced work in biophysical and human systems, from microbiology to the global climate, cybernetics, chemistry, anthropology, psychology, meteorology, history, and governance, including law.[6]

Dynamics, Interactions, and Human Choices

The particulars of complex systems ideas and applications vary from one field to the next. It matters, for example, whether the complex system includes humans making conscious choices. Where humans are involved, it matters whether they think the system has desirable qualities worthy of protection (e.g., watersheds with clean water or communities with amiable diversity) or regrettable qualities that need correction (e.g., industries with polluting emissions). Nonetheless, some basic insights apply widely.

Most fundamentally, the complexities of our world arise from dynamic interactions within and among system components at all scales from subatomic particles to cosmic radiation. Human individuals are themselves good examples. Each of us can be seen as a system with billions of resident bacteria, neural connections, and repair mechanisms plus flows of incoming and outgoing nutrients, air, ideas, and emotions, as well as cycles of maturation, reproduction, and expiration. Moreover, each of us participates in larger systems. We affect and are affected by systems centred on water and energy, food and shelter, communication and comprehension, production and consumption, economy and polity, custom and law—all of which are changing, overlapping, and mutually influential at many scales.

Some of these interactions follow identifiable rules, such as Newton's laws of motion or the laws governing chemical reactions. While the processes involved may be numerous and complicated, the results are predictable. That is why we can build rockets and fly to the moon. But most interactions in ecosystems, communities, and socio-ecological systems are beyond complicated. Complex systems feature mutually influential interactions among multitudes of linked factors, with positive and negative feedbacks, and unpredictable if not entirely surprising effects. Predictive difficulties arise in part because complex systems' responses to internal or external disruptions are often non-linear. Populations of species subject to heavy harvesting or predatory pressures (e.g., northern cod off the Canadian east coast) may decline

---

complex system   an identifiable grouping of many interacting components whose combined characteristics are affected by dynamic internal as well as external pressures and whose behaviour is at best imperfectly predictable

BOX 3.1 » Climate Change Complexities

For the past quarter century, global climate change has been among the world's most extensively studied scientific topics and most pressing public policy issues. The research, summarized by the Intergovernmental Panel on Climate Change (IPCC),[*] has established that human source greenhouse gas (GHG) emissions are the major cause of rising atmospheric concentrations, that the effects are already beginning to undermine the established patterns of global climate system behaviour, and that unless GHG emissions are sharply reduced, their adverse effects on future generations will be severe. Despite all the research, however, great uncertainty remains about many key concerns, including whether, where, and when climate changes will be gradual or abrupt.

The uncertainties persist mostly because global climate systems are highly complex. These systems involve vast numbers of interacting factors, great and small. The factors are too numerous and the interactions too poorly understood to permit adequate inclusion in even the most sophisticated computer models. Many of the interactions have non-linear effects, including **positive feedbacks**. For example, warmer arctic temperatures lead to increased melting of arctic ice and consequently less reflective surfaces, more melting of permafrost, more release of previously trapped methane (a potent GHG), even more melting, and on through the cycle again.[†]

Such positive feedbacks raise the potential for sudden climate shifts rather than gradual changes. Because we do not know what GHG loadings might take us across a regional or global climate system threshold into sudden or irreversible changes, we are left to make decisions on the basis of incomplete information about very serious and increasing risks.

So far, the international record of efforts to slow climate change has been typified by failures to meet modest objectives and revisions of commitments to facilitate additional delay. Some of the inaction can be attributed to complexity. There is no possible simple route to global agreement among nations on what needs to be done and how to allocate responsibility for action, especially when the looming effects are not precisely defined and mostly in the future.

But complexity can also serve effective climate change action. Many of the initiatives needed to avoid disastrous climate change would interact in mutually supporting ways and bring multiple benefits beyond climate change mitigation. For example, well-designed measures to curb urban sprawl and encourage urban densification would not only cut GHG emissions but also strengthen public transit, reduce servicing costs, facilitate protection of foodlands and ecosystems, spur a shift from car culture and, with a little creativity, give us more convivial places to live.[‡] And plenty of opportunities exist to combine those efforts with others (more efficient buildings, local energy generation from renewable sources, renewal of the urban forest, etc.) that would contribute similarly to virtuous circles of improvement.

---

[*]   IPCC reports are available at http://www.ipcc.ch/publications_and_data/publications_and_data_reports.shtml.

[†]   See, e.g., Susan Solomon, Dahe Qin, Martin Manning, Zhenlin Chen, Melinda Marquis, Kristen Averyt, Melinda Tignor, and Henry LeRoy Miller Jr., eds., *Climate Change 2007: Working Group I: The Physical Science Basis* (Cambridge: Cambridge University Press, 2007), at s. 8.7.2.4 Methane Hydrate Instability/ Permafrost Methane, http://www.ipcc.ch/publications_and_data/ar4/wg1/en/ch8s8-7-2-4.html.

[‡]   See, e.g., Pamela Blais, *Perverse Cities* (Vancouver: UBC Press, 2010); Andres Duany and Jeff Speck with Mike Lydon, *The Smart Growth Manual* (New York: McGraw-Hill, 2010); and Mark Roseland, *Toward Sustainable Communities*, 4th ed. (Gabriola Island, BC: New Society, 2012).

---

positive feedback   a cyclical process in which a complex system responds to a perturbation in ways that expand, intensify, and/or extend the initial effect only gradually until their **adaptive capacity** is exhausted, then collapse suddenly (see Figure 3.3).

Although a threshold between adaptability and collapse may be anticipated, it is usually difficult to locate until after it has been crossed. What happens after a collapse is often also beyond reliable prediction. Some systems go through more or less regular cycles of destruction and reorganization without much change in basic structure and function. Boreal forests recovering after fire can be like that. So can perennial gardens re-emerging after winter. In other cases, systems that are pushed beyond a threshold may reorganize in a quite different form, with different compon-

Figure 3.3   The Collapse of a Species

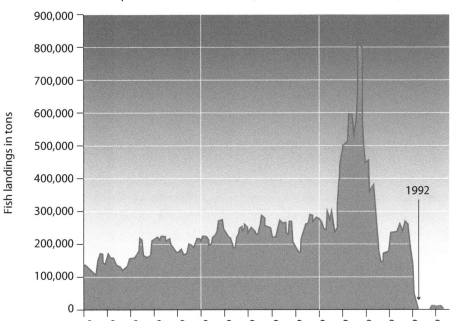

Collapse of Atlantic Cod Stocks (East Coast of Newfoundland), 1992

After 500 years of commercial fishing, northwest Atlantic cod stocks collapsed in the early 1990s, mostly due to overfishing. Despite a fishing moratorium since 1992, the stocks have not recovered.

Source: Adapted from Millennium Ecosystems Assessment.

---

adaptive capacity   the ability of a human and/or biophysical system to make adjustments in response to a potential or actual disturbance or its consequences without compromising the system's core characteristics

ents, relations, and behaviours. Atlantic aquatic ecosystems may reorganize with few northern cod. Coastal fishing communities may reorganize to harvest crab or serve whale-watching tourists. Or they may fall into decline as their most active members leave for jobs elsewhere.

What happens in complex systems is in part the biophysical working out of many linked interactions and effects. But human choices are also involved. The significance of human effects throughout the biosphere has now inspired proposals for the current geological epoch to be named the Anthropocene.[7] While many of our effects have been unintended, humans clearly can and do engage in intentional interventions to alter their biophysical, socio-economic, and cultural environments. We choose components and characteristics to encourage or suppress. We select valued places and qualities to protect, rehabilitate, or enhance. We identify current or emerging problems to correct and develop strategies to alter our environment and our own behaviour to deliver more desirable futures. In the past, we made many regrettable choices, perhaps most often out of ignorance. Recognizing that we live in a highly complex world in which most decisions must rely on incomplete information about the nature, even the existence, of key variables, does not excuse us from making tough decisions about how to live in such a world. It does not even provide an excuse for poor choices. It does, however, have major implications for the substance and process of decision-making.

Complexity Implications for Environmental Law

Environmental law is one of many tools for guiding decision-making. All of them can be designed and wielded poorly—with too much confidence, too little courage, or, most dangerously, too little understanding of the relevant factors and effects and too little awareness of what to do in the face of uncertainty. For environmental law, the most important implications of living with complexity fall under three imperatives: (1) respect uncertainty; (2) embrace complexity as a practical basis for understanding and action; and (3) foster both resilience and transformation. All three are a challenge for traditional law, including environmental law. Uncertainty does not fit well with expectations for proof beyond reasonable doubt. But the law can and must adapt.

Respect Uncertainty

Complexity entails uncertainty and uncertainty entails **risk**. One appropriate response is humility and associated restraint. Some risks can be calculated with considerable precision. In complex contexts, however, important risks may be open only to rough description, and what we do not know may be crucial.[8] Consequently,

---

risk the possibility of harming or losing something valuable; risk significance depends on the likelihood and severity of the harm or loss

where there is uncertainty and possibly significant risk (taking into account what little may be known or surmised about the likelihood and severity of potential harm and the importance of what may be harmed), prudent decision-making is precautionary. The **precautionary principle** favours risk avoidance or **mitigation** in the absence of scientific certainty.[9]

To lower risks in the face of uncertainty, decision-making processes may be designed to place the burden of "proof" (or at least the burden of presenting a convincing argument that there will be no appreciable risk of harm) on those who propose to introduce or continue the possibly significant risky behaviour in question (e.g., applying a new pesticide or growing a genetically modified crop). Other risk mitigation measures available in environmental law include incorporation of a substantial margin of safety (e.g., between permitted exposures to toxins and levels known to cause health or other damage). The safety margin is especially important where effects thresholds, especially for the most vulnerable, are not well understood. Law-based financial tools can also be effective. For example, measures that successfully impose full financial responsibility for any needed cleanup and rehabilitation (e.g., of mine tailings ponds) can shift proponent motivations enough to reduce risks of lasting damage and public cost.

Also, rather than trying to define a line between acceptable and unacceptable risk and determine whether a proposed product, project, or activity crosses that line, precautionary decision processes may require comparative evaluation of alternatives and favour options that present the lowest risks.[10] In such processes, preference for risk avoidance is incorporated in evaluation criteria. Criteria for comparing electrical energy system plan options, for instance, may include a preference for safe-fail options (e.g., energy demand reduction measures that can fail without significant risks to human health or the environment) over fail-safe options (such as nuclear generating facilities that require multiple shut down and containment features because a serious release of radioactive contaminants would be catastrophic). Similar preference can be given to options that are reversible, easy to monitor, simple to repair, accompanied by fallback alternatives, and/or sufficiently small and diverse that the system can function well enough if some raise unexpected problems and need to be taken out of service (e.g., a system with many small and different electricity generation sources is likely to be more adaptable in the face of minimally predictable accidents and demand changes than one that relies on a few very large hydro dams or nuclear plants).

---

precautionary principle   the proposition that caution should be paramount when an activity raises threats of harm to health or the environment, and that the proponent of the activity should bear the burden of proving that it is safe; a principle used to support the notion that where the threat of serious or irreversible damage exists, a lack of full scientific certainty should not be used as a reason for postponing measures to prevent environmental degradation

mitigation   the reduction of a problem or the risk of an undesirable effect

Dealing with risks in environmental law is, however, rarely a matter of simply avoiding potential perils. Often there are **trade-offs**. Avoiding one set of predictable negative effects and further risks may introduce other problems. For example, improved venting of workplace contaminants may reduce occupational health risks but raise contaminant exposures for children in the adjoining neighbourhood. Imposing strict environmental risk reduction measures may encourage some target companies to close facilities that have provided valued employment or to shift production to less well regulated jurisdictions with more vulnerable people and ecosystems.

Ideally, and in practice probably more often than we normally expect, we could find or develop alternatives that avoid undesirable trade-offs—by reducing risks to all receptors, providing both job security and environmental protection, etc. Such alternatives are, however, discoverable only if we look for them.[11] For environmental law, that underlines the importance of processes that require comparative evaluation of alternatives, favour risk avoidance and demand explicit identification of and justification for trade-offs.

Decisions about trade-offs are value-laden. They may be illuminated by technical studies of various kinds, but in the end they also involve the understanding, preferences, and priorities of the decision-makers. The same is true of many other choices in complex situations (e.g., what purposes should be served by a new undertaking? Which alternatives are most likely to be feasible and desirable? Which of the potentially infinite number of interacting factors are important enough to merit careful consideration?). Respecting uncertainty therefore entails special attention to participation and learning—finding fair, open, and credible ways of involving and representing people with an interest in the results (including future generations) and enhancing their understanding of the issues, options, information sources, and uncertainties.[12]

Strengthening understanding throughout society, not merely among decision-makers, is especially important because uncertainty can foster toxic forms of doubt. Perhaps inevitably, uncertainty undermines the foundations for confidence in scientific and other expertise. That is to some degree positive. Willingness to question received wisdom has often been a driver of change for the better. But problems arise when healthy skepticism declines into abandonment of rigorous efforts to understand the issues and to distinguish good evidence and logical analysis from mere opinion. This concern is not peculiar to law or environmental issues. It is, however, exacerbated when pervasive signs of complexity are accompanied by equally pervasive public conflicts—including ones before courts, tribunals, and other formal proceedings—where heavily credentialed experts line up on opposing sides of environmental and other controversies.

---

trade-off the sacrifice of something desirable to gain a different benefit or advantage

While the design of adversarial processes is a sensible means of testing evidence, the visible performance can be easy to interpret as an exercise of power and interest rather than an effort to enhance understanding. Such interpretations foster cynicism and resignation in the public and weaken defences against authorities who are willing to sacrifice careful adjudicative processes if that might serve an immediate political agenda. Neither result is compatible with a desirable future. The implications point to the second imperative.

Embrace Complexity as a Practical Base for Understanding and Action

Complexity is difficult. Dynamic, multi-scale interactions with non-linear results may be a common and inescapable feature of reality, but they are a managerial nightmare for organizations designed on simpler premises. In both the private and public sectors, organizations whose structure and culture favour clear rules and tidily arranged boxes of mandate and expertise can be expected to resist calls to address the interconnections and uncertainties of complex issues. Some private sector corporations facing complex demands for greater social and environmental responsibility have simply asserted an exclusive obligation to enhance shareholder value. Others have relied on public relations gestures as a cover for business as usual. Similarly, some governments have claimed to recognize complex challenges but have avoided effective action on climate change, biodiversity loss, and other outcomes of cumulative interactive effects. Other governments have gone further by restricting existing openings for attention to complexities (e.g., narrowing the scope and application of legislated obligations and restricting public engagement opportunities) in the name of regulatory manageability and affordability. These simplifying strategies are unlikely to be viable in the long term for corporations or governments. But even bodies willing to act on the demands of complex reality find the challenges daunting.

The challenges of complexity can be exaggerated, however. Embracing complexity has the great advantage of fitting with the actual world. At the conceptual level, a complex issue with a suite of potential response options is by common understanding more challenging than a simple issue with a single identified response. But that understanding applies practically only where core issues and suitable responses actually are simple. While that is sometimes the case, we have repeatedly found that treating complex issues as if they were simple tends to multiply consequent problems. For example, in the early 1970s, when government and industry interests chose to mitigate local air pollution by constructing tall emission stacks, their simple solution engendered regional-to-continental scale acidic precipitation demanding responses that consumed enormously greater resources and organizational capacities. More generally, embracing the complexities of early action to anticipate and prevent social injustices and environmental abuses is likely to be easier, cheaper, and more efficient in the long run than quick approvals that neglect key factors and connections and leave others to deal with the messy consequences.

Attention to complexities can also expand benefits. Because our world is actually complex, decision-making approaches that address complexities (e.g., endangered species laws that focus on maintaining ecosystems—see Chapter 11) are more realistic and consequently more likely to be effective. Similarly, approval processes that compare alternatives, consult stakeholders, recognize positive as well as adverse interactions, and favour precaution are likely to identify solutions that can help resolve multiple problems and avoid generating difficult new ones. This approach has been used to deal with garbage, for example. The standard approach was once simply to build new dumps when old ones were full. But the proliferation of dump grievances eventually pushed governments to introduce more demanding approval processes, including more serious consideration of alternatives. The results led to multi-faceted waste management with reduction, reuse, and recycling initiatives spreading back through product lifecycles and gradually enhancing resource efficiencies all along the way.

Similar stories can be drawn from experience in a variety of fields. In energy system and water management planning, for example, the standard practice was simply to provide additional conventional supply (new coal, hydro, and nuclear generating plants for energy or new dams, diversions, and aquifer tapping for water) to meet ever-rising demand. Advanced authorities are now moving to more complex integrated system planning with multiple linked components managing demand and providing incremental supply for diverse benefits (see Chapter 11). In forest management, as noted earlier, governments have reformed decision-making processes to do a better job of recognizing and accommodating multiple forest uses. In urban planning, rapidly growing metropolitan areas are moving from simply servicing development to much more ambitious efforts to encourage more density and public transit instead of cars and sprawl, again as the best way to address a range of current and looming issues.

All of these shifts have been difficult and slow. In most places, they are far from complete. They demand additional and unfamiliar capacities, and more public involvement and learning. In the absence of established traditions, they are also experimental and sometimes unsuccessful. But it is reasonable to expect that practice will improve with experience, and that by embracing the complexity of actual problems and opportunities, these more ambitious approaches will increasingly deliver a greater range of benefits while avoiding risks. Fewer risky undertakings and fewer unanticipated problems should reduce regulatory burdens. Perhaps counterintuitively, embracing complexity is a route to efficiency in the long run. Complexity-embracing processes will not be initially quicker or easier, but efficiency is about gaining the greatest enhancement of performance with the least expenditure of resources. Approaches designed for complex reality are more likely to do that than approaches that rest on simplistic assumptions and lead to a proliferation of problems.

Foster Both Resilience and Transformation

The dynamics of complex systems involve two main responses to pressures from internal and external sources: **resilience** and **transformation**. If a system can find ways to retain its basic structures and functions by deflecting or accommodating the new pressures, it is said to be resilient. If it is forced (or possibly, in human systems, if the participants choose) to abandon or alter some key structures and functions, the system has made a transition or has transformed. These are not either–or options. In their interactions with countless other systems at various scales, systems may exhibit both resilience and transformation.[13] The distinction between resilience and transformation is nonetheless important. We want to maintain and perhaps enhance the resilience of desirable systems. But we want undesirable systems to change for the better, and nudging a problematic system over a threshold into transformation entails overcoming the system's resilience.

Strategies to Enhance Resilience

A considerable literature now explains how to protect and enhance the resilience of valued ecosystems, vulnerable youth, communities facing economic decline or extreme weather events and other (partly) natural disasters, and many other systems that are assumed to be desirable. What works depends heavily on the peculiarities of context. Resilience experts have, however, identified generally applicable resilience-enhancing strategies that focus on strengthening adaptive capacity through greater flexibility, self-reliant components, diversity of resources, redundancies and fallback options, monitoring of changes, sharing of information, accountability and trust, mutual aid, fairness, and equity.[14] The key underlying idea is that sufficient adaptive capacity will allow human and ecological communities to act and adjust without being pushed across a threshold to major changes with minimally predictable and potentially adverse results.

For environmental law, means of enhancing adaptive capacity and resilience are important considerations in the rehabilitation and protection of desirable systems (e.g., in designing law-based incentives or penalties to encourage preservation of remaining wetlands, or using public participation provisions in existing laws to help disadvantaged neighbourhoods oppose noxious land uses). But while many environmental

---

resilience in complex systems, the ability to resist and/or accommodate disturbance and change while retaining identifying characteristics (including structure, functions, and processes)

transformation in complex systems, a shift from one set of identifying system characteristics to another, including more or less significant changes in structure, functions, and/or processes

law initiatives aim to protect and enhance desirable systems and system components, much of environmental law is devoted to halting and reversing undesirable practices, where reliance on goodwill and voluntary action has been insufficient.

Many of the problems addressed by environmental law are caused or maintained by deeply entrenched thinking and practices, perhaps located in or supported by powerful private and public sector organizations. The relevant systems of thought, motivation, organization, and practice may be highly resilient, in the sense of being well-equipped to resist change, but they are damaging to the environment and to the public interest. In such circumstances, the aim of environmental law is transformation, and appropriate strategies involve overcoming the resilience of the target systems, pushing them across thresholds of change, and helping them reform with structures and functions that are desirable as well as resilient.

Strategies for Transformative Change

Defining generally applicable strategies for transformative change in complex systems is more difficult than defining generic strategies for enhancing resilience. That is because of the great differences among needs for transformation, the common impossibility of knowing where a threshold for change lies, the complex interactions of intentional disruptions and accidental factors that can push systems across thresholds, and the exceptional openness of transforming systems to influences that could lead to a range of results, including regrettable ones. As we will see in the following discussion about (un)sustainability, significant transformations are clearly needed if we are to reverse dangerous current trends and enhance prospects for lasting well-being. That need, however, does not justify overconfident and ill-considered impositions. In environmental law as elsewhere, efforts to foster change need to be approached with care.

Where human organizations facing challenges choose to transform themselves, they can turn to guidance from several fields, including transition management and social innovation, which are informed by complex systems understanding. Common recommendations include humility and precaution, acceptance of gradual change, emphasis on long-term thinking, attention to influences at multiple scales, use of **backcasting** as well as **forecasting**, creation of openings for creative experimentation with alternatives, use of diverse motivations, and commitment to participatory engagement, fairness, and learning.[15]

---

backcasting a tool for future-oriented planning that centres on identifying a desired future objective or set of desired future characteristics and then seeking viable pathways from the present to the desired future; it is typically posed in contrast with forecasting; it is less tied to current systems and system dynamics than forecasting

forecasting a tool for future-oriented planning that centres on the projection of current trends into the future with adjustments for foreseeable influences

Some environmental law initiatives involve governments transforming their own behaviour, such as by requiring environmental assessments of their own projects or establishing rules for more open public access to government information. But probably the bulk of environmental law is passed by governments aiming to change the behaviour of others—municipalities, private corporations, landowners, citizens, etc. In these cases, the strategic recommendations listed above for internal transformations need to be accompanied by special emphasis on the engagement, fairness, and learning elements as well as on broadening and strengthening motivations to adopt the desired changes. That is because simply imposing new requirements on unwilling and ill-informed participants is rarely effective and almost never efficient. There are too many motives and openings for avoidance and never enough resources for monitoring and enforcement. Especially now that governments are widely thought to be at the limits of their managerial capacities, initiatives for change must be well understood, widely accepted, and supported by multiple encouragements for adoption, often including economic enticements as well as prohibitions and obligations.

Underlying all of these issues about strategies for protection and change is a larger and more fundamental question. How is desirability determined? How do we distinguish a desirable system whose resilience should be enhanced from an undesirable one in need of transformation? And how do we determine what characteristics should be sought in a transformed system? We might reasonably expect that minimally disturbed ecological systems are usually desirable, perhaps intrinsically and at least in their contributions to maintaining ecological goods and services for humans. But some of those systems include malaria, HIV, and the Ebola virus. We might also reasonably expect that evidently resilient human and socio-ecological systems have demonstrated desirability. But the Mafia has long been an impressively resilient human organization, and in recorded history the longest lasting particular socio-ecological system was probably the deeply inegalitarian civilization of Egypt in the time of the Pharaohs. While resilience qualities are crucial for maintaining desirable systems, they do not offer a sufficient basis for determining what is desirable now or in a transformed future. For that, it is helpful to turn to our other great contextual theme: sustainability.

Sustainability Basics

In its dictionary definition, *sustainability* sounds much like the objective of resilience. The difference lies in the concept's history and practical use. Sustainability and **sustainable development**, which for our purposes are essentially the same idea,

---

sustainable development "development that meets the needs of the present without compromising the ability of future generations to meet their own needs" (World Commission on Environment and Development, 1987); it involves improving the quality of human life and enhancing equity in the distribution of well-being while living within the carrying capacity of the planet's biophysical systems over the long term

arose in global deliberations about how to reconcile human advancement—especially the elimination of poverty—with stewardship of the biophysical environment. Sustainability has always been about what is desirable as well as lasting in a world where human well-being is ultimately and inevitably dependent on the biosphere. Also, in a world where human activities are pushing us into ever deeper unsustainability, reversing those trends is at the heart of what is desirable. Sustainability is therefore about transformation as well as resilience.

BOX 3.2 » The Blue Marble

"The Blue Marble" photograph was taken on December 7, 1972, by the crew of the *Apollo 17*.

Source: NASA/Goddard Space Flight Center.

Serious attention to sustainability issues would have been more difficult before 1972, when NASA released the first Blue Marble image showing earth from space.* The small, mostly blue ball floating in a black void captured the fundamental reality that this one planet is our home, and vast though it may seem to us on the surface, it is limited and vulnerable.

The notion of sustainability rests on attention to limits.[†] Lasting well-being is not possible unless we keep within the boundaries of what we can do without wrecking our basis for survival. Now that we have appropriated and are stressing the entire habitable planet, we have no alternative if we overreach.

Acceptance of limits has faced fierce resistance because the idea of limits clashes with current economic and political dependence on unending growth. While economic expansion can and should be defined and pursued in ways that reduce human pressures on the biosphere (and distribute the benefits much more equitably), that is not what the current economic systems deliver.

Not surprisingly, this resistance has led to great interest in defining the limits to planetary capacities. Unfortunately, none of the major limits is open to precise definition. With climate change, we know that atmospheric concentrations of carbon dioxide, which were never above 300 ppm before the modern era, are now 400 ppm and still rising.[‡] But as we have seen, specifying a precise point at which additional carbon dioxide and other GHG emissions will tip us over the brink into disastrous climate change is precluded by the complexities of the issue (and by different perspectives on what qualifies as "disastrous").

Most other limits are even further beyond precise identification. Unlike climate change, problems such as depletion of soils and groundwater, loss of biodiversity and wild fisheries, exposure to unprecedented mixes of synthetic and other chemicals, and demands for energy and materials are global only as the cumulative result of countless local and regional activities. They involve a wide diversity of the specific concerns and limits, and many of the local and regional limits are not absolute. Some repairs and replacements are possible (e.g., through introduction of new technologies to increase efficiencies of use or reduce extractive damage). Limits remain, and we are increasingly pressing them because repairing and replacing have only slowed the rate of damage. Moreover, the resulting problems interact through combined stresses (e.g., soil depletion rates are worsened by extreme weather events due to climate change) and trade-offs (e.g., protecting biodiversity in one place may add to development pressures elsewhere).

Better data and more sophisticated approaches to defining regional and planetary limits can reduce these difficulties. But precision about the limits is neither realistic nor necessary. The key realities are the evidence of ever-increasing demands upon the Blue Marble and the warning signs of systemic stress. We do not need a clearly defined limit to GHG emissions to know that today's unprecedented atmospheric concentrations are already dangerous and will have further delayed effects and that we need to move as quickly as possible to convert to non-GHG alternatives. For the cumulative regional stresses, it is perhaps easier to recognize and act on more localized problems and possibilities, collaborating where possible and working to ensure that effective responses will combine into global solutions just as continuing environmental abuses have accumulated into global problems.

Happily, we have plenty of openings for improving well-being while decreasing demands on the biosphere, especially by decoupling prosperity from material and energy expansion (at least for those already materially comfortable) and by greatly enhancing equity in the distribution of benefits.[§] The Blue Marble's limits are accompanied by endless opportunities for our creativity and advancement.

---

[*]   For the first Blue Marble images, see http://visibleearth .nasa.gov/view.php?id=57723. On the image's importance, see Libby Robin and Will Steffen, "History for the Anthropocene" (2007) 5:5 *History Compass* 1694.

[†]   Limits are emphasized in the most often-quoted definition of *sustainable development,* found in the report of the World Commission on Environment and Development, *Our Common Future* (Oxford: Oxford University Press, 1987):

> Sustainable development is development that meets the needs of the present without compromising the ability of future generations to meet their own needs. It contains within it two key concepts:
>
> • the concept of needs, in particular the essential needs of the world's poor, to which overriding priority should be given; and
> • the idea of limitations imposed by the state of technology and social organization on the environment's ability to meet present and future needs.

[‡]   See US Environmental Protection Agency, "Climate Change Indicators in the United States," May 2014, http://www.epa.gov/climatechange/science/indicators/ ghg/ghg-concentrations.html.

[§]   See, e.g., Tim Jackson, *Prosperity Without Growth: Economics for a Finite Planet* (London: Earthscan, 2009); Peter Victor, *Managing Without Growth: Slower by Design, Not Disaster* (Cheltenham, UK: Edward Elgar, 2008); Herman Daly, *Beyond Growth: The Economics of Sustainable Development* (Boston: Beacon Press, 1996); and Joan Martinez-Allier, Unai Pascual, Frank-Dominique Vivien, and Edwin Zaccai, "Sustainable De-growth: Mapping the Context, Criticisms and Future Prospects of an Emerging Paradigm" (2010) 69 *Ecological Economics* 1741.

Sustainability as a desirable agenda has two central components:

- concern for the well-being of future generations as well as those of the present, and
- comprehensive coverage of all the core issues of decision-making that affect lasting well-being.

Our understanding of these two central components has evolved over the past few decades as we have learned more about the nature and implications of complexity and about the unsustainability of important current trends. The goal of sustainability is now generally recognized to be a dynamic set of desirable characteristics rather than a fixed target with defined parameters. Also, we now see more clearly that the factors affecting progress toward sustainability are not well captured by separate attention to the social, economic, and ecological (or, more accurately, biophysical) pillars of sustainability. The links and interdependencies between and among these pillars are crucial. As the World Commission on Environment and Development (usually called the Brundtland commission) recognized in the 1980s, poverty cannot be overcome without also rehabilitating and securing the biophysical foundations for viable livelihoods, such as fertile soils and clean water.[16] The pursuit of sustainability is consequently not about balancing social, economic, and ecological objectives, but about seeing what is needed for lasting well-being and addressing all of these needs at once in ways that are mutually reinforcing.

In both theory and practice, the concept of sustainability has been explored as a desirable objective, a set of guides for decision-making, and a foundation for identifying appropriate indicators of advancement or decline. Some approaches have focused on top-down expert identification of broadly applicable principles. Others have favoured more participative bottom-up efforts centred on what matters in a particular situation. For most practical purposes, certainly for the development and application of environmental law in Canadian jurisdictions, both generic and specific understandings are needed.

The basics of what is required for progress toward sustainability can be drawn quite easily from the substantial record of global thought and experience on these matters. The specifics about what is desirable and feasible depend on the context of the application. The perils, possibilities, and preferences for sustainable community planning in Tuktoyaktuk differ from those in Toronto. Regulating the use of forests, fisheries, and other renewable resources that should be sustainable in perpetuity is different from regulating mining or hydrocarbon extraction activities that deplete their resources. Defining short- and long-term objectives, recognizing valued social and ecological qualities to maintain or strengthen, identifying undesirable stresses and trends, and determining what options for response are potentially realistic depend significantly on the particulars of the context. So does deciding what roles environmental law could usefully play, at what points in deliberation and action, in whose hands, and in combination with what other tools and resources.

The eight points presented in Box 3.3 summarize what is needed for progress toward sustainability everywhere. These core generic requirements reflect the most commonly recognized considerations in the sustainability literature and incorporate overlapping insights about respecting uncertainty and embracing complexity. Because of the direct focus on requirements for progress toward sustainability, the eight points are not organized under the commonly used social, economic, and ecological pillars. While the pillars fit well with existing government agency mandates and areas of academic expertise, they do not encourage attention to links and interdependencies. Not surprisingly, in a world of complex interactions, the core

BOX 3.3 » Core Generic Requirements for Progress Toward Sustainability

- *Socio-ecological system integrity.* Restore and strengthen the resilience of desirable systems and build the transformative capacities of systems needing significant change.
- *Livelihood sufficiency and opportunity.* Ensure for everyone sustainable livelihoods, including opportunities to enhance well-being that do not compromise options for future generations.
- *Intragenerational equity.* Close dangerous gaps in sufficiency and opportunity (e.g., in health, security, social recognition, and political influence) between the rich and the poor.
- *Intergenerational equity.* Preserve or enhance the opportunities and capabilities of future generations to live sustainably.
- *Resource maintenance and efficiency.* Reduce extractive damage, avoid waste, and cut overall material and energy use.
- *Socio-ecological civility and democratic governance.* Build public as well as institutional understanding of and commitment to respectful socio-ecological relations, and enhance capacities of all to participate effectively in governance for sustainability.
- *Precaution and adaptation.* Respect uncertainty, avoid risks of damage to the foundations for sustainability; plan to learn, design for surprise, and manage for adaptation.
- *Immediate and long-term integration.* Address all sustainability requirements at once, seeking mutually supportive benefits and multiple gains.

Source: Adapted from Robert B. Gibson et al., *Sustainability Assessment: Criteria and Processes* (London: Earthscan, 2005), chapter 5.

requirements for progress toward sustainability do not fit comfortably in the single pillars. All of them involve cross-pillar considerations.

For each practical application, these core requirements need to be integrated with the specific factors defining the case and place. Learning how to identify and integrate those factors is also important. But for the purposes of understanding sustainability imperatives as part of the big picture context for environmental law in Canada, a grasp of the core generic requirements in Box 3.3 is probably sufficient.

Sustainability Implications for Environmental Law

Fifty years ago, when the main components of contemporary environmental law were put in place, it was a bold step to give serious legal attention to air and water pollution, wilderness preservation, occupational health hazards, and resource stewardship. Introducing environmental law obligations meant recognizing a large new set of market system deficiencies that needed to be addressed by government intervention. Winning political support involved overcoming significant resistance from corporate interests unwilling to accept new costs or restrictions and from government authorities hesitant to take on new responsibilities. That it happened at all was due mostly to growing public awareness resulting from the efforts of non-governmental environmental groups, independent scientists, crusading reporters, and the first generation of environmental lawyers.

The initial rise of environmental law was, however, mostly an extension of conventional thinking. The objective was not fundamental change in the structure of decision-making or the direction of progress. Environmental law aimed merely to mitigate some of the undesirable side effects of economic advances, to set some special places aside, and to avoid costly mistakes by doing a better job of planning and resource management. Its most subversive elements were provisions for more transparency and opportunities for public participation in environmentally related decision-making.

The emerging role of environmental law in today's context of evident complexity and deepening unsustainability is considerably more ambitious largely because the old strategies have been insufficient. Despite the advances in environmental law (and associated improvements in, for example, technologies and policies for pollution abatement, energy and material efficiency, waste reduction, and protected area management), overall human pressures on the biosphere continue to rise. And despite the advances in wealth generation, huge numbers of people do not have the basic material requirements (e.g., adequate nutrition and clean water) for healthy lives. In this context, mitigation of adverse effects cannot be enough. Environmental law needs to participate in reversing the direction of change—lowering overall pressures on the biosphere while ensuring sufficiency and opportunity for all. The more ambitious agenda for environmental law (and for many other collaborating fields) entails rejection of many firmly entrenched economic and political ideas and practices. As noted above, progress toward sustainability is not compatible with reliance on ever-expanding use of materials and energy, trickle-down solutions to poverty, and market-driven technological fixes.

In the present context, the proper role for environmental law is transformational (recognizing the discussion above about humility and care in transformation initiatives). The basic substantive implications for environmental law's objectives and key provisions are the core generic requirements for progress toward sustainability set out in Box 3.3, as specified and elaborated for particular jurisdictions and applications. Relative to most if not all current environmental legislation, these core requirements are more demanding. They entail attention to a broader scope of considerations and options—system desirability and associated resilience and transformation implications, distributional effects within and between generations, expansion of opportunities while reducing material and energy demand, precaution, and collaboration and learning. They also emphasize recognizing connections, avoiding trade-offs, and finding the best options to deliver multiple, mutually reinforcing advances on all fronts.

Moreover, the core generic requirements have implications for decision-making processes: how objectives are set and issues defined, how criteria are specified and options compared, how legal and other tools are combined, how administration is organized, how effects are monitored, and how lessons are learned. Commitment to sustainability entails a renewed emphasis on open, participatory, and collaborative processes. This is in part because judgments about desirability are central in sustainability-based deliberations and such judgments are properly matters of public choice. But the main reason for active and informed engagement of citizens and civil society groups as well as government authorities and private sector interests is simply practical. The big transformations required for significant progress toward sustainability are not feasible without mobilization of multiple and diverse skills and perspectives, and development of widely shared awareness, understanding, and commitment. For everyone, progress toward sustainability will involve shared experiences in experimentation, deliberation, and learning. That is, appropriately, one of the places where the process and substance of sustainability merge.

Process and substance, or means and ends, also come together in expanding and extending the vision underlying environmental law's objectives and agenda. The context of sustainability and complexity is global and multi-generational. Some have called it "the big here and the long now."[17] Respecting that reality may be the most daunting implication of sustainability issues for environmental law. Current trends in many aspects of human activity, from communications to capital markets, appear to be running in the opposite direction, toward shorter attention spans and more individually focused self-interest. Even in this era of globalization, the concepts of planetary community and responsibility to future generations are rarely visible. We do, however, have unprecedented technological capacities for global collaboration and foresight, as well as unprecedentedly big and long obligations to meet. And environmental law with its role in addressing large-scale and multi-generational concerns such as climate change, biodiversity loss, and persistent toxic substances has a key role to play.

Finally, the challenges and opportunities raised by the need for progress toward sustainability are neither unique to environmental law nor well enough served by environmental law experts acting on their own. The law offers valuable tools that are useful for encouragement and compulsion, as well as facilitating agreement and strengthening parties' arguments in a conflict. But virtually all of these applications require, or benefit from, the involvement of other fields, players, and expertise in their design and implementation. As noted at the beginning of this chapter, the practice of law is well-suited to integrating ideas and experience from other fields. Dealing effectively with sustainability and complexity will require better efforts in all fields, including environmental law, to collaborate with one another and apply the available tools in mutually supporting ways.

Conclusion

The big picture context for environmental law in Canada is not something going on in the next room. It is directly present and has serious implications not only for how law needs to be designed and applied but also for how its role is defined. The most fundamental aspects of that context are complexity and unsustainability. We live in a highly complex world where prospects for the fair distribution of lasting human well-being are being undermined by increasingly unsustainable demands on the biosphere. These realities both dwarf and help to illuminate more commonly recognized contextual concerns, such as how to regenerate the global economy, overcome entrenched hatreds, and respond to continuing injustices. Although these too are important matters that frequently overlap with environmental law issues, they are just as unlikely to be addressed effectively unless complexity is embraced and unsustainability is reversed.

In this big context, environmental law is an agent of change toward more desirable futures, or at least more desirable future characteristics, possibilities, and options. Some of these changes involve maintaining or strengthening the resilience of desirable ecological and human systems. Others involve more fundamental transformations. In a world of uncertainty and surprise, all of these changes are risky. They should be initiated with care, as experiments backed by adaptive capacities and devoted to learning. To the extent possible, all should also be open and participative, mobilizing and building understanding, skills, and commitment. All should be informed by the full suite of requirements for progress toward sustainability, and all should seek to deliver multiple, mutually reinforcing gains.

In environmental law as in other fields, acting on the implications of complexity and unsustainability is and will be demanding, difficult, and time-consuming. The efficiencies will come through avoidance of more intractable future problems. The agenda will require vision and patience. Today's simplistic assumptions and unsustainable practices are firmly embedded in intertwined economic and political structures, habitual behaviours, and ways of thinking. The required changes will need to be incremental, but collectively and eventually they must transform a culture that supports deepening unsustainability into one with more cheerful prospects for all.

Peter Montague has identified three stages of change for the better:[18]

- Stage one involves individual local victories (e.g., stopping an ill-considered new dump and getting the municipality to do serious waste reduction, reuse, recycling, and composting) that may inspire others to seek similar gains.
- In the second stage, the new approaches are established at least temporarily in law and policy, or in other authoritative tools of government or corporate actors, signalling a shift in the way of doing business.
- Stage three is a cultural transformation, a change in "the climate of opinion" that entrenches more sustainable practice solidly in a new normal of thought

and behaviour, and relegates unsustainable practices to the realm of the unthinkable (e.g., as was accomplished in the abolition of slavery).

Environmental law has positive roles to play in all three stages.

Taken together, the implications for understanding and transformation may seem overwhelming. It is true that plenty of complexities are involved, and this chapter has merely skimmed the surface of the big picture context and what it entails. But this context is the world we all live in now. We are immersed in complexity every day, and most people have experienced enormous change in their own lifetimes. That is already familiar. Moreover, no one can be expected to know it all. The key lessons here are to respect uncertainty, embrace complexity, and seek positive change in ways that respect the core requirements for progress toward sustainability. Even highly imperfect efforts to apply these lessons in the multitudes of possible environmental law initiatives should bring great improvements over business as usual.

SUMMARY OF KEY POINTS

- Environmental law is affected by and in turn affects a vast range of concerns and opportunities—local to global, long-standing and emerging, desirable and catastrophic. The two contextual factors that are most fundamental and significant for the purposes of environmental law are complexity and unsustainability.

- While complexity is commonly recognized as a feature of modern life, it is rarely accepted and addressed as the key characteristic of life on earth. Dynamic human and ecological systems have trajectories and limits that are typically beyond confident prediction, in part because they interact constantly at multiple scales. Uncertainty and complex interconnections have important implications for understanding how to protect desirable but vulnerable systems, how to transform undesirable but entrenched systems, and how to combine action and precaution.

- Deepening unsustainability is the most serious failing of current human practices and the most significant challenge for environmental law. The concept of sustainability, informed by appreciation of complexity, is most useful as an integrated basis for defining what is desirable and potentially lasting. While sustainability language has been misused in many confusing ways, the core requirements for progress toward sustainability are easily identified, provide a sound basis for specification in particular cases and places, and offer a basis for environmental law and other fields to deliver multiple, mutually reinforcing and lasting gains.

KEY TERMS

adaptive capacity	mitigation	risk
backcasting	positive feedback	sustainable development
complex system	precautionary principle	trade-off
forecasting	resilience	transformation

DISCUSSION QUESTIONS

1. How should respect for uncertainty affect the application of environmental law? Would your answer be different for application to industrial innovation, urban planning, or raising a child?
2. How could environmental law be used to improve attention to positive and negative interactive effects within and among complex systems?
3. Describe a plausible environmental law initiative (or a non-law initiative that environmental law could support in various ways) that could serve all eight of the requirements for progress toward sustainability presented in Box 3.3.

SUGGESTED READINGS

Readings Focused Mainly on Complexity

Colander, David, and Roland Kupers. *Complexity and the Art of Public Policy: Solving Society's Problems from the Bottom Up*. Princeton, NJ: Princeton University Press, 2014.

Johnson, Neil. *Simply Complexity: A Clear Guide to Complexity Theory*. London: Oneworld, 2009.

Kay, James J., and Eric Schneider. "Embracing Complexity: The Challenge of the Ecosystem Approach." (1994) 20:3 *Alternatives* 32.

Meadows, Donella. *Thinking in Systems: A Primer*. White River Junction, VT: Chelsea Green, 2008.

Walker, Brian, and David Salt. *Resilience Practice: Building Capacity to Absorb Disturbance and Maintain Function*. Washington, DC: Island Press, 2012.

Waltner-Toews, David, James J. Kay, and Nina-Marie E. Lister, eds. *The Ecosystem Approach: Complexity, Uncertainty and Managing for Sustainability*, esp. chapters 1, 2, and 4. New York: Columbia University Press, 2008.

Readings Focused Mainly on Sustainability

Gibson, Robert B., with Selma Hassan, Susan Holtz, James Tansey, and Graham Whitelaw. *Sustainability Assessment: Criteria and Processes*, chapters 3-5. London: Earthscan, 2005.

Leach, Melissa, et al. "Transforming Innovation for Sustainability." (2012) 17:2 *Ecology and Society* 11, http://www.ecologyandsociety.org/vol17/iss2/art11/.

Ostrom, Elinor. "A General Framework for Analyzing Sustainability of Social-Ecological Systems." (2009) 325 *Science* 419.

World Commission on Environment and Development. "From One Earth to One World: An Overview." In *Our Common Future*, 1-23. Oxford: Oxford University Press, 1987.

Website

International Institute for Sustainable Development (IISD): http://www.iisd.org

NOTES

1. Lewis Carroll, *Through the Looking Glass* (London: Macmillan, 1871), chapter 2, http://www.gutenberg.org/files/12/12-h/12-h.htm.

2. See World Wildlife Federation, *Living Planet Report 2012* (Gland, Switzerland: WWF International, 2012), at 38, http://awsassets.panda.org/downloads/1_lpr _2012_online_full_size_single_pages_final_120516.pdf. The estimate that human pressures are 50 percent over planetary carrying capacity at current levels of human technology and administrative competence is debatable, but many studies have indicated that the estimate is plausible. See, e.g., Millennium Ecosystem Assessment, *Ecosystems and Human Well-Being: Synthesis* (Washington, DC: Island Press, 2005), available with various other reports at http://www.millenniumassessment.org/en/ index.aspx. The key concern is not the precise current level of unsupportable pressures but the continuing rise in these pressures.

3. Food and Agriculture Organization of the United Nations (FAO), *The State of Food Insecurity in the World 2013* (Rome: FAO, 2013), at 8, http://www.fao.org/ publications/sofi/en/.

4. Isabel Ortiz and Matthew Cummins, "Global Inequality: Beyond the Bottom Billion" (working paper, Social and Economic Policy, UNICEF, New York, 2011), at 11-16, http://www.unicef.org/socialpolicy/files/Global_Inequality.pdf.

5. Napoleonic scientist Pierre-Simon Laplace provided the most famous formulation of the notion:

   > An intelligence which at a given instant knew all the forces acting in nature and the position of every object in the universe—if endowed with a brain sufficiently vast to make all necessary calculations—could describe with a single formula the motions of the largest astronomical bodies and those of the smallest atoms. To such an intelligence, nothing would be uncertain; the future, like the past, would be an open book. [Quoted in Jacqueline D. Spears and Dean Zollman, *The Fascination of Physics* (San Francisco: Benjamin Cummings, 1986).]

   The statement has sometimes been condensed as "Give me the positions and velocities of all the particles in the universe, and I will predict the future."

6. Key figures include Ludwig von Bertalanffy and C.S. Holling in systems ecology, Lynn Margulis in microbiology, the Intergovernmental Panel on Climate Change in climate systems, Norbert Wiener in cybernetics, Ilya Prigogine in chemistry, Gregory Bateson in anthropology and psychology, Edward Lorenz in meteorology,

William Hardy McNeill and John Robert McNeill in history, and Elinor Ostrom in governance. For application of complex system thinking in legal studies see, e.g., J.B. Ruhl, "Panarchy and the Law" (2012) 17:3 *Ecology and Society* 31, http://www.ecologyandsociety.org/vol17/iss3/art31/.

7. Joseph Stromberg, "What Is the Anthropocene and Are We in It?" *Smithsonian Magazine*, January 2013, http://www.smithsonianmag.com/science-nature/what-is-the-anthropocene-and-are-we-in-it-164801414/.

8. Potential effects may be poorly understood not only because of the involvement of too many interactive factors but also because of practical and moral barriers to the necessary research (e.g., research into the effects of potential toxin combinations on children). Both of these difficulties qualify as complexity considerations.

9. The best recognized initial statement of the precautionary principle is in Principle 15 of the Rio Declaration on Environment and Development: "Where there are threats of serious or irreversible damage, lack of full scientific certainty shall not be used as a reason for postponing cost-effective measures to prevent environmental degradation." See United Nations Environment Programme, Rio Declaration on Environment and Development, 1992, http://www.unep.org/Documents.multilingual/Default.asp?DocumentID=78&ArticleID=1163. Some progress has been made toward the adoption of the precautionary principle in Canadian environmental law, e.g., in the *Canadian Environmental Protection Act, 1999* (see the preamble and ss. 2, 6, and 76.1) and the *Canadian Environmental Assessment Act, 2012*, at s. 4(2)). See also the discussion of the precautionary principle in Chapter 8.

10. Mary O'Brien, *Making Better Environmental Decisions: An Alternative to Risk Assessment* (Cambridge, MA: MIT Press, 2000).

11. Environmental assessment legislation in some Canadian jurisdictions requires comparative evaluation of alternatives. See Chapter 10.

12. Throughout its history, Canadian environmental law has often led steps to open government decision-making to more effective public engagement. Key steps have included loosening restrictions on who has "standing" to participate in quasi-judicial hearings and other legislated processes, introducing environmental bills of rights, and improving public access to government information. See Chapters 13-15.

13. Experts continue to debate the proper definition of *resilience* and how it relates to transformability in socio-ecological and mostly human systems. For an exploration focused on socio-ecological systems, see Carl Folke, Stephen R. Carpenter, Brian Walker, Marten Scheffer, Terry Chapin, and Johan Rockström, "Resilience Thinking: Integrating Resilience, Adaptability and Transformability" (2010) 15:4 *Ecology and Society* 20, http://www.ecologyandsociety.org/vol15/iss4/art20/.

14. See especially Brian Walker and David Salt, *Resilience Practice: Building Capacity to Absorb Disturbance and Maintain Function* (Washington, DC: Island Press, 2012). Note, however, that what we have listed here as strategies for enhancing resilience, Walker and Salt present (in a somewhat different version) as the "attributes" of resilient systems.

15. These points are drawn largely from Marina Fischer-Kowalski and Jan Rotmans, "Conceptualizing, Observing and Influencing Social-Ecological Transitions" (2009) 14:2 *Ecology and Society*, http://www.ecologyandsociety.org/vol14/iss2/art3/; Derk Loorbach and Jan Rotmans, "Managing Transitions for Sustainable Development," in Xander Olshoorn and Anna J. Wieczorek, eds., *Understanding Industrial Trans-formation: Views from Different Disciplines* (Dordrecht, Netherlands: Springer, 2006), 187-206; René Kemp, Saeed Parto, and Robert B. Gibson, "Governance for Sustainable Development: Moving from Theory to Practice" (2005) 8:1/2 *International Journal for Sustainable Development* 12; Geoff Mulgan with Simon Tucker, Rushanara Ali, and Ben Sanders, *Social Innovation: What It Is, Why It Matters and How It Can Be Accelerated* (Oxford: Said Business School, 2007), http://youngfoundation.org/wp-content/uploads/2012/10/Social-Innovation-what-it-is-why-it-matters-how-it-can-be-accelerated-March-2007.pdf; Geoff Mulgan, Julie Caulier-Grice, and Robin Murray, "How to Innovate: The Tools for Social Innovation" (working paper, Young Foundation, London, December 2008), http://youngfoundation.org/wp-content/uploads/2012/10/How-to-innovate-the-tools-for-social-innovation.pdf; and Frances Westley, "The Social Innovation Dynamic" (paper for Social Innovation Generation at Waterloo, Waterloo, ON, October 2008), http://sig.uwaterloo.ca/sites/default/files/documents/TheSocialInnovationDynamic_001_0.pdf.

16. World Commission on Environment and Development [WCED], *Our Common Future* (Oxford: Oxford University Press, 1987). This report is the source of the simple definition of *sustainable development* that is commonly adopted in public documents: "development that meets the needs of the present without compromising the ability of future generations to meet their own needs." Among the environmental laws that incorporate this definition is the *Canadian Environmental Assessment Act, 2012*, (see ss. 2(1) and 4(1)). For the longer version of the WCED definition, see Box 3.2, note †.

17. Brian Eno, "The Big Here and the Long Now," The Long Now Foundation, May 2000, http://longnow.org/essays/big-here-and-long-now/; and Libby Robin, "The Big Here and the Long Now: Agendas for History and Sustainability" (paper presented at the Conference on History and Sustainability, University of Cambridge, Cambridge, September 7, 2007).

18. Peter Montague, "#746—The Environmental Movement—Part 6: Changing the Climate of Opinion," *Rachel's Environment & Health Weekly*, March 14, 2002, http://www.rachel.org/?q=en/node/5508.

PART II

Aspects of Environmental Law

Courts, Tribunals, and Dispute Settlement

Introduction

The Canadian legal system can be a confusing maze of structures and terms. This should not be surprising since the Canadian system emerged from various other legal systems and has evolved over the past century. This chapter attempts to provide a very basic overview of how Canadian courts and tribunals operate. This overview is important since it forms the foundation for an understanding of the following chapters. The courts' application and interpretation of substantive environmental issues are discussed in Chapter 13. The role of tribunals is elaborated on in Chapter 14.

Civil Law and Common Law Jurisdictions

As we saw briefly at the beginning of Chapter 2, the Canadian legal system is largely based on common law, except in Quebec, where the civil law applies. Common law is a system of law based on the English legal tradition, which relies on precedent rather than on codified rules. Common law principles emerged from customary arrangements, have evolved over hundreds of years of court decisions, and continue to evolve as courts deal with new circumstances and new understandings. Common law principles stand as basic tenets of our legal regime, guiding behaviour among

CASE STUDY

The Application of Common Law Principles: Heyes v. City of Vancouver, 2009

Susan Heyes Inc. (the plaintiff) is a company that designs, manufactures, and sells maternity clothing on Cambie Street in Vancouver. A consortium of government agencies and other interests was constructing a rapid transit line (called the *Canada Line*) that would connect Vancouver, the City of Richmond, and Vancouver International Airport. The plaintiff's business is located on a street where an underground portion of the rapid transit line was to be constructed. The original plan was to use machinery that would bore a tunnel along the designated route. However, the approved tunnel would be constructed with a "cut and cover" method; essentially, the streets along the Canada Line route were to be excavated and then filled after the tunnel work was completed.

The plaintiff brought a legal action against the partners in the consortium alleging that the estimated four-year impact of the cut and cover construction along Cambie Street would result in a direct, negative economic impact to its business. In its legal action, the plaintiff relied on a number of common law torts to pursue its claim, including negligent misrepresentation, negligence, and nuisance.

The court dismissed the claims of negligent misrepresentation and negligence, but did grant the claim of nuisance against some of the defendants. The court defined *nuisance* as unreasonable interference with the use of land and noted:

> Consideration of the question of whether any particular use of land results in a nuisance must take into account the fact that in the modern world of multi-purpose land use, high density urbanization, and frequent if not continuous urban transformation and improvement, citizens and enterprises are expected to engage in a process of reasonable "give and take." The challenge is to identify the point at which give and take falls out of balance sufficiently to warrant a remedy.*

The court asked whether a small business should have to absorb a $500,000 loss in order for a construction company to find a less expensive way to construct a project. It found that the "nature, severity and duration of the impact" on the plaintiff resulting from the cut and cover construction outweighed "the social or public utility" of the project such that the plaintiff should be entitled to some compensation.

The case was appealed to the BC Court of Appeal. The BC Court of Appeal did not disagree with the lower court's finding that the construction of the transit project created a nuisance. However, the court found that the pertinent transit authority had the statutory authority to approve "the inevitable nuisance that would arise in the course of building rapid transit in this heavily-populated urban area." In other words, the defence of statutory authority suggests that a nuisance claim can be defeated where the activities that created the nuisance were legally approved by a government agency.†

Questions

How would you describe the common law principle of nuisance? What are the implications of this case for future transit projects? Would the decision of this case be binding or have to be followed in the courts of Ontario? Alberta? Nova Scotia? Are there instances where the defence of statutory authority would not defeat a nuisance claim?

---

*   *Heyes v. City of Vancouver*, 2009 BCSC 651.

†   *Susan Heyes Inc. (Hazel & Co.) v. South Coast BC Transportation Authority*, 2011 BCCA 77.

us as citizens and neighbours. For example, as discussed in Chapter 13, the common law establishes that we cannot undertake activity on our property if that activity unreasonably interferes with our neighbour's use of his or her property. Such interference constitutes the tort of nuisance. This idea is not written in any statute. Rather, it is a basic principle of common law.

When a court makes a decision applying the common law in a new case, that court sets a precedent. Its decision stands as a firm guide to courts making decisions about similar cases in the future. This principle is called ***stare decisis***. As one case builds on another case, a whole body of case law is developed. Reading through the succession of cases that address a particular area of conflict can provide a clear understanding of the state of the law in that area. A higher court, such as a court of appeal, can overrule a lower court and create a new precedent. In Canada, the final say goes to the Supreme Court of Canada.

The role of lawyers is to inform their clients about the state of the law on any given topic. Because of the importance of common law, it is not enough merely to know what is set out in statutes and regulations. Often it is the long succession of common law decisions that is most important. For example, what are the rights of an ardent organic farmer whose neighbours are spraying pesticides on their fields? Can the organic farmer argue that the neighbours are violating a common law principle of nuisance because the spray appears to be migrating across the property line and into the organic farm?

In such a case, the lawyer for the organic farmer might first look for similar cases that have been decided in the past. Even if no cases with identical issues exist, the lawyer might find analogous cases that show how the common law goals of equity and fairness have been applied in ways that favour protecting the organic farmer's interests in the present case. Of course, the lawyer for the neighbours would look for precedent-setting cases that favour the field-sprayers' position. The court would then have to apply the common law and make a decision. This decision would be binding for future cases.

The decision could, for example, become a precedent in a later case where a family is barbecuing meat every night next door to a vegetarian family. The vegetarians object, saying that the constant smell of burning meat spoils the enjoyment of their patio and that the barbecuers are committing an "unreasonable interference." Perhaps these neighbours can work out their differences. But if the conflict goes to court, and if the earlier decision had favoured the organic farmer over the pesticide sprayers, the vegetarian family could use the decision as a precedent. They could argue that the court should protect their patio enjoyment from barbecue odours just as the earlier court had protected the organic farmer's fields from pesticide spray.

---

stare decisis   principle that requires judges to follow decisions of higher courts in similar cases

The lawyer for the barbecuing family, however, could argue that the precedent does not apply because this case is fundamentally different from the earlier one. While spraying pesticides on a field serves the purpose of agricultural production, cooking is an essential human need. Hence, fumes from cooking do not create the same type of unreasonable interference complained of in the earlier lawsuit.

Common law jurisdictions must be distinguished from **civil law jurisdictions**. While most of Europe relies on civil law, only Quebec and Louisiana in North America are civil law jurisdictions. The basic principles and rules of law in civil law jurisdictions are derived from a civil code—*le droit civil*—that the courts interpret and apply on a case-by-case basis. Unlike common law, civil law does not rely on precedents. Civil law has no doctrine of *stare decisis*. While these are two different theories of law, there are many similarities.

Civil Law and Criminal Law Systems

Although the term *civil law* can refer to civil law jurisdictions such as Quebec, it also has another connotation. Within common law jurisdictions, an important distinction exists between **civil law systems** and **criminal law systems**. In most countries, including Canada, the civil law and criminal law systems work side by side. Civil law cases deal with disputes between parties—that is, between individuals in society, whether someone is collecting on money owed or neighbours are involved in a dispute over a fence. In a civil law case before a court, the party pursuing the claim, usually called the *plaintiff*, must establish that the *defendant* committed a wrong. Such a wrong is called a *tort* in common law jurisdictions and a *responsabilité civile* under the *Civil Code of Québec*. Unlike a criminal law case, in a civil law case a person (the plaintiff) brings a lawsuit against the defendant, alleging that the defendant is at fault for causing the wrong (or the tort) and, thus, must compensate the plaintiff in **damages** or a related remedy. For example, in the organic farmer versus the pesticide sprayers case described above, the organic farmer (the plaintiff)

---

common law jurisdictions   most of North America, with the exception of Quebec and Louisiana, where prior court decisions on similar facts may be binding law

civil law jurisdictions   most of Europe, but only Quebec and Louisiana in North America, where courts make decisions based on a civil code, not precedent, and there is no doctrine of *stare decisis*

civil law system   a system that deals with disputes between private parties, whereby the party pursuing the claim, usually called the *plaintiff*, must establish that the defendant committed a wrong (applies to both common law and civil law jurisdictions)

criminal law system   a system that deals with violations of the laws designed to protect the interests of society in general

damages   the monetary award that a defendant may be ordered by a court to pay to a successful plaintiff

would bring a claim in the tort of nuisance against the pesticide sprayers (the defendants). If the plaintiff is successful, the court may order the defendants to stop their spraying and/or require them to compensate the plaintiff with a payment of money (damages) and/or grant some other type of relief. In Chapter 13, we provide more information about environmental claims.

The criminal law system, in contrast, deals with those who break the laws designed to protect the interests of society in general. If one breaks a criminal law (e.g., a federal law against theft) or a quasi-criminal law (e.g., a provincial statute against dumping toxic chemicals), then the government (usually the attorney general or the Crown) can prosecute the lawbreaker. The violation of the law is not only a wrong against the victim of the crime, but a wrong against society in general. Hence, if the accused is convicted of the offence, the court may sentence the person to jail or require that a fine be paid to the government.

A key difference between the civil and criminal law systems involves the standard of proof that has to be met. In a criminal law case, the prosecutor must establish that the accused person is guilty beyond a reasonable doubt. Before convicting the accused person, the court must be satisfied that there are no reasonable grounds for thinking that the accused might not be guilty. In a civil matter, the standard of proof is much less onerous. The plaintiff must prove only that on a balance of probabilities the defendant is in the wrong. In other words, the court decides which party is more likely to be right and gives a judgment in that party's favour. In a criminal case, the accused, if convicted, is subject to incarceration and/or a fine. In a civil suit, the usual remedy is monetary damages.

The primary social policy in civil or tort law is to ensure that the party liable for a wrong compensates the person who was wronged. In the criminal law system, the primary objective is deterrence—that is, to send the signal that criminal and quasi-criminal behaviour are not tolerated in a civil society. In short, the purpose of the civil and criminal law systems is different in Canada: the former is to compensate the aggrieved party in a way that returns the party to the same position that the party was in before the wrong was committed; and the latter is to deter others from unacceptable behaviour.

It is important to re-emphasize that the civil and criminal law systems coexist. A person can be charged with a criminal or quasi-criminal offence *and* be subject to a civil lawsuit for damages. A classic example is the O.J. Simpson case in the United States, where a well-known football player was charged with the murder of his wife. At the criminal trial, the accused was found not guilty. However, the family of the deceased brought a civil action against the defendant and won a fairly large damages award. In this case, one can speculate that although the government could not prove "beyond a reasonable doubt" that Simpson caused the death of his wife under criminal law, the plaintiff family could prove that he was liable for her death on a "balance of probabilities."

An environmental example may shed some further light on how criminal or quasi-criminal and civil law systems work. If an individual allows a toxic chemical to leak into a groundwater source, one would expect the government to charge that person with some sort of offence. The individual, if convicted, may have to pay a fine to the government or even be sentenced to a jail term. The fine, however, would not help the homeowners who rely on the groundwater for their source of drinking water. Instead, the homeowners may have to bring a civil action for damages against that person in order to seek compensation for finding an alternative source of drinking water.

Courts and Tribunals

Courts may often seem to be the only major decision-making bodies in the Canadian legal system. However, the situation is much more complex, especially in environmental matters.

Courts have long played an adjudicative role in resolving disputes concerning environmental abuses. In fact, cases date back at least to the 1600s, when the courts in England ruled on issues involving contaminated drinking water or neighbourhoods poisoned by air emissions. Most cases today are considerably less dramatic, but the courts are still often called upon to rule on a wide range of environmental matters.

Since the Second World War, however, the courts have increasingly shared adjudicative tasks with other bodies. As a consequence of technological innovations, expanding pressures on limited resources, rising public expectations, and other related factors, environmental problems became more complex. In response, new regulatory regimes were developed, often with specialized **tribunals** established to deal with particular categories of concerns and conflicts. Some of the more important tribunals now carry much of the responsibility for adjudication of disputes in society. In many provinces, matters pertaining to landlord and tenant issues, immigration, human rights, licencing, property assessment, social benefits, to name but a few, are dealt with by tribunals. In the environmental realm, tribunals are particularly germane since they are often given legislative mandates in areas related to land use planning, sectoral regulation, pollution control, and assessment of new undertakings. While the courts retain advantages in breadth of authority and experience, key features of the tribunals can make them better equipped than courts to oversee and administer complex environmental regimes. An outline of Canada's court system appears in Figure 4.1.

---

tribunal   a specialized quasi-judicial board, commission, panel, or other decision-making body that makes decisions pursuant to particular statutes

Figure 4.1   Outline of Canada's Court System

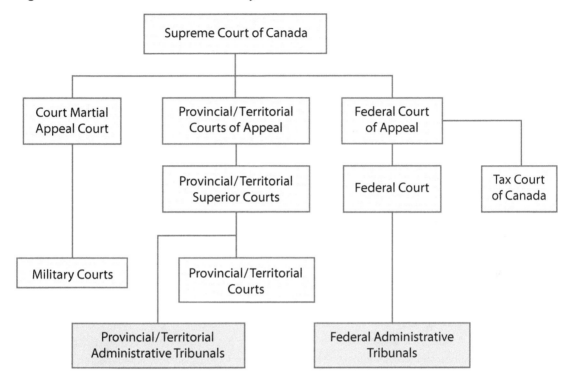

How Courts Work

Courts are an integral part of our democratic system and act as a foundation for the legal system. Their primary functions are to apply the law (e.g., by imposing sanctions through the criminal law), to provide a check on the use of government power (e.g., by protecting civil rights), and to adjudicate on matters of rights and liabilities (e.g., by ruling on disputes over property rights). In short, the courts attempt to deal with disputes in society.

The courts are, by design, adversarial in nature. The underlying theory is that the truth will emerge from the conflict of opposing positions. Accordingly, lawyers for each side are expected to represent their clients' interests fearlessly. Judges are appointed usually through a formal process and given a high degree of independence. In a civil matter, the result of a court case is a judgment in favour of a plaintiff or a defendant. In a criminal matter, the accused is either acquitted or found guilty of committing an offence. Table 4.1 outlines some of the differences between courts and tribunals.

Table 4.1 Differences Between Courts and Tribunals

	Courts	Tribunals
Purpose	Adjudicating rights among the parties	Overseeing a legislative framework
Mode of operation	Adversarial	Inquisitorial
Participants	• Judge adjudicates • Plaintiff brings action • Defendant defends action	• Tribunal members render decision • Proponent main player has onus to establish statutory tests for approval requested • Government officials may appear • Members of public may intervene
Nature of outcome	Judgment outlining winners and losers	Decision geared to further the public interest in administering the regime

How Tribunals Work

A tribunal is an administrative board, commission, panel, or some other decision-making body that carries out some sort of adjudicative, regulatory, or policy role in the implementation of a legislative scheme. Today hundreds of tribunals make decisions, ranging from the Canadian Radio-television and Telecommunications Commission granting licences to broadcasters to university adjudication bodies deciding what action to take when a student appeals a course mark. Generally, the public's first introduction to the Canadian legal system is through a tribunal (rather than through some court process).

Many tribunals have been established to implement statutory schemes that involve the granting (and withdrawal) of permits or that provide for hearings in planning or environmental assessment cases. Tribunals are meant to be less formal than courts and thus more accessible to the public. Although tribunal proceedings can be fiercely adversarial, often tribunals encourage the participation of many diverse parties beyond the immediate proponents and critics of the matter in question. Unlike courts, tribunals often take an active inquisitorial role, asking their own questions and perhaps even initiating their own research rather than relying solely on the emergence of information from opposing positions.

Two other important features of tribunals should be noted. First, unlike courts, tribunals do not have any "inherent" powers or authority. They only have the powers and jurisdiction granted to them by a statute. The court's role is to supervise tribunals to ensure that they act within the law and their jurisdiction. Environmental tribunals, because they are specialized and expert in nature, are often given deference by the courts—that is, the courts hesitate to interfere with the technical findings of

Table 4.2   Key Principles of Administrative Law

Administrative Principles	Brief Explanation
Right to notice	Parties to a proceeding have a right to be notified of the time and location of the hearing.
Right to counsel	Parties can be represented by a lawyer or other authorized representative.
Right to give evidence and cross-examine	Parties can give evidence relevant to the subject matter of the hearing and cross-examine the evidence of other parties.
Natural justice	Parties have the right to be heard and to have their case decided by an unbiased tribunal member(s) who heard the case.
Procedural fairness	Parties have the right to procedural protection that is suited to the type of proceedings being conducted. The content of the duty of fairness will vary across proceedings.
Jurisdiction	The tribunal will act only within the authority given to it by statute.
Discretion	The tribunal will exercise its discretion over its procedures and the merits of a case in a manner that is consistent with the applicable legislation.

Source: Adapted from Jerry V. DeMarco and Paul Muldoon. *Environmental Boards and Tribunals in Canada: A Practical Guide* (Toronto: LexisNexis, 2011), at 20.

environmental tribunals as long as such tribunals operate within their powers. The court's supervisory power in this regard is called **judicial review**, which is triggered when one party challenges whether the tribunal operated within its jurisdiction or followed the principles of natural justice and procedural fairness. In many jurisdictions, some of these principles are outlined in a statute, such as the *Statutory Powers Procedure Act*. Table 4.2 outlines some of the key principles of administrative law.

In Canada, many legislated regimes dealing with environmental matters include roles for tribunals. At the federal level, the boards of review can be set up under the *Canadian Environmental Protection Act, 1999* to deal with certain chemical assessments. Panels can also be set up under the *Canadian Environmental Assessment Act* to consider the potential effects and desirability of major proposed projects.

---

judicial review   a court's review of an administrative tribunal's decision to ensure that it acted within the powers granted under the legislation and respected the common law rules of natural justice and procedural fairness

Provincial examples of environmental tribunals include Ontario's Environmental Review Tribunal, which is mandated to examine and rule on undertakings subject to environmental assessment and to hear appeals about administrative orders (e.g., for pollution cleanup) or decisions to grant or refuse approvals (e.g., for new sources of air or water discharges). Alberta's Environmental Appeals Board is a tribunal that allows Albertans to appeal decisions of Alberta Environment and Sustainable Development under Alberta's *Environmental Protection and Enhancement Act* and *Water Act* regarding development approvals, water licences, reclamation certificates, and enforcement orders, for example.

Not all tribunals have final decision-making authority. Some (e.g., federal environmental assessment panels and water boards in the territories) are empowered only to make recommendations to the relevant government minister. And in other cases, a tribunal's ruling (such as a decision of the Joint Board in Ontario) may be appealed to the relevant federal or provincial Cabinet.

Dispute Resolution

It would be misleading to suggest that all disputes are resolved through the courts or tribunals. In fact, most matters are resolved through some sort of **alternative dispute resolution (ADR)** mechanism. ADR actually includes a number of related processes designed to resolve disputes. The most commonly used ADR processes are negotiation, facilitation, mediation, and arbitration. *Negotiation* is perhaps the most obvious process and involves an agreement between the parties to meet and attempt to resolve their issues outside of the court or tribunal setting. Negotiations may entail informal discussions among the concerned parties, or they may entail formal and structured meetings that include an exchange of documents, input from experts, and signed agreements. Through *facilitation*, the parties attempt to negotiate their dispute with the assistance of a third party (a facilitator) who is responsible for the communication process (e.g., scheduling meetings, preparing meeting agendas) and helping parties improve their mutual understanding. *Mediation* is a more structured process and also includes involvement of a third party (a mediator) to assist in negotiation of the issues. A mediator is a trained professional who understands how to encourage constructive discussion about the issues and find common ground to facilitate resolution to some or all of them. A mediator may meet with the parties before the formal mediation begins, assist the parties in identifying the real issues in the dispute, and ask the parties to exchange certain information. In *arbitration*, the parties choose a third person (an arbitrator) to help them resolve their dispute. The arbitrator also has the authority from the parties to make a final decision with

---

alternative dispute resolution (ADR)   a process other than the court system through which a conflict is settled; examples of ADR include negotiation, facilitation, mediation, and arbitration

respect to the dispute, and the parties agree that the arbitrator's decision is binding on the parties.

If a settlement is reached, the court or tribunal usually is given the authority to ensure that the terms of settlement are respected by the parties. It should be noted that the discussions within an ADR process remain confidential and cannot be used before courts or tribunals if the ADR process is unsuccessful.

Today, it is often difficult to become involved in a court or tribunal process without also becoming involved in an ADR process, particularly with respect to environmental matters. ADR processes are commonly involved in environmental disputes because many of the issues are so technical. Hence, it is far more cost-effective and timely to have experts in the field from all parties meet to discuss areas of common ground and differences in a collaborative setting rather than the formality of a court or tribunal setting. Apart from cost and time savings, ADR processes may also be more inclusive by allowing parties who may not have the resources to fully participate in a tribunal or court proceeding to have a role in an ADR process. In environmental matters, often no one "easy solution" to resolve a dispute exists, which suggests that cooperative, collective efforts may lead to more innovative approaches to a problem.

ADR is increasingly becoming incorporated in the day-to-day operation of courts and tribunals in their efforts to make the dispute resolution process more efficient and accessible. This trend is particularly pronounced in the complex and often protracted areas of environmental litigation, where the overriding public interest is to ensure both access to dispute resolution processes by those affected by environmental matters and the protection of the environment.

SUMMARY OF KEY POINTS

- Canada has two legal systems: common law and civil law (in Quebec). Common law is based on general principles of law that are applied by the courts, and set precedents are binding on subsequent cases. Civil law is governed by a civil code, and court decisions do not set precedents as in common law. Statutes and regulations govern both common law and civil law systems.

- Canada has both a civil and criminal legal system. Civil law, in this sense, pertains to disputes between people where one person (a plaintiff) brings an action against another person (the defendant). The key issue is whether the defendant is liable for a wrong (or a tort, such as nuisance) and, thus, must pay damages or provide related relief to the plaintiff. Criminal law involves the state (usually the attorney general or the Crown) laying a charge against a person (the accused) for breaking a criminal or quasi-criminal law. The court may impose a jail term or fine on the accused if the person is convicted of the offence. However, the government must prove its case "beyond a reasonable doubt" rather than on a "balance of probabilities," as is the case in a civil action.

- Courts remain the foundation of our legal system in that they decide both civil and criminal law matters. The court system is based on an adversarial approach. Tribunals are usually designed to implement a statutory scheme and tend to be inquisitorial and less formal than courts. Tribunals are supervised by the courts through judicial review, which is triggered when someone challenges a tribunal's process or to ensure that the tribunal followed the principles of natural justice and procedural fairness.

- In both courts and tribunals, great effort is being made to incorporate alternative dispute resolution methods to allow the public to resolve their disputes in ways that are less costly and more timely.

KEY TERMS

alternative dispute resolution (ADR)
civil law jurisdictions
civil law system
common law jurisdictions
criminal law system
damages
judicial review
stare decisis
tribunal

DISCUSSION QUESTIONS

1. Can you identify any strengths or weaknesses of the common law system as compared with the civil law system?
2. Describe a real situation dealing with an environmental problem and explain how the criminal law and civil law systems would apply. Identify the key differences between the two systems.
3. Under what circumstances would a court exercise its power over a tribunal even when the tribunal is a specialized environmental tribunal?
4. Why do you think legislatures throughout Canada are relying more on tribunals to further regulatory schemes? What are the attributes of tribunals that are beneficial in this regard?
5. What are the advantages and disadvantages of alternative dispute resolution?

SUGGESTED READINGS

Readings

Blake, Sara. *Administrative Law in Canada*, 4th ed. Markham, ON: LexisNexis, 2006.

DeMarco, Jerry V., and Paul Muldoon. *Environmental Boards and Tribunals in Canada: A Practical Guide*. Toronto: LexisNexis, 2011.

Stitt, Allan J. *Alternative Dispute Resolution for Organizations*. Toronto: Wiley, 1998.

Websites

Environment Review Tribunal: https://www.ert.gov.on.ca

United Nations Environment Programme, "Application of Environmental Law by National Courts and Tribunals—Resolving Environmental Disputes": http://www.unep.org/delc/Portals/119/10_RESOLVING %20ENVIRONMENTAL%20DISPUTES.pdf

CHAPTER 5

Aboriginal and Environmental Law

LEARNING OBJECTIVES

After reading this chapter, students will be able to:

- Identify key concepts and terminology in Aboriginal law.
- Describe the key constitutional, statutory, and treaty documents that provide the foundation for Aboriginal law.
- Discuss key court decisions that provide the foundation for Aboriginal law.
- Explain the connection between Aboriginal law and environmental law in Canada.
- Understand how to determine appropriate consultation in different contexts.

CHAPTER OUTLINE

Introduction

Aboriginal law is the body of laws that relate to **Aboriginal peoples** in any number of ways. Aboriginal law addresses the issue of whether someone is a **status Indian** under the *Indian Act* and how the individual rights of Aboriginal peoples under the *Canadian Charter of Rights and Freedoms* relate to the **collective rights** of Aboriginal peoples under the Constitution. Aboriginal law also addresses Aboriginal hunting

---

Aboriginal peoples Indians, Métis, and Inuit people, according to the *Constitution Act, 1982*

status Indian an Aboriginal person who is registered under the *Indian Act* on the Indian Register, which is maintained by Aboriginal Affairs and Northern Development Canada

collective rights rights held by a group (e.g., Aboriginal rights to hunt or gather) as opposed to rights held by an individual (e.g., voting rights)

CASE STUDY

The Northern Gateway Pipeline and First Nations

In 2010, Enbridge submitted a proposal for a twin pipeline between Bruderheim, Alberta and the port of Kitimat, British Columbia. The pipeline, known as the Northern Gateway, would extend over 1,770 kilometres in length (see Figure 5.1). As an energy project, it is subject to review by a Joint Review Panel of the National Energy Board and the Canadian Environmental Assessment Agency.

From the outset, the project has been criticized by several environmental and community groups as well as First Nations in British Columbia. Although views differ on whether the pipeline would be beneficial, little doubt exists that the issue of unresolved land claims along the pipeline route will affect whether or how it will proceed. Concerns raised by First Nations include potential impacts on hunting and fishing rights, particularly if a spill occurs. Another issue has been the extent to which consultation with First Nations is required.

In December 2013, the Joint Review Panel issued a recommendation that the project proceed, subject to numerous conditions. In June 2014, the federal government accepted the recommendation and approved the project, subject to 209 conditions. With respect to the concerns raised by First Nations, the Joint Review Panel stated: "[D]uring construction and routine operations, the project would not have a significant adverse effect on the ability of Aboriginal people to use the lands, waters, and resources in the project area for traditional purposes."* Further, if a major spill that affected First Nations' interests did occur, the panel "found that the adverse effects would not be permanent and widespread."† Within hours of the Joint Review Panel's announcement, the Lake Babine First Nation announced that it would seek judicial review of the Joint Panel's recommendation. Since then, a number of additional challenges to the project have been initiated by First Nations that will likely take years to resolve.

Questions

This case study raises a number of questions, including the following: Are presentations of concerns by First Nations during the environmental assessment process led by a Joint Review Panel sufficient? Or is an entirely separate process, involving "deep" and more direct consultation with First Nations required? Can the government approve a project over the objections of First Nations?

---

*   National Energy Board and Canadian Environmental Assessment Agency, *Report of the Joint Review Panel for the Enbridge Northern Gateway Project*, vol. 1 (Ottawa: National Energy Board, 2013), at 25, http://gatewaypanel.review-examen.gc.ca/clf-nsi/dcmnt/rcmndtnsrprt/rcmndtnsrprt-eng.html.

†   Ibid., at 21.

and fishing **rights**, and **title** to land. This chapter provides a broad summary of the law relating to Aboriginal rights and title. It is important to have some understanding of Aboriginal rights and title when studying environmental law because they relate to each other in law and in practice. In Canada, it is not possible to consider Aboriginal law without understanding environmental issues, and it is not possible to consider environmental law without understanding the law regarding Aboriginal title to land and Aboriginal rights to hunt, fish, and gather.

---

right   the constitutionally protected ability to carry out an activity

title   ownership of land; it is the right to the exclusive use and occupation of the land, and the right to choose the uses of the land, within constraints prescribed by law (such as zoning); Aboriginal title encompasses the right to exclusive use and occupation of the land for a variety of purposes, but the protected uses of the land must not be irreconcilable with the nature of the Aboriginal group's attachment to the land

Figure 5.1   Proposed Pipeline Route of the Northern Gateway

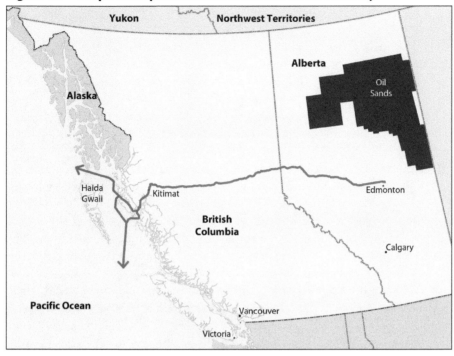

Key Constitutional, Statutory, and Treaty Documents

A number of key documents provide the foundation for Aboriginal law in Canada. The first is the *Royal Proclamation, 1763* issued by King George III. Among other provisions relating to the governance of the British North American colonies, the Royal Proclamation also recognized "several Nations or Tribes of Indians" and stipulated that "Indian lands" could only be surrendered to the Crown in order to avoid "frauds and abuses" by settlers.

The second is the *Constitution Act, 1867* (formerly known as the *British North America Act*), which outlines the jurisdiction of the federal and provincial governments. Section 91(24) provides that "Indians and land reserved for Indians" falls under federal jurisdiction.

BOX 5.1 » A Note on Terminology

Although the term *Indian* is seldom used in Canada today, it still exists in the *Constitution Act, 1867* and in the federal *Indian Act*. It is now common practice to use the term *First Nation* instead of the term *Indian*.

   Aboriginal peoples of Canada is defined in section 35(2) of the *Constitution Act, 1982* to include the Indian, Inuit, and Métis peoples of Canada.

Section 35(1) of the *Constitution Act, 1982* provides that the "existing aboriginal and treaty rights of the aboriginal peoples of Canada are hereby recognized and affirmed." These rights are collective, unlike other constitutional rights in Canada that are focused on the individual. Section 35 has been the subject of numerous court decisions attempting to interpret and explain what it means.

A number of **treaties** and other land claim agreements exist across Canada. They vary considerably in terms of breadth, specificity, and date, and many First Nations do not have treaties. Knowing whether a treaty is in place with a particular First Nation is important when considering applicable Aboriginal law and Crown obligations to consult with Aboriginal peoples.

Finally, a number of statutes are relevant to Aboriginal law. At the federal level, the key statutes are the *Indian Act*, other statutes relating to First Nations governance, and acts that enable development and revenue generation on Indian Reserve land. These include the *First Nations Commercial and Industrial Development Act* and the *First Nations Land Management Act*. Certain provincial statutes also apply because the provinces have jurisdiction over the matters covered in treaties, notably natural resources and provincial Crown land. As a result, provincial statutes have been used to outline processes and requirements for consultation with Aboriginal peoples in land use planning and in the implementation of treaties. For this reason, a modern treaty may have both a federal and a provincial statute giving it effect (e.g., the *Tsawwassen First Nation Act*[1] in British Columbia and the *Far North Act* in Ontario).

Common Law

A number of court cases have helped define what "title" to land is, what "rights" are, the obligations of the Crown in relation to Aboriginal peoples, and the test to be met before Aboriginal rights can be infringed. Many of these cases arose in response to government decisions. A number of cases arose to challenge a government decision to issue a permit (e.g., a logging permit) or approve a major project after an environmental assessment, on the basis that the decision infringed Aboriginal rights and title. Other cases arose because individuals were charged with an offence and their defence was that the law under which they were charged was unconstitutional because it infringed their Aboriginal rights.

Calder v. British Columbia (1973)

One of the earliest landmark cases that has helped define and shape Aboriginal rights in Canada is *Calder v. British Columbia*,[2] in which the Nisga'a First Nation

---

treaty (Aboriginal) a formal agreement between a First Nation and the provincial and federal governments regarding First Nations rights and title; treaties with First Nations are considered *sui generis* (unique) and are constitutionally protected.

claimed that it had title to about 2,600 square kilometres of land in northwestern British Columbia. In its decision, the Supreme Court of Canada addressed the issue of whether the title claimed by the Nisga'a had been extinguished. Part of the Nisga'a argument was that the *Royal Proclamation, 1763* applied to the Nisga'a territory and provided them with protection. Three justices decided that the Royal Proclamation did apply west of the Rocky Mountains and that once Aboriginal title is established, it is presumed to continue until the contrary is proven. However, three justices decided that the Royal Proclamation did not apply because the territory did not come under British sovereignty until 1846, and another justice ruled against the Nisga'a on unrelated grounds. Although the court did not reach a unanimous decision in this case, the *Calder* decision is significant in that it brought the issue of Aboriginal land claims to the attention of governments and launched the federal treaty process to attempt to reach agreements between the federal and provincial governments and First Nations.

R v. Sparrow (1990)

R v. Sparrow[3] was the first court decision to test the scope of section 35(1) of the *Constitution Act, 1982* and remains a key decision on Aboriginal and treaty rights. Ronald Edward Sparrow was a member of the Musqueam First Nation and was charged with violating the *Fisheries Act* requirements regarding maximum net length. His defence argued that the Aboriginal right to fish meant that net length restriction is unconstitutional. The Supreme Court of Canada interpreted "existing rights" in section 35 to mean those rights in existence on April 17, 1982, when the *Constitution Act, 1982* came into force. Rights that had been extinguished before that date are not recognized, and "existing" Aboriginal rights must be interpreted flexibly so as to permit their evolution over time. The court also decided that although Aboriginal rights are not absolute, regulations affecting Aboriginal rights must be constitutional and the infringement of rights must be justified. The court outlined a series of questions that must be addressed to determine whether a regulation

---

BOX 5.2 » What Is the "Extinguishment" of Aboriginal Title?

Extinguishment means that the Aboriginal title to land no longer exists. It can occur through surrender of the land to the Crown as part of a treaty or by a clear and competent legislative authority (e.g., *R v. Calder*). Aboriginal title may be extinguished by the Crown when the intention of the Crown is clear and plain. The onus of proving extinguishment lies with the Crown (e.g., *R v. Sparrow*).

---

extinguishment   the elimination of Aboriginal title to land; it can occur through surrender of the land to the Crown as part of a treaty or by a clear and competent legislative authority (e.g., *R v. Calder*).

infringes Aboriginal rights and whether the infringement can be justified. This set of questions is known as "the *Sparrow* test."

The first question in the *Sparrow* test is whether there is an existing Aboriginal right. In this part of the test, it is necessary to characterize the claimed right. It must be clear whether the right claimed is based on a practice, custom, or tradition integral to the Aboriginal culture in question. Also, it must be determined whether the practice, custom, or tradition that constitutes the Aboriginal right has continuity with that which existed prior to contact with Europeans. The court further stated that practices, customs, or traditions that are marginal to cultural identity are not rights. A case-by-case analysis is required because the response to this part of the test will vary from culture to culture.

The second question is whether the proposed regulatory action (e.g., a limitation on fishing net length, restrictions on hunting) interferes with the right because it is unreasonable, imposes undue hardship, or denies the holder of the right preferred means of exercising the right. The onus of proving infringement is on the group challenging the legislation.

The third question asks whether the infringement of an existing Aboriginal right is justifiable. Grounds for justification include, first, determining whether a valid legislative objective exists, and, second, whether the honour of the Crown has been upheld. Examples of valid legislative objectives are conservation and resource management. The *Sparrow* decision also stated that, depending on the context, the court may need to consider a number of additional questions. These questions include whether consultation has taken place, whether compensation is due, and whether there has been as little infringement as possible.

The *Sparrow* decision is about the concept of reconciliation. Federal power must be reconciled with federal duty, and the best way to achieve that reconciliation is to demand the justification of laws that infringe upon or deny Aboriginal rights. Laws that affect Aboriginal peoples are not automatically of no force and effect, but the process of working through the requirements of the *Sparrow* test are a way of reconciling Aboriginal rights with the authority of the Crown.

BOX 5.3 » The Sparrow Test

1. Is there an existing Aboriginal right?
2. Is the proposed regulatory action an interference with the right because it is
   - unreasonable,
   - imposes undue hardship, or
   - denies holder of the right preferred means of exercising the right?
3. If the right exists and is infringed, can this be justified because
   - there is a valid legislative objective, and
   - the honour of the Crown has been upheld?

Delgamuukw v. British Columbia (1997)

Delgamuukw v. British Columbia[4] is a key Supreme Court of Canada case that clarified what constitutes Aboriginal title. The case was spurred by a claim to 58,000 square kilometres by the Gitksan and Wet'suwet'en First Nations in British Columbia. The court stated that Aboriginal title is *sui generis* (unique) and not the same as other property interests. It also outlined the nature of Aboriginal title. Aboriginal title is a right to the exclusive use and occupation of the land, and the right to choose the uses of the land. Aboriginal title is inalienable and cannot be transferred, sold, or surrendered to anyone other than the Crown, and it is held communally rather than by individuals. Aboriginal title encompasses the right to exclusive use and occupation of the land for a variety of purposes, but the protected uses of the land must not be irreconcilable with the nature of the Aboriginal group's attachment to the land. Aboriginal title is a legal interest in the land itself, including timber, water, and minerals. Title has an economic component, which means that compensation is required if the title is infringed. Where Aboriginal title exists, so too does the duty of the Crown to consult with Aboriginal peoples who hold that title. The nature and scope of the consultation will vary, depending on the strength of the Aboriginal claim to the land, but it must always be conducted in good faith and with the intention of substantially addressing concerns. Finally, Aboriginal title is not absolute, and may be infringed if justified under the *Sparrow* test.

With respect to Aboriginal rights, the court determined that a spectrum of constitutionally protected Aboriginal rights exists, depending on the degree of connection with the land. At one end of the spectrum are practices, customs, and traditions integral to the distinctive Aboriginal culture of the people claiming the right, but where the use and occupation of the land for the activity is not close enough to claim title to the land. At the other end of the spectrum is title to the land itself, and that means that the land may be used for a variety of activities that are not individually protected as Aboriginal rights. In the middle of the spectrum are activities that out of necessity take place on land, and are site specific. Because Aboriginal rights can vary in terms of their degree of connection with the land, some Aboriginal peoples may not be able to establish title, but may still have constitutionally protected rights to activities on the land.

The Supreme Court of Canada also provided guidance on how Aboriginal title can be proven. First, the land must have been occupied prior to assertion of Crown sovereignty, which varies across Canada. In British Columbia, the province relevant to this case, the appropriate year is 1846. Second, the occupation must have been exclusive. Third, occupation must have been continuous. The court also recognized that oral histories have equal footing with other historical evidence, an important point considering that in establishing claims, Aboriginal peoples largely rely on oral rather than documentary evidence.

Taku River Tlingit First Nation v. British Columbia (Project Assessment Director) (2004)

Taku River Tlingit First Nation v. British Columbia (Project Assessment Director)[5] is an important case for understanding what constitutes adequate consultation. This case involved an environmental assessment process under the BC *Environmental Assessment Act* in which the project proponent planned to reopen a mine in northwestern British Columbia. One of the main issues was not the mine itself, but construction of the road to access the mine site. At the time, the *Environmental Assessment Act* provided for the establishment of a project assessment committee to review project proposals and make recommendations to applicable provincial ministers, who would then issue a project approval certificate if the project was approved. The Taku River Tlingit First Nation (TRTFN) was on the project assessment committee and received funding to participate in the process.

The TRTFN objected to the final recommendation of the committee, which was that the ministers should issue a project approval certificate. The ministers responsible accepted the recommendation of the committee and the TRTFN sought judicial review of that decision. Like other major cases in Aboriginal law, this case worked its way to the Supreme Court of Canada. The Supreme Court held that consultation was adequate in this case because the project approval certificate included measures to address the TRTFN's concerns, and because the environmental assessment was only one stage of the approval process, not the final decision for the project to go ahead, so there would be more opportunity for ongoing consultations. The issue of appropriate consultation on large projects subject to an environmental assessment process is ongoing. For example, several First Nations have stated publicly that neither the Crown nor Enbridge have adequately met their duty to consult or accommodate during the process of developing the Northern Gateway project.[6]

Haida Nation v. British Columbia (Minister of Forests) (2004)

The obligation to consult is closely related to the duty to accommodate. Accommodation refers to measures taken to address concerns related to Aboriginal rights and title, and includes the concept of reconciliation between the Crown and Aboriginal peoples. *Haida Nation v. British Columbia (Minister of Forests)*[7] is an important case with respect to consultation and accommodation. This case addressed the question of what is required to maintain the honour of the Crown and effect reconciliation. The court held that government (the Crown) has a constitutional duty to consult and, where appropriate, accommodate First Nations, even before rights or title are proven. The duty to consult arises when the Crown has real or constructive knowledge of the potential existence of a right or title and contemplates actions that might adversely affect that right or title. The scope and nature of the duty to accommodate are situation specific; they depend on an assessment of the strength of the claim and the seriousness of the potential adverse effect on the right or title of the First Nation. The Crown does not have to reach an agreement with the First Nation, but the Crown does have to commit to a meaningful process in good faith. Further, First Nations must participate in the consultation process. They cannot frustrate the Crown's efforts to consult in good faith, nor take unreasonable positions to thwart the Crown. In terms of what accommodation is, the court clarified that when the results of consultation suggest that the Crown should amend its policy and take steps to avoid irreparable harm or minimize infringement of rights or title, then those steps should be taken. The court further held that the obligations for consultation and accommodation lie with the Crown, not with third parties such as industry proponents of a project or permit holders. Third parties have no constitutional duty to consult or provide accommodation, but can be liable for breach of contract, negligence, or dishonest dealings.

Tsilhqot'in Nation v. British Columbia (2014)

On June 26, 2014, the Supreme Court of Canada released a decision regarding a land claim by the Tsilhqot'in Nation that had commenced in 1983 after the Tsilhqot'in objected to a commercial logging licence being issued in their traditional territory.[8] The Tsilhqot'in are a semi-nomadic group of six Indian bands in central British Columbia who share a common culture and history. The Supreme Court of Canada found, based on the evidence presented at the trial level, that the Tsilhqot'in had established title to the land they claimed and issued a declaration that British Columbia had breached its duty to consult with the First Nation. This is the first case in which the Supreme Court of Canada recognized title of a First Nation to a specific area of land, as previous decisions, such as *Delgamuukw v. The Queen*, had set out clarification of the law and sent the actual claim for title back for further negotiation between the Crown and the First Nation.

Aside from its significance to the Tsilhqot'in First Nation, this Supreme Court of Canada decision clarified a number of issues that will have more general application to Aboriginal rights and title claims in Canada. In *Delgamuukw v. The Queen*, the court had previously stated that the test for Aboriginal title was based on occupation prior to the assertion of European sovereignty and that the occupation must be sufficient, continuous, and exclusive. One issue in the *Tsilhqot'in* case was whether a semi-nomadic First Nation such as the Tsilhqot'in can meet the test for "occupation." In other words, is a semi-nomadic First Nation restricted to establishing title to specific settlements? The court decided that they are not, and that a claim for title can extend to tracts of land regularly used for hunting, fishing, and otherwise exploiting resources over which the First Nation exercised control prior to the assertion of European sovereignty. The court further held that in this case, the Tsilhqot'in had provided sufficient evidence of continuous and exclusive occupation over the broader territory they claimed.

Members of the Tsilhqot'in First Nation take part in a ceremony in downtown Vancouver to raise awareness of their land claims, prior to the Supreme Court of Canada's landmark ruling in their favour in June 2014.
Source: Harjap Grewal.

In determining whether the Tsilhqot'in had established title, the court looked at sufficiency of occupation, continuity of occupation, and exclusivity of occupation. With respect to sufficiency of occupation, the court stated the following:

> [W]hat is required is a culturally sensitive approach to sufficiency of occupation based on the dual perspectives of the Aboriginal group in question—its laws, practices, size, technological ability and the character of the land claimed—and the common law notion of position as a basis for title. ... [A] culturally sensitive approach suggests that regular use of territories for hunting, fishing, trapping and foraging is "sufficient" to ground Aboriginal title, provided that such use, on the facts of a particular case, evinces an intention on the part of the Aboriginal group to hold or possess the land in a manner comparable to what would be required to establish title at common law.[9]

With respect to certainty of occupation, the question was whether continuity exists between present and pre-sovereignty occupation. The court held that continuity does not require Aboriginal groups to provide evidence of an unbroken chain of continuity but that "the present occupation must be rooted in pre-sovereignty times."[10] On the issue of exclusivity, the court stated that exclusivity should be understood in the sense of intention and capacity to control the land.

The court further stated that once Aboriginal title is established, incursion on the land may only occur with the consent of the Aboriginal group with title to the land, or if the incursion is justified by a compelling and substantial public purpose and is not inconsistent with the Crown's fiduciary duty to the Aboriginal group.

Treaties

From 1871 to 1921, 11 "numbered treaties" were signed across Canada, where Aboriginal peoples were settled on reserves. Most numbered treaties include reserve land based on the number of Aboriginal people plus agreements for schooling, agricultural equipment, and training, gifts, and annuities. The numbered treaties extend more or less numerically from east to west, with Treaty No. 1 and Treaty No. 2 covering what is now Manitoba, Treaty No. 3 covering land in what is now Manitoba and Ontario, and Treaty No. 8 covering northwestern Alberta and northeastern British Columbia.

In addition to the colonial-era treaties, the provincial and federal governments have engaged in a number of more modern treaties. Treaties under the federal comprehensive land claims process launched in 1973 include the James Bay and Northern Quebec Agreement,[11] Yukon's Umbrella Final Agreement,[12] the Nunavut Land Claims Agreement,[13] the Nisga'a Treaty in northern British Columbia,[14] the Tsawwassen First Nation Final Agreement in southern British Columbia,[15] and the Maa-nulth First Nations Final Agreement on the west coast of Vancouver Island.[16] Other than Treaty No. 8 and some very early Douglas treaties (named after Governor James Douglas) on Vancouver Island, British Columbia has until recently had limited experience with treaty making compared with the rest of Canada.

Consultation Requirements Under Treaties

When determining what constitutes appropriate consultation and accommodation in a particular case, it is necessary to know whether a treaty applies. If a treaty does apply, it is important to review its provisions on the jurisdiction of the First Nation, the First Nation's rights under the treaty, and the depth of consultation required if a proposed Crown action may infringe on treaty rights. A treaty may include consultation requirements that differ from those in common law. Older treaties are usually vague, making common law guidance on consultation requirements important. However, modern treaties, such as those in British Columbia, have more extensive provisions. For example, the Tsawwassen Final Agreement includes a definition of "consult" and several sections specifying when consultation is required.[17] Another point to remember is that under some treaties, the *Indian Act* no longer applies to the First Nation party to the treaty. Therefore, standard practices for consulting with First Nations (or Indian bands) under the *Indian Act* are not directly transferrable. When working on a matter that involves a treaty, it is essential to carefully read the treaty's consultation requirements.

On July 11, 2014, the Supreme Court of Canada issued a decision regarding interpretation of Treaty No. 3.[18] This treaty was signed in 1873 between treaty commissioners acting on behalf of the Dominion of Canada and Ojibwe Chiefs in what is now northwestern Ontario and eastern Manitoba. Under the provisions of the treaty, the Ojibwe yielded ownership of their territory, except for certain lands reserved for them, and, in return, they received the right to harvest the non-reserve lands until such time as the lands were "taken up" for settlement, mining, lumbering, or other purposes by the Government of the Dominion of Canada.

In 2005, the Grassy Narrows First Nation challenged a forestry licence issued by the Government of Ontario to a pulp and paper manufacturer located within Treaty No. 3 territory. The central issue before the courts was whether Ontario had jurisdiction to issue the forestry licence, given that the treaty refers to the "Dominion of Canada." The Supreme Court of Canada determined that although Treaty No. 3 was negotiated between representatives of the federal government and the Ojibwe, it is an agreement between the Crown and the First Nation, and the Crown includes the provinces. The court held that both levels of government are responsible for fulfilling promises under the treaty, and because the provincial government of Ontario has jurisdiction over land and resources pursuant to sections 92(5), 92A, and 109 of the *Constitution Act, 1867*, the provincial government has jurisdiction over the resources in question. Further, the text of the provision regarding the "taking up" of lands supports the view that the right to take up land lies with the level of government that has jurisdiction to do so under the Constitution. The court found that the reference in the treaty to the "Dominion of Canada" simply reflected the fact that at the time, the lands were in Canada, not in Ontario as it is jurisdictionally defined today.

However, Ontario's authority to "take up" lands under Treaty No. 3 is not unconditional. The court further clarified that when a government exercises Crown power, the exercise of that power is burdened by the Crown's obligations to the Aboriginal people in question, and the Crown must exercise its power in conformity with the honour of the Crown and the fiduciary duties of the Crown in relation to Aboriginal interests.

The *Grassy Narrows* case illustrates both the similarities and differences between cases involving claims for Aboriginal title where there is no treaty, such as the *Tsilhqot'in* case and cases involving a treaty. The similarities are that the Crown is always subject to its duty to act honourably and consistently with its fiduciary duty toward Aboriginal people. The difference is that where there is a treaty, the specific terms and wording of the treaty are important in defining the obligations of the Crown.

Guidance on Consultation Obligations

In response to the growing body of Aboriginal law, federal and provincial governments have published a number of documents that summarize and explain the law and provide guidance on appropriate consultation with Aboriginal peoples. For example, the federal government published *Aboriginal Consultation and Accommodation: Updated Guidelines for Federal Officials to Fulfill the Duty to Consult* in

March 2011.[19] Similarly, the government of British Columbia issued *Updated Procedures for Meeting Legal Obligations When Consulting with First Nations* in May 2010,[20] and the government of Ontario issued *Draft Guidelines for Ministries on Consultation with Aboriginal Peoples Related to Aboriginal Rights and Treaty Rights*.[21] These documents are periodically updated to reflect developments in the law, are usually developed in consultation with Aboriginal people, and are made publicly available. However, consultation guides published by governments are interpretations of the law rather than the law itself.

Conclusion

A few themes emerge in Aboriginal law in Canada. One is that connection to the land and the right to hunt, fish, and gather are highly important to Aboriginal peoples. Another is that environmental law has developed alongside Aboriginal law. Conflicts in "Aboriginal law," therefore, are also often conflicts in "environmental law." The interconnection between Aboriginal law and environmental law means that activities that may affect the environment or resources (fisheries, water, forestry, mining) often must be undertaken in consideration of their potential effects on Aboriginal rights and title. The duty is on the Crown to consider Aboriginal rights and title prior to issuing permits for activities such as logging or mining. Another theme is that in Canada, major land use projects cannot proceed without consultation with Aboriginal peoples. Examples of such projects are fracking activities in several provinces, the development of the oil sands in Alberta, and the Northern Gateway pipeline and the use of groundwater in British Columbia. Even if consultation is not provided for in the applicable legislation or government policy, based on past court decisions, it is necessary to address Aboriginal rights and title claims. Consultation with Aboriginal peoples is a constitutional issue. Aboriginal law and environmental law will continue to evolve together. A complete understanding of environmental law requires keeping up to date with Aboriginal law.

SUMMARY OF KEY POINTS

- The Constitution recognizes existing Aboriginal and treaty rights (section 35 of the *Constitution Act, 1982*).
- The Crown has a special relationship with Aboriginal peoples and must behave honourably. Maintaining the honour of the Crown requires consultation with First Nations and, where appropriate, accommodation of First Nations concerns about impacts on their rights and title, even before rights or title are proven.
- Consultation with Aboriginal peoples is usually required when reviewing major projects or issuing permits that projects need to proceed. The *Haida*

Nation v. British Columbia (Minister of Forests) case clarified that the obligation to consult rests with the Crown (not third parties) and exists even before title is proven. The *Tsilhqot'in Nation v. British Columbia* case stated that where title is proven, it may only be impinged with the consent of the First Nation, or to meet a pressing and substantial public purpose.

- Treaties, where applicable, and the common law should be reviewed to determine the nature of consultation required on a project. Older treaties usually say very little or nothing of consultation, but recent ones such as the Tsawwassen First Nation Final Agreement or the Maa-nulth First Nations Final Agreement in British Columbia contain provisions identifying what matters trigger the need to consult with the First Nations signatory to the treaty.

KEY TERMS

Aboriginal peoples
collective rights
extinguishment
right
status Indian
title
treaty (Aboriginal)

DISCUSSION QUESTIONS

1. What are the key elements of the Supreme Court of Canada's interpretation of section 35 of the *Constitution Act, 1867*?
2. What is the difference between the terms *Indian, First Nation,* and *Aboriginal peoples*?
3. Suppose that you have been hired by a company to assist in the process of preparing a project for environmental assessment. The proposed activity may potentially affect the rights and title claims of First Nations in the area. What would you advise your employer to consider with respect to the following: (1) whether the company has an obligation to consult with First Nations; (2) whether you should determine if there is a treaty in place (and why or why not); and (3) the types of information the First Nation may provide to fulfill the required consultation.

SUGGESTED READINGS

Readings

British Columbia. *Updated Procedures for Meeting Legal Obligations When Consulting First Nations: Interim.* Victoria: Province of British Columbia, 2010, http://www2 .gov.bc.ca/gov/DownloadAsset?assetId=9779EDACB673486883560B59BEBE782E.

Canada. *Aboriginal Consultation and Accommodation: Updated Guidelines for Federal Officials to Fulfill the Duty to Consult.* Ottawa: Department of Aboriginal Affairs and Northern Development Canada, 2011, http://www.aadnc-aandc.gc.ca/DAM/ DAM-INTER-HQ/STAGING/texte-text/intgui_1100100014665_eng.pdf.

Delgamuukw v. British Columbia, [1997] 3 SCR 1010.

"Elsipogtog Anti-Fracking Protests Triggering Angry Online Backlash." *APTN National News,* December 2, 2013, http://aptn.ca/news/2013/11/15/elsipogtog-anti-fracking -protests-triggering-angry-online-backlash.

Haida Nation v. British Columbia (Minister of Forests), 2004 SCC 73, [2004] 3 SCR 511.

Hunter, Justine. "Northern Gateway Has Ottawa Scrambling to Avoid Lawsuits." *Globe and Mail,* December 23, 2013, http://www.theglobeandmail.com/news/british -columbia/northern-gateway-has-ottawa-scrambling-to-avoid-lawsuits/ article16096644/.

Ontario. *Draft Guidelines for Ministries on Consultation with Aboriginal Peoples Related to Aboriginal Rights and Treaty Rights.* Toronto: Secretariat for Aboriginal Affairs, 2006, https://www.ontario.ca/government/draft-guidelines-ministries -consultation-aboriginal-peoples-related-aboriginal.

Sinoski, Kelli. "Nestlé's Extraction of Groundwater Near Hope Riles First Nations." *Vancouver Sun,* August 22, 2013, http://www.vancouversun.com/life/Nestlé +extraction+groundwater+near+Hope+riles+First+Nations/8817969/story.html.

Sparrow, R v., [1990] 1 SCR 1075.

Taku River Tlingit First Nation v. British Columbia (Project Assessment Director), 2004 SCC 74, [2004] 3 SCR 550.

Tsilhqot'in Nation v. British Columbia, 2014 SCC 44.

Weber, Bob. "First Nations Ramp Up Challenge to Oilsands Development." *Vancouver Sun,* January 3, 2014.

Weber, Bob. "Lubicon vs. PennWest: Band Files Lawsuit Against Alberta Energy Firm Over Fracking." *Huffington Post Alberta,* December 2, 2013, http://www.huffingtonpost.ca/ 2013/12/02/lubicon-pennwest-lawsuit_n_4372856.html.

Websites

Aboriginal Affairs and Northern Development Canada: http://www.aadnc-aandc.gc.ca/eng

BC Treaty Commission: http://bctreaty.net

NOTES

1. *Tsawwassen First Nation Final Agreement Act*, SBC 2007, c. 39 (the provincial law giving the treaty effect) and the *Tsawwassen First Nation Final Agreement Act*, SC 2008, c. 32 (at the federal level).

2. *Calder et al. v. Attorney-General of British Columbia*, [1973] SCR 313.

3. *R v. Sparrow*, [1990] 1 SCR 1075.

4. *Delgamuukw v. British Columbia*, [1997] 3 SCR 1010.

5. *Taku River Tlingit First Nation v. British Columbia (Project Assessment Director)*, 2004 SCC 74, [2004] 3 SCR 550.

6. "Enbridge Northern Gateway Pipeline: Community Opposition and Investment Risk (Executive Summary)," *ForestEthics*, October 2010, http://wewillnotbesilenced.ca/downloads/Enbr_investor_summary_oct2010_print.pdf.

7. *Haida Nation v. British Columbia (Minister of Forests)*, 2004 SCC 73, [2004] 3 SCR 511.

8. *Tsilhqot'in Nation v. British Columbia*, 2014 SCC 44.

9. Ibid., at paras. 41 and 42.

10. Ibid., at para. 46.

11. The James Bay and Northern Quebec Agreement (JBNQA), 2004, http://www.gcc.ca/pdf/LEG000000006.pdf.

12. Umbrella Final Agreement Between the Government of Canada, the Council for Yukon Indians and the Government of the Yukon, 1993, http://www.eco.gov.yk.ca/pdf/umbrellafinalagreement.pdf.

13. Nunavut Land Claims Agreement, 1993, http://nlca.tunngavik.com.

14. Nisga'a Final Agreement, 1999, http://www.nisgaanation.ca/treaty-documents.

15. Tsawwassen First Nation Final Agreement, 2007, http://www.gov.bc.ca/arr/reports/down/tsawwassen_first_nation_final_agreement_implementation_report_0910.pdf.

16. Maa-nulth First Nations Final Agreement, 2006, http://www.bctreaty.net/nations/agreements/Maanulth_final_intial_Dec06.pdf.

17. British Columbia, "First Nations Negotiations," accessed July 14, 2014, http://www.gov.bc.ca/arr/firstnation/tsawwassen/down/final/tfn_fa.pdf.

18. *Grassy Narrows First Nation v. Ontario (Natural Resources)*, 2014 SCC 48.

19. Canada, *Aboriginal Consultation and Accommodation: Updated Guidelines for Federal Officials to Fulfill the Duty to Consult* (Ottawa: Department of Aboriginal Affairs and Northern Development Canada, 2011), http://www.aadnc-aandc.gc.ca/DAM/DAM-INTER-HQ/STAGING/texte-text/intgui_1100100014665_eng.pdf.

20. British Columbia, *Updated Procedures for Meeting Legal Obligations When Consulting First Nations: Interim* (Victoria: Province of British Columbia, 2010), http://www2.gov.bc.ca/gov/DownloadAsset?assetId=9779EDACB673486883560B59BEBE782E.

21. Ontario, *Draft Guidelines for Ministries on Consultation with Aboriginal Peoples Related to Aboriginal Rights and Treaty Rights* (Toronto: Secretariat for Aboriginal Affairs, 2006), https://www.ontario.ca/government/draft-guidelines-ministries-consultation-aboriginal-peoples-related-aboriginal.

CHAPTER 6

The Relationship Between Canadian and International Law

Introduction: How International Law Works

International law is a collection of rules governing countries. This simple definition should not disguise the complexity of international law. It is somewhat dangerous to compare international and **domestic law** (law within a particular country) because there are so many differences. Unlike domestic law in Canada, international law has no legislature that actually makes law, and it has no police force that can readily enforce the law. In fact, a constant challenge in international law is even identifying the precise obligations that states must fulfill.

The most fundamental precept of international law is that states are sovereign in nature. They can do what they want subject only to limits imposed by international law. In general terms, a state may be bound by conventional law or customary international law. How well this precept will serve in coming years is uncertain, in part because of the expanding challenges of environmental protection on a global scale. Many traditional environmental problems (e.g., resource degradation and overuse, habitat destruction, biodiversity loss, and exposure to toxic substances) are now

---

international law   a collection of rules governing countries

domestic law   the law within a particular country

CASE STUDY

Canada and the Stockholm Convention

A good example of the interplay between international and Canadian domestic law is the 2001 Stockholm Convention on Persistent Organic Pollutants,* an agreement in which Canada played a major role. The thrust of the convention is to phase out the "dirty dozen" most dangerous toxic substances in the world. Among other things, the Convention finally put in place a timeline to phase out DDT, an insecticide, which was identified as a damaging persistent toxin by Rachel Carson in her famous book *Silent Spring*.[†] The book appeared in 1962, nearly 40 years before the Stockholm Convention finally brought international action to this issue.

Negotiations for the Stockholm Convention began in 1996 in Montreal. In 2001, after five more negotiation sessions, the parties concluded the Convention in Stockholm, Sweden. The Stockholm Convention did not come into force until May 2004, when the last of the 50 countries required for it to enter into force ratified it.

Canada played a major role in the formation, and gradual implementation, of the Stockholm Convention. Its role was premised by the idea that in order to address the impacts of these substances within Canada, global action was required. Environment Canada noted that all Canadians may be exposed to these substances; "inhabitants of the far North are at increased risk to POPs [persistent organic pollutants] exposure due to a diet and culture that relies on foods harvested from their surrounding environment."[‡]

Although Canada had already regulated the uses of some of the substances of concern, it was required to take a number of legislative and policy actions to meet the obligations under the Stockholm Convention. In 2006, Canada submitted an action plan that would seek to implement the Stockholm Convention, and after consultation with

A peregrine falcon hunts among the office towers in Toronto, where it is nesting. It is one of the species of birds whose increase in numbers has been attributed to a ban on the pesticide DDT, which has been shown to thin the eggshells of many species.

Source: Carlos Osorio, GetStock.com.

the public, the final version was released in April 2013.§ Canada's action plan, which shows the interplay between international law obligations and domestic law and policy, indicates that its domestic laws and policies will fulfill its international obligations to reduce or phase out the substances listed in the Stockholm Convention.#

Questions

Why do you think that it took over 40 years for the international community to agree to phase out products like DDT? Do you have confidence that the obligations in the Stockholm Convention will be met, and, if not, what do you think can be done to promote compliance? Although Canada played an important role in the formation of the Stockholm Convention, what role should Canada play in the international environmental law arena?

---

*   *Stockholm Convention on Persistent Organic Pollutants*, 2001, http://chm.pops.int/Home/tabid/2121/mctl/ViewDetails/EventModID/871/EventID/514/xmid/6921/Default.aspx.

†   Rachel Carson, *Silent Spring* (Boston: Houghton Mifflin, 1962).

‡   Environment Canada, "Update to Canada's National Implementation Plan Under the Stockholm Convention on Persistent Organic Pollutants," April 2013, chapter 1, https://www.ec.gc.ca/lcpe-cepa/default.asp?lang=En&n=E0F02793-1&offset=2&toc=show.

§   The approved version: Environment Canada, "Update to Canada's National Implementation Plan Under the Stockholm Convention on Persistent Organic Pollutants," April 2013, https://www.ec.gc.ca/lcpe-cepa/default.asp?lang=En&n=E0F02793-1.

For a review of this action plan by a non-governmental group, see Fe de Leon, Anna Tilman, and Andrea Moher, Responding to Canada's National Implementation Plan Under the Stockholm Convention on Persistent Organic Pollutants (POPs) Consultation Draft February 2005, http://s.cela.ca/files/uploads/506_NIP.pdf.

cross-boundary issues and pose international threats to human and ecosystem well-being. Moreover, we now have fully global problems, the most serious of which is probably human-induced climate change. To deal effectively with these concerns, some further strengthening of international environmental law may be needed.

Conventional International Law

Conventional international law is established when two or more countries conclude a **treaty** or **convention**. These conventions bind only those countries that have signed them. Essentially, a treaty or convention is like a contract between two people. In a contract, one party agrees to do something (such as paint a house) if the other party agrees to some equally valuable action (such as paying a stated price for the work). Similarly, a country may agree to give up a small portion of its sovereignty

---

conventional international law   the body of international law contained in treaties or conventions versus customary international law or other types of international law

treaty (or convention)   an agreement between two or more sovereign states, binding only those states that sign it on particular matters within specified limits that are defined in the treaty. As might be expected, great efforts are usually made in treaty negotiations to determine precisely what the agreement covers and what obligations are involved.

Within conventional international law, various terms are used to describe the nature of an agreement. An international *convention* or *treaty* is usually regarded as the most formal form of international agreement and meant to signify that the parties to the convention are committed to its terms. A **protocol** is used for less formal agreements, as the following definition indicates:

> A protocol, in the context of treaty law and practice, has the same legal characteristics as a treaty. The term protocol is often used to describe agreements of a less formal nature than those entitled treaty or convention. Generally, a protocol amends, supplements or clarifies a multilateral treaty. A protocol is normally open to participation by the parties to the parent agreement. However, in recent times States have negotiated a number of protocols that do not follow this principle. The advantage of a protocol is that, while it is linked to the parent agreement, it can focus on a specific aspect of that agreement in greater detail.[1]

Most treaties and conventions take a long time to negotiate and implement. The basic steps of this process usually start when an international body (e.g., the United Nations Environment Programme) agrees to sponsor the negotiations among countries. If the international negotiating sessions are successful, an agreement is drafted and signed by the participating countries. However, the agreement does not take effect until a defined number of those countries have ratified the agreement within an allotted time.

Ratification simply means agreement to the terms of the convention by the national legislature of the countries signing the convention. On ratification, the agreement comes into effect, although most often there is a multi-year phase-in period. Once the agreement is in effect, the countries meet periodically in "conferences of the parties" to review the progress of the implementation.

Generally speaking, international conventions use a standard framework consisting of sections that set out

- the purposes of the convention,
- the general and specific obligations of the parties,
- reporting obligations,

---

protocol often used to describe an agreement of a less formal nature than a treaty or convention; generally, a protocol amends, supplements, or clarifies a multilateral treaty

ratification an agreement to the terms of a convention by the domestic legislatures of the countries signing the convention

- dispute settlement and compliance mechanisms, and
- review mechanisms for the convention.

Today, hundreds of **bilateral** and **multilateral treaties**, conventions, and agreements are in force pertaining to environmental protection and resource management. Hence, the first task in understanding the commitments of a particular state is to list the international agreements to which it is a party, and to understand the precise nature and scope of the obligations it has agreed to in each instrument.

There are over 1,100 international agreements dealing with the environment. Box 6.1 lists just a few of them.[2]

BOX 6.1 » Examples of United Nations Environment-Related Multilateral Treaties*

- Vienna Convention for the Protection of the Ozone Layer (Vienna, March 22, 1985)
- Basel Convention on the Control of Transboundary Movements of Hazardous Wastes and Their Disposal (Basel, March 22, 1989)
- United Nations Framework Convention on Climate Change (New York, May 9, 1992)
- Amendment to the Montreal Protocol on Substances that Deplete the Ozone Layer adopted by the Ninth Meeting of the Parties (Montreal, September, 17, 1997)
- Rotterdam Convention on the Prior Informed Consent Procedure for Certain Hazardous Chemicals and Pesticides in International Trade (Rotterdam, September 10, 1998)
- Stockholm Convention on Persistent Organic Pollutants (Stockholm, May 17, 2004)
- Minamata Convention on Mercury (Kumamoto, October 10, 2013)

---

* Adapted from United Nations, *Treaty Event 2014: Towards Universal Participation and Implementation* (New York: United Nations, 2014), https://treaties.un.org/doc/source/events/2014/Publication/publication-English.pdf; and United Nations, "Treaties Deposited with the Secretary-General Close to Universal Participation," May 2014, https://treaties.un.org/doc/source/events/2014/Treaties/list_global_english.pdf.

Customary International Law

Customary international law is the set of rules that has evolved over time and been accepted by states as effective law. Customary international law has two attributes: first, states must recognize a particular rule of law to be binding (this doctrine is called *opinio juris*), and second, states must in fact follow the rule.

---

bilateral treaty a treaty between two countries

multilateral treaty a treaty between more than two countries

customary international law the set of international rules that have evolved over time and been accepted by states as effective law

With respect to the environment, a number of important international customs are relevant, such as the following:

- *The good neighbour rule*. This principle requires a state not to cause damage to the environment of another state. It can be applied in situations such as dumping toxins into the Great Lakes, where a particular neighbour is affected, which is reminiscent of the tort of nuisance. It can also be applied to greenhouse gas emissions, where the scope of the neighbourhood is the entire planet.
- *Duty of equitable utilization*. This principle requires the fair sharing of resources outside national boundaries, such as in international waters. It involves an imperative to preserve and protect these resources with thought to the rights of others who also have the right to use them.
- *Duty to notify and consult*. This principle requires a state that is undertaking an activity that could result in harm to neighbouring nations to notify and consult with the governments of those nations. For example, if radioactive waste is to be shipped in international waters, any countries that could be affected by a spill should be notified in advance.

The Relevance of International Law to Canadian Environmental Law

The effect of international environmental law on domestic law varies. Arguably, international law influences domestic law by imposing requirements that must be carried out by Canada. In the case of the Great Lakes, the federal government has negotiated certain commitments with the province of Ontario to reduce phosphorous reductions. By and large, it is the province that has the bulk of constitutional authority to enact measures to reduce these kinds of pollutants. On the basis of these commitments, the federal government negotiated the first Great Lakes Water Quality Agreement with the United States.[3] In other words, the federal government knew exactly what commitments it could negotiate with the United States because it had secured specific commitments with the relevant province.

In other instances, the federal government may use international environmental law to encourage or promote provincial action on the basis that Canada has now made certain environmental commitments internationally and such commitments should be fulfilled. For example, Canada signed the United Nations Framework Convention on Climate Change in 1992, promising to stabilize greenhouse gas emissions at 1990 levels by the year 2000. It also signed the Kyoto Protocol in 1997, promising to cut Canadian emissions to 6 percent below our 1990 levels by 2012. But the Canadian Parliament did not formally ratify the Kyoto Protocol until late 2002, and in 2011, Canada formally pulled out of the accord. Far from reducing greenhouse gases, Canada's emissions grew 17 percent between 1990 and 2010;[4] even under the subsequent 2009 Copenhagen Accord, as of 2015 Canada remains far off the pace to reduce emissions to the target of 17 percent below 2005 levels by 2020. An interesting question is whether the federal government should have signed on to these international obligations without first securing the commitment of the provinces or whether the fact that the federal government did sign on had the benefit of initiating a robust debate within Canada on climate change and Canada's role with respect to this issue.

The United Nations Convention on Biological Diversity, which was signed and ratified by Canada in 1992, provides an example of another approach. Ten years later, in 2002, the *Species at Risk Act* was enacted, finally bringing Canada into compliance with its obligations under the convention. In that context, the federal government was very careful to design a law focused on areas of federal jurisdiction suggesting that the federal government did not intend to enter a controversial federal–provincial jurisdictional debate.

In other instances, Canada has influenced international law. The classic example is the expansion of Canada's rights over the oceans' resources. During the 1960s and early 1970s, Canada unilaterally extended its rights by establishing an exclusive economic zone stretching 200 nautical miles from the coast. This type of action was new; previously, states controlled only a very narrow belt of water adjacent to their coasts—approximately 3 to 12 nautical miles. Beyond this belt of **territorial waters**, the ocean was part of the high seas and open to use and exploitation by anyone. Before the new international regime introduced by Canada, two United Nations conferences on the law of the sea were unable to achieve consensus on extending jurisdiction to even a 12-mile territorial limit. Despite this history, Canada's initiative was embraced internationally, and the principle of an exclusive economic zone was accepted as a customary rule of international law. Later it was entrenched in the Law of the Sea Treaty. This treaty now provides all coastal nations with exclusive rights to a very important economic resource, including rich fishing and fossil fuel reserves.

Canada has not been a major player in the international environmental law scene. We have, however, made some significant contributions while at the same time being careful and not always consistent about the obligations we have been willing to take on through the negotiation of international agreements. In fact, in recent times, Canada has been obstructive in achieving more progressive international obligations under international law. For example, Canada has not taken proactive or progressive positions with respect to international negotiations on an international agreement to control mercury or on a proposal to add chrysotile asbestos to the Rotterdam Convention. Although Canada is often considered to be a leading member of the pack in international law, in practice, Canada has at times been criticized for trying to stall and failing to implement positive international environmental initiatives.[5]

---

territorial waters   the belt of water adjacent to a coast, over which the coastal state holds jurisdiction

SUMMARY OF KEY POINTS

- International law is a collection of rules that govern countries. Unlike domestic law, there is no international legislature or police force.
- Conventional international law is established when countries contract or agree to certain obligations expressly through an international agreement, treaty, convention, or protocol.
- Customary international law is the set of rules that has evolved over time and been accepted by states as law. States must recognize a particular rule of law to be binding (*opinio juris*) and states must follow the rule. Two examples of customary rules are the *good neighbour rule* and the *duty to notify and consult*.
- Numerous examples exist in which international environmental law has influenced domestic law and in which Canada has had an important influence on the establishment of new or emerging international environmental rules.

KEY TERMS

bilateral treaty
conventional international law
customary international law
domestic law

international law
multilateral treaty
protocol
ratification

territorial waters
treaty (or convention)

DISCUSSION QUESTIONS

1. Are conventional and customary international law really "law" in the way we understand law in Canada?
2. How effective do you think international law can be to protect the environment?
3. How would you characterize Canada's role in the international environmental arena? What role should it play in the future?

SUGGESTED READINGS

Readings

Birnie, Patricia, and Alan Boyle. *International Law and the Environment*, 2nd ed. New York: Oxford University Press, 2002.

Botts, Lee, and Paul Muldoon. *Evolution of the Great Lakes Water Quality Agreement*. East Lansing, MI: Michigan State University Press, 2005.

de Mestral, Armand, and Evan Fox-Decent. "Rethinking the Relationship Between International Law and Domestic Law." (2008) 53:4 *McGill Law Journal* 573-648.

Hughes, Elaine, Alastair Lucas, and William Tilleman. *Environmental Law and Policy*, 3rd ed., chapter 15. Toronto: Emond Montgomery, 2003.

United Nations. *Treaty Handbook*, rev. ed. New York: United Nations, 2012, https://treaties.un.org/doc/source/publications/THB/English.pdf.

Websites

Environment Canada, "Update to Canada's National Implementation Plan Under the Stockholm Convention on Persistent Organic Pollutants": https://www.ec.gc.ca/lcpe-cepa/default.asp?lang=En&n=E0F02793-1

Stockholm Convention on Persistent Organic Pollutants, Convention Text: http://chm.pops.int/TheConvention/Overview/TextoftheConvention/tabid/2232/Default.aspx

United Nations Environment Programme, "Treaties and Decisions": http://ozone.unep.org/en/treaties.php

NOTES

1. United Nations, *Treaty Handbook*, rev. ed. (New York: United Nations, 2012), at 69.

2. For more background on the number and nature of international environmental agreements, see International Environmental Agreements (IEA) Database Project, http://iea.uoregon.edu/page.php?file=home.htm&query=static.

3. See Lee Botts and Paul Muldoon, *Evolution of the Great Lakes Water Quality Agreement* (East Lansing, MI: Michigan State University Press, 2005), at 31.

4. The Conference Board of Canada, "Greenhouse Gas Emissions: Key Messages," January 2013, http://www.conferenceboard.ca/hcp/details/environment/greenhouse-gas-emissions.aspx.

5. See Tony Burman, "Canada's real international shame—and it's not Ford," *Toronto Star*, November 23, 2013, http://www.thestar.com/news/world/2013/11/23/canadas_real_international_shame_and_its_not_ford_burman.html, and Anna Johnston, "Canada Gutting Its International Reputation Along with Its Environmental Laws," *West Coast Environmental Law*, November 14, 2013, http://wcel.org/resources/environmental-law-alert/canada-gutting-its-international-reputation-along-its-environmenta.

PART III

Regulatory Regimes

CHAPTER 7

The Basic Structure of Environmental Protection Regimes

Introduction

This chapter outlines the basic structure of environmental law in Canada. Although significant differences exist among the various regimes at both the federal and provincial levels and from one province to another, some characteristics and features are common to all jurisdictions (environmental protection regimes are discussed further in Chapter 8).

The two basic categories of environmental law are private law and public law. **Private law** pertains to the protection or furtherance of personal or individual interests and property. Most environmental law is **public law**—that is, rules made and enforced by the state to protect the public interest and safeguard the public good. Table 7.1 provides a brief overview of the key components of private and public environmental law.

---

private law law pertaining to personal rights, such as the right to protect one's own property and interests

public law law enforced by the state against those who fail to abide by it

Table 7.1   Key Components of Environmental Law

	Private Law	Public Law
Description	Individuals exercise rights against others to protect their own property or interests	The state imposes regulatory frameworks that set environmental standards and consequences for non-compliance
Examples	Torts (e.g., nuisance, negligence), Ontario *Environmental Bill of Rights, 1993*	Federal *Environmental Protection Act, 1999* and the regulations passed under it; Ontario *Environmental Protection Act* and the regulations passed under it
Source	Common law or civil law and some statutory law	Statutes, regulations, administrative orders, and approvals

CASE STUDY

Can a Lawsuit Save a River? KVP Co. Ltd. v. McKie et al.

During the early 1940s, courtesy of the Great Depression, the Spanish River in Northern Ontario experienced a renewal and reprieve from many years of pollution. At the time, the pulp and paper mill that had caused serious environmental harm had been out of operation for ten years. The river had begun to heal itself. Its fish species had returned and were flourishing. Its waters had again become usable for swimming, fishing, and even human consumption. Nascent commercial fishing and tourism industries had sprung up. Then, suddenly, everything changed again.

In the summer of 1946, the pulp and paper mill was reopened by a new owner, the Kalamazoo Vegetable Parchment (KVP) Company. Following the industrial practice of the day, the company began discharging waste materials, large quantities of chemically laced wood fibres, into the river. Almost overnight, the water quality in the river became severely degraded and fisheries were devastated. Here is how Peter Best, a local lawyer and historian, described some of the impact:

> Soon the river began smelling like rotten cabbage right down and into Georgian Bay ... The water became unfit for drinking, cooking or washing and when it was heated the vapours given off were so offensive that "you could not stay in the house." The wild rice growing at the River's mouth was de-

stroyed eliminating a feeding ground for ducks. The river water could no longer be used to water farm animals or for any other domestic or agricultural purpose.*

Most residents in the area accepted the death of the river as the price that must be paid for the return of jobs and a measure of prosperity to an area that had been economically decimated by the closure of the mill in the early 1930s. However, the fishermen, tourist operators, and property owners who lived and worked along the river were angry. Their livelihood and use and enjoyment of their properties had been destroyed almost overnight. But what recourse did they have? In 1946, there was no such thing as an environmental statute in Ontario. Not a single law existed that could protect the river or its inhabitants from the impacts of industrial pollution.

These circumstances gave rise to a landmark legal challenge. The property owners on the Spanish River ("the riparian owners") pooled their resources and brought a private law suit against the KVP Company that made it all the way to the Supreme Court of Canada.† Their case relied on prior court decisions that had protected riparian property rights. Following a tough legal battle against the company, the riparian owners not only won their claim against the company but also obtained a ground-breaking court order, an injunction‡ that prohibited the company from "depositing foreign substances into the river waters which alter the character or quality of the water to the injury [of the riparian owners]." The case proved that a watercourse could be protected from environmental harm, without the need for environmental legislation or government action. The river had been saved by individuals following the old-school approach of suing one's neighbours in court to protect private property rights. Or so it seemed.

In the 1940s, the Ontario government did not pass laws to protect rivers from pollution. It was prepared, however, to pass a law to protect the jobs and perceived economic well-being of a one-industry northern Ontario community. In 1950, the *KVP Company Limited Act*§ came into force. This statute dissolved the injunction awarded by the courts against the KVP Company, thereby allowing the company to return to its previous polluting practices.#

Questions

What lessons can be drawn about the benefits and limitations of both public and private law as mechanisms to protect environmental resources and features from the KVP Company case? Are any of these lessons

still applicable today and, if so, how? Can the courts ensure long-term environmental protection for society through case-by-case adjudication of private law cases (i.e., legal disputes between companies and persons potentially wronged through environmental impacts of their industrial operations)? What are the strengths and limitations of the role of the courts in environmental protection?

---

* Peter Best, "KVP Trial History" (from articles appearing in the *Mid-North Monitor*), *Friends of the Spanish River* (offline as of October 2014).

† *KVP Co. Ltd. v. McKie et al.*, [1949] SCR 698, 1949 CanLII 8; aff'g. [1948] 3 DLR 201, [1948] OR 398, 1948 CanLII 93 (Ont. SC).

‡ See Chapter 13, which describes injunctions and other types of common law remedies applicable to environmental litigation.

§ *The KVP Company Limited Act, 1950*, SO 1950, c. 33.

The KVP Act did contain one unique and arguably progressive provision, a direction to the Research Council of Ontario to explore cleanup options for the river at the companies expense. KVP is reported to have taken some remedial actions in the aftermath of the court decision and legislative response, with positive consequences for the health of the Spanish River.

Private Law

Private law rights are the rights of private parties to seek compensation when they are harmed by others. Generally, private law rights are thought of as those derived from the common law (or the *Civil Code of Québec*), although various statutes further describe and augment common law rights.[1]

Common Law Rights

Common law rights are rights to sue for environmental harm (see Chapter 13 for details on the common law right to sue and environmental law causes of action). These rights were established over time, based on rulings by judges on a case-by-case basis, which become precedents for future cases.

For example, in the old and well-known case of *Rylands v. Fletcher*,[2] a reservoir burst and water escaped through an underground channel of which the reservoir owner was unaware, damaging a neighbour's property. The rule that arose from *Rylands v. Fletcher* provides that a person who has a dangerous thing on his or her land is liable for any damage to neighbouring lands caused by the escape of the thing. Over time, other judges followed the reasoning of the court in *Rylands*, applying it to new, similar fact situations, establishing a common law "cause of action" known as "the rule in *Rylands v. Fletcher*," or the "strict liability"[3] rule.

Other causes of action that address environmental harm and have developed through the common law include nuisance, negligence, trespass, and, as illustrated in the case study above, interference with riparian rights (water rights). These causes of action are discussed in more detail in Chapter 13.

Court decisions on environmental actions can have a broader impact on environmental behaviour that go beyond the case and litigants at hand. Sophisticated industries and industry associations track court rulings. Decisions on environmental law suits can deter potential polluters and set standards for environmental practices that industry will follow to avoid future liability.

At the same time, the court system and lawsuits based on common law causes of action have an obvious limitation as tools to advance broader environmental protection and pollution prevention objectives. The common law system is intended to allocate individual liability in specific disputes arising between private parties and to compensate identifiable victims, not to protect the environment generally for the benefit of the public and future generations.

Public Law

Public law consists of regulatory frameworks established by statutes, regulations, and policies. These regulatory frameworks create an often overlapping web of rules and processes that govern environmental behaviour.

Two underlying mechanisms are common to almost all of these regulatory frameworks: (1) a "command" function that involves setting standards for acceptable human behaviour regarding the protection of the environment; (2) and a "control" function that involves ensuring compliance with those standards. These two functions and how they operate are discussed in more detail in Chapter 8.

Beyond these two mechanisms, it is difficult to make general statements about how various regulatory systems aimed at environmental protection work. In Canada, this difficulty is due in part to the overlapping division of powers of the federal and provincial regimes created by the Canadian Constitution. In addition, as the next few chapters illustrate, governments approach the protection of the environment in different ways, depending on the situation. Some regulatory frameworks are more focused on one sector than another, and some are more sophisticated than others.

However, organizing concepts or themes can be discerned from a review of public law. In particular, three types of regulatory frameworks (or "regimes") have gained broad usage in many jurisdictions: (1) **media-based regimes**; (2) **sector-based regimes**;

---

media-based regimes   regulatory frameworks that apply to a particular environmental medium, such as air, water, or land

sector-based regimes   regulatory frameworks that apply to a particular sector or specific area, such as energy, endangered species, or agriculture and (3) **approval-based regimes**. Each type is introduced below and discussed in greater detail in subsequent chapters.

Regulatory Frameworks or Regimes

1. Media-Based Regimes

One very common approach to environmental law-making involves compartmentalizing legal regimes in accordance with the three basic media through which contaminants move: air, water, and land. In Canada, the federal government and virtually every province has a specific regime to protect air, water, and land from pollution.[4] For example, a single factory operating in Canada might be required to comply with the following separate media-based obligations:

- *Air.* Approval for air emissions.
- *Water.* Approval for discharge to water, approval to take water from a local water body, and compliance with sewer-use bylaws for discharge to sewers.
- *Land.* Approval for waste storage or processing onsite, and specific property use restrictions based on historical soil contamination.

Arguably the distinctions among media are artificial. For example, wastes stored on land can leach into groundwater, and sulphur emissions in the air cause acid rain and damage lakes. Although statutes with titles such as "Environmental Protection Act" suggest an integrated approach—where air and water emissions, and wastes from a particular facility are reviewed as a whole—the actual mechanics of the legislation continue to separate the environment into separate media. For example, in Ontario, air quality is addressed through approvals[5] and emission limits[6] are established under the *Environmental Protection Act*. Land contamination[7] and waste management[8] requirements are covered by the same Act but dealt with through very separate regulatory processes. Water issues are dealt with under entirely separate statutes: the *Ontario Water Resources Act*, *Clean Water Act*, and *Safe Drinking Water Act*.

The compartmentalization of the environment has historical roots that are based on the crisis–response development of environmental law. For example, when air pollution became recognized as a problem, legislatures dealt with it through specific legislation. When water pollution became recognized as a problem, legislation was then enacted to address the issues of the day, and so on. Many provinces in the 1960s and 1970s actually had separate air quality, water quality, and waste management statutes. Through the 1970s, the separate statutes were typically consolidated into a single "environmental protection" statute. However, a compartmentalized approach was maintained within these consolidated statutes.

---

approval-based regimes regulatory frameworks in which otherwise prohibited activities can occur if government permission or approval is obtained

As a result, Canadian jurisdictions tend to have a somewhat piecemeal, and at times fragmented, approach to environmental law. The practical effect of the current system is that one facility may require a whole host of approvals based on different statutes. Different parts of a facility, which emit different contaminants, often require different approvals. Provisions related to a single facility can contain overlapping and inconsistent requirements, while the potential impact from contaminants that move from one medium to the next (e.g., substances that are transported by air to nearby land and water resources) are missed.

Some advances have been made toward embracing an integrative approach to environmental regulation. Over the years, particularly in the United States, pilot projects and experiments have been undertaken to try to achieve a more integrative approach to environmental regulation. For example, **whole-facility permitting** involves a review of all the environmental exposures from a particular facility taken as a whole. Ontario has also been moving tentatively in the direction of whole-facility permitting through recent changes to the *Environmental Protection Act*,[9] although the administrative and decision-making processes to support this integrated approval process are still being worked out.

Overall, most jurisdictions continue to rely heavily on media-specific legislative frameworks, but some have started to build in more integrated structures. For example, in 2006 the Ontario Legislature passed the *Clean Water Act*, which includes a new approval and management regime for source water protection. This statute is focused on protecting a single medium (water), but the approach focuses on the regulation of existing and future land uses with implicit and explicit attention paid to the transmedia movement of contaminants through land and water.

In summary, the concept of media-based environmental protection applies generally to the control of air, water, and land pollution, although the specific requirements vary. The specifics for air, water, and waste legislation for individual provinces and territories would each take up a chapter, and another would be needed for the federal government—too much detail for our purposes and for an area that is continually changing. Chapter 8 outlines the common command and control framework of environmental protection and gives a general overview of media-based regimes. In addition, as introduced in the next section and discussed in more detail in Chapter 9, the media-based concept is also extended to specific sector-based regimes.

2. Sector-Based Regimes

Environmental laws can also be categorized into sector-based regimes—that is, laws and policies that apply to a particular sector or area, such as energy, endangered species, or agriculture. The framework for each sector-based regime is distinct

---

whole-facility permitting an approach to granting permits that involves a review of all the environmental exposures from a particular facility

because it is based on the nature of a specific sector. Sector-based regimes typically incorporate elements from the other two types of regulatory frameworks described in this chapter; that is, sector-based regimes typically target the protection of air, water, and land and use approvals to achieve regulatory objectives (see the next section). The laws, regulations, and policies of a sector-based regime, however, are customized to the area of regulatory interest within that sector. Sector-based regimes are described in more detail in Chapter 9.

3. Approval-Based Regimes

While many laws governing the protection of air, water, and land are prohibitory in nature, the prohibition is rarely absolute. The legislation may state that "no person shall discharge contaminants into the water" or "no one shall store, deposit, or dispose of wastes," but there is usually a proviso—an out-clause if you will—whereby the otherwise prohibited activity can occur if a government permission or approval is obtained. The prohibiting legislation, or its regulations, usually also establishes an approval process for such permissions overseen by a designated government agency. This process typically requires submission of an application and support studies to demonstrate that the activity for which approval is being sought can be carried out without harm to the environment. Often, an applicant has an opportunity to appeal a decision to an independent tribunal for a hearing if the application is refused.

Approvals vary significantly both in name and type. They may be called *certificates of approval, permits, environmental compliance approvals, licences,* or *authorizations.* The nature, scope, and content of the approval process are often complex and demanding for the applicant. These complications explain why helping individuals and companies obtain and maintain their approvals provides the bread and butter of many specialized planning, scientific, and engineering firms—not to mention environmental lawyers.

Approvals may be very simple, as in the case of permission to store waste containers on an individual's property. They may also be very comprehensive, as in the case of an air pollution approval for a large factory, which could include dozens of conditions dealing with such issues as monitoring, reporting, emission limits, emergency response and notification, and financial assurances. As Table 7.2 shows, "approvals" not only give permission to a facility to carry out an activity but also establish conditions of approval. Both the approval decision and the conditions are based on the scientific research and policy context within the standard-setting process. Once granted, the approval is enforceable and thus subject to compliance measures.

Both the standard-setting (or "command") and compliance (or "control") functions of public environmental law identified earlier in the chapter, and discussed in more detail in Chapter 8, are also part and parcel of approval-based regimes.

On the "command" side, government decision-makers set environmental standards both through the act of granting an approval to carry out a certain type of

Table 7.2   Component Goals of Environmental Legislation

	Standard Setting	**Approvals**	**Compliance**
Goals	Establish reasonable limits and restrictions to prevent environmental harm based on science and policy	Establish permissions and conditions/site specific rules for certain activities based on their potential environmental impacts	Establish penalties, if any, for non-compliance
Examples	Standards, objectives, guidelines, criteria	Permits, authorizations, licences, environmental compliance approvals	Prosecutions and fines, voluntary abatement

activity and, more specifically, by imposing detailed terms and conditions that set standards for the approved activity. Complex approvals with many pages of detailed conditions can operate like an individualized, facility-specific regulatory regime.

By what process do standards become incorporated into approval documents? Standards including specific regulatory limits, objectives, guidelines, criteria, and other instruments and documents guide government agencies in deciding whether an approval should be granted. These standards are also used by these agencies to draft the approvals themselves. While some standards found in approval documents are based in laws and regulations, many also include government-created policies, criteria, and guidelines that are not in and of themselves binding on individuals unless and until they are incorporated as terms and conditions in a specific approval instrument. In this way, an approval can turn otherwise unenforceable policies, guidelines, and criteria into enforceable standards.

This is where the "control" function of approvals comes into play. Once a government agency grants an approval, the approval and all of its various conditions become as legally binding and enforceable as a provision in a statute. Monitoring and reporting requirements are often built into conditions of licences and approvals. Measures to ensure compliance with environmental approvals can include consultations with agency staff, financial incentives, and inspections and enforcement actions if the overseeing regulatory agency determines these measures to be necessary. In other words, once the approval is issued, the person or organization holding the approval can be prosecuted, convicted, and sentenced to serious fines and other penalties if the terms and conditions of the approval are not met.

The Overlapping Nature of Environmental Regimes
The three types of environmental regimes described in the preceding sections rarely operate in isolation of one another. In most jurisdictions, approval requirements are

a building block component for media-based regimes and sector-based regimes. Most environmental laws (e.g., section 9 of the Ontario *Environmental Protection Act*) state that one cannot legally discharge any contaminant into the environmental media of air, water, or land without first seeking an approval from the government.

Conversely, government officials designated to issue approvals usually rely on the regime of regulations, policies, and guidance documents that govern the relevant medium (air, water, or land). By this means, approval-based regimes deploy a media-based approach. Similarly, sector-based regimes also involve environmental approvals (see Chapter 9).

More Integrated Environmental Assessment and Planning Approaches

The 1970s witnessed an effort to require developers to assess the possible environmental, social, and physical impacts of development. As a result, a body of laws and policies arose governing environmental assessment and planning. The objective was to take a more holistic, integrative, and preventive approach to environmental management than had been taken before. Today, every province and the federal government have an environmental assessment regime in place.

At the federal level, and in most provinces, regulatory frameworks also govern planning and management in areas such as urban planning, watershed management, parks, and endangered species. Environmental assessment and other types of planning-based regimes are explored in Chapters 10 and 11, respectively.

Participation Rights

As environmental law has evolved over the past half-century, it has been accompanied by public demand to participate directly in environmental decision-making. Government action to set and enforce standards has become the predominant approach to environmental protection in Canada, but it has not made the role of individuals and non-governmental organizations redundant or unnecessary. To the contrary, the importance of the **participation rights** of private citizens has grown and evolved alongside the public law processes as an essential component of environmental decision-making. In particular, participation rights continue to play an important role in environmental approvals.

Historically, government's role as the steward of the public interest translated into the power to make key decisions related to environmental protection on behalf of its constituents. This power exists in the legislature, made up of elected representatives of the people who pass statutes and regulations on behalf of the people, and extends to government officials and agencies that serve the elected representatives.

---

participation rights rights of private individuals to be informed and consulted as part of the environmental approval process

These government functionaries have been delegated important powers over the approval-based regimes described above: they have the power to approve activities and projects with environmental consequences.

Even today, it is common for government officials to negotiate with companies and individuals seeking environmental approvals with little or no public involvement. In many cases, not even those residents living beside a factory are consulted, or even informed, about the negotiations. After many decades of public effort, the nature, scope, and extent of public participation in environmental decision-making remains a vigorous point of discussion.

It is difficult to provide a single generic overview of public participation rights in Canada because they vary from province to province. They also vary within regulatory sectors. In other words, different rights exist in environmental assessment regimes and in relation to pollution approvals even within individual provinces.

Professors Peter Wiedemann and Susanne Femers provide a useful model for understanding the concept of participant rights in environmental decision-making with their ladder of public participation, reproduced in Table 7.3.

Following Wiedemann and Femers's hierarchy of public participation rights, the most basic public right is the **right to know**—that is, the right to be aware of what is being proposed. In the early 1990s, the right-to-know concept was used to establish the National Pollutant Release Inventory, a federal databank that outlines the release and transfer of pollutants of all major facilities in Canada. Moving up the ladder, the public has the right to be informed about, comment on, and object to proposals. Still higher up the ladder is the opportunity to participate more meaningfully in environmental decision-making.

How successful have Canadian jurisdictions been at incorporating public participation into environmental decision-making? Progress has been evolutionary rather than revolutionary. Initial efforts to establish an implied environmental right in the *Canadian Charter of Rights and Freedoms* through constitutional litigation were not successful. Further, the federal government has not enacted an omnibus law to legally define and enshrine the rights of Canadians to a clean and healthy environment.

The situation is changing, albeit slowly and gradually, at the provincial level with the passage of statutes that institute individual rights to both be informed of and participate in environmental decision-making. In Quebec, the profile and importance of environmental rights were raised by adding such rights to the Quebec *Charter of Human Rights and Freedoms*, which entrenches individual rights "to live in a healthful environment in which biodiversity is preserved."[10] In addition, beginning in the early 1990s, numerous provinces enacted laws and policies that strengthen

---

right to know the most basic of public participation rights—namely, the right to be aware of an issue that could be of public interest

Table 7.3   Weidemann and Femers's Ladder of Public Participation

Source: I. Weidemann and S. Femers, "Public Participation in Waste Management Decision-Making: Analysis and Management of Conflicts" (1993) 33 *Journal of Hazardous Materials* 355-68.

and entrench public participation rights in environmental decision-making. Some of these initiatives are outlined in Chapter 15. Of particular interest are statutes such as Ontario's *Environmental Bill of Rights, 1993*, which follow the Quebec example of entrenching individual rights to participate in, and potentially challenge, government environmental decision-making.

Public participation rights are never static. Moreover, the process of making a decision can be just as important as the decision itself. Democracies are not particularly cost-effective, but we are willing to pay the price to have our voices heard. Public participation is essential for ensuring that a wide spectrum of interests and concerns are considered, and to ensure that decisions have an air of legitimacy and are therefore respected by the public, even by those who are in disagreement with the result.

Overlap of Environmental Law with Other Areas of Law

Although "environmental law" is a recognized legal specialty, this branch of the law is highly interrelated with other areas. Environmental lawyers are often thought to have many specialties. Some of the areas of law that frequently overlap or connect with environmental law are examined briefly in the following sections.

Administrative Law

Administrative law pertains to the legal rules and processes that govern administrative decision-makers. These decision-makers include tribunals (also called *boards*, *commissions*, and *panels*), which make decisions after a hearing, as well as other administrative decision-makers, which make bureaucratic and ministerial decisions that grant or withhold a benefit without a hearing.

Administrative decisions must be made in conformance with the applicable legislative framework. The courts are empowered to review the decisions of tribunals to ensure that they are acting within the powers granted under the legislation, and to ensure that they respect the common law rules of fairness and natural justice. This process is called **judicial review**.

Criminal Law

Breaches of environmental statutes are **quasi-criminal offences**. They are not technically criminal matters since only the federal government has the constitutional powers to enact criminal law. However, the violation of environmental laws can lead to heavy fines and even jail time. Some provinces also have innovative initiatives that allow the courts to order restitution, cleanup, and other alternative measures.

In addition, as noted earlier in this chapter, most environmental approvals are legal instruments. This means that if their terms and conditions are not followed, the relevant environmental enforcement agency can prosecute the violators of those terms and conditions. Many prosecutions take place throughout Canada each year against companies, directors, and other individuals who have been charged with failing to comply with environmental laws, regulations, or approval requirements.

Civil Law

The chapter-opening case study provides an early example of a civil law action to stop pollution from destroying environmental resources. In civil law, an individual or corporation—the **plaintiff**—brings an action in court against another individual or corporation—the **defendant**. The plaintiff claims that the defendant caused harm to the plaintiff's health or property. Many environmental lawyers either practise civil law themselves or, when appropriate, refer their clients to lawyers who practise civil law.

---

administrative law   the legal rules and processes that govern administrative decision-makers

judicial review   a court's review of an administrative tribunal's decision to ensure that it acted within the powers granted under the legislation and respected the common law rules of natural justice and procedural fairness

quasi-criminal offences   provincial offences punishable by heavy fines and up to six months in jail

plaintiff   an individual or corporation that brings a civil action against another, called the defendant

defendant   an individual or corporation that is sued in a civil action by another, called the plaintiff

Municipal and Land Use Planning Law

A close connection has always existed between land use planning and environmental concerns. Urban boundaries, densities, and water and sewage infrastructure have a direct impact on the environment. Urban development on agricultural lands and development on wetlands, woodlots, and sensitive cultural or archeological resources have always been the subject of much debate and often litigation before both courts and tribunals.

The redevelopment of brownfields or deindustrialized land has also been the subject of much attention in recent years. The discussion has been driven both by the need to contain residential and commercial development within existing urban boundaries and by the high cost of real estate. The municipal and planning connections to environmental law are explored further in Chapter 11.

Corporate and Commercial Law

Corporate and commercial law is concerned with matters such as the rights and liabilities of shareholders, bankruptcy and insolvency, and directors' and officers' liability. Issues often arise about whether directors and officers are liable for the environmental wrongs of the company. Other issues involve what priority is given to environmental cleanup (as opposed to the interests of creditors) when a company goes bankrupt.

International Law

As Chapter 6 details, many international concepts and principles such as the precautionary principle were first recognized in international law. Slowly they have become accepted principles by both lawmakers and the courts in Canada.

Environmental Law and Societal Trends

Historically, environmental issues have been associated with members of upper- and middle-class society attempting to protect their health or property interests. However, over the years the development and implementation of environmental law and policy have become intimately connected to a broad range of other interests and values.

The environmental justice movement emerged in the United States in the 1970s when low-income communities predominantly comprising visible minorities organized and fought against the siting of hazardous landfills and other environmentally risky endeavours in their neighbourhoods. By the early 1990s, the environmental justice movement established that low-income, disadvantaged communities were disproportionately affected by environmental stress, such as air and water pollution, as well as proximity to landfills and incinerators. In 1994, President Bill Clinton issued an executive order requiring every federal agency to make achieving environmental justice part of its mission by identifying and addressing, as appropriate, disproportionately high and adverse human health or environmental effects of its programs, policies, and activities on minority populations and low-income populations.[11]

In the United States, environmental law is often connected to issues of social justice, public rights, and the protection of the public interest. In Canada, these connections also exist. A rich body of literature establishes these links and emphasizes, for example, the relationship between disadvantaged communities and environmental risks, and the relationship between Aboriginal rights and environmental management. Professor Morgan Gardner puts it this way in her book *Linking Activism: Ecology, Social Justice, and Education for Social Change*:

> Events contributing to this awakening of social justice-ecological linkages in the United States and Canada include the Brundtland Report's call for "sustainable development" and the United Nations conference on Environment and Development in Rio de Janeiro in 1992, the reaction to toxic waste in Love Canal, the rise of ecological feminism and the Fourth World Conference on Women, Equality, Development and Peace in Beijing in 1995, the creation of a Movement for Environmental Justice in the United States, the heated discourse pitting jobs versus the environment, and the continual struggle for justice by First Nations peoples in Canada and the United States. Together these forces are pushing these issues of gender, race, class, labor, health, democracy, geographical location, and North–South world power relations into the arena of environmental debate and concern. Their message is clear: we are not simply in this environmental challenge and solution together, we are also in it differently.[12]

SUMMARY OF KEY POINTS

- The two basic categories of environmental law are (1) private law—comprising common and civil law—which achieves environmental benefits indirectly through the protection of individual or property rights; and (2) public law, which is aimed at protecting the public interest in a healthy environment.
- Public law consists of regulatory frameworks established by statutes, regulations, and policies that govern environmental behaviour. Two underlying mechanisms that are common to almost all regulatory frameworks are (1) a "command" function that involves setting standards for acceptable behaviour as it pertains to the protection of the environment; and (2) a "control" function that involves ensuring compliance with those standards.
- Three regulatory frameworks (or "regimes") are found in many jurisdictions: (1) media-based regimes; (2) sector-based regimes; and (3) approval-based regimes.

- The participation rights of private citizens have grown and evolved into an essential component of environmental decision-making. In particular, they play an important role in environmental approvals. Certain provincial statutes assert the individual's fundamental right to a healthy environment and establish new opportunities for protecting these rights. Public participation ensures that public interests and concerns are considered and that decisions are legitimate and respected by the public.

- The current practice of environmental law has evolved from traditional sub-disciplines of legal practice premised on the protection of individual health and economic interests to societal reform movements that connect environmental protection to issues of social justice, public rights, and the protection of the public interest.

KEY TERMS

administrative law

approval-based regimes

defendant

judicial review

media-based regimes

participation rights

plaintiff

private law

public law

quasi-criminal offences

right to know

sector-based regimes

whole-facility permitting

DISCUSSION QUESTIONS

1. Referring back to the chapter-opening case study, if the courts do their job wisely and well in dealing with environmental litigation, is there any need for the arguably cumbersome, expensive, and intrusive use of government action to protect the environment?

2. What are the advantages of controlling environmental contamination by separately regulating the elemental media of air, water, and land? What are the limitations of this approach?

3. Given that elected government representatives and their specialized staff (the civil service) have traditionally been responsible for protecting the public interest in a healthy environment, what, if any, positive purpose can be served by further expanding the role and influence of individuals and special interest groups in environmental decision-making? What, if any, downside is there to this expanded role and influence?

4. Should political and societal movements that seek to redress perceived structural and economic inequities or empower disadvantaged groups (globally and/or locally) have any role in shaping environmental law? If so, why?

SUGGESTED READINGS

Readings

Alberta, *Water Act*, RSA 2000, c. W-3, http://www.qp.alberta.ca/1266.cfm?page
=w03.cfm&leg_type=Acts&isbncln=9780779733651.

Parson, Edward A. "Environmental Trends and Environmental Governance in Canada."
(2000) 26:2 *Canadian Public Policy* S123, http://qed.econ.queensu.ca/pub/cpp/
SE_english/Parson.pdf.

Website

British Columbia, "Air, Land, & Water": http://www2.gov.bc.ca/gov/theme.page?id
=A107794D5085039872470FDB7C7FE62D

NOTES

1. See, e.g., Part VI, ss. 82 to 93 of Ontario's *Environmental Bill of Rights*, SO 1993,
   c. 28, as amended, which expands the common law right to sue in the case of contravention of an environmental law that could cause harm to a public resource,
   creating a new cause of action: environmental harm. This point is discussed further
   in Chapter 15.

2. *Rylands v. Fletcher*, [1863] LR 1 Ex. 265.

3. Not to be confused with the term *strict liability offence*, which is used in the context
   of public law to describe a category offence in the case of a violation of an environmental statute. This concept is discussed in Chapter 8.

4. See, e.g., British Columbia's *Environmental Management Act*, SBC 2003, c. 53 and
   Alberta's *Water Act*, RSA 2000, c. W-3.

5. *Environmental Protection Act*, RSO 1990, c. E.19, as amended, s. 9.

6. O. Reg. 419/05 pursuant to the *Environmental Protection Act*.

7. *Environmental Protection Act*, supra note 5, Part XV.1; and O. Reg. 153/04, as
   amended.

8. *Environmental Protection Act*, supra note 5, Part V.

9. Part II.1 of the *Environmental Protection Act* now permits approval of a single
   instrument for a facility governing air and noise emission, water discharges, and
   waste management activities, whereas formally, three separate approval instruments would be required for these permissions.

10. See Quebec's *Charter of Human Rights and Freedoms*, s. 46.1, "Right to healthful
    environment."

11. US Department of Housing and Urban Development, "Executive Order 12898,"
    59:32 *Federal Register* (February 1994), http://portal.hud.gov/hudportal/
    HUD?src=/program_offices/fair_housing_equal_opp/FHLaws/EXO12898.

12. Morgan Gardner, *Linking Activism: Ecology, Social Justice, and Education for
    Change* (New York: Routledge, 2005), at 32-33.

CHAPTER 8

Environmental Protection Regimes: Command and Control

<table>
<tr><td>

LEARNING OBJECTIVES

After reading this chapter, students will be able to:

- Understand the general command and control framework most governments use to achieve environmental protection objectives.
- Describe the different instruments governments use to set environmental protection standards and limits on pollution.
- Identify the different approaches to environmental standard setting.
- Describe the range of tools governments use to ensure compliance with environmental protection standards.

</td><td>

CHAPTER OUTLINE

</td></tr>
</table>

Introduction

When governments regulate any sphere of activity, they traditionally employ a powerful one–two punch of state intervention known as **command and control**. The command function involves setting standards for acceptable human behaviour. The control function involves ensuring compliance with those standards. Almost all environmental protection regimes that have been established in Canada over the past 30 years generally follow this command and control structure.

In most environmental protection regimes, statutes that set out general prohibitions against polluting are the primary standard-setting mechanism. Most statutes also empower government officials, usually federal or provincial Cabinets, to establish regulations to set more specific standards for environmental behaviour. Environmental laws also typically give power to enforcement officers to carry out policing functions. Crown attorneys are usually charged with the task of prosecuting individuals and companies that fail to comply with the rules set out in environmental statutes and regulations.

---

command and control state intervention involving the creation of rules and the enforcement of those rules

The Rise and Decline of Command and Control in Ontario

By the early 1980s, most jurisdictions in North America had put in place tough-sounding laws to control pollution. In Ontario, the government had passed legislation called the *Environmental Protection Act*, which included a general prohibition against discharging contaminants into the environment and powers to pass specific regulatory limits on pollution. The problem was that the Ontario government had not yet dedicated either the resources or the expertise to the task of setting and ensuring compliance with environmental standards. As a result, (1) no specific, enforceable regulations had been passed for water pollution protection; (2) air pollution standards were weak and difficult to enforce; and (3) in general, no strategy or approach existed to enforce the pollution rules that were in place.

All of that changed in 1985 when two provincial political parties, who had been out of power for 40 years, signed a governing accord and formed a new minority government with an environmental mandate. This government ushered in a new "command and control" approach to environmental protection in Ontario. The new minister of the environment, the Honourable James Bradley, put in place tough new "control-at source" standards aimed at eliminating the discharge of industrial pollution into Ontario lakes and rivers: the Municipal Industrial Strategy for Abatement (MISA). The Bradley Ministry also created an environmental police force—an Ontario first. Resources were allocated to a professional law enforcement team (the Investigations and Enforcement Branch) comprising experienced provincial officers ("green cops") and lawyers with specific expertise and training in investigating and prosecuting polluters. Environmental legislation was amended to increase penalties from tens of thousands of dollars to hundreds of thousands of dollars and included potential imprisonment for violation of environmental offences. Environmental convictions skyrocketed with a success rate of over 90 percent.

Flash-forward 30 years, and a good deal of the air appears to have gone out of the environmental protection balloon. The Walkerton tragedy in Ontario in 2000, where a drinking water system contaminated with deadly bacteria led to 7 deaths and more than 2,300 reported illnesses, was attributed in part to a breakdown in Ontario's standard setting and enforcement system. In a special report to the Ontario Legislature in 2007, the Environmental Commissioner of Ontario (ECO; the province's environmental ombudsman) concluded that the Ontario Ministry of the Environment suffered from "chronic underfunding," with an operating budget that was 34 percent less than it was in 1992-93.* In its 2012-13 annual report, the ECO confirmed that the ministry's budget as well as the budget of its sister ministry with environmental protection responsibilities (the Ministry of Natural Resources) have continued to shrink: combined, the two ministries now represent 0.8 percent of the provincial budget, the smallest percentage in over 20 years.†

Who was the minister of the environment during the time the ECO report was released in October 2013? None other than the Honourable Jim Bradley, back for a second round as minister of the environment, over 25 years after implementing Ontario's groundbreaking environmental protection measures. Whither (wither?) command and control?

Questions

Do you think the changes made by the Ontario Ministry of the Environment in the mid-1980s strengthened environmental protection in the province, and if so, how? What factors have contributed to the decline in allocation of fiscal resources to environmental protection functions in Ontario over the past 20 years? Is this trend likely to continue? Assuming that governments are not able to dedicate sufficient resources to their environmental protection functions, what other options are available to fill the gap—and are they enough?

---

*   Environmental Commissioner of Ontario, *Doing Less with Less: How Shortfalls in Budget, Staffing and In-House Expertise Are Hampering the Effectiveness of MOE and MNR* (Toronto: Environmental Commissioner of Ontario, April 2007), http://www.eco.on.ca/uploads/Reports-special/2007-Less-with-Less/Less%20with%20Less%20report.pdf.

†   Environmental Commissioner of Ontario, *Serving the Public: Annual Report 2012/2013* (Toronto: Queen's Printer for Ontario, October 2013), http://www.eco.on.ca/uploads/Reports-Annual/2012_13/13ar.pdf.

This basic crime-and-punishment approach to environmental protection, however, does not begin to describe the complexities of environmental protection regimes. Environmental statutes also establish a broad range of management and decision-making powers, which serve the general policy objectives of environmental protection. For example, most environmental statutes provide for the licensing and approval of activities that could pose a risk to the environment.

Licensing and approvals incorporate elements of both command and control. On the command side, individuals and companies are prohibited from carrying out an identified activity unless they are able to obtain approval from a government agency. In addition, approvals often contain detailed standards in the form of conditions of approval. The licensing requirement, however, is itself also a control mechanism. It prohibits an individual or company from carrying out an environmentally risky activity unless it can be demonstrated that the impacts of the activity have been carefully studied and mitigated so that the risk of environmental damage is low.

This chapter outlines the inner workings of the command and control structure of environmental protection. It also explores other areas of government action that have grown up alongside the basic command and control structure. Specifically, it covers government regulation of environmental planning and management within specific environmental sectors. Taken together, these elements of an environmental protection regime constitute a formidable array of regulatory tools to implement a government's environmental protection objectives.

Command: Setting Standards for Environmental Behaviour

In this section, we explore different instruments used to set standards. We also compare various approaches to standard setting.

The Command Tool Box

Statutes, regulations, and site-specific legal instruments (e.g., environmental approvals and administrative orders) are legally enforceable, while policies and guidelines are not. What role does each play in protecting the environment?

Statutes

The primary tool available to government to command environmentally appropriate behaviour rests with elected officials. Parliament and the provincial legislators, our society's lawmakers, set the framework for the command and control model through the passage of statutes. For example, Ontario's *Environmental Protection Act* establishes the following general prohibition against polluting:

> No person shall discharge into the natural environment any contaminant, and no person responsible for a source of contaminant shall permit the discharge into the natural environment of any contaminant from the source of contaminant, in an amount, concentration or level in excess of that prescribed by the regulations.[1]

Of course, this provision will have no effect whatsoever unless a regulation has been put in place to prescribe specific standards establishing an unacceptable "amount, concentration or level" for a contaminant.

Regulations

Using our example above, the lieutenant governor in council is empowered to make such regulations pursuant to section 176(1)(e) of the *Environmental Protection Act* as follows:

> The Lieutenant Governor in Council may make regulations …
>   (e) prescribing maximum permissible amounts, concentrations or levels of any contaminant or combination of contaminants and any class of either of them.[2]

This section tells us who is responsible for setting the specific standards and regulations. As is common in most legislation, that power resides with the executive branch of government—that is, Cabinet.

As we dig deeper into the search for environmental standards, we find that Cabinet has passed regulations setting limits for the "amounts, concentrations or levels" of contaminants under the *Environmental Protection Act*. For example, e-Laws (www.e-laws.gov.on.ca), the Ontario government's complete listing of Ontario's laws and regulations, shows dozens of regulations passed under the *Environmental Protection Act*. These regulations set rules on a broad range of matters. Some regulations provide pollution control standards (e.g., general air pollution limits).[3] Others provide limits on effluent discharges to surface water, under the Municipal Industrial Strategy for Abatement (MISA) program, for nine industrial sectors.[4] A number of regulations govern waste management activities, including a general waste management regulation;[5] specific standards for construction of landfill sites;[6] rules for industrial, commercial, and institutional waste management;[7] municipal requirements for recycling and composting;[8] and rules for packaging reduction[9] and waste audits.[10]

In addition, a host of other standards governed by regulations under the *Environmental Protection Act* relate to specific issues such as the control of ozone-depleting substances;[11] monitoring and cleanup procedures and protocols;[12] rules governing spills and spill prevention;[13] emissions trading (discussed in Chapter 12);[14] and a myriad of other very specific and detailed rules governing a large range of activities and enterprise that could impact the natural environment.

We have now identified two important actors in the field of environmental standard setting: legislatures, which establish general provisions governing environmental conduct; and Cabinets, which can establish more specific rules and standards if granted this power by the legislatures. However, to understand the full range of legally binding standards affecting environmental behaviour, one must look beyond statutes and regulations.

Site-Specific Legal Instruments

Standards are also set on a case-by-case basis using site-specific legal instruments such as **environmental approvals** and **administrative orders**. The *Environmental Protection Act* delegates the power to issue environmental approvals and administrative orders to a government official known as a **director**. As its name implies, a site-specific legal instrument is specific to a particular site, plant, facility, individual, or company. However, it is legally binding in the same manner as a statute or regulation.

Environmental Approvals

Under the *Environmental Protection Act*, a document called an "environmental compliance approval," or ECA, is required if an individual or company wishes to engage in certain types of activities that have potential environmental consequences. For example, any person wishing to carry out an enterprise or activity that involves a discharge into the air must first obtain an ECA.[15] Similarly, solid and industrial waste treatment and disposal facilities or waste management systems all require ECAs.[16]

In order to obtain an ECA, the individual or company must make an application to the Ontario Ministry of the Environment. Part II.1 of the *Environmental Protection Act* outlines the process for how ECA applications are approved, the information needed to support the application, public consultation requirements,[17] the terms and conditions that can be imposed on the holder of the approval,[18] and the provisions for appealing approval decisions.[19] The conditions of approval typically include specific requirements for the construction, operation, monitoring, and performance level of pollution control equipment.

It is important to note that ECAs apply only to the specific individual or company to which an environmental approval has been issued. For that individual or company, the conditions of approval have the force of law, and failure to comply may lead to prosecution and serious fines and penalties.[20]

Administrative Orders

Under the *Environmental Protection Act*, a director may issue an administrative order under certain circumstances.[21] For example, where an investigation indicates

---

environmental approval   permission issued by a government agency or official to carry out an activity that may impact the environment, provided that certain conditions are met (see also *licences and approvals*)

administrative orders   orders made by government officials or authorized employees that impose specific requirements on individuals or companies, such as the requirement to investigate and clean up environmental contamination or control pollution discharges

director   an appointee under the Ontario *Environmental Protection Act* who may issue an administrative order in certain circumstances that a company is discharging a contaminant, an administrative order, called a *control order*, may be issued against the company to impose conditions and cleanup requirements. Administrative orders are discussed further later in this chapter.

Policies and Guidelines

Government officials may also establish policies and guidelines that are not legally enforceable. However, policies and guidelines can have a powerful impact on environmental behaviour, as in the case of the Blue Book guidelines. In the early 1980s, the Ontario Ministry of the Environment established guidelines that set specific limits on discharge to surface water for a long list of contaminants. These guidelines, known informally as "the Blue Book," were developed by ministry scientists and civil servants and were ultimately approved by the minister.

Because they were only guidelines, the Blue Book standards could not be enforced in the typical command and control sense. Charges could not be laid, and a company could not be convicted for failing to meet the Blue Book requirements. However, the Blue Book standards did affect environmental conduct in Ontario in two less direct ways:

1. They were adopted by the director for granting approvals for discharges to surface water under the *Ontario Water Resources Act*. As a result, the unenforceable ministry guidelines were implemented in a very meaningful way.
2. They were considered by the courts when determining whether an alleged offender was guilty of the prohibition against discharge of "a contaminant into the natural environment that causes or is likely to cause an adverse effect."[22]

The Blue Book standards are but one of many examples of how standards established in ministry policies and guidelines may play a powerful role in influencing environmental behaviour.

Approaches to Standard Setting

What choices are available to environmental rule-makers as they set about the task of establishing standards for environmental behaviour? What factors should be taken into account in establishing these rules? In this section, some of the basic options available to rule-makers are described.

Performance Versus Construction Standards

Rule-makers who want to control the amount of a particular contaminant entering the environment can do so by setting a performance standard or a construction standard.

A **performance standard** is a pollution limit imposed on a polluter. It is the responsibility of each operator to make sure that the standard is met. In this approach, the rule-maker is unconcerned about how the result is achieved. A company can bring discharge levels into line with an established performance standard in a variety of ways—for example, by installing state-of-the-art pollution control equipment, reducing its rate of production, or making changes to the input chemical materials.

Alternatively, rule-makers may prefer to establish a specific **construction standard**, which requires that a government-approved pollution control system be used for a particular activity or in a specific situation.

Most environmental regimes employ performance standards for some situations and construction standards for others. In Ontario, for example, performance-based standards have been set for the discharge of specific contaminants to surface water under the *Environmental Protection Act*,[23] while construction-based standards are imposed for sewage treatment systems through regulations under the *Building Code Act, 1992*.[24] It is not always clear how government rule-makers determine which of these two types of standards should apply to a particular situation.

Performance-based standards are often supported by industry associations because they give industries the flexibility to find their own solutions to pollution control objectives. Critics argue that construction standards entrench pollution control approaches and technologies that are not cost-effective and can quickly become obsolete. By contrast, performance-based standards encourage research and innovation, and they are more likely than construction standards to advance new, cheaper, and more effective technologies.

In certain situations, however, construction standards provide some advantages to both government and industry, particularly where the required technology is reliable. For government, such standards may be easier to enforce. Monitoring requirements can focus on ensuring that the required pollution control equipment has been properly installed and maintained. For industry, such standards may be a less worrisome alternative to the need to make operational changes to meet evolving, more restrictive performance-based standards.

Establishing Specific Limits

The task of establishing specific limits for the discharge or emission of contaminants into the environment may seem as though it should be an objective scientific process. In practice, however, the process of setting such standards requires a complex

---

performance standard a pollution limit imposed on a polluter, where the rule-maker is unconcerned with how the result is achieved

construction standard a government-approved pollution control system that is to be used for a particular activity or in a specific situation

balance of scientific and non-scientific factors. It requires consideration of societal goals and objectives, economic constraints, and occasionally controversial assumptions about the short- and long-term health, safety, and environmental consequences of industrial practices.

Environmental Quality-Based Standards

Traditionally, standards have been based on societal objectives for environmental quality. Mary Ann Franson, Robert Franson, and Alastair Lucas have described this approach as a five-step process:

- *Step 1*. Identify the objectives for pollution control, including the uses of the environmental resources to be protected.
- *Step 2*. Formulate specific criteria for meeting these objectives by collecting scientific information to answer questions such as "Is this water safe to drink?" or "Is this air safe to breathe?"
- *Step 3*. Based on these criteria, formulate specific ambient quality standards— that is, the quality of the air or water that is deemed necessary to achieve the desired objectives.
- *Step 4*. Translate the desired ambient quality standards into specific emission or effluent limits that are designed to control the amount of contaminants entering the environment.
- *Step 5*. Develop monitoring and other information-gathering programs to provide feedback on whether the environmental objectives are being met.[25]

Establishing standards using this approach has proven to be contentious, lengthy, and expensive. Given the room for disagreement and political and/or scientific judgments that need to be made at each stage of this process, one can begin to understand why.

Another type of environmental quality-based standard is the **health risk assessment standard**, which involves linking the standard under consideration to the health risks posed. This approach requires the use of risk assessment to determine the health risks associated with the level and duration of exposure to a contaminant.

A health risk assessment attempts to examine two controversial scientific relationships:

- the relationship between the release of a contaminant into the environment and the subsequent level of exposure to an individual, and
- the relationship between the release of a contaminant into the environment and the potential for health-related effects resulting from varying levels of exposure to the contaminant.

---

health risk assessment standard   a quality-based standard that involves linking the standard under consideration to the health risks posed

This analysis then leads to a risk calculation intended to determine the acceptable level of chemical exposure.

The health risk assessment approach to setting standards presents a number of problems. Because gathering health risk assessment information is expensive, little hard data are available on the long-term health impacts of many known contaminants. Scientists often suspect health effects that they are unable to prove because of a lack of data. In addition, the risk of long-term health effects is difficult to identify because of the time it often takes for health effects to become evident.

Many environmental scientists suspect that health risk assessments underestimate the real health costs of pollution. With persistent toxic contaminants, risks increase over time because these contaminants do not break down but bioaccumulate. These complicating factors mean that appropriate environmental standards for dangerous contaminants are rejected because time and resources are insufficient to draw the link between the contaminants and harm to health.

These problems suggest to some that a new approach is needed. Many scientists, environmental advocacy groups, and other stakeholders argue that the onus should be reversed.[26] Pollutants should not be assumed innocent until proven guilty. Individuals and companies proposing to release a contaminant into the environment should be required to demonstrate that the contaminant will not cause an adverse effect before any release is permitted. This approach reflects an important concept in environmental law: the **precautionary principle**.

The precautionary principle has emerged as an essential guiding principle of environmental law. It recognizes needs to act on potentially significant but not yet well delineated hazards, including the uncertain long-term consequences imposed by the discharge of human-made chemicals on human health and the natural environment. Precautionary approaches respond to the growing awareness of the complexity of interactions between natural and human-source substances and processes, and the consequent limits of the ability of current scientific knowledge to provide precise information about cause–effect relations as a basis for setting appropriate standards to prevent undesirable long-term consequences.

The precautionary principle has found its legal expression in: international agreements such as the Rio Declaration;[27] Canadian legislation including the *Canadian Environmental Protection Act*[28] and *Canadian Environmental Assessment Act*;[29] and environmental court cases, including a leading Canadian Supreme Court of Canada decision.[30] It has also become imbedded in the practices and policies of some

---

precautionary principle the proposition that caution should be paramount when an activity raises threats of harm to health or the environment, and that the proponent of the activity should bear the burden of proving that it is safe; a principle used to support the notion that where the threat of serious or irreversible damage exists, a lack of full scientific certainty should not be used as a reason for postponing measures to prevent environmental degradation

government environmental protection agencies. For example, as discussed in Chapter 15, pursuant to the Ontario *Environmental Bill of Rights*, Ontario government ministries are required to issue a Statement of Environmental Values that establishes environmental principles within which these ministries must operate. The Ontario Ministry of the Environment's Statement of Environmental Values[31] includes the following statement indicating a commitment to the precautionary principle in its environmental decision-making: "The Ministry uses a precautionary, science-based approach in its decision-making to protect human health and the environment." Thus, it can be seen that the precautionary approach to environmental protection has evolved from a persuasive, albeit not universally accepted, scientific principle to a legal principle integrated into international agreements, statutes, case law, and the policy underpinnings of government decision-making.

Technology-Based Standards

This standard-setting approach sidesteps many of the problems associated with developing environmental quality-based standards by asking a simple question: What is the best available technology for controlling a particular pollutant? If agreement can be reached on the answer to this question, it is a simple matter to impose a specific limit for this pollutant based on what the best available technology can achieve.

This approach has one obvious advantage: it removes many of the controversial political and scientific judgments that need to be made when establishing standards based on environmental objectives. Instead, the focus is on what limits to polluting are technologically possible.

Critics identify at least two important problems with technology-based standards. First, standards are developed without considering the needs of the environment. If a particular contaminant is having a catastrophic impact on unlimited environmental resources, why should a limit be based solely on current technology? Second, the approach entrenches prescribed technology and therefore discourages technological innovation to meet tougher standards linked to environmental quality-based objectives.

Practical experience with technology-based standards has led to mixed reviews. In 1986 the Ontario government initiated an ambitious technology-based standard-setting program for nine industrial sectors that discharge directly to surface water. The government initially focused on technology-based standards in the hope of gaining consensus among the industrial sectors on sector-wide effluent limits.

The MISA program (referred to in the chapter-opening case study) created nine separate industry–government working groups to develop standards using the criteria of "best available technology economically achievable." From 1988 to 1995, the program established specific effluent standards for all nine sectors. For the first time in the history of the province, Ontario had clear limits on specific pollutants on a province-wide basis.

However, the MISA process was slow and expensive. Representatives of industrial sectors and government officials debated for many months in an attempt to reach agreement on what "best available technology" and "economically achievable" should mean in a particular sector. The process demonstrated one of the problems with the technology-based approach: it opens the door to bargaining between industry and the standard-setting authority over what is practical, feasible, and "economically achievable." After spending so much time and effort to reach consensus on these standards, the provincial government appears to have little stomach for reviewing and updating these standards to reflect technological advancement. As a consequence, the hard-won MISA effluent limit standards, based on late 1980s to mid-1990s pollution control technologies, remain entrenched in Ontario to this day.

Point of Impingement Versus Control at Source

Another decision environmental rule-makers face is where to draw the spatial boundary for meeting discharge standards. Many environmental standards are still based on the human-centred principle that pollution is not significant until it crosses property boundaries. Air pollution standards are often based on **point of impingement** models that attempt to predict the impact of a pollutant once it reaches a property's boundaries, rather than at the end of the stack. For example, Ontario's general air pollution regulation[32] requires companies to apply a computer model that predicts the concentration of a contaminant that will occur at the property boundary of a facility based on information about discharge levels from the facility as well as weather data.

The conceptual flaw in this approach, of course, is that pollution does not respect property boundaries. Pollutants begin to have negative effects as soon as they are released into the environment. It is almost universally acknowledged that the surest means of preventing harm from air pollution is by controlling environmental contaminants at their source. Most jurisdictions (including Ontario), however, have been reluctant to base an air pollution standard-setting program entirely on this principle due to a variety of factors, including the economic and societal costs of imposing new standard-setting approaches on existing industries. Point of impingement standards have also come under scrutiny because they do not account for cumulative effects.[33] The Ontario model, for example, does not consider background contaminant levels or emissions produced by other facilities. Despite these limitations, the point of impingement model continues to be the primary standard-setting approach to air pollution control in Ontario as well as a number of other jurisdictions.

---

point of impingement   the point at which a pollutant contacts the airspace, ground, or a building at or beyond the property boundary of the source of the pollutant

Informational Standards

Some jurisdictions have used "informational standards" as an alternative, or supplement, to the traditional enforceable pollution control requirements. This approach involves imposing legal requirements on industries to disclose information about their environmental practices, such as level of pollutants discharged or emitted. Typically, these disclosure requirements exist in addition to imposition of standards for discharge of pollutants, and are intended to provide both (1) information that will assist regulators in the research and development of new standards, regulatory requirements, and guidelines, and (2) additional incentive for businesses to go beyond minimal compliance requirements. With respect to the latter point, companies faced with the requirement to provide public information about pollution practices are potentially exposed to pressure from both their investors and consumers of their products, in theory motivating them to do more to meet and exceed environmental standards.

An early example of a regulatory program based on informational standards is the Toxic Release Inventory (TRI) Program[34] administered by the United States Environmental Protection Agency. The program requires subject industries to submit regularly updated inventories of their toxic chemical emissions. Canada has followed suit with a similar program called the National Pollutant Release Inventory, a publically available inventory of pollutant releases as reported by industries and other facilities pursuant to the *Canadian Environmental Protection Act*.[35]

Pollution Prevention

Since the early 1990s, a new approach to standard setting, called **pollution prevention**, has been recognized and applauded, but formal acceptance and implementation have been slow. This approach changes the focus from *control* of the quantities of pollution at the end of the pipe to *prevention* of the use of potentially harmful substances in the first place. Pollution prevention involves avoiding the generation of pollution through techniques and methods such as the following:

- changes to manufacturing or production processes,
- product reformulation or substitution, and
- chemical substitution.

Pollution prevention is not about reducing levels of pollution; it is about examining why waste is being created in the first place and seeking to avoid it. Consider the example of a company that is discharging a problematic chemical. The traditional approach was to ask how much of the chemical the company can be allowed to discharge while still protecting human health and the environment. Pollution control

---

pollution prevention an approach emphasizing prevention rather than control of pollution using methods such as product reformulation, chemical substitution, and changes to processes

equipment was then installed to meet the discharge or effluent requirements. Pollution prevention, by contrast, requires an examination of the company's manufacturing process and asks why that chemical is being used or generated. Can the process be changed so that it will not be used or generated?

Some American states, such as Massachusetts, have enacted progressive and successful pollution prevention laws, which are called *toxic use reduction laws*. In Canada, considerable support exists for the principle behind such laws, although implementation has been slow.

The Canadian Council of Ministers of the Environment (CCME) formally committed to pollution prevention in 1993, and in 1996 it released the document *A Strategy to Fulfil the CCME Commitment to Pollution Prevention*.[36] It works in conjunction with the Canadian Centre for Pollution Prevention. Ontario had committed to introducing a comprehensive pollution prevention regime in late 2008.

Control: Compliance and Enforcement

We now turn to the "control" part of the command and control strategy of environmental protection. In this section, we explore the tools available to government for ensuring that environmental protection rules and standards (the commands) are followed.

The Control Tool Box

A full spectrum of tools are used to enforce environmental standards, from the carrot of positive incentives to the most punishing of sticks—that is, an aggressive policing approach with high fines and even jail terms for offences against the environment. These tools are summarized in Table 8.1 and discussed in the text that follows.

Table 8.1 Control Tools and Key Players

Tools	Key Players	Examples
Incentives and financial assistance	• Environmental abatement officers • Research and funding agencies	• Tax incentives • Sharing expertise and research
Licences and approvals	• Government environmental officials • Hearings tribunals (on appeal)	• A licence is obtained by a chemical plant to discharge treated wastewater into a local stream.
Administrative orders	• Enforcement officers • Government environmental officials • Hearings tribunals	• A company must thoroughly investigate and cleanup the pollution discharge. • A company must shut down operations until a solution is found.
Prosecutions	• Enforcement officers • Prosecutors • Criminal courts	• A company is charged, convicted, and fined for discharging pollutants into a river at levels that exceed provincial standards.

Incentives and Financial Assistance

Incentives and financial assistance are the least intrusive ways of encouraging good environmental behaviour. They involve establishing government programs to assist potential polluters in meeting government pollution control standards. For example, public funds could be allocated for grants to individuals and companies to assist them in upgrading their pollution control equipment and production processes.

However, governments may have a hard time explaining to their constituents why tax dollars should be spent subsidizing businesses. If producing a particular product requires expenditure of funds to protect the environment, why should those costs not be borne directly by the company and, ultimately, the consumers of the goods that are creating the risk to the environment? Grants are generally more popular with voters when they are directed toward the public at large, as when re-cycling containers are provided free of charge or rebates are available to offset the cost of making homes more energy efficient.

A less direct means of providing encouragement is the use of tax incentives, which reward companies for good environmental behaviour through a reduction in taxes. However, tax incentives are a close cousin of direct subsidies and, for the reasons cited in the above discussion, are unpopular with voters. Tax breaks have been allocated to give "green" companies an advantage over companies using older and dirtier pollution control technology in only a few instances.

Governments' taxation powers are more commonly used as a stick than a carrot. For example, in the United States, a special tax is imposed on chemical producers and tied into the volume of chemicals generated. This tax creates an incentive to reduce reliance on persistent toxins in production processes.

Another form of government incentive involves sharing expertise and research to help industries improve their environmental performance. In the early 1980s, for example, the Ontario Ministry of the Environment established the position of en-vironmental abatement officer. This government employee's sole function was to work with industries to develop programs to reduce the amount of pollution they generated. Abatement officers would meet with plant managers, inspect their oper-ations, and provide them with information and advice on how their companies could improve their environmental performance. Although the formal position of abatement officer no longer exists, government officials in Ontario and other juris-dictions are typically mandated to dedicate time and resources to assist industries in achieving voluntary compliance as an alternative to triggering more expensive enforcement mechanisms. Many governments make an effort to share research and to fund and share industry research on improving pollution control and production process methods. International treaties such as the Kyoto Protocol and the United Nations Framework Convention on Climate Change, described in Chapter 6, have motivated governments to fund this type of research.

Licences and Approvals

Licences and approvals are another important compliance tool available to government. The licensing of various types of facilities and projects that have potential environmental impacts combines both the carrot and the stick approach. On the carrot side, a particular environmental activity cannot proceed until an approval is granted. The approval authority must be satisfied that the project has been appropriately planned and studied, and that environmental risks are minimized. This requirement gives proponents of these projects the incentive to ensure minimal environmental impact.

On the stick side, most environmental approvals come with conditions attached. These conditions can spell out exactly how a facility must operate, setting out certain performance standards that must be met during the operating life of the facility. If these standards are not met, environmental officials usually have the power to take both administrative and enforcement action. Most environmental statutes give these officials enforcement options: the power to issue orders, and the power to commence prosecutions against companies that do not comply with conditions of approval.

Consider a chemical plant that obtains a licence to discharge treated waste water into a local stream. The conditions of approval may set standards for the quality of the water being discharged. It may also require ongoing self-monitoring and reporting to a regulatory authority such as the Ministry of the Environment. If the monitoring results show that discharge standards are not being met, the operator will be required to take certain actions. Some approval instruments even specify the particular remedial action that the company must take. If the specified action is not taken, charges can be laid, or an order can be issued requiring the company to shut down until the environmental problem is corrected. In this way, environmental approvals may be converted into direct and powerful enforcement tools.

As with all command and control mechanisms, a price tag is attached to the tool's effectiveness. In many jurisdictions, including Ontario, the Ministry of the Environment has insufficient resources for proactive monitoring. A great deal of reliance is placed on the operator to self-monitor, to report, and to address environmental issues before they become compliance problems.

In some cases, the final decision on environmental approvals and conditions of approval is made by a tribunal. With the care that these tribunals take in imposing conditions of approval, they can play an important role in addressing future potential compliance issues.

---

licences and approvals   permission issued by a government agency or official to carry out an activity that would not otherwise be permitted by law, typically accompanied by certain conditions/requirements that must be met by the individual or facility to which the permission has been granted (see also *environmental approval*)

Administrative Orders

Administrative orders are directives issued by government officials; they impose legal requirements on individuals or companies to take specific action to control pollution discharges, investigate and/or clean up environmental problems, repair damage caused to the environment, or take action to avoid future pollution problems.

Administrative orders can sometimes be more punishing for an individual or company than a conviction for an environmental offence. For example, an environmental administrative order could require a company to carry out extensive investigative and cleanup work that costs millions of dollars. Alternatively, an order could require a company to shut down operations until pollution control is brought into compliance with standards. Such an order could shut down a company for months, or even permanently, if a feasible solution cannot be found.

If convicted of an environmental offence, the offender eventually will have to pay a fine, but will not have any obligation to address the environmental problem unless ordered to do so by a court. In contrast, administrative orders are focused not on punishing offenders but rather on solving problems. An environmental order compels immediate direct and specific action to prevent spills or to clean up an environmental mess. Administrative orders may not carry the same stigma as a conviction for a crime against the environment but, as noted earlier, they may pack a financial punch. The cost of complying with an order could be as much of a deterrent as a conviction for an environmental offence. In many cases, orders and prosecutions are pursued concurrently.

Investigation and Report

The process of issuing provincial orders starts in a manner similar to the investigation of any environmental offence. An enforcement officer, given the title **provincial officer (PO)** under the Ontario *Environmental Protection Act*, is dispatched to the scene of a complaint or an environmental problem. The enforcement officer then begins to gather evidence about the incident. Once sufficient evidence is obtained, the officer prepares a report, which provides sufficient information to conclude that an environmental offence has occurred.

Given the potential consequences, it is easy to understand why the making of administrative orders must begin with an investigation and a report. For example, Ontario POs have the power to issue **provincial officers' orders (POOs)**, which

---

provincial officer (PO)   a government official who carries out enforcement functions such as investigating and gathering evidence about an environmental incident, preparing reports, and laying charges

provincial officers' orders (POOs)   orders issued by provincial officers (accompanied by a report following an investigation) that compel an individual or company to carry out certain actions to prevent or respond to an environmental problem

compel the individual or company receiving the order to carry out certain specified actions to prevent or respond to an environmental problem. These orders are accompanied by a PO's report, which provides a summary of the PO's rationale for the issuance of the order. In the case of most administrative orders, the PO must have "reasonable and probable grounds" to believe that an adverse environmental effect is associated with a particular undertaking or activity before the officer can issue the order.

Types of Orders

In Ontario, the two categories of environmental orders are POOs and director's orders. The actions that may be required by an administrative order are extensive and potentially extremely onerous.

POOs may be issued more quickly and with less administrative process than director's orders; therefore, POOs are more common. POOs may demand a broad range of actions, including the following:

- taking steps to stop contamination from entering the environment,
- removing waste material from a site,
- repairing injury from damage to the environment,
- providing alternative water supplies,
- submitting a plan to achieve compliance, and
- taking a range of preventive measures to prevent an adverse impact on the environment.[37]

POs have slightly less latitude than the director in issuing orders. POOs may be issued under the *Environmental Protection Act* if a PO has "reason to believe that the person is contravening a provision of the act or regulations, an existing administrative order, or the terms or conditions of an environmental approval."[38] POOs are also subject to review by directors.

Director's orders are typically, although not always, used for complex, large-scale environmental issues that require a more detailed and nuanced approach. The four types of director's orders specified under the *Environmental Protection Act* are as follows:

1. *Control orders.* These orders are issued when a contaminant is being discharged into the natural environment, and the person responsible for the source of the contamination needs to take steps to control it through improved pollution control measures.

2. *Stop orders.* These orders are issued in the more unusual and serious circumstance where a particular source is discharging a contaminant that the director believes constitutes an immediate danger to "human life, the health

of any persons, or to property." In this case, the director may issue an order requiring the discharge to stop entirely.

3. *Remedial orders.* These orders require the person who causes or allows the discharge of a contaminant to take action to repair or to prevent injury or damage to the environment.

4. *Orders for preventive measures.* These orders are issued when "reasonable and probable grounds" exist to indicate that preventive measures are necessary in order to prevent or reduce the risk of an impact on the environment from a contaminant.[39]

What do all of these administrative orders have in common? They all start with an investigation by an enforcement officer; they all involve tailored administrative responses to a particular environmental problem; and they all are based on evidence of a breach of an environmental law or regulation.

Administrative orders can have a broad scope. Before 1989, orders could be imposed only on the current owners of the source of a contaminant. This issue was debated at the Ontario Court of Appeal in *Canadian National Railway Co. v. Ontario (Director Under the Environmental Protection Act)*.[40] In this case, the ministry issued an order to investigate and clean up a serious environmental problem created by the manufacturing of railway ties. This process involved the use of creosote, a highly toxic preservative. The creosote plant was sold in 1982, and there was evidence of widespread offsite contamination of groundwater. The director issued an order not only against the current owner of the plant but also against the previous owner and Canadian National Railway.

When the order was challenged, the court found that the present owner was liable, leaving the former owner of the plant—that is, the company largely responsible for the pollution—with no liability. This decision triggered action by the provincial government. In 1989, amendments were made to Ontario's *Environmental Protection Act* that gave the director discretion to issue orders to previous or current owners of the property, and to previous or current persons in charge of management or control of a source of a contaminant.

Because of the serious consequences that may result from an order, most environmental legislation provides an avenue for appeal. In Ontario, a director's order, as well as POOs that have been reviewed by a director, may be appealed to the Environmental Review Tribunal. The tribunal then stands in place of the director to determine whether the issuance of the order was warranted.

Finally, to avoid the possibility that an appeal may be used as a stalling tactic to dodge cleanup responsibilities, many jurisdictions (including Ontario) have specifically provided that launching an appeal does not automatically trigger a **stay** of an

---

stay the temporary suspension of a court order, usually pending an appeal

order. In other words, while an appeal is in progress, the obligation to carry out the terms of the order remain, unless a motion is successfully brought for a stay.

Prosecutions

When it comes to controlling the behaviour of potential polluters, prosecution and financial incentives lie at opposite ends of the spectrum. Prosecution employs the full weight of government power to compel acceptable environmental behaviour. Unique among compliance tools, successful prosecutions cast a negative moral judgment on a particular environmental action or inaction by giving it a criminal connotation. Individuals and companies are effectively being told that, in the opinion of the prosecuting authority, their behaviour has run afoul of accepted societal standards.

If a decision is made by the enforcement branch of a Ministry of the Environment to prosecute an alleged environmental offence, the matter is turned over to a Crown counsel. The Crown counsel's job is to build a case that will lead to a conviction by a criminal court.

Considering the advantages of administrative orders, why would a decision be made to prosecute, particularly given that prosecutions are expensive and require a significant investment of public resources? There are at least two persuasive reasons:

1. *Specific deterrence.* A company that has been embarrassed by a public prosecution and conviction for violating environmental standards may be less likely to risk further damage to its reputation by offending again.
2. *General deterrence.* By prosecuting an individual or company that has caused environmental harm, the government makes a public statement that this behaviour will not be tolerated. Most companies are sensitive to public image. The message to potential polluters is that they risk public humiliation and financial consequences if they pollute.

Since the mid-1980s, the concept of treating breaches of environmental standards in the same way as any other alleged criminal activity has gained credence among government regulators. By associating harmful environmental behaviour with criminality, the government has an opportunity to send the message that polluting is not just a cost of doing business. Fines or penalties, without a criminal association, are simply another production expense that gets passed on to consumers. Once government becomes successful at branding a polluting company as a societal wrongdoer, it creates a much larger customer/consumer relations problem that can potentially threaten that company's economic viability.

In most Canadian jurisdictions, governments have established the equivalent of environmental police forces with a mandate to investigate potential violations of environmental standards and lay charges. As described in the chapter-opening case study, Ontario led the way in 1985 with the establishment of its Investigations and

Enforcement Branch, a centralized agency within the Ministry of the Environment that was responsible for carrying out high-profile investigations of alleged polluters.

As Ontario's "green cops," POs are responsible for investigating potential environmental offences. These officers have been given significant powers, equivalent to those of police officers, to investigate alleged environmental violations and gather evidence in preparation for prosecutions.

Inspections and Searches

In Ontario, the *Environmental Protection Act* gives POs a broad range of powers to help in an investigation, including the power to act in the following ways:

- Without a warrant or court order, a PO may enter private property or any other place where he or she has reason to believe that the environment may be adversely affected by an activity.
- During an inspection, a PO may carry out a range of activities, including excavating soils, requiring machinery to be operated under certain conditions, taking samples for analysis, conducting any tests or taking measurements, examining or copying any documents of data, taking photographs, video recordings, or other visual recordings, requiring production of any documents or data and removing such documentation for copying, and making "reasonable inquiries of any person either orally or in writing."
- By special order, a PO may protect the scene of a potential environmental offence by prohibiting entry onto public or private property, and by prohibiting the use of, interference with, destruction of, or disruption of anything during an inspection or during the time required to obtain a warrant.[41]

A PO also has the power to carry out a search, without a search warrant, of any place that is not a room used as a dwelling if the PO has reason to believe that

- an offence has been committed,
- the place to be searched will provide evidence of the offence, and
- it is impractical to obtain a search warrant.[42]

Seizing Evidence

A PO has the power to seize anything found in an inspection or search without a warrant under certain conditions. In the case of an inspection, the PO may seize anything that is produced to him or her or that is in plain view under any of the following conditions:

- the thing could be used as evidence of an offence,
- the thing is being used in connection with the commission of an offence, or

- the thing is discharging or likely to discharge a contaminant into the natural environment.[43]

During a search, a PO may seize anything without a warrant or court order under the following conditions:

- the PO reasonably believes that the thing could be used as evidence of an offence, or
- the thing is being used in connection with a commission of an offence and seizure is necessary to prevent the continuation of the offence.[44]

Like police officers, environmental POs often go to court to obtain search warrants or court orders to carry out an investigation, search, or seizure. In some cases, it is safer for a PO to obtain court sanction for a search in this way. The alternative is to risk a challenge launched on the basis that the investigation, search, or seizure violated the rights of the company or individual being investigated. If such a challenge is successful, a court could dismiss the pollution charges against the accused without having even considered the merits of the charges themselves.

Gathering Evidence

Gathering evidence of an environmental offence can be a highly technical exercise that requires scientific knowledge. Environmental enforcement officers usually require technical support from other experts and specialists in chemistry, air quality, or other disciplines. Enforcement officers must follow four practical steps to gather sufficient and accurate evidence to support a prosecution:

- *Step 1.* Take careful notes of observations during any inspection or search.
- *Step 2.* Take photographs, noting the time, date, and precise location of each picture. Videos may also be useful.
- *Step 3.* Take water, air, and soil samples based on established protocol and procedure, labelling them with the time, date, and precise location, and sealing the evidence and storing it properly. As in any criminal investigation, officers must be meticulous in cataloguing the chain of custody of samples from the moment they are obtained to their delivery to an accredited laboratory for analysis.
- *Step 4.* To prove the source of pollution, obtain comparative samples. For example, take water samples and visual evidence upstream and downstream of a release of effluent in water, or air samples upwind and downwind of a release into the air.

Cases are won or lost on the basis of whether or not these critically important steps are followed.

Standard of Proof

The prosecutor of any offence must prove the offence beyond a reasonable doubt. This **standard of proof** applies to *Criminal Code* offences, traffic violations, and environmental offences. It is a much heavier burden than the civil standard of proof—a **balance of probabilities**—which applies in civil cases, such as tort and contract lawsuits.

In civil cases, the intention of the law is to make things right between the parties, so the court rules in favour of the party with the stronger case. For example, if a person sues a neighbour for the loss of a tree allegedly caused by the neighbour's overuse of winter salt, he must prove the elements of the tort of nuisance on a balance of probabilities. This means that he must prove that his version of events is more probable than his neighbour's version.

By contrast, when a prosecutor is proving the elements of an offence against a defendant, the intention of the law is to punish an offender and to avoid convicting and punishing an innocent individual or corporation. Therefore, it is not enough for the prosecutor to prove that the defendant is probably guilty; rather, it is necessary to prove that the defendant is guilty **beyond a reasonable doubt**.

Strict Liability Offences

Although all offences must be proven beyond a reasonable doubt, the elements of an offence that must be proven by the prosecutor vary in accordance with the type of offence. Environmental offences are **strict liability offences**. To understand what this means, it is necessary to understand the meaning of criminal liability offences and absolute liability offences for the purpose of comparison.

The most serious offences under the *Criminal Code*—murder, for example—are known as **criminal liability offences** and are viewed by society most severely. The penal consequences are serious and include incarceration. The prosecutor must prove not only that an illegal action (the ***actus reus***) occurred but also that a mental

---

standard of proof the degree to which a party must convince a judge or jury that the allegations are true

balance of probabilities the standard of proof in a civil proceeding, whereby the plaintiff must convince the court that the allegations are more likely true than untrue

beyond a reasonable doubt the standard of proof in a criminal proceeding

strict liability offences offences in which proof that an accused performed the prohibited act is sufficient to sustain a conviction, regardless of intention, unless the accused demonstrates that he took all reasonable care to avoid committing the prohibited act

criminal liability offences serious offences under the *Criminal Code*, such as murder

actus reus an element of an offence—namely, the doing of the prohibited act

element (the ***mens rea***, or guilty mind) existed at the time of the crime. *Mens rea* reflects moral culpability on the part of the accused.

At the opposite end of the spectrum from criminal liability offences are the least serious offences, which are known as **absolute liability offences**. The prosecutor need only demonstrate that a particular illegal act occurred. The intention of the offender is not relevant. The consequences for the defendant on conviction are relatively minor: small fines or demerit points.

Environmental offences fall into a middle category of strict liability offences.[45] In these cases, the prosecutor's burden is greater than it is in an absolute liability offence but not as great as it is in a criminal liability offence. As is the case when prosecuting absolute liability offences, the prosecutor need not prove *mens rea*. Once the *actus reus* is proven—that is, once the prosecutor proves that the offence occurred and the defendant was responsible—the burden of proof shifts to the defendant. The defendant now carries the burden of proving that she took "all reasonable care" to prevent the offence. To escape liability, the defendant must prove **due diligence**—that is, the defendant must prove that she made serious efforts to become aware of the environmental risks and to prevent harm from occurring. The shift of the burden of proof to the defendant is necessary. Without it, the Crown would be put in the almost impossible position of trying to prove a negative: that the defendant did not take the reasonable steps needed to prevent the offence from occurring. Also, this shift of burden recognizes the reality that the defendant, not the Crown, is the party that has direct access to the evidence (if it exists) demonstrating that the defendant took "all reasonable care." The defendant must meet the less civil standard of proof: due diligence/reasonable care must be proven on a balance of probabilities rather than beyond a reasonable doubt.

Due diligence is a critically important concept in environmental law because it provides a significant incentive to businesses to use studies and regular monitoring to become aware of the potential environmental harm they may cause. It also encourages businesses to be proactive and focused on prevention in order to limit their exposure to prosecution.

---

mens rea   an element of a criminal offence—namely, a guilty mind or intention to commit the act

absolute liability offences   minor offences where the intention of the offender is not a required element

due diligence   the defence to a strict liability offence requiring the accused to demonstrate that he or she took all reasonable steps to avoid committing a prohibited act

SUMMARY OF KEY POINTS

- Environmental statutes establish a broad range of management and decision-making powers, which serve the general policy objectives of environmental protection.

- These powers can be generally categorized under two broad headings: "command" (setting standards for acceptable human behaviour) and "control" (ensuring compliance with those standards through measures and actions).

- Most environmental statutes provide for the licensing and approval of activities that could pose a risk to the environment.

- Governments use various legal tools to control pollution within their geographical jurisdictions, including statutes, regulations, site-specific legal instruments, and policies and guidelines. Each tool plays a different role in protecting the environment.

- Environmental rule-makers can choose among different approaches when setting standards for environmental behaviour. For example, a *performance standard* is used to impose a pollution limit on a polluter where the rule-maker is focused on ensuring that an operator meets a particular standard but is not concerned about how this result is achieved. By contrast, a *construction standard* requires that an operator use only government-approved pollution control systems.

- Some standards are developed based on the current "best available" pollution control technology. Others attempt to set standards to address environmental quality objectives.

- Rule-makers can also choose between general standards that use broad language to prohibit polluting activities or specific standards that set precise limits for specific types of contaminants, typically through detailed regulations.

- Specific standards can be established based on a range of approaches. Some approaches are preferred over others from an environmental protection perspective. Controlling contaminants at the source is generally favoured over measuring the impact of contaminants at property boundaries ("point of impingement"). Standards based on total loading of contaminants are usually preferred over those based on concentration limits.

- Regulators also have a choice as to how broadly or narrowly standards can apply. Some standards apply uniformly across an entire jurisdiction. Others are applied through site-specific approvals or orders to specific properties or facilities. Standards can also be applied to specific industrial sectors.

- A wide range of tools are available to ensure compliance with environmental protection standards, including incentives and financial assistance, licences and approvals, administrative orders, and prosecutions. These tools involve a number of key players, including environmental abatement officers and research and funding agencies (regarding incentives and financial assistance); hearing tribunals and government environmental officials (regarding licences and approvals and administrative orders); and criminal courts (regarding prosecutions).

KEY TERMS

absolute liability offences

actus reus

administrative orders

balance of probabilities

beyond a reasonable doubt

command and control

construction standard

criminal liability offences

director

due diligence

environmental approval

health risk assessment standard

licences and approvals

mens rea

performance standard

point of impingement

pollution prevention

precautionary principle

provincial officer (PO)

provincial officers' orders (POOs)

standard of proof

stay

strict liability offences

DISCUSSION QUESTIONS

1. Which of the environmental standard-setting instruments presented in this chapter do you think is the most effective? Why?

2. What factors are relevant in deciding whether a particular type of standard should be used?

3. Which approach to ensuring compliance with environmental standards do you think is most effective and why? Can you think of some strategies for ensuring compliance not covered in this chapter that might be more effective?

4. Given the breadth of activity and complexity of the command and control approach to government action, and taking into consideration the chapter-opening case study, is this approach to environmental protection economically sustainable?

5. What steps can be taken to maintain the effectiveness of the command and control approach in a political environment of fiscal restraint?

6. What other approaches (i.e., other than command and control) could be more effective and/or cost effective toward ensuring environmental protection? How would they work? Would they work better?

SUGGESTED READINGS

Readings

Environmental Commissioner of Ontario. *Losing Our Touch: Annual Report 2011/2012—Part 2*. Toronto: Queen's Printer for Ontario, 2012, http://www.eco.on.ca/uploads/Reports-Annual/2011_12/Losing%20Our%20Touch.pdf.

Environmental Commissioner of Ontario. *Losing Touch: Annual Report 2011/2012—Part 1*. Toronto: Queen's Printer for Ontario, 2012, http://www.eco.on.ca/uploads/Reports-Annual/2011_12/Losing%20Touch%20I%20EN.pdf.

Environmental Commissioner of Ontario. "The MISA Wastewater Regulations:
A Review Is Overdue." In Environmental Commissioner of Ontario, *Engaging
Solutions: Annual Report, 2010/2011*, 124-27. Toronto: Queen's Printer for Ontario,
2010, http://www.eco.on.ca/uploads/Reports-Annual/2010_11/Final-English
-Bookmarked-2010-AR.pdf.

Environmental Commissioner of Ontario. *Serving the Public: Annual Report 2012/2013*.
Toronto: Queen's Printer for Ontario, 2013, http://www.eco.on.ca/uploads/
Reports-Annual/2012_13/13ar.pdf.

Environmental Protection Act, RSO 1990, c. E.19.

Keenan, Karyn. "Environmental Tool Kit: Private Prosecutions." (2000) 25:3/4 *Intervenor*.
http://www.cela.ca/article/environmental-tool-kit-private-prosecutions.

MacDonald, Elaine, and Anastasia Lintner. "Summary of Concerns: Municipal Industrial
Strategy for Abatement (MISA) Regulations." Ecojustice, January 2010,
http://www.ecojustice.ca/files/submissions/EBR%20AfR%20MISA
%20Regulation%20Summary%20of%20Concerns.pdf/view.

Saxe, Dianne. *Ontario Environmental Protection Act Annotated*. Aurora, ON: Canada
Law Book, 2014.

Swaigen, John, Albert Koehl, and Charles Hatt. "Private Prosecutions Revisited: The
Continuing Importance of Private Prosecutions in Protecting the Environment."
Paper presented at a Symposium on Environment in the Courtroom (II):
Environmental Prosecutions, University of Ottawa, Ottawa, March 2013,
http://cirl.ca/files/cirl/john_swaigen_and_albert_koehl_and_charles_hatt-en.pdf.

Websites

Air Quality Ontario: http://www.airqualityontario.com

Canadian Environmental Law Association: http://www.cela.ca

Ecojustice: http://www.ecojustice.ca

e-Laws—Ontario laws and regulations: http://www.e-laws.gov.on.ca

Environment Canada: http://www.ec.gc.ca

Ontario, "Environment and Climate Change": http://www.ontario.ca/ministry-environment

Ontario, "Environmental Approvals": https://www.ontario.ca/environment-and-energy/
environmental-approvals

Ontario, "Great Lakes and Watersheds": http://www.ontario.ca/environment-and-energy/
great-lakes-protection

NOTES

1. *Environmental Protection Act*, RSO 1990, c. E.19, as amended, October 31, 2011, s. 6(1).

2. Ibid., s. 176(1)(e).

3. O. Reg. 419/05.

4. O. Reg. 560/94; O. Reg. 215/95; O. Reg. 561/94; O. Reg. 64/95; O. Reg. 214/95; O. Reg. 562/94; O. Reg. 63/95; O. Reg. 537/93; and O. Reg. 760/93.

5. RRO 1990, Reg. 347, as amended.

6. O. Reg. 232/98.

7. O. Reg. 103/94.

8. O. Reg. 101/94.

9. O. Reg. 104/94; and RRO 1990, Reg. 357, Refillable Containers for Carbonated Soft Drink.

10. O. Reg. 102/94.

11. O. Reg. 143/10.

12. For example, O. Reg. 127/01, Airborne Contaminant Discharge Monitoring and Reporting Protocol.

13. RRO 1990, Reg. 360, as amended; and O. Reg. 224/07.

14. O. Reg. 397/01.

15. *Environmental Protection Act*, supra note 1, s. 9.

16. Ibid., ss. 25 to 47.

17. Ibid., ss. 20.2, 20.3, and 20.7 to 20.14.

18. Ibid., s. 20.6.

19. Ibid., ss. 20.1 to 20.16.

20. Ibid., s. 186(3).

21. Ibid., s. 7 (control orders), s. 8 (stop orders), s. 17 (remedial orders), s. 18 (order for preventative measures), and s. 157 (provincial officer's orders).

22. Ibid., s. 14(1).

23. See supra note 4 for a series of regulations that set performance standards for discharge to surface water. They were generated by Ontario's Municipal Industrial Strategy for Abatement (MISA) standard-setting program, developed in the late 1980s and early 1990s. This program is discussed later in the chapter.

24. *Building Code Act, 1992*, SO 1992, c. 23, as amended, s. 10.1; and O. Reg. 332/12, Building Code, s. 1.1.2.3 and Part 8, Division B.

25. Mary Ann Franson, Robert T. Franson, and Alastair Lucas, *Environmental Standards: A Comparative Study of Canadian Standards, Standard Setting Processes and Enforcement* (Edmonton: Environment Council of Alberta, 1983).

26. See, e.g., Science and Environmental Health Network, "Wingspread Conference on the Precautionary Principle," January 26, 1998, http://www.sehn.org/wing.html. Scientists participating in this conference formulated the concept as follows: "When an activity raises threats of harm to human health or the environment, precautionary measures should be taken even if some cause and effect relationships are not fully established scientifically."

27. See Chapter 3, note 9.

28. See *Canadian Environmental Protection Act, 1999*, SC 1999, s. 2(1)(a) which states: "In the administration of this Act, the Government of Canada shall … exercise its powers in a manner that protects the environment and human health, applies the precautionary principle that, where there are threats of serious or irreversible damage, lack of full scientific certainty shall not be used as a reason for postponing cost-effective measures to prevent environmental degradation, and promotes and reinforces enforceable pollution prevention approaches."

29. See *Canadian Environmental Assessment Act, 2012*, SC 2012, c. 19, s. 4(2), which states: "The Government of Canada, the Minister, the Agency, federal authorities and responsible authorities, in the administration of this Act, must exercise their powers in a manner that protects the environment and human health and applies the precautionary principle."

30. *114957 Canada Ltée (Spraytech, Société d'arrosage) v. Hudson (Town)*, 2001 SCC 40, [2001] 2 SCR 241, at paras. 31 and 32, where the Supreme Court of Canada cites the precautionary principle in a case involving a challenge by a pesticide company to a municipal bylaw banning the use of pesticides. In its decision, upholding the municipal pesticide ban, the Court outlines the international law basis of the pre-cautionary principle: "In the context of the precautionary principle's tenets, the Town's concerns about pesticides fit well under their rubric of preventive action."

31. Ontario Ministry of the Environment, Statement of Environmental Values, http://www.renaud.ca/public/Environmental-Regulations/MOE Statement of Environmental Values.pdf.

32. O. Reg. 419/05, as amended.

33. See, e.g., *Dawber v. Ontario (Director, Ministry of Environment)*, [2007] Environ-mental Review Tribunal, Case Nos. 06-160 to 06-181/06-183. The Ontario En-vironmental Review Tribunal found that the point of impingement standards established under O. Reg. 419/05 are not consistent with the precautionary principle established under the Ontario Ministry of the Environment's Statement of Environ-mental Values in part because they do not require consideration of cumulative impacts.

34. *Emergency Planning and Community Right-to-Know Act*, Title 42, c. 116, US Code, s. 313 administered by the United States Environmental Protection Agency. The program requires subject industries to regularly submit inventories of their toxic chemical emissions.

35. *Canadian Environmental Protection Act, 1999*, SC 1999, c. 33, as amended, s. 46.

36. Canadian Council of Ministers of the Environment (CCME), *A Strategy to Fulfil the CCME Commitment to Pollution Prevention* (Winnipeg: CCME, 1996).

37. *Environmental Protection Act*, supra note 1, s. 157(3).

38. Ibid, s. 157(1).

39. Ibid., Part II.

40. *Canadian National Railway Co. v. Ontario (Director Under the Environmental Protection Act)* (1992), 7 OR (3d) 97, 87 DLR (4th) 603, 1992 CanLII 7705 (CA).

41. *Environmental Protection Act*, supra note 1, Part XV.

42. Ibid.

43. Ibid., s. 160.

44. Ibid.

45. The leading case establishing the principle of strict liability for environmental offences is *R v. Sault Ste. Marie*, [1978] 2 SCR 1299, 85 DLR (3d) 161, 7 CELR 53.

CHAPTER 9

Sectoral Regulatory Regimes

LEARNING OBJECTIVES

After reading this chapter, students will be able to:

- Describe the environmental regulation of fossil fuels at the provincial and federal levels and identify the federal statutes that affect fossil fuel exploration and development.
- Identify the role of the Canadian Nuclear Safety Commission and summarize the nuclear activities that are affected by federal governance.
- Understand the negative effects of mining and aggregate extraction on the environment, and explain how they should be addressed.
- Describe key Canadian laws on fisheries management and conservation and the international obligations that have influenced them.
- Discuss the environmental problems that may arise from agriculture and aquaculture, and the role of regulations in mitigating environmental harm.
- Identify the conflicts that arise from attempts to regulate pesticides, which are believed to cause unintended damage to non-target species.
- Describe the legal and regulatory framework that governs Canada's biotechnology strategy.

Introduction

This chapter examines the regulatory regimes governing several important sectors: fossil fuels, nuclear energy, mining and aggregates, fisheries, agriculture and aquaculture, pesticides, and biotechnology and genetic engineering. The governance of a single sector often involves the overlapping jurisdictions of international law, federal law, provincial law, and municipal law. Several statutes and numerous regulations apply to each jurisdiction.

CASE STUDY

Bees and Neonics: Class Action Lawsuit Targets Pesticides

In September 2014, two Ontario beekeeping companies filed a class action lawsuit against two pesticide manufacturers. The lawsuit alleges that *neonicotinoids*, a widely used class of pesticides manufactured by the defendants, caused widespread bee deaths in the province. The lawsuit claims $450 million in compensation. Neonicotinoids (also referred to as *neonics*) are used to coat soybean and corn seeds and act by affecting the nervous system of pests. The plaintiffs claim that the pesticide has permeated the air, water, soil and plants, and that it has poisoned bees and resulted in the collapse of bee colonies.

The first step in this lawsuit is to ask the court to "certify" (approve) the lawsuit as a class action lawsuit, in which all beekeepers in the province will participate unless they opt out. In Ontario, a lawsuit may be certified as a class action if there is an identifiable class of two or more persons in a claim, the claim raises common issues, and a class proceeding would be the preferred method of resolving the common issues.* A class proceeding may be the preferred method of proceeding if, for example, it would be repetitive and inefficient to require plaintiffs to each launch an individual claim. If successful in obtaining certification, the lawsuit could potentially represent over 1,600 beekeepers in Ontario,[†] who would share any compensation awarded.

The background to this claim is the alarming collapse of bee colonies across Ontario and several other parts of Canada as well as worldwide over the past several years. The collapse of bee colonies is a significant issue not only because of the impact on honey production and the economic loss to beekeepers, but also because of the critically important role bees play in pollinating crops, which is essential in maintaining our food supply.

The Canadian Association of Professional Apiculturists (CAPA) issues an annual report on honey bee colony losses. An average loss of 15 percent is the normal mortality rate reported by beekeepers each winter, but the winter loss has been significantly higher for the past few years. For example, in 2011-12, 2012-13, and 2013-14, the average honey bee wintering losses across Canada were 29 percent, 28.6 percent, and 25 percent, respectively.[‡] In the winter of 2013-14,

Believing that neonicotinoids are responsible for high mortality rates in their bee colonies, a number of Ontario beekeepers have launched a class action suit against pesticide manufacturers.

Source: Carlos Osorio/GetStock.

Ontario experienced a particularly high loss of 58 percent of its honey bees.[§] A variety of reasons have been offered for the collapse: climate change, mites, parasites, cellphone radiation, the thinning ozone layer, habitat loss, and poor management by beekeepers. Nevertheless, the results of studies have raised sufficient concern among scientists that the use of neonics today has been compared with the use of DDT in the 1960s.[#]

In 2013, the European Union announced a two-year ban on the use and sale of neonics. The European Food Safety Authority referred to studies indicating that neonics can affect human health and recommended that exposure to two types of neonicotinoids be reduced pending further studies.** Then, in November 2014, the Ontario government announced an aggressive policy to reduce the acreage of neonic-treated seeds by 80 percent by 2017, making it the first province or state in North America to take such a step.[††] It also pitted grain farmers against apiculturists: grain farmers objected to the restriction, saying it was tantamount to a ban and that they would face lower crop yields due to pests, which would place them at a competitive disadvantage with other jurisdictions. For their part, pesticide producers maintain that their products are safe if used properly and that the newer generation of chemicals they have developed are less harmful than older generations. (It is also worth noting that this policy was enacted by a recently elected Liberal majority government; had the Progressive Conservatives won the 2014 Ontario provincial election, it is highly unlikely that such a bold step would have been taken.)

Questions

The outcome of the beekeepers' class action lawsuit, if it proceeds, could have a significant impact on the liability of producers of pesticides and on the responsibility of regulators in approving pesticides for use. (Please see this text's website for updates on this class action lawsuit: emp.ca/enviro2e.) This case raises a number of questions, aside from whether neonics actually cause the death of bees:

- *Is it possible to meet the legal standard to establish causation?* Consider that the law requires the plaintiffs to establish a causative link between pesticides and bee deaths. Given the multiple potential causes of the deaths and the interaction between them, is it possible to reconcile the standard of proof required by a court with scientific uncertainty?
- *What should the role of governments be in regulating pesticides for use, and what standards should governments use for issuing approvals?* Related to these questions is the *precautionary principle.* Was the European Union restriction on neonics, pending further study, a sensible step or an unwarranted action, given uncertain scientific evidence? Should the European

Union, the Ontario government, the federal government of Canada, and others have taken more precautionary steps sooner in relation to neonics, to prevent any adverse effects their use might cause?

---

* *Class Proceedings Act, 1992*, SO 1992, c. 6, s. 5(1).

† The Ontario Beekeepers' Association states that its information reaches at least 1,600 beekeepers in the province. See Ontario Beekeepers' Association, *Annual Report 2013* (Milton, ON: OBA, 2013), http://www .ontariobee.com/sites/ontariobee.com/files/OBA _AnnualReport_2013_Final.pdf.

‡ Eric Atkins, "More Than Half of Ontario Honey Bees Did Not Survive the Winter," *Globe and Mail*, July 23, 2014, http://www.theglobeandmail.com/report-on-business/ more-than-half-of-ontario-honey-bees-did-not-survive -the-winter/article19721276/; and "CAPA Statement on Honey Bee Wintering Losses in Canada (2014)," July 24, 2014, http://www.capabees.com/content/uploads/ 2013/07/2014-CAPA-Statement-on-Honey-Bee -Wintering-Losses-in-Canada.pdf.

§ "CAPA Statement," supra note ‡.

\# Terry Pedwell, "Neonicotinoid Pesticides Responsible for Bee Deaths, Scientists Say," *Toronto Star*, June 25, 2014, http://www.thestar.com/news/canada/2014/06/25/ neonicotinoid_pesticides_responsible_for_bee_deaths _scientists_say.html.

** European Food Safety Authority, "EFSA Assesses Potential Link Between Two Neonicotinoids and Developmental Neurotoxicity," news release, December 17, 2013, http://www.efsa.europa.eu/en/press/news/131217.htm.

†† Eric Atkins, "Ontario to Restrict Use of Pesticide Linked to Bee Deaths," *Globe and Mail*, November 26, 2014, B5, http://www.theglobeandmail.com/report-on-business/ ontario-first-in-n-america-to-restrict-use-of-pesticide -linked-to-bee-deaths/article21747328/.

Fossil Fuels

Fossil fuels include oil, natural gas, and coal, all of which contain **hydrocarbons**, the organic compound of hydrogen and carbon atoms that produces energy when burned.

Located mainly in western Canada and the Atlantic offshore region, the fossil fuel exploration and extraction industries are Canada's largest private sector investors. On average, oil exports represent 30 percent of Canada's total net exports, and nearly all trade is with the United States.[1] Canada is the world's fifth-largest producer and

---

hydrocarbons the organic compound of hydrogen and carbon atoms that produces energy when burned; found in fossil fuels such as oil, natural gas, and coal

fourth-largest exporter of natural gas.[2] As well, Canada is the largest foreign supplier of both natural gas and crude oil to the United States.[3]

Oil and gas revenues have fuelled economies in western and Atlantic Canada and in the Arctic, where major natural gas pipelines have been proposed over the last 40 years.[4] Coal is also important, accounting for nearly 20 percent of Canadian electricity generation, mainly in Alberta, Saskatchewan, and Nova Scotia. Ontario, however, has seen a dramatic decrease in its use of coal in the last decade, and by 2015 it had become the first jurisdiction in North America to eliminate coal from its list of power sources. This shift was a major factor in the reduction in officially recognized "smog days" in Ontario from 53 in 2005 to none in 2014.[5] The oil sands of Alberta may be the largest remaining source of fossil fuels in North America, and their importance to Canada's economy has become momentous as other fossil fuel sources have been depleted.[6]

The environmental and health effects of fossil fuel operations are significant. Consider the following:

- Exploration, development, and production, often in remote areas, are major land uses. They have the potential to create serious effects on land, wildlife, air, water, local communities, and Aboriginal peoples.[7]
- Environmental and human health risks exist from the development of "sour" natural gas—that is, gas that has a high sulphur content.[8]
- The oil and gas industry produces 25 percent of Canadian greenhouse gas emissions.[9] Annual emissions increased from 101 megatonnes in 1990 to 173 megatonnes in 2012.[10] Greenhouse gas emissions have a substantial impact on the environment and human health, including air pollution, global warming, and extreme weather events.[11]
- With the decline in conventional oil and gas reserves in Canada, recent industry developments—particularly oil sands and coal bed methane extraction in western Canada—have resulted in new land use effects and environmental risks.[12]
- Greenhouse gas emissions from coal-fired electricity generation are a major problem in Alberta. These emissions have attracted federal regulation.[13]

Environmental regulation of fossil fuels occurs primarily at the provincial level.[14] The direct effects of exploration, development, production, and transportation within the provinces are regulated by both provincial environment departments and regulators of energy and natural resources.[15]

Direct federal environmental regulation of oil and gas activities within provinces is limited to interprovincial and export pipelines.[16] However, on Crown land north of latitude 60°N, the federal government is responsible for the management of oil and gas resources, under the *Canada Oil and Gas Operations Act* and the *Canada Petroleum Resources Act*.[17] In the Atlantic offshore area, federal and provincial environmental regulation is harmonized through the Canada–Nova Scotia Offshore Petroleum Board and the Canada–Newfoundland and Labrador Offshore Petroleum Board.[18] There are federal and provincial moratoria on west coast offshore hydrocarbon activities that date from the 1970s.[19] Constitutional jurisdiction over the most promising offshore drilling areas remains uncertain, although British Columbia's interest in developing these resources has declined in recent years.[20]

The most sophisticated hydrocarbon regulator is the Alberta Energy Regulator (AER). It is a quasi-independent government agency responsible for providing "efficient, safe, orderly and environmentally responsible development of energy resources in Alberta."[21] British Columbia[22] and Saskatchewan[23] have similar oil and gas tribunals.

The AER applies environmental criteria to licensing of the following:

- oil and gas wells;[24]
- facilities such as natural gas processing plants, oil sands mines, and upgrading plants;[25]
- intraprovincial pipelines;[26] and
- coal mines.[27]

The environmental criteria used by the AER are elaborated in the relevant statutes: the Alberta *Oil and Gas Conservation Act*,[28] the *Oil Sands Conservation Act*,[29] the *Pipeline Act*,[30] and the *Coal Conservation Act*.[31] Additional environmental criteria are also included in the regulations under these Acts.[32]

Until 2013, Alberta's licensing of hydrocarbon activities involved a coordinated process with Alberta's Environment and Sustainable Resources Development for environmental impact assessment under the *Environmental Protection and Enhancement Act*.[33] If an approval application went to a hearing because objections were filed by affected persons, the environmental assessment reports and studies were part of the evidence before the Energy Resources Conservation Board (ERCB), the AER's predecessor. The board and Alberta Environment cooperated in setting terms of reference and reviewing the environmental assessment documents.

For applications that required ERCB approval as well as approval for contaminant discharge under the *Environmental Protection and Enhancement Act*, the ERCB and Alberta Environment operated together as a "single window" under a memorandum of understanding. Reviews of applications were coordinated, and an Alberta Environment official might sit as an acting ERCB member. Section 2 of the now repealed *Energy Resources Conservation Act*, the board's empowering statute, gave the ERCB discretionary power to determine whether a proposed development was in the public interest, "having regard to the social and economic effects of the project and the effects of the project on the environment."[34]

All of this changed with the enactment in 2012 of the *Responsible Energy Development Act*,[35] which replaced the ERCB with the Alberta Energy Regulator and established the regulator's mandate, structure, and powers. The AER issues approvals under both energy and environmental statutes. It also acts as an appeal tribunal for environmental approvals[36] that were previously heard and determined by the Alberta Environmental Appeals Board. The structure and processes of the new regulator have been controversial.[37] Issues have centred around the regulator's independence[38] and the transparency and fairness of its proceedings.[39] Whether the new legislation decreases the number and possibility of public hearings on approval applications[40] and narrows the standing of concerned persons and non-governmental organizations to participate[41] have been active issues.

Oil and Gas

Alberta is Canada's largest producer of oil and gas.[42] In Alberta, specific prohibitions exist against hydrocarbon releases to land, water, and air, including detailed performance standards for natural gas flaring from oil and gas facilities.[43] The AER enforces these requirements through an **enforcement ladder system** of inspections and progressively more serious warnings, monetary penalties, shutdowns, and prosecutions.[44]

The AER has authority over the licensing of wells for waste disposal as well as oil and gas wells and the approval of processing plants, pipelines, and storage facilities. The regulator pays special attention to proposed wells in the sensitive montane region of the Rocky Mountains' eastern slopes[45] and to proposed sour gas wells.[46] Sour gas wells produce gas that is high in sulphur and hydrogen sulphide (H_2S), a gas that can be lethal, even in small doses. Companies proposing to drill for sour gas must prepare detailed emergency response plans. They must also ensure that minimum distance requirements between sour gas pipelines and human settlements are met.[47]

The AER also regulates contaminated oil and gas sites, including the reclamation of **orphaned sites**—that is, wells and other facilities abandoned by oil and gas operators.[48] An orphan well program manages a fund generated by means of a levy on well operators and well licence fees for new companies. Companies pay sums based on their proportionate share of estimated liability compared with total industry liability. This program is now operated by the non-profit Orphan Well Association as an authorized delegate of the AER.[49]

In addition, the AER uses a complex **licensee liability rating system** that "applies to all upstream oil and gas wells, facilities, and pipelines included within the scope of

---

enforcement ladder system   approach to responding to environmental law violations that increases in intensity, and involves inspections and progressively more serious warnings, monetary penalties, shutdowns, and prosecutions

orphaned sites   oil wells and other facilities abandoned by oil and gas operators

licensee liability rating system   a system for ensuring that a company can pay for the costs of possible contamination before a licence is granted for a new facility, by comparing the assets of the company with the estimated risk of contamination liability

BOX 9.1 » The Politics of Fracking

Perhaps the most dynamic and controversial area of energy policy in recent years is the practice of hydraulic fracturing, or **fracking**. This process has revolutionized the way in which gas and oil reserves are extracted from the ground. Its success in the United States has allowed that country to target energy independence by 2030—that is, to end any reliance on Middle Eastern oil imports—which has significant consequences for geopolitics, economics, and environmental and climate change policy. However, it has also raised alarm because this practice is now being shown to increase seismic activity (i.e., earthquakes).*

In Canada, various provinces have taken different policy approaches. In New Brunswick, fracking policy became a major issue in the 2014 provincial election:

> An issue that galvanized this election, shale gas and the method used to extract it—hydraulic fracturing or fracking—shows a province divided over its future course, as illustrated by the results of a close, albeit troubled, vote.
>
> On one side, Liberal Premier-designate Brian Gallant vowed to impose a moratorium on the controversial practice "until risks to the environment, health and water are fully understood."
>
> [T]he Progressive Conservatives made shale gas development a linchpin in their plans to help bring the province out of debt and create jobs to keep skilled workers in the province, rather than heading to Alberta to make a living.
>
> Nearly one year ago tensions over the future of shale gas development in New Brunswick reached a tipping point, as the RCMP broke up a protest encampment near Elsipogtog First Nation.
>
> Mounties, acting on a court injunction, used tear gas and reportedly used rubber bullets to disperse demonstrators, after protesters blocked Route 134 for weeks in opposition to shale gas exploration in the area—a hot-button issue across the province. ...
>
> [Carleton University Professor] Lori Turnbull ... said shale gas and fracking have been a "polarizing" issue throughout the campaign.
>
> She said voters may have been willing to sacrifice other priorities to side with the leader that best suited their views on fracking.
>
> "It's a difficult issue in the sense that it asks voters to weigh potential economic growth against potential environmental costs—and there are a lot of unknown variables on both sides."†

---

* Maria Galluci, "Kansas Earthquakes Likely Tied to Rise in Fracking Wastewater, State Geologists Say," *International Business Times*, January 28, 2015, http://www.ibtimes.com/kansas-earthquakes -likely-tied-rise-fracking-wastewater-state-geologists-say-1797652.

† Nick Logan, "NB Election: Did Shale Gas and Fracking Sway the Vote?" September 23, 2014. http://globalnews.ca/news/1577434/n-b-election-did-shale-gas-and-fracking-sway-the-vote/.

---

fracking derived from the term *hydraulic fracturing*; method of extracting oil or natural gas by injecting highly pressurized liquid into subterranean rock

the expanded Orphan Fund."[50] The rating system is used to compare the assets of a company seeking a licence with the estimated risk that the company will incur contamination liability during its proposed activities.[51] The AER may approve, approve with conditions, or deny a licence transfer application as a result of the rating.[52]

Oil Sands

The AER also regulates oil sands development. The **oil sands** are crude bitumen deposits found in an area of northern Alberta and part of Saskatchewan that is approximately the size of New Brunswick. Production occurs by means of large-scale mining of surface deposits and *in situ* thermal recovery through wells for deeper deposits. When oil sands are taken into account, oil reserves in Canada rank third only behind those of Saudi Arabia and Venezuela. Production from oil sands has passed 1.9 million barrels of oil per day. In 2013, total investment in new and existing oil sands projects exceeded $514 billion, although the unexpected drop in global oil prices that occurred in late 2014 has begun to have a major impact on investment, jobs, and the feasibility of new oil sands projects.[53]

The environmental impact of oil sands development is significant. It includes vast land surface disturbances, water use, pollution, and air emissions (including major greenhouse gas releases).[54] The AER regulates oil sands mining and *in situ* development, primarily under the *Oil Sands Conservation Act* and the *Oil Sands Conservation Rules*.[55] It also administers the *Water Act*[56] as it applies to oil sands activities, which is significant because of the large quantities of water required to upgrade the bitumen from oil sands to crude oil. The AER has environmental jurisdiction over oil sands activities under the *Environmental Protection and Enhancement Act*. In 2010, Syncrude Canada Ltd. was prosecuted successfully under section 155 of the Act after 1,600 ducks died on a Syncrude tailings pond.[57] Section 155 requires "[a] person who keeps, stores or transports a hazardous substance or pesticide [to] do so in a manner that ensures that the hazardous substance or pesticide does not directly or indirectly come into contact with or contaminate any animals, plants, food or drink." Under the *Climate Change and Emissions Management Act*[58] and *Specified Gas Emitters Regulation*,[59] which are administered by Alberta Environment, major emitters of greenhouse gas emissions—including oil sands facilities—must meet **emission intensity reduction** limits based on emissions per unit of production.[60]

The pace of oil sands exploitation has highlighted substantive environmental and process concerns, including the following:[61]

---

oil sands   crude bitumen deposits found in an area of northern Alberta and part of Saskatchewan that is approximately the size of New Brunswick

emission intensity reduction   emission limits based on emissions per unit of production, rather than a set limit

- lack of comprehensive planning for oil sands development,
- undue jurisdictional and regulatory complexity,
- lack of transparency, and
- limited opportunities for public participation.

Coal

Both federal and provincial governments regulate coal. The federal government regulates interprovincial and international trade and commerce, manages non-renewable resources on federal lands, and has jurisdiction over interprovincial and international emissions. The provinces govern exploration, development, conservation, and management of non-renewable resources, as well as electricity. On April 1, 2014, the federal government devolved responsibility for Northwest Territories resources (including coal) to the Government of the Northwest Territories.[62]

Although regulatory regimes for coal development vary across the provinces, they have similar features and address common issues.[63] Each jurisdiction requires reclamation of surface-mined land and containment or treatment of acidic drainage. Coal used for electricity generation is a major source of air emissions. Standards are enforced for air contaminants, particularly sulphur dioxide (SO_2). Federal greenhouse gas emission regulations establish emission limits for coal-fired electricity generation plants and provide for the phasing out of coal-fired generation units by 2030.[64]

In Alberta, where coal-fired plants produce approximately 47 percent of provincial greenhouse gas emissions, limits are set under the *Climate Change and Emissions Management Act*. Although some provinces have reduced or plan to reduce coal-fired generation, Alberta continues to rely on coal for more than half of its electricity generation. The AER regulates coal mines,[65] while the Alberta Utilities Commission regulates coal-fired electricity-generating plants.[66]

Federal Regulation

A number of federal statutes and associated regulations affect the environmental impacts of fossil fuel exploration and development. In particular:

- Under the federal *National Energy Board Act*,[67] the National Energy Board (NEB) considers potential environmental effects in certificate applications for major interprovincial and international pipelines, and regulates the direct environmental effects of operating pipelines.
- The *Fisheries Act* prohibits discharge of "deleterious substances" into "water frequented by fish."[68] Under the *Migratory Birds Convention Act*, no person "shall deposit a substance that is harmful to migratory birds … in waters or an area frequented by migratory birds."[69]
- The *Canadian Environmental Protection Act, 1999* imposes pollution prevention plan requirements and contaminant release reporting.

- The *Canadian Environmental Assessment Act* (CEAA)[70] requires environmental assessments of oil and gas facilities that are located on federal lands or that need an approval under a federal statutory power listed in the regulations. The Act also regulates activities in the northern territories and offshore, as well as major interprovincial and international pipelines.
- The NEB must provide an environmental impact assessment of a proposed export of natural gas as a result of *Quebec (Attorney General) v. Canada (National Energy Board)*,[71] a 1994 decision of the Supreme Court of Canada. The NEB has ruled that greenhouse gas emissions by upstream oil sands extraction and upgrading are outside its jurisdiction (and thus within provincial jurisdiction) in considering facilities applications for major interjurisdictional pipelines.[72] However, whether the outcome of *Quebec (Attorney General)*—that NEB gas export approvals cannot be conditional on future successful environmental assessment of power plants to generate the exported electricity—can be applied to interprovincial oil pipelines is unclear. The electricity export context is different. But there is a strong analogy to support an argument that the legal principle should be the same. This issue has been raised in judicial review applications concerning the proposed Northern Gateway Pipeline[73] that was recommended positively by a joint review panel[74] and approved by the governor in council[75] in 2014.

Federal and provincial statutes provide for joint environmental review and approval processes in relation to oil, gas, and coal exploration, as well as energy development and production activities. Joint panels of Alberta ERCB (now AER) members and representatives of the Canadian Environmental Assessment Agency have reviewed and assessed major proposed oil sands facilities and coal mines.[76] But since the repeal and re-enactment of the CEAA in 2012, the NEB is the sole decision-maker for interjurisdictional pipelines, with authority under both the *National Energy Board Act* and the CEAA.

Climate Change

In 2010, Canada subscribed to the Copenhagen Accord target of a 17 percent reduction in greenhouse gas emissions from 2005 levels by 2020.[77] The federal approach acknowledges the present 80 percent and potentially larger, longer-term contribution to greenhouse gas emissions by fossil fuels used for energy purposes.[78] Currently, approximately 44 percent of greenhouse gas emissions are from stationary sources such as electricity generation fossil fuel industries, and mining; 27 percent are from domestic transportation; 9 percent are from fugitive sources such as gas flaring and venting; and the remainder are from non-energy sectors (industrial processes, agriculture, and waste).[79]

The federal government's action plan on climate change follows a sectoral approach, and it is based on its regulatory authority under the *Canadian Environmental Protection Act, 1999:*[80]

- *Transportation:* In 2014, it issued regulations to reduce emissions from cars and light trucks[81] and heavy-duty vehicles.[82]
- *Electricity:* In 2012, it issued regulations to reduce emissions from coal-fired electricity generation and requires "intensity-based" emissions reductions and the phase out of generation units by 2030.[83]
- *Renewable fuels:* As of 2010, motor fuels must contain a minimum percentage of renewable fuel content.[84]
- *Hydrofluorocarbons (HFCs):* In 2014, it announced its intention to regulate HFCs and reduce these emissions over the next 10 to 15 years.[85]

Several provinces have developed climate change policies and passed their own climate change statutes. Alberta, first among provincial greenhouse gas emitters—mainly because of its energy and coal-fired electricity activities—passed its *Climate Change and Emissions Management Act* in 2003. The Act provides for **emission intensity**–based greenhouse gas reduction targets for large emitters that are linked to the provincial gross domestic product (GDP).

The Alberta targets are intended to reduce greenhouse gas emissions per unit of production by 50 percent below 2005 levels by 2050. Under this emission intensity–based approach, while emissions from specific sources should decrease, economic growth in the province—particularly in relation to projected oil sands development—is likely to result in increased total emissions in the near term. Nevertheless, the Alberta government projects real reductions of greenhouse gas emissions by 14 percent below 2005 levels by 2050. Included in its *Climate Change and Emissions Management Act* is the structure for an emissions-trading system, mandatory emissions reporting, and a climate change and emissions management fund. Property rights in **carbon sinks**—which are created by "sequestering" carbon by growing trees, reducing soil tillage, and injecting carbon dioxide (CO_2) into depleted hydrocarbon formations—can be traded as **carbon offsets**.

---

emission intensity a measure of the amount of carbon emitted per barrel of oil produced, or the relationship between emissions and economic activity. As the technology for accessing and consuming energy improves, the emissions intensity decreases. However, this approach is controversial because the amount of actual carbon entering the atmosphere can still increase, even as efficiency rises.

carbon sinks areas created by removing or "sequestering" carbon dioxide by growing trees, reducing soil tillage, and injecting carbon dioxide into depleted hydrocarbon formations; used in emissions-trading systems

carbon offsets the use of carbon sinks to offset emissions of carbon dioxide; used in emissions-trading systems

Alberta's approach to reducing greenhouse gas emissions is sensitive to potential developments in federal law and makes provision for agreements with other jurisdictions.[86] British Columbia addresses greenhouse gas emissions reduction through the *Greenhouse Gas Reduction Targets Act*.[87] Ontario addresses greenhouse gas emissions reduction through regulations under its *Environmental Protection Act*.[88] In addition, British Columbia[89] and Quebec[90] have implemented carbon taxes (see Chapter 12).

Nuclear Energy

Nuclear power regulation is complex and controversial, perhaps not surprisingly in light of the history of the technology. Originating in the United States during the Second World War, it was further developed throughout the Cold War. Subsequent events, such as the Chernobyl reactor accident in 1986, the attacks on the United States on September 11, 2001, and the Great East Japan Earthquake and tsunami that caused meltdowns and radioactive releases from at least three nuclear power units at the Fukushima Daiichi Nuclear Power Station in 2011 have prompted reviews of the safety and security of nuclear power sources. Nuclear power as a technology differs markedly from other forms of power generation in terms of the types of accidents that may occur, the longevity of the hazardous radioactive wastes generated, and the potential for reactor-grade plutonium to be used in weapons.

Many special rules and approaches have been developed in Canada and elsewhere to enable and continue the use of nuclear power. The presence of these rules sets nuclear energy apart from natural gas, coal, hydroelectricity, wind, solar, geothermal, and other sources of power. The adequacy of these rules is constantly being tested and questioned, and this situation will continue as long as nuclear power forms part of the electricity supply in Canada.

Canada plays a highly significant role in nuclear power generation internationally. It is the world's second-largest uranium exporter, providing 15 percent of the global supply in 2012.[91] Canada exports almost 85 percent of its uranium production, currently from mines in northern Saskatchewan.[92] As of 2013, nuclear power accounted for about 17 percent of Canadian electricity.[93] The largest user of nuclear energy is Ontario, where nuclear power constitutes more than 50 percent of the total power used in the province.[94]

In the 1950s and 1960s, Canada developed the CANDU nuclear power generation technology. **CANDU technology** is used in nuclear generating stations in Ontario and New Brunswick, and was used in Quebec.[95] The technology was also exported to India, Pakistan, China, South Korea, Argentina, and Romania for power

---

CANDU technology   a nuclear power generation technology that uses heavy water to moderate the uranium fuel fission reaction and requires fast, redundant shutdown systems to be available in various circumstances

generation. CANDU technology uses heavy water to moderate the uranium fuel fission reaction and requires fast, redundant shutdown systems to be available in case of various events. This fusion reaction produces large amounts of energy, which is harnessed through steam to power large turbines for power generation. Nuclear power plants must be located on large bodies of water, which play a role in thermal cooling and provide an outlet for some of the emissions, bypasses, and spills discharged from the plants.

Nuclear facilities involve an immense capital cost. For example, $14.4 billion was spent building the Darlington Nuclear Generating Station, Ontario's newest plant, between 1981 and 1993. The Ontario government has estimated that tens of billions of dollars will be required between 2018 and 2043 if the existing Ontario nuclear power plants are to be refurbished and remain operational until 2043. The Ontario government had been proposing to build new nuclear power plants at the Darlington nuclear generation site but announced in 2013 that it was no longer pursuing new-build nuclear plants and instead was intending to focus on refurbishing existing nuclear power reactors in the province. As of 2014, the cost estimate for refurbishing the four aging Darlington units was $13 billion.[96] Federal and provincial approvals are required before refurbishment could proceed at that location. In November 2014, the Federal Court ruled against a legal challenge that sought to overturn the environmental assessment of that project based on the assertion that it was inadequate under the *Canadian Environmental Assessment Act*.[97]

The debate over continued nuclear power generation in Canada centres on four main areas of concern:

- the enormous financial cost of nuclear-generated power;
- the risks of a nuclear power plant accident;
- the long-term disposal of nuclear wastes, which are highly radioactive and hazardous, and continue to be toxic for hundreds of thousands of years; and
- the risk of nuclear weapons proliferation and other human and national security risks, such as terrorist attacks on nuclear plants.

In addition, there have been long-standing debates over the location of nuclear power generation plants and related facilities, such as low-level, medium-level, and high-level radioactive waste disposal sites; the transportation of radioactive fuel and waste; and the importing of used fuel, including plutonium fuel, from countries such as Russia and the United States.

International Law

The United Nations Atomic Energy Commission was established in 1946 "to deal with the problems raised by the discovery of atomic energy."[98] In 1957, it formed the International Atomic Energy Agency. One of the agency's first steps was the imposition of safeguards for a Canadian supply of uranium to Japan in 1959. Around the same time, EURATOM was established in Europe. EURATOM regulated all non-military nuclear activities of the member states, including France and Britain, and theoretically provided for collective ownership of nuclear materials by member states.

In 1968 the Treaty on the Non-Proliferation of Nuclear Weapons was signed by the United Kingdom, the United States, and the Soviet Union. Today, all members of the United Nations are signatories except for India, Pakistan, Israel, and Cuba. The treaty attempts to limit further development of nuclear weapons by additional states.

International treaties that play a significant role in Canadian nuclear regulatory obligations arose as a consequence of events such as the development of nuclear power production and the capacity of various countries for nuclear technology. The various stages of the Cold War and the occurrence of serious accidents, such as the tragedies at Chernobyl in 1986 and at Fukushima Daiichi in 2011, have also resulted in the adoption and amendment of international nuclear treaties and their instruments. Canada is a signatory to international agreements in the following areas:

- nuclear safety (1986);
- safety of spent fuel management and radioactive waste management, including transboundary movement of these materials (1997 and 1990);
- third-party liability, civil liability, and supplementary compensation for nuclear damage (various conventions, annexes, amendments, and supplements adopted in 1960, 1963, 1964, 1982, 1997, 1998, and 2014);
- physical protection of nuclear material (1979);
- early notification of nuclear accidents (1986);
- assistance in the event of nuclear accident and radiological emergency (1986); and
- prevention of nuclear explosions or disposal of nuclear waste in Antarctica (1959).

Despite being a signatory, Canada is not always in compliance with these international agreements—for example, Canada has so far failed to comply with the treaties covering nuclear liability in the event of an accident. The 1976 federal *Nuclear Liability Act* exempted nuclear power generators and suppliers from the normal rules of civil liability by capping liability at $75 million in the event of a serious accident and by exempting suppliers from any liability even if at fault. This exemption is controversial because it is a significant subsidy that is not available to generators of other types of electrical power. However, as of 2014, the federal government had introduced proposed legislation in Parliament four times over recent years intending to change the liability limit and other matters. As of the date of writing, the latest proposed legislation, Bill C-22, which would increase the liability limit to $1 billion by operators (but still exempt suppliers), is still before Parliament but is expected to pass.

Federal Regulation

Jurisdiction over nuclear power and activities such as the production of nuclear energy and research on nuclear energy is primarily federal because atomic energy was stated in the *Nuclear Energy Act* to be "[f]or the general advantage of Canada," which brought it under jurisdiction of section 92(10)(c) of the *Constitution Act, 1867*. The Canadian *Nuclear Safety and Control Act* sets out obligations that are overseen by the Canadian Nuclear Safety Commission (CNSC), which reports to the minister of natural resources. In Canada, those who wish to carry out activities that use nuclear technology must obtain a licence to do so from the CNSC. Separate licences are required for various activities, including uranium exploration, uranium mine development and operation, siting of power plants, construction of plants, operation of plants, research facilities, medical facilities, and production of products using radioactive materials.

The CNSC may take different approaches when determining the level of safety and safeguards that the applicant must meet to obtain a licence. The industry approach, traditionally adopted by the CNSC, has been to reduce risks to a level "as low as reasonably achievable" (commonly referred to by the acronym **ALARA**). This approach has been controversial in Canada. Recent initiatives by the regulator have included the development of criteria for decisions regarding the siting of new nuclear power plants and design standards, more rigorous requirements for onsite emergency response, and additional requirements for offsite emergency planning and readiness, including pre-distribution of potassium iodide pills to all residents in the "primary" zone (generally 10 to 13 kilometres for Canadian nuclear power plants).

Other areas of federal governance affect nuclear activities:

- Health Canada maintains a registry to monitor the lifelong radiation doses of all workers exposed to radioactive materials.
- A federal–provincial–territorial radiation committee makes recommendations by way of guidelines to governments on practices and standards regarding radiation exposure in Canada; the provincial and territorial governments are responsible for the actual standards adopted.
- The *Transportation of Dangerous Goods Regulations* control the transport of radioactive materials in Canada. They incorporate the technical instructions of the Convention on International Civil Aviation for air transport, including provisions pertaining to the specifications of packages and labelling.
- The federal government provides national drinking water guidelines. All of the provinces as well as Yukon Territory have implemented binding drinking water standards for municipal drinking water, often patterned on the national

---

ALARA   acronym for "as low as reasonably achievable" with respect to risk, which is the approach to safety used in the nuclear industry

guidelines, although the actual standards adopted may be more or less stringent than the guidelines. In Ontario, public attention to the issue of appropriate standards for tritium (a radioactive isotope) in drinking water two decades ago resulted in some reduction in the allowable amount, but a recommendation by that province's Drinking Water Advisory Committee to lower the standard even further has not been acted on by the province.

Provincial Regulation

Each province has jurisdiction over the mixture of electricity sources within the province. For example, the Ontario Energy Board reviews the rate requirements of Ontario Power Generation (OPG), which operates nuclear power plants in Ontario at Pickering and Darlington, and the Ontario Power Authority enters into procurement contracts for electricity supply with other operators such as Bruce Nuclear, which leases the nuclear plants near Kincardine from OPG.

Some provinces, such as Saskatchewan and Quebec, also apply their provincial environmental assessment legislation to the nuclear industry within the province. Quebec decided to close its Gentilly-2 nuclear power plant in 2012 and has no plans to pursue nuclear generation in the future. While Ontario is less involved in regulating nuclear power sources through its general environmental assessment legislation as compared with other provinces, matters of general application may apply to the nuclear industry—for example, the need for a permit before withdrawing water from ground or surface water sources.

Mining and Aggregates

Mining

Canada is one of the most mineral-rich countries in the world, and mining has always been important to Canada's economy. Non-metal mining (for salt and quartzite) and energy-related coal mining are also significant industries. In 2012, Canada's mining and mineral-processing industries contributed $52.6 billion to the economy;[99] this figure represents just over 3 percent of Canada's GDP.[100] In 2012, mining-related industries employed over 400,000 people.[101]

Despite its economic benefits, mining causes severe environmental effects that may damage and pollute the landscape for years after a mining activity concludes. The following environmental effects are typical in mining:

- obliteration of the natural habitat of wildlife and fish;
- generation of large amounts of waste, noise, and dust;
- contamination of water, land, and air with organic chemicals, cyanide, and heavy metals that leach from acid mine drainage; and
- continued pollution of the environment for decades after a mine closes, if it is not properly rehabilitated.

Table 9.1 Jurisdiction Over Mining

Federal Jurisdiction	Provincial Jurisdiction
All mines on federal lands	All mines on provincial lands except uranium mines
All uranium mines	

The federal government is responsible for mines on federal lands, as well as uranium mining regardless of where it is undertaken. Provincial governments are responsible for all other types of mines on provincial lands. Table 9.1 sets out federal and provincial jurisdiction over various types of mines.

Rules and requirements are associated with each stage of the mining process. The key stages of mining exploration and development are as follows:

- mineral exploration and prospecting;
- claim staking;
- environmental assessment and approvals;
- operation and production, which includes waste management; and
- monitoring and closure/site rehabilitation.

The staking of a mining claim is required to explore for mineral deposits. A mining claim gives a prospector the exclusive right to conduct an exploration in a specific area, and exploration work must actually be carried out to maintain the claim.

A prospector is allowed to explore for (but not extract) minerals under a mining claim. Prior to 2009 amendments to Ontario's *Mining Act*, prospectors could stake mining claims and explore on land where the Crown owned the subsurface mineral rights, even if another person owned the rights to the surface land. That right has now been limited. Private lands in southern Ontario have been withdrawn from claim staking,[102] and lands may be withdrawn from staking in northern Ontario.[103]

When exploration leads to the discovery of valuable mineral deposits, mining almost always goes ahead. To proceed with mining, the holder of a mining claim must negotiate a mining lease with the provincial government and pay annual rent. Once a mining lease has been granted, the claim holder must follow the requirements of the *Mining Act* and other relevant laws. In Ontario, mining is subject to a class environmental assessment process that applies to decisions of the Ministry of Northern Development and Mines (MNDM) with respect to surface rights, mining rights, and **chattels**, as well as MNDM mine hazard rehabilitation activities.[104] (It should

---

chattels any building, structure, machinery, personal property, ore, slimes, tailings, or other effects not otherwise privately owned and on mining lands that have reverted to the Crown (definition taken from Class Environmental Assessment for Activities of the Ministry of Northern Development and Mines)

BOX 9.2 » The Ring of Fire

The "Ring of Fire" is an area of Ontario's Far North with mining potential for minerals such as nickel, chromite, copper, zinc, and gold.* Many mining claims have been staked over an area of approximately 2,250 square kilometres, which includes undisturbed boreal forest, species at risk, and the traditional lands of 38 First Nations. The Ontario government passed the *Far North Act, 2010* to govern land use planning in the Far North. However, concern exists that the current environmental assessment and land use planning regimes that apply to this region are not adequate to address the potential negative effects of the transportation and energy infrastructure that will be required for the Ring of Fire, in addition to the impact of the proposed mines themselves.

Question

As of 2015, development plans for the region had stalled for various reasons, but it is likely that it will eventually become a viable project once again. How should Ontario balance the desire to extract these natural resources with the need to protect the environment?

---

*   Cheryl Chetkiewicz, and Anastasia M. Lintner, *Getting It Right in Ontario's Far North—The Need for a Regional Strategic Environmental Assessment in the Ring of Fire* (Thunder Bay, ON: Wildlife Conservation Society Canada and Ecojustice Canada, 2014), http://www.ecojustice.ca/publications/getting-it-right-in-ontarios-far-north-the-need-for-a-regional-strategic-environmental-assessment-in-the-ring-of-fire-wawagajing/attachment; Environmental Commissioner of Ontario, "Making Informed Decisions for the Far North and the Ring of Fire," last modified October 10, 2013, http://ecoissues.ca/index.php/Making_Informed_Decisions_for_the_Far_North_and_the_Ring_of_Fire.

---

be noted that while Ontario is the example being discussed here, all provinces have their own required environmental assessment processes for any proposed mining activity within their jurisdiction.)

Under the *Mining Act*, a mine closure plan must be prepared before mining operations can begin.[105] The plan must explain how the mine will be rehabilitated and how environmental problems will be addressed when the mine is eventually closed. The mining company must also offer some financial assurance to cover the future costs of mine rehabilitation. In the past, many mines across Canada were abandoned and required rehabilitation at public expense.

Aggregates

Aggregates include sand, gravel, and crushed stone, and are extracted from pits and quarries in areas that contain these natural resources. Aggregates are used in highway construction, in building dams and airports, and in some manufactured products. While new aggregates are often used in these projects, it is possible to recycle and reuse aggregate products in order to better conserve existing aggregate resources.

The provinces are responsible for regulating aggregate pits and quarries. For example, in Ontario, an aggregate operator must obtain a licence under the *Aggregate Resources Act*, and this process requires consideration of environmental effects.

However, applications for new and expanded aggregate operations are often successful despite concerns about environmental effects. Approvals are also required under the *Planning Act* to address land use planning issues.

Many of the best-quality aggregate deposits are located in areas that are ecologically unique and important, such as the Niagara Escarpment and the Oak Ridges Moraine in the Greenbelt of Ontario. Moreover, aggregate operations are often permitted in sensitive areas like wetlands, raising issues related to source water protection. Many are calling for new processes that better balance environmental protection with aggregate extraction. In 2013, the Standing Committee on General Government of the Ontario Legislative Assembly held hearings and prepared a *Report on the Review of the Aggregate Resources Act*. The committee made recommendations on developing planning tools to reduce land use conflicts between aggregate extraction and other uses, such as rural residential, agricultural, and natural activities.[106]

The Ontario government has addressed the rehabilitation of pits and quarries differently than it has the rehabilitation of mines. All aggregate operators must contribute money to both their own site-specific fund (that serves as financial assurance for the site) and a common fund that may be used to rehabilitate orphan sites.

Fisheries

The role of fisheries in Canada is substantial. According to Fisheries and Oceans Canada, the value of the commercial catch in Canada was over $2 billion in 2012; this figure excludes the value of aquaculture, which exceeded $800 million. Recreational fisheries exist throughout Canada and also have economic and social significance.

The importance of Canadian fisheries is not limited to coastal communities. The per capita consumption of fish products in Canada in 2013 was 8.12 kilograms. The exploitation of these fisheries has a direct effect on the environment within Canada, as well as neighbouring countries and international waters. This impact is evident in the frequent appearance of fishery-related stories in Canada's national newspapers.

Many Canadian laws on fisheries management and conservation derive from Canada's international obligations. The following are a few examples:

- The *Coastal Fisheries Protection Act* was enacted, among other reasons, to manage and protect sedentary species on the continental shelf beyond Canadian fisheries water.[107] It also prohibits fishing in the Northwest Atlantic Fisheries Organization Regulatory Area. The Northwest Atlantic Fisheries Organization has 12 member states, including Canada.[108]
- Conservation and management measures are also included in the Convention on Future Multilateral Co-operation in the Northwest Atlantic Fisheries.[109] This convention, which was signed in Ottawa on October 24, 1978, is the governing convention for the Northwest Atlantic Fisheries Organization.

Pursuant to this convention, Canada's portion of the northwest Atlantic Ocean is subject to a fisheries management regime.

- Federal law regarding pollution of the marine environment in the **exclusive economic zone** is based on the United Nations Convention on the Law of the Sea. This convention contains a variety of articles relating to conservation and management—for example, articles 60 to 70 and 116 to 120 as well as part XII, which covers the protection and preservation of the marine environment.[110] It also gives coastal states jurisdiction over the marine environment in the exclusive economic zone.

- Federal provisions relating to conservation and management of fisheries are implemented through an agreement generally known as the United Nations Fishing Agreement (UNFA).[111] This agreement creates regional organizations to manage and protect straddling and migratory stocks of marine species both within and beyond the exclusive economic zone.

- Article 3(1)(a) of the Agreement to Promote Compliance with International Conservation and Management Measures by Fishing Vessels on the High Seas[112] and article 18(1) of UNFA require Canada to take measures necessary to ensure that fishing boats comply with international conservation and management measures.

The federal government has primary jurisdiction over both seacoast and inland fisheries in Canada, although it interacts closely with the provinces on many matters. The provinces may dispose of the fisheries they own, but may not trespass on the federal power to regulate fisheries. This jurisdictional decision was reached in 1914 in the case of *Attorney General of British Columbia v. Attorney General of Canada*.

Federal jurisdiction creates no right of property, but it confers the exclusive right to impose restrictions or limitations to control public fishing. Thus, the statutory conservation obligations rest with the federal government.

The primary legislation that governs fisheries law in Canada is the *Fisheries Act*. The Act applies to all waters in the fishing zones of Canada, all waters in the territorial seas of Canada, and all internal waters of Canada.

The habitat protection and pollution prevention provisions of the *Fisheries Act*, combined with the Act's broad application to internal waters—including rivers and streams—made the *Fisheries Act* a frequent choice for prosecution of environmental offences. Section 35 provides that "No person shall carry on any work, undertaking or activity that results in serious harm to fish that are part of a commercial, recreational or Aboriginal fishery, or to fish that support such a fishery"; however, these works and undertakings can be conducted if a permit or authorization is issued in advance.

---

exclusive economic zone   the area of ocean adjacent to the coastline belonging to the coastal state

Previously, section 35 addressed "harmful alteration, disruption or destruction of fish habitat." Amendments to the Act in 2012 introduced the requirement for "serious harm" and limited this provision to a commercial, recreational, or Aboriginal fishery. A new section 2(2) was also added to the Act, which specifies that "serious harm to fish is the death of fish or any permanent alteration to, or destruction of, fish habitat." The impact of these legislative changes is not yet evident, but the addition of the requirement for serious harm is certainly a weakening of these habitat protection provisions.

Many activities have the potential to affect fish habitat. Builders and others involved in construction are well advised to review sites for streams or other areas of potential fish habitat. Section 20 of the Act authorizes the minister to require the construction of "fishways" around obstacles.

Decisions to grant permits or authorization pursuant to the *Fisheries Act* can trigger a requirement for an environmental assessment pursuant to the *Canadian Environmental Assessment Act, 2012*. The CEAA 2012 requires the minister to make a decision whether a screening or an environmental assessment will be required for a designated project or activity under the *Regulations Designating Physical Activities*. While the issuance of a permit or approval by the minister of fisheries and oceans does not itself trigger a screening or environmental assessment, many of the activities listed in the regulations include matters that would require permits or approvals issued by the minister of fisheries and oceans.

Section 36(3) of the *Fisheries Act* provides that "no person shall deposit or permit the deposit of a deleterious substance of any type in water frequented by fish or in any place under any conditions where the deleterious substance or any other deleterious substance that results from the deposit of the deleterious substance may enter any such water." The phrase "deleterious substance" is defined broadly and includes most substances that would degrade or alter the quality of water, making it deleterious to fish. In *Fletcher v. Kingston (City)*, the Ontario Court of Appeal held that this section does not require actual harm.[113] In other words, the *potential* of a deleterious substance to cause harm to fish once discharged may be sufficient, even without proof that the substance actually caused harm to the fish. Section 38 of the Act provides broad powers for inspectors. Section 40 provides that offences are punishable by fines of up to $12 million and imprisonment for up to three years, with varying levels of fines depending upon the individual or corporate status of an offender, whether the conviction is summary or by indictment and whether the offence is a first offence. In all cases, there are minimum levels of fines that vary from $5,000 for an individual on a summary conviction for a first offence to $1,000,000 for a corporation on an indictment for a second conviction.

Some provincial legislation governs aspects of the fisheries, predominantly licensing and management. Limited environmental provisions are also included in certain provincial legislation—for example, section 28 of the British Columbia *Fisheries*

Act requires the installation of fish-protective devices around dams or hydraulic projects. The federal government has entered into memoranda of understanding with provinces regarding management of aquaculture; this has resulted in various provincial statutes on this subject—for example, the Nova Scotia *Fisheries and Coastal Resources Act*. However, a recent judicial decision in British Columbia, *Morton v. British Columbia (Agriculture and Lands)*,[114] declared the province's regulatory regime for aquaculture constitutionally invalid and resulted in federal assumption of regulatory jurisdiction for aquaculture in British Columbia through enactment of the *Pacific Aquaculture Regulations* under the *Fisheries Act* in 2010. To date, British Columbia is the only province where aquaculture is federally regulated and the jurisdictional issue has not yet been brought before the Supreme Court of Canada.

Agriculture and Aquaculture

Agriculture and **aquaculture** (the farming of fish and aquatic plants) have long been important industries and ways of life in Canada. Both continue to be significant to our economy and livelihoods. In 2012, Canada's agriculture and agri-food system generated $103.5 billion, 6.7 percent of the country's GDP, and provided work for over 2.1 million Canadians.[115] Although agriculture and aquaculture provide many benefits, they can also damage biodiversity and contaminate air, water, soil, and sediment quality.

Agriculture

A major trend in agriculture in recent years has been the growth of intensive **industrial farming**. In the past 50 years, the size of the average Canadian farm has tripled but, at the same time, the number of farms in Canada has steadily declined. Much larger numbers of livestock, particularly pigs, are being kept close together on much smaller areas of land than were traditionally used to farm livestock. By 2006, average pig herd sizes on Canadian farms had increased by 150 percent over the previous ten years.

Manure

Besides creating increased odour problems, intensive farming of livestock has caused other major effects on the environment. The ever-growing quantities of manure produced by intensive livestock operations must be disposed of. Farmers have usually disposed of manure by spreading it as fertilizer on farm fields. However, if manure is not properly handled, stored, and distributed, it can harm the air, soil, and water.

---

aquaculture   fish farming

industrial farming   large farms operated by corporations, distinct from traditional family-run farms

Too much manure may run off into nearby streams or leach through the soil into groundwater, causing contamination and infections such as E. coli poisoning. The result can be surface water that is unsafe for drinking or swimming, and groundwater that is unsafe for drinking. In May 2000, such a situation led to the deaths of seven people and made many others seriously ill in Walkerton, Ontario.

In the past, it has been difficult to address some of these environmental effects because of the economic importance of agriculture. For example, Ontario's *Farming and Food Production Protection Act* notes that intensive agriculture may cause "discomfort and inconveniences" to others and purports to balance agriculture with concerns about health, safety, and the environment. It protects farmers from legal liability for nuisances, such as odour, dust, flies, and noise, caused by standard farming practices.

The federal and provincial governments share responsibility for the regulation of agriculture. The federal government has developed programs to address the environmental effects of pig farming in particular. However, in 2005 the federal Commissioner of the Environment and Sustainable Development noted that the government was not yet certain about whether these programs were successfully reducing problems or not. A 2006 case study of hog farming prepared for the federal government noted the benefits of compliance with environmental regulations both to hog producers and broader society. These benefits include improved water quality, soil quality, and biodiversity.[116]

Following the tragedy in Walkerton, the Ontario government developed new laws to better protect water from intensive agricultural practices. In 2002 the *Nutrient Management Act* established provincial rules for the appropriate application of manure and other **nutrients** to help ensure both sustainable agriculture and environmental protection. The *Clean Water Act* was passed in 2006 to assist communities in developing plans to protect their watersheds from threats to drinking water, including potential threats from agriculture. In response to threats to the Great Lakes from manure and agricultural runoff, a Great Lakes Nutrient Initiative was developed in connection with the Canada–United States Great Lakes Water Quality Agreement in 2012, and Ontario proposed a *Great Lakes Protection Act* in 2013.

Other Issues

Other environmental issues related to agriculture include the following:

- The use of chemical pesticides is a concern managed by both the federal and the provincial governments. Pesticides are assessed and approved before they are used in Canada, but questions about their effects on environmental and

---

nutrients materials, including fertilizer, manure, compost, sewage biosolids, and pulp and paper biosolids, that can be applied to land to improve the growth of agricultural crops (definition modified from *Nutrient Management Act*)

human health persist. Pesticide regulation is discussed in detail later in this chapter.

- Many concerns have also been raised about the use of genetically modified organisms (GMOs) in agricultural production. The use of GMOs is not heavily regulated, and no requirement exists that products containing GMOs be labelled.
- The routine feeding of antibiotics to pigs, cows, and chickens, and the feeding of growth-promoting hormones to beef cattle pose a threat to human health. Contaminants in pharmaceuticals excreted by farm animals are often carried into water through runoff from manure; this may also have harmful effects on the environment, including wildlife.
- Laws have been used to protect prime agricultural lands from residential and commercial development. British Columbia established a special land use zone known as the "agricultural land reserve" in 1973 to protect agricultural land from increasing development. In 2005, the Ontario government enacted the *Greenbelt Act* to protect agricultural land and rural communities around the rapidly growing Greater Toronto Area from urban development and sprawl. However, the loss of natural habitat to the initial conversion to agriculture was likely the greatest source of harm.

Aquaculture

Aquaculture may contribute to a range of harmful environmental effects, including the following:

- water and sediment pollution by nutrients from fecal material and waste feed;
- depletion of wild fish as a result of diseases such as fish lice that escape into the wild population;
- depletion of wild fish that are caught to feed farmed fish; and
- negative effects on biodiversity when a non-native species escapes from an aquaculture cage in open water.

Like Canadian laws governing agriculture, Canadian laws governing aquaculture attempt to balance the economic value of the fisheries industry with the need to protect the environment. The federal and provincial governments share regulatory responsibility for aquaculture, but gaps in regulation remain. The federal government is involved in aquaculture management planning throughout Canada and has joined with the provinces in a National Aquaculture Strategic Action Plan Initiative, which involves action plans for sustainable aquaculture development.[117] Provincial governments may require that licences be obtained before an applicant engages in aquaculture; for instance, both Ontario and British Columbia have instituted licensing procedures. It is important that all licensing decisions be made with possible environmental effects in mind. Ontario's environmental commissioner has expressed concerns about a lack of oversight of environmental effects from the farming of fish in floating net cages in open water.[118]

In 2004, the Commissioner of the Environment and Sustainable Development reported on gaps in program coordination between the federal and provincial governments concerning salmon aquaculture. The commissioner also highlighted gaps in scientific knowledge about potential environmental effects that need to be addressed.

Figure 9.1   Which Seafood Species Are Sustainably Managed?

Many consumers are uncertain about the sustainability of the seafood options available in restaurants and grocery stores and are unsure about what species they should eat. Some conservation groups have attempted to augment the amount of information available from governments by offering their own rating systems for consumers looking for well-managed and sustainable seafood stocks, whether wild or farmed. These three labels are an example of one system used to indicate sustainable seafood choices.

Source: SeaChoice.org.

Pesticides

The term **pesticide** covers a range of products that are "means for directly or indirectly controlling, preventing, destroying, mitigating, attracting or repelling any pest."[119] These products function by a variety of mechanisms and are commonly categorized according to the pest that they target. They are known, for example, as *insecticides*, *fungicides*, *herbicides*, and *rodenticides*. Some pesticides work by killing the target organism by affecting its nervous system; others work by affecting the organism's ability to reproduce; others work as predators of the target organism; and still others affect living conditions to make the area less attractive for the target pest.

Pesticides are used for a variety of reasons. The most popular uses are for crop and forestry production. They are also used in an attempt to protect property such as wood structures. They may be employed for aesthetic reasons—for example, to maintain a weed- or grub-free lawn. Pesticides may be synthetic or natural in origin, and may take the form of a powder, liquid, or spray, or they may be a living creature such as a nematode.

---

pesticides a range of products that have in common the control of living organisms

In the 1960s, a number of pesticides historically manufactured in Canada and elsewhere were found to be persistent in the environment and to be causing adverse population effects and a decline in wildlife. A group of one dozen such chemicals were termed **persistent organic pollutants (POPs)** because of their long-lasting toxicity. POPs were the subject of debate and discussion in Canada and internationally; they were eventually banned for use in many countries, including Canada.

As a result of these efforts, contamination levels of some pesticides have declined. Benefits include the recovery of the bald eagle and peregrine falcon populations in the Great Lakes lowlands, where these species had become nearly extinct. Because of this experience, pesticide accumulation, persistence, and magnification in the food chain is now examined when registration of a new pesticide is considered.

Of course, new generations of pesticides can bring new challenges. Since the mid-1990s, a new class of synthetic pesticides chemically similar to nicotine, known as neonicotinoids, or neonics, have come to dominate the field crop, horticulture, nursery, and urban forestry markets (see also the case study at the beginning of this chapter). Neonics can be sprayed on leaves, drenched into soil, injected into trees, applied to tree bark, or coated on seeds to protect against insects. Neonics are neurotoxins that kill insects by attacking receptors in nerve synapses. However, they are also highly toxic to bees and persistent in soil and, because they are water soluble, can end up in runoff to local watercourses. Recently, neonics have been subject to a temporary ban in Europe and to increasing research and control in Canada and the United States.

The law regulating the manufacture and use of pesticides comes from a variety of sources: international law, federal law, provincial law, and municipal law. Each source is examined separately below.

International Regulation

Canada is a party to many international conventions, agreements, statements, declarations, and initiatives. The following international instruments have influenced Canada's approach to pesticide regulation:

- The Commission for Environmental Cooperation (CEC) is an international organization created by Canada, Mexico, and the United States in 1994 under the North American Agreement on Environmental Cooperation. The purpose of the CEC is to prevent trade and environmental conflicts and to promote the effective enforcement of environmental law.
- The precautionary principle, which is embodied in the 1990 Bergen Ministerial Declaration on Sustainable Development, states: "Where there are threats of

---

persistent organic pollutants (POPs) about a dozen chemicals identified as having long-lasting toxicity

serious or irreversible damage, lack of full scientific certainty should not be used as a reason for postponing measures to prevent environmental degradation."[120] The precautionary principle is referenced in federal pesticides legislation and in judgments of the Supreme Court of Canada pertaining to municipal pesticides regulation.

- The Stockholm Convention on Persistent Organic Pollutants was signed by nearly 200 countries and came into force in 2004. Since that time, several provinces recalled POPs and buried them in bulk in landfill locations.
- The Organisation for Economic Co-operation and Development (OECD) brings together the governments of free-market democracies to share information and expertise for common purposes such as sustainable economic growth. The OECD created its Pesticide Programme in 1992 to help OECD countries harmonize pesticide review, share work on pesticide evaluation, and reduce the risks of using pesticides.[121]

In addition, Canada's pesticide registration agency, the Pest Management Regulatory Agency, has developed a policy of harmonizing some of its pesticide re-evaluations with the US *Food Quality Protection Act*; it follows the same timelines and uses the same information base that is used in the United States. Pesticide re-evaluations are critical because so many pesticides in use in Canada and elsewhere were used or approved long ago on the basis of erroneous risk assessment criteria; under amendments to the *Pest Control Products Act* in 2006, all pesticides must now be re-evaluated every 15 years to determine whether they meet today's standards.[122]

Federal Regulation

In order for a pest control product to be used in Canada, it must be registered by Health Canada through the Pest Management Regulatory Agency. In response to public pressure and a report of the Standing Committee on Environment and Sustainable Development, a new *Pest Control Products Act* was enacted in 2002. This legislation allows the minister of health to register a pesticide in Canada if the following criteria are satisfied:

- the pesticide is of value and effective, and
- requirements to safeguard health and the environment are met.

There are also authorized departures from full registration under the *Pest Control Products Act*, known as conditional registrations. A conditional registration allows commercial sale and use of a pesticide for a three-year period while further information is gathered and tests and monitoring are conducted by the registrant. This information is reported to the Pest Management Regulatory Agency to confirm assessments of risk. A conditional registration may be renewed, but cannot become a full registration until all data requirements of the Pest Management Regulatory

Agency have been met. However, the federal Commissioner of the Environment and Sustainable Development (in the office of the Auditor General of Canada) and a Senate agriculture committee have recently raised concerns with the conditional registration program due to repeated renewals of some pesticides while data required by the Pest Management Regulatory Agency remain outstanding. Neonics are one class of pesticide that has been conditionally registered for years in Canada.

An important component of the pesticides registration process is re-evaluation of already-registered pesticides. Currently, an enormous backlog exists of older pesticides that were never considered under present-day registration standards. So far, many pesticides that have undergone the re-evaluation process have had stringent restrictions imposed on their use or have been withdrawn from use altogether. Re-evaluation of older pesticides is therefore a high priority. Despite the recent amendments and improvements to the *Pest Control Products Act*, some pesticides not allowed in other OECD countries are registered for use in Canada.

A further mechanism for addressing problematic pesticides is the "special review," designed to examine pesticides with potentially unacceptable health and environmental risks, or value, registered under the *Pest Control Products Act*. The Federal Court of Canada has held that, in certain circumstances, a special review and a re-evaluation of a pesticide can take place at the same time.

The *Pest Control Products Act* provides important opportunities for public participation in pesticides registration, re-evaluation, and other processes. Specifically, members of the public are invited to participate in the following ways:

- review notices of applications for registration,
- comment on proposals,
- review lists of substances undergoing re-evaluation,
- seek special review, and
- review studies and data in special reading rooms.

The registration of a pesticide, if granted, is conditional on compliance with labelling requirements. Labels must clearly outline the proper use of the pesticide, including restrictions on its use and requirements for protective gear, such as masks and gloves. Pursuant to the *Pest Control Products Act* and the *Competition Act*, manufacturers, distributors, and retailers must not misrepresent the health and safety risks associated with the use of pesticides.

Provincial Regulation

In addition to the federal requirement that pesticides be registered before they can be used or sold, the provinces and territories regulate pesticide use. The requirements and provisions vary among the provinces and territories, but many contain the following:

- a classification system for pesticides;
- training and licensing requirements for pesticide vendors;
- provisions regarding the sale of certain classes of pesticides; and
- training and licensing requirements for agriculture, forestry, and commercial pesticide applicators.

Additional requirements may be specified for pesticides, such as use restrictions, storage, transportation, and disposal. In 2008, Ontario passed legislation that authorized a province-wide ban on listed cosmetic pesticides (i.e., pesticides that are used primarily for aesthetic purposes, such as lawn maintenance; the ban does not apply to the use of such products on golf courses, in agriculture, or in forestry). This provincial standard now displaces municipal bylaws restricting cosmetic pesticides.

Ontario also has recently announced intentions to enhance the health of pollinators (e.g., butterflies, bumblebees, and honey bees) because of their importance to food production, by developing requirements under the *Pesticides Act* to reduce the use of neonics in the province.

Municipal Regulation

Beginning with a few Quebec communities in the early 1990s, a growing number of municipalities in Canada have passed bylaws to control and reduce the use of pesticides within their boundaries. Most of these bylaws have been directed at the non-essential or aesthetic use of pesticides (e.g., on lawns and in gardens).

The municipal jurisdiction to pass pesticide control bylaws was unsuccessfully challenged by the pesticide and applicator industries in Hudson, Quebec. All three levels of courts within Quebec and the Supreme Court of Canada upheld the bylaw and the municipality's authority to pass it under the Quebec *Cities and Towns Act*. The City of Toronto passed a similar bylaw, which was also unsuccessfully challenged by an industry organization. The courts have agreed that municipalities have an important role to play in environmental regulation and are trustees of our local environment. The Supreme Court of Canada has also confirmed that Canada's international commitments to the precautionary principle are to be respected in municipal rule-making as well as in federal and provincial decisions.

Biotechnology and Genetic Engineering

Biotechnology is commonly defined as "any technological application that uses biological systems, living organisms, or derivatives thereof, to make or modify products or processes for specific use."[123] Biotechnology is not a new phenomenon.

---

biotechnology any technological application that uses biological systems, living organisms, or derivatives thereof, to make or modify products or processes for specific use

Fermentation in the making of beer and bread, selective breeding of farm animals to increase certain traits, and the biological processes used in sewage treatment plant all fall within the definition. However, modern biotechnology focuses on **genetic engineering**, which is the genetic modification of a microbe, plant, or animal to serve a new or enhanced purpose.

DNA (deoxyribonucleic acid), the genetic code of all livings things, is what makes each species, and each member of each species, unique. For decades, scientists have been able to take genetic material from one species and implant it into another for the purpose of adding very specific characteristics or traits to plants and animals. This genetic engineering can, in effect, create a new life form that can then pass these characteristics on to its offspring.

Applications of Genetic Engineering

Genetic engineering has a variety of applications. Consider the following examples:

- *Transgenic crops.* Perhaps the best-known examples of genetic engineering are **transgenic crops**, which have been given specific characteristics to improve taste, appearance, nutritional value, and rate of growth. Some plants are engineered to increase resistance to specific pesticides and herbicides, so that these pesticides and herbicides can be used to kill weeds around the transgenic crops.
- *Microbes.* **Microbes** are single-celled organisms such as bacteria, algae, and fungi. Genetically modified microbes can be sprayed on temperature-sensitive plants and crops to aid in preventing frost damage, which allows for a longer growing season. Genetically altered microbes are also being developed in the mining industry to assist in leaching minerals from ores and tailings. In addition, they are used in the cleanup of spills and the detoxification of wastes. Microbes also facilitate the efficient degradation of sludges from sewage treatment processes and serve many other purposes.
- *Hormones.* Hormones have been developed to enhance growth or prevent disease and to substantially increase the milk production of cows.

Hundreds, if not thousands, of biotechnology products exist or are under development around the world. Over a quarter of Canada's biotechnology companies focus on the development of agriculture and agri-food products. Although "old" biotechnology has provided many environmental and human health benefits, the risks posed by products created by means of modern biotechnology have raised concerns.

---

genetic engineering   genetic modification of a microbe, plant, or animal to serve a new or enhanced purpose

transgenic crops   genetically engineered crops given specific characteristics to improve taste, appearance, nutritional value, and rate of growth

microbes   single-celled organisms such as bacteria, algae, and fungi

Risks

Concerns about modern biotechnology generally reflect the fact that seldom is enough information available to understand how a new life form will interact in the natural environment. It is difficult to evaluate all the contingencies involved in putting the new technologies into use. As is suggested in a 2001 expert panel report on the future of food biotechnology, the "potential risk is most often stated to be of a 'low probability, high consequence risk.' In other words, although the chance of something going wrong may be very slight, if something does go wrong, the ecological consequences may be tremendous."[124]

Consider the following risks associated with biotechnology:

- *Reduction of biodiversity.* Several genetically modified crops produce their own pesticide (*Bt* varieties; *Bt* refers to *Bacillus thuringiensis*, a bacterium used as a pesticide) or are made resistant to conventional chemical pesticides. Genetic engineering thus contributes to an increased presence of pesticides in agricultural fields, which are used by wildlife, including several species of useful insects (e.g., bees) and birds. The increased presence of pesticides in agricultural fields, enabled by the considerable increase in the use of genetically engineered cultivars by farmers, is suspected of endangering several species.
- *Disruption of the food chain.* When a new invasive or exotic species is introduced from one ecosystem into another, it can have devastating effects by disrupting the food chain. This problem occurred with the introduction of the lamprey, the zebra mussel, and the goby from European waters into the Great Lakes system. With no natural predators in the new environment, the population of any new species can grow unchecked and consume the food supply relied on by native species.
- *Competitive advantage.* Similarly, GMOs could expand beyond their niche to disrupt the natural ecological balance. This could happen if they are resistant to certain diseases and thus establish a competitive advantage over natural species.
- *Uncontrolled reproduction.* GMOs may survive and reproduce after the completion of their intended use. Once they are let loose in the environment, it is nearly impossible to contain them.
- *Cross-pollination.* **Transgenes**—that is, genetically modified genes—may find their way into wild plant populations as a result of pollination with genetically engineered plants. The results are unpredictable.

The concerns listed above raise an important question: Are all biotechnology applications and products appropriate, or should ethical and policy issues be raised and discussed before new technologies or products are developed and introduced?

---

transgenes genetically modified genes

The Legal Framework

The federal government's 1983 national biotechnology strategy determined that biotechnology would be governed within the existing framework of legislation and regulatory agencies. If the product of genetic engineering is food, food safety regulations will apply. If the food product uses a genetically engineered crop, the *Seeds Act* will also apply. The Canadian regulatory framework for biotechnology was originally designed to conform with the product-based approach promoted by the OECD, which rests on a patchwork of regimes that are based on the nature of the products involved. This approach is often contrasted with the process-based approach adopted by the European Union, which regulates the process of genetic engineering.

The rationale behind the approach adopted in Canada is that regulatory agencies—such as Health Canada, the Canadian Food Inspection Agency, and Environment Canada—have acquired expertise in their respective product areas; therefore, they are well suited to expand their safety mandate to assess the risks of bioengineered products. An overview of the legal framework governing biotechnology appears in Table 9.2.

Consider the functions of the following agencies:

- *Canadian Food Inspection Agency.* The Canadian Food Inspection Agency is the lead agency responsible for agricultural products, including seeds, plants, animal fertilizers, and feeds. The agency enforces the food safety and nutritional quality standards that are set by Health Canada. It also carries out inspections and enforces standards for animal health and plant protection. As part of its functions, the agency assesses new products to ensure that they meet the applicable standards under the relevant legislation, such as the *Seeds Act* and the *Feeds Act.* Information that must be provided by the person or business seeking to introduce a new product into Canada includes the nature and type of the new product, test data with respect to environmental and human health risks, mitigation measures, and contingency plans. The assessment is the same regardless of whether the product is bioengineered.

- *Health Canada.* Health Canada is the lead agency responsible for traditional and novel foods under the *Food and Drugs Act,* including genetically modified food sold in Canada. Novel foods are dealt with under a separate section of the *Food and Drug Regulations.* In a manner that resembles the Canadian Food Inspection Agency process, persons wanting to introduce novel foods into the Canadian market must provide information to Health Canada, including data establishing that the food is safe for consumption. Once Health Canada is satisfied that it has sufficient information, it then determines whether the food may be sold.

- *Environment Canada.* Environment Canada is charged with certain responsibilities regarding biotechnology under the *Canadian Environmental Protection*

Act, 1999. The Act and its *New Substances Notification Regulations* ensure that no product escapes assessment by requiring an assessment of any biotechnology product that is not regulated by other legislation.

The three agencies listed above are responsible for assessing all new or novel products within their areas of expertise.

Table 9.2   Overview of Federal Laws and Agencies Regulating Biotechnology*

Nature of Product	Statute and Regulations†	Agency
Food, drugs (human and veterinary), cosmetics, and medical devices, including those derived through biotechnology	*Food and Drugs Act* and regulations	Health Canada
Pest control products	*Pest Control Products Act* and regulations	Pest Management Regulatory Agency, Health Canada
Fertilizer supplements, including novel supplements (microbial and chemical)	*Fertilizers Act* and regulations	Canadian Food Inspection Agency
Feeds and feed additives	*Feeds Act* and regulations	Canadian Food Inspection Agency
Plants and seeds	*Seeds Act* and regulations	Canadian Food Inspection Agency
Plant pests	*Plant Protection Act* and regulations	Canadian Food Inspection Agency
Fish products of biotechnology	*Canadian Environmental Protection Act, 1999‡* and Health Canada regulations	Environment Canada, HealthCanada
All animate products of biotechnology for uses not covered under other federal legislation (the legislative/regulatory "safety net")	*Canadian Environmental Protection Act, 1999* and Health Canada regulations	Environment Canada, HealthCanada
Chemical products	*Canadian Environmental Protection Act, 1999* and Health Canada regulations	Environment Canada, HealthCanada

*   Adapted from Canadian Food Inspection Agency, "Legislative Responsibility for the Regulation of Biotechnology," last modified March 6, 2014, http://www.inspection.gc.ca/plants/plants-with-novel-traits/general-public/overview/eng/1338187581090/1338188593891.

†   Industry Canada, Agriculture and Agri-Food Canada, and Natural Resources Canada (NRCan) do not regulate products; however, they do provide an important advisory function in biotechnology regulatory policy development. In addition, NRCan provides scientific advice related to environmental safety decision-making for products such as plants with novel traits that are trees.

‡   The *Canadian Environmental Protection Act, 1999* is a critical legislative component of this framework. CEPA 1999 defines the criteria of notification and assessment that are the basis for the exemption of other acts from the notification and assessment requirements of CEPA 1999. CEPA 1999 currently provides coverage for aquatic organisms, livestock, or production organisms derived through biotechnology.

Novelty Threshold

Seeds, animal feed, human food, and similar products are subject to an assessment if they are considered novel. The novelty test applies to all products regardless of whether they are genetically modified. A **novel product** (or **novel food**) "exhibits characteristics that were not previously observed or no longer exhibits characteristics that were previously observed."[125] In conformity with international standards, the government of Canada claims to use the principles of familiarity (for seeds) and substantial equivalence (for food) to compare plants and food in risk assessment processes, rather than as tools to decide on novelty. As a result, all GMOs authorized in Canada would have been subjected to strict regulatory oversight, whether deemed familiar or substantially equivalent to existing products or not.

The *Seeds Act* and its regulations apply to plants with "novel traits" that are intended for release into the environment. The *Feeds Act* and its regulations deal with livestock feeds, including novel feeds.

The assessment of all new or novel products in the same way, regardless of whether they result from cross-breeding or from genetic modification, is a controversial matter. Many experts suggest that a separate and more robust review of biotechnology products should be in place. A 2001 Royal Society of Canada report argued that the use of **substantial equivalence** as the threshold to exempt genetically modified agricultural products from a more rigorous scientific assessment was scientifically unjustifiable and inconsistent with the precautionary regulation of technology.[126] The panel recommended a four-stage diagnostic assessment of transgenic crops and foods. Following this report, the government assured Canadians that its use of substantial equivalence was for comparative purposes only, and not a way to authorize genetically modified products without adequate risk assessment.

---

novel product (or novel food) product that exhibits characteristics that were not previously observed or no longer exhibits characteristics that were previously observed

substantial equivalence the concept that a new food product that is found to be substantially equivalent to an existing food or food component can be judged similarly in terms of safety; critics find this principle unscientific, arbitrary, and overly permissive in favour of food producers

SUMMARY OF KEY POINTS

- Environmental regulation of fossil fuels occurs mainly at the provincial level. Direct federal regulation of oil and gas activities within provinces is limited to interprovincial and export pipelines. The Alberta Energy Regulator (AER) is a quasi-independent government agency responsible for providing "efficient, safe, orderly and environmentally responsible development of energy resources in Alberta." Similar oil and gas tribunals exist in British Columbia and Saskatchewan.

    Federal and provincial statutes provide for joint environmental processes in relation to oil, gas, and coal exploration, as well as energy development and production activities. Joint panels of Alberta Energy Resources Conservation Board (now AER) members and representatives of the Canadian Environmental Assessment Agency have reviewed and assessed major proposed oil sands facilities and coal mines.

- Several provinces have developed climate change policies and passed their own climate change statutes (Alberta passed its *Climate Change and Emissions Management Act* in 2003).

- Nuclear power and activities such as production of nuclear energy and research into nuclear energy are mainly under federal jurisdiction because atomic energy was stated in the *Nuclear Energy Act* to be "[f]or the general advantage of Canada," which brought it under section 92(10)(c) of the *Constitution Act, 1867*. The *Nuclear Safety and Control Act* sets out obligations that are overseen by the Canadian Nuclear Safety Commission (CNSC), which reports to the minister of natural resources.

- Mining causes severe environmental effects that may damage and pollute the landscape for years after a mining activity concludes. The federal government is responsible for mines on federal lands (as well as all uranium mines, regardless of location), and provincial governments are responsible for all other types of mines on provincial lands.

- Federal provisions relating to conservation and management of fisheries are implemented through an agreement generally known as the United Nations Fishing Agreement. This agreement creates regional organizations to manage and protect straddling and migratory stocks of marine species both within and beyond the exclusive economic zone. The *Fisheries Act* applies to all waters in the fishing zones of Canada, all waters in the territorial seas of Canada, and all internal waters of Canada.

- Intensive industrial farming has caused major environmental effects. The ever-growing quantities of manure produced by intensive livestock operations must be properly disposed of. If manure is not properly handled, stored, and distributed, it can harm the air, soil, and water. Too much manure may run off into nearby streams or leach through the soil into groundwater, causing contamination and infections such as E. coli poisoning. The federal government has developed programs to address the environmental impacts of pig farming in particular. Ontario passed the *Nutrient Management Act* in 2002 to address the appropriate application of manure and other nutrients. It passed the *Clean Water Act* in 2006 to assist communities in developing plans to protect their watersheds from threats to drinking water.

- Canada's biotechnology sector is governed by the existing framework of legislation and regulatory agencies. If the product of genetic engineering is food, food safety regulations will apply. If the food product uses a genetically engineer crop, the *Seeds Act* will also apply. The rationale behind the approach adopted in Canada is that regulatory agencies—such as Health Canada, the Canadian Food Inspection Agency, and Environment Canada—have acquired expertise in their respective product areas; therefore, they are well suited to expand their safety mandate to assess the risks of bioengineered products.

KEY TERMS

ALARA
aquaculture
biotechnology
CANDU technology
carbon offsets
carbon sinks
chattels
emission intensity
emission intensity reduction
enforcement ladder system
exclusive economic zone
fracking
genetic engineering

hydrocarbons
industrial farming
licensee liability rating system
microbes
novel product (novel food)
nutrients
oil sands
orphaned sites
persistent organic pollutants (POPs)
pesticides
substantial equivalence
transgenes
transgenic crops

DISCUSSION QUESTIONS

1. Describe and outline the role of the Alberta Energy Regulator (AER).
2. Summarize and provide a brief description of the federal statutes that affect fossil fuel exploration and development in Canada.
3. Under the *Nuclear Liability Act*, nuclear power generators and suppliers are exempt from the normal rules of civil liability by capping liability at $75 million in the event of a serious accident and by exempting suppliers from any liability even if at fault. Although the federal government has now introduced proposed legislation to increase the liability limit to $1 billion by operators (still exempting suppliers), this subsidy is not available to generators of

other types of electrical power. Do you think the federal government should make this subsidy available to all other power generators?

4. What recent steps has the Ontario government taken to address the environmental effects of mining and aggregate extraction?

5. Fish stocks do not respect international boundaries. What, if anything, can Canada do to help protect fish stocks in international waters that are being fished by other nations?

6. What negative effects can livestock farming have on the environment? What impact can governments have when attempting to implement policies that may be largely targeted at private landowners?

7. What unique policy challenges might be presented by the rise of aquaculture, or the "fish farm" industry? What role can, or should, NGOs such as conservation groups play in this sector?

8. Consider the debate surrounding with the regulation of pesticides—specifically, neonics. Who are the direct, as well as the indirect, stakeholders in this matter? What larger issues are at stake, beyond the livelihoods of beekeepers and grain farmers?

9. Can the Canadian product-based approach to regulating genetic engineering be said to be less rigorous than the process-based approach common in Europe?

10. To what extent can the concept of novelty be delineated from the principles of substantial equivalence and familiarity?

SUGGESTED READINGS

Readings

Aggregate Resources Act, RSO 1990, c. A.8.

Agriculture and Agri-Food Canada. *Environmental and Economic Impact Assessments of Environmental Regulations for the Agriculture Sector: A Case Study of Hog Farming.* Ottawa: Minister of Public Works and Government Services Canada, 2006.

Environmental Commissioner of Ontario. "Missing in Action: Ontario's Oversight of Cage Aquaculture." *Engaging Solutions, ECO Annual Report, 2010/11.* Toronto: Queen's Printer for Ontario, 2011, http://www.ecoissues.ca/index.php/ Missing_in_Action:_Ontario's_oversight_of_cage_aquaculture.

Fisheries and Oceans Canada. *Aquaculture in Canada 2012: A Report on Aquaculture Sustainability*, http://www.dfo-mpo.gc.ca/aquaculture/lib-bib/asri-irda/pdf/ DFO_2012_SRI_AQUACULTURE_ENG.pdf.

Legislative Assembly of Ontario. *Report on the Review of the Aggregate Resources Act.* Toronto: Standing Committee on General Government, 2013, http://www.ontla .on.ca/committee-proceedings/committee-reports/files_pdf/Legislative %20Assembly%20Aggregate%20English%20Readable.pdf.

Mining Act, RSO 1990, c. M.14.

Nutrient Management Act, 2002, SO 2002, c. 4.

Ontario Ministry of Northern Development and Mines. *A Class Environmental Assessment for Activities of the Ministry of Northern Development and Mines under the Mining Act*. Toronto: Ministry of Northern Development and Mines, 2012, http://www.mndm.gov.on.ca/sites/default/files/mndm_class_environmental _assessment_pdf.pdf.

Royal Society of Canada. *The Royal Society of Canada Expert Panel: Environmental and Health Impacts of Canada's Oil Sands Industry*. Ottawa: Royal Society of Canada, 2010.

Websites

"The Alberta Energy Regulator": http://www.aer.ca/documents/about-us/ AER_Brochure.pdf

(Ontario) Mining Act Modernization: http://www.mndm.gov.on.ca/en/mines-and -minerals/mining-act/mining-act-modernization

Royal Society of Canada: http://rsc.ca

NOTES

1. Natural Resources Canada, "Trade," 2014, http://www.nrcan.gc.ca/energy/ fuel-prices/15816.

2. Ibid.

3. US Energy Information Administration, "Canada," September 30, 2014, http://www.eia.gov/countries/cab.cfm?fips=CA.

4. See Canadian Environmental Assessment Agency, *Foundation for a Sustainable Northern Future: Report of the Joint Review Panel for the Mackenzie Gas Project* (Ottawa: Minister of Environment, 2009), http://www.acee-ceaa.gc.ca/default.asp ?lang=En&n=155701CE-1.

5. Canadian Electricity Association, *Power Generation in Canada: A Guide* (Ottawa: CEA, 2006), http://www.electricity.ca/media/pdfs/EnvironmentallyPreferrablePower/ 2-powergenerationincanada.pdf, and Ontario Ministry of the Environment and Climate Change, "Summary of Smog Advisories: 2003-2015," http://www.airquality ontario.com/press/smog_advisories.php.

6. Canadian Association of Petroleum Producers, *Crude Oil: Forecast, Markets and Transportation* (Calgary: CAPP, 2014), executive summary and chapter 2, http://www.capp.ca/getdoc.aspx?DocID=247759&DT=NTV.

7. Royal Society of Canada, *The Royal Society of Canada Expert Panel: Environmental and Health Impacts of Canada's Oil Sands Industry* (Ottawa: RSC, 2010), http://rsc.ca/sites/default/files/pdf/RSC%20Oil%20Sands%20Panel%20Main %20Report%20Oct%202012.pdf.

8. Allan Ingelson, ed., "Sour Gas Well Licensing," *Canada Energy Law Service* (Toronto: Carswell, 1999) (loose-leaf), at paras. 212-213a.

9. Environment Canada, *National Inventory Report 1990-2012: Greenhouse Gas Sources and Sinks in Canada—Executive Summary* (Gatineau, QC: Environment Canada, 2014), at 8, http://www.ec.gc.ca/ges-ghg/3808457C-9E9E-4AE3 -8463-05EE9515D8FE/NIR2014-Exec%20Sum-Web-Final.pdf.

10. Ibid.

11. Environment Canada, "Impacts of Greenhouse Gas Emissions," last modified July 11, 2013, http://www.ec.gc.ca/indicateurs-indicators/default.asp?lang=en&n =D4C4DBAB-1.

12. John Cotter, "Environmental Health Risks of Alberta Oil Sands Likely Underesti-mated: Study," *Globe and Mail*, February 3, 2014, http://www.theglobeandmail .com/news/national/environmental-health-risks-of-alberta-oilsands-probably -underestimated-study/article16667569/; and Mary Griffiths and Chris Severson-Baker, *Unconventional Gas: The Environmental Challenges of Coalbed Methane Development in Alberta* (Drayton Valley, AB: Pembina Institute, 2003), http://www.pembina.org/reports/CBM_Final_April2006D.pdf.

13. *Reduction of Carbon Dioxide Emissions from Coal-Fired Generation of Electricity Regulations*, SOR/2012-167.

14. Based on exclusive provincial legislative jurisdiction under the *Constitution Act, 1867* in relation to property and civil rights in the province (s. 92(13)), local works and undertakings (s. 92(10)), management and sale of public lands (s. 92(5)), and non-renewable natural resources (s. 92A).

15. See, e.g., Alberta, *Enhancing Assurance: Developing an Integrated Energy Resource Regulator—A Discussion Document* (Edmonton: Government of Alberta, 2011), http://www.energy.alberta.ca/Org/pdfs/REPEnhancingAssuranceIntegrated Regulator.pdf.

16. Under *Constitution Act, 1867*, s. 92(10)(a); and *National Energy Board Act*, RSC 1985, c. N-7.

17. *Canada Oil and Gas Operations Act*, RSC 1985, c. O-7; *Canada Petroleum Resources Act*, RSC 1985, c. 36 (2d Supp.). See Canada, *Northern Oil and Gas Annual Report 2013* (Ottawa: Aboriginal Affairs and Northern Development, 2014), http://www .aadnc-aandc.gc.ca/eng/1398800136775/1398800252896.

18. *Canada–Nova Scotia Offshore Petroleum Resources Accord Implementation Act*, SC 1988, c. 28; Canada–Nova Scotia Offshore Petroleum Board, online: http://www .cnsopb.ns.ca/environment. *Canada–Newfoundland Atlantic Accord Implementa-tion Act*, SC 1987, c. 3; Canada–Newfoundland and Labrador Offshore Petroleum Board, online: http://www.cnlopb.ca.

19. Natural Resources Canada, "Offshore British Columbia: Review of the Federal Moratorium on Oil and Gas Activities Offshore British Columbia," last modified November 16, 2013, http://www.nrcan.gc.ca/energy/offshore-oil-gas/5843.

20. "BC Offshore Drilling No Longer a Priority," *CBC News*, May 8, 2011, http://www.cbc.ca/news/canada/british-columbia/b-c-offshore-drilling-no -longer-a-priority-1.1082525.

21. *Responsible Energy Development Act*, SA 2012, c. R-17.3, s. 2(1)(a).

22. The Oil and Gas Commission, which gets its powers from the *Oil and Gas Activities Act*, SBC 2008, c. 36.

23. The Oil and Gas Conservation Board, which was established by *The Oil and Gas Conservation Act*, RSS 1978, c. O-2.

24. *Responsible Energy Development Act*, supra note 21, s. 2 (mandate) and part 2; and *Oil and Gas Conservation Act*, RSA 2000, c. O-6, parts 5, 6.

25. *Oil Sands Conservation Act*, RSA 2000, c. O-7, ss. 5-15; *Oil and Gas Conservation Act*, supra note 24, s. 1(w) "facility," parts 5, 6.

26. *Pipeline Act*, RSA 2000, c. P-7, parts 2, 4, 6.

27. *Coal Conservation Act*, RSA 2000, c. C-17, ss. 4, 9, part 4.

28. *Oil and Gas Conservation Act*, supra note 24, s. 10(1)(b); Alta. Reg. 151/1971, s. 1.100, parts 3, 7, 8.

29. *Oil Sands Conservation Act*, supra note 25, s. 20; Alta. Reg. 76/1988, ss. 1.1(2)(d), 7(1)(b), 19(c).

30. *Pipeline Act*, supra note 26; Alta. Reg. 91/2005, ss. 60(9), 82(3)-(9).

31. *Coal Conservation Act*, supra note 27, ss. 4(e), 9(1)(c.1); Alta. Reg. 270/1981, ss. 2(d), 4(1)(e), 14(1)(j), 19(e), part 2, ss. 26-30.

32. Alta. Reg. 270/1981, ibid.; Alta. Reg. 151/1971, supra note 28; Alta. Reg. 76/1988, supra note 29; and Alta. Reg. 91/2005, supra note 30.

33. *Canada Energy Law Service*, supra note 8, at para. 93.

34. *Energy Resources Conservation Act*, RSA 2000, c E-10, s. 3.

35. *Responsible Energy Development Act*, supra note 21; and Alberta Energy Regulator, "The Alberta Energy Regulator," 2014, http://www.aer.ca/documents/about-us/ AER_Brochure.pdf.

36. *Responsible Energy Development Act*, supra note 21, part 2, division 3, "Regulatory Appeals."

37. Nickie Vlavianos, "A Single Regulator for Oil and Gas Development in Alberta? A Critical Assessment of the Current Proposal" (2012) 113 *Canadian Institute of Resources Law*.

38. Shaun Fluker, "Amended Rule of Practice for the Alberta Energy Regulator: More Bad News for Landowners and Environmental Groups" *ABlawg* (blog), December 11, 2013, http://ablawg.ca/2013/12/11/amended-rules-of-practice-for-the-alberta -energy-regulator-more-bad-news-for-landowners-and-environmental-groups/.

39. Ibid.

40. Shaun Fluker, "The Right to Public Participation in Resources and Environmental Decision-Making in Alberta" (2015) 52:3 *Alberta Law Review* (forthcoming).

41. Nigel Bankes, "Directly and Adversely Affected: The Actual Practice of the Alberta Energy Regulator," *ABlawg* (blog), June 3, 2014, http://ablawg.ca/2014/06/03/4447/.

42. Canadian Association of Petroleum Producers, "Alberta," 2014, http://www.capp.ca/canadaIndustry/industryAcrossCanada/Pages/Alberta.aspx.

43. Alberta Energy Regulator, *Directive 060: Upstream Petroleum Industry Flaring, Incinerating, and Venting* (Calgary: AER, 2014), http://www.aer.ca/documents/directives/Directive060.pdf.

44. Alberta Energy Regulator, *Directive 019: Compliance Assurance* (Calgary: Energy Resources Conservation Board, 2010), https://www.aer.ca/documents/directives/Directive019.pdf.

45. Alberta Energy Regulator, *Directive 056: Energy Development Applications and Schedules* (Calgary: Energy Resources Conservation Board, 2011), http://www.aer.ca/documents/directives/Directive056_April2014.pdf; Energy Resources Conservation Board, Bulletin 2011-25 (Calgary: ERCB, 2011), http://www.aer.ca/documents/bulletins/Bulletin-2011-25.pdf; and *Canada Energy Law Service*, supra note 8, at para. 111a.

46. *Canada Energy Law Service*, supra note 8, at paras. 541-550.

47. Ibid., at para. 542; Alberta Energy Regulator, *Directive 026: Setback Requirements for Oil Effluent Pipelines* (Calgary: Energy Resources Conservation Board, 2005), https://www.aer.ca/documents/directives/Directive026.pdf.

48. *Canada Energy Law Service*, supra note 8, at paras. 398a, 398b.

49. Alberta Oil and Gas Orphan Abandonment and Reclamation Association, Orphan Well Association 2013/14 Annual Report, at 1, http://www.orphanwell.ca/OWA%202013-14%20Ann%20Rpt%20Final.pdf.

50. Alberta Energy Regulator, *Directive 006: Licensee Liability Rating (LLR) Program and Licence Transfer Process* (Calgary: Energy Resources Conservation Board, 2013), http://www.aer.ca/documents/directives/Directive006_May2013.pdf.

51. Ibid.; and Alberta Energy Regulator, *Directive 011: Licensee Liability Rating (LLR) Program: Updated Industry Parameters and Liability Costs* (Calgary: AER, 2014).

52. Alberta Energy Regulator, supra note 50, at 10.

53. Canadian Energy Institute, *Canadian Economic Impacts of New and Existing Oil Sands Development in Alberta (2014-2038)* (Calgary: Canadian Energy Research Institute, 2014), at ix, http://www.ceri.ca/images/stories/CDN_Economic_Impacts_of_New_and_Existing_Oil_Sands_Development_in_Alberta_-_November_2014_-_Final.pdf.

54. Royal Society of Canada, supra note 7.

55. Alta. Reg. 76/1988, supra note 29.

56. *Water Act*, RSA 2000, c. W-3.

57. *R v. Syncrude Canada Ltd.*, 2010 ABPC 229.

58. *Climate Change and Emissions Management Act*, SA 2003, c. C-16.7.

59. Alta. Reg. 139/2007.

60. Ibid., ss. 2-6. Emission reduction beyond intensity limits creates emission perform-ance credits, which, along with certain offset credits and fund payment credits ($15 per tonne), may be used to meet emission target requirements (ss. 7-9).

61. Nickie Vlavianos, *The Legislative and Regulatory Framework for Oil Sands Develop-ment in Alberta: A Detailed Review and Analysis*, CIRL Occasional Paper #21 (Calgary: Canadian Institute of Resources Law, 2007), 57-75, http://dspace.ucalgary .ca/bitstream/1880/47188/1/OP21Oilsands.pdf.

62. Aboriginal Affairs and Northern Development Canada, "Mining & Minerals in Nunavut and on Crown Lands Under the Administration of AANDC in the North-west Territories," last modified April 1, 2014, https://www.aadnc-aandc.gc.ca/eng/ 1100100036000/1100100036004.

63. See, e.g., the Alberta *Coal Conservation Act*, supra note 27; the British Columbia *Mines Act*, RSBC 1996, c. 293; the Ontario *Mining Act*, RSO 1990, c. M.14; and the Nova Scotia *Mineral Resources Act*, SNS 1990, c. 18.

64. *Reduction of Carbon Dioxide Emissions from Coal Fired Generation of Electricity Regulations* (under the *Canadian Environmental Protection Act, 1999*, SC 1999, c. 33), with certain exemptions, provided carbon capture and storage technologies are used to sequester CO_2.

65. *Coal Conservation Act*, supra note 27.

66. *Hydro and Electric Act*, RSA 2000, c. H-16.

67. *National Energy Board Act*, RSC 1985, c. N-7.

68. *Fisheries Act*, RSC 1985, c. F-14, s. 36(3).

69. *Migratory Birds Convention Act, 1994*, SC 1994, c. 22, s. 5.1. In *R v. Syncrude*, supra note 57, Syncrude was also convicted under this section.

70. *Canadian Environmental Assessment Act*, SC 2012, c. 19, ss. 52, 2(1) "designated project," 13, 14.

71. *Quebec (Attorney General) v. Canada (National Energy Board)*, [1994] 1 SCR 159.

72. Canada, *Reasons for Decision: TransCanada Keystone Pipeline GP Ltd., OH-1-2009, Facilities and Toll Methodology* (Calgary: National Energy Board, 2010), at 74, https://docs.neb-one.gc.ca/ll-eng/llisapi.dll/fetch/2000/90464/90552/418396/ 550305/604643/604441/A1S1E7_-_OH-1-2009_Reasons_for_Decision.pdf? _gc_lang=en&nodeid=604637&vernum=0&redirect=3.

73. See *ForestEthics Advocacy, Living Oceans Society and Raincoast Conservation Foun-dation v. A-G Canada and Northern Gateway Pipelines*, Notice of Application under s. 28 of *Federal Courts Act*, FCA file no. A-56-14, January 17, 2014, https://www.ecojustice.ca/files/noa-northern-gateway-jrp-jr/at_download/file.

74. Enbridge Northern Gateway Project Joint Review Panel, *Considerations: Report of the Joint Review Panel for the Enbridge Northern Gateway Project* (Calgary: National Energy Board, 2013), http://gatewaypanel.review-examen.gc.ca/clf-nsi/dcmnt/ rcmndtnsrprt/rcmndtnsrprt-eng.html.

75. Order in Council PC 2014-809, June 17, 2014, *Canada Gazette* Part 2, vol. 48, no. 20, June 28, 2014.

76. See *Alberta Wilderness Assn. v. Cardinal River Coals Ltd.*, [1999] 3 FCR 425 (FCTD) (DFO approval based on Joint Review Panel report on proposed coal mine quashed).

77. Canada, "Canada's Action on Climate Change," last modified September 19, 2014, http://climatechange.gc.ca. The Copenhagen Accord is merely an "agreement" by the heads of state at the 2009 Copenhagen UN Climate Change Conference of which the UNFCC Conference of the Parties "takes note" (Decision/CP. 15, 18 December 2009). It is not a binding international obligation.

78. Canada, "Canada's Action on Climate Change: Greenhouse Gas Emissions," last modified September 28, 2012, http://www.climatechange.gc.ca/default.asp?lang=en&n=21654B36-1.

79. Ibid.

80. Greenhouse gases are listed as toxic substances that may then be subject to regulations (*Canadian Environmental Protection Act, 1999*, supra note 64, ss. 90(1), 330(3.2), 332(11).

81. *Passenger Automobile and Light Truck Greenhouse Gas Emission Regulations*, SOR/2010-201.

82. *Heavy-Duty Vehicle and Engine Greenhouse Gas Emission Regulations*, SOR/2013-247.

83. *Reduction of Carbon Dioxide Emissions from Coal-Fired Generation of Electricity Regulations*, supra note 13.

84. *Renewable Fuels Regulations*, SOR/2010-189.

85. "Canada's Action on Climate Change," supra note 78.

86. *Environmental Protection and Enhancement Act*, RSA 2000, c. E-12, s. 19.

87. *Greenhouse Gas Reduction Targets Act*, SBC 2007, c. 42.

88. Including O. Reg. 452/09, *Greenhouse Gas Emissions Reporting Regulation*.

89. *Carbon Tax Act*, SBC 2008, c. 40.

90. *An Act Respecting Implementation of the Quebec Energy Strategy*, SQ 2008, c. 46.

91. Natural Resources Canada, "About Uranium," last modified October 6, 2014, http://www.nrcan.gc.ca/energy/uranium-nuclear/7695.

92. Ibid. Former uranium mines exist in the Northwest Territories, Saskatchewan, and Ontario. See World Nuclear Association, "Uranium in Canada," December 2014, http://www.world-nuclear.org/info/Country-Profiles/Countries-A-F/Canada--Uranium/.

93. Canadian Nuclear Association, *The Canadian Nuclear Factbook 2013* (Ottawa: CNA, 2013), https://cna.ca/wp-content/uploads/2014/07/CNA-Factbook-2013.pdf.

94. Ontario Power Generation, "Nuclear Power," accessed December 6, 2014, http://www.opg.com/generating-power/nuclear/Pages/nuclear.aspx.

95. The Gentilly-2 Nuclear Generating Station, Quebec's remaining nuclear reactor, was shut down in 2012. See Government of Canada, "Gentilly-2 Nuclear Generating Station," last modified June 27, 2014, http://nuclearsafety.gc.ca/eng/reactors/power-plants/nuclear-facilities/gentilly-2-nuclear-generating-station/index.cfm;

and "Quebec to Shut Down Its Only Nuclear Reactor," *CBC News*, September 11, 2012, http://www.cbc.ca/news/canada/montreal/quebec-to-shut-down-its-only -nuclear-reactor-1.1177555.

96. John Spears, "Cost of Power from Darlington Will Jump After Overhaul," *Toronto Star*, February 10, 2014, http://www.thestar.com/business/2014/02/10/cost_of _power_from_darlington_will_jump_after_overhaul.html.

97. Ecojustice, "Statement on Federal Court Ruling on Life-Extension of Darlington Reactors," news release, November 27, 2014, http://www.ecojustice.ca/ statement-on-federal-court-ruling-on-life-extension-of-darlington-reactors.

98. United Nations, "Global Issues: Atomic Energy," accessed December 9, 2014, http://www.un.org/en/globalissues/atomicenergy.

99. Mining Association of Canada, *Facts and Figures of the Canadian Mining Industry 2013* (Ottawa: MAC, 2013,) at 11.

100. Ibid., at 10.

101. Ibid., at 10.

102. *Mining Act*, supra note 63, s. 35.1(2).

103. Ibid., s. 35.1(8).

104. Class Environmental Assessment for Activities of the Ministry of Northern Development and Mines, approved under the *Canadian Environmental Assessment Act* on December 12, 2012 and amended on July 3, 2014.

105. *Mining Act*, supra note 63, part VII.

106. Standing Committee on General Government, *Report on the Review of the Aggregate Resources Act* (Toronto: Legislative Assembly of Ontario, 2013), http://www.ontla .on.ca/committee-proceedings/committee-reports/files_pdf/Legislative %20Assembly%20Aggregate%20English%20Readable.pdf.

107. Fisheries and Oceans Canada, "A Practical Guide to the Fisheries Act and to the Coastal Fisheries Protection Act," part II, http://www.dfo-mpo.gc.ca/Library/ 282791.pdf.

108. Northwest Atlantic Fisheries Organization, "Northwest Atlantic Fisheries Organization," accessed December 7, 2014, http://www.nafo.int/about/frames/about.html.

109. Convention on Future Multilateral Cooperation in the Northwest Atlantic Fisheries, http://www.nafo.int/about/frames/convention.html.

110. United Nations Convention on the Law of the Sea, http://www.un.org/depts/los/ convention_agreements/convention_overview_convention.htm.

111. Agreement for the Implementation of the Provisions of the United Nations Convention on the Law of the Sea of 10 December 1982 relating to the Conservation and Management of Straddling Fish Stocks and Highly Migratory Fish Stocks, http://www.un.org/depts/los/convention_agreements/convention_overview_fish _stocks.htm.

112. Agreement to Promote Compliance with International Conservation and Management Measures by Fishing Vessels on the High Seas, http://www.fao.org/docrep/MEETING/003/X3130m/X3130E00.HTM.

113. *Fletcher v. Kingston (City)*, (2004) 7 CELR (3d) 198 (Ont. CA).

114. *Morton v. British Columbia (Agriculture and Lands)*, 2009 BCSC 136.

115. Agriculture and Agri-Food Canada, "An Overview of the Canadian Agriculture and Agri-Food System 2014," last modified April 15, 2014, http://www.agr.gc.ca/eng/about-us/publications/economic-publications/alphabetical-listing/an-overview-of-the-canadian-agriculture-and-agri-food-system-2014/?id=1396889920372.

116. Agriculture and Agri-Food Canada, *Environmental and Economic Impact Assessments of Environmental Regulations for the Agriculture Sector: A Case Study of Hog Farming* (Guelph, ON: Agriculture and Agri-Food Canada, 2007), http://www.georgemorris.org/publications/file.aspx?id=c26ddcdb-c3ff-4f56-bb47-ed7a06bd0ba1.

117. Fisheries and Oceans Canada, *Aquaculture in Canada 2012: A Report on Aquaculture Sustainability* (Ottawa: Fisheries and Oceans Canada, 2013), http://www.dfo-mpo.gc.ca/aquaculture/lib-bib/asri-irda/pdf/DFO_2012_SRI_AQUACULTURE_ENG.pdf.

118. Environmental Commissioner of Ontario, "Missing in Action: Ontario's Oversight of Cage Aquaculture," *Engaging Solutions, ECO Annual Report, 2010/11* (Toronto: Queen's Printer for Ontario, 2011), http://www.ecoissues.ca/index.php/Missing_in_Action:_Ontario's_oversight_of_cage_aquaculture.

119. Health Canada, "The Regulation of Pesticides in Canada," 2009, http://www.hc-sc.gc.ca/cps-spc/pubs/pest/_fact-fiche/reg-pesticide/index-eng.php.

120. Bergen Ministerial Declaration on Sustainable Development in the ECE Region, 1990, UN Doc. A/CONF.151/PC/10, at para. 7.

121. Organisation for Economic Co-operation and Development, *OECD Survey on the Collection and Use of Agricultural Pesticide Sales Data: Survey Results* (Paris: OECD, 1999).

122. Health Canada, "Statutory Review of the Pest Control Products Act," May 16, 2013, http://www.hc-sc.gc.ca/cps-spc/pest/part/consultations/_pcpa_review-examen_lpa/index-eng.php.

123. Food and Agriculture Organization of the United Nations, "FAO Statement on Biotechnology," March 2000, http://www.fao.org/biotech/fao-statement-on-biotechnology/en/.

124. Royal Society of Canada, *Elements of Precaution: Recommendations for the Regulation of Food Biotechnology in Canada* (Ottawa: Royal Society of Canada, 2001), https://rsc-src.ca/sites/default/files/pdf/GMreportEN.pdf.

125. *Food and Drug Regulations*, CRC, c. 870.

126. Royal Society of Canada, supra note 124.

PART IV

Integrated Approaches to Environmental Law

Environmental Assessment

Introduction

The story of **environmental assessment law** in Canada is similar to the larger story of progressive legislation here and in many other jurisdictions. Environmental assessment law originated in response to the evident need for legislated intervention in decision-making on important undertakings to ensure that they are a little more farsighted and broadly informed. Environmental assessment law's history has been characterized not only by major advances in understanding and application but also by continuing inadequacies and persistent resistance from those required to think and act differently. Its present is a struggle between ambition and constraint. And

---

environmental assessment law law requiring careful attention to environmental considerations in the planning and approval of new undertakings

CASE STUDY

Wreck Cove Hydroelectric Power Project: An Example of the Beginnings of Environmental Assessment

In the mid-1970s, one of the first formal environmental assessment reviews in Canada examined the potential environmental effects of a hydropower project at Wreck Cove in Nova Scotia's Cape Breton highlands. The project included multiple dams, river diversions, and reservoirs adjacent to Cape Breton Highlands National Park. However, the assessment review was not initiated until after the project had been approved, and by the time the review findings were available, much of the project work had been completed.*

The Wreck Cove environmental assessment review, undertaken under a non-legislated federal Cabinet directive, set a low benchmark for subsequent assessments. Today, most assessment practices embody great advances over the Wreck Cove effort. Every major Canadian jurisdiction now has environmental assessment law. Moreover, some applications have been admirable examples of open, participative processes that are initiated early in planning, that effectively integrate consideration of biophysical and socio-economic factors, and that aim to ensure that proposed undertakings represent the best option for serving the public interest.

Unfortunately, major deficiencies remain. Environmental assessment requirements and their implementation remain highly uneven across Canada. No Canadian environmental assessment law incorporates all that we have learned about what should be done, and some important players in industry and government are convinced that existing processes are too demanding.

As a result, environmental assessment law remains a field of conflict. The considerable accomplishments of the past decades are often obscured by battles over the handling of particular controversial projects and opposing initiatives to extend or prune existing laws.

Question

A question to consider as you read through this chapter: What have been the major improvements to environmental assessment law since the Wreck Cove case?

_____

*   D. Paul Emond, *Environmental Assessment Law* (Toronto: Emond Montgomery, 1978), 251-59.

its future in a world of expanding environmental challenges and limited capacities to address them promises to be, depending on your perspective, deeply unsettled or marvelously exciting.

The regulatory regimes discussed in Chapters 7, 8, and 9 continue to play an important role in limiting environmental damage and forcing corrective action. They protect the air, water, and soil against specific anticipated threats from particular activities and certain sectors. This protection is crucial and will remain so. However, regulatory regimes are not now, and never will be, sufficient guardians of the environment. That is because standard regulatory approaches work best on problems that are basically simple, and many of our most significant environmental challenges are profoundly complex. Regulatory regimes could be adequate guardians of the environment only if the world were simpler than it actually is.

To be convenient for regulatory purposes, all environmental threats would have to be separate, measurable, and targeted at individual receptors. The economy would have to be divided tidily into well-defined sectors, all engaging in predictable activities with specific and well-known environmental effects. The effects would have to be either clearly bad or cheerfully benign, and the detrimental effects would have to be correctable with available technology and finances.

For better or worse, the real world is not like this. It is complicated, variable, full of tangled interconnections, ever changing, and often puzzling. Moreover, circumstances—such as ecosystem stresses, community needs, cultural preferences, and economic conditions—often vary dramatically from one place to the next.

Environmental effects also tend to mix with one another, as in the case of chemical soups of air pollutants, and to mix with other factors, as in the case of poor communities economically dependent on a polluting employer. These combinations make decisions challenging. And when environmental damage is done, it is often very difficult and very costly to repair, if repair is possible at all.

These insights are not new. Jurisdictions in Canada and most other industrialized countries began to recognize the limitations of conventional regulatory regimes nearly half a century ago, and have since been gradually adjusting and supplementing them, using a variety of tools. Very generally, the evolution of environmental law beyond environmental regulation has centred on the following themes:

- recognition of the complexity of environmental threats,
- awareness of and respect for the diversity of circumstances,
- facilitation of a larger public voice in decision-making, and
- emphasis on anticipation and prevention of environmental damage rather than on corrective action when a crisis emerges.

Initial steps taken to address these matters included the introduction of certificates of approval for new emission or discharge sources, site-specific requirements for particular polluters, and anticipatory protection of vulnerable areas. Also important have been broader planning efforts, the provision of public access to environmental information, the granting of environmental rights, and the use of public hearings. Among the most significant advances was the introduction and gradual expansion of environmental assessment law.

The Origins and Evolution of Environmental Assessment Law

Environmental assessment law began as an attempt to avoid, or at least minimize, environmental damage by changing the nature of project planning, design, and implementation. The central idea was that the proponents of environmentally significant undertakings should take environmental considerations into account in the same way that they already took financial and technical matters into account.

Clearly this was not happening. Private sector proponents, such as corporations developing new industrial facilities, tended to see environmental protection as a cost to be avoided if possible. Similarly, public sector proponents, such as transportation departments planning new highways or municipal officials seeking new landfill sites, tended to focus on their immediate mandate. Sometimes a particularly enlightened proponent would worry about liability for environmental damage, possible costs of cleanup, or loss of public trust. However, such enlightenment was not common or reliable enough to ensure careful attention to environmental factors in project decision-making. A formalized system for considering these factors and imposing obligations was needed.

The US National Environmental Policy Act of 1969

The first step was taken in the United States. The *National Environmental Policy Act of 1969* (NEPA) included a short section requiring proponents of environmentally significant new undertakings to carry out environmental assessments before finalizing decisions to proceed. These assessments were to centre on anticipatory prediction of environmental impacts and identification of various means of mitigating or avoiding significant adverse effects.

Unlike traditional regulatory approaches, the assessments were to cover a wide range of environmental considerations, including social as well as biophysical effects, in an integrated way. NEPA required proponents to compare the predicted effects of their favoured project option with those of alternatives (e.g., for a proposed garbage landfill, alternatives could include different landfill sites, waste incineration, and waste reduction at source or through reuse, diversion, recycling, and composting). As well, NEPA required reporting of the assessment findings in a publicly available document, and failure to do assessments properly could be challenged in court.

NEPA's environmental assessment requirements proved to be powerful and controversial. In part because the legal provisions were brief and general, some years and many court cases were needed to clarify the requirements. A potentially major role for the courts made authorities in other jurisdictions nervous. The Canadian federal government, for example, was under considerable public pressure to establish its own environmental assessment process but did not want to have its decision-making authority constrained by law or subject to litigation.

BOX 10.1 » **The Purposes of the United States' National Environmental Policy Act of 1969**

The purposes of this Act are: to declare a national policy which will encourage productive and enjoyable harmony between man and his environment; to promote efforts which will prevent or eliminate damage to the environment and biosphere and stimulate the health and welfare of man; to enrich the understanding of the ecological systems and natural resources important to the Nation; and to establish a Council on Environmental Quality.

Source: *National Environmental Policy Act of 1969*, 42 USC 4321, § 2.

The Establishment of Environmental Assessment Law in Canada

The Canadian government tried to have its cake and eat it too by deciding in 1972 to introduce a policy-based assessment process. All federal departments and agencies would be required to undertake environmental assessments of new projects that might have significant effects, but implementation was left largely to the discretion of the relevant authorities. No penalties existed for non-compliance and, not surprisingly, mostly poor compliance was the result.

Over the years, the federal Environmental Assessment and Review Process (EARP) was gradually clarified and strengthened. But few federal departments took steps to ensure effective implementation. Even the major early cases that proceeded to public hearings before specially appointed review panels revealed the weakness of the federal commitment. In the first EARP review, which examined the proposed Point Lepreau nuclear generating station in New Brunswick, assessment requirements were watered down to avoid conflict with the project's financing and construction schedules. The second EARP review was the ill-fated review of the Wreck Cove hydroelectric power project, which is discussed in the chapter-opening case study.

An internal government audit in 1982, ten years after the government's initial policy commitment, found continuing disregard for environmental assessment obligations in many departments and agencies. In response, the government issued what it thought was merely a stronger policy statement. The 1984 Environmental Assessment and Review Process Guidelines Order under the *Government Organization Act* was an awkward creation designed to serve conflicting objectives. The government wanted to give the appearance of strengthening a notoriously weak assessment process. However, at the same time, the government wished to retain flexibility and avoid imposing difficult obligations on itself. The resulting guidelines order was self-contradictory—guidelines are discretionary, while orders are mandatory.

In 1989 an unexpected court decision changed all of that. It established that the guidelines order had the force of law. In a case involving the controversial Rafferty-Alameda dams in southern Saskatchewan, lawyers for the Canadian Wildlife Federation argued that federal authorities were legally obligated to apply the guidelines order. To the surprise of many, Justice Cullen of the Federal Court of Canada agreed. His April 1989 ruling that the guidelines order was legally binding essentially meant that the noun prevailed over the adjective: an order was an order.[1] The ruling was upheld by the Federal Court of Appeal[2] and confirmed by the Supreme Court of Canada in 1992 in a case involving the proposed Oldman River dam in Alberta.[3]

After the Rafferty-Alameda decision, federal authorities immediately began to design an intentionally legislated environmental assessment process. A bill to establish a *Canadian Environmental Assessment Act* was introduced in 1990, strengthened through amendments in 1992, and amended further by a new government in 1994. It was finally proclaimed in force along with a set of key regulations in 1995, a quarter century after the pioneering US environmental assessment law was enacted.[4]

The move to legislate environmental assessment was quicker in other Canadian jurisdictions. Ontario's *Environmental Assessment Act*, passed in 1975, was based on the US NEPA model but was in some ways stronger. Most significantly, its process led to an enforceable decision.

Under NEPA, proponents doing assessments were required to identify purposes and alternatives, predict environmental effects (social, economic, cultural, and biophysical), consider mitigation options, and justify the preferred alternative in an assessment document subject to public review. Although addressing these matters was mandatory, the assessment and its review were intended to inform government decisions rather than be an approval process. The findings were merely to be taken into account in final decisions and implementation. Under Ontario's 1975 *Environmental Assessment Act*, in contrast, assessments led to a rejection or approval of the proposed undertaking, and approvals were typically accompanied by formal terms and conditions, with possible fines for non-compliance.

Gradually over the years that followed, environmental assessment laws of general application were put in place in every province and territory in Canada. Particular assessment processes were also incorporated in a variety of other venues:

BOX 10.2 » Standard Contents of an Environmental Assessment Under the Ontario Environmental Assessment Act

6.1(2) Subject to subsection (3), the environmental assessment must consist of,

(a) a description of the purpose of the undertaking;

(b) a description of and a statement of the rationale for,

(i) the undertaking,

(ii) the alternative methods of carrying out the undertaking, and

(iii) the alternatives to the undertaking;

(c) a description of,

(i) the environment that will be affected or that might reasonably be expected to be affected, directly or indirectly,

(ii) the effects that will be caused or that might reasonably be expected to be caused to the environment, and

(iii) the actions necessary or that may reasonably be expected to be necessary to prevent, change, mitigate or remedy the effects upon or the effects that might reasonably be expected upon the environment, by the undertaking, the alternative methods of carrying out the undertaking and the alternatives to the undertaking;

(d) an evaluation of the advantages and disadvantages to the environment of the undertaking, the alternative methods of carrying out the undertaking and the alternatives to the undertaking; and

(e) a description of any consultation about the undertaking by the proponent and the results of the consultation.

Source: *Environmental Assessment Act*, RSO 1990, c. E.18, s. 6.1(2).

- Provisions in many land claim agreements with First Nations and Inuit groups have introduced environmental assessment processes. The pioneering example was the James Bay and Northern Quebec Agreement of 1975, covering traditional Cree and Inuit lands in Quebec. Provisions in land claim agreements now provide the foundations for assessment laws in the Yukon, the Northwest Territories, and Nunavut.[5]
- The official planning processes of many municipalities include environmental assessment as a prerequisite for certain approvals.
- Many sectoral regulatory regimes—for example, those covering aggregates extraction in Ontario—incorporate environmental assessment processes.
- Laws establishing or guiding specific agencies—for example, the law governing the activities of Export Development Canada[6]—also often include an environmental assessment process tailored to the work of the agency.

No two environmental assessment laws in Canada are identical, and the variations among their requirements and processes are great. Indeed, the variety and inconsistency of assessment requirements in Canada have been continuing sources of aggravation for project proponents and others responsible for making the processes work. Nevertheless, environmental assessment regimes in Canada (and elsewhere) reflect the broad acceptance and adoption of many of the well-recognized, basic components of effective environmental assessment law. A few Canadian regimes also include more advanced components recommended in the environmental assessment literature.

Basic and Advanced Components of Environmental Assessment Laws

Environmental assessment is essentially a form of logical step-by-step deliberation and decision-making that takes environmental factors into account. It is meant to ensure that environmentally informed logic is incorporated throughout the process of conceiving, selecting, designing, reviewing, and implementing any proposed undertaking that could have important effects. However, laws that include environmental assessment requirements typically focus on assessment efforts during the approval stage of an undertaking, although they usually require evidence that the deliberations leading to a formal proposal have given serious attention to environmental considerations and that the results are integrated into overall planning and approvals.

---

environmental assessment   the identification and evaluation of actual or potential effects (positive and adverse) of an undertaking on the environment; "undertakings" may include policies, plans, and programs as well as projects, and "environment" may include social, economic, and cultural as well as biophysical effects, and the interactions among these effects; environmental assessments may also involve a critical review of purposes, comparative evaluation of alternatives, and a follow-up examination of effects

Most assessment processes require the proponent of the undertaking to do the bulk of the assessment work. This is often a practical necessity because the proponent is best placed to integrate the environmental findings into the usual consideration of technical, financial, and perhaps political factors in the overall planning. Because proponents had rarely done this voluntarily, environmental assessment law imposed clear obligations for serious environmental studies and application of the findings.

A fundamental difficulty with the proponent-centred approach is that proponents tend to focus on their own interests and to be biased in favour of their established ways of doing things. These understandable factors tend to undermine the quality of their assessment work. It is therefore necessary for environmental assessment laws to ensure that the proponent's work is checked by government agencies with environmental mandates and by public interest organizations and individuals who have some motivation for careful and critical review.

Recognizing these basic considerations, environmental assessment laws are generally built around a framework for addressing four key questions:

- What undertakings will be subject to assessment obligations?
- What is the nature and scope of factors that must be addressed?
- How will effective government and public review of the assessment findings be ensured?
- How will the results influence decision-making on final design, approval, and implementation?

In addition, all environmental assessment laws define administrative mandates, set out process and procedures, and provide for details to be specified in regulations.

Virtually all environmental assessment processes include different streams. Most common are two basic streams: one to provide for relatively quick assessments with modest assessment and review requirements for undertakings that are unlikely to pose serious environmental threats if implemented properly, and a second that imposes more demanding assessment obligations and review procedures for undertakings with potentially significant adverse effects.

All serious environmental assessment laws require the work to be completed before irrevocable decisions are made. They are centred on the submission and review of a formal assessment report that precedes a decision on whether to proceed with the undertaking. Nevertheless, most environmental assessment laws at least suggest that environmental assessment should be seen as a series of deliberations and decisions through the full life of an undertaking from initial conception to final decommissioning.

Beyond these common elements, actual environmental assessment requirements, including review and approval provisions, vary considerably. Most laws apply only to physical projects, but some also provide for assessment of plans, programs, and policies. Some laws require integrated assessment of social, economic, cultural, and biophysical effects and their interactions. Others limit attention wholly or largely to the "natural environment," although they may include discretionary openings for applying the more comprehensive approach in certain circumstances.

In some cases, proponents are encouraged to identify the best option by defining the needs and purposes to be served, and comparing reasonable alternative approaches to meeting these needs and purposes. In other cases, proponents are required only to assess their preferred option. Environmental assessment laws also differ on whether to

- require consideration of **cumulative effects**;
- draw attention to uncertainties;
- foster enhancement of positive effects as well as mitigation of adverse ones;
- facilitate public consultation throughout the process;
- provide for formal public hearings with funding for intervenors; and/or
- require implementation, monitoring, and decommissioning plans.

Existing environmental assessment processes in Canada represent a modest improvement over the old regulatory approaches. They are a little more anticipatory, a little more comprehensive, and a little more open to public scrutiny. But the key question they seek to answer is still whether the proposed undertaking is "acceptable."

Because no set standard defines an "acceptable" undertaking, the decision typically turns on whether "significant" adverse effects are anticipated and, if so, whether these effects can be "justified in the circumstances." As might be expected, a good deal of scientific and judicial deliberation has gone into clarifying what should and should not qualify as significant. Determining when significant adverse effects may be justified has also involved profound difficulties.

The problem of defining *acceptability* is partially resolved in more advanced and ambitious assessment processes, which require a comparative evaluation of the reasonable alternative ways of meeting a public interest need or purpose. This approach requires a broad scope and integrated consideration of potential effects—including social, economic, cultural, and biophysical effects—but it also sets a higher standard than merely requiring an acceptable undertaking. The comparative approach seeks to identify the option that promises the greatest overall contribution to long-term well-being, which includes the avoidance of adverse environmental effects.

The key differences between environmental assessment law provisions that aim for acceptability and those that seek the best alternative are set out in Table 10.1.

---

cumulative effects changes to the environment that are caused by an action in combination with other past, present, and future human actions, as well as changing natural conditions

Table 10.1   The Components of Basic and Advanced Assessment Laws

Component	Basic Assessment Laws	Additions in Advanced Assessment Laws
Application rules	Specify the sorts of undertakings that are subject to assessment requirements, so that planners and proponents know from the outset that they will have to address environmental factors in the planning and design of the proposed undertaking	Ensure assessment of all undertakings—including strategic-level policies, programs, plans, and projects—that might have significant environmental effects, individually or cumulatively
Levels of assessment	Provide more and less demanding assessment streams (for more and less significant kinds of undertakings), with suitable guidance and procedures for determining the level of assessment and review required in particular cases	Provide authoritative links so that broader strategic assessments can guide and be guided by individual project assessments
Conception of environmental considerations	Define clearly the range of environmental considerations to be addressed, preferably including socio-economic, cultural, and biophysical factors, but emphasizing adverse effects	Adopt a broad conception of the environment as linked complex systems with intertwined social, economic, cultural, and biophysical/ecological factors at multiple scales; include positive as well as adverse effects; emphasize attention to cumulative effects
Breadth of analysis: undertaking	Require identification and evaluation of the potentially significant effects of each proposed undertaking in light of existing environmental conditions, pressures, and trends	Ensure critical review of public interest purpose of each undertaking; require identification and comparative evaluation of the reasonable alternatives—including different general approaches and different designs—with justification for selection of the preferred alternative as the proposed undertaking
Breadth of analysis: effects	Provide for setting reasonable case-specific boundaries and focusing assessment work on the most important issues raised by a proposed undertaking	Require integrated consideration of related undertakings as well as interactive and cumulative effects of existing, proposed, and reasonably anticipated future activities
Knowledge	Emphasize expert opinion and scientific and technical findings based on application of accepted methods of research and analysis; recognize the importance of public opinion on matters such as identification of valued environmental components	Incorporate different kinds of knowledge and analysis, including informal, traditional, and Aboriginal knowledge as well as conventional science
Evaluation of predicted effects	Require evaluation of the effects of proposed undertakings including mitigation measures, with particular attention to residual significant adverse environmental effects	Require identification and evaluation of the significance of predictable effects, uncertainties (about effect predictions, mitigation, and enhancement effectiveness) and associated risks; apply explicit sustainability-based criteria for evaluation, recognizing differences in cases and contexts

Component	Basic Assessment Laws	Additions in Advanced Assessment Laws
Public participation	Provide for public and technical review of the proposed undertaking and the assessment work to evaluate both the proposed undertaking and the adequacy of efforts to incorporate attention to environmental considerations in developing the proposal, including review through public hearings in especially significant cases	Include provisions, including funding support, to ensure effective public as well as technical notification and consultation at significant points throughout the proposal development and assessment process and in the post-approval monitoring
Compliance and follow-up	Provide means of ensuring that assessment and review findings are incorporated in approvals and permits, and in provisions for monitoring and compliance with approval conditions	Establish enforceable decision-making powers requiring compliance with conditions, monitoring of actual effects, and timely response to emerging problems and opportunities
Role in overall approval decision-making	Require documented identification and evaluation of potential negative effects and the best means of avoiding or mitigating them, with particular attention to any residual significant adverse environmental effects; provide for the incorporation of assessment findings in overall approval decision-making (typically outside the assessment process)	Treat environmental assessment as the main venue for comprehensive evaluation and public review of purposes of and rationale for proposed undertakings, based on a comparative evaluation of options, considering positive as well as adverse effects
Core decision criteria	Require that the proposed undertaking be acceptable, including though mitigation of significant adverse effects; reject the proposed undertaking if significant adverse effects cannot be justified in the circumstances	Require that the proposed undertaking represent the most beneficial option, with the greatest contribution to lasting gains while avoiding significant adverse effects; favour precaution and adaptability; aim to avoid trade-offs and reject all trade-offs that displace significant adverse effects to future generations
Broader links	Encourage monitoring to check effect predictions, with open reporting to encourage learning from experience	Provide for integration of assessment work, including monitoring, into a broader regime for setting, pursuing, and re-evaluating public objectives and guiding future undertakings
Additional process efficiency measures	Establish clear process rules including explicit criteria for evaluations and decisions; encourage early application in proponent deliberations; provide well-defined steps for the more and less demanding assessment streams; encourage cooperation among overlapping assessment jurisdictions	Use strategic-level assessments to guide and streamline individual project assessments; clarify relations with specific permitting and licensing processes; harmonize the central components of Canadian environmental assessment regimes to facilitate multi-jurisdictional assessments

The existing environmental assessment laws and associated processes in Canada do not fall neatly into the two general categories that appear in Table 10.1. Also, the most recent laws are not necessarily the most advanced. Globally and in Canada, environmental assessment has generally evolved toward adoption of more advanced and ambitious components, but there have also been reversals where existing provisions have been eliminated or narrowed under the guise of process efficiency improvements. Many existing environmental assessment laws feature a combination of basic and advanced components.

Both the Canadian federal process under the *Canadian Environmental Assessment Act* and the Ontario process under the *Environmental Assessment Act* provide illustrative examples of advances and retreats in environmental assessment law, as the next two sections show.*

Canadian Environmental Assessment Act and Process

The first *Canadian Environmental Assessment Act* (CEAA) was passed in 1992, came into effect in 1995, was adjusted modestly in 2003, and was replaced by a substantially different law in 2012. The original law, usually referred to as CEAA 1995, was a mix of basic and advanced components. It featured quite broad application (although only to projects), mandatory attention to cumulative effects, some funding for public participation in major assessment reviews, and encouragement of follow-up monitoring. Unfortunately, some of the law's provisions led in many cases to assessment requirements being imposed and specified too late to be incorporated effectively in project planning. Also, while the law allowed authorities to require attention to the need for alternatives to the project, and to the full suite of broadly environmental considerations, use of these powers was discretionary and typically initiated too late to influence early project planning. As a result, application of some of the most advanced aspects of CEAA 1995 was uncertain or less effective than it could have been.

Under the 1995 law, federal environmental assessment was frequently criticized by project proponents for unnecessarily delaying desirable development. The fairness of these criticisms was a matter of debate.[7] The uncertainties mentioned above probably did contribute to avoidable confusions and delays. Most inefficiency complaints, however, focused on the apparent duplication of effort where individual projects were subject to both federal and provincial assessment requirements, and the complainants favoured reliance on provincial processes alone. While inefficiencies were involved in some of these cases, despite federal–provincial cooperation agreements, the underlying problem was not duplication but overlap between different but interconnected areas of federal and provincial responsibility, and these areas could not

---

* Flow charts depicting examples of various environmental assessment processes are included in the instructor PowerPoint slides accompanying this text.

be abandoned without creating serious assessment gaps. Moreover, provincial assessment processes were and are wildly divergent and sometimes clearly weaker than the federal process. Consequently, a shift to provincial-only assessments could be as much about weakening assessment obligations as about reducing inefficiencies.

The tensions between efficiency and effectiveness became especially apparent with the introduction of the current Canadian environmental assessment law, CEAA 2012. The new law's most dramatic component was the elimination of "screenings"—the modest reviews of small projects that had constituted well over 90 percent of assessments under the old law. In addition, the new law focuses more narrowly on matters of exclusive federal jurisdiction, consolidates decision authority in three agencies,[8] specifies time limits for particular review process components, and provides for the substitution of provincial processes. At the same time, it adds new provisions for the exercise of ministerial discretion and, consequently, new openings for process uncertainties.

CEAA 2012 strengthened federal environmental assessment only by introducing an enforceable decision in which conditions of approval may be specified.[9] As well, the new law retained some important advanced components, including participant funding, a useful public registry, and a formal purpose to "promote sustainable development."[10] Attention to cumulative effects is also retained and modestly supplemented by a provision for establishing advisory committees to consider regional cumulative effects.[11] The new law does not, however, follow other jurisdictions in providing a legislated foundation for **strategic-level assessments** (covering government policies, plans, programs, and other broad-scale initiatives) where attention to the cumulative effects of multiple undertakings is likely to be much more effective and efficient.[12]

Since 1990, the federal government has had a non-legislated strategic assessment process for proposals that need ministerial or Cabinet approval and may have significant environmental effects.[13] The Cabinet directive on strategic assessment requires the integration of environmental assessment findings in broader evaluations of strategic options, covers positive as well as adverse and cumulative and individual effects, and is framed as a tool to contribute to **sustainable development**. It is also meant to streamline project-level planning and assessment. Unfortunately, the process is inaccessible to public scrutiny and lacks the credibility and authority to

---

strategic-level assessments   application of environmental assessment requirements to government policies, plans, programs, and other broad-scale initiatives

sustainable development   "development that meets the needs of the present without compromising the ability of future generations to meet their own needs" (World Commission on Environment and Development, 1987); it involves improving the quality of human life and enhancing equity in the distribution of well-being while living within the carrying capacity of the planet's biophysical systems over the long term; see Chapter 3, especially Box 3.2, footnote †

provide effective guidance of project-level planning and assessment.[14] CEAA 2012 does nothing to address these deficiencies.

Early critics of the new law argued that, overall, the changes would weaken federal environmental assessment as a means of driving better environmental performance while not delivering much more streamlined decision-making.[15] The results in practice, however, are likely to be affected not only by the provisions of CEAA 2012 but also by other factors including growing scientific and public concerns about the sustainability of current trends (e.g., rising greenhouse gas emissions, declining biodiversity, and deepening economic inequities) and the expanding legal recognition of Aboriginal rights and interests, which are unavoidably matters of federal jurisdiction.

BOX 10.3 » The Purposes of the Canadian Environmental Assessment Act, 2012

4(1) The purposes of this Act are

(a) to protect the components of the environment that are within the legislative authority of Parliament from significant adverse environmental effects caused by a designated project;

(b) to ensure that designated projects that require the exercise of a power or performance of a duty or function by a federal authority under any Act of Parliament other than this Act to be carried out, are considered in a careful and precautionary manner to avoid significant adverse environmental effects;

(c) to promote cooperation and coordinated action between federal and provincial governments with respect to environmental assessments;

(d) to promote communication and cooperation with aboriginal peoples with respect to environmental assessments;

(e) to ensure that opportunities are provided for meaningful public participation during an environmental assessment;

(f) to ensure that an environmental assessment is completed in a timely manner;

(g) to ensure that projects, as defined in section 66, that are to be carried out on federal lands, or those that are outside Canada and that are to be carried out or financially supported by a federal authority, are considered in a careful and precautionary manner to avoid significant adverse environmental effects;

(h) to encourage federal authorities to take actions that promote sustainable development in order to achieve or maintain a healthy environment and a healthy economy; and

(i) to encourage the study of the cumulative effects of physical activities in a region and the consideration of those study results in environmental assessments.

Source: *Canadian Environmental Assessment Act, 2012*, SC 2012, c. 19, s. 52.

The Ontario Environmental Assessment Act and Process

The first environmental assessment law in Canada was passed by the province of Ontario in 1975 and amended in 1996. It applies automatically to all undertakings—including both plans and projects—of the provincial and municipal governments, unless they are exempted. It can also be applied to designated private sector undertakings, although it has been commonly applied only to waste disposal and some electricity projects. Overall, the Ontario law's greatest strength lies in its application to the public sector. Its greatest deficiency may be its failure to apply often or reliably to significant private sector undertakings, including major mines.

Under the Ontario law, *environment* is broadly defined to include biophysical, social, economic, and cultural factors and their interrelations. Proponents are generally required to justify the purposes of their undertaking and carry out a comparative evaluation of alternatives to establish that their proposed undertaking is environmentally preferable to other reasonable options. Since 1996, however, proponents have been allowed to propose narrower terms of reference for "scoped" assessments that avoid some of the general requirements.

Submitted assessments are subject to public as well as government reviews, which may be followed by formal quasi-judicial hearings before a decision-making board, although these have become very rare and funding of public interest intervenors was eliminated at the time of the 1996 amendments. In every case, a decision is rendered under the environmental assessment law, and approvals are typically subject to enforceable terms and conditions.

Ontario uses a more streamlined **class environmental assessment** process for various categories of mostly moderately significant, repetitive undertakings, including municipal road and sewer projects and flood protection work by watershed-based conservation authorities. The class processes, which guide the vast majority of assessments in the province, require proponents to go through the following basic series of logical assessment steps:

- *Step 1:* Identify purposes and alternatives.
- *Step 2:* Select a preferred alternative on the basis of an initial review of potential effects.
- *Step 3:* Carry out detailed design incorporating measures to mitigate possible negative effects.
- *Step 4:* Prepare a report on the process, findings, and conclusions.

---

class environmental assessment   (1) in Ontario, an assessment document that covers a category of undertakings (e.g., municipal road and water projects or forest management planning) and sets out a streamlined process for assessments of proposed undertakings in the category; (2) under the *Canadian Environmental Assessment Act* (1992), a streamlined generic environmental assessment (also called a "model class screening"), which was used, perhaps with case-specific adjustments, for proposed undertakings in a particular category (e.g., small-scale fish habitat restoration or enhancement projects)

Public notices and opportunities for comment are provided at key points. Those with continuing serious concerns after the report is issued may request a minister's order to bump up the case to full assessment. Although these requests are almost never granted, they can lead to useful negotiations about the concerns raised and may result in additional conditions in project approvals. Unless a bump-up request (formally a Part II order) is granted, the proposed undertaking is approved once the final public comment period is over.

Ontario's class environmental assessment process and its inclusion of plans as undertakings for individual assessments have sometimes provided valuable vehicles for public assessment of broad policy and planning options. In regional waste management, forest management on **Crown land**, and electricity demand and supply management, assessments under the Ontario law have played a crucial role in encouraging broader thinking and facilitating important transitions (e.g., planning for multi-use forests rather than only for timber, working to reduce waste rather than focusing only on new landfills, and expanding energy efficiencies and use of renewables rather than accepting demand growth and building more nuclear plants). But in Ontario, as elsewhere, plenty of room remains for more such applications of the environmental assessment process.

The Future of Environmental Assessment

As suggested at the beginning of this chapter, the environmental assessment story so far reflects basic tensions between what we need for responsible decision-making in a dynamic and complex world and what our governance systems feel willing and able to provide. Just how these tensions will affect the future of environmental assessment is beyond reliable prediction. Much will depend on the influence of developments in other areas, including governance shifts, advances in scientific understanding, the effects of climate change and other stresses on the biosphere, and the nature of other demands on our attention and capacity. Moreover, even in the realm of environmental assessment, many changes are likely to emerge beyond the usual ambit of formal environmental assessment regimes.

For many years now, requirements and processes established under environmental assessment law have been expanding into and overlapping with laws related to **land use planning** and activities in the resource and industrial sectors, as well as interacting with a diversity of factors pushing corporate responsibility initiatives. Even in this broader context, however, it is safe to assume that effectiveness and

---

Crown land public land held under the administration and control of the provincial or federal government

land use planning determining how a parcel of land will be used by defining objectives, collecting information, identifying problems, and analyzing alternatives

manageability issues will continue to be important considerations in environmental assessment and that the best options will involve innovative ways of serving both imperatives at the same time.

On the effectiveness side, lessons learned from experience will continue to push environmental assessment law and practice to be more demanding. As is evident from Table 10.1, expectations for advanced assessment law include a diversity of components that extend the reach and ambitions of environmental assessments to address evident deficiencies, incorporate new understandings, and respond to emerging problems and opportunities. Many environmental assessment process experts and practitioners have been advocating new or greater emphasis on assessment of strategic-level undertakings, more effective attention to cumulative and interactive effects, increased respect for complexity and uncertainty, greater reliance on informed public engagement, greater recognition of knowledge sources beyond conventional science, and expanded application of sustainability-based criteria to the assessment of proposed undertakings, including critical consideration of their purposes and comparative evaluation of alternatives.

On the manageability side, many assessment regimes have been criticized, especially by project proponents, for being too onerous and too slow. As noted above, the most common complaints have focused on the application of both federal and provincial assessment requirements to individual projects where one properly designed and managed process would seem possible and sensible. While some calls for greater efficiency have been thinly disguised efforts to lighten environmental obligations, opportunities certainly exist for significant improvements in efficiency, including through steps that would also enhance effectiveness.

Many of the efficiency initiatives introduced in recent revisions of environmental assessment law have treated environmental assessment as a project approval process and have focused on how to make it quicker and easier. The Ontario and federal law reforms, for example, have included measures to exempt more projects, narrow the scope of assessments, impose time limits for reviews, and restrict public participation. These changes streamline assessment more by weakening it than by making it more efficient.

The preferable alternative would be to treat environmental assessment as a process for planning better undertakings in the long-term public interest and to focus on gaining efficiencies by strengthening assessment where it can bring major improvements. Such an approach to efficiency and effectiveness might focus on three big opportunities for improvement: upward harmonization of assessment processes across Canada; serious application of assessment requirements to cumulative effects and strategic undertakings; and transition to integrated, sustainability-based assessment to replace the currently ill-defined and fragmentary approach to decision-making wherein environmental assessment is still a poorly integrated component.

Upward Harmonization

The constitutional reality of Canada includes overlapping federal and provincial jurisdiction in many areas, including a wide range of matters relevant to the socio-economic and biophysical environment. As well, Canada has three territories with some devolved authority and Aboriginal peoples with constitutional rights that must be recognized in the design and practice of environmental assessment. One consequence of this constitutional complexity is that Canada has a multitude of differing and overlapping federal, provincial, territorial, and Aboriginal environmental assessment regimes. Moreover, many jurisdictions have established assessment-like requirements in other legislation (e.g., concerning land use planning, resource management, and sectoral regulation). Especially at the project level, these assessment processes also overlap with more specific regulatory permitting and licensing requirements. Often at least two sets of formal assessment requirements and several major regulatory processes apply to the same undertaking. Coordinating these multiple overlapping processes represents a significant and intractable challenge for environmental assessment effectiveness as well as efficiency.

Overlapping obligations and oversight have advantages. Few real-world concerns fit tidily in separate boxes. Mobilizing multiple sources of expertise and different perspectives enhances the potential quality of advice and cuts the risk of bad decisions by insufficiently informed and independent authorities. A mix of authorities operating at different scales can combine knowledge of local and regional specifics with consistent broader overviews. In environmental assessment in Canada, the problem is not the fact of overlap but the poor fit, conflicting demands, and diverse weaknesses of the overlapping requirements.

No two environmental assessment laws and associated processes in Canada take the same approach to the basic assessment requirements set out in Table 10.1. Moreover, no one law meets all of the expectations for advanced environmental assessment set out in that table and the inadequacies of each law differ from one jurisdiction to the next. These divergences make assessment process coordination difficult and leave highly uneven assessment results across the country. Expertise that should be devoted to improving our understanding of environmental effects and deciding how to incorporate them in decision-making is instead occupied with wrestling over the conflicting details of many different processes. Proponents and other assessment participants are burdened with needs to understand and meet the expectations of authorities with different rules, procedures, and responsibilities.

Efforts to reduce multiple process problems have enjoyed some successes. Several jurisdictions allow consolidation of hearings when a proposed undertaking is subject to two or more laws that include environmental hearing provisions. Agreements on assessment cooperation, including joint hearings for those few projects that proceed to a public hearing, have been signed between the federal government and various provincial territorial and Aboriginal authorities.[16] Although the cooperating authorities have parted ways in some cases,[17] the cooperation efforts have often succeeded in bridging the divides between and among government agencies. The disparities and inefficiencies and missed opportunities resulting from very different and highly uneven assessment regimes in Canada remain, nonetheless.

The most attractive approach to reducing process integration difficulties and increasing the consistency of environmental assessment requirements across Canada is upward harmonization.[18] In effect, upward harmonization would require broad agreement among jurisdictions on a common high standard for environmental assessment law and processes in Canada and revision of existing regimes to incorporate the core components in at least roughly compatible ways. Both agreement on and incorporation of such changes would have to be voluntary. The resulting laws and processes would still vary, if only to respect the distinct cases and contexts for assessment in different jurisdictions. While the challenges would be great, the objective is highly appealing as a means of enhancing effectiveness and efficiency simultaneously.

Although it seems unlikely that Canadian jurisdictions will soon agree on a common high standard for environmental assessment, eventual success is certainly conceivable. The possibility was tested back in the late 1990s, when the Canadian Standards Association hosted an initiative to develop a best practices guide for environmental assessment process design as a basis for harmonization. The technical committee appointed for the task included representatives of federal, provincial, territorial, and Aboriginal authorities, as well as proponents and other stakeholders. Despite the contrasting perspectives of these participants, the committee came very close to agreement on the 14th draft, which incorporated most of the advanced components in Table 10.1. Although the proposed "guideline standard" demanded no commitments for application and the effort failed in the end, it did reveal the potential for broad multi-stakeholder agreement on advanced assessment.

Cumulative Effects and Strategic-Level Assessments

Environmental assessments are often the key venue for public debate and conflict involving matters of great public controversy. Recent assessments in Canada have dealt with proposals for additional bitumen extraction (called "oil sands projects" by proponents and "tar sands projects" by detractors) and associated pipelines, fracking, uranium mining, large hydropower projects in undisturbed watersheds or on waterways already significantly manipulated, hydrocarbon exploration in important fishing grounds, and highways to facilitate urban growth. All such undertakings raise big policy issues as well as immediate project-specific concerns. Common big policy issues include whether there are adequate ecological, social, and administrative capacities to deal with the cumulative effects of multiple undertakings in an area, and whether we should permit initial or further development along a questionable path when attractive alternative strategies may exist (e.g., promoting energy efficiencies and renewable energy sources rather than facilitating more extraction and use of hydrocarbons).

Especially in open public reviews, requirements to recognize cumulative effects and to ensure comparative evaluation of alternatives in project-centred environmental assessment processes have been useful means of identifying the larger policy implications of major undertakings. Often, such requirements have also been effective means of pushing authorities to give serious attention to progressive new options (e.g., getting waste reduction considered alongside landfills in waste project assessments). But project-level proceedings are predictably ill-equipped to evaluate issues and options beyond the project scale. These matters usually lie beyond the mandate and expertise of the usual project proponents and government reviewers, and perhaps also beyond the authority of the immediate decision-makers.

Despite these limitations, project assessment reviews remain lightning rods for public debate about the larger implications of major undertakings because they provide the only available open, potentially impartial, and authoritative venue for discussion. Debates on these matters in project assessments can have positive results. Big issue considerations are often crucial in the comparative evaluation of project alternatives. Many public review panels have made recommendations encouraging governments to address larger issues in concert with project approval. In some cases, the evidence of public concern and possibly more attractive alternatives has led governments to establish broader inquiries in the contested area. But debating big issues through project assessments is at best inefficient and rarely more than indirectly effective.

The evident need is for formal, authoritative assessment at the strategic level of policies, plans, programs, and other broad scale issues and initiatives. For well over a decade now, strategic assessment has been the liveliest area of environmental assessment theory and practice internationally.[19] The Canadian government's formal approach to strategic environmental assessment remains weak—it is based only in policy, has very limited public involvement, and has apparently inspired little effort to ensure compliance. Most provincial and territorial assessment laws also neglect strategic assessment or merely allow for ad hoc applications. However, practical Canadian experience with strategic-level assessments is surprisingly extensive.

Some past and current efforts under legislated environmental assessment processes qualify as major formal strategic assessment efforts. These include Ontario's class environmental assessment of timber management (1994), British Columbia's assessment of salmon aquaculture regulation (1997), and Quebec's reviews of industrial hog farms (2003) and shale gas exploitation (ongoing since 2010). Many strategic assessments under other titles and mandates have also taken place. Tiers of public processes for developing strategic policies and plans that then guide more specific plan and project decisions have long been common in urban and regional planning. Illuminating examples of strategic assessment in planning include the growth management strategy development work undertaken by regional municipalities in British

Columbia, including the Capital Regional District (2003). Applications in other areas include Saskatchewan's Great Sand Hills Regional Environmental Study (2007) and Nova Scotia's inquiry into Bay of Fundy tidal power issues and implications for governance (2008). Although these initiatives were diverse, with different methods and procedures, all were major public policy and planning exercises that involved evaluation of alternatives as well as ecological, social, and economic factors at a scale beyond what was possible in project-level exercises.

Strategic assessment is both an expansion of environmental assessment practice and a link with similar public deliberations with different roots and legislative mandates. In environmental assessment regimes, it can offer much more direct and potentially effective attention to the major issues and options that represent our most significant future concerns and opportunities. As well, by providing credible venues for addressing policy-level matters, strategic assessment can guide and streamline project-level assessment work without compromising effectiveness.

Complexities of application are inevitable. The great range of policy, plan, and program initiatives, deficiencies, and contexts means that strategic assessment law and policy must combine firm principles with adaptive flexibility. Also, ensuring the necessary transparency and openness to public engagement can involve confronting entrenched traditions of secrecy. While the essentials of good strategic assessment law and policy are easily identified[20] and the potential benefits are great, establishing strong strategic assessment processes that can be harmonized for collaborative application across Canada is likely to remain a challenge well into the future.

Sustainability-Based Assessment

Perhaps the most promising examples of positive harmonization with important strategic and project significance have come from cases involving environmental assessment review panels jointly established by some combination of federal, provincial, territorial, and Aboriginal authorities. In five notable cases, the joint panels applied a contribution to sustainability test that entails a comprehensive assessment of the positive and negative effects and the long-term legacy of the proposed undertakings.[21] Typically, environmental assessment decision-makers have aimed only to ensure that the proponents took environmental effects issues into account and avoided or mitigated any serious predicted damages. As noted earlier in this chapter, relatively advanced assessment regimes have gone further by requiring comparative evaluation of alternatives and justification for the selection of one option as the preferred alternative. In theory, that approach should lead to the best option, not just mitigation of the most serious adverse effects. But in practice, most assessment work has focused on mitigation, not on how to enhance the lasting benefits of the proposed undertaking.

The contribution to sustainability test requires lasting net gains. In 1997, in the first explicit application of this higher test in a Canadian environmental assessment, the joint panel examining the proposed Voisey's Bay Nickel Mine and Mill on the north coast of Labrador stated that it wanted to know "the extent to which the Undertaking may make a positive overall contribution towards the attainment of ecological and community sustainability, both at the local and regional levels."[22]

Similar expectations imposed by subsequent assessment panels were increasingly accompanied by explicit sustainability-based criteria for judging whether the high test was met. In 2007, two joint federal–provincial panels—one reviewing a proposed quarry and marine terminal at White's Point in Nova Scotia and the other reviewing the Kemess North copper-gold mine case in British Columbia—applied the contribution to sustainability test and recommended against approval of the proposed projects because they would not provide lasting net gains.[23] These were followed by the 2009 joint panel report on the Mackenzie Gas project (involving development of three fields and a 1,000 kilometre pipeline in the Mackenzie Valley of the Northwest Territories) and the 2011 Lower Churchill joint panel report on a proposal for two new hydropower dams in southern Labrador.[24] In each of the latter cases, the panel developed, applied, and published a set of context-specified sustainability criteria to assist its own deliberations and to inform the analysis of the final decision-makers in the collaborating governments.

It is not yet clear how soon this more demanding approach will be broadly adopted in Canada for project and strategic-level assessments. Sustainability-based assessment processes are spreading quickly around the world,[25] and it is reasonable to expect further applications here too.

Taken together, upward harmonization, strategic assessments, and consistent adoption of sustainability-based assessment approaches could help establish an admirably advanced next generation of environmental assessment law and practice. The resulting processes would be more demanding, but they would also be more respectful of assessment complexities and support more efficient and effective decision-making. The challenges lie in pushing and facilitating the necessary changes and in establishing confidence that both the transition and the results can be managed with existing resources and capacities. But as has been seen already in this text and will be evident as well in Chapter 11's discussion of planning and management regimes, these challenges are widely shared in and beyond the many fields of environmental law.

SUMMARY OF KEY POINTS

- Environmental assessment law began well over 40 years ago with the basic idea that environmental considerations should be integrated equally with the usual financial and technical concerns in decision-making about important undertakings. This area of law has been evolving gradually and unevenly in Canada ever since.

- In the evolution of environmental assessment law, the most positive steps have made (or would make) environmental assessment more ambitious. They have aimed to cover more undertakings (at the strategic as well as the project level), to integrate attention to more issues (socio-economic as well as biophysical, cumulative as well as individual), to apply a higher test (choosing the option with the best contribution to sustainability rather than merely mitigating most significant adverse effects), and to be more open and participative.

- At the same time, assessment obligations have been resisted for being unfriendly to business as usual, and assessment processes have been criticized for being inefficient, especially where two or more processes (e.g., federal and provincial) apply to the same undertaking.

- The record of environmental assessment law design, application, and amendment in Canada illustrates major differences in approaches as well as common tensions between effectiveness and manageability.

- The future promise of environmental assessment law likely centres on initiatives that can enhance both effectiveness and manageability. Key efforts would aim for upward harmonization of environmental assessment law in Canada's many overlapping jurisdictions in ways that facilitate application of assessment obligations more consistently and rigorously to influential strategic-level undertakings (policies, plans, and programs) and establish positive contributions to sustainability as the standard to be met.

KEY TERMS

class environmental assessment	environmental assessment law
Crown land	land use planning
cumulative effects	strategic-level assessments
environmental assessment	sustainable development

DISCUSSION QUESTIONS

1. What have been the greatest strengths of environmental assessment law in Canada so far, and what potential future advances offer the greatest promise?
2. What have been the greatest weaknesses and continuing deficiencies of environmental assessment in Canada? Why have they persisted and what would you want done about them?
3. What one environmental assessment law reform initiative would you most want to be hired to work on for a future federal, provincial, territorial, or Aboriginal authority in Canada, and what would be the main challenges to be faced in designing, gaining approval for, and implementing that initiative?

4. What would be the advantages and risks of seeking upward harmonization of the great diversity of environmental assessment laws and processes in Canada, and what would be the key characteristics of the desired result?

SUGGESTED READINGS

Readings

Canadian Environmental Assessment Act, 2012, SC 2012, c. 19, s. 52.

Gibson, Robert B., with Selma Hassan, Susan Holtz, James Tansey, and Graham Whitelaw. *Sustainability Assessment: Criteria and Processes.* London: Earthscan, 2005.

Noble, Bram F. *Introduction to Environmental Impact Assessment: A Guide to Principles and Practice*, 2nd ed. Toronto: Oxford University Press, 2010.

World Commission on Environment and Development. *Our Common Future.* Oxford: Oxford University Press, 1987.

Websites

Canadian Environmental Assessment Agency: http://www.ceaa-acee.gc.ca

Canadian Environmental Assessment Registry: http://www.ceaa-acee.gc.ca/050/index-eng.cfm

International Association for Impact Assessment: http://www.iaia.org/publications -resources/downloadable-publications.aspx

NOTES

1. *Canadian Wildlife Federation Inc. v. Canada (Minister of Environment)*, [1989] 3 FC 309 (TD).

2. *Canadian Wildlife Federation Inc. v. Canada (Minister of Environment)*, [1989] 99 NR 72, 2 WWR 69 (FCA).

3. *Friends of the Oldman River Society v. Canada (Minister of Transport)*, [1992] 1 SCR 3.

4. For details on the federal government's slow progress toward legislated environmental assessment requirements, see Stephen Hazell, *Canada v. the Environment: Federal Environmental Assessment 1984-1998* (Toronto: Canadian Environmental Defence Fund, 1999); and Robert B. Gibson, "From Wreck Cove to Voisey's Bay: The Evolution of Federal Environmental Assessment in Canada" (2002) 20:3 *Impact Assessment and Project Appraisal* 151-59.

5. For example, the *Yukon Environmental and Socio-economic Assessment Act* of 2003 satisfied a commitment in the 1993 umbrella final agreement with the Council of Yukon Indians.

6. *Export Development Act*, RSC 1985, c. E-20.

7. Arlene Kwasniak, "Environmental Assessment, Overlap, Duplication, Harmonization, Equivalency, and Substitution: Interpretation, Misinterpretation, and a Path Forward" (2009) 20:1 *Journal of Environmental Law and Practice* 1-35.

8. Under the *Canadian Environmental Assessment Act, 2012*, SC 2012, c. 19, s. 52 (CEAA 2012), s. 15, the three authorities are the Canadian Environmental Assessment Agency, the National Energy Board, and the Canadian Nuclear Safety Commission.

9. CEAA 2012, ss. 31, 54, 97-102.

10. Ibid., s. 4(1)(h).

11. Ibid., ss. 73-77.

12. See Peter N. Duinker and Lorne A. Greig, "The Impotence of Cumulative Effects Assessment in Canada: Ailments and Ideas for Redeployment" (2006) 37:2 *Environmental Management* 153-61.

13. The current version is Canada, "Strategic Environmental Assessment: The Cabinet Directive on the Environmental Assessment of Policy, Plan and Program Proposals," Privy Council Office and the Canadian Environmental Assessment Agency, 2010, http://www.ceaa-acee.gc.ca/default.asp?lang=en&n=B3186435-1.

14. Robert B. Gibson, Hugh Benevides, Meinhard Doelle, and Denis Kirchhoff, "Strengthening Strategic Environmental Assessment in Canada: An Evaluation of Three Basic Options" (2010) 20:3 *Journal of Environmental Law and Practice* 175-211.

15. Doelle, Meinhard, "CEAA 2012: The End of Federal EA as We Know It?" (2012) 24 *Journal of Environmental Law and Practice* 1-17.

16. For details of the agreements, see Canadian Environmental Assessment Agency, "Environmental Assessment Agreements," last modified May 14, 2012, https://www.ceaa-acee.gc.ca/default.asp?lang=en&n=CA03020B-1.

17. One notable example is the case of the proposed Prosperity Mine in British Columbia, where the proponent reportedly did not want a cooperative federal–provincial process. The province carried out its review quickly and issued an early approval. In contrast, the federal government chose review by public panel and, on the panel's advice, rejected the proposal. The proponent then revised and resubmitted its proposal. The second federal review also held hearings and identified significant problems. Despite provincial lobbying in favour of the project, the federal government rejected it again.

18. See Deborah Carver, Robert B. Gibson, Jessie Irving, and Erin Burbidge, *Interjurisdictional Coordination of EA: Challenges and Opportunities Arising from Differences Among Provincial and Territorial Assessment Requirements and Processes*, Report for the Environmental Planning and Assessment Caucus, Canadian Environmental Network, 2010; Canadian Environmental Network, "Environmental Planning and Assessment Caucus," 2014, http://rcen.ca/caucus/environmental -planning-and-assessment/resources; and Next Generation Environmental Assessment Project: Dissertations, Theses, Monographs, and Major Projects, accessed July 14, 2014, https://uwaterloo.ca/next-generation-environmental-assessment/ research-contributions/dissertations-theses-monographs-and-major-reports.

19. See Barry Dalal-Clayton and Barry Sadler, *Strategic Environmental Assessment: A Sourcebook and Reference Guide to International Experience* (London: Earthscan, 2005).

20. Gibson, Benevides, Doelle, and Kirchhoff, supra note 14.

21. The reports of the five sustainability-based reviews panel are as follows: Canadian Environmental Assessment Agency, *Voisey's Bay Mine and Mill Environmental Assessment Panel Report*, 1999, http://www.ceaa-acee.gc.ca/default.asp?lang=En&n=F06E8BD3-1; Canadian Environmental Assessment Agency, *Environmental Assessment of the Whites Point Quarry and Marine Terminal Project*, 2007, http://www.ceaa-acee.gc.ca/default.asp?lang=En&n=CC1784A9-1; Canadian Environmental Assessment Agency, *Kemess North Copper-Gold Mine Project: Joint Review Panel Report*, 2007, http://www.ceaa-acee.gc.ca/052/details-eng.cfm?pid=3394 (CEAA, *Kemess*); Canadian Environmental Assessment Agency, *Foundation for a Sustainable Northern Future: Report of the Joint Review Panel for the Mackenzie Gas Project* (Canada: Minister of Environment, 2009), http://www.acee-ceaa.gc.ca/default.asp?lang=En&n=155701CE-1 (CEAA, *Foundation*); Canadian Environmental Assessment Agency, *Report of the Joint Review Panel: Lower Churchill Hydroelectric Generation Project*, 2011, http://www.ceaa.gc.ca/052/details-eng.cfm?pid=26178.

22. Canadian Environmental Assessment Agency, *Environmental Impact Statement Guidelines for the Review of the Voisey's Bay Mine and Mill Undertaking*, 1997, s. 3.3.

23. CEAA, *Kemess*, supra note 21.

24. CEAA, *Foundation*, supra note 21.

25. Barry Dalal-Clayton and Barry Sadler, *Sustainability Appraisal: Sourcebook and Reference Guide to International Experience* (Oxford: Routledge, 2014).

CHAPTER 11

Planning and Management Regimes

Introduction

Planning and management regimes are important where long-term planning is needed to preserve, renew, or manage an important resource—such as timber, fish, or electricity—and to consider all competing interests and needs. Land use planning laws and policies also play a critical role in managing urban growth and ensuring that development pressures do not overwhelm the need to protect and wisely manage environmental resources.

This chapter explores current approaches to planning and management that seek to achieve environmental protection and conservation objectives in the face of a variety of growth and development pressures. As discussed in Chapter 9, the sectoral approach continues to dominate the regulatory landscape. However, a slow but steady transition to a more comprehensive and integrated approach to the planning and management of Canada's environmental future is taking place.

CASE STUDY

The Calgary Flood of 2013

"At first it was just intense, pretty powerful, an amazing thing to watch. As daylight came, it just got bigger and bigger and wider and wider. And it's still getting bigger and bigger and wider and wider. All you can hear is, like, boulders and trees. I watched a refrigerator go by, I watched a shed go by, I watched couches go by. It's insane." (Canmore, Alberta resident Wade Graham)*

On June 19, 2013, as the waters of the Bow and Elbow rivers began their unstoppable rise, Calgary and other parts of Southern Alberta were on the verge of one of the most devastating natural disasters in Canadian history. By the time the waters subsided several days later, it had become the costliest natural disaster in Canadian history, with damage estimated at $1.7 billion. Four lives were also lost.

All of Canada's major cities are built adjacent to water, and some, including Winnipeg and Toronto, are built on actual flood plains—geographical features that are prone to flooding and are less-than-ideal locations to build a city. Winnipeg's Red River Floodway opened in 1968, and it has played a major role in diverting water that would have otherwise inundated the city. Toronto is currently "re-naturalizing" the mouth and banks of the Don River in order to mitigate future flooding. The Toronto flood of July 2013—occurring only days after the Calgary flood—was the most expensive natural disaster in Ontario's history, estimated at $850 million by the Insurance Bureau of Canada.†

The emerging pattern is that a "flood of the century" happens far more often than that. Canadian cities, towns, farms, and infrastructure—and people themselves—are

The Bow River and the Centre Street Bridge in downtown Calgary, June 22, 2013.

Source: Rosanne Tackaberry, Alamy.

increasingly vulnerable to natural disasters. Some of the vulnerability may be attributable to the fact that we have built many of our cities beside water. But there is also a strong indication that extreme weather events are becoming more commonplace, just as climate scientists have been predicting for years.

In the wake of the 2013 Alberta flood, the City of Calgary and the provincial governments understood that similar events were very likely to occur again in years to come. The flood called for not only a better understanding of the emergency measures required for responding to such events but also an assessment of land use policies and watershed management, which are intended to mitigate the impact of floods in the first place. In June 2014, the city released *Calgary's Flood Resilient Future: Report from the Expert Management Panel on River Flood Mitigation*, which drew on the expertise of scores of specialists, including engineers, climate scientists, economists, hydrologists, and conservation authorities. The report explored many themes, from event forecasting to measures to conserve natural riparian features, while also acknowledging that certain options, such as moving all new development in Calgary out of the flood plain, were simply not possible. The overall message of the report was an emphasis on mitigation and adaptation, which requires a focus on better land use planning, conservation, understanding of risks, and building resiliency into various systems. Some notable passages from the report:

Managing Development in the Flood Plain

Calgary, like many other communities in Canada and around the world, has historically developed within the floodplain. As a consequence, portions of the city are inherently vulnerable to flood impacts from extreme events. The downtown core and several communities within the city are built in low-lying areas that are prone to surface flooding, high groundwater levels and sewer back-up during river floods. Since 1985, limited new development has been permitted in the floodway and flood resilience requirements guide new development in the flood fringe. At times these limitations are relaxed for development. The amount of development in the floodplain has a significant impact on Calgary's vulnerability to flood events. Development along riverbanks also limits the protection that can be provided to entire neighbourhoods as land is unavailable for The City to construct either permanent or temporary flood barriers in these locations.[‡]

Leaving the Floodplain

In Alberta, the communities of Fort MacLeod, Medicine Hat, High River and Edmonton have all relocated development away from specific areas with high flood risk. Houses in flood risk areas may be raised above flood levels rather than removed. Across the United States, homes that are substantially damaged by a flood are required to be raised above the flood safety level, as mapped by the Federal Emergency Management Agency (FEMA). Homes in designated flood zones that are not raised above this level have significantly higher rates for mandatory flood insurance. Some states are providing grants to help homeowners raise houses that were damaged by Hurricane Sandy.[§]

Looking back on the flood of 2013, the panel also recalled the response of Calgary's citizens:

> As the recovery process proceeded, Calgarians asked many questions, such as: How can we prevent this from happening again? What could we have done differently? When will it happen again? Is this normal or caused by a changing climate? How can I protect myself from future flooding?[#]

Questions

Consider the questions posed by Calgarians, above. How much impact can urban planning and watershed management policies have in addressing these sorts of environmental problems? Governments are often unable to implement certain measures because they would involve incursions onto private property. What responsibility do private landowners have to mitigate risks? Is it realistic to undertake large-scale changes to current development patterns?

---

*   "Calgary Flood: Alberta Residents Describe What They're Seeing," *CBC News*, June 21, 2013, http://www.cbc.ca/news/canada/calgary/calgary-flood-alberta-residents-describe-what-they-re -seeing-1.1301234.

†   Carys Mills, "Toronto's July Flood Listed as Ontario's Most Costly Natural Disaster," *Toronto Star*, August 14, 2013, http://www.thestar.com/business/2013/08/14/july_flood_ontarios_most_costly _natural_disaster.html.

‡   Expert Management Panel on River Flood Mitigation, *Calgary's Flood Resilient Future* (Calgary: City of Calgary, 2014), at 20, http://www.calgary.ca/UEP/Water/Documents/Water-Documents/Flood -Panel-Documents/Expert-Management-Panel-Report-to-Council.PDF.

§   Ibid., at 23.

Ibid., at 3.

Crown Land Management

Crown land management is the management of land owned by the federal and provincial governments. Governments, particularly provincial governments, have often relied heavily on revenues from the sale and development of public lands. Not surprisingly, financial priorities centred on revenues from major economic uses, such as timber harvesting, have tended to take priority over less economically rewarding land uses.

Crown Land

Crown land, also called *public land*, is land owned by a provincial or federal government, which controls its use and sale. All land that has not been legally granted to private persons is Crown land; it includes the vegetation, soil, and minerals on and under the surface of the land. Much of Canada's wilderness is Crown land—for example, 85 percent of Ontario remains Crown land.[1]

Crown land public land held under the administration and control of the provincial or federal government

The Canadian Constitution divides Crown land between the federal government and provincial governments.[2] Provinces generally own public land within their boundaries, with the exception of a few areas specially designated as federal land. Examples of federal land include national parks, harbours, defence properties, lands reserved for First Nations,[3] and coastal marine belts.

The northern territories are subject to federal jurisdiction, except to the extent that responsibilities have been delegated to territorial governments or allocated to First Nations under land settlement agreements. Some areas are also subject to un-resolved Aboriginal land claims, where title to the lands is in dispute. See Chapter 5 for further information on Aboriginal land claims and treaties.

Sectoral Resource Development Law

Legislation concerning public lands has largely taken the form of sectoral natural resource development laws. Sectors include the following:

- forestry,
- minerals,
- water,
- grazing, and
- wildlife (hunting and fishing).

Each sector provides a stage for the recurring drama of development versus protection. This conflict is played out in a variety of different ways as a result of the competing values and interests concerning public land and resource use.

The historical focus on sectoral natural resource development has resulted in several major problems. Consider the following:

- *Fragmented decision-making.* Separate legal frameworks for particular sectors—such as minerals, forestry, and recreation—have resulted in fragmented decision-making that does not take cross-purposes into account. For example, the noise and pollution caused by mining may interfere with camping or skiing on nearby land.
- *Incrementalism.* Decision-making on a project-by-project basis without a clear consideration of long-term objectives can send us down an undesirable path. Each additional undertaking continues the development momentum and sets a new baseline level of disturbance and expectation. The succession of individual approvals sooner or later degrades vulnerable lands, eliminates opportunities for non-exploitive land uses, undermines ecological functions, and reduces the environmental legacy of future generations.
- *Pre-emption effect.* When a project such as a mine is proposed, roads and power lines may be built before the environmental assessment process begins. Building of this nature may raise a community's expectations regarding employment

and other economic benefits; this situation creates a strong economic imperative that is likely to influence the approval decision. Once a project is approved, the resulting public land allocation, infrastructure construction, and development initiatives establish an irreversible commitment to more of the same kind of economic activity. Thus, one development opens the door for other similar or related public land uses in the area.

- *Cumulative effects.* The combined effects of multiple land uses and developments are not anticipated and therefore not considered by decision-makers. The cumulative result is often negative, unexpected, and irreversible.

Because of these serious problems inherent in sectoral natural resource development law, the trend in law-making is toward a more forward-looking and comprehensive approach.

Public Land Planning and Management

Comprehensive public land planning and management takes into account the many competing demands and long-term possibilities for public land use. Environmental assessments are a first step, but they are largely project-specific. Assessments of cumulative effects are sometimes performed. However, they are severely limited by a lack of information and an inability to deal with individually innocuous, but cumulatively significant, actions. Cumulative-effects assessments also suffer from a failure to establish workable and generally accepted significance criteria.

Some jurisdictions, such as British Columbia, have initiated a variety of high-profile regional and subregional land use planning processes that bring together representatives of the main land use interests and attempt to forge a consensus on land allocations and management principles. If the parties reach a consensus, their consensus can then help guide particular decisions under sectoral legislation.

In other cases, sectoral laws may be used to accommodate attention to competing land uses. Ontario, for example, uses the class assessment provisions of its *Environmental Assessment Act* in combination with its *Crown Forest Sustainability Act, 1994* to provide a framework for forest management planning that includes public consultation. The planners are required to "have regard for" a broad range of social, economic, and ecological values beyond the interests of the forest products industry. Whether non-timber values are given adequate attention and whether the practices resulting from the decisions are sustainable remain subjects of debate. However, Ontario's forest management regime is clearly a step toward a more comprehensive approach.

Public Engagement

Planning and managing public lands is unavoidably difficult. Huge areas are involved, with many different resources, ecosystems, exploitive and non-exploitive users, cultures, and livelihoods. As the competing pressures on public lands and their resources increase, there are growing political tensions and higher expectations for transparent, participative, and fair decision-making. It also becomes harder to find ways to satisfy present demands without undermining future opportunities. Gradually, public land planning practices have moved toward more comprehensive and better-integrated means of wrestling with these challenges, although not all attempts have been entirely successful.

In the 1990s, British Columbia's Commission on Resources and Environment (CORE) integrated public land and resource management policy and law with an open and extremely inclusive public process to develop plans for contested public regions of the province. A regional stakeholder negotiation process was created to empower interested parties and to formulate recommendations on legislation, policies, and practices. CORE's work provided a valuable base for the subsequent subregional land resource management planning processes in several areas, and some of CORE's recommendations were implemented. However, major recommendations—such as the enactment of a sustainability statute—were never put into practice, and regional land and resource management plan development and implementation remained incomplete, although the province has executed a number of strategic land and resource plans across the province.[4]

As noted above, the Ontario forest management process is also consultative, although less ambitiously so than CORE's, and it became more firmly established and authoritative. However, it too failed to eliminate tensions and doubts about the sustainability of its results. Experience elsewhere confirms that public engagement provides no miracle solution. Competing interests do not easily reach consensus. In some circumstances—for example, when joint management bodies comprise government officials and Aboriginal people—there may be a wide gulf to bridge in terms of culture, language, and world view.

Land use management is more likely to be accepted as legitimate and potentially trustworthy if it includes direct engagement of the relevant interests. Even if all parties do not reach agreement in the end, they at least gain some understanding of one another's positions and concerns.

Complexity

The second major lesson to emerge from public land planning and management experience centres on the challenges of working in complex systems. The ecologies and socio-economic activities on public lands are intricately interwoven and constantly changing. Well-informed management decisions need to be based on a solid understanding of these interrelationships and the factors that influence them. But any such understanding is always highly imperfect and must be continually reconsidered.

The modern science of complex dynamic systems suggests that wise management must accept uncertainty and anticipate surprise. It must recognize that human well-being depends on ecosystem services, which in turn depend on maintenance of the ability of ecosystems to deal with stresses (most human economic activities) and catastrophes (e.g., major forest fires).

Because we cannot know enough about these systems to predict the effects of our activities accurately, it is important to take a precautionary approach, rather than try to identify the point of maximum sustainable yield. The key is to ensure that our activities do not compromise the resilience of ecosystems and linked socio-economic systems. If we are to preserve these systems' ability to accommodate and recover from disturbance, we must favour small-scale, diverse, and adjustable activities rather than single, big, inflexible ones. It also means combining planning and management with monitoring and adaptation.

Public land planning and management that applies this type of thinking is not yet common, but it is increasingly influential. It is perhaps best demonstrated in park management under the *Canada National Parks Act*, which sets maintenance of ecological integrity as the key management objective. It also informs some management practices in the Ontario forestry regime discussed above and under New Brunswick's *Crown Lands and Forests Act*.

Remaining Challenges

If public land law is to integrate public participation and an understanding of complex systems more fully, it should involve the following actions:

- Include a legislated set of clear purposes and decision criteria that are centred on sustainability objectives and precaution, and that recognize the importance of maintaining the integrity of ecosystems and the socio-economic systems that depend on them.
- Address the full range of potentially competing land values and uses, including social, cultural, ecological, and economic uses.
- Combine the engagement of the many concerned parties with a means of representing and protecting the broader public interest in ecosystem integrity and the well-being of future generations.
- Impose direct requirements for specific decisions—for example, under sectoral laws and in environmental assessments and approvals of individual projects—that comply with overall planning guidance.
- Link the application of the sustainability objectives achieved through consultative planning to continuous monitoring, regular review, and adaptive management.

Parks and Other Protected Areas

The establishment and maintenance of parks and other protected areas are among the most well-known means of protecting natural habitats and scenic areas. While the word *park* denotes the most well-known type of protected area, many other terms are used to signify a degree of protection, including the following:

- reserve,
- sanctuary,
- wildlife or wilderness area, and
- conservation land.

The degree of protection offered in various protected areas may differ widely.

International Law

At the international level, the International Union for Conservation of Nature sets out six categories of protected areas that range from strictly protected areas in category 1 (examples include designated wilderness areas and nature reserves) to sustainable use areas in category 6. Two of the key international agreements that address protected areas are the following:

- the United Nations Convention on Biological Diversity, which encourages parties to establish protected area systems to conserve biological diversity; and
- the United Nations World Heritage Convention, which addresses some of the most important cultural and ecological sites on the planet.

Canada harbours over a dozen world heritage sites, such as the parks in the Rocky Mountains of British Columbia and Alberta; Gros Morne National Park in Newfoundland; and Wood Buffalo National Park in Alberta and the Northwest Territories.

Federal Parks

Canada's protected areas system is subject to a long list of laws and regulations. At the federal level, national parks are the cornerstone of the system. They typically protect representative natural areas of Canadian significance.

The *Canada National Parks Act*, which sets aside parks for public benefit, appreciation, and enjoyment, requires that the parks be maintained in an unimpaired state for future generations. Some of Canada's oldest national parks, such as Banff, date back to the late 1800s. National parks include landscapes and the resident wildlife that constitute iconic symbols of Canada itself.

In the most recent amendments to the *Canada National Parks Act*, the emerging concept of **ecological integrity** was adopted as the guiding vision for Canada's national parks. Managing for ecological integrity essentially involves considering the needs of nature as the first priority. This approach differs from other approaches that put the human use of parks above the needs of the park's natural inhabitants.

---

ecological integrity an approach adopted for national parks that considers the needs of nature as the first priority

With the authority of the *Canada National Parks Act* and its regulations, national parks prohibit most large-scale extractive uses, such as commercial forestry, mining, and hydroelectric development. Other federal designations, such as migratory bird sanctuaries and national wildlife areas, also offer some protection for natural areas. These latter two types of protected areas total more than 12 million hectares across Canada (for comparison purposes, the land mass of Newfoundland is just over 11 million hectares). The majority of those hectares are devoted to bird sanctuaries, in which there are prohibitions against the hunting of birds, the taking of bird eggs, and destroying or tampering with bird nests.

Provincial Parks

The national parks of Canada are a key component of Canada's protected areas system; however, other types of protected areas, many of which are administered by the provinces and territories, actually account for more protected land area than the national parks system. Perhaps the best-known and most widely used designation is the provincial park. Like national parks, provincial parks have a long history. For example, Ontario's Algonquin Provincial Park originated in the late 1800s, the same era in which Banff National Park was founded.

Ontario's recent parks and conservation reserves legislation, which covers hundreds of protected areas, embraces ecological integrity as a guiding principle. Like the *Canada National Parks Act*, Ontario's parks legislation and that of many other jurisdictions excludes large-scale industrial uses, subject to certain exceptions.

Aboriginal Partnerships

In recent years, a much greater emphasis has been placed on Aboriginal involvement in the creation and management of protected areas. Indeed, entirely new protected area designations and systems are arising from partnerships between Aboriginal governments and federal, provincial, and territorial governments. These approaches can help to maintain natural features and traditional activities, while prohibiting industrial activities. One example of this partnership approach is Gwaii Haanas National Park Reserve, National Marine Conservation Reserve, and Haida Heritage Site, an archipelago of islands off the coast of British Columbia (formerly known as the Queen Charlotte Islands). After a lengthy series of protests and political battles to limit logging and other forms of natural resource extraction, an accord was struck that eventually led to the protection of the park as well as a cooperative management agreement between the Haida Nation and the Government of Canada.

Private Landowners

Private landowners, such as the Nature Conservancy of Canada, contribute to Canada's system of protected areas as well. Privately owned and managed areas may not be covered by legislated designations such as parks; however, legislative provisions

Figure 11.1 Canada's Protected Areas, 2014

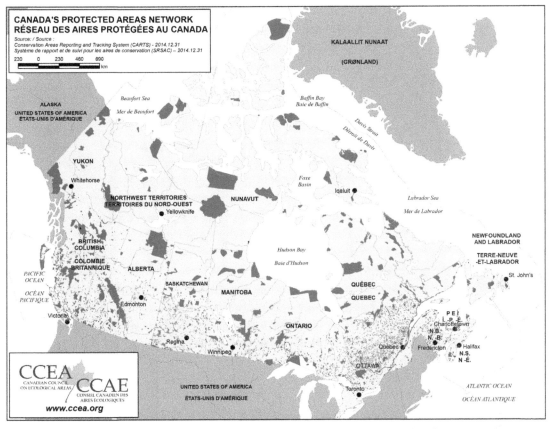

Source: Conservation Areas Reporting and Tracking System (CARTS), 2014.12.31. Canadian Council on Ecological Areas.

that offer significant incentives to private stewardship often facilitate the creation of these areas. Legislated tax incentives, exceptions, and rebates—as well as innovative legal tools such as **conservation easements**—are among the many means that are used to encourage the protection of privately owned natural habitats.

Marine Areas

While terrestrial, or land-based, protected areas are the most well known, a great deal of recent attention has been placed on marine protected areas. The federal government has set aside some marine parks or conservation areas and has committed itself to creating new marine protected areas in the future. Some provinces have also

---

conservation easement a legal tool used to protect natural habitats on privately owned land

begun work on systems of water-based protected areas. Under the international Convention on Biological Diversity (CBD), which came into force in 1993, Canada is committed to protecting at least 17 percent of land and inland waters and 10 percent of coastal and marine areas by 2020.[5]

Remaining Challenges

Parks and protected areas, especially those offering the highest degree of protection from harmful activities, are a key part of biodiversity conservation. These areas typically maintain the integrity of the natural environment in areas that would otherwise have been subjected to extractive uses or other types of development. While they are often considered to be the backbone of landscape-level protection, it is important to note that they typically occupy only a small percentage of the total land base. It is therefore imperative that the so-called working landscape outside the protected areas be managed sustainably so that the protected areas do not become isolated islands of green in an otherwise degraded environment.

Endangered Species

The plight of endangered species across the world is well publicized. Current rates of extinction are much higher than historical rates of extinction. In response to the endangered species crisis, various international, national, and provincial systems have been created, with varying degrees of effectiveness.

Species at Risk

Canada has over 700 officially recognized **species at risk**.[6] This collective term includes the five categories used by the scientific body known as the Committee on the Status of Endangered Wildlife in Canada (COSEWIC):

1. *Extinct.* Extinct species no longer exist. For example, the passenger pigeon, which was once North America's most common bird, is now considered extinct.
2. *Extirpated.* A species is extirpated when it no longer exists in the wild in Canada but still exists elsewhere—in a zoo or in an another country, for example.
3. *Endangered.* A species is endangered if it is facing imminent extirpation or extinction.
4. *Threatened.* A species is threatened when it is likely to become endangered if limiting factors are not reversed.

---

species at risk   a collective term that includes five categories: extinct, extirpated, endangered, threatened, and special concern

5. *Special concern.* Special concern status is given to a species that may become threatened or endangered because of a combination of biological characteristics and identified threats.

In a non-technical sense, extirpated, endangered, threatened, and special concern species are collectively known as *endangered species*. As more studies are undertaken and more types of species are assessed, and as more threats to species and habitats manifest themselves, Canada's list of species at risk grows longer.

In order to address the fact that protecting endangered species requires cooperation among governments, a national accord—Accord for the Protection of Species at Risk—was signed in 1996. This accord committed Canada's governments to establishing complementary legislation and programs that provide for effective protection of species at risk throughout Canada. Implementation of the accord has been inconsistent across Canada. Some provinces (e.g., Ontario) developed new legislation and programs to reflect the commitments in the accord, while others did not do so (e.g., Alberta).

Despite the disturbing trend faced by Canada's endangered species as a whole, certain species have benefited greatly from species protection and recovery efforts. The American white pelican, for example, has been removed from COSEWIC's endangered species list. Unfortunately, over 35 Canadian species have already been found by COSEWIC to be extinct or extirpated.

International Trade

The international trade in endangered species, such as wild parrots, and products derived from endangered species, such as ivory, has long been a concern to the international community. Canada is a party to the 1973 Convention on International Trade in Endangered Species of Wild Fauna and Flora (CITES). This convention seeks to ensure that international trade in specimens of wild animals and plants does not threaten their survival.

To implement CITES, Canada passed the *Wild Animal and Plant Protection and Regulation of International and Interprovincial Trade Act*. This Act aims to protect Canadian and foreign species of animals and plants that may be at risk of exploitation because of illegal trade. It controls the international trade and interprovincial transport of listed endangered species and their derivatives through various restrictions and permit requirements. However, Canada has come under criticism in recent years for often showing a lack of support for existing trade bans on numerous endangered species.[7]

Habitat Loss

While international trade is a threat to many well-known species across the world, by far the greatest modern threat to biological diversity in Canada, and in many other countries, is habitat loss. Simply put, without the places they call home, species cannot survive.

The decline of biological diversity from habitat loss is partly addressed in the 1992 United Nations Convention on Biological Diversity. It calls on countries to pass laws to better protect threatened species. Canada has attempted to address threats to endangered species within its borders, including some aspects of habitat loss, through the *Species at Risk Act*. This Act addresses those aspects of endangered species protection and recovery that are within federal jurisdiction. Implementation of the Act has been disappointing, however. Academic studies and court decisions have found that the federal government has failed to take proper actions to implement this important legislation.

By virtue of their constitutional powers, Canada's provinces have a significant role to play in protecting and restoring the habitat of endangered species. Many provinces have passed endangered species acts (ESAs). The approaches they use vary widely. Some provinces leave the decision to list species for protection to politicians, while others employ independent scientists to create the list. Some make habitat protection mandatory, while others leave this critical issue to government discretion. Some ESAs provide assistance to private landowners to protect habitat, while others focus on a regulatory approach. Very few ESAs include all the elements necessary to provide effective legal protection for endangered species.

Ontario's *Endangered Species Act, 2007*, which replaced its 1971 predecessor, is the first Canadian legislation to include both scientific listing and mandatory habitat protection. It also includes important provisions for recovering endangered and threatened species, addressing Aboriginal concerns, and promoting habitat stewardship. Like most environmental laws, however, it still leaves room for the government to create exemptions from the general protections offered to endangered species. Ontario's extensive use of the exemption provision, coupled with other implementation shortcomings, has led to significant criticism from that province's environmental commissioner. No matter how strongly any ESA is worded, the real test is whether it is implemented in such a way that existing endangered species recover and that new species do not become endangered. Judged against this standard, all ESAs have yet to accomplish their lofty objectives. As a whole, Canada's endangered species problem has grown larger over time, despite some examples of progressive legislation.

By their very nature, ESAs often focus on the urgent measures required to bring individual species back from the brink of extinction. Nonetheless, the shortcomings of the typical single-species management approach of current ESAs are well known to conservation biologists. Often the endangerment of a single species is simply an early warning sign that an entire natural community or ecosystem is under threat. To be effective in the long term, ESAs will need to go beyond addressing the loss of biological diversity at the species, subspecies, or population level. Certain ESAs, including the Ontario and federal Act, offer some opportunities for implementing multi-species and ecosystem approaches. Prairie grassland conservation planning is a recent example of the multi-species approach. The use of such approaches may increase in the future.

Climate Change

Endangered species protection regimes largely predated attempts to address climate change. Consequently, the ability of ESAs, as currently written, to provide for the long-term protection of species such as the polar bear in the face of large-scale climate change is questionable. As with many areas of environmental law, the successful accomplishment of the goals of ESAs will require effective action in many areas not typically covered within the four corners of endangered species legislation.

Urban Planning, Growth Management, and Brownfields

Human decisions about the use made of land occupied by many species are fundamental to environmental integrity. Poor planning decisions on land use can lead to the physical destruction of the natural environment, the wasteful consumption of agricultural land, the loss of habitat for native species, and the contamination of air, land, and water. Therefore, land use planning regimes, with their control of urban planning, growth management, and brownfields redevelopment, serve a critical role in environmental protection.

Land Use Planning

Land use planning involves the use of a set of assessment tools for making decisions about land use. Professional planners gather information and apply certain principles to make recommendations about how land should be used and where certain types of uses should be located. However, this description makes the procedure sound like a scientific exercise, and it presents only part of the picture.

Land use planning also encompasses the public—and often very contentious—process of decision-making. Decision-makers attempt to weigh and balance various competing interests such as the following:

- private and public interests,
- different private interests, and
- present and future needs.

---

land use planning   determining how a parcel of land will be used by defining objectives, collecting information, identifying problems, and analyzing alternatives

For example, a land use decision typically involves a contest between the long-term protection of environmental resources and proposals by private interests to maximize the income-generating value of property. Often no clearly right or wrong answers exist. Land use planning therefore requires not only the application of planning principles in a scientific way but also a fair and open decision-making process that considers the different stakeholders' needs and values.

Land use planning regimes typically carry out four functions, each of which will be discussed in more detail below:

1. They establish broad land use planning policies, including the designation of geographical areas for certain uses and settlement patterns through the establishment of land use plans or "official plans."
2. They impose specific rules to control the use of land, including the form and location of buildings and structures on the land through zoning bylaws or ordinances.
3. They control the division or partitioning of lands into smaller parcels by making decisions on land severances and plans of subdivision.
4. They create procedures, including public consultative and adjudicative processes, to ensure that stakeholders and other affected individuals and agencies have a role in land use decision-making.

Roles and Responsibilities

Municipalities have primary responsibility for land use decision-making in most Canadian jurisdictions. In Ontario, for example, the *Planning Act* confers a number of powers on municipal governments for controlling land use, including approval of official plans, the passage of zoning bylaws, subdivision control, site plan control, and demolition.

Most provincial governments retain an important overriding role with respect to matters of broader importance to the province. In Ontario, the province maintains responsibility for matters considered of "provincial interest." The *Planning Act* empowers Cabinet, through the Ministry of Municipal Affairs, to establish provincial policies that are intended to guide all planning decisions made by municipalities. All land use planning decisions must be "consistent with" any provincial policies that are approved by the province.[8]

Under this authority, Ontario's Cabinet issued the Provincial Policy Statement (PPS) in 1996, since updated in 2005 and 2014. The PPS outlines the province's land use planning vision and reflects the government's attempt to balance development interests with the protection of natural resources. The present version of the PPS[9] includes policies that give direction to planning authorities (such as municipalities and the Ontario Municipal Board) on planning decisions in the following key areas:

- building strong and healthy communities, which includes growth management and development patterns, housing, employment, parks and open spaces, public services and infrastructure, energy conservation, air quality, and climate change;[10]
- natural resource management, which includes land use restrictions to protect and enhance "natural heritage systems" such as wetlands, woodlands, plant and animal life, and water features and systems;[11]
- preservation of foodlands and agricultural resources through restrictions on lot creation and prohibitions on urban development on prime agricultural lands;[12] and
- the long-term protection of mineral aggregate resources and petroleum as well as extraction that is undertaken in a way that minimizes the effects on human health and the environment.[13]

Notably, for the first time, the 2014 PPS directed planning decision-makers to support climate change adaptation in their land use planning decisions.[14]

Land Use Plans

Both the provincial and municipal governments may produce plans that establish the framework and planning rules within which land use planning decisions can be made.

Provincial Plans

While the role of establishing planning policies has historically been given to local municipalities, provincial governments sometimes create planning documents of broader application. Consider the following plans of the government of Ontario, which provide broad planning policy direction across southern Ontario:

1. The Niagara Escarpment Plan[15] imposes land use planning controls across the Niagara Escarpment, a geologically and ecologically significant landform with a lateral extent of over 750 kilometres that has been designated by the United Nations as an international biosphere reserve.
2. The Oak Ridges Moraine Conservation Plan[16] provides a similar level of provincial land use control over a large moraine feature that runs 165 kilometres from Peterborough to Brampton across the Greater Toronto Area and requires protection as a recharge area for drinking water for many communities north of Toronto.
3. The Greenbelt Plan[17] builds on the land use planning protections provided by the Niagara Escarpment and Oak Ridges Moraine plans. It establishes strict land use policies in rural areas across the land known as the "Golden Horseshoe," which rings Lake Ontario from Toronto to Fort Erie.

Regional and Municipal Official Plans

Regional and municipal official plans establish general land use policies across large geographical areas, which are usually based on municipal boundaries. These differ from plans such as the Niagara Escarpment and Oak Ridges Moraine plans, which are based on ecological features and landforms. In most provinces, land use plans arose from the need to establish municipal jurisdiction over settlement patterns and land use control. The official plan therefore generally encompasses the whole of the municipality that has formulated the plan. Where there are two tiers of municipal government, there may be larger regional official plans that provide overall guidance for more specific municipal plans. The Capital Regional District in British Columbia, for example, has a regional growth strategy that must be followed by the official plans of Victoria, Saanich, Esquimalt, and the other municipalities in that regional district.[18] In Ontario, this hierarchy is enshrined in the *Planning Act*, which requires that lower-tier municipalities ensure that their official plans and zoning bylaws conform to the official plan of the upper-tier municipality.[19]

PURPOSE AND FUNCTION   Official plans establish a formal set of policies and principles governing the nature, pattern, extent, and timing of future growth and development within a municipality. The plans are developed with a time frame or "planning horizon" in mind, usually about 20 years. An official plan typically sets out a series of policies concerning key areas that affect growth and development within a municipality, including the following:

- range and types of housing;
- settlement patterns;
- industrial and commercial development;
- provision of necessary services, including transportation and highways, public utilities such as water and sewage treatment, and waste management;
- protection of environmental resources, including flood plains, wetlands, and aggregate extraction;
- conservation and protection of agricultural lands and activities;
- provision of health, policing, and school services;
- restrictions on land severance and subdivision;
- economic development; and
- rules governing public participation in land use planning decisions.

Most important, the document serves as a blueprint for guiding land use across the municipality and managing the estimated population growth. Thus, one of the most important aspects of any official plan is the land use map attached to the plan.

---

regional and municipal official plans   plans that establish general land use policies across large geographical areas delineated by political boundaries

This map indicates the lands on which urban growth and redevelopment are intended to occur and designates the ultimate land use or function that the municipality considers appropriate for each geographical area within its boundaries.

AMENDMENT   Official plans, like all planning tools, are not cast in stone. Mechanisms are in place to amend official plans to respond to changing information, ideas, and desires about how land development should occur. In Ontario, for example, four mechanisms are available to amend official plans:

1. *Municipality-initiated amendments.* Municipalities may initiate amendments to their own plans.[20] In Ontario, although most official plans are designed for at least a 20-year planning horizon, the *Planning Act* requires municipalities to review and update their official plan once every five years.[21] Typically, this update involves a comprehensive municipal review of relevant information about population growth projections, the demand for municipal services, industrial and commercial growth projections, and the status of environmental resources within the municipality. On the basis of this information, the municipality determines what, if any, changes are required to the plan and initiates a public process for developing and approving a new official plan.

2. *Secondary plans.* Municipalities, particularly in urban areas, sometimes identify the need for detailed planning policies within an official plan. **Secondary plans** cover specific areas within a municipality. For example, if an official plan designates an area for residential use, a secondary plan may provide additional detailed policies and mapping to show areas where high-, medium-, and low-density residential development is permitted.

3. *Private amendments.* Amendments to an official plan may be initiated at any time to permit specific development projects that do not conform with the existing plan.[22] Typically, this type of amendment is initiated by private landowners or developers and is accompanied by applications to establish zoning and/or plans of subdivision to permit a particular development to proceed. For example, a developer who wishes to build a shopping mall in a residential area must apply to the municipality to change the official plan designation from residential to commercial, and to establish specific policies to govern the commercial uses.

4. *Provincial amendments.* The provincial government has the power to amend an official plan to address a matter of provincial interest.[23] In Ontario, such provincial interventions in local planning decisions are rare but not unprecedented.

---

secondary plans plans that cover specific areas within a municipality and provide more detailed planning policies for those areas

LEGAL FORCE AND EFFECT   Regional and official plans set out policies that guide municipal councils and other government decision-makers. Policies are not generally considered by the courts to be legally enforceable against individuals. For example, official plans do not directly impose legal requirements on property owners. A municipality may not lay charges against a property owner for carrying out a land use that does not conform to the official plan.

In many jurisdictions, however, official plans indirectly impose property use restrictions on individuals. In Ontario, for example, no municipality may pass a zoning bylaw that does not conform to its official plan.[24] (Zoning bylaws are discussed in greater detail below.) Unlike official plan policies, zoning bylaws are legally enforceable instruments that restrict land use activities and impose planning rules on individual property owners. If an individual seeks a zoning amendment to change the existing rules or to expand the permissible uses on his or her property, the municipality is legally bound to refuse the amendment if it does not conform to the official plan. This example demonstrates how official plans can exert significant planning control over the way individuals can use their property, albeit indirectly.

Multiple Land Use Plans

Some areas are governed by two, or even three, land use plans. In the city of Burlington, for example, in order to determine the land use policies governing a particular property, a landowner might need to look first at the Niagara Escarpment Plan and/or the Greenbelt Plan, then the Halton Region Official Plan, and finally the City of Burlington Official Plan.

In cases where more than one plan governs land use, a hierarchy is typically established. For example, the Niagara Escarpment Plan creates land use designations to protect escarpment features, to which all regional and local official plans must conform. The Halton Region Official Plan also provides a general policy direction, including direction on permitted land uses to which the local (City of Burlington) official plan must conform. Finally, the city's official plan provides still more specific direction on permissible land uses and the other aspects of land use planning described above. In the event of conflict between the city and regional plans, the policies of the regional plan govern.

Zoning Bylaws

Official plans establish general policies and direct the locations where growth and development will occur. **Zoning bylaws** provide the specific, legally enforceable rules and requirements for the use of land, and for the use and location of buildings and structures on land. Zoning bylaws influence how buildings are constructed by

---

zoning bylaws legally enforceable rules and requirements for the use of land and for the use and location of buildings and structures on land

setting rules about the height, bulk, location, size, floor area, spacing, and general character and use of buildings or structures.

Functions

Generally, local municipalities are responsible for passing zoning bylaws, which have the following functions:[25]

- *Land use.* Zoning bylaws may restrict the specific land uses permitted on certain lands. For example, a zoning bylaw may prohibit the commercial or industrial use of a particular property.
- *Setback requirements.* Zoning bylaws may establish rules for locating buildings by means of setback requirements. For example, zoning bylaws typically establish the amount of frontage required for each building within a zone, the spacing between buildings through side yard zoning, the depth of lots, and the size of front and rear yards.
- *Density control.* Zoning bylaws usually control density by establishing minimum lot sizes and the number of dwelling units permitted on each lot within a zone. Within a particular zone, for example, a zoning bylaw could permit individual dwelling units in one area, medium-density townhouse development in a second area, and high-density apartment buildings in a third area.
- *Building height.* Zoning bylaws may establish the maximum height permitted for buildings within a zoning category. Through this mechanism, the municipality has the ability to establish a range of community types and densities.
- *Parking requirements.* Zoning bylaws may set parking requirements, which raise important considerations for residential, commercial, and industrial development.

Zoning bylaws provide a mechanism for detailed regulatory control over land use. They implement and give the force of law to the environmental and land use planning protections that municipalities seek to establish through official plan policies.

Factors Considered

Factors considered in the drafting of zoning bylaws primarily include the following:

- whether the zoning conforms to the policies and land use designations set out in the official plan, and
- whether land use conflicts might be created by the bylaw.

For example, a decision to rezone in order to permit a high-density development within a residential area typically involves consideration of the development's impact on the neighbourhood, including the adjacent properties. Studies might be required to determine the probable effects, and whether they are acceptable, before a zoning change is approved.

Legal Non-Conforming Uses

It is common, particularly in older areas, to find land or buildings that are being used for purposes other than those permitted by the current zoning bylaw. This situation arises when a zoning bylaw is imposed after an existing use is already established. Hardship would result for users of land if they were suddenly required to cease using their property in the legal manner in which they had been using it. Rather than disrupting businesses or residents in this way, governments give property owners relief from latterly imposed planning rules through a concept called **legal non-conforming uses**.

According to this principle, a pre-existing use on a property is allowed to continue, even if it does not conform to the existing zoning requirements, provided that the use is maintained uninterrupted. If the use is discontinued temporarily, the current zoning requirements come into effect. In most jurisdictions, a legal non-conforming use cannot be expanded without permission.[26]

Subdivision and Land Severances

A critically important tool available to government to protect environmental resources and manage growth is the regulation of the subdivision of land. The potential environmental effects of permitting unchecked division of properties into increasingly smaller individually owned parcels are obvious. Therefore, municipalities are empowered to decide whether new lots may be created and built on. In Ontario the *Planning Act* establishes the following two mechanisms for lot creation:

- grant of consent to sever,[27] and
- approval of plans of subdivision.[28]

Generally, owners apply for **consent to sever** if a proposal involves the creation of only one or two lots. In cases involving more complex lot creation patterns, such as a new housing development, a **plan of subdivision** is required.

During the 1980s, a number of rural Ontario municipalities permitted residential growth through the granting of severances. In Grey County, for example, the number of severances rose from several hundred per year in the early 1980s to almost 2,000 in 1989. Consider the problems that were created:

---

legal non-conforming uses pre-existing uses of a property that are allowed to continue, even though they do not conform to existing zoning requirements

consent to sever permission to divide a lot into usually two lots that may be separately sold and bought

plan of subdivision a plan for dividing a parcel of land into many lots to be sold and bought separately

- The government agencies responsible for reviewing severance decisions and key issues, such as the adequacy of septic systems and the impacts on water supply and wetlands, were not able to respond in a timely way.
- Lots were established on major concession roads, and not through the use of internal secondary road systems, leading to traffic and safety issues.
- The creation of lots adjacent to agricultural operations created the potential for land use conflicts arising from the effects associated with standard farming activities, such as odour, dust, and noise.
- Continuing severances caused gradual fragmentation of farmland, mounting pressure on environmental resources as a result of incremental decision-making, and ultimately the loss of high-quality farmland.

In most municipalities, the granting of severances is closely regulated, particularly in rural areas. In Ontario, the current provincial policy dramatically limits the potential for lot creation of any kind on agricultural lands. New residential lots in prime agricultural areas are permitted only in very limited circumstances.[29] In accordance with this provincial direction, most municipalities in Ontario place significant restrictions on the number of severances that may be granted in rural areas.

In contrast to severances, plans of subdivision provide the opportunity for a more comprehensive community-planning approach. For example, the creation of a series of residential lots through a plan of subdivision requires consideration of the overall impact: the adequacy of utilities, such as drinking water and sanitary sewage treatment; the need for infrastructure, such as roads; and the provision of municipal services, such as policing, education, and health services.

Consents to sever remain useful in the context of existing areas, where severances sometimes provide an opportunity for further development of a particular lot within an established neighbourhood. This procedure is consistent with the policy of increasing residential density in urban areas, an undertaking known as **residential intensification**.

Decision-Making Processes

On the one hand, land use decision-making lends itself to rational policy and rule-making. On the other hand, decisions about land use can involve high drama and high stakes. Behind many planning or zoning decisions are judgments about how best to reconcile or balance private property rights, economic objectives, larger community interests, and long-term environmental land stewardship.

Many stakeholders have an intense interest in the outcome of this balancing act. Consider the following examples:

---

residential intensification redevelopment to add density in residential areas

- Private developers want a return on their investment in lands that they have purchased or acquired rights to. Restrictive planning policies or zoning rules can mean a loss of revenue.
- Neighbouring property owners may object if a vacant lot is turned into an apartment building complex that fundamentally alters the nature and character of the community and creates traffic, noise, and visual changes.
- Municipalities are concerned because planning decisions affect municipal resources, demands on municipal services, and the municipal vision for community-building.
- A planning decision may have broad implications for the mandate of provincial government agencies. For example, the decision to permit a golf course in an ecologically important wetland complex would run directly against the mandate of the Ontario Ministry of Natural Resources to protect these provincially significant natural features.[30]

Given the potential tensions and conflicts associated with land use planning decisions, and the environmental and economic issues at stake, it is important that the decision-making process be seen as accessible, rational, and fair to all stakeholders. Because land use decisions are generally associated with local decision-making, local political accountability is also an important component of the process.

The Decision-Making Process in Ontario

Ontario is used here as an example of how the decision-making process works at the municipal level. Land use planning decisions are triggered in the following two ways:

1. by municipal action to establish new land use policies or zoning rules,[31] or
2. by private action through an application to change land use rules to permit a land development project on a specific property.[32]

The approval processes for municipally and privately initiated proposals are similar, although some differences exist. A land use change triggered by a municipal action—such as a proposed new official plan, secondary plan, or municipality-wide comprehensive zoning bylaw—begins with extensive studies to establish the need for the new planning rules. By contrast, private amendments tend to involve studies specific to a proposed development and property.

MUNICIPAL PROPOSALS   In developing a new official plan, a municipality may be required to carry out municipality-wide studies concerning the following matters:

- population growth projections;
- current demands on municipal and other services, including policing, hospitals, schools, and municipal sewage treatment and water supply facilities;

- transportation needs and current traffic levels on municipal roads;
- inventories of current environmental resources within the municipality, including wetlands, aggregate resources, and agricultural lands;
- inventories of existing employment lands and employment opportunities in the municipality;
- market studies to determine the existing and future need for retail stores and services within the municipality; and
- existing and projected future settlement patterns.

All of this information is analyzed by municipal planners on behalf of the municipality and then translated into a series of policy objectives.

Municipalities usually consult various stakeholders before and during the development of a proposed new official plan or comprehensive zoning bylaw. Stakeholders include businesses, prominent environmental and neighbourhood interest groups, as well as a long list of government agencies responsible for various environmental and public resources that could be affected by land use planning changes.

The *Planning Act* presents formal opportunities for both written and oral submissions. For example, the Act gives members of the public an opportunity to make submissions directly to municipal councils at public meetings.[33]

PRIVATE PROPOSALS   Private development proposals go through a similar process, most often on a smaller scale, because the proposed land use changes typically relate to a specific property or group of adjoining properties. Developers or landowners are required to apply to the municipality to seek the amendments to the official plan that are necessary to allow a particular development to proceed.[34]

Municipalities generally require studies to support these applications. Under the *Planning Act*, a municipality may refuse to review a planning application if sufficient information is not provided.[35] If a private development involves a significant land use change, such as a plan of subdivision or a major industrial or commercial proposal, applications must be accompanied by technical studies covering a range of disciplines.

For example, a residential subdivision usually requires a study to show that the new homes to be built in the subdivision will be adequately serviced with water, sanitary sewage treatment, and traffic access. If the project involves potential effects on environmental resources—such as wetlands, woodlots, or the natural habitat of significant wildlife or plant species—studies must be provided to show that unacceptable effects will not occur.

The level of study and the amount of detail required by the municipality depend on the nature and scale of the development proposal. For example, a consent to sever one or two lots does not generally require as extensive a study as a plan of subdivision that will create a new residential community with 100 homes.

Once a municipality determines that the information provided in support of a study is acceptable, it begins the circulation process to relevant government agencies.[36]

The developer has an opportunity to respond to agency concerns and to make changes to the development or proposal to address these concerns. The municipality also makes the application material available to the public, and gives the public a chance to make submissions, either in writing or orally before council at a public meeting.

COUNCIL DECISION   The municipal council makes a decision on a proposed land use change after reviewing a report from its planning staff on the application and all of the public comments. Notice of the decision is provided to the public.[37]

APPEAL TO THE ONTARIO MUNICIPAL BOARD   Ontario, unlike most jurisdictions in Canada, provides an opportunity for stakeholders who are unhappy with council's decision to appeal to an independent tribunal—the Ontario Municipal Board (OMB). The OMB hears appeals of land use planning decisions by municipal councils with respect to the following:

- official plans and official plan amendments,[38]
- zoning bylaws and amendments,[39]
- approval of consents,[40]
- approval of severances and plans of subdivision,[41] and
- other municipal and planning-related issues.[42]

Hearings at the OMB are less formal than in the courts, but they are run in accordance with specified rules and procedures. Most parties are represented by lawyers, and witnesses are subject to cross-examination.

Tribunals other than the OMB may also have a mandate related to land use and environmental matters. For example, in Ontario the Niagara Escarpment Hearing Office hears appeals of development permit applications and conducts Niagara Escarpment Plan amendment proceedings under the *Niagara Escarpment Planning and Development Act*.[43]

Land Use Planning as a Growth Management Tool

In some parts of Canada, provincial and municipal planning regimes have focused on one critically important function for government-led land use planning: the proper management of growth and development.

Urban Sprawl

A particular concern for jurisdictions is the impact of **urban sprawl**, a product of unchecked urban growth that can have serious long-term adverse consequences. Detrimental effects of urban sprawl include the following:

---

urban sprawl low-density residential growth in rural areas

- loss of prime agricultural land;
- encroachment of human development on natural habitats;
- wasteful public expenditures on infrastructure, such as roads, electricity, water, and sewers, to support low density; and
- unnecessary overreliance on cars and road systems for transportation to serve low-density populations with its attendant negative environmental and economic consequences.

In most Canadian jurisdictions, the current preferred planning approach to growth management is to focus population growth within existing urban areas and adjacent lands. This approach is a response to the economic inefficiencies, wasteful use of land and natural resources, and environmental effects of sprawling low-density residential growth in rural areas.

Intensification

Focusing growth within existing urban areas, through redevelopment and intensification, allows more people to live within the current urban boundaries, helps support improvements in public transit, and better uses other existing services and infrastructure. Redevelopment through intensification also reduces the need to accommodate growth through additional land consumption, thereby avoiding the loss of good agricultural lands and the extension of human activities into natural areas.

Ontario has taken specific steps to manage population and growth at the macro level through the following regulatory and related policy initiatives:

- creation of the Greenbelt Plan,[44] which imposes restrictive land use policies on rural areas across a portion of southern Ontario, in conjunction with the Niagara Escarpment Plan[45] and the Oak Ridges Moraine Plan;[46]
- passage of the *Places to Grow Act, 2005*, which allows the province to establish growth management plans that identify where and how growth should occur in the province;[47] and
- preparation of Ontario's first **growth plan**, the Growth Plan for the Greater Golden Horseshoe (GPGGH), which establishes growth management policies for a broad and populous urban band in southern Ontario and encompasses the Greater Toronto Area, Hamilton, and other surrounding urban municipalities.[48]

All of the measures above direct population and employment growth to existing urban areas. For example, the GPGGH establishes a series of growth management requirements, including intensification objectives, to which the official plans of municipalities within the Greater Golden Horseshoe must conform.[49]

---

growth plan a plan that identifies where and how growth should occur

Placing controls on the expansion of existing settlement area boundaries is a priority in Ontario. For example, the GPGGH states that a settlement boundary expansion can occur only as part of a "municipal comprehensive review" that clearly demonstrates the need for such an expansion. This review must show, among other things, that insufficient opportunities currently exist to accommodate forecasted growth through intensification within the existing settlement boundary.[50]

Growth plans also identify urban growth areas within which municipalities must ensure that certain density targets for both residence and jobs are met.[51] Municipalities are mandated to plan urban growth centres as the focal points for investment in public services as well as commercial, recreational, cultural, and entertainment uses.[52] The GPGGH also directs municipalities to bring jobs closer to where people live by allocating an adequate supply of lands for employment uses.[53]

These new policies are largely focused on a single objective: to reverse the trend of urban sprawl that has emerged in Ontario over the last 40 years and reduce or eliminate the pressure on environmental and agricultural land resources in rural areas.

Future Challenges

Planning direction at the provincial level ushered in through the *Places to Grow Act, 2005* and the *Greenbelt Act, 2005* is unprecedented. Ontario is clearly aiming to close loopholes that led to inefficient and environmentally expensive development in the rural parts of the province. It remains to be seen whether these measures will be effective.

For example, although it has been about ten years since the passage of the *Places to Grow Act, 2005*, we do not yet know what will happen if municipalities fail to meet the provincially set growth targets or veer away from provincial policies. There is no clear enforcement mechanism.

Further, there may yet be a backlash against the restrictive nature of these policies. Some development interests have argued that the policies are unfair to rural communities included in the Greenbelt Plan area and artificially limit the availability of a full range of housing types and locations because of the focus on urban redevelopment and intensification (see the case study at the beginning of Chapter 3).

Brownfields Redevelopment

One principle of land use policy that has won broad acceptance in recent years is the value of brownfields redevelopment. **Brownfields** are abandoned, underused,

---

brownfields   abandoned, underused, or derelict sites of previous human activity, such as crumbling factories, old railway yards, and condemned apartments

or derelict sites of previous human activity. They may include crumbling factories, old railway yards, or condemned apartments. These sites are often located within or near urban centres.

From the perspective of efficiency and resource management, it makes more sense to explore opportunities to redevelop lands that have already been subject to the long-term stresses of human activity than to expand the human footprint into greenfield locations. Within Canada's existing urban areas, an estimated 30,000 to 100,000 brownfield sites could be redeveloped. While the concept seems sound—even obvious—implementation has proven to be a great challenge.

Environmental Liability

The key challenge facing the redevelopment of brownfields is the risk of environmental liability. Before obtaining land use planning approvals from a municipality, a developer must conduct investigations to assess the environmental quality of a site by testing soils and groundwater.[54] Few developers are willing to take on the unknown risks associated with ownership of sites that may be seriously contaminated. Consider the following:

- *Unforeseen contamination.* Investigation can be expensive, and the level of thoroughness required is usually difficult to assess at the outset. For example, a routine investigation of an abandoned apartment complex might, on closer inspection, reveal that the lot had also been used as a dumping ground for toxic chemicals.
- *Unforeseen cleanup costs.* The result of an investigation can impose new financial obligations on a developer and landowner. For example, if contamination in groundwater is found to be affecting neighbouring properties, the current property owner may be ordered by the Ministry of the Environment to clean it up.[55]
- *Unforeseen legal claims.* The potential for offsite contamination also raises the possibility of private legal claims from neighbours whose properties are affected.

In order to redevelop brownfield sites, developers must initiate a process that has much cost, risk, and uncertainty associated with it. All of these costs, risks, and liabilities come with no guarantee that the redevelopment will even be approved. It is not surprising that developers prefer fresh, clean sites.

Ironically, when developers are deterred from brownfields redevelopment, not only is the opportunity for redevelopment lost, but buried environmental problems are also left unaddressed, and greater harm may result from the migration of contaminants. As time goes on, it becomes even less likely that the original polluter will be found and required to pay any of the cleanup costs.

Ontario Initiatives to Encourage Brownfields Redevelopment

Most governments recognize both the value of brownfields redevelopment and the circumstances that discourage private investment. Consequently, governments wishing to advance brownfields redevelopment have been moving to reduce the costs and risks of environmental liability. Ontario has taken a number of steps to reduce them:

- *Records of site condition.* Records of site condition must be filed with an environmental site registrar to certify that a development site meets appropriate standards for soil and groundwater quality.[56] A regulatory process has been put in place for obtaining records of site condition that could involve detailed and very expensive investigations and cleanup measures.[57] However, once a record of site condition is registered, it provides current and future owners with limited protection from orders made by the Ministry of the Environment.[58]
- *Grants and loans.* The Ontario *Planning Act* gives municipalities the power to establish "Community Improvement Plans" under which grants and loans can be made available to developers to defray the costs of cleanup of brownfield sites.[59]
- *Tax cancellation.* The *Municipal Act* permits the passage of bylaws cancelling property taxes on contaminated properties under certain conditions.[60]
- *Mortgage incentives.* The *Environmental Protection Act* provides incentives for mortgages to extend funding to developers of brownfield properties by protecting them from orders made by the Ministry of the Environment.[61]

Innovative developers, in cooperation with forward-looking municipalities, have succeeded in a few cases in advancing major redevelopment projects. In most cases, however, the risks of incurring environmental liability, the costs of investigation, and the costs of cleaning up contamination have discouraged positive action. To encourage redevelopment, conditions have to be right: the site must have a high revenue-generating potential, and the risks of environmental liability must be known and manageable.

While governmental measures provide some relief from risks, they are not likely to lead to significant private sector investment in brownfields redevelopment. Ultimately, the willingness of private developers to reclaim lands saddled with historical contamination will likely depend upon the market value of the land in its redeveloped and environmentally improved state.

Watershed Planning and Source Water Protection

As discussed in the previous section, in Canadian jurisdictions land use planning and management decisions are usually based on municipal boundaries. Local governments have primary responsibility for producing the planning rules that govern decisions on land use and the protection of environmental resources, subject to any constraints that exist within provincial or federal environmental legislation. However, alternative planning models that are not based on political boundaries exist. One of the most important of these is watershed planning.

A **watershed** is an area of land from which all water drains into a common body of water, such as a lake or river. **Watershed planning** refers to a scale of planning that is based on natural watershed boundaries and hence extends beyond political boundaries.

The traditional municipality-by-municipality approach to land use planning has a long history in Canada and works well for many types of planning decisions. Its principle advantage is that it is convenient and time-efficient for each municipality to conduct its affairs independently and irrespectively of what neighbouring municipalities are doing. The effectiveness of the approach starts to break down, however, when one considers the challenges of protecting surface and groundwater resources.

Water does not respect political boundaries, and when individual municipalities make decisions in isolation, they are unable to factor in the needs of the watershed as a whole or the needs of neighbouring municipalities. For example, if upstream Town A is experiencing a rapid growth in its economy and population, its heavy water usage and growing tendency to pollute may endanger Town B downstream. The situation will continue to degenerate unless the two towns can enter into a joint planning structure whereby they become aware of, and take into account, the effects of their actions on each other and the environment as a whole. If watershed planning were put into practice, the two towns would benefit by

- sharing the information and expertise necessary to assess the overall health of, and broader impacts on, the watershed; and
- gaining access to a planning structure in which the towns' councils could work collaboratively with other councils and stakeholders to develop appropriate land use policies and controls, taking into account not only their own needs, but also the ecological needs of the watershed itself.

Since the effects of human consumption and pollution are experienced across the whole watershed, it makes sense that the planning process should be conducted on the same scale. Additionally, if the ecological integrity of key watershed features—such as wetlands, forests, and shorelines—falters, the water resource is threatened.

---

watershed an area of land from which all water drains into a common body of water, such as a lake or river

watershed planning a scale of planning that is based on natural watershed boundaries and hence extends beyond political boundaries

Watershed Planning in Ontario

Although Ontario's land use planning regime generally follows the traditional approach based on municipal boundaries, it also has a lengthy experience and history with watershed management. In 1946, in response to the concerns of farmers, naturalists, and others regarding the degradation of the environment through poor land, water, and forestry management practices,[62] the Government of Ontario passed the *Conservation Authorities Act*. This Act created watershed-based entities called *conservation authorities*. Conservation Ontario defines **conservation authorities** as "local, community-based environmental agencies … [that] represent a grouping of municipalities on a watershed basis and work in partnership with others to manage their respective watersheds."[63]

Southern and central Ontario is now blanketed by 36 conservation authorities, each with jurisdiction over one or more watersheds. While the primary impetus for the creation of conservation authorities was flooding and erosion issues caused by deforestation, over the years, their roles and responsibilities have grown. In addition to their role in physically managing watercourses to control flooding and prevent erosion,[64] conservation authorities have been granted regulatory responsibility for floodplain protection and approval authority over development proposal that could affect wetlands and other environmental features within watersheds or along shorelines.[65]

Conservation authorities are also relied upon by many municipalities to provide input into municipal land use planning decisions with respect to floodplains and hazardous lands and the protection of environmental features.

Despite the increased role of conservation authorities, watershed planning continues to take a back seat to planning based on municipal boundaries in Ontario. Until recently,[66] conservation authorities were not allocated any direct authority over long-term land use planning decisions within their watershed boundaries; that power remained principally within the jurisdiction of municipal governments.[67]

The Walkerton Tragedy

In 2000 the contamination of drinking water in Walkerton, Ontario stunned the province and devastated the small town, which suffered the death of 7 residents and the illness of 2,300. The source of the problem was E. coli contamination that originated from manure spread on farmland mere metres from a municipal well. The owner of the farm, who followed best management practices, was unaware that the municipal well was situated so close to his property.[68]

---

conservation authorities local watershed management agencies that deliver services and programs that protect and manage water and other natural resources in partnership with government, landowners, and other organizations

Shortly after the tragedy, Justice Dennis O'Connor was appointed commissioner of the Walkerton Inquiry. Following an in-depth investigation of the incident, Justice O'Connor released a two-volume report. The second volume includes 93 recommendations that comprise a broad-ranging strategy for regulatory reform to ensure safe drinking water.[69] The report criticized the weak environmental laws that had allowed the municipality's source of drinking water to become contaminated. One of Justice O'Connor's primary recommendations was that "[d]rinking water sources should be protected by developing watershed-based source protection plans. Source protection plans should be required for all watersheds in Ontario."[70]

Over the next six years, the Government of Ontario began the daunting task of implementing Justice O'Connor's recommendations. The initial changes involved new legislation governing the treatment of drinking water and concentrated on operator licensing and training, laboratory requirements, and standards for drinking water quality.[71] However, it was not until 2006 that one of the final (and potentially most important) pieces of legislation was passed: the Ontario *Clean Water Act*,[72] which was designed to protect the *sources* of drinking water on a watershed scale.

Ontario's Clean Water Act

Ontario's *Clean Water Act* introduced a process for assessing threats to drinking water sources and, where necessary, reducing these threats through land use restrictions and other protective policies set out in "source protection plans."[73] The process is guided by multi-stakeholder "source protection committees" composed of representatives from municipalities; the agricultural, commercial, and industrial sectors; and other interested parties such as environmental groups, health groups, and the general public.[74]

Conservation authorities have an important role to play under the *Clean Water Act*. Following the recommendations of the Walkerton Inquiry, the legislation directs that source protection activities be organized on a watershed-planning scale, roughly adhering to the existing watershed-based boundaries of the province's conservation authorities.[75] Conservation authorities designated under the Act as "drinking water source protection" authorities are charged with the responsibility of establishing the source water protection committees and overseeing the development of source water protection plans. They provide scientific and administrative support and resources, and ensure that key documents are made available to the public.[76]

Once approved, source protection plans have the potential to become powerful planning tools. In the case of conflict between significant threat policies of source protection plans and other planning requirements such as municipal official plans, zoning bylaws, and provincial policy statements, the source protection policies prevail. All planning decisions made in the province must also conform with these significant threat policies.[77] In addition, Part IV of the Act allocates enforcement responsibilities to municipalities including responsibility to regulate existing uses that pose a threat to drinking water sources. Specifically, municipalities are required to appoint "risk management officials" and inspectors who are empowered to impose and enforce risk management plans on businesses and properties which pose a significant risk to drinking water.[78]

The *Clean Water Act* is a potential advancement in the way governments protect the environment because of the inclusion of three innovative elements. First, it introduces the concept of "three-dimensional" land use planning rules that extend below the ground surface to protect underground water resources. Second, the approach gives greater clout to watershed planning rules that extend beyond municipal boundaries. Finally, one of the most revolutionary, and potentially controversial, components is the authority given to municipal risk management officers to impose restrictions on existing uses that are posing a significant threat to drinking water, including the authority to effectively shut down pre-existing businesses.

Remaining Challenges

The *Clean Water Act* is a groundbreaking piece of legislation because it brings together stakeholders, conducts assessments, and plans responses on a watershed scale. It also provides municipalities with the additional powers needed to implement a range of risk management measures to reduce significant threats. Despite these progressive and innovative features, the *Clean Water Act* is not without its drawbacks. Specifically, its approach falls short of true watershed planning in three important ways:

1. *Human-centred assessment and risk-management measures.* Because the core rationale for the Act is to protect source water for the specific needs of human populations, the resulting source water planning does not necessarily consider the broader needs of the ecosystem. The assessment, planning, and risk-management measures are therefore all tied to drinking water protection objectives with little or no consideration of plant life, fisheries, wildlife, or their habitat.

2. *Geographical limitations.* Although it made sense to use the existing boundaries of the conservation authorities as a foundation for the source protection regions, the effect of this decision has been to exclude a large geographical portion of the province. Conservation authorities cover only southern Ontario and select parts of central and northern Ontario. As a result, the northern portions of the province that do not have conservation authorities do not enjoy the legislative protection that is available in southern Ontario.

3. *The exclusion of First Nations water systems and private wells.* The Act does not automatically encompass First Nations water systems or non-municipal water systems.[79] A First Nations band council must make a request to Cabinet that its system be included by regulation, and a non-municipal water system

can only be included by a resolution of a municipal council or a ministerial amendment.[80]

The challenges of implementing the *Clean Water Act* are evident from its slow regulatory rollout. The Act has been in force for almost ten years, and only 3 of 36 source protection plans are in place.[81] While it is expected that the remaining source protections plans will finally be in effect in 2015, municipalities are bracing for the complex, potentially contentious, but crucially important implementation tasks that lay ahead: putting in place risk management measures to ensure municipal drinking water threats are addressed.

Future Challenges

Watershed planning is becoming an increasingly popular approach to water protection. Although Ontario is considered to be a leader in source water protection, other jurisdictions are making progress in watershed planning in a variety of areas. A central challenge facing planners and legislators is the need to coordinate planning across national, regional (provincial and/or state), and local jurisdictions.

BOX 11.1 » The Navigation Protection Act

At the federal level, one of the most significant and controversial changes to the regulation of water resources occurred in 2012 with the passage of the *Navigation Protection Act* (formerly the *Navigable Waters Protection Act*, which dates to 1882). Part of the controversy stemmed from the fact that this important piece of legislation was buried along with many others in the second of a massive, two-part omnibus bill (Bill C-45, the *Jobs and Growth Act, 2012*, part of the Conservative government's federal budget), which allowed for little if any debate on the issues involved. Such significant legislative changes relating to environmental matters are not typically found in a budget bill.

While it is intended to reduce red tape, many First Nations and environmental groups maintain that the vast majority of Canada's lakes and rivers will be left with no protection under the Act and subject to varied and shifting provincial regulations, and that only 10 of Canada's 37 heritage rivers will retain federal protection. The Act's new name is also noteworthy: the change from "navigable waters" to "navigation protection" suggests a new emphasis on various human uses of waterways, instead of a focus on environmental protection for its own sake.

Critics are concerned that this policy shift opens the door for industries to have much easier access to water resources to meet their needs, without the usual oversight. For instance, major pipeline and interprovincial power line projects are now exempt from previous regulations that had required industry to show that their proposals would not damage navigable waterways.

Proponents of the changes say that the existing environmental assessment and review process had grown vastly complex, resulting in unnecessary delays and costs, and that a "one project, one review" approach was required. Critics note, however, that while it is entirely normal and acceptable for industry groups to lobby the government with policy recommendations, in the case of the *Navigation Protection Act*, industry's goals were enshrined in legislation without sufficient consultation or debate.

Source: Sarah Stenabaugh, "Bill C-45: What's All the Fuss?" *The Northern Times*, January 16, 2013, http://www.kapuskasingtimes .com/2013/01/16/bill-c-45-whats-all-the-fuss; and Heather Scofield, "Documents Reveal Pipeline Industry Drove Changes to Navigable Waters Act," *CTV News*, February 20, 2013, http:// www.ctvnews.ca/politics/documents-reveal-pipeline-industry -drove-changes-to-navigable-waters-act-1.1164476.

Consider the joint effort by Canada and the United States to address significant issues facing the Great Lakes through the Great Lakes Water Quality Agreement. The Great Lakes Water Quality Agreement Review Working Group, which is charged with reviewing aspects of the Agreement, created a subgroup to address watershed planning and land use. This subgroup has recognized the challenges that are inherent in implementing watershed planning in the Great Lakes, given the disconnect that exists between local governments (which are typically responsible for land use planning) and federal governments (which are parties to the Great Lakes Water Quality Agreement). One of the subgroup's recommendations states that:

> Canada and the U.S. should cooperate to address the issue [the effects of land use patterns on chemical, biological and physical integrity of the waters of the Great Lakes ecosystem] by pursuing policies and common goals that improve the consistency of watershed planning across the Basin, and by increasing the role that watershed planning can have on local development decisions, on watersheds, and, ultimately, on the water quality of the Great Lakes.[82]

Electric Power Systems

Not long ago, governments and electricity generators thought that ensuring a reliable supply of electricity simply meant anticipating growth in demand and responding by planning for and building more generating units—usually big new plants powered by hydroelectricity, nuclear technology, or fossil fuels—and expanding the grid of transmission lines. Now, virtually everyone understands that each of the three conventional generation options is problematic. Big hydro projects disrupt watershed ecosystems and associated livelihoods. Nuclear plants require extraordinary safety efforts in operation and leave highly toxic radioactive wastes. And fossil fuel plants discharge smog-producing emissions and contribute to climate change. Moreover, reliance on a transmission grid with only a few big generating sources makes electric power systems inflexible and vulnerable to system failure if one component runs into difficulty.

In response, most jurisdictions are shifting their approach to electrical energy to include two new components: promoting electricity conservation and demand management, rather than simply meeting growing electricity demand, and gradually converting to a diversity of small-scale renewable energy sources. These changes have been accompanied by a third innovation. To manage the transition and to facilitate coherent design and operation of the more complex results, progressive jurisdictions have moved toward more integrated and somewhat more open electric power system planning. The objective is power systems that are more cost-effective, less threatening to climate stability and human health, more compatible with environmental integrity, more flexible and adaptable, less vulnerable to catastrophic breakdown, and as a result more viable over the long run.

Conservation and Demand Management

Electricity **conservation and demand management** approaches are based on recognition that every kilowatt-hour reduction of demand for electricity is a kilowatt-hour that does not have to be generated and transported through the transmission system. Governments and electricity providers in many jurisdictions have found that it is often cheaper to encourage investment in reducing electricity demand—overall and at particular times to match generating capacity—than it is to build more generating plants and transmission lines to service inefficient use.

Efficiencies in electrical energy use can be achieved in many ways. Major options include the following:

- energy conservation, often achieved through simple waste reduction such as turning off lights in unoccupied rooms and buildings;
- conversion of industry, offices, and homes to new, more energy efficient technologies, lighting, and products (such as high-efficiency appliances), as well as more efficient generation and transmission in the electricity system itself;
- peak shaving, which involves shifting a portion of electricity demand to off-peak times to make better use of existing generating capacity; and
- energy source shifting (sometimes called *fuel substitution*) to non-electricity sources for efficiency gains, which could include (1) switching from electricity to natural gas usage (e.g., for water heating) to avoid the costly expansion of the electricity generating system; (2) replacing electrical energy from the grid with energy from other resources, such as wood or agricultural waste, for on-site co-generation of steam and electricity; and (3) matching energy quality to end-use needs, which favours using high-quality electrical energy for purposes that only electricity can serve effectively (e.g., powering computers) rather than purposes that can be served effectively by lower-quality energy sources (e.g., heating indoor spaces to comfortable ambient temperatures using solar or geothermal heat).

While conservation and demand management initiatives require public and private expenditures in education and promotion, incentives, and the adoption of technologies, they avoid the often much higher costs of new supply. In 2013, Ontario calculated that it had avoided about $2 in electricity system costs for every $1 of energy efficiency investment.[83] In addition to cost savings, efficiency initiatives avoid the increased resource demands, contaminant emissions, waste production, and land

conservation and demand management   initiatives aimed at reducing overall electricity demand or reducing demand at particular times to match generating capacity, recognizing that reducing demand can be much less expensive than building new generation and transmission capacity

disturbances that accompany new generation and transmission projects. Often they also have beneficial side effects such as more dispersed employment, higher productivity, and reduced dependency on electricity supply systems that may fail.

Measures to promote energy efficiency and conservation have been facilitated, encouraged, or required through law-based actions by all levels of government. The federal *Energy Efficiency Act*, for example, allows the federal government to make regulations prescribing efficiency and labelling requirements and to initiate programs fostering efficiency research and education. The federal government established a non-legislated model building code that provincial governments have used, with adjustments and expansions, under provincial law to require efficiency improvements in new construction. Both levels of government have imposed minimum appliance efficiency regulations and have adjusted tax policies to encourage the purchase of energy-efficient products.

Provincial governments have more direct authority than the federal government over electricity systems, and provincial Crown corporations are major players or monopolies in many provincial electricity markets. Therefore, the provinces have a greater ability to set pricing regimes and use other tools to encourage conservation and demand management steps in electricity generation and transmission by industrial, commercial, and residential consumers.

Renewable Energy Sources

In much of Canada, electric power planning now also places greater emphasis on smaller-scale renewable energy sources for new supply. These renewable energy options include the following:

- wind energy,
- solar arrays,
- small-scale hydroelectricity plants, and
- thermal generators burning biomass wastes or landfill gases.

While all of these sources have some undesirable aspects, they are generally much less damaging to the environment than the conventional large-scale hydro, nuclear, and fossil fuel options. Especially when combined with conservation and demand management initiatives, inclusion of small-scale renewable generation makes electric power systems more flexible and adaptable. The increased number and diversity of generation sources allows quicker response to changes in demand, avoids dependence on a few big power sources, and reduces risks of system failure. Compared with conventional large-scale generating facilities, the smaller renewable options generally require less up-front capital, can be located in a broader range of places, and are more likely to provide employment opportunities in or near existing population centres.

Federal, provincial, territorial, and even municipal governments have a wide variety of law-based tools available to facilitate and encourage greater electricity production from renewable sources. They can, for example, require utilities to include at least a minimum percentage of renewable-sourced electricity in their portfolios, introduce subsidies, ensure secure base prices for renewable energy suppliers, contract directly for construction of renewable energy facilities, or purchase electrical power from these facilities.

In addition, governments can support the transition to renewable energy sources indirectly. For example, initiatives to address the full costs of conventional energy sources reduce their advantages relative to small-scale renewable sources. Since 2007, British Columbia has required all fossil-fuel fired thermal-generating facilities to have no net greenhouse gas emissions.[84] Ontario, recognizing the costs of health damage due to smog as well as climate change effects, chose to phase out its existing coal-burning power plants, which once supplied 25 percent of the province's power.[85] Both provinces' efforts have opened the field for more emphasis on renewable energy sources.

Energy System Transition

It is not easy to move from the relatively simple practice of building big, new supply plants to meet rising demand, to planning and managing a more complex system that combines conventional sources with a wide range of conservation and demand management efforts and small-scale renewable energy generation. Several levels of government and a variety of legal, financial, and other tools are involved. Moreover, the electricity-focused purposes overlap with other considerations. In addition to objectives related to energy efficiency and climate change, electricity systems are often expected to enhance economic competitiveness, regional development, provincial self-sufficiency, and international trade.

Electricity system planning needs to respect consumer concerns about near-term electricity rates but also look ahead several decades or more. Many individual electricity options require many years from initial conception to practical implementation, and overall energy system transition is a necessarily gradual process that needs a long-term target. The shifts move ahead over time as older facilities (e.g., nuclear power plants) reach the end of their useful lives, newer renewable technologies (e.g., wind and solar photovoltaic energy) advance through testing and innovation, and consumers achieve increasing levels of efficiencies. Energy system transitions are also buffeted by shifting political winds and challenged by uncertainties surrounding many factors that may influence the growth or decline in electricity demand and the speed of technological change (e.g., How soon will governments be driven to act decisively on cutting greenhouse gas emissions? How quickly will the costs of solar and wind options decline? Will there be a major shift to electric vehicles? Will the proliferation of industrial robotics and consumer electronics lead to more overall efficiencies or more overall demand for electricity?).

To address all of these matters at once, many provincial electricity authorities have been pushed into integrated system planning—choosing among various possible combinations and interdependencies involving many generation, conservation, and demand management components—to determine which evolving package will best serve all the multiple objectives and minimize undesirable trade-offs. The work is technically difficult not only because of the number of complex components but also because of the complex interrelations among the components. At the same time, however, much of the decision-making is about preferences. It involves weighing priorities and making decisions in the face of uncertainty.

For environmental law, the move to integrated system planning has implications for the nature of decision-making processes as well as for the authority, structure, and substance of the resulting system plans. The relevant legislation and regulations must establish and assign responsibility to undertake integrated system planning, include some specifics about what is to be incorporated (e.g., renewable generation plus conservation and demand management as well as more conventional generation and transmission), and set some rules about how key concerns (e.g., appropriate financing, electricity rates, and system reliability) are to be addressed. But no less important are the provisions affecting the processes of planning, review, and decision-making.

Integrated electricity system planning is generally accepted as a task of government. The particular structures, however, vary considerably across the country. While ultimate authority typically rests with the provincial or territorial Cabinet, the main planning work may be assigned to the ministry with responsibility for electric power matters, the public electricity utility (if there is one), a public utility planning agency, an electricity regulator or commission, or some combination of these entities.

In most if not all cases, a major and contentious issue for law and practice is whether the decision-making is subject to arm's-length public review. Ontario and British Columbia, for example, have both wavered between having public reviews of integrated system plans and retreating into the less open exercise of political authority. In both cases, public reviews have identified serious deficiencies in proposed plans and have encouraged rethinking in the provinces' best interests. But the experiences did not leave the provincial authorities well pleased, and neither province now has an established process of independent oversight and public review for its energy system planning.[86]

As with decision-making in many of the other areas discussed in this book, planning and managing a transition to more sophisticated and sustainable electrical energy demand and supply systems involve choices that can be informed by experts and facilitated by well-structured decision-making processes. However, they are ultimately matters of public preference. The laws that ensure public access to information and effective opportunities to participate in the deliberations can be just as important as the laws that support regulatory requirements and pricing rules.

SUMMARY OF KEY POINTS

- Legislation concerning public lands has largely taken the form of sectoral natural resource development laws. The result has been major problems such as fragmented decision-making, incrementalism, the pre-emption effect, and cumulative effects. Competing pressures on public lands and their resources have increased, and so too have political tensions and higher expectations for transparent, participative, and fair decision-making. Gradually, public land planning practices have moved toward more comprehensive and better-integrated means of coping with the associated challenges of meeting present demands without undermining future opportunities. The ecologies and socio-economic activities on public lands are dynamic and interrelated and, therefore, good management decisions need to be based on understanding these interrelationships and the factors that influence them.

- Canada's protected areas system is subject to many laws and regulations. The *Canada National Parks Act*, which sets aside parks for public benefit, appreciation, and enjoyment, requires that the parks be maintained in an unimpaired state for future generations.

- Many laws work to protect animal and plant species when their survival is threatened or endangered by human development. A national accord was signed in 1996 in recognition of the fact that protecting endangered species requires cooperation among governments. This accord committed Canada's governments to establishing complementary legislation and programs that provide for effective protection of species at risk throughout Canada. The *Species at Risk Act* addresses those aspects of endangered species protection and recovery that are within federal jurisdiction.

- Land use planning requires not only the application of planning principles in a scientific way but also a fair and open decision-making process for all stakeholders. Professional planners use a set of assessment tools for making decisions, but land use planning also encompasses the public, and this often leads to very contentious debate. Decision-makers attempt to weigh and balance various elements, including private and public interests, economic versus environmental goals, and present and future needs. Often no clearly right or wrong answers exist.

- While land use planning decisions are usually based on municipal boundaries, alternative planning models that are not based on political boundaries exist. One of the most important of these is watershed planning, which refers to a scale of planning based on natural watershed boundaries, not political boundaries. Because water does not respect political boundaries, individual municipalities cannot make decisions in isolation, but need to factor in the needs of the watershed as a whole, and the needs of neighbouring municipalities.

- It is widely understood that conventional methods for producing electricity—hydroelectric projects, nuclear technology, burning fossil fuels—are problematic. In response, most jurisdictions are promoting electricity conservation and demand management, and converting to various small-scale renewable energy sources. Some jurisdictions are also developing more integrated system planning. The goal is to create power systems that are more cost-effective, flexible, and adaptable; pose less of a threat to climate stability and human health; and are less vulnerable to catastrophic breakdown.

KEY TERMS

brownfields
consent to sever
conservation and demand management
conservation authorities
conservation easement
Crown land
ecological integrity
growth plan
land use planning
legal non-conforming uses

plan of subdivision
regional and municipal official plans
residential intensification
secondary plans
species at risk
urban sprawl
watershed
watershed planning
zoning bylaws

DISCUSSION QUESTIONS

1. What are some of the current challenges involved in managing Crown land, and how are approaches to it evolving in Canada?

2. Single-species protection and recovery efforts may have been well-suited to species suffering from relatively straightforward threats such as over-hunting. As more species are put at risk by habitat loss and climate change, how should approaches to biological conservation change?

3. What role can land use planning play in the protection of environmental features and functions?

4. What are the pros and cons of allowing municipalities to have primary control over land use decisions? Should other levels of government (federal or provincial) control certain aspects of this decision-making process? If yes, which aspects and why?

5. This chapter identifies a number of barriers to the cleanup and redevelopment of brownfield sites, even though some governments have made efforts to encourage this type of redevelopment. What tools and approaches can you think of to surmount those barriers?

6. What are the advantages and challenges of basing a land use planning regime on a watershed rather than municipal boundaries?

7. What challenges do you foresee in implementing legislation aimed at protecting sources of drinking water, such as Ontario's *Clean Water Act*? How would you meet those challenges?

8. Integrated electricity system planning is generally accepted as a task of government and that decision-making and many of the key options are matters of public preference as much as technical analysis. What are the most important choices to be made, and what are the advantages and disadvantages of open public reviews of proposed integrated electricity system plans?

SUGGESTED READINGS

Readings

Dunsky, Philippe. *The Role and Value of Demand-Side Management in Manitoba Hydro's Resource Planning Process* [testimony to the Manitoba Public Utilities Board]. Montreal: Dunsky Energy Consulting, 2014, http://www.pub.gov.mb.ca/nfat/pdf/demand_side_management_dunsky.pdf.

Makuch, Stanley M., Neil Craik, and Signe B. Leisk. *Canadian Municipal and Planning Law*, 2nd ed. Toronto: Carswell, 2004.

O'Connor, Hon. Dennis R. *Report of the Walkerton Inquiry, Part One: The Events of May 2000 and Related Issues.* Toronto: Queen's Printer for Ontario, 2002, http://www.attorneygeneral.jus.gov.on.ca/english/about/pubs/walkerton/part1/.

O'Connor, Hon. Dennis R. *Report of the Walkerton Inquiry, Part Two: A Strategy for Clean Drinking Water.* Toronto: Queen's Printer for Ontario, 2002, http://www.attorneygeneral.jus.gov.on.ca/english/about/pubs/walkerton/part2/.

Rian, Allen, and Philippa Campsie. *Implementing the Growth Plan for the Greater Golden Horseshoe: Has the Strategic Regional Vision Been Compromised?* Toronto: Neptis Foundation, 2013, http://www.neptis.org/publications/reports.

Rowlands, Ian H. "Renewable Electricity: Provincial Perspectives and National Prospects." In Debora L. VanNijnatten, ed., *Canadian Environmental Politics and Policy: The Challenges of Austerity and Ambivalence*, 4th ed. Don Mills, ON: Oxford University Press, forthcoming.

Websites

Biodivcanada.ca: http://www.biodivcanada.ca/default.asp?lang=en&n=DABC84B3-1

Environment Canada, "Comprehensive Approach to Clean Water": http://www.ec.gc.ca/eau-water/default.asp?lang=En&n=B1128A3D-1

Ontario, "Crown Land": https://www.ontario.ca/rural-and-north/crown-land

Ontario Ministry of Municipal Affairs and Housing, "Land Use Planning": http://www.mah.gov.on.ca/Page186.aspx

NOTES

1. Ontario, "Crown Land," 2014, https://www.ontario.ca/rural-and-north/crown-land.

2. *Constitution Act*, 1867, 30 & 31 Vict., c. 3., ss. 91, 92, 92A.

3. Ibid., s. 91(24).

4. See British Columbia, "Strategic Land and Resource Planning," 2014, http://www
.for.gov.bc.ca/tasb/SLRP/.

5. Biodivcanada, "Draft 2020 Biodiversity Goals and Targets for Canada," last modified
July 4, 2014, http://www.biodivcanada.ca/default.asp?lang=En&n=00248250-1.

6. Canada, Committee on the Status of Endangered Wildlife in Canada, "Widespread
Species in Canada Losing Ground," news release, December 1, 2013, http://www
.cosewic.gc.ca/eng/sct7/sct7_3_23_e.cfm.

7. "Canada Opts Not to Block International Trade in 76 Endangered Species," *CBC
News*, December 10, 2014, http://www.cbc.ca/news/technology/canada-opts-not
-to-block-international-trade-in-76-endangered-species-1.2867437.

8. *Planning Act*, RSO 1990, c. P.13, as amended, s. 3.

9. Ontario Ministry of Municipal Affairs and Housing, *Provincial Policy Statement*
(Toronto: Queen's Printer for Ontario, 2014), http://www.mah.gov.on.ca/
AssetFactory.aspx?did=10463.

10. Ibid., part V, s. 1.0.

11. Ibid., part V, ss. 2.1, 2.2.

12. Ibid., part V, s. 2.3.

13. Ibid., part V, ss. 2.4, 2.5.

14. Ibid., part V, s. 1.8.

15. Niagara Escarpment Commission, "Niagara Escarpment Plan," 2014,
http://escarpment.org/landplanning/plan; established pursuant to the *Niagara
Escarpment Planning and Development Act*, RSO 1990, c. N.2, as amended.

16. Ontario Ministry of Municipal Affairs and Housing, "Oak Ridges Moraine Conservation Plan," last modified November 8, 2010, http://www.mah.gov.on.ca/
Page1707.aspx; established pursuant to the *Oak Ridges Moraine Conservation Act,
2001*, SO 2001, c. 31.

17. Ontario Ministry of Municipal Affairs and Housing, "The Greenbelt Plan," last
modified January 9, 2013, http://www.mah.gov.on.ca/Page189.aspx; established
pursuant to the *Greenbelt Act, 2005*, SO 2005, c. 1, as amended.

18. Capital Regional District, *State of the Region Report: 2008 Regional Growth Strategy
Five-Year Monitoring Review* (Victoria: Planning and Protective Services, 2008), at
1, https://www.crd.bc.ca/docs/default-source/regional-planning-pdf/RGS/
2008-state-of-the-region-report.pdf?sfvrsn=0.

19. *Planning Act*, supra note 7, s. 27.

20. Ibid., s. 21.

21. Ibid., s. 26.

22. Ibid., s. 22.

23. Ibid., s. 23.

24. Ibid., s. 24(1).

25. See, e.g., *Planning Act*, supra note 7, s. 34(1).

26. See, e.g., ibid., s. 45(2).

27. Ibid., s. 53.

28. Ibid., s. 51.

29. Ontario Ministry of Municipal Affairs and Housing, supra note 9, s. 2.3.4.1.

30. This was the subject of an Ontario Municipal Board decision: *Re: Ontario Ministry of Municipal Affairs and Housing and Stella Ziff et al.*, OMB Case No. PL050640 (August 14, 2008). The OMB refused planning applications to establish a golf course based on the golf course's predicted effects on a wetland that had been identified by the Ministry of Natural Resources as provincially significant.

31. *Planning Act*, supra note 7, ss. 17, 21, 34(1).

32. Ibid., ss. 22, 34(10).

33. Ibid., ss. 17(15)-(21), 34(12)-(14).

34. Ibid.

35. Ibid., ss. 22(6), (6.1)-(6.6).

36. Consultation with public agencies for official plans and official plan amendments is required pursuant to s. 17(15)(b) of the *Planning Act*, supra note 7.

37. See *Planning Act*, supra note 7, ss. 17(23), 34(18).

38. Ibid., s. 17(36) or 17(40).

39. Ibid., s. 34(11) or 34(19).

40. Ibid., s. 53(19).

41. Ibid., s. 51(34) or 51(39).

42. Ibid., s. 33(4), for example.

43. *Niagara Escarpment Planning and Development Act*, RSO 1990, c. N.2 as amended, ss. 10(3), 25(8).

44. Ontario Ministry of Municipal Affairs and Housing, supra note 17; see also the *Greenbelt Act, 2005*, supra note 17.

45. Niagara Escarpment Commission, supra note 15.

46. Ontario Ministry of Municipal Affairs and Housing, supra note 16; see also the *Oak Ridges Moraine Conservation Act*, supra note 16.

47. *Places to Grow Act, 2005*, SO 2005, c. 13.

48. Ontario Ministry of Infrastructure, *Growth Plan for the Greater Golden Horseshoe* (Toronto: Queen's Printer for Ontario, 2012), http://www.placestogrow.ca/content/ggh/plan-cons-english-all-web.pdf.

49. *Places to Grow Act*, supra note 47, s. 12.

50. Ontario Ministry of Infrastructure, supra note 48, s. 2.2.8.2.

51. See, e.g., ibid., s. 2.2.4.

52. Ibid., s. 2.2.4.4.

53. Ibid., s. 2.2.6.

54. For example, pursuant to s. 168.3.1(1) of Ontario's *Environmental Protection Act*, RSO 1990, c. E.19, as amended, a developer cannot change the use of an industrial property to a commercial or residential use without first carrying out the study and cleanup required to obtain a "record of site condition."

55. See Chapter 8, which outlines the powers of the Ontario Ministry of the Environment to issue Director's orders pursuant to s. 17 ("Remedial orders") and s. 18 ("Order by Director re preventive measures") of Ontario's *Environmental Protection Act*, supra note 54.

56. *Environmental Protection Act*, supra note 54, Part XV.1.

57. O. Reg. 153/04, as amended.

58. *Environmental Protection Act*, supra note 54, s. 168.3(3).

59. *Planning Act*, supra note 7, s. 28.

60. *Municipal Act, 2001*, SO 2001, c. 25, s. 365.1.

61. *Environmental Protection Act*, supra note 54, Part XV.2.

62. Conservation Ontario, "History of Conservation Authorities," 2013, http://www.conservation-ontario.on.ca/about-us/conservation-authorities/history.

63. Conservation Ontario, "What Is a Conservation Authority?" 2013, http://www.conservation-ontario.on.ca/about-us/faqs#what_is_CA.

64. *Conservation Authorities Act*, RSO 1990, c. C.27, s. 22.

65. Ibid., s. 28 and individual regulation passed for each conservation authority granting each the approval powers for any development that could alter wetlands or alter watercourses or shorelines within its watershed(s).

66. As discussed later in this chapter, conservation authorities now have an expanded planning role under the *Clean Water Act*.

67. See the discussion of Ontario's *Planning Act* in the previous section.

68. Hon. Dennis R. O'Connor, *Report of the Walkerton Inquiry, Part One: The Events of May 2000 and Related Issues* (Toronto: Queen's Printer for Ontario, 2002), http://www.attorneygeneral.jus.gov.on.ca/english/about/pubs/walkerton/part1.

69. Hon. Dennis R. O'Connor, *Report of the Walkerton Inquiry, Part Two: A Strategy for Clean Drinking Water* (Toronto: Queen's Printer for Ontario, 2002), at 18-32, http://www.attorneygeneral.jus.gov.on.ca/english/about/pubs/walkerton/part2.

70. Ibid., at 92.

71. *Safe Drinking Water Act, 2002*, SO 2002, c. 32.

72. *Clean Water Act*, SO 2006, c. 22.

73. Ibid., Part II.

74. Ibid., s. 7.

75. Ibid., ss. 4-6.

76. Ibid., Part II.

77. Ibid., Part III.

78. Ibid., Part IV.

79. See s. 15(1) of the *Clean Water Act*, supra note 72, which requires assessment reports to "municipal drinking water systems" but does not explicitly require consideration of private wells. It only requires consideration of First Nations drinking water supplies if prescribed by regulation.

80. Ibid., s. 8(3).

81. See the listing of source protection plans at the Conservation Ontario website: http://www.conservation-ontario.on.ca/uncategorised/143-otherswpregionsindex.

82. Agreement Review Committee, *Great Lakes Water Quality Agreement Review Report—Volume 2: Review Working Group Reports*, 2007, at 419.

83. Ontario Ministry of Energy, "Ontario's New Energy Vision Puts Conservation First," news release, July 16, 2013, http://news.ontario.ca/mei/en/2013/07/ontarios-new -energy-vision-puts-conservation-first.html.

84. The rules applied all new facilities immediately. Existing facilities were given until 2016 to comply. See British Columbia, *The BC Energy Plan: A Vision for Clean Energy Leadership* (Victoria: Ministry of Energy, Mines and Petroleum Resources, 2007), http://www.energyplan.gov.bc.ca/PDF/BC_Energy_Plan.pdf.

85. Ontario, "Ontario—First Place in North America to End Coal-Fired Power," news release, November 21, 2013, http://news.ontario.ca/opo/en/2013/11/ontario---first -place-in-north-america-to-end-coal-fired-power.html.

86. George Hoberg and Ian Rowlands, "Green Energy Politics in Canada: Comparing Electricity Policies in BC and Ontario," paper prepared for the American Political Science Association annual meeting, New Orleans, August 30-September 2, 2012, http://papers.ssrn.com/sol3/papers.cfm?abstract_id=2108967; for Ontario, see also Mark Winfield, *Blue-Green Province* (Vancouver: UBC Press, 2011), at 163-69, 181-82, 189.

CHAPTER 12

Corporations and Harnessing Market Forces

Introduction

This chapter examines corporate law as it relates to environmental protection and considers some approaches that attempt to work with, rather than against, market forces. It also considers economic instruments that have been adapted for environmental purposes, such as subsidies to assist companies in developing or purchasing new environmentally friendly equipment. This chapter concludes with a discussion of voluntary non-regulatory instruments used by the corporate sector (and encouraged by governments) and their linkages with the law.

Corporate Law

It is often the activities of corporations that cause harm to the environment. Corporate law is generally viewed as unfriendly to environmental concerns for two primary reasons:

1. It protects shareholders from liability.
2. It mandates that corporations operate in their own best interests.[1]

CASE STUDY

Alberta's Carbon Pricing Regime: Advancing or Impeding the Move to Lower Emissions?

In 2014, Alberta's oil sands industry and the Alberta government were very nervous. Proposed bitumen export pipelines had stalled in Canada and the United States because of opposition from citizens (and celebrities—Neil Young and Leonardo DiCaprio), and because of legal actions by First Nations and non-governmental organizations. Oil sands have been a significant and rapidly increasing source of greenhouse gas (GHG) emissions.

"We get it—we are a large source of emissions," said Eric Newell, chair of Alberta's Climate Change and Emissions Management Corporation (CCEMC),[*] the clean energy technology fund established by the government to support its emission reduction regulations. The CCEMC finances corporate technology projects aimed at cutting GHG emissions. The fund is based on $15 per tonne payments by GHG emitters under Alberta's cap and trade climate change and emissions management scheme.[†] Emitters can meet their reduction targets by cutting their own emissions, buying "offset" credits generated by other emission reductions (such as biosequestration by agriculturalists changing tillage practices or planting trees), or paying $15 per tonne of emissions.

According to the Pembina Institute,[‡] however, this scheme is unlikely to achieve its emission reduction goals because the $15 per tonne price is too low to induce companies to make substantial cuts to GHG emissions. The low price also affects the quality and supply of offset credits. The result is a "price cap on the system" that removes the incentive to invest in abatement that costs more than $15 per tonne.[§]

In 2013, an Alberta government 40/40 proposal under which large emitters would be required to reduce GHG emissions by 40 percent and pay $40 per tonne of CO_2 above that level was rejected by the industry. A price as high as $150/tonne may be necessary for a viable offset market.[#] A further problem is that the emissions targets for large emitters are based not on real quantitative reductions but on "emission intensity"—that is, emissions as a function of firm output.[**]

Questions

Is Alberta's cap and trade climate change and emissions management scheme a subsidy program? Is it a carbon tax? What changes would you recommend to make the scheme work effectively as a cap and trade system with a real market for emission offsets? What is the prospect for voluntary GHG reduction commitments by industry? Alternatively, would you recommend amending the relevant environmental statutes to simply prescribe quantified emission limits that are legally enforceable? Is there a potential for a federal cap and trade scheme or a cooperative federal–provincial scheme? As of 2014, no federal GHG cap and trade legislation existed.

---

[*]   Yadullah Hussain, "Oil Sands Titans See Promise in Rising Carbon Emissions," *Calgary Herald*, May 2, 2014, http://www2.canada.com/calgaryherald/news/business/story.html?id=1d46cf74-6bf5-458d-8d62-39108a99a16d.

[†]   *Climate Change and Emissions Management Act*; and *Specified Gas Emitters Regulation*, Alta. Reg. 139/2007.

[‡]   P.J. Partington, "Getting Back in Gear: Oil Sands Climate Performance," Pembina Institute (blog), April 17, 2014, http://www.pembina.org/blog/788.

[§]   Ibid.

[#]   Hussain, supra note [*].

[**]   Ibid.; and Andrew Read, "Backgrounder: Climate Change Policy in Alberta," Pembina Institute, 2014, http://www.pembina.org/docs/oil-sands/sger-climate-policy-backgrounder.pdf.

However, there are exceptions to these general precepts, which are discussed in the following section. In addition, the corporate mandate of self-interest may even be used to advance environmental protection.

Liability and the Corporate Veil

Mitchell Crusto has described corporate law as "a shell that does not address environmental protection."[2] Corporate law protects shareholders from liability for torts committed by a corporation. In essence, this means that owners of corporations may avoid personal liability for corporate activities because lawsuits must be directed at the corporation itself. If a corporation has no assets, those who bring lawsuits against it may find themselves unable to recoup losses caused by the corporation.

Despite these challenges, environmental law has chipped away at the protective shell of corporate law. The corporate veil does not protect against environmental liability in certain circumstances:

- *Personal liability for officers and directors.* Environmental statutes hold corporate officers and directors personally liable for environmental offences committed by corporations in some circumstances, whether or not the corporation is convicted or even charged with an offence.[3]
- *Vicarious liability for acts of employees.* Corporations have **vicarious liability** for the environmentally damaging acts of their employees if the action occurs on the site of employment. They are also liable when one of their agents (such as a lawyer or consultant) commits an environmentally damaging action in the exercise of his or her authority or the performance or his or her duties.[4]
- *Parent corporation's liability for acts of a subsidiary.* A parent corporation may be liable for contamination caused by the actions of a **subsidiary**, a corporation whose controlling interest is owned by the parent company.
- *Owner's liability for a contaminated site.* Environmental legislation may impose liability on the owner of a contaminated site.[5]

Corporate Mandate

The **corporate mandate** requires corporations to operate in their own best interests; this requirement is legislated in statutes such as the *Canada Business Corporations*

---

vicarious liability the legal responsibility of one party for the actions of another—for example, an employer is responsible for the actions of an employee

subsidiary a corporation whose controlling interest is owned by the parent company

corporate mandate the statutory requirement that corporations operate in their own best interests

Act.[6] Corporations must operate in a self-serving manner and maximize returns for shareholders.

This rule has a very important purpose—namely, to protect minority shareholders from officers, directors, or controlling shareholders who might otherwise use the corporation to further their own financial or other personal interests. However, the duty to serve the corporation's best interests may also curtail activities that benefit the environment. Any such secondary activities must always serve the ultimate corporate objective of profit maximization.

This mandate does not necessarily prevent corporations from behaving in an environmentally responsible manner. In fact, responsible and sustainable[7] environmental behaviour may best advance the corporation's interests in many circumstances. For example, it is generally in a corporation's best interests to achieve environmental protection objectives,[8] including the following:

- complying with environmental laws and regulations to avoid fines and lawsuits,
- conserving energy to reduce costs,
- participating in emissions reduction programs to qualify for tax reductions and subsidies, and
- preserving and promoting an environmentally friendly image to satisfy customers and clients.

All of these objectives are often brought under the rubric of "corporate social responsibility." But voluntary sustainability pledges create no liability for corporations or their directors.[9] A related concept is that of "social licence to operate," which refers to the level of acceptance obtained from local communities and other persons affected by corporate activities. This "licence" is conceptual only, not a legal authorization.[10]

Some corporations, such as The Body Shop, BCE, TELUS, and Ben & Jerry's, have made support of environmental causes part of their successful marketing campaigns. For example, Box 12.1 presents BCE's corporate social responsibility statement on its environmental mandate. As environmental issues become more urgent, consumers may become more inclined to support environmentally friendly businesses and even demand minimum standards of environmental responsibility from the businesses that they patronize. In some small measure, consumers' concerns could begin to align market forces with environmental goals.[11]

Corporate codes of environmental conduct have been proposed as part of self-regulatory corporate governance codes.[12] In the United States, citizens and some politicians have even called for the revocation of the corporate charters of companies that have failed to comply with environmental laws.[13] Revocation of a corporate charter essentially dismantles a corporation and prevents it from continuing to operate if it fails to comply with the law.

BOX 12.1 » BCE's Corporate Social Responsibility Statement on the Environment

Caring for future generations

Minimizing our environmental impact in everything we do

A deep commitment to environmental protection is essential to Bell's corporate goal to be recognized by customers as Canada's leading communications company. It aligns with our sustainability vision and with our strategic imperative to achieve a competitive cost structure. Just as important, the commitment to minimize our carbon footprint and instil stewardship of the environment into every aspect of our operations reflects Bell's values. And finally, it is simply the right thing to do for our fellow Canadians and for our planet.

We make every effort to be environmentally responsible when deploying and maintaining networks, building our offices and consuming energy and other resources. Bell team members save energy and reduce greenhouse gas emissions by minimizing the time our vehicles are left on idle, increasing energy efficiency at Bell facilities and using Smart Meeting tools such as VideoZone an alternative to travel. As well, we are visible supporters of broader environmental initiatives such as Earth Hour when most Bell buildings across Canada go dark, along with signs on major venues such as the Bell Centre in Montréal.

For more than 20 years, Bell has implemented and maintained numerous programs to reduce the environmental impact of our operations. Bell has achieved ISO 14001 certification for our environmental management system, the only Canadian telecommunications company to be so certified. Bell also receives many commendations every year for our environmental performance.

We maintained our ISO 14001 certification for Environmental Management System for the 5th straight year.*

Quick facts:

- Since 2008, the Bell team has prevented the release of nearly 40 kilotonnes of CO_2 equivalent emissions by reducing electricity consumption at Bell facilities, improving fuel efficiency in company vehicles, and using phone-, video- and web-conferencing tools to curtail business travel.
- In 2013, Real Estate, Network and IT energy efficiency projects saved 40.36 million kWh of electricity at Bell facilities, enough energy to heat 4,340 homes for a year.
- In 2013, we achieved a 2% decrease in net vehicle energy consumption compared to 2012, amounting to 627,000 fewer litres of fuel consumed. That was due in part to consolidation of our fleet which removed 329 net vehicles from the road.
- Our 2013 anti-idling campaign resulted in a reduction of 2% in idling rates, representing a saving of 220,000 litres of fuel, or about 386,000 kg of reduced CO_2 emissions.
- Through consolidation and virtualization, we optimized 50% of physical servers; 30% were transformed into virtual machines and an additional 20% were decommissioned.
- We reused and recycled 150 tonnes of computers and peripherals and 9.9 tonnes of toner cartridges, an increase of 43% and 25% respectively over 2012. In 2013, we donated to charitable organizations a total of 101 tonnes of recovered furniture valued at $186,290.[†]

ISO 14001:2004
EMS 545959

---

* The International Organization for Standardization (ISO) is a private international standards organization that provides management system requirements for developing and implementing policies to address legal and other perceived requirements and information about environmental aspects of operations. It does not specify environmental performance criteria or certify compliance. See http://www.iso.org/iso/home.htm.

† BCE, "Environment: Caring for Future Generations," 2011, http://www.bce.ca/responsibility/environment/.

Economic Instruments

Externalities are the public costs of environmental degradation.[14] For example, the environmental and health costs of smokestack emissions are borne by the public, not by the factory that pollutes or the customers who purchase the factory's products. As a result, businesses are subsidized by the public and by future generations, who are forced to shoulder the burden of present-day environmental harm.

When the cost of doing business, such as the cost of manufacturing a product, is measured without considering environmental costs, the rational behaviour assumed by free market economics does not occur. For example, imagine that it costs Smokestack Inc. $4 to produce a widget. Every year 200,000 customers are willing to pay $10 per widget, providing Smokestack with a generous $6 profit per widget and a total annual profit of $1,200,000. What no one has thought about is the externalized costs of widget production. A closer look reveals that the cost to the environment of widget production approximates $3 per widget.

If these externalized costs are absorbed by Smokestack, what is likely to happen?

- Smokestack may pass on the additional cost to the consumer, and charge $13 per widget. In this case, fewer customers will be willing to pay the higher price. If only 100,000 customers remain, Smokestack's profits will be reduced by half to $600,000.
- Smokestack may continue to charge $10 per widget and retain its customer base; however, its profit will drop to $3 per widget, and its overall profit will again be reduced by half to $600,000.

Given these numbers, which are based on an accurate and full picture of all costs, Smokestack may alter its business choices. It may spend more money on research and development to improve its processes. It, or one of its competitors, may develop a substitute for the widget that satisfies customers and does less harm to the environment.

Public costs can be reduced or eliminated by regulating or prohibiting an activity that is causing damage, and by imposing penalties for non-compliance. This is the standard command and control model, which is discussed in Chapter 8. However, many economists argue that the same goal can be reached most effectively by using **economic instruments** that provide companies with flexibility and permit them to minimize costs, and allow these costs to be reflected in the market.

---

externalities   the public costs of environmental degradation

economic instruments   fiscal and other economic incentives and disincentives designed to encourage companies to absorb at least some of the environmental costs of doing business

Types

Economic instruments require that companies absorb at least some of the environmental costs of doing business. The two primary types of economic instruments are shown in Table 12.1. **Fixed-price measures** use tax and subsidy incentives to reduce pollution. **Tradeable emission rights**, which are also called "**cap and trade**," create "rights" to pollute up to a prescribed limit or cap, and permit the trading of these rights at a price established by supply and demand.

Table 12.1   Economic Instruments

	Fixed-Price Measures	Tradeable Emission Rights ("Cap and Trade")
Description	Tax and subsidy incentives to reduce pollution. Two types: 1. Emission taxes: Taxes are charged on units of contaminants released into the environment (e.g., BC and Quebec carbon taxes). 2. Subsidies: Grants, loans, or tax breaks are provided to polluters for reducing discharge, with the size of the subsidy based on the amount of the reduction.	Rights representing specified quantities of emissions that are issued to polluters and that may be traded. • An aggregate cap on allowable emissions (baseline) is set, and it is divided into units. • Units are allocated to polluters on the basis of previous polluting history, by auction, or by a combination of these two methods.
Criticism	They do not provide for a limit or cap on the total amount of pollution discharged.	The baseline is often set too high, thereby redistributing pollution but not reducing it.

Fixed-Price Measures

The two types of fixed-price measures are emission taxes and subsidies. The amount of tax or subsidy is fixed by the government per unit of pollution.

Emission taxes are taxes charged on units of contaminants released into the environment. These taxes encourage polluters to discharge less by increasing the total costs of production. The taxes collected can be used by the government for other environmental protection initiatives. Examples are the carbon taxes prescribed in British Columbia[15] and Quebec.[16]

---

fixed-price measure   tax and subsidy incentives to reduce pollution; a type of economic instrument

tradeable emission rights   rights representing specified quantities of emissions that are issued to polluters and that may be traded; a type of economic instrument

cap and trade   a policy and legal tool for controlling emissions from a group of sources; a maximum limit on emissions is set, and emitters covered by the program are authorized to emit based on the emission allowance of the cap; emitters must meet reduction requirements, and may sell or purchase allowances to do so

emission taxes   taxes charged on units of contaminant released into the environment; a type of fixed-price measure

BOX 12.2 » Taxing Carbon: An Idea Whose Time Has Come?

In 2008, Stephane Dion's Liberal Party, running on a "green shift" environmental platform that featured a carbon tax, lost the federal election to the Conservatives. Clearly, most Canadians were not yet ready to embrace such policies. But that same year, British Columbia implemented a provincial carbon tax. Instead of being a "job killer," as critics had predicted, new statistics show it has been a success, and is now touted as a model for Ontario and other jurisdictions in Canada and internationally. Typically, environmental policy matters are framed as a choice between ensuring jobs or helping the environment; Ross Beaty and colleagues, however, say that BC is proving this to be a false choice:

> BC now has the lowest personal income tax rate in Canada (with additional cuts benefiting low-income and rural residents) and one of the lowest corporate rates in North America. ... At the same time, it's been extraordinarily effective in tackling the root cause of carbon pollution: the burning of fossil fuels. Since the tax came in, fuel use in BC has dropped by 16 per cent; in the rest of Canada, it's risen by 3 per cent (counting all fuels covered by the tax). To put that accomplishment in perspective, Canada's Kyoto target was a 6-per-cent reduction in 20 years. And the evidence points to the carbon tax as the major driver of these BC gains. Further, while some had predicted that the tax shift would hurt the province's economy, in fact, BC's GDP has slightly outperformed the rest of Canada's since 2008.
>
> With these impressive results, BC's carbon tax has gained widespread global praise as a model for the world—from organizations such as the OECD, the World Bank and The Economist. ... It shows that Canada can be competitively ambitious in shaping a 21st century economy that internalizes the real costs of pollution. And that is important, because carbon and other emissions from burning fossil fuels impose heavy costs on us all—as BC knows well. The mountain pine beetle infestation, resulting from warming winters, has devastated the province's interior forest industry, closing mills and costing thousands of jobs. Similarly, air pollution, caused mainly by burning fossil fuels, costs thousands of lives and more than $8-billion a year to Canada's economy. These problems will only get worse if we don't get serious about tackling the causes of carbon emissions.
>
> BC's example shows that we can do that, while also building a prosperous economy, if we use smart policies. And it's not alone in doing so. Both Alberta and Quebec, for example, have also put a price on carbon emissions, using different policy approaches. All three provinces offer instructive, made-in-Canada lessons for spurring clean innovation, advancing energy efficiency, and preparing Canada's economy to compete with other nations that are already making this shift.

Questions

Why is taxation emerging as a way to reduce emissions? Critics call carbon taxes a government "cash grab" that means higher prices for the average person buying food, gas, and almost all other goods. Is this a reasonable criticism? What are the pros and cons of such taxes?

Source: Ross Beaty, Richard Lipsey, and Stewart Elgie, "The Shocking Truth About BC's Carbon Tax: It Works," *Globe and Mail*, July 9, 2014, http://www.theglobeandmail.com/globe-debate/the-insidious-truth-about-bcs-carbon-tax-it-works/article19512237/. Reprinted by permission.

Subsidies are grants, loans, or tax breaks provided to polluters for reducing discharge by basing the size of the subsidy on the amount of the reduction. Like the pollution tax, subsidies provide a direct financial incentive to reduce pollution. It is a "carrot" approach in contrast to the "stick" approach of emission taxes.

Both emission taxes and subsidies work by raising the relative cost of producing the polluting product. When this cost is passed on to the consumer, the demand for the product may decrease. Customers will either use less of the product or find cheaper alternatives to it. Emission taxes and subsidies also cause polluters to research and invest in new methods of reducing pollution—for example, by acquiring new technology.

A criticism of fixed-price measures is that they do not provide for a limit or cap on the total amount of pollution discharged. It is possible to impose a cap on allowable discharge for individual businesses by using regulation in addition to fixed-price measures; however, it is not possible to impose a cap on the aggregate levels within a jurisdiction or industry. Polluters may choose to pay the tax or forgo the subsidy rather than curb emissions.

Tradeable Emission Rights

Tradeable emission rights are rights representing specified quantities of emissions that are issued to polluters and that may be traded. The keys, as John Dales explained in 1968, are property rights that are priced in the market.[17] An aggregate cap on allowable emissions, called a **baseline**, is set and divided into units. The units are allocated to polluters on the basis of their previous polluting history, by auction, or by a combination of these two methods.

Once an emission right is owned by a polluter, it may be used to discharge pollutants, traded at a price determined by the marketplace, or saved for later use. Businesses with the lowest abatement costs actually reduce emissions. Those with higher abatement costs purchase pollution rights. The objective is to meet emissions reduction targets by setting a sufficiently low baseline, and to ease the burden on industry by facilitating pollution abatement where it is least expensive. In theory, provided that a market is competitive, an industry's overall abatement costs are minimized, and the baseline objective can be achieved.

A criticism of this model is that the baseline is often set too high, thereby redistributing pollution but not reducing it.[18] How rights are allocated can also be problematic. If rights are assigned to established businesses on the basis of their pollution history,

---

subsidies grants, loans, or tax breaks provided to polluters for reducing discharge, with the size of the subsidy based on the amount of the reduction; a type of fixed-price measure

baseline an aggregate cap on allowable emissions, which is divided into units that may be traded

an unintended consequence is that new businesses are at a disadvantage when entering a market because they are forced to purchase emission allowances to operate.

When used wisely, economic instruments may be important tools; unfortunately,
they are not a panacea for environmental challenges.

Non-Regulatory Instruments

For decades, regulatory requirements of various kinds have been the main political
means of getting industry to improve its environmental performance. This is still
the case. However, beginning in the 1990s, a variety of non-regulatory "voluntary"
instruments were introduced through government–industry cooperation.

Types

Non-regulatory instruments are sometimes used as supplements to regulation and
sometimes as alternatives to regulation. The most important types are as follows:

- *Organizational operations.* Companies may adapt their organizational operations—that is, energy use, production processes, etc.—to conform to an
  environmental management system.[19] Placing greater emphasis on environmental issues can achieve not only environmentally desirable outcomes but
  also strengthen organizational capabilities.
- *Pollution reduction agreements.* Agreements to reduce pollution may be negotiated between governments and either industries or industrial sectors.[20]
  These agreements commit industry to environmental protection actions that
  exceed prevailing regulatory requirements.
- *Industry association performance obligations.* Industry associations may push
  their members to meet higher environmental standards. Marketing by an
  association on behalf of its members may include reference to these goals or
  achievements. One high-profile example is the Chemistry Industry Association of Canada's Responsible Care® program.[21]
- *Sectoral abatement challenges.* Governments may set informal targets or
  "challenges," often in cooperation with polluting industries in a particular
  sector, and encourage businesses within the sector to meet these targets without regulatory obligation.[22]
- *"Profit from pollution prevention" educational programs.* Educational programs,
  usually initiated by government, are intended to inform businesses of opportunities to reduce pollution while saving money; an example of such a program
  is one that advocates the reduction of waste materials and energy use.
- *Eco-labelling programs.* Eco-labelling programs involve labelling the products
  and services of businesses that comply with specified environmental standards.[23] Such programs provide a competitive advantage to participants when
  marketing to environmentally concerned customers and clients.

- *Green consumer education programs.* Green consumer education programs focus on educating consumers and can work in conjunction with eco-labelling programs. Consumers are given information about various products and are encouraged to choose those whose manufacture involves fewer negative environmental effects, and whose use or disposal is less environmentally dangerous. By raising consumer awareness and encouraging environmentally conscious purchasing decisions, governments hope that informed consumers will affect corporate behaviour.

Many of these non-regulatory instruments are likely to increase in importance as environmental issues become more urgent, and as growing numbers of consumers appreciate this urgency. New programs and approaches are likely to arise as well.

Voluntariness

Non-regulatory instruments are often called "voluntary," which is technically correct. None of them involves direct regulatory obligation. However, measures such as pollution reduction agreements are effective only in conjunction with an implicit threat of more stringent and less flexible regulation in the event that the voluntary initiative fails.[24]

Likewise, industry associations that push their members to improve environmental performance beyond regulatory requirements are acting voluntarily in the sense that they are not required to do so by regulation. However, these initiatives are usually driven by fear of tough regulations or other financial consequences if the sector does not take action to improve its environmental behaviour. For example, the Chemistry Industry Association of Canada introduced its Responsible Care® program after a series of nasty chemical industry accidents had darkened the industry's reputation, made investors and insurers nervous, and inspired calls for tougher regulation.[25]

Indirect regulatory pressures may also encourage compliance with voluntary measures. Indirect pressures include concerns about liability if a serious environmentally damaging event occurs. In order to prove due diligence and avoid penalties under environmental protection statutes, businesses must demonstrate that they have taken every reasonable precaution to avoid these damaging incidents. Proving due diligence is much easier when an offending business can show that it had an environmental management system in place.[26]

The law and voluntary initiatives are interconnected in various ways:[27]

- Voluntary initiatives can be referentially incorporated in law. For example, voluntary emissions reduction commitments have been incorporated by energy regulators as terms and conditions of regulatory approvals that can be enforced by regulators.[28]

- Voluntary codes may elaborate or refine legal requirements.
- Voluntary codes can be used in private legal actions to establish liability—for example, by informing the identification of duties of care in negligence actions.
- Voluntary compliance may train firms and their employees in quantification and reporting techniques in advance of legal requirements.[29]

Perhaps the only initiatives that are truly voluntary are the ones that focus on profitable pollution-reducing actions. These rely on the core financial motives that private sector firms are expected to apply. We might expect profit-driven companies to be naturally good at finding ways to cut expenses in environmentally desirable ways. However, unless a company is organized to look for these opportunities, it may well miss them.

Consider the example of Nortel Networks. Some years ago, Nortel invested $1 million in an initiative to eliminate use of an environmentally damaging solvent. As a result of the process changes involved, the company saved $4 million in three years. This initiative was undertaken in anticipation of a regulatory requirement, and the fact that it was a cost-saving opportunity was recognized only later.

Advantages and Disadvantages

Non-regulatory instruments are flexible, may raise overall environmental performance at a lower cost than regulatory action, can be easier to implement than regulations, and may help persuade businesses that environmental improvements can serve their economic self-interest. They also make use of a wide range of motivations and pressures—from bankers, insurers, employees, and consumers, as well as governments.

At the same time, non-regulatory instruments tend to be less well-defined, more difficult to test for adequacy and effectiveness, less open to public scrutiny, and less evenly applied than regulations.[30] They are most problematic when adopted as alternatives to regulatory action, since the threat of effective regulation and the indirect influence of legal obligations are probably the most powerful motivators of voluntary action.

We are likely to see continued, and perhaps increasing, use of non-regulatory instruments in combination with government's continuing core reliance on regulation. The two primary reasons for this trend are as follows:

1. *Regulatory initiatives are not enough.* Governments increasingly recognize that regulatory initiatives may benefit from the contribution of economic instruments.[31] Regulatory authorities are facing increasing challenges as technologies become more ambitious and as economic activities develop more complex linkages from local producers to global trade systems. Most governments are under pressure to do more in many areas while not increasing tax burdens, and this situation creates a powerful impetus for experimentation with combinations of regulatory and non-regulatory instruments.

2. *Pressure from public interest groups has grown.* Public interest or "civil society" organizations have gained prominence in recent years. Governments are no longer the only significant source of pressure for better corporate performance on environmental matters.[32] Public interest organizations have become much more numerous and influential. They use the Internet and other modern technologies to organize effective coalitions that exert direct pressure on the private sector to improve environmental performance.[33] Campaigns by these groups have included boycotts of targeted environmentally undesirable products or environmentally irresponsible companies and have increased public awareness of the unsustainability of current practices. Citizen groups have adopted strategies that involve opposition to particular projects that become proxies for broader environmental goals.[34] Examples include a loose coalition of groups opposed to the Keystone XL Pipeline and Northern Gateway Pipeline projects. Their ultimate objectives are shutting down "dirty" bitumen production from the Alberta oil sands and promoting early progress toward low carbon energy futures. Another example is the broad-based—even global—opposition to hydraulic fracturing (or "fracking") in oil and gas production. These groups have made effective use of sophisticated websites along with social media tools. Public interest groups have greatly contributed to the rising public expectations that are pushing industry to adopt at least the green mantle of corporate social and environmental responsibility if they wish to maintain consumer respect, investor confidence, and employee loyalty.

Drivers of Change

The direct influence of environmental regulation has combined with non-regulatory instruments and civil society actions to establish a number of drivers of change that are shaping corporate environmental performance. In addition to simple command and control obligations and penalties, these drivers now include the following:

- incentives to reduce costs, especially by cutting resource use and waste generation;
- desire to avoid, or at least delay, additional regulatory action that would impose undesirable administrative and compliance costs;
- concern about negative reaction from environmentally informed consumers;
- fear of damage to public image and associated consumer and investor confidence (or desire to enhance public reputation and associated consumer and investor confidence);
- desire to minimize risk of costly surprises;
- expectation of competitive advantage through exclusion of new competitors and access to new markets;

- requirements imposed by banks and/or insurers that do not wish to inherit environmental liabilities;
- demands of suppliers and consumers who wish to avoid environmental costs and liabilities;
- pressure from staff or other industry members; and
- personal commitment of corporate leaders.

So far, few steps have been made to approach regulatory and non-regulatory initiatives in a coordinated way that mobilizes all of these drivers effectively and ensures that each strengthens the other. Indeed, we still have only an incomplete understanding of how regulatory efforts must be designed and focused to provide a firm foundation for a larger and more powerful environmental regime. But increasingly the building blocks are being put in place.

SUMMARY OF KEY POINTS

- Corporate law does not protect against environmental liability in certain circumstances, including personal liability for officers and directors, vicarious liability for acts of employees, and corporate parents' liability for the acts of subsidiaries.
- Legal corporate mandates do not prevent corporations from acting environmentally responsibly. Relevant non-legal concepts are "corporate social responsibility" and "social licence to operate."
- Economic instruments have been used to achieve environmental objectives and hold potential for the future.
- Economic instruments used to achieve environmental objectives include fixed-price measures (emission taxes and subsidies) and tradeable emission rights (cap and trade systems; emission offset schemes).
- Non-regulatory instruments can be important supplementary initiatives to achieve environmental objectives. These include government–industry pollution reduction agreements, sectoral abatement "challenge" programs, educational programs, and eco-labelling programs.

KEY TERMS

baseline
cap and trade
corporate mandate
economic instruments

emission taxes
externalities
fixed-price measure
subsidiary

subsidies
tradeable emission rights
vicarious liability

DISCUSSION QUESTIONS

1. What are the pros and cons of emission tax instruments?
2. What are the key elements of cap and trade systems?
3. From a corporate standpoint, what are some best-bet voluntary environmental initiatives? Can you think of statutory provisions that can be designed to facilitate or enhance voluntary initiatives?
4. What key factors should be included in a federal cap and trade system that targets greenhouse gas emissions? What about a federal cap and trade system that targets sulphur dioxide (consider the sources)?
5. Is some form of linkage among cap and trade systems (e.g., the provinces and US states) critical to success of the systems? What about cap and trade systems beyond North America, including the greenhouse gas reduction system under the Kyoto Protocol (see Chapter 6)?

SUGGESTED READINGS

Readings

Barrera-Hernández, Lila K. "Consumer Behaviour and the Environment: An Environmental Law and Policy Approach." (1995) 5:2 *Journal of Environmental Law and Practice* 161.

Dales, John H. *Pollution, Property, and Prices*. Toronto: University of Toronto Press, 1968.

Doern, G. Bruce, ed. *The Environmental Imperative: Market Approaches to the Greening of Canada*. Toronto: C.D. Howe Institute, 1990.

Gunningham, Neil, and Darren Sinclair. *Leaders and Laggards: Next Generation Environmental Regulation*. Sheffield, UK: Greenleaf, 2002.

Hahn, Robert W., and Robert N. Stavins. "Incentive-Based Environmental Regulation: A New Era from an Old Idea." (1991) 18 *Ecology Law Quarterly* 1.

Stavins, Robert N. "Lessons from the American Experiment with Market-Based Environmental Policies." KSG Working Paper No. PWP01-032; FEEM Working Paper No. 30.2002, April 2002, http://ssrn.com/abstract=285998.

United Nations Environment Programme (UNEP). *The Use of Economic Instruments in Environmental Policy: Opportunities and Challenges*. New York: UNEP, 2004, http://www.unep.ch/etb/publications/EconInst/econInstruOppChnaFin.pdf.

Website

World Health Organization, The Health and Environment Linkages Initiative (HELI), "Economic Instruments as a Lever for Policy": http://www.who.int/heli/economics/econinstruments/en/

NOTES

1. That is, in the best interests of the shareholders: see *Smith v. Hanson Tire Company Ltd.*, [1927] 3 DLR 786 (Sask. CA).

2. Mitchell Crusto, "Green Business: Should We Revoke Corporate Charters for Environmental Violations?" (2003) 63 *Louisiana Law Review* 175, at 181.

3. See, e.g., *Canadian Environmental Protection Act, 1999*, SC 1999, c. 33, s. 280.1; and Ontario *Environmental Protection Act*, RSO 1990, c. E.19, s. 194.

4. See, e.g., Ontario *Environmental Protection Act*, s. 192.

5. On previous owners of the sites and owners of contaminant substances, see Alberta *Environmental Protection and Enhancement Act*, SA 1992, c. E-12, ss. 107(1), 129; and BC *Environmental Management Act*, SBC 2003, c. 53, ss. 45-48.

6. *Canada Business Corporations Act*, RSC 1985, c. C-44, s. 122(1) requires corporate officers and directors to act "with a view to the best interests of the corporation."

7. See Jeffrey Bone, "The Consideration of Sustainability by Corporate Directors" (2013) 26:1 *Journal of Environmental Law and Practice* 1, which focuses on corporate sustainability pledges.

8. Sanjay Sharma and Harrie Vredenburg, "Proactive Corporate Environmental Strategy and the Development of Competitively Valuable Organizational Capabilities" (1998) 19 *Strategic Management Journal* 729; Brenda Kenny, Alastair A. Lucas, and Harrie Vredenburg, "The New Role of Law in Stimulating Industrial Innovation and Regional Development: The Canadian Experience with Reflexive Law in Reconciling Economic Development, Environmental Protection and Entrepreneurship in the Energy Industry" (2012) 4 *Journal of Innovation and Regional Development* 8.

9. Bone, supra note 7, at 5-6.

10. See Leeora Black, "The Social Licence as a Framework for Managing Cumulative Impacts: A Case Study of the Upper Hunting Mining Dialogue," Australian Centre for Corporate Social Responsibility, presented at the International Association of Impact Assessment Conference, Calgary, May 14, 2013, http://www.accsr.com.au/pdf/ACCSR_IAIA2013_Black.pdf.

11. Lila Barrera-Hernández, "Consumer Behaviour and the Environment: An Environmental Law and Policy Approach" (1995) 5:2 *Journal of Environmental Law and Practice* 161.

12. Stepan Wood, "Voluntary Environmental Codes and Sustainability," in Benjamin Richardson and Stepan Wood, eds., *Environmental Law for Sustainability* (Oxford: Hart, 2006), at 229-76.

13. Crusto, supra note 2.

14. Ronald Coase, "The Problem of Social Cost" (1960) 3 *Journal of Law and Economics* 1.

15. *Carbon Tax Act*, SBC 2008, c. 40.

16. *An Act Respecting Implementation of the Quebec Energy Strategy*, SQ 2006, c. 46.

17. John H. Dales, *Pollution, Property, and Prices* (Toronto: University of Toronto Press, 1968).

18. For example, essentially this is the problem with Alberta's greenhouse gas emissions reduction scheme. Firm targets are based on emission intensity—emissions as a function of output. The means of meeting targets include the option of paying a prescribed per-tonne sum into a fund. See Yadullah Hussain, "Oil Sands Titans See Promise in Rising Carbon Emissions," *Calgary Herald*, May 2, 2014, http://www2.canada.com/calgaryherald/news/business/story.html?id=1d46cf74 -6bf5-458d-8d62-39108a99a16d.

19. Sharma and Vredenburg, supra note 8.

20. See Barry Barton, Robert Franson, and Andrew Thompson, *A Contract Model for Pollution Control* (Vancouver: University of British Columbia, Westwater Research Centre, 1984).

21. Chemical Industry Association of Canada, "Responsible Care®," accessed September 10, 2014, http://www.canadianchemistry.ca/responsible_care.

22. See Alastair Lucas, "Voluntary Initiatives for Greenhouse Gas Reduction: The Legal Implications" (2000) 10 *Journal of Environmental Law and Practice* 89.

23. Mario F. Teisl, Brian Roe, and Robert L. Hicks, "Can Eco-Labels Tune a Market? Evidence from Dolphin-Safe Labeling" (2002) 43:3 *Journal of Environmental Economics and Management* 339.

24. Neil Gunningham and Darren Sinclair, *Leaders and Laggards: Next Generation Environmental Regulation* (Sheffield, UK: Greenleaf, 2002), at 39.

25. John Moffet, François Bregha, and Mary Jane Middelkoop, "Responsible Care: A Case Study of a Voluntary Environmental Initiative," in Kernaghan R. Webb, ed., *Voluntary Codes: Private Governance, the Public Interest and Innovation* (Ottawa: Carleton University Research Unit for Innovation, Science and Environment, 2004), 177.

26. *R v. Bata Industries Ltd.*, [1992] 7 CELR (NS) 245, at 287-88 (Ont. Prov. Ct.).

27. See Kernaghan Webb and Andrew Morrison, "The Law and Voluntary Codes: Examining the 'Tangled Web,'" in Webb, supra note 25, at 98-99.

28. Alastair Lucas, "Voluntary Commitment and Rule Development: Canada's VCR Inc. Greenhouse Gas Limitation Program and the Energy Sector" (2004) 12 *Environmental Liability* 229.

29. Ibid., at 235.

30. Jamie Benedickson, *Environmental Law*, 4th ed. (Toronto: Irwin Law, 2013), at 370.

31. Ibid., at 386.

32. Frank de Bakker and Frank den Hond, "Activists Influence Tactics and Corporate Policy" (2008) 71 *Business Communication Quarterly* 107.

33. Alastair Lucas, Theresa Watson, and Eric Kimmel, "Regulating Multistage Hydraulic Fracturing in a Mature Oil and Gas Jurisdiction," in Donald Zillman, Aileen McHarg, Lila Barrera-Hernández, and Adrian Bradbrook, eds., *The Law of Energy Underground* (Oxford: Oxford University Press, 2014), 127-45.

34. Ibid., at 143.

PART V

Protecting Environmental Rights

Using the Courts to Protect the Environment

Introduction

The very first environmental protection court cases were civil lawsuits based on private property rights. Neighbours sued neighbours for damage caused to their land.

After providing a historical context of private actions, this chapter examines the current role that civil actions play in protecting the environment. It also addresses some of the key challenges encountered in civil litigation, such as obtaining standing (the right to sue), identifying a cause of action, proving causation, proving damages, and suffering the costs consequences of losing a case.

Smith v. Inco Limited: Applying the Torts of Private Nuisance and Strict Liability

Residents in Port Colborne, Ontario who lived near a nickel refinery that had operated for 66 years brought a class action against the refinery, alleging that their property values had not increased compared with those of local municipalities because of public concerns over nickel deposits in the soil of their properties.* The class action was based on trespass, public and private nuisance, and strict liability (sometimes called "the rule in *Rylands v. Fletcher*" [[1868] UKHL 1]). The trial judge dismissed the trespass and public nuisance claims but found the nickel refinery liable to property owners on the basis of private nuisance and strict liability. Consequently, the refinery was ordered to pay $36 million in damages to the claimants. The Court of Appeal, however, overturned the lower court ruling and dismissed the case.

It should be noted that the class action, as originally constituted, involved a number of other defendants and included allegations of health impacts arising from the nickel emissions. Various procedural challenges and court rulings took place, spanning a number of years. When the matter went to trial, the nickel refinery was the only defendant at trial, and the claims at trial related solely to damages to property values.

The Court of Appeal accepted the trial court's findings of fact that until the refinery had closed its doors, no significant public health concerns were associated with nickel levels in the soil around the refinery. However, once a Ministry of Environment study in 2000 discovered higher levels of nickel in the soil than previously recorded, health impacts became a significant community concern.

With respect to the tort of private nuisance, the court provided the following analysis:

> People do not live in splendid isolation from one another. One person's lawful and reasonable use of his or her property may indirectly harm the property of another or interfere with that person's ability to fully use and enjoy his or her property. The common law of nuisance developed as a means by which those competing inter-

ests could be addressed, and one given legal priority over the other. Under the common law of nuisance, sometimes the person whose property suffered the adverse effects is expected to tolerate those effects as the price of membership in the larger community. Sometimes, however, the party causing the adverse effect can be compelled, even if his or her conduct is lawful and reasonable, to desist from engaging in that conduct and to compensate the other party for any harm caused to that person's property. In essence, the common law of nuisance decided which party's interest must give way. That determination is made by asking whether in all the circumstances the harm caused or the interference done to one person's property by the other person's use of his or her property is unreasonable: *Royal Anne Hotel Co. v. Village of Ashcroft*, [1979] B.C.J. No. 2068, 95 D.L.R. (3d) 756 (C.A.), at pp. 760-61 D.L.R.†

The Court of Appeal noted that interference may take the form of "physical injury to land" or "substantial interference with the plaintiff's use or enjoyment of his or her land" (sometimes referred to as "amenity nuisance").‡ It added that the case deals with physical injury to land and not amenity nuisance, since the property owners did not argue that the nickel deposits interfered with their use and enjoyment of their property.

The Court of Appeal indicated that when amenity nuisance is claimed, the reasonableness of the interference with the use of land must be assessed by balancing certain competing factors. However, such balancing does not occur when the nuisance alleged is a physical injury to land.

With the "physical injury to land" form of nuisance, the Court of Appeal held that the plaintiffs would have to show that the nickel levels posed some risk to health. In other words, the plaintiffs would have to establish that nickel particles in the soil caused "actual, substantial, physical damage to their properties."§ The court explained this finding as follows:

> [W]e think the trial judge erred in finding that the nickel particles in the soil caused actual, substantial, physical damage to the claimants' lands. In our view, a mere chemical alteration in the content of soil, without more, does not amount to physical harm or damage to the property. For instance, many farmers add fertilizer to their soil each year for the purpose of changing, and enhancing, the chemical composition of the soil. To constitute physical harm or damage, a change in the chemical composition must be shown to have had some detrimental effect on the land itself or rights associated with the use of the land. For example, in *Russell Transport Ltd.* [*Russell Transport Ltd. v. Ontario Malleable Iron Co.*, [1952] OR 621, 4 DLR 719], the authority relied on by the claimants, it was not the mere emission of the iron oxide particles onto the plaintiff's property that constituted the nuisance.#

After ruling that the claim in private nuisance failed, the Court of Appeal discussed the application of the rule in *Rylands v. Fletcher*. The traditional understanding of the rule is that it imposes strict liability (i.e., liability without having the plaintiff to establish any fault) for damages caused to a plaintiff's property by the escape from the defendant's property of a substance that can cause harm as a result of the defendant's "ultra-hazardous activities."

The Court of Appeal found that there is no common law rule imposing strict liability on activities only because they are "ultra hazardous." The court noted that environmental regulation is designed to protect the community from hazardous activities and that the refinery's emission levels did not contravene any regulations. It added that strict liability in the context of the rule in *Rylands v. Fletcher* is triggered by "damage occurring from a user inappropriate to the place where it is maintained."** The plaintiff needed to establish that the defendant's nickel refinery was a "non-natural use" of its property.

The Court of Appeal found no basis on which to argue that the nickel refinery's operations or its emissions of nickel particles were "extra hazardous" and that the operation of the facility was a "non-natural use" in that the refinery was operating in an industrial area and was not creating risks beyond what one would expect in such areas.

Finally, the Court of Appeal also found that the plaintiffs did not establish that the claimants' properties had reduced values because of public concerns over the nickel deposits in the soil in the claimants' properties.

Questions

Applying the reasoning of the Court of Appeal, what do you think the outcome of the case would have been if lead (rather than nickel) emissions were involved? Do you think the case would have had a different outcome if the plaintiffs were in a position to establish health impacts on the local residents? What evidence would have been needed to support a winning case for the plaintiffs?

---

*   *Smith v. Inco Limited*, 2011 ONCA 628.

†   Ibid., at para. 39.

‡   Ibid., at para. 43.

§   Ibid., at para. 58.

Ibid., at para. 55.

**   Ibid., at para. 91.

Environmental Issues and Private Actions

Canadians are blessed with a wide array of rights and freedoms. However, these rights and freedoms are not unlimited, and ultimately it is up to the courts to determine what the limits are. In the environmental context, the courts must reconcile the rights of owners and occupiers of property to use and enjoy the property with the rights of their neighbours to do the same. Consider the following issues:

- Can you build a tall fence to create privacy in your backyard if your fence deprives your neighbour's award-winning rosebush of sunlight?
- Can a factory near your home continue its manufacturing process if the noise it emits at night is so loud that you have problems sleeping?
- What can a farmer do when the groundwater she uses for irrigation is being contaminated by a neighbouring landfill?
- What can residents do when tunnels dug by a mining company under their land begin to cave in?
- Can a factory emit a pollutant that affects the health of residents downwind?
- What can residents do if their drinking water smells bad and is discoloured?
- Can residents stop the migration of contaminants from an abandoned site?

Similar issues were litigated as far back as the 1800s, although they were not called "environmental matters" at that time. There was scant, if any, legislation on these subjects. The courts were therefore required to apply general principles of the common law to the particulars of each case.

The Challenges of Environmental Litigation

In Canadian society, civil lawsuits are common. The courts are there to assist in the resolution of disputes. A homeowner may bring a lawsuit against the builder of a house because the basement leaks; a patient may sue his doctor because an operation went wrong; or a customer of a grocery store may sue because she slipped and fell on a wet floor. There are hundreds of examples of "typical" lawsuits. Each lawsuit, of course, has its own challenges. In many ways, environmental civil lawsuits are legal actions like all others where one party (the plaintiff) is seeking some relief (such as damages or an injunction) against another party (the defendant) for some wrong the defendant did against the plaintiff (the civil wrong, or the "tort").

Today, environmental court actions occur on a regular basis. Most do not make the front pages of newspapers. Many environmental court actions apply traditional legal principles, while others attempt to forge new principles, such as some of the cases that apply the *Canadian Charter of Rights and Freedoms* (see Box 13.1). It is important to note that each and every one of them adds to the growing body of law that governs the environment. While the courts remain the primary forum for the adjudication of environmental rights in lawsuits initiated by individuals, litigants face many challenges in pursuing environmental claims in the courts.

Standing

Not just anyone may go to court to bring a lawsuit. A person must have **standing**, or the right to sue. Under traditional rules, it was always difficult for persons who wanted

---

standing   the right to sue

BOX 13.1 » **The Role of the Canadian Charter of Rights and Freedoms in Environmental Protection**

In 1982, the *Canadian Charter of Rights and Freedoms* entrenched a number of profoundly important rights and freedoms. For example, section 7 states the following:

> 7. Everyone has the right to life, liberty and security of the person and the right not to be deprived thereof except in accordance with the principles of fundamental justice.

However, no case as of yet has been successful in invoking a Charter claim, especially under section 7. In many of the cases, the challenge has been evidentiary; that is, the plaintiff must provide evidence that the harm complained of leads to a judicial finding that it is a deprivation of "the right to life, liberty, and security of the person."

Some believe that, over time, the Charter will be applied and interpreted in a manner that will enhance environmental and natural resource protection. As one professor noted, "[F]ortunately, no amendment is required in order to import ecological rights into the *Canadian Charter of Rights and Freedoms*. The protections provided within that document are broad enough, and our traditions of judicial interpretation robust enough, to allow these crucial interests to benefit from the protection of the supreme law of the land."*

---

*   Lynda M. Collins, "An Ecologically Literate Reading of the Canadian Charter of Rights and Freedoms" (2009) 26 *Windsor Review of Legal and Social Issues* 7, at 19.

to protect the environment to attain status to sue, but over the years the courts have broadened the rules and have developed rules for public interest standing.

The Traditional Standing Rule

Courts are generally willing to hear only from people who are directly involved in or affected by the matter in dispute. To open the courthouse doors to anyone who wants to be heard would be cumbersome and very costly. Therefore, standing is reserved only for people with a recognized legal interest. Intervention, discussed below, is a procedural device that allows individuals to participate in an ongoing lawsuit.

The traditional **"three p" rule** for determining whether a person has standing requires would-be litigants to demonstrate that they have one of the following three interests:

1. *Property interest.* The person's property has allegedly been harmed.
2. *Personal (health) interest.* The person's health has allegedly been harmed.

"three p" rule a traditional rule for determining whether a person has standing, requiring the person to demonstrate a property interest, a personal (health) interest, or a pecuniary interest

3. *Pocketbook or pecuniary (financial) interest.* The person's business or economic interests have allegedly been harmed.

The "three p" rule limits standing to those individuals with a direct and measurable interest in the dispute. The rationale for the "three p" rule is rooted in the understanding that the traditional role of the courts is to resolve disputes between its members of society. Hence, one side is to argue its position to the best of its ability; the other side is given the opportunity to present its position, and through this adversarial approach, the court is best able to discern "the truth."

However, sometimes it is appropriate to allow wider participation in a lawsuit, and this matter is explored in the following sections.

Public Interest Standing

Consider the following cases where groups and individuals want to bring a legal action to protect a common or public interest:

- A community member is concerned about city council's decision to build fire stations in local parks, thus removing valuable green space from neighbourhoods.
- A passerby notices that trees are being cut down on lands owned by the province, and wants to have it stopped.
- A conservation group wants to challenge a bureaucratic decision to allow the draining of a wetland.

In all of these cases, the groups and individuals who want to bring an action do not satisfy the traditional "three p" standing rule because their property, health, and pocketbooks are not directly affected.

The standing rule has often stood in the way of environmentalists who seek redress in court. This issue was raised in the US Supreme Court in the early 1970s, when an environmental group tried to bring an action to prevent a development activity near a national park. One of the submissions, a law review article by Christopher Stone entitled "Should Trees Have Standing?," remains a persuasive treatise about why rules of standing should be relaxed for environmental litigation.

Since that time, the courts have carved out an exception to the traditional standing test by applying a **public interest standing** test in certain circumstances. This new, broader test requires that three questions be answered in the affirmative:

---

public interest standing a new and broader test for determining whether a person has standing, requiring that the person either have a genuine interest in the litigation or be in a better position to bring the action than anyone else

1. Is a serious issue being raised?
2. Does the applicant have a "genuine interest" in the litigation, as demonstrated by
   a. his or her having worked on the issue for a long time, and
   b. his or her being knowledgeable about it?
3. Is the applicant in a better position to bring the action than anyone else—that is, is there no other way to bring the issue before the court?

Public interest standing is now well recognized in Canadian courts. However, the granting of public interest standing remains discretionary. Hence, in each case the proposed public interest plaintiff must make a very persuasive argument for standing.

Class Actions

A **class action** is a procedural mechanism that is used when large numbers of plaintiffs sue over the same event or set of facts. Class actions do not give plaintiffs any additional rights; rather, they are intended to facilitate the efficient progress of the case. The chapter-opening case study gives a real-life glimpse into the nature of a class action. However, it is possible to give many other examples.

Assume, for example, that a company negligently allowed a contaminant to leak from its facility and affected over 40 landowners in the immediate vicinity such that their groundwater was contaminated.

Using the traditional lawsuit method, every landowner affected by the contaminated groundwater would bring a separate action. However, in a class action, one plaintiff (called the **representative plaintiff**) brings one action on behalf of all the affected landowners. Usually a notice is posted in newspapers informing the public of the class action. In our example, the notice would ask the affected landowners to contact the plaintiff's lawyer.

The representative plaintiff must have the class certified, or approved, by the court. The lawsuit then carries on in much the same way as any other. The difference is that the result of the action by the representative plaintiff binds all members of the class. The win or loss by the representative plaintiff is a win or loss for all of the members of the class. Rules of court procedure usually permit plaintiffs to opt out of the class at the beginning of the process if for any reason they do not want to be bound by the class action. A plaintiff might opt out if he or she wanted to start a separate action, for example.

---

class action   a procedural mechanism used when a large number of plaintiffs sue over the same event or set of facts

representative plaintiff   in a class action, the plaintiff who brings the action on behalf of the class of plaintiffs

Class actions also require that it be demonstrated that some issues are in common to all class members' claims and a demonstration that the class action approach is the best way of dealing with the claims in dispute.

The courts have taken a cautious approach with respect to class actions involving environmental claims. In 2001 in *Hollick v. Toronto (City)*, the Supreme Court of Canada concluded that a class action concerning a claim by 30,000 residents living near a landfill site should not be certified.[1] The claim was based on complaints by the residents that the landfill produced fumes and noise such that it interfered with the use and enjoyment of their properties. The Supreme Court of Canada stated essentially that a class action was not the preferred approach because the diversity and complexity of individual claims overshadowed any one common claim.

However, as the chapter-opening case study shows, class actions are still possible. In the case study, the original class action included health claims. However, the claim was narrowed to claims to property in order to avoid the issues that arose in the *Hollick* case.

Interventions

Once a legal action is already under way, other interested parties may want to become involved. These parties may wish to intervene in the case to protect their interests or to have their concerns and points of view heard by the court.

Intervention is a procedural device that allows persons or organizations that are not plaintiffs or defendants to participate in a legal proceeding. Intervention is particularly relevant in environmental law cases since businesses, environmental groups, community organizations, and others may want to participate in cases that could set binding precedents or raise important policy implications for the present and future of environmental law.

Most of the provinces have the same general procedural rules and tests for intervention. The two types of intervention are *intervention as an added party* and *intervention as a friend of the court*. Each type of intervention has its own common law heritage and its own test for status. An intervenor as an added party becomes a party to the legal action and is thus afforded greater rights than an intervenor as a friend of the court. An intervenor as a friend of the court remains a non-party to the proceeding, but enjoys limited participation rights. In practice, the distinction between these two types of intervention may become blurred. Because courts carefully define the rights of each intervenor, some intervenors may be given rights that are broader than a friend of the court but narrower than an added party. There are also specific rules for interventions at appeal courts, federal courts, and the Supreme Court of Canada.

---

intervention   a procedural device that allows persons or organizations that are not plaintiffs or defendants to participate in a legal proceeding as added parties or friends of the court

Added Party

A person or organization may apply to a court to gain intervenor status as an added party. If the application is successful, the person or organization becomes a party to the proceeding with a fairly broad array of rights, including the right to file pleadings, introduce evidence, examine and cross-examine witnesses at trial, present arguments, and appeal an adverse ruling. These rights are attractive to prospective intervenors who want to present evidentiary material. However, with the rights of a party come the potential risks, such as an adverse costs order if the case is unsuccessful.

To attain the status of an intervenor as an added party, the rules usually require that applicants establish that they have an interest in the subject matter of the proceeding or that they may be adversely affected by a judgment in the proceeding.

Traditionally, the interest test required that the applicant's direct legal interests would be affected—for example, when a case involves the interpretation of a forestry licence held by a company and a First Nations wants to intervene to protect its land claim or treaty rights or when the applicant would be directly affected commercially. Gradually, courts widened the test to include a less direct interest in the subject matter of the case by using terms such as "vital," "legitimate," or "substantial" interests. This broader interpretation of the rule is important since it creates the possibility of adding public interest litigants—such as community groups or environmental organizations—as parties to the litigation.

The second test deals with whether the prospective intervenor will be "adversely affected." Courts have not made much of an effort to distinguish between having a "direct interest" and being "adversely affected." However, it is usually safe to assume that if applicants meet the direct interest test, they will also be directly affected by the outcome of the proceeding.

Friend of the Court

If a person is granted the status of an intervenor as a **friend of the court**, which is sometimes known as an *amicus curiae*, the person does not become a party. Rather than having the full rights of a party, this type of intervenor has the right to present oral and/or written submissions to the court.

To gain intervenor status as a friend of the court, the applicant must demonstrate that he or she will assist the court in resolving the issues before it. Historically, a friend of the court would assist the court by informing it of a relevant fact or circumstance or by advising it on a point of law. It is fair to say that this narrow notion of "assistance" has widened. It now involves a consideration of whether the applicant can address an issue that the parties are not fully canvassing, bring a different or

---

friend of the court an intervenor with the right to present oral and/or written submissions to the court, but without the full rights of a party (also called an *amicus curiae*)

unique perspective to the issues at hand, or add expertise or specialized knowledge that will make the ultimate decision more informed.

Public Interest

At times, the categories of added party and friend of the court become blurred because of a gradual trend to broaden the scope of both types of intervention in recognition of the need to consider the public interest. As a result, **public interest intervention**, for all practical purposes, has become a category in itself.

Public interest intervention is commonly recognized where a provision of the *Canadian Charter of Rights and Freedoms* is being interpreted and applied and the court would benefit from submissions about the implications of various interpretations. Apart from Charter cases, many environmental law cases have intervenors since so many of the cases have broad public interest implications.

Public interest intervention allows different stakeholders in society—such as environmental groups, business associations, and informed individuals—to participate in important litigation that may have implications far beyond the four corners of the dispute.

Causes of Action

Not all grievances can be litigated. For example, if the smell of your neighbour's barbecue disturbs you, it is unlikely that you have grounds to sue. Causes of action are categories of grievances that are recognized by the common law and can be litigated. These "causes of action" are sometimes called "civil wrongs" or "torts." In short, the activity complained of that leads to the harm must be recognized by the court as a civil wrong in order to be granted relief.

Causes of action are distinguished from criminal offences, which are prosecuted by the state. In a civil lawsuit, the onus is on the plaintiff to prove that

- the defendant did something that falls within an established cause of action, and
- the defendant's action caused harm to the plaintiff.

The most recognized and relevant causes of action in environmental matters are nuisance, trespass, negligence, and strict liability.

---

public interest intervention   a category of intervention that blurs the added party and friend of the court categories, and which is commonly recognized where the Charter is an issue in the case

Nuisance

Nuisance occurs when one person unreasonably interferes with the use and enjoyment of someone else's property. What is reasonable in one circumstance may be unreasonable in another. Courts consider such circumstances as the gravity of the harm and the nature of the neighbourhood. The annoyance of occasional barbecue smells is not a serious enough harm to amount to nuisance. However, a neighbour who is raising pigs in his backyard might be liable for nuisance (as well as guilty of violating zoning bylaws).

As noted in the chapter-opening case study, a nuisance may not only be an unreasonable interference with one's land, but also something that has caused injury or harm to the land.

One of the defences to a nuisance claim is that the government authorized the activity that led to the nuisance by issuing a permit or an approval. Hence, a person living beside a factory would have a major hurdle to overcome in bringing a successful civil action against the company if the emissions are squarely within the terms of the approval issued by the government.

Trespass

Trespass is traditionally defined as an "invasion" of property; however, simply walking over property without the owner's permission may amount to trespass. Examples of trespass include fences encroaching past a property line, snowmobilers crossing into private property to find a trail, and advertisers posting flyers on someone else's property. In most other causes of action, plaintiffs must establish that they suffered harm in order to collect damages (monetary compensation). However, the mere act of trespass is sufficient to give rise to damages, and plaintiffs are not required to establish that any real harm occurred. Plaintiffs may be awarded only nominal damages in trespass cases where the act of trespass is of a minor nature.

Whether pollution can be considered a trespass is a contentious issue. The decisions of some cases suggest that a trespass must involve an invasion by a "physical mass" rather than invisible pollutants.

Public Nuisance

A public nuisance occurs when a whole community, rather than merely one person, is annoyed by the actions of a party. It may be prompted by the release of noxious or offensive smells, or exposure to a serious infectious disease. Generally, a public nuisance is defined as "an injury inflicted on or an interference with the rights of the community at large rather than individual members."[2]

---

nuisance   tort in which the defendant interferes with the use and enjoyment of the plaintiff's property

trespass   a physical presence on someone else's property, without permission

A typical example of a public nuisance would be a company dumping something into a waterway and thereby polluting an entire beach. It could be argued that no person in particular has suffered any more than another in the sense that everyone is precluded from using the beach until the contamination is cleaned up.

The challenge posed by a public nuisance action is that the government (usually represented by the attorney general) can stay the action—that is, prevent the litigation from going forward. In this sense, a public nuisance action can only proceed with the express or implicit permission by the relevant government authority.[3] Hence, public nuisance is typically not seen as a cause of action, but as a barrier for members of a community to bring an action. While some debate exists about the relevance of this concept, a number of jurisdictions have established laws to remove public nuisance as a barrier to bringing a lawsuit.[4]

Negligence

Negligence is the basis of many environmental lawsuits. Several elements must be proven by the plaintiff to establish negligence:

- *Duty of care.* The defendant had an obligation to the plaintiff to act reasonably.
- *Standard of care.* The defendant did not act reasonably in the circumstances.
- *Foreseeability.* The harm suffered by the plaintiff was a foreseeable consequence of the defendant's breach of the standard of care.

Negligence occurs when someone fails to act reasonably and, thus, causes harm to someone to whom a duty of care is owed. The harm suffered by a plaintiff must be foreseeable—for example, a bleach manufacturer would not be held liable if a purchaser used the bleach to poison a neighbour's tree. This result is too remote from the actions of the manufacturer.

Generally, everyone has a **duty of care**—the legal obligation to act reasonably so that harm does not occur to others. For example, if you are driving your neighbour to an environmental convention, you owe a duty of care to your neighbour to drive in a reasonable manner. You also owe a duty of care to other drivers, bicyclists, and pedestrians.

What is *a reasonable manner*? The standard of care owed to others varies depending on the circumstances. For example, a taxi driver who solicits a fee for riding in a taxi may be held to a higher **standard of care** than a neighbour who does you a favour. Similarly, the standard of care required with respect to storing chemicals may be lower for a homeowner than for a major industrial facility.

---

negligence   failure to act reasonably, with the result being harm to someone else

duty of care   the legal obligation to act reasonably so that harm does not occur to others

standard of care   the degree or level of care that is required—what is reasonable in the circumstances

Strict Liability

Another cause of action commonly cited in environmental lawsuits is **strict liability**, sometimes called "the rule in *Rylands v. Fletcher.*" The general principle is that "people who bring onto their land for their own use anything likely to do harm if it escapes do so at their own peril."[5] If the potentially harmful material escapes and harm ensues, the defendant is liable even if the defendant took all reasonable precaution and was not negligent in the activities. Sometimes strict liability is referred to as "absolute liability," in that the plaintiff may not have to prove that the defendant did anything wrong. The usual application of this principle in the environmental context is when someone undertakes an abnormal use of land, has some extra-hazardous material on the land, or uses the land for some environmentally risky business. As one commentator noted, "noxious gases, effluent discharges, mercury, radioactivity, lead, and the like might, under some circumstances, be caught by this rule."[6] However, as noted in the chapter-opening case study, the Court of Appeal found the defendant's nickel refinery not subject to strict liability because its emissions were not considered "extra hazardous" and the operation of its refinery was not a "non-natural use" of the industrial land on which it was located.

Statutory Causes of Action

The causes of action mentioned above are grounded in common law—that is, legal principles that have evolved through case law. In some cases, legislatures create new causes of action to give people the specific right to commence a lawsuit if certain conditions are met. For example, the *Canadian Environmental Protection Act, 1999* and the Ontario *Environmental Bill of Rights, 1993* both create statutory causes of action. The causes of action enacted by these statutes are narrow and limited in scope. They are also essentially the same and can be summarized as follows:

- Any person may bring an action if someone has violated an identified environmental law.
- Before bringing an action, litigants must request an investigation in accordance with the procedures outlined in the statute.
- Defendants will not be found liable if they can prove due diligence—that is, that they took reasonable care to prevent the incident.
- No damages are available to the plaintiffs.
- Remedies may be ordered to address any harm done.

Because of the limited scope of these causes of action, the federal and the provincial statutory causes of action have rarely been used to date.

---

strict liability   a liability incurred by a party who undertakes a hazardous activity on a property and allows harmful material to escape that harms others; the party is liable even if he or she took all reasonable precaution and was not negligent in the activities

Causation: Establishing the Cause–Effect Relationship

In most environmental lawsuits, the most difficult obstacle to success is causation—establishing that the injury or harm complained of was the direct result of the actions of the defendant. The rule of **causation** is usually expressed as follows: causation is established when the harm suffered by the plaintiff would not have occurred "but for" the defendant's action. Causation must be established on a balance of probabilities—that is, that the defendant's activities probably caused the harm complained of by the plaintiff.

Demonstrating causation is a complex matter. In a negligence action, can the plaintiff prove that a company defendant was negligent in not maintaining pipes and valves that caused a leak into a local waterway? In a nuisance action, can plaintiffs living near a lead smelter establish that they suffer from a higher rate of cancer than the general population? It is exceedingly difficult to prove that a particular case of cancer would not have occurred "but for" the existence of the smelter. In this instance, the plaintiffs will have to establish that their cancer arose directly from the conduct of the defendant. When one thinks about it, it is difficult to establish generally how and why one gets cancer, and now sufficient evidence must be provided that establishes a cancer was caused by the defendant's emissions.

Many environmental cases have travelled through the various levels of courts for years, owing to the complexity of both the law and the facts. The case profiled in Box 13.2 illustrates how a family was successful in proving causation and negligence in a lawsuit against the Ontario government.

Damages and Remedies

Generally speaking, court cases are divided into two parts: liability and remedy. Liability involves proof of the elements of the cause of action, and **remedy** relates to compensation. What form of remedy is appropriate? If a remedy involves damages (monetary compensation), how much money is adequate?

Most often, plaintiffs want monetary compensation and therefore must attach a monetary value to the harm they have suffered. In other circumstances, plaintiffs may simply want a court to order a defendant to do or to refrain from doing something.

Monetary Damages

Establishing the appropriate amount of monetary damages to compensate a plaintiff is often very challenging. The plaintiff may need to bring evidence through expert witnesses and documentation to prove the amount of damages.

---

causation   the evidentiary link between the conduct of the defendant and the damages complained of in a lawsuit such that the damages complained of would not have occurred but for the actions of the defendant

remedy   court-ordered redress to a plaintiff in a civil case, such as monetary compensation

Berendsen v. Ontario: Establishing Causation and Negligence in a Land Contamination Case

In *Berendsen v. Ontario*,* a farming family was successful in proving causation, as well as the other elements of negligence, in its lawsuit against a provincial government that refused to take responsibility for road waste dumped on the farm. In the mid-1960s, the Ontario Ministry of Transportation undertook roadwork near a small town in Ontario. The ministry's contractor buried truckloads of the road surface waste of concrete and asphalt beside a watercourse on a nearby farm. A family bought the farm and ran a dairy operation close to the place where the waste was buried. Soon after they started the farming operation, the family noticed that their cattle and other farm animals were refusing to drink water from a creek near the barn. As a result, the cattle became dehydrated and ill, which resulted in poor milk production. Some of the cattle, as well as chickens and rabbits, died prematurely. Some family members also experienced health problems. Eventually the family moved to another farm. Since the family was unable to sell the property with its suspected environmental problems, the land remained vacant and abandoned.

The family brought a lawsuit against the province of Ontario, claiming that the buried road waste contributed to the damages that occurred. They sued the province in negligence for burying potentially toxic wastes near a source of water and failing to remediate the situation once the problem became known.

The province denied all liability. It challenged several of the elements of negligence, and made the following claims:

- It owed no duty of care to the family, and it was not liable for the acts of an independent contractor.
- It did not breach the standard of care because the burial of waste material on rural property was a common practice in the 1960s.
- No causal connection existed between the road waste and the water contamination. The health problems experienced by the cattle were the result of poor farm management.
- It was not foreseeable that burying the waste would cause harm to cattle and humans.

The court ruled in favour of the plaintiff, and found that the plaintiff had established all the elements of negligence and causation on a balance of probabilities.

The defendant did owe a duty of care to the plaintiff. There was a clear relationship of proximity (a relationship that gives rise to a duty of care) between the defendant that deposited the waste materials and the occupiers of the land on which the waste was deposited.

Policy considerations favoured upholding a high standard of care. The public obviously derived a benefit from the defendant's road maintenance and repair activities, and these activities included the incidental disposal of waste materials. The defendant breached the standard of care both by depositing and burying the harmful waste close to a natural watercourse and dairy farm well and residence, and by conducting an inadequate investigation and remediation of the harmful environmental effects of the buried waste.

The harm was foreseeable. The defendant knew or ought to have known that asphalt was a petroleum-based product containing potentially harmful residue. The defendant would have known that care and common sense had to be exercised both in the placement of the waste on private lands and in its duty to investigate and eliminate the continuing harmful effects in the 1980s, when it was called on to remedy the situation.

The deposit of the roadside waste was the cause of the harm suffered by the plaintiff. The expert evidence presented at trial was reviewed extensively in the court's decision. The court noted that not only was there evidence of a substantial connection between the buried materials and the contamination of the well water, but also the evidence persuasively eliminated other potential causes of contamination. For example, the dioxin detected in the water would not have emanated from other sources on the farm, such as debris from fires or residue from chemical storage.

In the end, the court held the defendant liable for business loss, loss of farm property value, economic loss, and other damages totalling over $1.7 million.

The lower court ruling was overturned by the Ontario Court of Appeal.[†] The Court of Appeal expressed concern about the trial judge's finding on causation because of the trial judge's "wholesale rejection of one side's experts" and the "wholesale acceptance of the other side's experts."[‡] However, the Court of Appeal stated that its concern, by itself, "does not undermine" the lower court's finding on causation. Instead, the Court of Appeal found that the case of negligence was not established by the plaintiff: the defendant did not breach the standard of care in that the damage that occurred from the burying of waste in the 1960s was not foreseeable. The Court of Appeal noted that the plaintiff had the onus of establishing that the harm was a reasonably foreseeable risk and that "foreseeability of harm had to be assessed when the conduct in issue occurred, in the 1960s, not today when we know so much more about the risks of toxicity from waste material."[§]

---

*   *Berendsen v. Ontario*, 2008 CanLII 1416 (Ont. SCJ).

†   *Berendsen v. Ontario*, 2009 ONCA 845.

‡   Ibid., at para. 34.

§   Ibid., at para. 62.

Imagine, for example, that a company is found liable for spilling a toxic chemical and contaminating the groundwater under your property. However, if your water source is the municipal system, and you do not use the groundwater, what are your damages? You may argue that the value of your property has suffered depreciation, although a new buyer may neither notice nor care about the state of the groundwater. In the case, you will have to establish that in fact the groundwater contamination did affect the value of your property.

Now imagine the situation of a farmer who is complaining about dust and odour from a nearby landfill. However, the nuisance affects neither the farmer's ability to farm nor the farmer's enjoyment of his land. The farmer's monetary damages may be very small even though a nuisance has been established.

Generally speaking, there are three categories of damages: special damages, general damages, and punitive damages.

- **Special damages** are damages directly caused by the defendant's behaviour, and are easily and objectively quantifiable. Examples include costs of repair, remedial measures, and cleanup; costs of monitoring and testing water; and medical bills. They are out-of-pocket expenses incurred by the plaintiff.
- **General damages** are subjective and not as easily quantified. They include loss of enjoyment; pain and suffering; future effects, such as future monitoring and testing of water; depreciation of land value; and loss of business. Expert witnesses are often required to make a convincing case regarding the appropriate amount of general damages. When determining the size of damages awards, courts consider the size of awards in similar cases.

---

special damages   damages directly caused by the defendant's behaviour that are easily and objectively quantifiable, such as the costs of repair

general damages   damages that are subjective and not easily quantified, such as pain and suffering

- **Punitive damages** go beyond the usual purpose of damages—that is, putting the plaintiff back into the position she was in before the event. Instead, they focus on punishing the defendant and setting an example. Punitive damages are rarely awarded because they are warranted only when a defendant acts in a particularly malicious, grossly reckless, or violent manner, and when the defendant has not been punished by other means, such as by fines.

Equitable Relief

Equitable relief may be available at the discretion of a court when monetary compensation is inadequate or inappropriate. For example, a plaintiff who is suffering from a nuisance caused by his neighbour may be more interested in having the nuisance stop than in receiving monetary compensation.

An **injunction** is a court order that requires a defendant either to do something (a mandatory injunction) or to refrain from doing something (a prohibitory injunction). For example, a mandatory injunction may be employed to order a polluter to install a pollution control system, and a prohibitory injunction may be employed to order a polluter to stop its environmentally harmful activities.

Injunctions are ordered at the discretion of the court and are not granted routinely. One of the barriers encountered by plaintiffs who apply for injunctions is the possibility that courts may require them to provide security for costs. In the event that the defendant is successful at trial, the costs arising from the imposition of the injunction will be paid to the defendant out of the amount that the plaintiff has posted as security.

Another form of equitable relief is a declaration. A **declaration** is simply a finding of a court. For example, a court may make a declaration that a defendant has not complied with an environmental assessment process or has not provided proper monitoring data. Although in and of itself a declaration may not provide relief to a plaintiff, it may assist in further private or public action.

Costs

In Canada, the costs of a lawsuit are awarded to the winning party. This means that the losing party must pay the costs of the winner. The purpose of this rule is to protect defendants against frivolous lawsuits and to encourage parties to settle their differences before expending court resources. However, a costs award usually represents only a portion of the total costs incurred. Furthermore, a court has the

---

punitive damages damages intended to punish the defendant and set an example

injunction a court order that requires a defendant either to do something (a mandatory injunction) or to refrain from doing something (a prohibitory injunction)

declaration a finding of the court, given without other relief

discretion not to award costs—for example, in a test case or a case that raises a matter of general public interest. Obviously many environmental groups attempt to bring their cases within these exemptions. However, the matter always remains within the discretion of the court.

Mediation

Mediation (a form of alternative dispute resolution; see Chapter 4) and pretrial negotiations are almost always attempted for the purpose of resolving a matter before it is necessary to incur the expense and expend the energy involved in a lengthy trial. By far, the majority of cases are settled before trial begins.

In some jurisdictions, mediation and pretrial negotiations are mandatory. Trained mediators attempt to find common ground among the parties and resolve the dispute. Only if this process is exhausted without a successful resolution may the matter proceed to trial.

Court Action as an Environmental Protection Tool: Its Limits and Potential

One would assume that increased environmental concern in recent times would make court actions the instrument of choice to pursue environmental causes. However, many of the challenges that arise in any court action are compounded in environmental matters. Indeed, legal commentators have highlighted the uphill battles in pursuing environmental lawsuits. In terms of lawsuits related to toxic chemicals, Professor Jamie Benedickson noted that litigation remains "a source of continuing fascination for those interested in the inherent limitations of common law proceedings."[7] David Boyd, an environmental law scholar, gives an equally challenging view of environmental litigation by stating that the judicial system's contribution to furthering environmental protection goals is undermined for a variety of reasons, including "a historical bias toward private rather than public interests, the absence of constitutional environmental rights, a lack of access to the courts, the high costs of litigation, judicial deference to government decision makers, and low penalties for environmental offences."[8]

Causal Links and Quantifying Damages

It is easy to understand why environmental lawsuits are challenging. Plaintiffs are faced with the age-old problem of attempting to establish the causal link between the damaging conduct and the resultant harm. Establishing such a link can be a

---

mediation a structured dispute resolution process that involves a third party (a mediator) to assist in the confidential negotiation of the issues in hope of settling all or part of the dispute and thus avoid or shorten the litigation process

daunting task since the impact of environmentally damaging activities can be affected by other factors. The other problem is quantifying damages. The legal system has not yet evolved to be able to recognize or measure the inherent value of nature or its pristine water, natural heritage features, or old-growth forests. Instead, it has concentrated on nature's market value. As noted above, the time, costs, and evidentiary hurdles of court actions suggest that the role of the judicial system as an environmental protection tool is limited to all but the most clear cases.

Generally, it can be said that the court system may simply not be equipped in many circumstances to respond to environmental protection challenges. Indeed, many individuals and groups across Canada can well describe their frustration with the process. Nevertheless, it would be unwise to give up. Over the years, many courts have slowly become sensitized to the environmental plight. The Supreme Court of Canada, for example, has described the environment as "one of the major challenges of our time" and environmental stewardship as a "fundamental value" of Canadian society.[9]

Despite the growing sensitivity of the courts, however, legal rules concerning standing, causation, and costs may require further changes to better respond to the challenges of environmental protection litigation.

SUMMARY OF KEY POINTS

- In Canada, civil lawsuits are common, and issues were litigated as far back as the 1800s. Little legislation related to environmental matters existed at the time, and the courts were therefore required to apply general principles of the common law to the particulars of each case. Environmental lawsuits present a number of challenges.

- One of the challenges for environmental lawsuits is standing or status to sue. Usually, lawsuits involve a plaintiff suing a defendant because his or her property, financial status, or personal health has been negatively affected by the actions of the defendant. However, when a person wants to defend the interests of the environment generally, achieving standing becomes more difficult. In this instance, the person has to argue that public interest standing should be granted in that the person has a genuine interest in the matter and no one is in a better position to bring the lawsuit.

- Class actions and interventions are procedural mechanisms that allow persons to gain access to the courts. A class action allows a representative plaintiff to act on behalf of the entire class of plaintiffs in a single action. Class actions, although they further judicial economy, do not create substantive rights. An intervention is a procedural device that allows persons to participate in a legal action in situations where they have a direct interest or would be substantially affected by the outcome of the proceeding. An intervention can be made as an added party or a friend of the court.

- Once the standing hurdle is overcome, the plaintiff must plead a relevant cause of action. The most common causes of action in environmental matters are nuisance, negligence, trespass, and strict liability. Nuisance is an unreasonable interference with the use and enjoyment of another's property. Trespass entails someone putting something on or travelling through another's property without permission. Negligence is a failure to show a duty of care owed to another person. Finally, strict liability is a liability incurred by a party who undertakes a hazardous activity on a property and allows harmful material to escape that harms others.

- One of the challenges in environmental lawsuits is establishing causation—that the harm endured by the plaintiff would not have occurred "but for" the actions of the defendant.

- If standing, causes of action, and causation have been established, the plaintiff is entitled to various forms of damages or injunctive relief. It should be recalled that in Canada, the "loser pay" rule is in effect; that is, the party who loses the lawsuit has to pay both his or her costs and the costs of the other party.

- Increasingly, mediation is playing a role in litigation. In mediation, through the assistance of a third party (the mediator), the parties try to resolve various issues in hope of arriving at the settlement of all or part of the lawsuit.

- Environmental lawsuits remain an important tool for persons to be compensated for harm to their health, their property, or natural resources. However, such lawsuits present a number of challenges.

KEY TERMS

causation	mediation	special damages
class action	negligence	standard of care
declaration	nuisance	standing
duty of care	public interest intervention	strict liability
friend of the court	public interest standing	"three p" rule
general damages	punitive damages	trespass
injunction	remedy	
intervention	representative plaintiff	

DISCUSSION QUESTIONS

1. Using the reasoning in the *Smith v. Inco Limited* (see the chapter-opening case study), would the outcome have been different if the substances emanating from the plant were different? Give some examples of substances that may result in a finding by the court that the emissions were a nuisance.
2. What is meant by "an environmental lawsuit"?
3. What are the key challenges of environmental litigation?
4. Do you think popular legal movies, such as *A Civil Action*, reflect the reality of environmental lawsuits?
5. If the groundwater you rely on for drinking water was affected by a nearby landfill, what causes of action would you rely on in your lawsuit?
6. Why is causation one of the most significant hurdles for environmental litigation? In what situations would causation be a particular issue? And what are some techniques or ways you think causation could be dealt with in those situations?
7. Do remedies in civil actions actually address environmental harm? If endangered species are adversely affected by someone's actions, what remedies would you pursue, and how effective would they be?
8. What role and degree of success do you think mediation can play in environmental litigation? Would mediation have more or less chances of success in environmental matters?
9. What reforms would you suggest to ensure the public has greater access to the courts in order to protect public natural resources?

SUGGESTED READINGS

Benedickson, Jamie. "Environmental Law Survey (1980-92), Part 1." (1992) 24 *Ottawa Law Review* 733, at 763.

Collins, Lynda M. "An Ecologically Literate Reading of the Canadian Charter of Rights and Freedoms" (2009) 26 *Windsor Review of Legal and Social Issues* 7.

Collins, Lynda M., and Heather McLeod-Kilmurray. "Material Contribution to Justice? Toxic Causation After *Resurfice Corp. v. Hanke*." (2010) 48 *Osgoode Hall Law Journal* 411.

Elgie, Stewart, and Anastasio Lintner. "The Supreme Court's *Canfor* Decision: Losing the Battle but Winning the War for Environmental Damages." (2005) 38 *UBC Law Review* 223.

Estrin, David, and John Swaigen. *Environment on Trial: A Guide to Ontario Environmental Law and Policy*, 3rd ed., chapter 6. Toronto: Emond Montgomery, 1993.

Stone, Christopher D. *Should Trees Have Standing? Law, Morality, and the Environment*, 3rd ed. New York: Oxford University Press, 2010.

Taylor, Matthew, Patrick Field, Lawrence Susskind, and William Tilleman. "Using Mediation in Environmental Tribunals: Opportunities and Best Practices." (1999) 22 *Dalhousie Law Journal* 51.

NOTES

1. *Hollick v. Toronto (City)*, 2001 SCC 68, [2001] 3 SCR 158.

2. See Paul Muldoon and Richard Lindgren, *The Environmental Bill of Rights: A Practical Guide* (Toronto: Emond Montgomery, 1995), at 168.

3. See West Coast Environmental Law, "Common Law—Public Causes of Action," last modified July 7, 2011, http://www.bcwatersheds.org/wiki/index.php?title =Common_Law_%E2%80%93_Public_Causes_of_Action.

4. See, e.g., s. 103 of Ontario's *Environmental Bill of Rights, 1993*, SO 1993, c. 28.

5. David Estrin and John Swaigen, *Environment on Trial: A Guide to Ontario Environmental Law and Policy*, 3rd ed. (Toronto: Emond Montgomery, 1993), at 118.

6. Ibid.

7. Jamie Benedickson, "Environmental Law Survey (1980-92), Part 1" (1992) 24 *Ottawa Law Review* 733, at 764.

8. David Boyd, *Unnatural Law—Rethinking Canadian Environmental Law and Policy* (Vancouver: UBC Press, 2003), at 267.

9. *Friends of the Oldman River Society v. Canada (Minister of Transport)*, [1992] 1 SCR 3; and *R v. Hydro-Québec*, [1997] 3 SCR 213, at para. 127.

CHAPTER 14

Using Administrative Decision-Making Processes to Protect the Environment

Introduction

Many years ago, a story appeared in a Vancouver newspaper by a reporter who attended a **public hearing** of the British Columbia Pollution Control Board (the environmental regulatory tribunal of the day).[1] The hearing concerned an application by a mining company for an approval to discharge copper mine waste into

public hearing a formal meeting where members of the public provide facts and opinion on a proposed government action to a decision-making body

Rupert Inlet, in northern Vancouver Island. The reporter described how company experts were questioned about and explained scientific and technical issues, while nobody else in the community hall "understood a thing." Environmental groups, whose members included knowledgeable specialists, had not been granted **standing** to participate in the hearing. These specialists were reduced to whispering questions to several citizens who had been permitted to participate, and who tried to put the specialists' questions to the company's experts. It was bad theatre and a very ineffective public hearing. Many participants in various kinds of public hearings in different parts of Canada can relate to this frustrating procedure.

This story illustrates the kind of public participation issues that administrative law can potentially address. Procedural fairness in administrative law, discussed below, requires that decision-makers provide affected persons with a full and fair opportunity to be heard. But the standing of environmental groups, as opposed to affected citizens, to participate may still be in doubt, also discussed below. However, citizen participants have played a major role in hearings, and their contributions have influenced decision outcomes, as the Northern gas pipelines saga case study shows.

Through environmental assessment public review processes, citizen participants have contributed to more complete and better balanced environmental assessments. For example, environmental groups have promoted the idea of assessment of cumulative effects in a number of panel hearings under the *Canadian Environmental Assessment Act, 1999*. Although results are mixed,[2] these interventions have assisted developments in the scope of cumulative-effects assessment under the Act. In Alberta, citizens have been active participants in hearings on well licence applications that were denied by the Energy and Utilities Board. Noteworthy cases include applications by Amoco Canada Ltd.[3] and Polaris Resources Ltd.[4] In the latter case, the board noted the potential environmental impacts in the sensitive montane region of Alberta's Rocky Mountain eastern slopes and the corporation's failure to address community concerns, including cumulative environmental effects.

Much environmental law, including the Amoco and Polaris cases, involves administrative decision-making. It is therefore worthwhile to acquire a basic understanding of the principles and practices of administrative law. This chapter explains different types of administrative decisions, placing particular attention on decision-making by tribunals. It introduces the environmental public hearing process and the common law concept of procedural fairness, along with its attendant safeguards. As well, it emphasizes the importance of understanding the statute that governs each administrative decision-maker and the role of the courts in overseeing administrative decision-making.

---

standing the right to sue

The Northern Gas Pipeline Saga

The processes for reviewing and analyzing proposals for large diameter pipelines to move natural gas from the Canadian Arctic to southern North American markets have had an important influence on the development of Canadian environmental law. The regulatory reviews and judicial review cases that arose out of the pipeline review proceedings have been particularly significant. They resulted in milestone decisions on critical procedural matters, including community hearings to receive Aboriginal traditional knowledge, intervenor funding, and decision-maker impartiality.

The northern gas pipeline story spans more than 35 years and involves two separate sets of pipeline proposals.* The first set of pipeline plans, which included two competing proposals—one following a Mackenzie Valley route and the other an Alaska Highway route—was advanced in the early 1970s. Approval then, as now, was required by the National Energy Board (NEB). The first proposal that was announced, the Mackenzie Valley Pipeline, created sufficient public controversy that the federal government established a commission of inquiry under Justice Thomas Berger. Justice Berger's mandate was to study the project's environmental, social, and economic impact regionally, to hold hearings, and to report to the responsible federal minister.

Hearings took place from 1974 to 1976. The inquiry's procedure, rulings, and final report produced a number of Canadian environmental law firsts. One was the structured, yet open, procedure adopted. Formal hearings involving the applicant (Canadian Arctic Gas Pipeline Ltd.), an expert panel funded by the applicant, Aboriginal and environmental intervenors, and a competing pipeline company were held in Yellowknife and other communities. But, significantly, dozens of informal hearings were held in small communities. Justice Berger was determined to hear from the people along the route of the proposed pipeline, and he did. The informal hearings were a preview of the important role that traditional Aboriginal knowledge would have in subsequent regulatory proceedings. Intervenors in the formal hearings received funding from the inquiry to participate. Justice Berger was adamant that although public interest groups "do not represent the public interest ... it is in the public interest that they should be heard."[†] After hearing representation from the parties, he ruled that interest groups seeking funding had to meet the following criteria:

Justice Thomas Berger's commission visited numerous remote communities in the Northwest Territories from 1974 to 1976. Here, Dene Chief Jim Thom visits remote fishing villages to inform people of Berger's upcoming hearings on the proposed Mackenzie Valley Pipeline.

Source: PWNHC / Michael Jackson.

1. A clearly ascertainable interest that ought to be represented at the inquiry.
2. It should be established that separate and adequate representation of that interest would make a necessary and substantial contribution to the inquiry.
3. Those seeking funds should have an established record of concern for, and should have demonstrated their own commitment to, the interest they sought to represent.
4. It should be shown that those seeking funds did not have sufficient financial resources to enable them adequately to represent that interest, and that they would require funds to do so.
5. Those seeking funds had to have a clearly delineated proposal as to the use they intended to make of the funds, and had to be sufficiently well-organized to account for the funds.[‡]

These funding criteria have become the gold standard for guiding participant funding decisions.

Justice Berger recommended that the pipeline should not proceed until Aboriginal land claims were settled in the region—precisely the same argument made by the Aboriginal intervenors. This recommendation and its supporting evidence provided an important basis for northern land claims negotiations that proceeded over the next 25 years. The inquiry also witnessed considerable collaboration between the Aboriginal and environmental group intervenors—a preview of the complex issues that have emerged around environmental law and the broadly similar, but not always consistent, objectives of First Nations and environmental groups.

Justice Berger stated in his report that for environmental protection, land use regulations based on the concept of multiple use were insufficient.[§] Land preservation was necessary to protect wilderness, wildlife species, and critical habitat. He also recognized basic ecological values. Thus, he ruled out northern Yukon and Mackenzie Delta pipeline routes and recommended that a wilderness park be established in northern Yukon. He did not use the term "precaution" in his reporting letter to the minister. But the idea of a precautionary principle, now

common currency in Canadian environmental law, comes through clearly. A similar precautionary approach was taken by the environmental coalition in the inquiry. The coalition argued that the proposed buried pipelines with chilled gas (to prevent problems resulting from discontinuous permafrost melting) amounted to experimenting on the North and should not be permitted.

Ultimately, the NEB approved both the Canadian Arctic Gas Pipeline and the competing Foothills Pipeline (Yukon) projects,[#] but not before two major events occurred.

First, the environmental intervenors raised a bias allegation against the NEB chair (who chaired the hearing panel), which they fought all the way to the Supreme Court of Canada.[**] The chair had been appointed six months before the NEB received the Canadian Arctic Gas Pipeline application. He had been president of the Canada Development Corporation, a member of the pipeline consortium, and had participated in planning and routing decisions. In a decision that has become the leading Canadian case on bias by administrative decision-makers, the Supreme Court ruled that participation by the NEB chair created a "reasonable apprehension of bias." This ruling voided the NEB process. The resulting delay, along with deteriorating national economic conditions, ensured that the pipelines did not proceed.

Fast forward to the early 2000s. A new Mackenzie Valley gas pipeline proposal emerged. In many ways it was remarkably similar to its 1970s predecessor. An NEB application for this $16 billion project was filed by the project consortium in 2004. Hearings, which included 15 Arctic communities, began in 2006 and led to approval in 2010, subject to 264 specific conditions concerning the environment, engineering, and other matters.[††]

Along the way, a unique cooperative regulatory assessment process was carried out based on a "Cooperation Plan" among ten federal, territorial, and First Nation agencies that had some type of regulatory or consultative process. This plan involved a joint federal–territorial–First Nation Environmental Review Panel and separate NEB hearings. An NEB panel member, who also sat on the Joint Review Panel, provided a critical link.

Not all First Nations were in agreement with the consultation process and filed judicial review applications, including a challenge to the Cooperation Plan. For example, the Dene Tha' First Nation argued that the federal government had not included them in the consultation that led to the Cooperation Plan, which infringed on constitutional Aboriginal consultation rights. The litigation contributed to the considerable overall length of the consultation process, but was ultimately settled in the Dene Tha' First Nation's favour. The action confirmed the procedural rights of First Nations and underlined the significance of the duty to consult,[‡‡] particularly in relation to large linear projects that affect the environment and Aboriginal rights.

The regulatory assessment process introduced innovative cooperative arrangements. But the result was a replay of the 1970s in the sense that the late 2000s recession, coupled with rapid development of shale gas in both Canada and the United States, resulted in the project not proceeding.

Ultimately, the 35-plus-year northern gas pipeline saga has shaped Canadian environmental and Aboriginal law in a number of ways. Procedural fairness and Aboriginal consultation principles were advanced. Perhaps most important, basic values, including early articulations of sustainability, precaution, and ecological integrity—values that underpin much of modern Canadian environmental law—were affirmed.

Questions

Can we look forward to project review, environmental decisions, and environmental decision processes continuing to advance fundamental environmental law principles? Why or why not?

---

[*]   Thomas Berger, *Northern Frontier, Northern Homeland: The Report of the Mackenzie Valley Pipeline Inquiry* (Ottawa: Minister of Supply and Services Canada, 1977).

[†]   Parliament of Canada, "Statements by Members," November 1, 1995, http://www.parl.gc.ca/HousePublications/Publication.aspx?DocId=2332511&Language=E&Mode=1.

[‡]   Berger, supra note *, vol. 2, appendix, at 225-26.

[§]   Ibid., at xi.

[#]   National Energy Board, *Reasons for Decision—Northern Pipelines* (Ottawa: Minister of Supply and Services Canada, 1977).

[**] *Committee for Justice and Liberty et al. v. National Energy Board et al.*, [1978] 1 SCR 369.

[††] Joint Review Panel for the Mackenzie Gas Project, *Foundation for a Sustainable Northern Future: Report*, vol. 1 (Ottawa: Minister of Environment, 2010), http://www.reviewboard.ca/upload/project_document/EIR0405-001_JRP_Report_of_Environmental_Review_Executive_Volume_I_1263228660.PDF.

[‡‡] Kirk Lambrecht, *Aboriginal Consultations, Environmental Assessment and Regulatory Review in Canada* (Regina: University of Regina Press, 2013).

Types of Administrative Decision-Making

Administrative decisions are decisions made by government officials or tribunals pursuant to a statute, which sets out the requisite decision-making process. They differ from judicial decisions, which are made by courts. There are two basic types of administrative decisions:

1. decisions made by a government employee or Cabinet minister; and
2. decisions made by a relatively impartial decision-maker (usually called a *tribunal* or a *board*), involving some form of hearing.

---

administrative decisions   decisions made pursuant to a statute, which sets out the requisite decision-making process

Environmental statutes often provide for administrative decisions. For example, initial decisions about whether to approve projects are usually delegated to environment ministries or sometimes to ministers, who make decisions on the basis of the advice of ministry personnel.[5] Applicants for approvals are usually required to inform and engage interested members of the public and provide their feedback to the decision-maker; however, public hearings are not commonly held at this stage. There is usually no formal process beyond applicants providing specific information and decision-makers exercising procedural fairness by receiving and considering the information submitted, and by providing reasons for their decision to affected persons. No general legal obligation exists to allow public participation through hearings in administrative law; public hearings are required when an applicable statute affords parties that right.[6]

The procedure at a public hearing is similar to the procedure in a court, and is often called *quasi-judicial*. Anyone who walks into a public hearing by some environmental tribunals—and most energy and natural resource tribunals, which have the statutory power to grant approvals for natural resource and energy developments—will think he or she is in a courtroom. Tribunal members sit at the front on a raised dais, and participants rise when members of the tribunal enter and exit the hearing room. Lawyers formally examine and cross-examine witnesses, make objections, and present arguments. Nevertheless, the process is less formal than the process of a court, with relaxed rules of procedure and evidence. Non-governmental organizations and members of the public are generally permitted to participate in some manner. Typically, decisions are based on statutory powers to decide whether proposed developments are in the public interest.[7]

Other tribunals are less formal. Hearings are conducted in the manner of a meeting or seminar with an agenda, interactive proceedings, and sometimes a round-table format. Often the degree of formality is determined by statutory requirements. Some tribunals, such as environmental appeal boards, may be required to hold oral hearings in accordance with the legal dictates of procedural fairness. Others, such as review panels under the *Canadian Environmental Assessment Act, 2012*, conduct their proceedings relatively informally.[8]

Tribunal Procedures

The law governing the procedures of administrative tribunals attempts to balance two competing interests: efficiency and fairness. An informal process is much quicker and less expensive than a formal court process, and it allows for the admission of a broader range of evidence from a wider scope of sources. However, too much informality may compromise fairness and the impartiality of the decision-maker by not, as a formal legal requirement, providing affected citizens with notice, information, and an opportunity to respond.

Natural Justice and Procedural Fairness

The fundamental procedural concept is **natural justice** or, as it has become more commonly known in the last two decades, **procedural fairness**.[9] This common law concept was developed by the English courts in the early 18th century. Elements of procedural fairness have since been codified in many statutes; however, unless a statute is clear and explicit in changing or excluding one of the common law rights of procedural fairness, the common law rights continue to apply and fill any gaps. For example, a statute may state that "personal written notice is not required" for a particular decision; however, the common law may still require that some form of notice—through advertising, for example—be given to persons affected by the decision.

A tribunal must employ three main elements of procedural fairness:

1. reasonable notice of a proposed decision and key issues against affected parties;[10]
2. a fair opportunity to be heard, orally[11] or in writing;[12] and
3. an impartial and independent decision-maker.[13]

Whether specific formal procedural rights—such as cross-examination, questioning of witnesses, or representation by legal counsel—apply depends on the circumstances, including the mandate of the empowering statute and the procedure that is followed. For example, the right to cross-examine may exist when a formal quasi-judicial procedure is used, but no such right may exist when a hearing assumes an informal meeting-type format.

Evidence

Evidence refers to facts, objects, and (in some circumstances) opinions that are presented to a decision-maker for the purposes of reaching a decision. To be admissible, evidence must be relevant to the subject of the decision, and it must be reasonably reliable.

---

natural justice   a doctrine originally developed by English judges; the common law procedural rights of a person affected by an administrative or quasi-judicial decision that include reasonable notice of a decision, a fair hearing, and an impartial decision-maker; it involves procedures that are more formal and less flexible than the doctrine of procedural fairness

procedural fairness   the modern doctrine of natural justice; the common law procedural rights of a person affected by an administrative or quasi-judicial decision, which include reasonable notice of a decision, a fair hearing, and an impartial decision-maker; specific procedures depend on the nature of the decision, the nature of the statutory scheme, the importance of the decision to the affected person, the reasonable expectations of the affected person, and the decision-maker's choice of procedures

evidence   facts, objects, and opinions that are presented to a decision-maker for the purpose of making a decision

Tribunals do not usually observe the stringent rules of evidence that apply in courts. This means that tribunals often receive **hearsay** evidence (statements about what a witness heard from another person) and opinions, even though a witness may not be formally qualified as an expert on the subject about which he expresses the opinion. Tribunals are generally less concerned than courts about assessing the relevance of evidence when deciding whether it is admissible. Often tribunals prefer to listen to the evidence and assess its relevance later when they decide how much weight, if any, to give to it.

Tribunals may also have the coercive powers to summon witnesses and compel production of evidence. These powers may be derived either from the statute governing a particular tribunal[14] or from the general powers of commissions of inquiry under public inquiries statutes. To compel the appearance of witnesses and documents, tribunals may issue subpoenas, usually on the application of a party to the proceeding.

Record

The **record** of proceedings includes the decision challenged and all evidence and arguments presented at a hearing. Decisions are usually required to be based on the record, and not on extraneous information.[15] For example, members of the tribunal may not base decisions on their own independent research, unless they invite input and response from hearing participants by requesting written comments or reopening the oral hearing. However, tribunals may take **official notice** of obvious and well-accepted facts—such as the fact that the Don River flows into Lake Ontario—without requiring formal proof.

The importance of a record is less obvious in proceedings such as **public inquiries**—that is, investigative proceedings that result in recommendations to government.[16] Recommendations may be based on the record of any hearings that such an inquiry decides to hold or on the results of its own investigations. This broad-ranging mandate makes sense because public inquiries result merely in recommendations to government, rather than in enforceable decisions.

Parties

In the context of administrative law, a party is a person or organization that is recognized by a tribunal as a participant in a decision-making process. Obtaining party

---

hearsay statements about what a witness heard from another person

record all evidence and arguments presented at a hearing

official notice the allowance of obvious and well-accepted facts by an administrative decision-maker, without the need for proof

public inquiry investigative proceedings that result in recommendations to government

status may depend on meeting a statutory test, such as being "directly affected" by a decision. If there is no statutory test for obtaining party status, tribunals may create their own tests or categories, provided that the principles of procedural fairness are respected. They may, for example, invite persons to decide whether they want to be full parties—that is, participants who are present throughout the hearing, submit evidence and arguments, and question witnesses—or whether they merely want to make a presentation or file a written submission. The tribunal then decides who can participate and in what capacity.[17]

Decisions and Reasons

Tribunals must, as their statutes require, reach explicit final decisions. In making their decisions, they must give due consideration to written and oral evidence that the parties have provided. Although not a general requirement, they usually issue written reasons for their decision, at least if directly requested to do so by persons significantly affected by it. This duty is particularly strong if affected persons are seriously impacted or need reasons to exercise a right to appeal the decision.[18]

Costs

Funding for hearing participation by members of the public and non-governmental organizations is often essential to ensure full and effective involvement.[19] Like courts, some tribunals have the authority to force unsuccessful parties to pay the **costs** of successful parties. The National Energy Board, for example, may award "actual costs reasonably incurred to any person who made representations" in a board hearing.[20] Similarly, the Alberta Energy Regulator has the power to award participation costs to participants, whether they win or lose; participants include persons who are likely to be directly and adversely affected by a decision of the regulator, have a tangible interest in the subject matter of the hearing, and will "materially assist" the regulator in deciding the matter at hand.[21] The Ontario Energy Board can order a person to pay all or part of another person's costs of participating in a processing before the board.[22] It is necessary to examine the empowering statutes to determine the extent of the cost-awarding powers of a particular tribunal.

Environmental tribunals, such as environmental appeal boards, often have powers to award costs after appeal hearings.[23] In assessing cost requests, a major criterion is whether the costs applicant has made a substantial contribution to the appeal and focused on the important issues that needed to be addressed.

Participant funding, by contrast, is funding made in advance of a hearing to assist parties in the participation of the hearing process and is not usually tied to the

---

costs part of legal expenses that a court or tribunal may order the losing party to pay to the winning party at the conclusion of the case

outcome of a hearing.[24] Participant funding is available in some types of proceedings, such as environmental assessments under the *Canadian Environmental Assessment Act, 2012*. In assessing funding requests, tribunals have tended to consider criteria such as the following:

- whether a funding applicant is in a position to make a substantial contribution to the hearing;
- whether the funding sought is directly related to the specific issues in the hearing or to broader environmental issues; and
- whether the applicant is in financial need.

The application of these criteria has often resulted in the drastic reduction of costs claims, particularly the costs of legal and other professional assistance. A limited-budget participant funding program, based on a federal government fund, has been developed for environmental assessment processes under the *Canadian Environmental Assessment Act*.[25]

Appeals

No automatic right to appeal an administrative decision exists, whether that decision is made by a government official or results from a formal hearing. A right of appeal must be provided by statute, and if no statutory right to appeal exists, there may be no appeal.

Where a statute does provide a right to appeal, it sets out the particulars of that right: what body hears the appeal, what issues are to be considered by the appellate decision-maker, and what preconditions must be met before the appeal is heard. Sometimes, particularly in appeals to courts, it is necessary to obtain permission, or leave, to appeal before presenting a case.[26] The court hears arguments and decides whether a serious arguable point has been raised with a reasonable prospect of success.

Two possible forums for appeals are as follows:

1. appeals to another administrative tribunal, such as an environmental appeal board, established by a provincial government; and
2. appeals to a court.

Statutes dictate whether it is necessary to appeal an administrative decision to a court or an appellate tribunal. It may be necessary to "exhaust" appeal remedies before pursuing judicial review in a court.[27]

The two types of appeal processes are as follows:

1. *Appeals de novo*. These appeals are new hearings in which a court or an appeals tribunal rehears and reconsiders everything that was before the original decision-maker, as well as any fresh evidence or new arguments.

2. *Appeals on questions of law and jurisdiction.* These appeals are limited to legal arguments; no new evidence is submitted.

Again, the scope of the appeal depends on the wording of the applicable statutory appeal provision.

Environmental Appeal Boards

A number of specialized tribunals have been established under provincial environmental legislation to hear appeals from administrative decisions. They include the following:

- Alberta's Environmental Appeals Board;[28]
- British Columbia's Environmental Appeal Board;[29] and
- Ontario's Environmental Review Tribunal.[30]

These appeal boards are required to hold hearings *de novo*.

Appeals may sometimes consist of written submissions only. They may include reconsideration of decisions to grant or deny approvals or to make enforcement orders. Administrative decisions suspending or revoking approvals, requiring cleanup or remediation, or imposing monetary penalties are typical subjects of appeal.

Operators against whom orders have been made and individuals who meet statutory standing requirements have a right to appeal. The test for standing varies from

---

BOX 14.1 » Ontario's Environmental Review Tribunal

Ontario's Environmental Review Tribunal (ERT) is an independent and impartial tribunal established by provincial legislation. The ERT holds public hearings on appeals mainly arising from decisions regarding the issuance, alteration, or revocation of an order, approval, licence, or permit under the *Clean Water Act, 2006*, the *Environmental Protection Act*, the *Nutrient Management Act, 2002*, the *Ontario Water Resources Act*, the *Pesticides Act*, the *Safe Drinking Water Act, 2002* and the *Toxics Reduction Act, 2009*.

The ERT derives its authority from the *Environmental Bill of Rights, 1993*, and conducts hearings to decide whether to grant a person permission to appeal certain types of decisions made by a "director" under the *Environmental Protection Act*, the *Ontario Water Resources Act*, and the *Pesticides Act*.

The ERT's jurisdiction arises in part from the following environmental review tribunal statutes of Ontario:

- *Clean Water Act, 2006*
- *Environmental Assessment Act*
- *Environmental Bill of Rights, 1993*
- *Environmental Protection Act*
- *Greenbelt Act, 2005*
- *Nutrient Management Act, 2002*
- *Oak Ridges Moraine Conservation Act, 2001*
- *Ontario Water Resources Act*
- *Pesticides Act*
- *Safe Drinking Water Act, 2002*
- *Toxics Reduction Act, 2009*

Source: Adapted from Environmental Review Tribunal, "About the Environmental Review Tribunal," 2013, http://www.ert.gov.on.ca/english/about/ert/index.htm.

jurisdiction to jurisdiction. For example, in Alberta, a person has standing to appeal when he or she is "directly affected" (provided that he or she files a notice of objection to the original decision).[31] In British Columbia, a "person aggrieved" has standing to appeal.[32] And in Ontario, standing to initiate an appeal to the Environmental Review Tribunal is granted to a "person to whom an order was directed."[33] As well, others can seek leave to appeal certain environmental decisions on the basis that a decision is unreasonable with regard to government policies or could result in significant harm to the environment.[34]

Environmental appeal boards have significant advantages over courts. Their members have a range of environmental expertise. As well, their procedures are less formal than those of courts and usually include well-developed mediation processes that make it possible for appellants to negotiate satisfactory results without resorting to hearings. Boards review negotiated settlements and approve them as board decisions. Even if appeals do go to hearings, the process is likely to be faster and less costly than court proceedings.

However, there may be a disadvantage to environmental appeal board appeals if, as in Alberta, they are subject to approval by environment ministers.[35] Ministers may even have power to vary or rescind appeal board decisions.[36] Although ministers do not often reverse or modify board decisions, they nevertheless have the power to do so. Parties do not have the right to make submissions to the minister, but reasons for a ministerial decision may be required in some circumstances.

In *Fenske v. Alberta (Minister of Environment)*,[37] Alberta's Environmental Appeals Board allowed an appeal by local residents challenging an Alberta Environment decision to approve the massive expansion of a rural landfill. The board sent the matter back to the department for a proper environmental assessment, with a request for additional information to be submitted by the developer. However, the minister stepped in and granted the approval, with conditions requiring additional studies and information. A lower court overturned the minister's decision on procedural fairness grounds, but the Alberta Court of Appeal upheld it. The Court of Appeal ruled that the decision was neither outside the minister's jurisdiction nor procedurally unfair, even though the minister failed to hear from the local residents. By contrast, the provisions of certain statutes may require decision-makers to provide some rationale for key elements of their decision.[38] Failure to give adequate reasons may also be a breach of the duty of procedural fairness.[39]

Substantive Judicial Review

While it is possible to challenge board decisions in court, it is not easy. In judicial review applications to provincial superior courts (as opposed to appeals) questions of standing to bring actions may arise. As the following section demonstrates, grounds for standing that could lead to judicial review are narrow. Courts give great weight to the expertise of environmental appeal boards and to ministerial expertise, which derives from departmental staff experts. Considerable deference is given to environmental decision-makers.

Standing

If there is no statutory right to appeal either to an environmental appeal board or to a court, anyone with standing may still challenge an environmental decision in a judicial review application. Historically, standing has required that the applicant establish that he or she is "aggrieved," "specially affected," or "suffering loss over and above the rest of the community."[40]

In recent decades, however, standing requirements have been liberalized. The Supreme Court of Canada has approved a standing test derived from constitutional law test cases.[41] This test requires that the applicant establish the following:

1. that there is a serious legal issue to be determined that affects the applicant directly,
2. that the applicant has a "genuine interest as a citizen" in the decision, and
3. that there is no other reasonable and effective manner in which the issue may be brought before the court.[42]

This test is not a legal rule. It is a matter of judicial discretion that involves considering the factors listed.

The result has been that in many cases, the matter of standing is not raised at by any of the parties. However, denial of standing has been upheld by the courts. An example is *Canadian Council of Churches v. Canada (Minister of Employment and Immigration)*.[43] In this case, the council sought a declaration that amendments to the federal *Immigration Act* concerning Convention Refugees violated the *Canadian Charter of Rights and Freedoms*. The Attorney General of Canada argued that the council lacked standing. Ultimately, the Supreme Court of Canada agreed, concluding that there is another reasonable and effective manner of bringing this issue before the court—namely, judicial review actions by the Convention Refugee claimants themselves. The court stressed that recognition of public interest standing "does not amount to a blanket approval to grant standing to all who wish to litigate an issue."[44] Consequently, standing remains an issue that must be addressed in many environmental judicial review cases.

Alternative Remedies

Courts may deny judicial review when they are satisfied that an adequate alternative remedy such as a statutory appeal to an environmental appeal board exists and has not been pursued. This decision is a matter of judicial discretion based on the courts' assessment of the nature and capacity of the appeal tribunal and the likelihood of a fair hearing.[45]

Reviewing the Merits of a Decision: The Standard of Review and Grounds for Judicial Review

Reviewing the merits of a decision is the most complicated category of judicial review. It involves the application of one of two standards of review: correctness or reasonableness.[46] It also involves an examination of the grounds for judicial review. Generally, it is not the role of a court to second-guess administrative decision-makers.

The Standard of Review

Courts have developed sometimes complex and confusing theory and methodology for deciding to what extent they will review the decisions of regulatory tribunals and officials. Where the application for judicial review is based on an allegation that an error was made in the substantive "correctness" of a decision, the court must first determine the **standard of review**—that is, the intensity of the review. The court asks itself how much deference it must give to the administrative decision-maker. Fortunately, this process was simplified by the Supreme Court of Canada in *Dunsmuir v. New Brunswick*.[47] In this case, the court reduced the standards of review from three to two:

1. *Correctness.* Correctness involves an intense probing review in which the reviewing court does not show deference to the decision-maker's reasoning process. Rather, it substitutes its own analysis of the issues and legal principles, and makes its own decision.[48]
2. *Reasonableness.* Reasonableness involves a less probing review that focuses on the reasonableness of the decision-making process used by the decision-maker. A court does not engage in its own assessment and reasoning; rather, it reviews the decision-maker's reasoning to evaluate the analytic method, logic, and consistency applied. It then determines whether the decision falls "within a range of possible, acceptable outcomes, having regard to the facts and the law, which are defensible in respect of the facts and law."[49] The court considers whether the decision exhibits principles such as justification, transparency, and intelligibility.[50] Thus, the court may defer to a decision it does not agree with, provided that the decision is not unreasonable.

To determine which standard of review applies in a case, courts look in particular at whether the tribunal interpreted its empowering statute and at any relevant cases.[51] The court considers the following factors when determining the standard of review:[52]

---

standard of review   the scope of a judicial review—the broader correctness standard (Was the tribunal's decision correct?), or the stricter reasonableness standard (Was the tribunal's decision reasonable?)

- *Privative clause.* A **privative clause** is a provision that is sometimes included in a governing statute that specifically limits judicial review of administrative decisions made under that statute.
- *Expertise of the decision-maker.* Expertise does not refer to the academic achievements or other formal qualifications of tribunal members; rather, it refers to the statutory responsibilities of tribunal members and the experience and "field sensitivity" that they develop.
- *Policy versus technical issue.* Looking at the statutory scheme and the particular provision under which the decision-maker acted, a court asks itself whether the decision is technical or based on policy. Administrative decision-makers, rather than courts, should make policy decisions.
- *Law versus fact.* Is the issue a matter of law—for example, how a common law principle should be applied or how an ambiguous statutory provision should be interpreted? Alternatively, does the matter involve finding and assessing facts—for example, who put what contaminant in the water, when, and how? The courts are the experts on questions of law, while environmental regulators, who are closer to what happened and have heard directly from the parties, are better placed to decide factual questions.

The court then weighs these factors and decides whether the standard of review should be correctness or reasonableness, as illustrated in Table 14.1.

Because procedural fairness involves legal rights rather than tribunal expertise or policy, the standard for review associated with judicial reviews based on procedural fairness is always correctness.[53]

Table 14.1 Two Standards of Review

Least deference ⬅ ➡ Greatest deference	
Correctness	**Reasonableness**
The court uses legal analysis to determine whether the administrative decision is legally correct. If the court concludes that the decision was not correct, it sets the decision aside.	The court determines whether the decision was within a range of possible acceptable outcomes defensible on the facts and law, with regard to factors including justification, transparency, and intelligibility.

privative clause a provision that is sometimes included in a governing statute that specifically limits judicial review of administrative decisions made under that statute

Substantive Legal or Jurisdictional Grounds for Judicial Review

On judicial review, a court may find that an environmental decision-maker made a reviewable error on grounds asserted by the applicant, such as the following:

- substantive *ultra vires* (making decisions or acting outside its statutory powers);
- failing to consider relevant matters or considering irrelevant matters;
- unlawful fettering of discretion;
- real or apprehended bias;
- breach of procedural fairness;
- exercising a discretion for an improper purpose or in bad faith;
- unlawful subdelegation of a discretionary power; and
- errors of law and/or fact (in restricted circumstances).[54]

Limited constitutional grounds exist for judicial review. These include acting outside constitutional authority (federalism) (see Chapter 2) or, potentially, infringing rights protected by the *Canadian Charter of Rights and Freedoms*. Charter grounds have gained little environmental law traction. An example is *Kelly v. Alberta (Energy and Utilities Board)*,[55] in which the applicants alleged that the risk to their personal health from proposed sour oil wells infringed their section 7 Charter rights to "life, liberty and security of the person and the right not to be deprived thereof except in accordance with the principles of fundamental justice." The trial judge concluded that the Charter ground was at least arguable and granted leave to appeal to the Alberta Court of Appeal. But the Alberta Energy and Utilities Board allowed the oil company to withdraw its licence application. The Court of Appeal then ruled that the matters at issue were moot and dismissed the appeal.

Public Inquiries

Public pressure may cause a government to establish a public inquiry into an environmentally sensitive matter. However, public inquiries are rare. They occur only in the case of significant proposed developments that catch the attention of both governments and the public. A famous example is the Berger inquiry of the early 1970s, discussed in the chapter-opening case study, which held hearings on proposals to build major natural gas pipelines from the Arctic.[56]

Public inquiries are more commonly used to investigate and provide recommendations to government when environmental problems emerge or when disasters, such as the Walkerton water system tragedy,[57] occur. Public inquiries operate independently of governments and usually hold public hearings that provide a public forum for discussion about the environmental problems under investigation. The creation of public inquiries is entirely a matter of government discretion.

SUMMARY OF KEY POINTS

- Environmental decisions under statutory power are often made by government officials (such as Cabinet ministers) or by boards or tribunals following some type of hearing. Persons who meet statutory standing requirements are entitled to participate in hearings.

- Boards and tribunals must comply with the principles of procedural fairness: affected persons are entitled to reasonable notice of a proposed decision, a fair opportunity to be heard, and an impartial and independent decision-maker. Some procedural fairness requirements at the lower end of a spectrum (hearings are normally not required) also apply to ministers and Cabinets.

- Funding (including advance funding) for hearing participants may be available if it is provided for by statute or based on a tribunal's policy.

- Persons may have a right to appeal environmental decisions to an environmental appeal board or the equivalent provided that a statutory right to appeal exists.

- Appeals of environmental decisions, including environmental appeal board decisions, may be taken directly to court, provided that a statutory right to appeal exists.

- If no statutory right to appeal exists, environmental decisions can still be challenged by judicial review, provided that applicants meet common law standing tests or the criteria for discretionary public interest standing.

- Substantive judicial review challenges the court to determine whether the appropriate standard of review should be correctness (no deference to the decision-maker) or reasonableness (deference to the decision-maker).

- In addition to the standard of review, decisions may be challenged in judicial review and appeals on substantive legal or jurisdictional grounds, such as misinterpretation of statutory requirements or failing to take relevant matters into consideration.

KEY TERMS

administrative decisions	official notice	record
costs	privative clause	standard of review
evidence	procedural fairness	standing
hearsay	public hearing	
natural justice	public inquiry	

DISCUSSION QUESTIONS

1. Is environmental law a set of organic customary principles that have developed in Canadian society?
2. In what ways might environmental decisions be unfair? How can unfairness be prevented?
3. What are the key factors likely to be in determining the standard of review applicable to environmental regulatory decisions?
4. What grounds may be available for judicial review of specific environmental decisions?
5. At this stage, what are your ideas for priority environmental regulatory law improvements?

SUGGESTED READINGS

Readings

Bryden, Philip. "New Developments in Tribunal Reform: Lessons from British Columbia." Paper presented at The Future of Administrative Justice Symposium, Toronto, January 18, 2008, https://www.law.utoronto.ca/documents/conferences/adminjustice08_bryden.pdf.

Doelle, Meinhard, and Chris Tollefson. "Judicial Review of Environmental Decision-Making." In Meinhard Doelle and Chris Tollefson, eds., *Environmental Law: Cases and Materials*, 2nd ed. Toronto: Carswell, 2013.

Hughes, Elaine, Alastair Lucas, and William Tilleman. "Environmental Assessment." In Elaine Hughes, Alastair Lucas, and William Tilleman, eds., *Environmental Law and Policy*, 3rd ed. Toronto: Emond Montgomery, 2003.

Jones, David. *Principles of Administrative Law*, 5th ed. Toronto: Thomson Carswell, 2009.

Mullan, David. *Essentials of Canadian Administrative Law*. Toronto: Irwin Law, 2001.

Van Harten, Gus, Gerald Heckman, and David J. Mullan, eds. *Administrative Law: Cases, Text, and Materials*, 6th ed. Toronto: Emond Montgomery, 2010.

Websites

ABlawg: the University of Calgary Faculty of Law Blog on Developments in Alberta Law, Environmental Category: http://ablawg.ca/category/environmental/

AdminLawBC: http://www.adminlawbc.ca

BC Council of Administrative Tribunals, "Publications": http://bccat.net/publications/publications

Canadian Environmental Law Association, "CELA in the Courts": http://www.cela.ca/collections/celacourts

Canadian Institute for the Administration of Justice: http://www.ciaj-icaj.ca

Council of Canadian Administrative Tribunals: http://www.ccat-ctac.org

Environmental Law Centre, University of Victoria: http://www.elc.uvic.ca

Ontario Ministry of the Attorney General, "Guidelines for Administrative Tribunals":
http://www.attorneygeneral.jus.gov.on.ca/english/justice-ont/french_language
_services/services/administrative_tribunals.asp

Supreme Court of Canada, "Administrative Tribunals and the Courts: An Evolutionary
Relationship" (Speech by Chief Justice Beverley McLachlin): http://www.scc-csc
.gc.ca/court-cour/judges-juges/spe-dis/bm-2013-05-27-eng.aspx

NOTES

1. Alastair R. Lucas and Patrick A. Moore, "The Utah Controversy: A Case Study of
Public Participation in Pollution Control" (1973) 13 *Natural Resources Journal* 36.

2. *Alberta Wilderness Assn v. Cardinal River Coals Ltd.*, [1999] 3 FC 425; and *Friends of
the West Country Assn. v. Canada (Minister of Fisheries and Oceans)*, [2000] 2 FC 263.

3. Alberta Energy Resources Conservation Board, *Decision D 94-8, Application for an
Exploratory Well—Amoco Canada Petroleum Company Limited—Whaleback Ridge
Area*, September 6, 1994.

4. Alberta Energy and Utilities Board, *Preliminary Decision 2003-030*, December 16,
2003.

5. See Alastair Lucas, ed., *Canadian Environmental Law*, 2nd ed. (Toronto: LexisNexis)
(looseleaf), at paras. 8.19-8.21.

6. *Canadian Association of Regulated Importers v. Canada (Attorney General)*, [1993]
3 FC 199 (TD); rev'd. [1994] 2 FC 247 (CA).

7. Terminology differs. The *National Energy Board Act*, RSC 1985, c. N-7, s. 52, concerning interjurisdictional pipeline approval, refers to "public interest" and "public
convenience and necessity." Manitoba's *Environment Act* refers to a "high quality of
life including social and economic development, recreation and leisure for this and
future generations (s. 1(1)). Purposes sections, in both Alberta's *Environmental
Protection and Enhancement Act*, RSA 2000, c. E-12, s. 2(a) and Nova Scotia's *Environment Act*, SNS 1994-95, c. 1, s. 2(a), use similar language concerning environmental protection as "essential to the integrity of ecosystems and human health and
the socio-economic well-being of society." Ontario's *Environmental Assessment Act*,
RSO 1990, c. E 18, s. 2, identifies the "betterment of the people of the whole or any
part of Ontario."

8. See *Canadian Environmental Asessment Act, 2012*, SC 2012, c. 19, s. 52, ss. 42-44.

9. See Gus Van Harten, Gerald Heckman, and David J. Mullan, eds., *Administrative
Law: Cases, Text, and Materials*, 6th ed. (Toronto: Emond Montgomery, 2010),
part II. The leading case is *Baker v. Canada (Minister of Citizenship and Immigration)*,
[1999] 2 SCR 817, in which the Supreme Court of Canada established a template
for determining procedural fairness rights. Factors for assessing the relative
strength of procedural fairness rights include the relative judicial nature of the
decision, the terms of the statutory power, the importance of the decision to the

individual affected, (perhaps) the legitimate expectations of that person, and the decision-maker's choice of procedure.

10. In *Pembina Institute v. Alberta (Environment and Sustainable Resources Development)*, 2013 ABQB 567, one issue raised by the NGO Pembina Institute and addressed by the court was the failure of the Alberta Environment Director to disclose to Pembina a "Briefing Note" by Alberta Environment staff to the minister in a water licence application by the operator of a proposed oil sands project. The note stated that Pembina and the Oil Sands Environmental Coalition (of which Pembina was a member) had been disallowed as statement of concern filers (a requirement for participant status) and explained that the groups were "now less inclined to work cooperatively" and that Pembina had published "negative media on the oil sands." The judge said that the Department of the Environment was "apparently operating under an undisclosed policy" that contradicted stated Alberta Environment policies encouraging public participation in the regulatory process. Also see Shaun Fluker, "The Smoking Gun Revealed: Alberta Environment Denies Environmental Groups Who Oppose Oil Sands Projects the Right to Participate in the Decision-Making Process," *ABlawg* (blog), October 3, 2013, http://www.ablawg.ca.

11. *Pembina Institute v. Alberta (Environment and Sustainable Resources Development)*, supra note 10. Pembina said that Justice Marceau, was "not told about the 'Briefing Note' and consequently could not have answered the allegation that Pembina was regarded as uncooperative" (at 34).

12. An oral hearing may be required where credibility of individuals is at issue: see *Khan v. Ottawa (University of)*, [1997] 34 OR 3d 535 (CA).

13. *Committee for Justice and Liberty et al. v. National Energy Board et al.*, [1978] 1 SCR 369, at 394-95, in which the newly appointed NEB chair who had led one member of the applicant pipeline consortium and sat on the management and ownership and routing committees during preparation of the application, was disqualified for reasonable apprehension of bias. The test adopted by the court (Justice de Grandpré quoting the Federal Court of Appeal, at 395) was "what would an informed person, viewing the matter realistically and practically—and having thought the matter through—conclude?" See also *Wewaykum Indian Band v. Canada*, 2003 SCC 45, [2003] 2 SCR 259, at para. 60.

14. For example, review panels under the *Canadian Environmental Assessment Act*, supra note 8, s. 45.

15. David Mullan, *Essentials of Canadian Administrative Law* (Toronto: Irwin Law, 2001), at 297.

16. See Allan Mason and David Mullan, eds., *Commissions of Inquiry* (Toronto: Irwin Law, 2003); and Russell Anthony and Alastair Lucas, *A Handbook on the Conduct of Public Inquiries in Canada* (Toronto: Butterworths, 1985).

17. For example, National Energy Board (NEB), *Trans Mountain Pipeline ULC: Trans Mountain Expansion Project* (Hearing Order OH-001-2014), April 2, 2014,

https://docs.neb-one.gc.ca/ll-eng/llisapi.dll/fetch/2000/90464/90552/548311/956726/2392873/2449981/2445930/A15-3_-_Hearing_Order_OH-001-2014_-_A3V6I2.pdf?nodeid=2445615&vernum=-2, and attached Ruling on Participation. Parties allowed to participate are commenters (file one letter of comment) and intervenors (file written evidence, ask written questions about Trans Mountain's and other intervenors' evidence, and present written and oral argument); Aboriginal traditional evidence may be presented orally.

18. *Baker v. Canada (Minister of Citizenship and Immigration)*, supra note 9.

19. Alastair Lucas, "Canadian Participatory Rights in Mining and Energy Resource Developments: The Bridges to Empowerment," in Donald Zillman, Alastair Lucas, and George Pring, eds., *Human Rights in Natural Resource Development* (Oxford: Oxford University Press, 2002), 305-54, at 322.

20. *National Energy Board Act*, RSC 1985, c. N-7, s. 39.

21. Alberta, *Responsible Energy Development Act: Alberta Energy Regulator Rules of Practice* (Edmonton: Alberta Queen's Printer), ss. 9, 58, 58.1, http://www.qp.alberta.ca/documents/Regs/2013_099.pdf.

22. *Ontario Energy Board Act*, SO 1998, c. 15, Sched. B, s. 30.

23. See, e.g., the Ontario *Environmental Protection Act*, RSO 1990, c. E.19, s. 20.15(7), and Alberta's *Environmental Protection and Enhancement Act*, supra note 7, s. 96.

24. Lucas, supra note 19, at 323.

25. Ibid. See also Justice Berger's MacKenzie Valley Pipeline inquiry funding criteria in Thomas Berger, *Northern Frontier, Northern Homeland: The Report of the Mackenzie Valley Pipeline Inquiry* (Ottawa: Minister of Supply and Services Canada, 1977), vol. 2, appendix.

26. For example, leave by the Alberta Court of Appeal is required to appeal from a decision of the Alberta Energy Regulator based on the *Responsible Energy Development Act*, 2012, s. 45.

27. The issue is whether the administrative appeal would provide an "adequate alternative remedy." The appeal tribunal's relative expertise, expeditiousness, and costs are factors: see *Harelkin v. University of Regina*, [1979] 2 SCR 561.

28. *Environmental Protection and Enhancement Act*, supra note 7, Part 4, ss. 90-106.1.

29. *Environmental Management Act*, SBC 2003, c. 53, Part B; and *Environmental Review Tribunal Act, 2000*, SO 2000, c. 26, Sched. F.

30. *Ontario Energy Board Act*, supra note 22.

31. *Environmental Protection and Enhancement Act*, supra note 7, s. 91.

32. *Environmental Management Act*, supra note 29, s. 100.

33. *Environmental Protection Act*, supra note 23, Part XIII, ss. 138-140.

34. Ontario *Environmental Bill of Rights, 1993*, SO 1993, c. 28, s. 41. See *Dawber v. Ontario (Director, Ministry of the Environment)* (2007), 28 CELR (3d) 281 (Ont. ERT);

aff'd. (2008), 36 CELR (3d) 191 (Ont. Div. Ct.) (leave to appeal granted on ground of failure to consider impacts cumulative on entire ecosystem affected by water permit where water quality standards met).

35. *Environmental Protection and Enhancement Act*, supra note 7, ss. 99, 100.

36. Ibid., s. 100; *Environmental Management Act*, supra note 29, s. 97 (minister may "in the public interest, vary or rescind an order or decision of the appeal board").

37. *Fenske v. Alberta (Minister of Environment)*, 2002 ABCA 135.

38. *Imperial Oil Resources Ventures Limited v. Canada (Fisheries and Oceans)*, 2008 FC 598 (joint review panel failure to provide rationale for conclusion that intensity-based mitigation would reduce greenhouse gas emissions from oil sands plant to insignificance).

39. *Newfoundland and Labrador Nurses' Union v. Newfoundland and Labrador (Treasury Board)*, 2011 SCC 62, [2011] 3 SCR 708.

40. Van Harten, Heckman, and Mullan, supra note 9, at 1090.

41. *Finlay v. Canada (Minister of Finance)*, [1986] 2 SCR 607.

42. *Minister of Justice (Can.) v. Borowski*, [1981] 2 SCR 575, at 598.

43. *Canadian Council of Churches v. Canada (Minister of Employment and Immigration)*, [1992] 1 SCR 236.

44. Ibid., at 263.

45. *Harelkin v. University of Regina*, supra note 27; and *Canadian Pacific Ltd. v. Matsqui Indian Band*, [1995] 1 SCR 3.

46. British Columbia is unique in having codified the standard of review in the *Administrative Tribunals Act*, SBC 2004, c. 45 (ATA). Because the codification occurred before the *Dunsmuir* decision, that statute contains three, not two, standards of review. Practitioners in British Columbia should consult the tribunal's enabling legislation and the ATA in order to understand standard of review in that province.

47. *Dunsmuir v. New Brunswick*, 2008 SCC 9, [2008] 1 SCR 190.

48. Issues and legal principles can include constitutional questions (such as division of powers, environmental jurisdiction, and possible *Canadian Charter of Rights and Freedoms* issues), questions of fact, questions of procedural fairness, issues of general law that are "of central importance to the legal system as a whole and outside the [adjudicator's] specialized area of expertise," and perhaps certain narrow questions of whether the decision-maker had legal authority to decide particular issues at all: *Dunsmuir*, supra note 47, at paras. 58-60.

49. Ibid., at para. 47.

50. Ibid.

51. On questions closely related to the tribunal's function and within its particular expertise, see ibid., at para. 54; and *Western Canada Wilderness Committee v. Manitoba*, 2013 MBCA 11. Interpretation of the empowering statute creates a presumption that the standard of review is reasonableness: *Alberta (Information and Privacy*

Commissioner) v. Alberta Teachers' Association, 2011 SCC 61, [2011] 3 SCR 654, at para. 39. But the Federal Court of Appeal in *Georgia Strait Alliance v. Canada (Minister of Fisheries and Oceans)*, 2012 FCA 40 rejected application of this reasonableness presumption to interpretation by the minister or his own administrative powers.

52. *Georgia Strait Alliance v. Canada (Minister of Fisheries and Oceans)*, supra note 51, at paras. 51-56. See *Sierra Club Canada v. Ontario (Natural Resources & Transportation)*, 2011 ONSC 4655, at paras. 29-35.

53. *Alberta (Information and Privacy Commissioner) v. Alberta Teachers' Association*, 2011 SCC 61, [2011] 3 SCR 654, at para. 82.

54. Chris Tollefson, "Public Participation and Judicial Review," in Elaine Hughes, Alastair Lucas, and William Tilleman, eds., *Environmental Law and Policy*, 3rd ed. (Toronto: Emond Montgomery, 2003), at 255, 261.

55. *Kelly v. Alberta (Energy and Utilities Board)*, [2009] ABCA 161; Nickie Vlavianos, "Charter and Oil and Gas Issues to Await Another Day: A Disappointing End to the Kelly Appeal?" *Ablawg* (blog), June 3, 2009, http://www.ablawg.ca.

56. Berger, supra note 25. The project was not built, the victim of low gas prices and developing Aboriginal rights and environmental concerns. More than 30 years later, a similar pipeline project was approved by the Minister of the Environment and the NEB: see Joint Review Panel for the Mackenzie Gas Project, *Foundation for a Sustainable Northern Future: Report*, vol. 1 (Ottawa: Minister of Environment, 2010), http://www.reviewboard.ca/upload/project_document/EIR0405-001_JRP _Report_of_Environmental_Review_Executive_Volume_I_1263228660.PDF. This project too has not proceeded.

57. Justice Dennis O'Connor, *Report of the Walkerton Inquiry: The Events of May 2000 and Related Issues*, part 1, January 18, 2002 (Toronto: Ministry of the Attorney General, 2002), http://www.attorneygeneral.jus.gov.on.ca/english/about/pubs/ walkerton/part1/; and part 2, *A Strategy for Safe Drinking Water*, May 23, 2002, http://www.attorneygeneral.jus.gov.on.ca/english/about/pubs/walkerton/part2/.

CHAPTER 15

Environmental Bill of Rights and Access to Information

LEARNING OBJECTIVES

After reading this chapter, students will be able to:

- Discuss the appropriate role of public and stakeholder participation in environmental decision-making by government.
- Discuss the relationship between environmental rights, government accountability, and access to information.
- Describe how the Ontario *Environmental Bill of Rights, 1993* and federal and provincial access to information legislation provide the public with opportunities to participate in environmental decision-making.
- Evaluate the effectiveness of the Ontario *Environmental Bill of Rights, 1993* in delivering on the promise of increased public access to environmental decision-making.
- Describe how lawmakers attempt to balance the public's right to government-held information on environmental decision-making and the protection of privacy.

CHAPTER OUTLINE

Introduction

Does every Canadian have a fundamental right, and obligation, to take action when an activity or decision threatens the air, land, and drinking water that sustains them? The traditional view of environmental law is that when individuals cast their ballots, they effectively delegate these rights and obligations of environmental stewardship to government decision-makers. This chapter examines two types of legislation that counter this trusting, government-centred approach to environmental protection by granting members of the public increased access to environmental decision-making: (1) environmental bills of rights such as the Ontario *Environmental Bill of Rights, 1993*, and (2) access to information statutes.

A Toxic Plume and the Right to a Hearing

The village of Elmira, Ontario is entirely dependent on groundwater for its drinking water. For many years, Elmira was also home to a large chemical manufacturing plant owned by Uniroyal Chemical Ltd. By the late 1980s, there was strong evidence indicated that a chemical plume emanating from Uniroyal property was posing a substantial risk to the town's drinking water supply.* The plume was a result of buried wastes beneath the Uniroyal property. The fastest-moving contaminant, a carcinogen known by the acronym NDMA, had already reached two of Elmira's drinking wells. One of the key voices of concern regarding this drinking water threat was a group of ratepayers, APTE, that had served as the *de facto* local environmental watchdog for a number of years.

Under the Ontario *Environmental Protection Act*, the Ministry of the Environment (MOE) has the legislated power to address this problem. This power includes the right to impose orders against the company, requiring it to remove the buried waste, clean up the contamination, remediate the groundwater, and, if necessary, even provide a replacement drinking water supply.

In 1990 a regional MOE director issued a series of orders requiring Uniroyal to conduct further study, clean up the existing contamination, and remove the buried waste.[†] The company immediately appealed these orders, triggering a public hearing process before the Environmental Appeal Tribunal (EAB), an independent board. APTE did not trust either Uniroyal or the MOE to address the problem. APTE, the local municipality of the Township of Woolwich, and the Regional Municipality of Waterloo (which is responsible for the municipal water supply wells in the area, the Region of Waterloo) all sought and obtained party status at the hearing. In describing the role of the residents' group, the EAB wrote:

> The members of APTE were simply concerned that the other public authorities might not fully present their interests and bring out all of the evidence required to protect their health and well-being. Their

experience in dealing with government agencies convinced them that they needed separate representation.[‡]

The hearing was lengthy and highly contested on all sides. After 13 months, the EAB had heard over 41 hearing days of detailed evidence, some of it unflattering to the MOE's role as regulator, and no end was in sight. Then suddenly, without the involvement of APTE or the other parties, MOE and Uniroyal announced that they had struck a deal designed to end the hearing. Under this agreement, Uniroyal withdrew its appeal of the previous orders, while MOE issued a new replacement order acceptable to Uniroyal. Even though the other parties were far from satisfied with the new order, both the MOE and Uniroyal took the position that the EAB had no jurisdiction to continue the hearing and that the participation right of the other parties ended with the withdrawal of the appeal and the order under appeal.[§]

They had a point. It was far from clear that the other parties had a right to a hearing once Uniroyal had withdrawn its appeal. The statute that empowered the issuance of the orders, the Ontario *Environmental Protection Act*, does not provide a right of appeal to anyone other than an individual against whom the order was issued. It was only Uniroyal's decision to appeal and trigger a public hearing that had given the two municipalities and the residents' group any toehold in the decision-making process on the MOE orders in the first place.

APTE and the two municipalities did not back down. They returned to the EAB and advised it that the settlement between the MOE and Uniroyal did not satisfy their concerns and that that they were prepared to call evidence that the new MOE order did not adequately protect either the public interest or the environment. They urged the EAB to reject the settlement and continue the hearing.

In an important decision, the EAB ruled that it did have both the jurisdiction to review the settlement agreement and the authority, although not a duty, to continue the hearing.[#] The EAB held that, where the rights of other parties are affected by a settlement, the board has a limited power to strengthen orders and decisions, notwithstanding that the appeal that was the basis for the EAB's involvement in the matter has been withdrawn. Part of the rationale for this ruling was the finding that the EAB, while a creature of statute, had inherent powers to both exercise control over its own process and protect the public interest. This ruling had a positive result. It forced all the parties back to the negotiating table to arrive at a more acceptable settlement that addressed the formerly excluded parties' concerns and strengthened the replacement order.

This case raises some fundamental questions about the role of the public in environmental decision-making. If the MOE and Uniroyal had made their deal before Uniroyal appealed, the township, region, and the residents' group (under the Ontario law at that time) would have had no hearing. The most directly affected stakeholders would have had no say in the outcome. They would have had to rely entirely on the MOE to protect their interest in a safe drinking water supply.

Questions

When the Ontario legislature passed the statute empowering the MOE to issue environmental cleanup orders against companies such as Uniroyal, why do you think it decided to allow an appeal right (and hearing opportunity) to the individual or company to which the order applies, but not to potentially impacted residents or the municipalities? Do you think that APTE, the Township of Woolwich, and the Regional Municipality of Waterloo should have been allowed a right to a hearing in this case even if the MOE and Uniroyal were satisfied with the environmental order? What does this case, which occurred before Ontario put in place environmental bill of rights legislation in 1993, teach us about the role individuals and other stakeholders should play in environmental decision-making?

---

* *Re Uniroyal Chemical Ltd.* (1992), 9 CELR (NS) 151, at 156.

† Ibid., at 155.

‡ Ibid., at 156.

§ Ibid., at 161.

Ibid., at 172.

One common impetus behind these two types of legislation is the notion that individuals should have the legal right to hold governments accountable if they fail to deliver on their mandate to prevent pollution and protect environmental resources. Another common impetus is the relationship between environmental rights and access to information, one encapsulated by the famous quote by Jean Rostand, French biologist and philosopher: "The obligation to endure gives us the right to know."

Canada's History of Environmental Rights

In the early 1970s, a number of new, non-governmental groups had formed across Canada to respond to the lack of public involvement in government decisions about the environment. Groups that spearheaded the movement toward more transparency and accountability in government decisions about the environment included the following:

- Canadian Environmental Law Association
- Pollution Probe
- West Coast Environmental Law Association
- Environmental Law Centre (Alberta) Society

Various proposals were published for new and bold initiatives to increase public participation. Perhaps one of the best-known proposals was for an environmental bill of rights. The environmental bill of rights movement called for recognition in the Canadian Constitution of the fundamental right of all citizens to a healthy environment[1] and/or recognition of this right in legislation passed by provincial governments. Once entrenched, it was hoped and supposed that this fundamental right could serve as the basis to empower individuals and stakeholder groups to have increased say in the way governments protect the environment and manage natural resources.

Support for constitutionally protected environmental rights, however, has never gained political traction in Canada. During the political and public debate leading up to the 1982 passage of the *Canadian Charter of Rights and Freedoms*, a Special Joint Committee considered but ultimately rejected inclusion of a specific reference to a "clean and healthy environment" alongside the political and legal rights that were ultimately included in the Charter.[2] Since then, many environmental groups and legal scholars have continued to argue persuasively for a constitutional right to a clean environment, but the road to any constitutional amendment is slow and politically arduous, and the proposition continues to be controversial in many sectors.

After missing out on the opportunity for constitutional entrenchment, however, environmental rights advocates focused on trying to establish environmental rights through federal or provincial legislation. In the 1970s and early 1980s, led by the environmental organizations noted in the list above, there was a push for legislative reform that expanded the individual environmental rights to a concrete set of provisions, including the following:

- access to information legislation;
- whistle-blower legislation;
- the right to notice and to comment on new environmental approvals, policies, laws, and environmental impact assessments; and
- the right to sue when environmental requirements are violated.

At the time, these were wide-ranging and progressive reforms—a wish list for environmentalists, community leaders, and others who felt excluded from environmental decision-making.

In 1984 the federal minister of the environment, Charles Caccia, supported the enactment of an environmental bill of rights for Canada. However, he was unable to gain adequate political support before the 1984 election, and his aspiration was not translated into concrete action.[3]

At the provincial and territorial government level, the story is different. The Quebec government was the first to recognize in provincial law an individual's right to a healthy environment in a 1978 statute, the *Environmental Quality Act*.[4] This right was limited, however, by the phrase "to the extent provided for by this act and the regulations, orders, approvals and authorizations issued under any section of this act."[5] Quebec has since incorporated a slightly expanded concept of environmental rights into its *Charter of Human Rights and Freedoms*,[6] but has not passed an environmental bill of rights.

In other provinces, progress has been even slower. In Ontario, at least six private members' bills to establish environmental rights legislation were put forth by opposition parties between the late 1970s and the late 1980s. Although private members' bills are rarely enacted, they do serve to create an atmosphere for discussion and debate.

By the early 1990s, no environmental bill of rights had yet been passed by a provincial or federal government, but two territorial governments (the Yukon and the Northwest Territories) had enacted environmental bill of rights laws.[7] As well, numerous provinces had made progress in responding incrementally to some of the proposals. Many provinces enacted laws or adopted policies throughout the mid-1970s, 1980s, and early 1990s to incrementally provide either limited and specific environmental rights or broader public rights. Consider the following examples in Ontario:

- in 1983, environmental laws were enacted to create whistle-blower legislation to protect workers who exposed the environmental violations of their employers;
- access to information legislation was enacted in 1987; and
- a class action statute was passed in 1992.

Many other provinces also made incremental reforms on a variety of issues. By the early 1990s, most jurisdictions had some sort of environmental assessment regime in place.

In 1990 the New Democratic Party formed the government in Ontario after campaigning for environmental rights. Shortly after the election, Ruth Grier was appointed environment minister. In the spring of 1991, she appointed an Environmental Bill of Rights Task Force that comprised environmentalists, industry, and government to draft a new rights bill. The Ontario *Environmental Bill of Rights, 1993* (EBR) was introduced into law in February 1994.

While all three territorial governments have passed legislation with different forms of enforceable environmental rights, Ontario is still the only province with an environmental bill of rights. Given this fact, it is worth exploring Ontario's approach to protecting environmental rights in more detail.

Ontario's Approach to Protecting Environmental Rights

Ontario's EBR begins with a broad and expansive purposes section that sets an ambitious set of objectives, including the following:

- protecting, conserving, and, where reasonable, restoring the integrity of the environment;
- providing sustainability of the environment;
- protecting the right to a healthful environment;[8]
- preventing, reducing, and eliminating the use, generation, and release of pollutants that pose an unreasonable threat to the integrity of the environment;
- protecting and conserving biological, ecological, and genetic diversity;
- protecting and conserving natural resources, including plant life, animal life, and ecological systems;
- encouraging the wise management of our natural resources; and
- identifying, protecting, and conserving ecologically sensitive areas and processes.[9]

In order to achieve these broad objectives, the EBR promises to provide four basic avenues of public empowerment:

1. *Public participation rights*: providing the means for participation by Ontario residents in government decisions about the environment (Part II).
2. *Court access*: increasing legal opportunities for residents to initiate law suits for the protection of the environment (Part VI).
3. *Whistle-blower protection*: enhancing protection against employer reprisal for employees who take action on environmental harm (Part VII).
4. *Accountability*: increasing the transparency and accountability of government action (or inaction) in protecting the environment (Part I).

How does the EBR attempt to deliver on these four areas of promised public empowerment? The specifics for each are discussed next.

Public Participation Rights

The EBR established four new rights to expand the ability of Ontario residents to participate in government decisions about the environment:

- the right to receive notice and comment on proposed statutes, regulations, policies and instruments (approvals or environmental orders) issued by government officials (sections 12-37);
- the right to request leave to appeal the approval of an instrument (sections 38-48);
- the right to request a review of an existing law or instrument (sections 61-67); and
- the right to request an investigation into a potential violation of environmental law (sections 74-81).

The Right to Receive Notice and Comment
on Proposals and Instruments

One of the key rights provided in the EBR is the right of the public to receive notice of and provide comment on any government proposal to change Ontario's environmental laws. This right applies not only to environmentally significant proposed changes to legislation, regulations, and policies ("proposals") but also to specific legal "instruments." The term **instruments**, in this context, refers to various types of approvals and environmental orders issued by government. These could include environmental compliance approvals (ECAs), permits and licences issued by government officials under various environmental statutes, or environmental orders such as the orders issued by the MOE in the chapter-opening case study. Some important examples of the approval instruments for which public notice and comment is required include ECAs for air emissions, waste management sites, and sewage works; permits for taking water from the ground for bottled water or other purposes; and licences for mineral extraction. Environmental orders covered by the EBR include orders for environmental cleanup and orders for taking preventive measures under the *Environmental Protection Act.*[10]

The public is notified of proposals and instruments through information posted on the Environmental Registry,[11] an online registry maintained by the MOE. Generally, the EBR establishes a minimum 30-days' notice/comment period for all proposals and instruments, and requires the responsible ministry[12] to take into account comments submitted. As required by the EBR, the MOE posts the final decision on the Environmental Registry and summarizes the comments made. It also includes responses that explain how the comments were or were not addressed in the final decision.

Most, *but not all*, significant government proposals and instruments related to the environment must be placed on the Environmental Registry. Whether a particular government proposal or instrument is subject to EBR requirements, including the requirement to give public notice and receive comment, will depend on whether the responsible ministry for that proposal or instrument is listed in the authorizing regulation of the EBR.[13] This regulation lists the ministries and the specific Acts that are subject to public participation and notice requirements under the EBR.

The MOE and the Ministry of Natural Resources are subject to all public participation requirements for proposals, key instruments, applications for review, and applications for investigations. Other ministries may be exempt from some or all EBR requirements. One source of long-standing criticism of the EBR is its exemption of the Ontario Ministry of Finance from all requirements of the EBR through

instruments approvals, permits, licences, or other authorizations issued by government, as defined in the *Environmental Bill of Rights, 1993*

the passage of regulation[14] in 1995. This exemption was the subject of a special report of the Environmental Commissioner of Ontario (ECO) in January 1996.[15]

Proposals are treated differently than instruments under the EBR. The EBR requires the responsible ministry to post notice of any proposal for an Act, policy, or regulation that its minister determines "could, if implemented, have a significant effect on the environment," and sets out specific factors that the minister must consider making this determination.[16]

By contrast, the EBR requires each ministry to classify the various instruments for which it is responsible into one of three types based on a number of considerations related to the level of risk and potential harm to the environment involved, and whether or not a hearing would be required. Depending on the classification, different process rights could be granted to members of the public; however, a minimum 30 days' notice and the comment requirement applies to all three types of instruments.[17]

The Environmental Registry system is periodically updated in an effort to keep pace with new technology. Having the registry accessible online has contributed significantly to greater public awareness of and participation in government decisions about the environment. A 2006 case study by Allan Gunn and Jim Lewis reported approximately 10,000 site visitors per month with over 3,400 postings per year, over 3,100 of which are postings for proposals and decisions.[18] Readers are encouraged to explore Ontario's Environmental Registry website (www.ebr.gov.on.ca) to evaluate its effectiveness in fulfilling the EBR objective of providing public access to government decisions about the environment.

The Right to Seek Leave to Appeal a Decision on an Instrument

Before the EBR was enacted, in most cases only the person seeking an environmental or natural resource approval was allowed to appeal a decision by the MOE to a tribunal such as the Environmental Review Tribunal (ERT). In addition, as illustrated in the chapter-opening case study, only persons or companies who were the subject of environmental orders had the right to appeal an order and have the matter considered by an independent tribunal at hearing. The EBR has now extended the opportunity to trigger a hearing to other members of the public impacted by a decision on an approval or environmental order. Specifically, section 38 of the EBR gives any Ontario resident who has an interest in a decision on an instrument the right to seek leave to appeal to the relevant administrative tribunal for a full hearing on the matter.

The question of whether a hearing will actually be granted is left to the appellant tribunal that would hear the appeal if sought by an applicant or orderee. The tribunal must consider a somewhat onerous three-part test set out in the EBR:

1. Does the person have an interest in the decision—that is, a relationship, history, or involvement with the subject matter of the decision?

2. Does it appear that there is good reason to believe that the decision is unreasonable, having regard to the relevant law and government policies?
3. Does it appear that the decision could result in significant harm to the environment?[19]

Before deciding a leave application, the tribunal first receives and considers written submission on whether this three-part test has been met, not only from the person seeking leave but also from the government official who made the decision as well as the applicant (in the case of an approval decision) or orderee (in the case of an environmental order).

Thus, while the EBR gives members of the public the possibility to seek a hearing on approvals and orders that could significantly impact the environment, there is no absolute right to such a hearing. Members of the public must still seek permission from the tribunal that would hear the appeal, based on the challenging three-part test.

According to information provided by the ECO, 285 applications for leave to appeal were made pursuant to the EBR between April 1, 1995 and March 31, 2014.[20] Hearings were granted for approximately 20 percent of the applications received.[21]

The Right to Request a Review of an Existing Law

The right to request a review gives the public an opportunity to voice concerns about existing laws and instruments. Any two residents of Ontario may file an application for review, requesting that a law, policy, or instrument be reviewed by the appropriate ministry.[22] This right is discretionary. The decision of whether to grant a review is left to the ministry responsible for the laws that are the subject of the request. In practice, this has meant that relatively few requests for a review are granted. The ECO has tracked a total of 305 applications for review submitted between April 1, 1995 and March 31, 2014. The vast majority of these requests were refused by the responsible ministry. Similarly, a ten-year review (from 2000 to 2010) released by the ECO found that only 17 percent of the applications received resulted in the responsible ministry undertaking a review.[23]

Nevertheless, a number of applications for review have been accepted and had influential results. Three examples are noteworthy:

- In 2001, residents of Hamilton, Ontario sent a request to review ministry approvals for a local incinerator; the provincial government granted the review, at least in part, and then amended the approvals for the incinerator. As a result of the amendments, the city decided that the new requirements were too onerous and decommissioned the incinerator.[24]
- In 2003, two Ontario residents requested a review of the efforts of the Ontario aggregate industry to rehabilitate pits and quarries under the *Aggregate Resources Act*. The Ministry of Natural Resources agreed to a review that

exposed shortcomings and resulted in increased monitoring and enforcement requirements.[25]

- In 2007, two University of Toronto law students requested a review by the MOE of restrictive rules that were preventing some homeowners from using outdoor clotheslines to dry their laundry, an activity that supports energy conservation. The ministry agreed to conduct a review. The result has been the passage of new laws that make it illegal to prohibit restrictive covenants and agreements that ban the use of outdoor clotheslines.[26]

One other request for review is worthy of mention. In 2010, the Canadian Environmental Law Association filed an application to review the EBR itself. In March 2011, the MOE agreed that this review was warranted and began a review. As of the time of writing of this book, the MOE review was not complete and the approach and scope of the review was still under development.[27]

The Right to Request an Investigation

The EBR also establishes the right of any two Ontario residents to ask a responsible ministry to investigate the violation of environmental statutes, regulations, or instruments.[28] The Act only requires the responsible ministry to consider the request. If it chooses not to investigate, however, it must provide an explanation. If the request is successful, the ministry then investigates and decides whether to prosecute.

The ECO reported in 2004 that 141 requests for investigation were made between 1995 and 2003.[29] Since that time, the rate of requests for investigation has declined. Between April 1, 2004 and March 31, 2013, only 86 requests had been made.[30] Most requests for investigation are also refused by responsible ministries. The ECO 2000-2010 review reported that 27 of the 111 investigation requests made to responsible ministries (i.e., about 24 percent of such requests) resulted in an investigation.[31]

Again, some success stories exist in which individuals have been able to initiate an investigation that led to an environmental response. For example, a 2004 application by a farmer and a trailer park owner triggered action by government officials to obtain required approvals and issue remedial order to repair a poorly designed drainage system that was causing environmental harm.[32] Another application for investigation by two Hamilton residents in 2012 led the MOE to investigate and take action on an asphalt manufacturing and storage facility that was operating without the required air emission approval.[33]

It is interesting to note that the right to request an investigation is closely mirrored in the *Canadian Environmental Protection Act, 1999.*[34]

Court Access

The EBR also expands the ability of individuals to use the civil courts to bring a private lawsuit to protect the environment. It provides (1) the right to sue for "Harm to Natural Resources," and (2) less restrictive rules around the common law action of "public nuisance."

The Right to Sue for Harm to Natural Resources

In the United States, most environmental laws have provisions that allow the public to bring a civil lawsuit to enforce the provisions of the statute. In Canada, by contrast, most jurisdictions must rely on the common law to establish the basis to sue for environmental harm (see Chapters 2, 4, and 13 for more about the role of the common law in environmental law). The EBR, however, establishes a statutory right allowing any resident to bring a legal action against a person where a public resource in Ontario is at risk of harm as a result of the contravention of a statute, regulation, or instrument by that person.[35]

Taking advantage of this right, however, is not straightforward: before the action can begin, the plaintiff must both request an EBR investigation as described in the preceding section and demonstrate that either the responsible ministry has failed to respond or the response has been "unreasonable.[36] Another challenge for plaintiffs is the availability of the defence of due diligence. If the defendant is able to demonstrate that all reasonable care and precautions were taken to avoid the alleged transgression, it has a valid defence to the claim.[37] The EBR provides for a broad range of other remedies[38] that could be awarded if an action is successful, including an injunction to stop an activity causing environmental harm and an order requiring the parties to negotiate a plan to restore environmental resources that have sustained environmental harm (a "restoration plan") and to order the restoration plan if the parties cannot agree on one.[39] The EBR does not allow the court to award damages (see Chapter 13) to individuals for harm to natural resources, although it does not forestall an individual from seeking damages in the case where the harm caused falls under the category of public nuisance causing personal injury or loss. Like the right to request an investigation, the right to sue for harm to natural resources is closely mirrored in the federal *Canadian Environmental Protection Act, 1999* by provisions that create a right to commence an "environmental protection action."[40] Probably because of the complexity of the governing provisions, the statutory right to sue has not been used often either under the EBR or under the *Canadian Environmental Protection Act, 1999*.

Lowered Restrictions on Public Nuisance

Historically, the common law has prevented private nuisance claims by individuals who suffered the same harm as the harm suffered by the rest of the community. In cases of public nuisance, only the government could bring a claim, and this restriction raised a significant barrier against environmental nuisance claims. The EBR removes this barrier; now any person who suffers a direct loss as a result of public nuisance is entitled to bring a claim without permission from the government.[41]

Whistle-Blower Protection

Whistle-blowers are people who report information about violations of the law to enforcement agencies or the media. Often they are people with inside information, such as employees of a polluting company or employees of a government agency that is not doing its job properly.

Whistle-blowers are often concerned about reprisals by employers, colleagues, or others who stand to lose when incriminating information is disclosed. Threats by employers of discipline or dismissal may prevent many potential whistle-blowers from coming forward. To address these concerns and encourage whistle-blowers to disclose important information, some—although not all—environmental protection statutes include provisions to protect whistle-blowers. For example, employees who act in compliance with the Ontario *Environmental Protection Act*[42] or the *Canadian Environmental Protection Act, 1999*[43] are protected against unjust dismissal or coercive action by their employers.

Ontario's EBR is more specific. It prohibits employer reprisals (e.g., through dismissal, harassment, or intimidation) against employees who have exercised any right established under the EBR. It also expressly protects employees who seek enforcement of environmental statutes, give information to enforcement agencies, or give evidence in environmental proceedings.[44]

Accountability

The EBR establishes two specific mechanisms to make the government more accountable for its environmental decision-making: the office of the ECO, and the requirement that government ministries put in place a statement of environmental values to govern their activities and decisions.

The Environmental Commissioner of Ontario

One of the most important changes brought about in Ontario through the passage of the EBR was the creation of a high-profile watchdog charged with auditing the effectiveness of the Ontario government in protecting the environment.[45] The environmental commissioner is an independent officer who reports directly to the Legislative Assembly of Ontario and is appointed for a five-year term.[46] The commissioner's role is to review the implementation of the EBR to ensure that ministries comply with its requirements and report annually to the legislature, and thus to the public.[47] Examples of the issues reported on by the commissioner include the following:

---

whistle-blowers insiders, such as employees, who report information about violations of the law to enforcement agencies or the media

- the exercise of discretion by ministers under the EBR
- appeal rights under the EBR
- the receipt, handling, and disposition of applications for review and applications for investigation under the EBR

The commissioner's office produces and publishes an annual report online (www .eco.on.ca) through which its evaluations of the EBR's implementation, and the ministries' compliance, are shared with the public. The commissioner's office also handles more than 1,600 inquiries per year from the public.[48]

Statements of Environmental Values

EBR also establishes a unique legislative requirement intended to improve accountability and transparency in government decision-making with respect to the environment. Designated ministries who are subject to the EBR are required to develop a statement of environmental values (SEV).[49] Once an SEV is in place for a ministry, the EBR requires ministers to "take every reasonable step to ensure that [the SEV] is considered whenever decisions that might significantly affect the environment are made in the ministry."[50]

The legal status of the SEV has been canvassed by the courts in an important decision: *Lafarge Canada Inc. v. Ontario (Environmental Review Tribunal)*.[51] A coalition of environmental groups sought and obtained leave to appeal a 2006 MOE decision to issue approvals to a large cement manufacturing company, Lafarge Canada Inc., to burn tires, plastics, and other waste materials at its cement plant near Kingston, Ontario. Lafarge and the MOE challenged the ERT's decision to proceed to a hearing in court, arguing that the ministry's decision to issue approvals was reasonable and did not require a consideration of the MOE's SEV. This was important for the environmental group appellant's case: the MOE's SEV requires it to consider two important environmental concepts that the MOE had failed to address in its decision to grant the Lafarge approvals: the precautionary principle and cumulative effects. The court held that the tribunal was reasonable in finding that the SEV was part of government policies developed to guide decisions of that kind.

While the SEVs are now in place for 15 Ontario government ministries that make environmentally related decisions, there are two notable exceptions: the Ministry of Finance and the Ministry of Infrastructure. As noted above, the ECO is on record, as early as 1996, as supporting the inclusion of the Ministry of Finance under the EBR.[52]

Access to Information

The old saying that "knowledge is power" is particularly true in the case of complex environmental issues that deal with specialized information and expertise. The capacity of an individual to participate meaningfully in government decisions about the environment is often critically linked to that individual's ability to tap into reports, communications, and other information housed within the halls of government.

Access to any information held by government agencies, however, is not automatic. Businesses generally have the right to protect information such as trade secrets, manufacturing processes, customer lists, and financial data. Individuals have privacy rights that protect their personal and health information. Governments are required to protect confidential information in many circumstances.

The decision about whether information should be available to the public requires a balancing of competing rights: the right to protect information must be weighed against the rights of interested parties to obtain it. Some kinds of information are very difficult to acquire independently, and often good reasons exist why they should be shared.

Three kinds of access to information rights are applicable to environmental information:

1. *Notice and disclosure.* In civil and criminal proceedings, the parties have the right to notice and disclosure of the case against them. In civil cases, these procedural rights are available only to persons who meet the relevant legal standing test.
2. *Environmental statutes.* Federal and provincial environmental statutes include general rights of any resident to have access to specified kinds of environmental information. A procedure usually exists for determining whether particular information must be disclosed.
3. *Access to information statutes.* Federal and provincial access to information statutes give general rights of access to all residents, regardless of whether they have a direct personal stake in the issue. Canadian citizens may even have information access rights under the US *Freedom of Information Act.*

Access to information granted to the general public by statutes often involves exceptions under which information need not be disclosed. It is important to keep in mind that these exceptions do not apply to the common law procedural rights of litigants—rights that are necessary for reasonable notice and a fair opportunity to be heard.

Access to Information Statutes

Under the federal *Access to Information Act,*[53] members of the public may request disclosure of environmental information held by the government and its agencies. Provincial statutes, such as the freedom of information acts of Alberta,[54] British Columbia,[55] and Ontario,[56] are broadly similar to the federal statute.

Difficulties sometimes arise in exercising rights to information. The need to clearly identify the information requested, the difficulties of delay, and the high cost of photocopying may all be problematic for those who seek to exercise their access rights. Most significant, however, are the broad categories of exemptions in the Act.

Access to Information Exemptions and Exceptions to Exemptions

General exemptions from the government's obligation to disclose under the federal *Access to Information Act* can be sweeping. The Act exempts

- advice or recommendations developed by or for a government,
- confidential private business information, and
- information relevant to the economic interests of Canada.[57]

Typical exemptions from disclosure in the provincial statutes include

- advice and recommendations to government (but not facts or statistical information), Cabinet records, and information that may harm law enforcement, intergovernmental relations, or government economic interests;
- unreasonable interference with personal privacy; and
- potential harm to private economic interests.[58]

The exemptions become even more complicated as a result of the exceptions. For example, public health and safety exclusions do not apply to heritage conservation and endangered or threatened species in the legislation of the provinces of Alberta,[59] British Columbia,[60] and Ontario.[61]

The **public interest override** is another important exception to the exemptions. The exemptions may be overridden where it is in the public interest to do so. Examples of cases in which the override may be used include situations where public health, safety, or protection of the environment outweighs potential financial, competitive, or other consequences of disclosure.

The public interest override may permit disclosure of private information, such as that collected by environmental regulators, even if confidentiality is claimed. Under the federal statute, the public interest override does not apply to government information; therefore, the government may refuse access. The Ontario *Freedom of Information and Protection of Privacy Act*, however, provides that access can be refused only in the case of Cabinet documents and law enforcement information where it is in the public interest not to disclose.[62]

Finally, the British Columbia statute[63] and the Ontario statute[64] create an exception to the economic interest exemption for the results of product or environmental testing. Unless the testing is done as a service for someone outside government for a fee or for the purpose of developing methods of testing, the exception applies.

---

public interest override a provision in the *Access to Information Act* that allows for disclosure of confidential information where public health, safety, or protection of the environment outweighs the consequences of disclosure

With these categories of exemptions and exceptions to exemptions, it is not hard to imagine the kinds of disclosure disputes that can arise. For example, imagine that a statute contains exemptions from disclosure for "advice or recommendations to government" as well as "economic interests of the province"; it also contains no exception from the exemption for environmental test results. Are the toxicity test data produced by private consultants for a government committee developing environmental standards exempt from disclosure? Would it make any difference if there is a provision indicating that "public interest outweighs likely public harm"? Most access to information legislation creates a mechanism to resolve these issues of interpretation, typically through the vehicle of an information commission.

Information and Privacy Commissioner

In the four access to information statutes discussed in this section, information seekers who are unsuccessful in obtaining the information they want are provided the right to file a complaint to an information and privacy commissioner. The commissioner may investigate. Under the federal legislation, the commissioner may make non-binding recommendations to departments.[65] By contrast, commissioners under the Alberta[66] and Ontario statutes[67] may make binding rulings.

Information and privacy commissioners are called on to interpret exemptions and exceptions to exemptions. Examples of rulings by Alberta's information and privacy commissioner include the following:

- A report about the effects of oil and gas activities on the cattle industry, prepared by a consultant for the Alberta Environmental Law Centre (a government agency), was not exempt from disclosure, even though the consulting contract contained a confidentiality clause.
- Information about the operation of a natural gas processing plant was not exempt from disclosure, although it contained only facts and no advice to a public body.

SUMMARY OF KEY POINTS

- Two types of legislation counter the government-centred approach to environmental protection by granting members of the public greater access to participate in environmental decision-making: (1) the Ontario *Environmental Bill of Rights, 1993*, and (2) federal and provincial access to information statutes.
- In the early 1970s, non-governmental groups organized the movement toward more transparency and accountability in environmental decision-making by government. This movement called for recognition in the Canadian Constitution of the fundamental right of all citizens to a healthy environment and/or legislation passed by provincial governments.

- Canadian lawmakers have increased the role of individuals in environmental decision-making with legislative reform that expanded the individual environmental rights to a concrete set of provisions. The three territorial governments have passed laws with different forms of enforceable environmental rights, and Ontario is currently the only province with an environmental bill of rights.

- The Ontario *Environmental Bill of Rights, 1993* established four new rights for Ontario residents to participate in environmental decision-making by government: (1) the right to receive notice and comment on proposed statutes, regulations, policies, and instruments (approvals or environmental orders) issued by government officials; (2) the right to request leave to appeal the approval of an instrument; (3) the right to request a review of an existing law or instrument; and (4) the right to request an investigation into a potential violation of environmental law.

- The decision about whether information should be available to the public requires a balancing of competing rights: the right to protect information must be weighed against the rights of interested parties to obtain it. Lawmakers have attempted to maintain the balance between the public's right to government-held information on environmental decision-making and the protection of privacy through notice and disclosure, environmental statutes, and access to information statutes.

KEY TERMS

instruments
public interest override
whistle-blowers

DISCUSSION QUESTIONS

1. If governments are elected to protect the public interest, including the public interest in a healthy environment, why would we need an environmental bill of rights? What more can an EBR provide?

2. Which provisions in the Ontario EBR do you think are the most effective in protecting an individual's right to a healthy environment, and why?

3. The Ontario EBR is sometimes criticized for leaving too much discretion for various EBR decisions in the hands of government officials. Identify some examples of this discretion in the EBR. What are the pros and cons of removing this discretion for each of the examples you have found?

4. How could the Ontario EBR be strengthened to improve its effectiveness in serving the objectives of (1) encouraging public participation in environmental decision-making, (2) making public participation more meaningful, and (3) improving government accountability in protecting the environment?

5. What factors must be balanced in granting increased public access to information? Have the access to information statutes discussed in this chapter struck the right balance?

SUGGESTED READINGS

Readings

Boyd, David R. Right to a Healthy Environment: A Series of Discussion Papers. David Suzuki Foundation, 2013, http://www.davidsuzuki.org/publications/reports/2013/right-to-a-healthy-environment-papers.

Environmental Commissioner of Ontario (ECO). *Ontario's Environmental Bill of Rights and You*. Toronto: ECO, 2013, http://www.eco.on.ca/uploads/EBR%20Documents/The%20EBR%20and%20You%202013.pdf.

Muldoon, Paul, and Richard Lindgren. *The Environmental Bill of Rights: A Practical Guide*. Toronto: Emond Montgomery, 1995.

Websites

Canadian Environmental Law Association: http://www.cela.ca

Ecojustice: http://www.ecojustice.ca

Environmental Commissioner of Ontario: http://www.eco.on.ca

Environmental Law Centre (Alberta) Society: http://elc.ab.ca

Environmental Registry, Ontario Ministry of the Environment: http://www.ebr.gov.on.ca

Pollution Probe: http://www.pollutionprobe.org

West Coast Environmental Law Association: http://wcel.org

NOTES

1. See, e.g., Noel Lyon, "Testimony Before the Special Joint Committee of the Senate and the House of Commons on the Constitution of Canada," *Minutes of Proceedings and Evidence*, November 26, 1970, Issue no. 16, at 40-41.

2. Special Joint Committee of the Senate and the House of Commons on the Constitution of Canada, *Minutes of Proceedings and Evidence*, January 30, 1981, Issue no. 49, at 8.

3. See also David R. Boyd, The History of the Right to a Healthy Environment in Canada: Executive Summary (David Suzuki Foundation, 2013), http://davidsuzuki.org/publications/2013/11/DSF%20White%20Paper%202--2013.pdf.

4. *Environment Quality Act*, SQ 1978, c. 15, s. 19.1.

5. Ibid.

6. *Charter of Human Rights and Freedoms*, CQLR c. C-12, s. 46.1. The full provision reads: "Every person has a right to live in a healthful environment in which biodiversity is preserved, to the extent and according to the standards provided by law."

7. *Environment Act*, RSY 2002, c. 76, as amended (see in particular ss. 6-36); and *Environmental Rights Act* RSNWT (Nu) 1988, c. 83, as amended.

8. *Environmental Bill of Rights, 1993*, SO 1993, c. 28, Part I, s. 2(1).

9. Ibid., Part I, s. 2(2).

10. See O. Reg. 681/94, as amended. It establishes the instruments that are classified as Class I, II, and III instruments, which are subject to the notice and commenting rights under the EBR. The approvals and orders listed as examples are all under Part II, which prescribes instruments under Ministry of the Environment legislation.

11. *Environmental Bill of Rights, 1993*, supra note 8, s. 5(1); and O. Reg. 73/94, as amended, ss. 13-14, which prescribe that the Environmental Registry be operated by the Ontario Ministry of the Environment. See the Environmental Registry here: http://www.ebr.gov.on.ca.

12. The term *responsible ministry* is used in this chapter to refer to any Ontario ministry subject to the EBR requirements.

13. O. Reg. 73/94.

14. O. Reg. 482/95.

15. Eva Ligeti, *Ontario Regulation 482/95 and the Environmental Bill of Rights: A Special Report to the Legislative Assembly of Ontario* (Toronto: Environmental Commissioner of Ontario, January 1996).

16. *Environmental Bill of Rights, 1993*, supra note 8, ss. 12-18.

17. Ibid., ss. 19-37; and O. Reg. 681/94.

18. Allan Gunn and Jim Lewis, "Ontario's Environmental Registry: A Case Study in Public Participation," November 12, 2006, PowerPoint presentation.

19. *Environmental Bill of Rights, 1993*, supra note 8, s. 41.

20. Office of the Environmental Commissioner of Ontario, email message to author, November 3, 2014.

21. Based on an interview with a colleague, 2013.

22. *Environmental Bill of Rights, 1993*, supra note 8, s. 61.

23. Environmental Commissioner of Ontario, *Ministries' Handling of EBR Applications: A Ten-Year Statistical Retrospective (2000-2010)* (Toronto: ECO, 2012), at 8.

24. Environmental Commissioner of Ontario, "Review of the SWARU Incinerator," in Environmental Commissioner of Ontario, *Developing Sustainability: Annual Report 2001-2002* (Toronto: ECO, 2002), at 123-26.

25. Environmental Commissioner of Ontario, *Reconciling Our Priorities: Annual Report 2006-2007 Supplement* (Toronto: ECO, 2007), at 177-85.

26. Environmental Commissioner of Ontario, *2008/2009 Annual Report Supplement* (Toronto: ECO, 2009), at 117-18.

27. Environmental Commissioner of Ontario, *Serving the Public: Annual Report 2012/2013 Supplement* (Toronto: ECO, 2013), at 165.

28. *Environmental Bill of Rights, 1993*, supra note 8, ss. 74-81.

29. Environmental Commissioner of Ontario, "Annual Reports & Supplements," 2004-2012, http://www.eco.on.ca/index.php/en_US/pubs/annual-reports-and -supplements. See the annual reports from 1994-95 to 2003-4.

30. Office of the Environmental Commissioner of Ontario, supra note 20.

31. Environmental Commissioner of Ontario, supra note 23.

32. Environmental Commissioner of Ontario, *Neglecting Our Obligations: Annual Report 2005-2006 Supplement* (Toronto: ECO, 2005), at 290-95.

33. Environmental Commissioner of Ontario, supra note 27, at 235-36.

34. *Canadian Environmental Protection Act, 1999*, SC 1999, c. 33, as amended, s. 17.

35. *Environmental Bill of Rights, 1993*, supra note 8, Part VI.

36. Ibid., s. 84(2).

37. Ibid., s. 85.

38. Ibid., s. 93.

39. Ibid., ss. 95-98.

40. *Canadian Environmental Protection Act, 1999*, supra note 34, ss. 22-40.

41. *Environmental Bill of Rights, 1993*, supra note 8, s. 103.

42. *Environmental Protection Act*, RSO 1990, c. E.19, as amended, s. 94.

43. *Canadian Environmental Protection Act, 1999*, supra note 34, s. 16(4).

44. *Environmental Bill of Rights, 1993*, supra note 8, Part VII.

45. Ibid., Part III.

46. Ibid., s. 49(3).

47. Ibid., s. 58.

48. Yazmin Shroff, Public Information and Outreach Officer, ECO, personal communication, November 3, 2014.

49. *Environmental Bill of Rights, 1993*, supra note 8, ss. 7-11.

50. Ibid., s. 11.

51. *Lafarge Canada Inc. v. Ontario (Environmental Review Tribunal)*, [2008] CanLII 30290 (Ont. Dist. Ct.).

52. Ligeti, supra note 15, at 2.

53. *Access to Information Act*, RSC 1985, c. A-1.

54. *Freedom of Information and Protection of Privacy Act*, RSA 2000, c. F-25, as amended.

55. *Freedom of Information and Protection of Privacy Act*, RSBC 1996, c. 165, as amended.

56. *Freedom of Information and Protection of Privacy Act*, RSO 1990, c. F.31, as amended.

57. *Access to Information Act*, supra note 53, ss. 18, 20, and 21.

58. See, e.g., *Freedom of Information and Protection of Privacy Act* (Ont.), supra note 56, ss. 12-23.

59. *Freedom of Information and Protection of Privacy Act* (Alta.), supra note 54, s. 28.

60. *Freedom of Information and Protection of Privacy Act* (BC), supra note 55, s. 18.

61. *Freedom of Information and Protection of Privacy Act* (Ont.), supra note 56, s. 21.1.

62. Ibid., ss. 12-14.

63. *Freedom of Information and Protection of Privacy Act* (BC), supra note 55, s. 17(3).

64. *Freedom of Information and Protection of Privacy Act* (Ont.), supra note 56, s. 18.

65. *Access to Information Act*, supra note 53, ss. 32-37.

66. *Freedom of Information and Protection of Privacy Act* (Alta.), supra note 54, ss. 72-73.

67. *Freedom of Information and Protection of Privacy Act* (Ont.), supra note 56, s. 54.

Bibliography

Statutes and Regulations

Federal

Access to Information Act, RSC 1985, c. A-1.

Antarctic Environmental Protection Act, SC 2003, c. 20.

Arctic Waters Pollution Prevention Act, RSC 1985, c. A-12.

Bill C-32, *An Act Respecting the Sustainable Development of Canada's Seacoast and Inland Fisheries*, 2nd Sess., 39th Parl., 2007.

Canada Business Corporations Act, RSC 1985, c. C-44.

Canada Consumer Product Safety Act, SC 2010, c. 21.

Canada Foundation for Sustainable Development Technology Act, SC 2001, c. 23.

Canada National Parks Act, SC 2000, c. 32.

Canada Oil and Gas Operations Act, RSC 1985, c. O-7.

Canada Petroleum Resources Act, RSC 1985, c. 36 (2nd Supp.).

Canada Water Act, RSC 1985, c. C-11.

Canada Wildlife Act, RSC 1985, c. W-9.

Canadian Charter of Rights and Freedoms, Part I of the *Constitution Act, 1982*, being Schedule B to the *Canada Act 1982* (UK), 1982, c. 11.

Canadian Environment Week Act, RSC 1985, c. E-11.

Canadian Environmental Assessment Act, SC 1992, c. 37.

Canadian Environmental Assessment Act, 2012, SC 2012, c. 19, s. 52.

Canadian Environmental Protection Act, 1999, SC 1999, c. 33.

Coastal Fisheries Protection Act, RSC 1985, c. C-33.

Competition Act, RSC 1985, c. C-34.

Constitution Act, 1867, 30 & 31 Vict., c. 3, reprinted in RSC 1985, Appendix II, No. 5.

Constitution Act, 1982, being Schedule B to the *Canada Act 1982* (UK), 1982, c. 11.

Criminal Code, RSC 1985, c. C-46.

Department of the Environment Act, RSC 1985, c. E-10.

Energy Efficiency Act, SC 1992, c. 36.

Environmental Contaminants Act, RSC 1985, c. E-12.

Environmental Enforcement Act, SC 2009, c. 14.

Export Development Act, RSC 1985, c. E-20.

Federal Sustainable Development Act, SC 2008, c. 33.

Feeds Act, RSC 1985, c. F-9.

Fertilizers Act, RSC 1985, c. F-10.

First Nations Commercial and Industrial Development Act, SC 2005, c. 53.

First Nations Land Management Act, SC 1999, c. 24.

Fisheries Act, RSC 1985, c. F-14.

Food and Drugs Act, RSC 1985, c. F-27.

Hazardous Products Act, RSC 1985, c. H-3.

Indian Act, RSC 1985, c. I-5.

International River Improvements Act, RSC 1985, c. I-20.

Lake of the Woods Control Board Act, 1921, SC 1921, c. 10.

Migratory Birds Convention Act, 1994, SC 1994, c. 22.

National Energy Board Act, RSC 1985, c. N-7, as amended by SC 2012, c. 19.

National Wildlife Week Act, RSC 1985, c. W-10.

Nuclear Energy Act, RSC 1985, c. A-16.

Nuclear Liability Act, RSC 1985, c. N-28.

Nuclear Safety and Control Act, SC 1997, c. 9, as amended by SC 2012, c. 19.

Pest Control Products Act, RSC 1985, c. P-9.

Plant Protection Act, SC 1990, c. 22.

Quebec Act, 1774, 14 Geo. III, c. 83 (UK).

Royal Proclamation, 1763, RSC 1985, c. I-7.

Seeds Act, RSC 1985, c. S-8.

Species at Risk Act, SC 2002, c. 29.

Statutory Instruments Act, RSC 1985, c. S-22.

Transportation of Dangerous Goods Act, 1992, SC 1992, c. 34.

Tsawwassen First Nation Final Agreement Act, SC 2008, c. 32.

Weather Modification Information Act, RSC 1985, c. W-5.

Wild Animal and Plant Protection and Regulation of International and Interprovincial Trade Act, SC 1992, c. 52.

Yukon Environmental and Socio-economic Assessment Act, SC 2003, c. 7.

Alberta

Alberta Land Stewardship Act, SA 2009, c. A-26.8.

Climate Change and Emissions Management Act, SA 2003, c. C-16.7.

Department of the Environment Act, SA 1971, c. 24.

Environmental Protection and Enhancement Act, RSA 2000, c. E-12.

Freedom of Information and Protection of Privacy Act, RSA 2000, c. F-25.

Oil and Gas Conservation Act, RSA 2000, c. O-6.

Oil Sands Conservation Act, RSA 2000, c. O-7.

Pipeline Act, RSA 2000, c. P-7.

Responsible Energy Development Act, SA 2012, c. R-17.3.

Water Act, RSA 2000, c. W-3.

British Columbia

Administrative Tribunals Act, SBC 2004, c. 45.

Carbon Tax Act, SBC 2008, c. 40.

Environment and Land Use Act, RSBC 1996, c. 117.

Environmental Assessment Act, SBC 2002, c. 43.

Environmental Management Act, SBC 2003, c. 53.

Export Development Act, RSC 1985, c. E-20.

Fisheries Act, RSBC 1996, c. 149.

Freedom of Information and Protection of Privacy Act, RSBC 1996, c. 165.

Greenhouse Gas Reduction Targets Act, SBC 2007, c. 42.

Tsawwassen First Nation Final Agreement Act, SBC 2007, c. 39.

Waste Management Act, RSBC 1996, c. 118.

Manitoba

The Environment Act, CCSM c. E125.

The Sustainable Development Act, CCSM c. S270.

New Brunswick

Crown Lands and Forests Act, SNB 1980, c. C-38.1.

Northwest Territories and Nunavut

Environmental Rights Act, RSNWT (Nu) 1988, c. 83 (Supp.).

Nova Scotia

Environment Act, SNS 1994-95, c. 1.

Fisheries and Coastal Resources Act, SNS 1996, c. 25.

Ontario

Aggregate Resources Act, RSO 1990, c. A.8.

Building Code Act, 1992, SO 1992, c. 23, as amended.

Clean Water Act, 2006, SO 2006, c. 22.

Conservation Authorities Act, RSO 1990, c. C.27.

Crown Forest Sustainability Act, 1994, SO 1994, c. 25.

Endangered Species Act, 2007, SO 2007, c. 6.

Environmental Assessment Act, RSO 1990, c. E.18.

Environmental Bill of Rights, 1993, SO 1993, c. 28.

Environmental Protection Act, RSO 1990, c. E.19.

Environmental Review Tribunal Act, 2000, SO 2000, c. 26, sch. F.

Far North Act, SO 2010, c.18.

Farming and Food Production Protection Act, SO 1998, c. 1.

Freedom of Information and Protection of Privacy Act, RSO 1990, c. F.31.

Greenbelt Act, 2005, SO 2005, c. 1.

KVP Company Limited Act, 1950, SO 1950, c. 33.

Mining Act, RSO 1990, c. M.14.

Municipal Act, SO 2001, c. 25.

Niagara Escarpment Planning and Development Act, RSO 1990, c. N.2.

Nutrient Management Act, 2002, SO 2002, c. 4.

Oak Ridges Moraine Conservation Act, 2001, SO 2001, c. 31.

Ontario Energy Board Act, SO 1998, c. 15.

Ontario Water Resources Act, RSO 1990, c. O.40.

Pesticides Act, RSO 1990, c. P.11.

Places to Grow Act, 2005, SO 2005, c. 13.

Planning Act, RSO 1990, c. P.13.

Safe Drinking Water Act, 2002, SO 2002, c. 32.

Statutory Powers Procedure Act, RSO 1990, c. S.22.

Toxics Reduction Act, 2009, SO 2009, c. 19.

Quebec

An Act Respecting Implementation of the Québec Energy Strategy, SQ 2006, c. 46.

Charter of Human Rights and Freedoms, CQLR c. C-12.

Cities and Towns Act, CQLR c. C-19.

Civil Code of Québec, CQLR c. C-1991.

Environment Quality Act, SQ 1978, c. 15.

Environment Quality Act, CQLR c. Q-2.

Yukon

Environmental Act, RSY 2002, c. 76.

Agreements and Conventions

A Canada-Wide Accord on Environmental Harmonization: http://www.ccme.ca/files/Resources/harmonization/accord_harmonization_e.pdf.

The James Bay and Northern Quebec Agreement (JBNQA): http://www.gcc.ca/pdf/LEG000000006.pdf.

Nisga'a Final Agreement: http://www.nisgaanation.ca/treaty-documents.

Nunavut Land Claims Agreement: http://nlca.tunngavik.com.

Stockholm Convention on Persistent Organic Pollutants—Convention Text: http://chm.pops.int/TheConvention/Overview/Textofthe Convention/tabid/2232/Default.aspx.

Yukon Land Claims Agreement: http://www.gcc.ca/pdf/LEG000000006.pdf.

Cases

114957 Canada Ltée (Spraytech, Société d'arrosage) v. Hudson (Town), 2001 SCC 40, [2001] 2 SCR 241.

Canadian Environmental Law Association v. Canada (Minister of the Environment) (1999), 30 CELR (NS) 59 (FCTD); aff'd. 2000 CanLII 15579 (FCA) and 2001 FCA 233.

Canadian Wildlife Federation Inc. v. Canada (Minister of Environment) (1989), 99 NR 72, 27 FTR 159; [1990] 2 WWR 69 (FCA).

Crown Zellerbach Canada Ltd., R v., [1988] 1 SCR 401.

Delgamuukw v. British Columbia, [1997] 3 SCR 1010.

Fowler v. The Queen, [1980] 2 SCR 213.

Friends of the Oldman River Society v. Canada (Minister of Transport), [1992] 1 SCR 3.

Haida Nation v. British Columbia (Minister of Forests), 2004 SCC 73, [2004] 3 SCR 511.

Heppner v. Alberta (Environment, Minister), 1977 ALTASCAD 206.

Hydro Québec, R v., [1997] 3 SCR 213.

Northwest Falling Contractors Ltd., R v., [1980] 2 SCR 292.

Sparrow, R v., [1990] 1 SCR 1075.

Taku River Tlingit First Nation v. British Columbia (Project Assessment Director), 2004 SCC 74, [2004] 3 SCR 550.

Tsilhqot'in Nation v. British Columbia, 2014 SCC 44.

Books and Reports

Agriculture and Agri-Food Canada. *Environmental and Economic Impact Assessments of Environmental Regulations for the Agriculture Sector: A Case Study of Hog Farming.* Ottawa: Minister of Public Works and Government Services Canada, 2006.

Birnie, Patricia, and Alan Boyle. *International Law and the Environment*, 2nd ed. New York: Oxford University Press, 2002.

Blake, Sara. *Administrative Law in Canada*, 4th ed. Markham, ON: LexisNexis, 2006.

Botts, Lee, and Paul Muldoon. *Evolution of the Great Lakes Water Quality Agreement.* East Lansing, MI: Michigan State University Press, 2005.

British Columbia. *Updated Procedures for Meeting Legal Obligations When Consulting First Nations: Interim.* Victoria: Province of British Columbia, 2010, http://www2.gov.bc.ca/gov/DownloadAsset?assetId=9779EDACB673486883560B59BEBE782E.

Canada. *Aboriginal Consultation and Accommodation: Updated Guidelines for Federal Officials to Fulfill the Duty to Consult.* Ottawa: Department of Aboriginal Affairs and Northern Development Canada, 2011, http://www.aadnc-aandc.gc.ca/DAM/DAM-INTER-HQ/STAGING/texte-text/intgui_1100100014665_eng.pdf.

Carver, Deborah, Robert B. Gibson, Jessie Irving, and Erin Burbidge. *Inter-jurisdictional Coordination of EA: Challenges and Opportunities Arising from Differences Among Provincial and Territorial Assessment Requirements and Processes.* Report for the Environmental Planning and Assessment Caucus, Canadian Environmental Network, 2010.

Colander, David, and Roland Kupers. *Complexity and the Art of Public Policy: Solving Society's Problems from the Bottom Up.* Princeton, NJ: Princeton University Press, 2014.

Dalal-Clayton, Barry, and Barry Sadler. *Strategic Environmental Assessment: A Sourcebook and Reference Guide to International Experience.* London: Earthscan, 2005.

Dalal-Clayton, Barry, and Barry Sadler. *Sustainability Appraisal: Sourcebook and Reference Guide to International Experience.* Oxford: Routledge, 2014.

Dales, John H. *Pollution, Property and Prices.* Toronto: University of Toronto Press, 1968.

DeMarco, Jerry V., and Paul Muldoon. *Environmental Boards and Tribunals in Canada: A Practical Guide.* Toronto: LexisNexis, 2011.

Doern, G. Bruce, ed. *The Environmental Imperative: Market Approaches to the Greening of Canada.* Toronto: C.D. Howe Institute, 1990.

Dunsky, Philippe. *The Role and Value of Demand-Side Management in Manitoba Hydro's Resource Planning Process* [testimony to the Manitoba Public Utilities Board]. Montreal: Dunsky Energy Consulting, 2014, http://www.pub.gov.mb.ca/nfat/pdf/demand_side_management_dunsky.pdf.

Emond, D. Paul. *Environmental Assessment Law.* Toronto: Emond Montgomery, 1978.

Environmental Commissioner of Ontario. *Losing Touch: Annual Report 2011/2012—Part 1.* Toronto: Queen's Printer for Ontario, 2012, http://www.eco.on.ca/uploads/Reports-Annual/2011_12/Losing%20Touch%20I%20EN.pdf.

Environmental Commissioner of Ontario. *Losing Our Touch: Annual Report 2011/2012—Part 2.* Toronto: Queen's Printer for Ontario, 2012, http://www.eco.on.ca/uploads/Reports-Annual/2011_12/Losing%20Our%20Touch.pdf.

Environmental Commissioner of Ontario. "The MISA Wastewater Regulations: A Review Is Overdue." In Environmental Commissioner of Ontario, *Engaging Solutions: Annual Report, 2010/2011,* 124-27. Toronto: Queen's Printer for Ontario, 2011, http://www.eco.on.ca/uploads/Reports-Annual/2010_11/Final-English-Bookmarked-2010-AR.pdf.

Environmental Commissioner of Ontario. "Missing in Action: Ontario's Oversight of Cage Aquaculture." In Environmental Commissioner of Ontario, *Engaging Solutions: Annual Report, 2010/2011,* 32-33. Toronto: The Queen's Printer for Ontario, 2011, http://www.ecoissues.ca/index.php/Missing_in_Action:_Ontario's_oversight_of_cage_aquaculture.

Environmental Commissioner of Ontario. *Ontario's Environmental Bill of Rights and You.* Toronto: Enviornmental Commissioner of Ontario, 2013, http://www.eco.on.ca/uploads/EBR%20Documents/The%20EBR%20and%20You%202013.pdf.

Environmental Commissioner of Ontario. *Serving the Public: Annual Report 2012/2013.* Toronto: Queen's Printer for Ontario, 2013, http://www.eco.on.ca/uploads/Reports-Annual/2012_13/13ar.pdf.

Estrin, David, and John Swaigen, eds. *Environment on Trial: A Guide to Ontario Environmental Law and Policy,* 3rd ed. Toronto: Emond Montgomery, 1993.

Fisheries and Oceans Canada. *Aquaculture in Canada 2012: A Report on Aquaculture Sustainability.* Ottawa: Fisheries and Oceans Canada, 2012, http://www.dfo-mpo.gc.ca/aquaculture/lib-bib/asri-irda/pdf/DFO_2012_SRI_AQUACULTURE_ENG.pdf.

Forsey, Eugene. *How Canadians Govern Themselves.* Ottawa: Parliament of Canada, 2012, http://www.parl.gc.ca/About/Parliament/SenatorEugeneForsey/book/preface-e.html.

Gibson, Robert B., with Selma Hassan, Susan Holtz, James Tansey, and Graham Whitelaw. *Sustainability Assessment: Criteria and Processes.* London: Earthscan, 2005.

Gunningham, Neil, and Darren Sinclair. *Leaders and Laggards: Next Generation Environmental Regulation.* Sheffield, UK: Greenleaf, 2002.

Hazell, Stephen. *Canada v. the Environment: Federal Environmental Assessment 1984–1998.* Toronto: Canadian Environmental Defence Fund, 1999.

Hughes, Elaine, Alastair Lucas, and William Tilleman, eds. *Environmental Law and Policy,* 3rd ed. Toronto: Emond Montgomery, 2003.

Johnson, Neil. *Simply Complexity: A Clear Guide to Complexity Theory.* London: Oneworld, 2009.

Jones, David. *Principles of Administrative Law,* 5th ed. Toronto: Thomson Carswell, 2009.

Legislative Assembly of Ontario. *Report on the Review of the Aggregate Resources Act.* Toronto: Standing Committee on General Government, 2013, http://www.ontla.on.ca/committee-proceedings/committee-reports/files_pdf/Legislative%20Assembly%20Aggregate%20English%20Readable.pdf.

Lucas, Alastair R., and Chidinma Thompson. *Canadian Environmental Law.* Toronto: LexisNexis, 2009.

MacDonald, Elaine, and Anastasia Lintner. "Summary of Concerns: Municipal Industrial Strategy for Abatement (MISA) Regulations." Ecojustice, January 2010, http://www.ecojustice.ca/files/submissions/EBR%20AfR%20MISA%20Regulation%20Summary%20of%20Concerns.pdf/view.

Makuch, Stanley M., Neil Craik, and Signe B. Leisk. *Canadian Municipal and Planning Law,* 2nd ed. Toronto: Carswell, 2004.

McKenzie, Judith. *Environmental Politics in Canada.* Oxford: Oxford University Press, 2002.

Meadows, Donella. *Thinking in Systems: A Primer.* White River Junction, VT: Chelsea Green, 2008.

Muldoon, Paul, and Richard Lindgren. *The Environmental Bill of Rights: A Practical Guide.* Toronto: Emond Montgomery, 1995.

Mullan, David. *Essentials of Canadian Administrative Law*. Toronto: Irwin Law, 2001.

National Energy Board and Canadian Environmental Assessment Agency. *Report of the Joint Review Panel for the Enbridge Northern Gateway Project*. Ottawa: National Energy Board, 2013, http://gatewaypanel.review -examen.gc.ca/clf-nsi/dcmnt/rcmndtnsrprt/ rcmndtnsrprt-eng.html.

Noble, Bram F. *Introduction to Environmental Impact Assessment: A Guide to Principles and Practice*, 2nd ed. Toronto: Oxford University Press, 2010.

O'Connor, Hon. Dennis R. *Report of the Walkerton Inquiry, Part One: The Events of May 2000 and Related Issues*. Toronto: Queen's Printer for Ontario, 2002, http://www.attorneygeneral.jus .gov.on.ca/english/about/pubs/walkerton/part1/.

O'Connor, Hon. Dennis R. *Report of the Walkerton Inquiry, Part Two: A Strategy for Safe Drinking Water*. Toronto: Queen's Printer for Ontario, 2002, http://www.attorneygeneral.jus.gov.on.ca/ english/about/pubs/walkerton/part2/.

Ontario. *A Class Environmental Assessment for Activities of the Ministry of Northern Development and Mines Under the Mining Act*. Toronto: Ministry of Northern Development and Mines, 2012, http://www.mndm.gov.on.ca/ sites/default/files/mndm_class _environmental_assessment_pdf.pdf.

Ontario. *Draft Guidelines for Ministries on Consultation with Aboriginal Peoples Related to Aboriginal Rights and Treaty Rights*. Toronto: Secretariat for Aboriginal Affairs, 2006, https://www.ontario.ca/government/draft -guidelines-ministries-consultation-aboriginal -peoples-related-aboriginal.

Reich, Charles. *The Greening of America*. New York: Random House, 1970.

Rian, Allen, and Philippa Campsie. *Implementing the Growth Plan for the Greater Golden Horseshoe: Has the Strategic Regional Vision Been Compromised?* Toronto: Neptis Foundation, 2013, http://www.neptis.org/ publications/reports.

Royal Society of Canada. *Royal Society of Canada Expert Panel: Environmental and Health Impacts of Canada's Oil Sands Industry*. Ottawa: Royal Society of Canada, 2010.

Saxe, Dianne. *Ontario Environmental Protection Act Annotated*. Aurora, ON: Canada Law Books, 2014.

Stitt, Allan J. *Alternative Dispute Resolution for Organizations*. Toronto: Wiley, 1998.

Stone, Christopher D. *Should Trees Have Standing? Law, Morality, and the Environment*, 3rd ed. New York: Oxford University Press, 2010.

United Nations. *Treaty Handbook*, rev. ed. New York: United Nations, 2012, https://treaties .un.org/doc/source/publications/THB/ English.pdf.

United Nations Environment Programme (UNEP). *The Use of Economic Instruments in Environmental Policy: Opportunities and Challenges*. New York: UNEP, 2004, http://www.unep.ch/etb/publications/EconInst/ econInstruOppChnaFin.pdf.

Van Harten, Gus, Gerald Heckman, and David Mullan, eds. *Administrative Law: Cases, Text, and Materials*, 6th ed. Toronto: Emond Montgomery, 2010.

Walker, Brian, and David Salt. *Resilience Practice: Building Capacity to Absorb Disturbance and Maintain Function*. Washington, DC: Island Press, 2012.

Waltner-Toews, David, James J. Kay, and Nina-Marie E. Lister, eds. *The Ecosystem Approach: Complexity, Uncertainty and Managing for Sustainability*. New York: Columbia University Press, 2008.

Webb, Kernaghan. *Pollution Control in Canada: The Regulatory Approach in the 1980s*. Ottawa: Law Reform Commission of Canada, 1988.

World Commission on Environment and Development. *Our Common Future*. Oxford: Oxford University Press, 1987.

Articles

Barrera-Hernández, Lila. "Consumer Behaviour and the Environment: An Environmental Law and Policy Approach." (1995) 5:2 *Journal of Environmental Law and Practice* 161.

Benedickson, Jamie. "Environmental Law Survey (1980-92), Part 1." (1992) 24 *Ottawa Law Review* 733.

Boyd, David R. Right to a Healthy Environment: A Series of Discussion Papers. David Suzuki Foundation, 2013, http://www.davidsuzuki.org/publications/reports/2013/right-to-a-healthy-environment-papers.

Bryden, Philip. "New Developments in Tribunal Reform: Lessons from British Columbia." Paper presented at The Future of Administrative Justice Symposium, Toronto, January 18, 2008, https://www.law.utoronto.ca/documents/conferences/adminjustice08_bryden.pdf.

Canada, "Strategic Environmental Assessment: The Cabinet Directive on the Environmental Assessment of Policy, Plan and Program Proposals." Privy Council Office and the Canadian Environmental Assessment Agency, 2010, http://www.ceaa-acee.gc.ca/default.asp?lang=en&n=B3186435-1.

Collins, Lynda M. "An Ecologically Literate Reading of the Canadian Charter of Rights and Freedoms." (2009) 26 *Windsor Review of Legal and Social Issues* 7.

Collins, Lynda M., and Heather McLeod-Kilmurray. "Material Contribution to Justice? Toxic Causation After *Resurfice Corp. v. Hanke*." (2010) 48 *Osgoode Hall Law Journal* 411.

de Mestral, Armand, and Evan Fox-Decent. "Rethinking the Relationship Between International Law and Domestic Law." (2008) 53 *McGill Law Journal* 573.

Doelle, Meinhard. "CEAA 2012: The End of Federal EA as We Know It?" (2012) 24 *Journal of Environmental Law and Practice* 1.

Doelle, Meinhard, and Chris Tollefson. "Judicial Review of Environmental Decision-Making." In Meinhard Doelle and Chris Tollefson, eds., *Environmental Law: Cases and Materials*, 2nd ed. Toronto: Carswell, 2013.

Duinker, Peter N., and Lorne A. Greig. "The Impotence of Cumulative Effects Assessment in Canada: Ailments and Ideas for Redeployment." (2006) 37:2 *Environmental Management* 153.

Elgie, Stewart, and Anastasio Lintner. "The Supreme Court's *Canfor* Decision: Losing the Battle but Winning the War for Environmental Damages." (2005) 38 *UBC Law Review* 223.

"Elsipogtog Anti-Fracking Protests Triggering Angry Online Backlash." *APTN National News*, December 2, 2013, http://aptn.ca/news/2013/11/15/elsipogtog-anti-fracking-protests-triggering-angry-online-backlash.

Gibson, Robert B. "From Wreck Cove to Voisey's Bay: The Evolution of Federal Environmental Assessment in Canada." (2002) 20:3 *Impact Assessment and Project Appraisal* 151.

Gibson, Robert B., Hugh Benevides, Meinhard Doelle, and Denis Kirchhoff. "Strengthening Strategic Environmental Assessment in Canada: An Evaluation of Three Basic Options." (2010) 20:3 *Journal of Environmental Law and Practice* 175.

Hahn, Robert W., and Robert N. Stavins. "Incentive-Based Environmental Regulation: A New Era from an Old Idea." (1991) 18 *Ecology Law Quarterly* 1.

Hughes, Elaine, Alastair Lucas, and William Tilleman. "Environmental Assessment." In Elaine Hughes, Alastair Lucas, and William Tilleman, eds., *Environmental Law and Policy*, 3rd ed. Toronto: Emond Montgomery, 2003.

Hunter, Justine. "Northern Gateway Has Ottawa Scrambling to Avoid Lawsuits." *The Globe and Mail*, December 23, 2013, http://www.theglobeandmail.com/news/british-columbia/northern-gateway-has-ottawa-scrambling-to-avoid-lawsuits/article16096644/.

Kay, James J., and Eric Schneider. "Embracing Complexity: The Challenge of the Ecosystem Approach." (1994) 20:3 *Alternatives* 32.

Keenan, Karyn. "Environmental Tool Kit: Private Prosecutions." (2000) 25:3/4 *Intervenor*. http://www.cela.ca/article/environmental-tool-kit-private-prosecutions.

Kwasniak, Arlene. "Environmental Assessment, Overlap, Duplication, Harmonization, Equivalency, and Substitution: Interpretation, Misinterpretation, and a Path Forward." (2009) 20:1 *Journal of Environmental Law and Practice* 1.

Leach, Melissa, et al. "Transforming Innovation for Sustainability." (2012) 17:2 *Ecology and Society* 11, http://www.ecologyandsociety.org/vol17/iss2/art11/.

M'Gonigle, R. Michael, T. Lynne Jamieson, Murdoch K. McAllister, and Randall M. Peterman. "Taking Uncertainty Seriously: From Permissive Regulation to Preventive Design in Environmental Decision Making." (1994) 32 *Osgoode Hall Law Journal* 53.

Ostrom, Elinor. "A General Framework for Analyzing Sustainability of Social-Ecological Systems." (2009) 325 *Science* 419.

Parson, Edward A. "Environmental Trends and Environmental Governance in Canada." (2000) 26:2 *Canadian Public Policy* S123, http://qed.econ.queensu.ca/pub/cpp/SE_english/Parson.pdf.

"Raw Sewage Flows into Halifax Harbour." *CBC News*, May 12, 2011, http://www.cbc.ca/news/canada/nova-scotia/raw-sewage-flows-into-halifax-harbour-1.1059448.

Rowlands, Ian H. "Renewable Electricity: Provincial Perspectives and National Prospects." In Debora L. VanNijnatten, ed., *Canadian Environmental Politics and Policy: The Challenges of Austerity and Ambivalence*, 4th ed. Don Mills, ON: Oxford University Press, forthcoming.

Shaw, Rob. "Greater Victoria Politicians Debate Sewage Project Deadline Extension." *Times Colonist*, January 8, 2014, http://www.timescolonist.com/greater-victoria-politicians-debate-sewage-project-deadline-extension-1.783170.

Sinoski, Kelli. "Nestlés Extraction of Groundwater Near Hope Riles First Nations." *Vancouver Sun*, August 22, 2013, http://www.vancouversun.com/life/Nestl%C3%A9+extraction+groundwater+near+Hope+riles+First+Nations/8817969/story.html.

Stavins, Robert N. "Lessons from the American Experiment with Market-Based Environmental Policies." KSG Working Paper No. PWP01-032; FEEM Working Paper No. 30.2002, April 2002, http://ssrn.com/abstract=285998.

Swaigen, John, Albert Koehl, and Charles Hatt. "Private Prosecutions Revisited: The Continuing Importance of Private Prosecutions in Protecting the Environment." Paper presented at the Symposium on Environment in the Courtroom (II): Environmental Prosecutions, University of Ottawa, Ottawa, March 2013, http://cirl.ca/files/cirl/john_swaigen_and_albert_koehl_and_charles_hatt-en.pdf.

Taylor, Matthew, Patrick Field, Lawrence Susskind, and William Tilleman. "Using Mediation in Environmental Tribunals: Opportunities and Best Practices." (1999) 22 *Dalhousie Law Journal* 51.

Weber, Bob. "First Nations Ramp Up Challenge to Oilsands Development." *Vancouver Sun*, January 3, 2014.

Weber, Bob. "*Lubicon vs. PennWest*: Band Files Lawsuit Against Alberta Energy Firm Over Fracking." *Huffington Post Alberta*, December 2, 2013, http://www.huffingtonpost.ca/2013/12/02/lubicon-pennwest-lawsuit_n_4372856.html.

Wood, Stepan, Georgia Tanner, and Benjamin Richardson. "Whatever Happened to Canadian Environmental Law?" (2010) 37 *Ecology Law Quarterly* 981.

Glossary

Aboriginal peoples: Indians, Métis, and Inuit people, according to the *Constitution Act, 1982*

absolute liability offences: minor offences where the intention of the offender is not a required element

*actus reus***:** an element of an offence—namely, the doing of the prohibited act

adaptive capacity: the ability of a human and/or biophysical system to make adjustments in response to a potential or actual disturbance or its consequences without compromising the system's core characteristics

administrative decisions: decisions made pursuant to a statute, which sets out the requisite decision-making process

administrative law: the legal rules and processes that govern administrative decision-makers

administrative orders: orders made by government officials or authorized employees that impose specific requirements on individuals or companies, such as the requirement to investigate and clean up environmental contamination or control pollution discharges

ALARA: acronym for "as low as reasonably achievable" with respect to risk, which is the approach to safety used in the nuclear industry

alternative dispute resolution (ADR): a process other than the court system through which a conflict is settled; examples of ADR include negotiation, facilitation, mediation, and arbitration

approval-based regimes: regulatory frameworks in which otherwise prohibited activities can occur if government permission or approval is obtained

aquaculture: fish farming

assimilative capacity: the ability of air, water, or soil to receive contaminants and cleanse itself without deleterious effects

backcasting: a tool for future-oriented planning that centres on identifying a desired future objective or set of desired future characteristics and then seeking viable pathways from the present to the desired future; it is typically posed in contrast with forecasting; it is less tied to current systems and system dynamics than forecasting

balance of probabilities: the standard of proof in a civil proceeding, whereby the plaintiff must convince the court that the allegations are more likely true than untrue

baseline: an aggregate cap on allowable emissions, which is divided into units that may be traded

beyond a reasonable doubt: the standard of proof in a criminal proceeding

bilateral treaty: a treaty between two countries

bill: a draft statute, subject to change and not yet passed into law

biotechnology: any technological application that uses biological systems, living organisms, or derivatives thereof, to make or modify products or processes for specific use

brownfields: abandoned, underused, or derelict sites of previous human activity, such as crumbling factories, old railway yards, and condemned apartments

bylaws: legally enforceable rules created by municipalities according to the powers given to them by municipal statutes

CANDU technology: a nuclear power generation technology that uses heavy water to moderate the uranium fuel fission reaction and requires fast, redundant shutdown systems to be available in various circumstances

cap and trade: a policy and legal tool for controlling emissions from a group of sources; a maximum limit on emissions is set, and emitters covered by the program are authorized to emit based on the emission allowance of the cap; emitters must meet reduction requirements, and may sell or purchase allowances to do so

carbon offsets: the use of carbon sinks to offset emissions of carbon dioxide; used in emissions-trading systems

carbon sinks: areas created by removing or "sequestering" carbon dioxide by growing trees, reducing soil tillage, and injecting carbon dioxide into depleted hydrocarbon formations; used in emissions-trading systems

causation: the evidentiary link between the conduct of the defendant and the damages complained of in a lawsuit such that the damages complained of would not have occurred but for the actions of the defendant

causes of action: legal grounds for a civil lawsuit

chattels: any building, structure, machinery, personal property, ore, slimes, tailings, or other effects not otherwise privately owned and on mining lands that have reverted to the Crown (definition taken from Class Environmental Assessment for Activities of the Ministry of Northern Development and Mines)

civil law: in Quebec, a system based on the Custom of Paris and later codified using French civil law and Code Napoléon, which applies to private disputes between citizens; the term can also be used to refer

to the law between citizens, even in a common law jurisdiction (as opposed to public law, or the law between state and citizens)

civil law jurisdictions: most of Europe, but only Quebec and Louisiana in North America, where courts make decisions based on a civil code, not precedent, and there is no doctrine of *stare decisis*

civil law system: a system that deals with disputes between private parties, whereby the party pursuing the claim, usually called the *plaintiff*, must establish that the defendant committed a wrong (applies to both common law and civil law jurisdictions)

class action: a procedural mechanism used when a large number of plaintiffs sue over the same event or set of facts

class environmental assessment: (1) in Ontario, an assessment document that covers a category of undertakings (e.g., municipal road and water projects or forest management planning) and sets out a streamlined process for assessments of proposed undertakings in the category; (2) under the *Canadian Environmental Assessment Act* (1992), a streamlined generic environmental assessment (also called a "model class screening"), which was used, perhaps with case-specific adjustments, for proposed undertakings in a particular category (e.g., small-scale fish habitat restoration or enhancement projects)

cleanup laws: laws designed to minimize discharge of human and industrial waste into the environment

collective rights: rights held by a group (e.g., Aboriginal rights to hunt or gather) as opposed to rights held by an individual (e.g., voting rights)

command and control: state intervention involving the creation of rules and the enforcement of those rules

common law: a system of law based on the English legal tradition, which relies on precedent rather than on codified rules; may also refer to (1) decisions by courts exercising their "common law" jurisdiction as opposed to their "equitable" jurisdiction based on broad principles of fairness, or (2) case law generally as opposed to legislation

common law jurisdictions: most of North America, with the exception of Quebec and Louisiana, where prior court decisions on similar facts may be binding law

complex system: an identifiable grouping of many interacting components whose combined characteristics are affected by dynamic internal as well as external pressures and whose behaviour is at best imperfectly predictable

consent to sever: permission to divide a lot into usually two lots that may be separately sold and bought

conservation and demand management: initiatives aimed at reducing overall electricity demand or reducing demand at particular times to match generating capacity, recognizing that reducing demand can be much less expensive than building new generation and transmission capacity

conservation authorities: local watershed management agencies that deliver services and programs that protect and manage water and other natural resources in partnership with government, landowners, and other organizations

conservation easement: a legal tool used to protect natural habitats on privately owned land

constitution: a document that establishes the basic framework under which all other laws are created and the basic principles to which all laws must conform

construction standard: a government-approved pollution control system that is to be used for a particular activity or in a specific situation

conventional international law: the body of international law contained in treaties or conventions versus customary international law or other types of international law

corporate mandate: the statutory requirement that corporations operate in their own best interests

costs: part of legal expenses that a court or tribunal may order the losing party to pay to the winning party at the conclusion of the case

criminal law system: a system that deals with violations of the laws designed to protect the interests of society in general

criminal liability offences: serious offences under the *Criminal Code*, such as murder

Crown land: public land held under the administration and control of the provincial or federal government

cumulative effects: changes to the environment that are caused by an action in combination with other past, present, and future human actions, as well as changing natural conditions

customary international law: the set of international rules that have evolved over time and been accepted by states as effective law

damages: the monetary award that a defendant may be ordered by a court to pay to a successful plaintiff

declaration: a finding of a court, given without other relief

defendant: an individual or corporation that is sued in a civil action by another, called the plaintiff

dilution solution: the idea that air or water pollutants do not pose a problem if they are spread out widely enough, such as by the wind or ocean currents

director: an appointee under the Ontario *Environmental Protection Act* who may issue an administrative order in certain circumstances

discretionary decisions: decisions whereby the decision-maker has considerable latitude concerning the basis for a particular decision and the factors that can be taken into account in reaching the decision

domestic law: the law within a particular country

due diligence: the defence to a strict liability offence requiring the accused to demonstrate that he or she took all reasonable steps to avoid committing a prohibited act

duty of care: the legal obligation to act reasonably so that harm does not occur to others

ecological integrity: an approach adopted for national parks that considers the needs of nature as the first priority

economic instruments: fiscal and other economic incentives and disincentives designed to encourage companies to absorb at least some of the environmental costs of doing business

emission intensity: a measure of the amount of carbon emitted per barrel of oil produced, or the relationship between emissions and economic activity. As the technology for accessing and consuming energy improves, the emissions intensity decreases. However, this approach is controversial because the amount of actual carbon entering the atmosphere can still increase, even as efficiency rises.

emission intensity reduction: emission limits based on emissions per unit of production, rather than a set limit

emission taxes: taxes charged on units of contaminant released into the environment; a type of fixed-price measure

enforcement ladder system: approach to responding to environmental law violations that increases in intensity, and involves inspections and progressively more serious warnings, monetary penalties, shutdowns, and prosecutions

environmental approval: permission issued by a government agency or official to carry out an activity that may impact the environment, provided that certain conditions are met (see also *licences and approvals*)

environmental assessment: the identification and evaluation of actual or potential effects (positive and adverse) of an undertaking on the environment; "undertakings" may include policies, plans, and programs as well as projects, and "environment" may include social, economic, and cultural as well as biophysical effects, and the interactions among these effects; environmental assessments may also involve a critical review of purposes, comparative evaluation of alternatives, and a follow-up examination of effects

environmental assessment law: law requiring careful attention to environmental considerations in the planning and approval of new undertakings

environmental law: the body of legislated statute and common law that can be used to protect and improve environmental conditions

environmental regulatory law: law governing the discharge of harmful substances into the air and water and onto land

evidence: facts, objects, and opinions that are presented to a decision-maker for the purpose of making a decision

exclusive economic zone: the area of ocean adjacent to the coastline belonging to the coastal state

externalities: the public costs of environmental degradation

extinguishment: the elimination of Aboriginal title to land; it can occur through surrender of the land to the Crown as part of a treaty or by a clear and competent legislative authority (e.g., *R v. Calder*).

fixed-price measure: tax and subsidy incentives to reduce pollution; a type of economic instrument

forecasting: a tool for future-oriented planning that centres on the projection of current trends into the future with adjustments for foreseeable influences

fracking: derived from the term *hydraulic fracturing*; method of extracting oil or natural gas by injecting highly pressurized liquid into subterranean rock

friend of the court: an intervenor with the right to present oral and/or written submissions to the court, but without the full rights of a party (also called an *amicus curiae*)

general damages: damages that are subjective and not easily quantified, such as pain and suffering

genetic engineering: genetic modification of a microbe, plant, or animal to serve a new or enhanced purpose

governor in council: a federal member of Cabinet vested with power to create regulations and rules pursuant to a statute

growth plan: a plan that identifies where and how growth should occur

health risk assessment standard: a quality-based standard that involves linking the standard under consideration to the health risks posed

hearsay: statements about what a witness heard from another person

hydrocarbons: the organic compound of hydrogen and carbon atoms that produces energy when burned; found in fossil fuels such as oil, natural gas, and coal

industrial farming: large farms operated by corporations, distinct from traditional family-run farms

injunction: a court order that requires a defendant either to do something (a mandatory injunction) or to refrain from doing something (a prohibitory injunction)

instruments: approvals, permits, licences, or other authorizations issued by government, as defined in the *Environmental Bill of Rights, 1993*

international law: a collection of rules governing countries

intervention: a procedural device that allows persons or organizations that are not plaintiffs or defendants to participate in a legal proceeding as added parties or friends of the court

judicial review: a court's review of an administrative tribunal's decision to ensure that it acted within the powers granted under the legislation and respected the common law rules of natural justice and procedural fairness

jurisdiction: the power to legislate or make a decision

land use planning: determining how a parcel of land will be used by defining objectives, collecting information, identifying problems, and analyzing alternatives

laws of general application: laws that apply to everyone and to all activities

legal non-conforming uses: pre-existing uses of a property that are allowed to continue, even though they do not conform to existing zoning requirements

liability: legal obligations and responsibilities

licences and approvals: permission issued by a government agency or official to carry out an activity that would not otherwise be permitted by law, typically accompanied by certain conditions/requirements that must be met by the individual or facility to which the permission has been granted (see also *environmental approval*)

licensee liability rating system: a system for ensuring that a company can pay for the costs of possible contamination before a licence is granted for a new facility, by comparing the assets of the company with the estimated risk of contamination liability

lieutenant governor in council: a provincial member of Cabinet vested with power to create regulations and rules pursuant to a statute

media-based regimes: regulatory frameworks that apply to a particular environmental medium, such as air, water, or land

mediation: a structured dispute resolution process that involves a third party (a mediator) to assist in the confidential negotiation of the issues in hope of settling all or part of the dispute and thus avoid or shorten the litigation process

mens rea: an element of a criminal offence—namely, a guilty mind or intention to commit the act

microbes: single-celled organisms such as bacteria, algae, and fungi

mitigation: the reduction of a problem or the risk of an undesirable effect

multilateral treaty: a treaty between more than two countries

natural justice: a doctrine originally developed by English judges; the common law procedural rights of a person affected by an administrative or quasi-judicial decision that include reasonable notice of a decision, a fair hearing, and an impartial decision-maker; it involves procedures that are more formal and less flexible than the doctrine of procedural fairness

negligence: failure to act reasonably, with the result being harm to someone else

novel product (or novel food): product that exhibits characteristics that were not previously observed or no longer exhibits characteristics that were previously observed

nuisance: tort in which the defendant interferes with the use and enjoyment of the plaintiff's property

nutrients: materials, including fertilizer, manure, compost, sewage biosolids, and pulp and paper biosolids, that can be applied to land to improve the growth of agricultural crops (definition modified from *Nutrient Management Act*)

official notice: the allowance of obvious and well-accepted facts by an administrative decision-maker, without the need for proof

oil sands: crude bitumen deposits found in an area of northern Alberta and part of Saskatchewan that is approximately the size of New Brunswick

orphaned sites: oil wells and other facilities abandoned by oil and gas operators

paramountcy: overriding, chief in importance, supreme; in Canada, the doctrine of paramountcy holds that where there is a conflict, federal laws prevail over provincial laws

participation rights: rights of private individuals to be informed and consulted as part of the environmental approval process

performance standard: a pollution limit imposed on a polluter, where the rule-maker is unconcerned with how the result is achieved

persistent organic pollutants (POPs): about a dozen chemicals identified as having long-lasting toxicity

pesticides: a range of products that have in common the control of living organisms

plaintiff: an individual or corporation that brings a civil action against another, called the defendant

plan of subdivision: a plan for dividing a parcel of land into many lots to be sold and bought separately

planning and management regimes: legislative schemes that govern a sector, such as forests, fisheries, farmlands, and watersheds, with the purpose of maximizing the long-term benefits obtainable from the resource while minimizing the detrimental effects of its exploitation

point of impingement: the point at which a pollutant contacts the airspace, ground, or a building at or beyond the property boundary of the source of the pollutant

pollution prevention: an approach emphasizing prevention rather than control of pollution using methods such as product reformulation, chemical substitution, and changes to processes

positive feedback: a cyclical process in which a complex system responds to a perturbation in ways that expand, intensify, and/or extend the initial effect

precautionary principle: the proposition that caution should be paramount when an activity raises threats of harm to health or the environment, and that the proponent of the activity should bear the burden of proving that it is safe; a principle used to support the notion that where the threat of serious or irreversible damage exists, a lack of full scientific certainty should not be used as a reason for postponing measures to prevent environmental degradation

private law: law pertaining to personal rights, such as the right to protect one's own property and interests

privative clause: a provision that is sometimes included in a governing statute that specifically limits judicial review of administrative decisions made under that statute

procedural fairness: the modern doctrine of natural justice; the common law procedural rights of a person affected by an administrative or quasi-judicial decision, which include reasonable notice of a decision, a fair hearing, and an impartial decision-maker; specific procedures depend on the nature of the decision, the nature of the statutory scheme, the importance of the decision to the affected person, the reasonable expectations of the affected person, and the decision-maker's choice of procedures

protocol: often used to describe an agreement of a less formal nature than a treaty or convention; generally, a protocol amends, supplements, or clarifies a multilateral treaty

provincial officer (PO): a government official who carries out enforcement functions such as investigating and gathering evidence about an environmental incident, preparing reports, and laying charges

provincial officers' orders (POOs): orders issued by provincial officers (accompanied by a report following an investigation) that compel an individual or company to carry out certain actions to prevent or respond to an environmental problem

public hearing: a formal meeting where members of the public provide facts and opinion on a proposed government action to a decision-making body

public inquiry: investigative proceedings that result in recommendations to government

public interest intervention: a category of intervention that blurs the added party and friend of the court categories, and which is commonly recognized where the Charter is an issue in the case

public interest override: a provision in the *Access to Information Act* that allows for disclosure of confidential information where public health, safety, or protection of the environment outweighs the consequences of disclosure

public interest standing: a new and broader test for determining whether a person has standing, requiring that the person either have a genuine interest in the litigation or be in a better position to bring the action than anyone else

public law: law enforced by the state against those who fail to abide by it

punitive damages: damages intended to punish the defendant and set an example

quasi-criminal offences: provincial offences punishable by heavy fines and up to six months in jail

ratification: an agreement to the terms of a convention by the domestic legislatures of the countries signing the convention

reasonable person: a hypothetical person recognized as having a level of maturity and responsibility common to most people in the community and used as an objective standard for determining liability

record: all evidence and arguments presented at a hearing

regional and municipal official plans: plans that establish general land use policies across large geographical areas delineated by political boundaries

regulations: legally enforceable rules created by the governor in council (federal) or lieutenant governor in council (provincial) providing practical details of how a statute is to be implemented

remedy: court-ordered redress to a plaintiff in a civil case, such as monetary compensation

representative plaintiff: in a class action, the plaintiff who brings the action on behalf of the class of plaintiffs

residential intensification: redevelopment to add density in residential areas

resilience: in complex systems, the ability to resist and/or accommodate disturbance and change while retaining identifying characteristics (including structure, functions, and processes)

right: the constitutionally protected ability to carry out an activity

right to know: the most basic of public participation rights—namely, the right to be aware of an issue that could be of public interest

risk: the possibility of harming or losing something valuable; risk significance depends on the likelihood and severity of the harm or loss

secondary plans: plans that cover specific areas within a municipality and provide more detailed planning policies for those areas

sector-based regimes: regulatory frameworks that apply to a particular sector or specific area, such as energy, endangered species, or agriculture

sectoral laws: laws dealing with a resource sector such as water or forests, or an industrial sector such as fisheries or waste management

special damages: damages directly caused by the defendant's behaviour that are easily and objectively quantifiable, such as the costs of repair

species at risk: a collective term that includes five categories: extinct, extirpated, endangered, threatened, and special concern

standard of care: the degree or level of care that is required—what is reasonable in the circumstances

standard of proof: the degree to which a party must convince a judge or jury that the allegations are true

standard of review: the scope of a judicial review—the broader correctness standard (Was the tribunal's decision correct?), or the stricter reasonableness standard (Was the tribunal's decision reasonable?)

standing: the right to sue

stare decisis: principle that requires judges to follow decisions of higher courts in similar cases

status Indian: an Aboriginal person who is registered under the *Indian Act* on the Indian Register, which is maintained by Aboriginal Affairs and Northern Development Canada

statutes: codified laws passed by legislatures

stay: the temporary suspension of a court order, usually pending an appeal

strategic-level assessments: application of environmental assessment requirements to government policies, plans, programs, and other broad-scale initiatives

strict liability: a liability incurred by a party who undertakes a hazardous activity on a property and allows harmful material to escape that harms others; the party is liable even if he or she took all reasonable precaution and was not negligent in the activities

strict liability offences: offences in which proof that an accused performed the prohibited act is sufficient to sustain a conviction, regardless of intention, unless the accused demonstrates that he took all reasonable care to avoid committing the prohibited act

subsidiary: a corporation whose controlling interest is owned by the parent company

subsidies: grants, loans, or tax breaks provided to polluters for reducing discharge, with the size of the subsidy based on the amount of the reduction; a type of fixed-price measure

substantial equivalence: the concept that a new food product that is found to be substantially equivalent to an existing food or food component can be judged similarly in terms of safety; critics find this principle unscientific, arbitrary, and overly permissive in favour of food producers

sustainable development: "development that meets the needs of the present without compromising the ability of future generations to meet their own needs" (World Commission on Environment and Development, 1987); it involves improving the quality of human life and enhancing equity in the distribution of well-being while living within the carrying capacity of the planet's biophysical systems over the long term; see Chapter 3, especially Box 3.2, footnote †

territorial waters: the belt of water adjacent to a coast, over which the coastal state holds jurisdiction

"three p" rule: a traditional rule for determining whether a person has standing, requiring the person to demonstrate a property interest, a personal (health) interest, or a pecuniary interest

title: ownership of land; it is the right to the exclusive use and occupation of the land, and the right to choose the uses of the land, within constraints prescribed by law (such as zoning); Aboriginal title encompasses the right to exclusive use and occupation of the land for a variety of purposes, but the protected uses of the land must not be irreconcilable with the nature of the Aboriginal group's attachment to the land

tort: civil wrong other than a breach of contract, for which damages may be sought to compensate for any harm or injury sustained

toxics control laws: laws designed to control the manufacture, use, sale, transport, storage, and disposal of toxic substances

trade-off: the sacrifice of something desirable to gain a different benefit or advantage

tradeable emission rights: rights representing specified quantities of emissions that are issued to polluters and that may be traded; a type of economic instrument

tragedy of the commons: an ethical problem in which the consumption of a shared resource by rational individuals pursuing their own needs leads to the depletion or loss of that resource for the community as a whole

transformation: in complex systems, a shift from one set of identifying system characteristics to another, including more or less significant changes in structure, functions, and/or processes

transgenes: genetically modified genes

transgenic crops: genetically engineered crops given specific characteristics to improve taste, appearance, nutritional value, and rate of growth

treaty (Aboriginal): a formal agreement between a First Nation and the provincial and federal governments regarding First Nations rights and title; treaties with First Nations are considered *sui generis* (unique) and are constitutionally protected.

treaty (or convention): an agreement between two or more sovereign states, binding only those states that sign it

trespass: a physical presence on someone else's property, without permission

tribunal: a specialized quasi-judicial board, commission, panel, or other decision-making body that makes decisions pursuant to particular statutes

urban sprawl: low-density residential growth in rural areas

vicarious liability: the legal responsibility of one party for the actions of another—for example, an employer is responsible for the actions of an employee

voluntary compliance: an approach that relies on industry and individuals to do the right thing, motivated by conscience, public relations, or a desire to avoid regulation

waste control laws: laws designed to control discharge of waste using permits and approvals

watershed: an area of land from which all water drains into a common body of water, such as a lake or river

watershed planning: a scale of planning that is based on natural watershed boundaries and hence extends beyond political boundaries

whistle-blowers: insiders, such as employees, who report information about violations of the law to enforcement agencies or the media

whole-facility permitting: an approach to granting permits that involves a review of all the environmental exposures from a particular facility

zoning bylaws: legally enforceable rules and requirements for the use of land and for the use and location of buildings and structures on land

Index

Taste of ISRAEL

A MEDITERRANEAN FEAST

Taste of

ISRAEL

A MEDITERRANEAN
FEAST

✶

AVI GANOR
RON MAIBERG

with Zachi Bukshester and Kenneth R Windsor

STEIMATZKY

Israeli edition: Steimatzky Ltd.
11 Hakishon Street, P.O. Box 1444 Bnei-Brak; Tel 03-579.4.576

Photography & Art Direction   *Avi Ganor*
Text & Recipes   *Ron Maiberg*
Design   *Kenneth R Windsor, Metamark International*
Food Stylist & Consultant   *Zachi Bukshester*
Production   *Arnon Orbach*
Research   *Stella Korin-Liber*
Administrative Assistant   *Sarah Elergant*
Ceramics   *Dafna Botzer*

Printed in Hong Kong by Imago

British Library Cataloguing in Publication Data
Maiberg, Ron
   Taste of Israel
   1. Jews, Food - Recipes
   I. Title
   641.5676
ISBN 1 85375 041 7

PHOTOGRAPHS, PAGES 1-8

1. Jaffa oranges, Israel's ambassadors of goodwill. In the background a stretch of seascape in Jaffa.

2. Onion fields in the Golan. Abundance from a fertile land.

3. Labaneh cheese balls in olive oil. Stored in olive oil, labaneh keeps for a long time.

4. Granite mountains in the Judean desert.

5. A colorful display of summer and winter squash.

6. Almond trees in full bloom in Central Galilee.

7. Traditional preparation of zhoug, a fiery Yemenite relish.

8. Strawberries forever. Each year the season is longer and the strawberries bigger.

Above: Goat's cheese with mint and carrots.

C ONTENTS

$\mathscr{I}$ NTRODUCTION

Whenasked to write about Israeli cuisine, foreign food critics usually resort to the Israeli breakfast. It is a subject they can be enthusiastic about without compromising their integrity. In most instances, the setting

13

for this much admired meal is a kibbutz - the pioneering spirit is somehow a fitting backdrop for it. In a kibbutz, the foreign food critic finds himself caught up in an experience which is at once esthetic and gastronomic. He is impressed with the rich display of creams, cheeses, yogurts and buttermilks, set off by a

lush barrage of vegetables. It is an attractive sight, wholesome and full of vitality. It is hard not to respond to it. This, then, is the archetypal scene that has made breakfast, in the eyes of more than one critic, "Israel's main contribution to world cuisine." While in Israel, recommended one critic, eat once a day. Preferably breakfast. Preferably in a kibbutz.

◆ Lahuhua,

Yemenite

spongy

pancakes.

Most of the food we eat in Israel is not indigenous to the Eastern Mediterranean, but it is Israeli by virtue of the fact that it is grown, prepared and eaten here. However, an educated palate can easily identify the major influences at work in Israeli kitchens. There is the North African or Mahgrebi influence. Jews have lived in North Africa for centuries and few surveys of Moroccan food fail to mention the contribution made by the Jewish population. Other influences come from Eastern Europe, where Jews once flourished and prospered. Israel's Arab population has contributed yet other influences. But Arabs and Jews have not assimilated in Israel. They represent two opposing and sometimes hostile cultures, each with its distinctive flavour.

What is Israeli cuisine? To some Israelis, the question is meaningless. How can one describe something which is neither homogeneous nor coherent? But this attitude completely misses the point. Israeli cuisine is unique and deserving of attention precisely because of the plurality of ethnic and cultural influences that compose it. All of these influences - Moroccan, Yemenite, Russian, Arab, Polish - are equally important and the existence of such a wide selection of cuisines in such a small country is what makes Israeli food worthy of discussion.

The existence of an Israeli cuisine is much debated in Israel today. The population is just about equally divided into those who believe there is no such thing and those who believe there is. Giving world-renowned dishes Hebrew names is not Israeli cuisine. Filet mignon with blue cheese under a new name is still filet mignon with blue cheese. But those brave chefs who are slowly teaching us to be proud of what we have achieved claim that they are "Israeli" when they combine avocados, oranges and biblical hyssop. They feel they are breaking new ground with their version of St. Peter's fish with *tahini*.

◆ A Yemenite dancer in the robe traditionally worn on festive occasions such as weddings.

In fact Israeli cuisine went nouvelle before it had a chance to define itself. Local experts claim, for example, that Israel's main contribution to world cuisine is not breakfast but barbecued *foie gras*. We were the first to expose this expensive and rare delicacy to the rigors of open fire. Since *foie gras* is largely fat, its preparation is classically conservative and careful. If not watched like a hawk, it can easily melt away. Usually it is made into pâté or cooked whole and served warm or cold. Grilling goose liver on a spit is therefore either a demonstration of courage or an act of defiance against the order of the old world. And what could be more outrageously Israeli than serving *foie gras* in *pita* bread?

At this particular moment, Israel is in culinary ferment, still assimilating the influx of new cuisines - French, Italian, American - introduced in the early eighties, but beginning to realize that it has its own character. Anomalies abound. We have, for instance, a white desert truffle which is inedible. We have an artichoke named after Jerusalem, which is not an artichoke

◆ *Head shot*

of a carp,

Israel's

national

fish.

and has nothing to do with Jerusalem. Hyssop, an herb mentioned in the Bible, is now a protected plant, so nobody is allowed to pick it. We now raise more lamb than we can eat, so we are having to educate Jews to like chops, roast leg of lamb and lamb fries rather than beef. Until five years ago, we had only sweet red wine and respectable table wines were termed "sour" and shunned.

Our grandmothers did more than most to formulate an Israeli cuisine, although recent influences have obscured their achievement. They cooked according to their respective backgrounds but adapted their creativity to local produce and weather conditions.

My Russian grandmother used to bake a brown and fragrant *cholent*, a substantial casserole of meat and potatoes, beans and barley, in the oven of our family bakery. It was a large commercial oven, built of red bricks, and my grandmother knew to a fraction of a degree when the temperature was right for her *cholent*. She would put it in, covered with a kitchen towel, just after the last Sabbath *challah* loaf was taken out early on Friday morning and let it cook until the next morning. She tended her *cholent* all through the night as if it were a child. Every hour, on the hour, she would wake up, march briskly to the bakery, pull the pot out of the deep oven, remove the towel carefully so as not to wake the *cholent*, and measure the amount of liquid left in the pot. Her nightmare was that her *cholent* would dry up. Having raised three children against terrific odds, she had no intention of this happening.

Nothing that I have ever eaten compares with the *cholent* that came out of that old blackened pot. Aided by plain water, smartly added, the potatoes turned golden and soft, the beans tied up with the barley, and the meat blended with the bone marrow until it was impossible to tell them apart. It took dedication and stamina, and

◆ Early morning in Safed, an ancient hilltop town famous for its clear air, occasional snow and its devout residents.

my grandmother had both. Even her hand-made eggplant salad remains, to my mind, more typically Israeli than anything we eat today. She burnt the eggplants over an open fire, peeled them, mashed them with a fork, then added garlic, lemon juice, mayonnaise and hot peppers. Her pickles were excellent. Even her simple breakfast omelets were memorable.

My Polish grandmother, who came from Cracow, had standards every bit as tough and rigid as those of my Russian grandmother. She did not fry, and she never used glowing charcoals, let alone grilled over them. She used to cook meat with sour cream and capers - strictly non-kosher. Her carp, very sweet and totally inedible to the modern Israeli palate, used to quiver in a molded prison of jelly. Her cucumber salad with fresh dill and cream was very good, though. She also in-  troduced me to my first artichoke, which was almost as erotic and exciting as my first girlfriend. She showed me how to remove the outer leaves and nibble the flesh from the stem end, and how to pluck away the thistle- down, and how to slice the heart and dip each tasty morsel in white sauce. I am no expert on sauces, but I can improvise a sauce for artichokes based on what I remember of my grandmother's. She also bought us our first whole goose liver, a round and massive ball wrapped in foil, and taught us how to eat it. That was in the early sixties, when *foie gras* was as foreign as lobster and pheasant, both by the way still unavailable. Unlike my Russian grandmother, who was an extrovert, my Polish grandmother never ate at the table. She never really served either, in the sense of dispensing food to others. She shoved food in front of us and commanded us to eat. She would not relax until everything was finished and was furious if something was left untouched. I always hoped, for her sake, that she sneaked something in the kitchen, but people who knew her better told me not to count on it.

The world's great cuisines were formed during lengthy periods of peace and fun. One might almost say that stability and parties are prerequisites for true gastronomy. Such prerequisites have seldom been the lot of Jews or Israelis. We have scarcely had time for leisure, no time to play enjoyable games, and the dietary laws of *kashrut* have discouraged us from mixing meat with milk and eating seafood. So, all things considered, it is a wonder that so many tasty things have emerged from the Israeli kitchen. In the early years we had to make do with very little. Now we have found our culinary voice. It is high time that it was heard.

◆ *At the end of a day of harvest, bales of hay await collection in the Jezreel Valley.*

Taste of
ISRAEL

A MEDITERRANEAN
FEAST

$\mathcal{S}$ TARTERS &

HOT STUFF

◆ Hummus, *an aerial view. One of Israel's national foods,* hummus *is filling, nutrititious and cheap. No knives or forks are needed, just* pita *bread and an expert wrist. In view: whole chickpeas, olive oil, paprika, parsley, pickled turnips and raw onion for added pungency.*

$\mathcal{M}$*ezze* can be translated as appetizers, starters, hors d'oeuvres, snacks. But none of these words conveys the range of delicacies, cooked and uncooked, which constitute the start of a meal in

21

◆ *A eucalyptus*

tree in sand

dunes near

Nitzana, on the

desert borders of

the northern

Negev.

Israel and throughout the Middle East.

Although going to restaurants is not always the best way to learn about or judge the food of a country, in the case of *mezze* I thoroughly recommend it. You will encounter, in one sitting, an enormous variety of dishes, far more than any single household can muster. Even a modest restaurant runs to at least twenty different items.

The portions are small, but they are an ideal introduction to the exotic and unfamiliar. There are crudités, served with various dips, *hummus*, *tahini*, lemony *labaneh* cheese, cheese in cubes, grilled chicken livers, eggplants prepared in a variety of ways, salads laced with turmeric and cumin, pickled vegetables, fried *kibbeh* or meat patties, stuffed vine leaves, small pastries filled with meat or cheese or spinach, and fiery relishes such as *harissa* and *zhoug*. In fact any dish can be considered part of the *mezze* table if it has a strong individual taste and comes in small portions.

This diversity reveals something else about Israeli food. We shy away from eating our meals as set courses served in sequence, with each course calculated to feed a given number of people. We like to spread our food out on the table so that we can help ourselves. Although variety is the spice of life, an indiscriminate jumble of *mezze* piled on the same plate is frowned upon. One is supposed to pick and choose rather than eat everything in sight, simultaneously.

The fiery concoctions served with *mezze* are as invigorating as they look. *Zhoug, shatta, hreimeh, harissa* and *madbuha* are all based in varying degrees on green and red chili peppers, all locally grown. Fresh horseradish is tame by comparison. Chili-based relishes are a staple of Israeli food. No meal is complete without them. At most restaurants you do not have to ask for them. They are always on the table. They perk up any and every *mezze*, can be blended with *hummus* and *tahini*, squirted over *falafel*, and added to casseroles and grilled meats. They cross ethnic barriers with the same ease as the aroma of baking bread, and even if they were once the prerogative of Yemenite and Moroccan immigrants, they are now consumed by all and considered common property. To the novice diner, they are dangerous and part of a game Israelis love to play on the unwary. Beware of Israelis bearing hot peppers.

◆ *Sunset over the Judean desert.*

Yemenite Jews claim that *zhoug* and *shatta*, two of the most explosive of these condiments, have the power to ward off all sorts of diseases, from the common cold to blocked coronary arteries. There have even been scientific studies that tried to establish cause and effect between hot food and rude health, but they were inconclusive. The ability of various communities to eat *harissa* and its relatives without flinching is an indication of health in itself.

On the face of it, the appeal of the red hot chili pepper is hard to reconcile with the agony it causes. The taste is difficult to describe, for it is not so much a taste as a sensation of great heat applied to a small area. It is wise to have *pita* or some other bread within reach, bread being the only food that seems to soothe chili burns.

The truth is that chili paste is a macho game even deadlier than poker. You never let on when you're down. You never admit that your

◆ *Traditional preparation of Yemenite zhoug. Hot peppers and garlic are crushed and ground by hand, then mixed with coriander and spices.*

mucous membranes hurt like hell. A man's suffering can only be judged by the sweat on his brow. He never makes a dash for the restroom to stick his head in a sink of cold water. He keeps scooping until the last fragment of *pita* is finished.

Commercially grown chili peppers are regarded, by purists, as lacking in virtue. They lose some of their potency during transport and handling, they say. They would rather pluck the peppers that grow in their grandmother's garden than spend money on store-bought peppers.

Chili peppers are shrouded in folklore. Small jars of home-made chili paste are sold in local markets and those which have an old, old woman standing behind them are thought to have extra potency and

◆ *A typical Israeli chili pepper. There are only a few kinds and this is the most common.*

authenticity. In the old Yemenite quarter of Tel Aviv, *zhoug* and *shatta* are still prepared by hand. The preparation is quite simple, but one has to wear gloves and protect the eyes and other sensitive areas. Fresh, crisp chili peppers are ground by hand on a large flat stone, or chopped up and pounded on a stone mortar, then mixed with spices and herbs. Stored in jars with tightly fitting lids, the mixture keeps for months.

Other Jewish communities have their own hot and not so hot stuffs. Moroccans use *harissa* and *hermulla*, also based on chili peppers and mixed with salt and garlic. Rumanians like to use freshly minced garlic, mixed with vinegar and other liquids, on their meat, serving it like any other condiment.

Chili peppers are second nature to many Israelis, and eaten with all meals, even with breakfast. Bitter comments are made if they are not hot and fiery enough. Regretfully, there are seasons when they are less potent.

STARTERS &
HOT STUFF

◆ *A selection of* mezze, *the traditonal Israeli and Middle Eastern starters.*

Recipes

STUFFED GRAPE LEAVES

8 oz/225g fresh or preserved grape/vine leaves
1 1/3 cups/250g long-grain rice
2 or 3 tomatoes, skinned and chopped
1 large onion, finely chopped
2 tablespoons finely chopped fresh parsley
1 tablespoon dried crushed mint
1/4 teaspoon ground cinnamon
1/2 teaspoon ground allspice
salt and freshly ground black pepper
2 tomatoes, sliced (optional)
1/2 cup/100ml olive oil
1/4 teaspoon powdered saffron (optional)
1 teaspoon sugar
juice of 1 lemon
lemon wedges, to garnish

If you are using grape leaves preserved in brine, the excess salt must be removed. Put them into a large bowl and pour boiling water over them, making sure the water penetrates between the layers. Let the leaves soak for 20 minutes, then drain them and soak them in fresh cold water. Drain and repeat the process.

If you are using fresh grape leaves, soften them by plunging them into boiling water for a few minutes, then shave off the harder part of the stem.

Wash the rice, soak it for 10 minutes, then drain it. Add boiling water, stir the rice around, then drain it and rinse under cold running water.

Mix the rice with the chopped tomatoes, onion, parsley, mint, spices, salt and pepper. Place a generous spoonful of this mixture near the stem end of each grape leaf. Fold the stem end over the stuffing, fold both sides towards the middle, then roll up the package like a small cigar. Squeeze lightly in the palm of your hand. The process gets easier once you have rolled a few!

Pack the stuffed leaves tightly in a large, shallow pan lined with sliced tomatoes and any torn or imperfect grape leaves. Add a clove of garlic here and there if you like.

Mix the olive oil with the water, saffron (if used), sugar and lemon juice, and pour it over the stuffed leaves. Put a plate on top of the leaves to prevent them unwinding, cover the pan, and simmer very, very gently for at least 2 hours, adding water from time to time as the liquid in the pan is absorbed. Leave the stuffed leaves in the pan to cool. Serve cold with lots of lemon wedges.

Serves 5 or 6

TABBOULEH
A salad of cracked wheat, vegetables & herbs

1 cup bulgur/cracked wheat
4 tablespoons chopped fresh flat-leaved parsley
2 tablespoons chopped mint
1 cucumber, diced
1 bell pepper
1 onion/6 scallions, diced
1 large tomato, diced
grated rind of 1 lemon
juice of 2 lemons
1/3 cup/80 ml olive oil
salt and pepper
pinch ground allspice

Soak the bulgur/cracked wheat in cold water for 30 minutes, then drain in a fine sieve, squeezing out the excess moisture. In a salad bowl, combine all ingredients.

Serve as a tangy starter, but not before refrigerating for 1 hour.

◆ *Stuffed grape leaves are eaten in most Eastern Mediterranean countries, including Greece, Turkey, Lebanon and Cyprus. The filling can be rice or meat or both.*

TAHINI SAUCE
A savoury sauce based on sesame seeds

1/2 cup/100g sesame paste
1/4 cup/60ml water
1/4 cup/60ml fresh lemon juice
1/4 teaspoon salt
1 teaspoon finely minced garlic

Using a fork, blend together the sesame paste and water, then add the lemon juice, parsley and garlic, mixing well after each addition. Alternatively, mix all the ingredients together in a blender. The mixture will thicken later in the refrigerator.

A *mezze* version of *tahini* sauce calls for lots of fresh, finely chopped coriander or parsley as well. Keeps in the refrigerator for up to 10 days.

CUCUMBER AND FENNEL SALAD

1 large cucumber, peeled and finely chopped
1/4 bulb fennel, finely chopped
pinch of salt
1/4 teaspoon freshly ground black pepper
3 tablespoons sour cream
1 tablespoon olive oil
2 tablespoons fresh lemon juice
2 scallions/spring onions, finely chopped

Thoroughly combine all the ingredients, and chill well before serving. Serves 4.

EGGPLANT SALAD
Three versions out of many

1 lb/450g eggplants/aubergines

5 tablespoons fresh lemon juice
scant teaspoon minced garlic
1 teaspoon salt
or
1/2 cup/100ml tahini sauce
(see recipe opposite)
coarsely chopped parsley, to garnish
or
1/2 cup mayonnaise
2 tablespoons chopped onion
1 tablespoon diced red pepper
2 tablespoons olive oil
1 tablespoon chopped dill

Prick the eggplants a few times with a fork, then bake over charcoal until the skins are blistered and black. This is usually done after grilling meat, while the barbecue is still hot. Otherwise it can be done under the broiler/grill, or in the oven, but the smoky aroma will be missing. Allow the eggplants to cool, then remove the skins. Mash the flesh in a food processor (connoisseurs never use anything but a fork!), then stir in one of the three flavorings listed above. Serve cold, with hot *pita* bread.

JELLIED CALF'S FOOT

3 - 4 lbs/1.4-1.9kg calf's feet
10 cups/2.0 liters water
6 cloves garlic
1 carrot
2 medium size onions
1 celery
fresh thyme
4 bay leaves
salt and black pepper to taste
2 hard-boiled eggs, sliced
lemon wedges, to garnish

Blanch the calf's feet (plunge them into boiling water, bring the water to a boil again, then remove the feet and wash them). Cut each one into 3 or 4 pieces, put the pieces into a saucepan with the 10 cups/2 liters of water, then bring to a boil and skim. Add all the other ingredients, except for the eggs, and simmer until the slices of calf's foot are tender - this takes about 4 hours.

Strain the broth, taste it, and add salt and pepper to taste. At this stage some cooks clarify the broth as for consommé, using egg whites and egg shells. Pick the celery, bay leaves, thyme and bones out of the strainer - this should be done by hand, even though the contents of the strainer are very sticky. Grind/mince whatever is left in the strainer and return it to the broth.

To see whether the broth will gel or not, put a spoonful on a plate and put the plate in the freezer for 10 minutes. If necessary, add 1/2 oz/15g unflavored gelatin to the broth.

Arrange the slices of hard-boiled egg in a shallow dish, ladle the broth over them, and put the dish in the refrigerator for several hours.

When ready to serve, cut the jelly into 8 portions, transfer it to a serving plate and garnish with lemon wedges.

◆ *Jellied calf's foot is a traditional Jewish dish from Eastern Europe. It is eaten with generous helpings of lemon juice.*

◆ *Moroccan*

cigars are rolled

sheets of filo

dough, deep-

fried, with

different

fillings. They

are a favorite on

festive

occasions.

Moroccan Cigars

In Israel *filo* dough is often made into filled "cigars." Several variations on the theme are given below. The fillings are spread on half-leaves of *filo*, then the edges of the *filo* are folded over and the dough is rolled up into a cigar shape. The edges are sealed with egg white or with a mixture of flour and water. The cigars are then fried in deep oil for 2 minutes until they turn golden. Plan on 6-8 cigars per person as a starter.

Filling for Meat Cigars
1 onion, chopped
1 tablespoon oil
6 oz/180g ground/minced meat
1 teaspoon chopped parsley
1/4 teaspoon ground cumin
pinch of cinnamon
salt and pepper to taste

Fry the onion in the oil, then add the meat, parsley, spices and seasoning. For a real treat, add a little finely chopped goose liver too.

Filling for Potato Cigars
1 onion, chopped
1 tablespoon vegetable oil
5 oz/150g boiled potatoes, mashed
salt, white pepper and nutmeg to taste

Fry the onions in the oil, then mix well with the mashed potato and seasoning.

Filling for Cheese Cigars
4 oz/125g cheese, grated
fresh mint leaves

Put two leaves of mint into each cigar before you roll it up.

CHOPPED LIVER

1 cup/225ml oil
2 large onions, sliced
1 lb/450g chicken livers
5 or 6 hard-boiled eggs
salt and pepper
radishes and tomato slices, to garnish

◆ *Chopped liver,*

pickles, and

beer at a

Levinsky

Street diner

in Tel Aviv.

Heat the oil and fry the onions until they are golden brown, then drain them on paper towels/kitchen paper. Set aside 1/4 cup/ 60ml of the oil and fry the chicken livers in the rest. Drain the livers on paper towels and allow them to cool. Discard the oil in which they were cooked.

Grind/mince the chicken livers, the fried onions and the hard-boiled eggs, then mix them all together, adding pepper and salt to taste. Slowly blend in the reserved oil until the mixture is the consistency of a smooth spread. Serve garnished with radishes and slices of tomato. Chopped liver is traditionally eaten with a fork or spread onto a slice of *challah* (see recipe p. 90).

◆ *One of the*

wonders of

Jewish cuisine -

chopped liver,

on toasted

challah.

MOROCCAN CARROT SALAD

1 1/2 lbs/700g carrots
1 bulb garlic, finely chopped
1/2 cup/100ml vegetable oil
1 tablespoon finely chopped chili peppers
1 teaspoon sweet paprika
3/4 cup/180ml water
salt
ground turmeric
1/3 cup/80ml vinegar
1 tablespoon lemon juice
1 tablespoon chopped parsley

Wash and peel the carrots, and boil or steam them until they are tender but still firm. Drain them and allow to cool. Gently fry the garlic in the oil until it is soft and transparent - this takes about 12 minutes. Now add the chili peppers and paprika to the pan and fry for 1 minute. Pour in the water, then add the cooked carrots, salt, turmeric, vinegar and lemon juice. Simmer for 5 minutes, then remove from the heat, allow to cool, cover, and refrigerate for 24 hours. Stir well before serving, sprinkled with parsley. Serve as cold starter or to accompany *couscous* (see photograph p. 108).

◆ *Chicken*

livers,

egg, onion,

and a

meat grinder

spell...chopped

liver.

ONIONS WITH VINEGAR

2 large mild/Spanish onions
salt
2 or 3 tablespoons white wine vinegar
1 tablespoon dried mint or
chopped fresh parsley

Peel and slice the onions into half rings and sprinkle them with a little salt. Combine them with the vinegar and mint, and allow to stand for at least 1 hour before serving. They will become soft, lose much of their pungency, and absorb the other flavors. Serve them as an appetizer or as a relish with a main dish.

PICKLED TURNIPS

2 lbs/450g turnips
1 raw beet/beetroot
juice of 1/2 lemon
1 1/2 heaped tablespoons salt
6 cups/1.4 liters water

Wash the turnips and the beet, but do not peel them. Cut both into slices 1/4 inch/ 0.5cm thick. Sprinkle the slices of beet with the lemon juice and lay them in the bottom of a squat glass jar (they will give the turnips a reddish tinge). Now pack the turnip slices on top and add salted water to cover. Seal and keep in a cool place for 7 days. Serve with other *mezze* dishes.

◆ *Some people*

pickle everything

- turnips,

carrots,

cucumbers, red

peppers, whole

lemons, olives,

garlic...

HOT OLIVE SALAD

1 lb/450g green olives, pitted
2 large ripe tomatoes, skinned and grated
1/3 cup/80ml vegetable oil
6 cloves garlic, crushed
1 tablespoon tomato paste/purée
3 slices unpeeled lemon
1 teaspoon chili powder
1 teaspoon red pepper
salt and freshly ground black pepper

Put the olives into a saucepan, cover them with water, and bring to a boil. Drain, cover with water again, and repeat the process. In another saucepan, mix the tomatoes with the oil, garlic and tomato paste, and simmer together for a few minutes. Now add the olives, lemon slices, spices, salt and pepper, and mix well together. Add a little water and simmer over a low heat until the water is absorbed. Remove the lemon and set aside to cool. Serve cold as a *mezze* dish.

◆ *A feast of olives: cracked olives, and hot red peppers.*

ZHOUG
Chili paste with parsley and coriander

*1 cup/225g puréed fresh chili peppers,
green or red
8 tablespoons chopped fresh parsley
8 tablespoons chopped fresh coriander
1 1/2 tablespoons minced garlic
1 teaspoon salt
1 teapoon pepper
1 teaspoon ground cumin
pinch of ground cardamom*

Use a food processor to purée the chili peppers. Then add the parsley and coriander and blend again. Add the garlic, salt, pepper, cumin, and cardamom.

Re-blend, spoon into a glass jar, seal, and refrigerate. *Zhoug* will keep for several months in the refrigerator.

The red version uses *only* red chili peppers and no herbs and though more common it lacks the typical Yemenite flavor of the green version.

Zhoug is served with Yemenite dishes such as *chilbe* or *mlawach*, with a small bowl of freshly puréed tomatoes.

HUMMUS
Chickpea dip with garlic and *tahini*

*1 1/2 cups/350g dry chickpeas
1 teaspoon baking soda
3 or 4 cloves garlic, minced
1 teaspoon salt
1/2 teaspoon ground cumin
1/2 cup/100ml tahini sauce (see p. 30)
juice of 2 lemons
olive oil*

Soak the chickpeas in water overnight, with the soda. Cook them until soft, then drain them, reserving a little of the cooking liquid. Reserve a few whole chickpeas for garnishing.

Mash all the ingredients together, but not too finely. If the consistency is too dry, add a little of the chickpea cooking liquid. Spoon the mixture onto a plate and make a well in the center. A skilled hummus artist can make a perfect crater with a thin film of paste in the middle in one swift, circular movement. Put a little olive oil, and the reserved chickpeas, into the well and serve. Some cooks like to add extra *tahini*.

◆ *The twin towers of Yemenite cuisine: green zhoug and red zhoug, two fiery condiments which are chiefly responsible for the flavor of Yemenite food.*

◆ *The Dead Sea is the lowest place on earth. It is rich with minerals and phosphates, and nothing ever grows in it.*

HAZERET/HREIN
Horseradish relish

3 oz/100g fresh horseradish
10 oz/275g fresh beets/beetroot
1/2 cup/100ml vinegar
1 teaspoon salt
2 tablespoons sugar

Peel the horseradish. Wash the beets, then boil them for 15 minutes. When cool, peel them. Now grate the horseradish and the beets using a fine grater or a food processors - do this near an open window! Mix the grated horseradish and beets with the other ingredients and refrigerate in a glass jar. Use as a condiment with any traditional Eastern European savoury dish, and never ever attempt to serve gefilte fish without it.

HARISSA
A North African condiment

18 fresh red chili peppers
2 red bell peppers
4 cloves garlic
1 teaspoon ground cumin
1 teaspoon coriander seeds
1/2 teaspoon hot chili powder
1 teaspoon coarse salt
3 tablespoons white vinegar
2 tablespoons olive oil

Remove the stalks and seeds from the chili peppers - make sure you wear gloves to do this. Using a pestle and mortar (or a food processor, which is less fun), grind the peppers up with the garlic and spices. Deseed the bell peppers and deep-fry or broil/grill them; remove the skins. Add the flesh to the chili paste, with the rest of the ingredients, and grind for another minute or two. Keep a week's supply in the refrigerator and freeze the rest.

HREIMEH
Spicy Moroccan fish

3 tablespoons vegetable oil
2 tablespoons chopped parsley
1 onion, chopped
8 cloves garlic, chopped
2 tablespoons tomato paste/purée
1/2 teaspoon salt
2 tablespoons lemon juice
1/4 teaspoon black pepper
ground coriander or cumin, to taste
1/2 teaspoon paprika
1 1/2 cups/350ml water
1 lb/450g fresh fish (sea bass,
gray mullet or carp)

In a saucepan, heat the oil and fry the onion and parsley for 5 minutes. Add the garlic, tomato paste, salt, lemon juice, black pepper and coriander or cumin. Add the water, mix well, and cook for 5-10 minutes over a medium heat.

Lay the fish in the saucepan, cover, and poach in the spicy broth for 25 minutes.

◆ *Horseradish sauce, flavored with beets, is the sole hot contribution to Israeli cuisine by Eastern European Jews. A customary condiment of Passover, it is eaten as a reminder of a harsh and bitter past.*

D AIRY & CHEESE

◆ *Shultza, the*
shepherd, tends
his flock of
goats in the
northern region
of the country.
The milk is
used to make
rich, fatty
cheese.

I n Byniamina, along a narrow

passageway called Cypress Road,

in the back room of Shomron Dairy, a

shop as fragrant as its name is musical,

Moshe Bachar cuts into a burnished-

brown wheel of Turkish *kachkavel* with

a small knife shaped like a spade. Using the knife as a wedge, he cracks open the huge, damp, moldy cheese into two craggy halves, then bends down and squints at its texture.

"Horef" he says. "Winter."

Abu-Mussa, an Arab who makes his living tapping the sides of thousands of wheels of *kachkavel* each year, nods in agreement. He taps the cheeses with a tiny steel hammer, listening carefully for evidence of unwanted holes in their moist interior. "Too white, not yellow straw," he comments, referring to the color the cheese should have been if the goats that provided the milk for it had eaten the deep green grass and alfalfa of summer.

Moshe Bachar is a third-generation cheese-maker and a native-born Israeli. The huge 45-lb/20-kg wheel of 1988 vintage cheese has been made from the milk of goats fed on winter fodder. It is a winter cheese, too white, too young, a bit too acid to eat as a dessert with red wine. But it will be a wonderful cheese for cooking with vegetables, perfect for grating over pasta.

A 1987 vintage wheel, a rare cheese to have since demand is such that Bachar cannot allow his cheeses to age properly and gracefully, is described as "a little elder sister." It is tinged with yellow inside, and its texture is more moist, a sign that it possesses more style and breeding. It was made from the milk of spring. Bachar forgets his dismay over the young and restless *kachkavel* and takes a bite of its elder sister. It deserves its appellation. Just look at its golden color and the ragged veins running through it like a mother lode! "Like silk," Bachar breathes.

◆ Shultza tending his flock near a water hole.

◆ For a fixed price, the Ein Kamonim roadside inn, in the Upper Galilee offers a tray of assorted cheeses, country-style bread, vegetables, homemade wine, pickles, vinegar, and olive oil. Fire crackles in the fireplace in winter.

◆ *Fresh ricotta*

cheese in cheese-

cloth, still

dripping whey,

Shomron Dairy,

Byniamina.

Kachkavel, also known as *kasseri*, is an aristocratic cheese, the people of Byniamina say, the king of cheeses, made by hand and with love, just as it has been for a hundred years. It is also produced in a few villages on the

Golan Heights, Druze villages that have never stopped making it. Their *kachkavel* is stronger and sharper than Bachar's. Byniamina's citizens boast of the strawberries, oranges and zucchini that grow in the rich fields around their city, but most of all they revel in their cheese. Goats are imported and bred specially for the richness and quantity of their milk, the milk that will become *kachkavel*. Cheese-making in Byniamina is considered a high calling, an art not taught in any other way than by father to son, mother to daughter. The whey that is the by-product of the cheese-making process becomes food for Byniamina's cows and Byniamina swears that its beef is wonderful only because the milk of its goats is so rich.

Before the cheese-making process begins, two collections of milk are needed, and these must be blended carefully. Cheese-making begins at about five o'clock each morning and ends at about noon, "and it must be done three hundred and sixty-five days a year" Bachar explains "because goats do not know about holy days."

The evening's milk is brought in, poured into shallow stainless steel tanks, and left overnight. It separates into two components, heavy cream that sinks to the bottom and lighter skim milk. The next morning the skim milk,

◆ *Dairy produce being delivered in the early morning hours from the back of a truck, Tel Aviv.*

46

containing virtually no fat, is drained from the tanks and mixed in copper cooking kettles with that morning's collection of fresh, whole milk. Combining the two milks is an arduous business. The copper kettles hold 240 gallons/1,100 liters each and although the milks can be and are mixed by giant beaters, the cheese-makers insist on mixing them partly by hand. They like to feel and touch the milk. "It is our way of making the cheese ours" says Bachar.

A portion of the whey from the previous day is added to the milk mixture and the heat is turned on under the kettles. The whey, Bachar explains, is rich in lactic acid, the perfect ingredient for beginning the ripening process. As the milk is heated to 95°F/35°C, Abu-Mussa keeps reaching for and reading the temperature on a special thermometer immersed in the milk. When the correct temperature is reached, he turns off the heat and adds a bit of rennet to each kettle. Rennet, from the stomachs of calves, will curdle the milk.

And so the process goes on, fresh milk at one end and ripened cheese at the other. But not so long ago, when Bachar's cheese had a chance to age gracefully, most Israelis subsisted on fresh white cheese. It was the only kind made. It was never aged and had no taste or aroma to speak of. It was spread on bread or used in cakes and cooking. It contained 5-9 percent fat and freshness was all. The only milk product with a hint of maturity to it was *labaneh*, made from curdled yogurt, and that was an Arab invention. *Labaneh*, a thick

◆ *Cows grazing in lush winter pasture, Byniamina.*

lemony paste traditionally stored in glass jars filled with olive oil, keeps for a long time without refrigeration. No one grated cheese - there was no cheese worth grating - and no one served cheese as a separate course.

As with other aspects of Israeli food and cooking, it was foreign travel that brought about a change of taste. New demand created new products. Matured cheese has been with us for ten years or so now, but blue-veined cheese, of which we have only one variety, is still viewed with suspicion unless it is disguised in a dip. We are past wine-and-cheese get-togethers as a means of introducing new cheeses, but only just. We have still not assimilated the culinary possibilities of cheese. Of course the Jewish dietary laws forbid the mixing of milk products and meat, so cooking meat with butter or cream is out

◆ *Stacks of kachkavel wheels drying in Shomron Dairy. The hard yellow cheese is also known as* kasseri.

of the question. This is one of the reasons why Israeli cuisine makes such limited use of dairy products in cooking. Margarine is substituted for butter and ersatz cream for the real thing.

Even in this age of refrigerators and well stocked supermarkets, a disappointing number of "new" offerings are really old products under new names. Many varieties of cream cheese are sold which are not really cheese at all, but dips which start off as white cheese which is then mixed with various flavorings and colorings. Fortunately, however, not everyone is content with pseudo cheese. There are farms with small dairy herds and flocks which choose to produce the real thing and we now have a reasonable, although limited, range of bries, chèvres and cheddars, and even a little ricotta and mozarella. These are still a far cry from the great originals, but they hold their own. If you sample them in their own right, and do not make too many comparisons, they are acceptable.

DAIRY & CHEESE

◆ *If it's* labaneh, *it must be* breakfast. *Labaneh* in *olive oil with* za'atar *and* scallions, is *morning fare.*

Recipes

GRILLED PEPPERS WITH YOGURT

3 red bell peppers, halved lengthwise and cored
7 oz/200g pecans, shelled and halved
vegetable oil
2 1/2 cups/600ml thick plain yogurt
2 teaspoons salt

Lightly brush the peppers with vegetable oil and cook them under a pre-heated broiler/grill until soft. Fry the pecans in a little oil until golden, then drain on paper towels/kitchen paper. Stir the salt into the yogurt.

For a hearty Sephardic breakfast, lay the peppers on top of the yogurt and top with nuts and a sprinkling of mint. Serves 4.

CHILLED CUCUMBER & YOGURT SOUP

1 large cucumber
salt
2 1/2 cups/600ml plain yogurt
1/2 cup/100ml fresh tomato paste/purée
1 clove garlic, chopped very fine
pinch ground coriander
chopped fresh mint and paprika, to garnish

Wash the cucumber, but do not peel it. Chop it coarsely, sprinkle it with salt, and set aside for 30 minutes - this removes some of the bitter taste. Rinse and drain the cucumber, put it in the food processor with the rest of the ingredients, and blend until smooth and creamy.

Serve well chilled, sprinkled with mint and paprika. Serves 4.

◆ *Red peppers roasted on an open fire, with yogurt, chopped mint and pecan nuts.*

CHEESE BLINTZES
Cheese-filled pancakes

BATTER
1 cup/100g all-purpose/plain flour
1 tablespoon sugar
1/4 teaspoon salt
1 cup/225ml milk
4 large eggs, lightly beaten
1 teaspoon unsalted butter, softened or melted
2 tablespoons/40g extra butter for frying

CHEESE FILLING
1 1/2 cups/350g cottage cheese
2 cups/450g cream cheese, softened
2 large egg yolks
3/4 cup/175g sugar
1/2 teaspoon salt
1/2 teaspoon vanilla extract/essence
1 teaspoon grated lemon peel
1/4 cup/60g unsalted butter

2 cups/450ml sour cream
3 cups/500g strawberries

In a blender, mix all the batter ingredients to a smooth consistency and chill for 10 minutes.

Lightly butter a small non-stick skillet/frying pan and heat it thoroughly. Pour 2 tablespoons of batter into it, tilting the pan so that the batter forms a thin, even layer.

As soon as the batter has solidified, remove the skillet from the heat, flip the blintz over using a spatula and slide it onto a warm dish. Repeat until all the batter is used up.

Beat together the filling ingredients. Fill each blintz with 2 tablespoons of filling, fold the sides over the filling and roll up. To serve, fry 2 blintzes per person for 2 minutes on each side, seam-side down first. Serve with sour cream and strawberries. To be polite, offer sifted confectioner's/icing sugar too.

◆ *A household*

staple: labaneh

cheese balls in

olive oil, with

rosemary and

chili peppers.

LABANEH CHEESE BALLS

2 teaspoons salt
2 pints/1 liter plain sheep's milk yogurt
olive oil
coarsely ground black pepper
crushed dried mint or paprika

Mix the salt and yogurt together, then tie it in fine cheesecloth/muslin, and leave it to drain over a bowl or sink for 48 hours. This gets rid of the excess moisture. (In this form it can be eaten spread on bread, with a little chopped fresh mint or wild thyme, or used to make the salad below.)

Chill the cheese in the refrigerator, then roll it into balls about the size of plums and store in olive oil with a sprig of rosemary and 1-2 dried chili peppers. When you want to eat them, remove them from the oil, drain, and roll in pepper and mint/paprika.

LABANEH & CUCUMBER SALAD

8 oz/225g labaneh *cheese*
(see recipe above)
2 tablespoons milk
4 baby cucumbers, unpeeled and finely diced
2 cloves garlic, crushed
1 teaspooon dried mint
salt
1 tablespoon olive oil

Mash the cheese to a smooth paste with the milk, then add the cucumber, garlic, mint and salt, and mix well. Add the olive oil. Serve as a *mezze* dish, with warm *pita* bread.

SAMBUSAK
Cheese-filled pastry crescents

DOUGH
1/4 cup/80g butter, melted
1/4 cup/80g olive or vegetable oil
1/4 cup/80g water
1 teaspoon salt
2 cups/225g all-purpose/plain flour
1 egg yolk, or milk, to glaze
1 teaspoon sesame seeds

CHEESE FILLING
1 oz/225g white cheese (feta is ideal)
pepper
1 hard-boiled egg, diced

Mix the butter, oil, water and salt together in a bowl. Add the flour a tablespoon at a time, mixing thoroughly. Any lumps will gradually disappear. The consistency is right when pieces of dough flake away from the sides of the bowl and it can be shaped into a smooth ball. Pre-heat the oven to 375°F/ 190°C.

To make the filling, simply mix the cheese and other ingredients together.

To make the *sambusak*, break off walnut-size pieces of dough and roll them into circles about 3 inches/8cm across. Put a teaspoon of filling onto each circle, fold the dough over the filling, and crimp the edges together with finger and thumb. Take care not to overfill - the cheese mixture tends to expand during cooking.

Lay the *sambusak* side by side on an oiled baking sheet, brush with egg yolk or milk, and bake for 30 minutes or until golden brown. Makes about 20.

CARROT & SOUR CREAM COLD SOUP

3 tablespoons butter
1 onion, coarsely chopped
1 clove garlic
2 lbs/900g carrots, sliced
1/2 tablespoon each of ground turmeric,
coriander, ginger and chili
2 cups/500ml vegetable stock
2 cups/500ml sour cream
1 cup/225g plain yogurt
scant 1/2 teaspoon salt
fresh chives, to garnish

Put the butter, onion, garlic, carrots and spices into a pressure cooker and simmer for 10 minutes. Add the stock, put the lid on and pressure cook for 15 minutes. Allow to cool, then liquidize and strain through a fine sieve. Add the sour cream, yogurt and salt, and chill well. Serve with a sprinkling of snipped chives.

◆ Sambusak *can make a hearty meal. Feta cheese gives* sambusak *a tangy taste and each bite is dipped in za'atar, a mixture of hyssop and spices.*

◆ *Freshly baked* sambusak *in one of many small, busy bakeries in Jaffa.*

FRIED GOAT'S CHEESE WITH MINT SALAD

12 oz/350g goat's cheese in a log, well chilled
flour
1 egg, lightly beaten and seasoned with thyme
and nutmeg
vegetable oil
garlic
1 small onion, finely chopped
1 tablespoon olive oil
1 tablespoon wine vinegar
dash tabasco
6 heaped tablespoons chopped fresh mint

Slice the cheese and dip the slices first in flour, then in beaten egg, then in flour again. Heat the oil in a skillet/frying pan until it just begins to smoke, then slide the cheese slices into the pan and cook on both sides until golden brown.

Rub the inside of a bowl with garlic, and mix together the chopped onion, olive oil, vinegar, tabasco and mint. Spoon the mixture onto individual plates and place the cheese slices on top. Makes 4 portions.

◆ *Goats*

grazing by

an olive tree

near Harduf,

in northern

Israel.

AVOCADO ORANGE CHEESECAKE
Unusual but delicious

7 oz/200g graham crackers/digestive biscuits
1/4 cup/50g melted butter
3 oranges
1 large avocado
juice of 1/2 lemon
3 oz/75g cream cheese
2 eggs, separated
2/3 cup/150ml sour cream
1/2 oz/15g gelatin
2 tablespoons sugar

Crush the crackers/biscuits, stir in the melted butter and press the mixture into the bottom of a 7-inch/18-cm cake pan. Grate the rind of one orange, squeeze the juice from two, and prepare a few peeled orange segments from the third. Remove several slices from the avocado and put them in water to a little lemon juice has been added - this prevents them blackening.

In a food precessor, blend together the rest of the avocado and lemon juice, the cream cheese, egg yolks, sour cream, orange rind and orange juice. Dissolve the gelatin in a little water and add it to the mixture, beating well. Whip/whisk the egg whites with the sugar until stiff, then fold them into the creamy orange/avocado mixture. Spoon the mixture into the cake pan, garnish with the orange segments and drained avocado slices, and refrigerate. Makes 12 generous servings.

◆ *Fried goat's*

cheese with

mint.

GREEK SALAD

As with watermelon and feta, this salad
has become a "native" of Israel.

1 romaine/cos or crisphead/iceberg lettuce
4 cucumbers
4 large, juicy tomatoes
1 onion, peeled
salt and pepper to taste
wine vinegar
olive oil
11 oz/300g feta cheese
1 teaspoon dried thyme
black olives, to garnish

Wash all the vegetables. Cut the lettuce
into 1-inch/2.5-cm cubes. Slice the onions
into rings. Cut all the other vegetables into
cubes or chunks the same size as the lettuce
(leave the cucumbers unpeeled). Divide
the lettuce among 4 big soup bowls, then
arrange the other vegetables on top. Season
with salt, pepper, vinegar and oil to taste.
Cut the cheese into cubes and put it on top.
Add the onion rings and a sprinkling of
dried thyme. Decorate each bowl with 4 or
5 black olives.

◆ *Feta cheese*

salad, an

Israeli version

of a Greek

recipe.

◆ *Waiting for a*

breeze. A slice of

sweet, juicy

watermelon is com-

plemented by feta

cheese and black

olives.

F I S H

◆ Yuki, a trout

farmer, raises trout

in the choppy waters

of the Banias River.

The cold clear

waters originate in

the melted snow of

Mount Hermon.

No one ever forgets, even if he or she has enjoyed it only once, the aroma and flavor of freshly caught Mediterranean fish grilled over charcoal. The fish are not more exciting or flavorful than those caught in Boston or Le Havre or Hydra - in all honesty Israel's territorial waters offer a poor catch compared with other Mediterranean countries - but the direct and intense heat of the open fire, the nutty perfume of the smoke and the crispiness of the fish's skin seem to make all the difference. Charcoal-grilled fish can be sampled in any of thousands of restaurants from Alexandria to Athens, from Algiers to Istanbul, but the taste of Jaffa is unique. Here fish need only a hint of garlic, lemon juice and red pepper to be perfect.

◆ *Fisherman's wharf in the port of Acre, one of Israel's biblical towns.*

As you drive south along Tel Aviv's renovated Riviera, the ramparts of the old city of Jaffa rise from the tranquil sea. Jaffa is untouched by time. The city planners keep their distance. There is a quality of age and grace about the place that is better left untouched.

A few years ago a fisherman called Benny Raba came ashore and opened a fish restaurant. He is short and stocky and not at all the slim, trim fellow he was in his fishing days, but in the few years he has been in dry dock

he has become a walking status symbol. He drives a brand-new Mercedes with a car phone and wears gold bracelets and chains. He sits at his table facing the sea and holds court.

Benny's favourite pastime is recalling his seafaring days, when the sea was fierce and the fish were feisty. He cuts the air with chubby, leathery hands to illustrate his points, and as he sails down memory lane an attentive waiter covers the table with *mezze*, small colorful plates of appetizers such as *hummus, tahini, labaneh, tabbouleh*, eggplant purée, pickles, red hot peppers and other delights. Benny pushes a plate of fat, shiny olives towards his guests, urging them to try one, waiting anxiously for the verdict. The olives are meaty and tasty, and they blend well with the moist chunks of feta cheese.

Benny's religion is fresh fish. He will show you the eyes and say, "You can tell a fresh fish by its eyes." His fish are firm of body and bright of color, and do not flake and fall apart when they are deep-fried. No, Benny is not ashamed to deep-fry his fresh fish, although it seems that Israel is, in general, past its deep-frying days. Why fry a fish to a crisp if you can flirt with it? With a charcoal grill going full blast at every street corner, is it not a shame and a sin to fish & chip your fish?

◆ *A fisherman mends a net torn by rocks off Jaffa harbor.*

When he is in the mood or when the restaurant is quiet, Benny dons an apron and goes into his kitchen. Taking an ax to a huge gray mullet, he reduces it to bite-size pieces and grills them on skewers over an open fire. Before he serves them, he flambés them in arak, the local version of ouzo or Pernod.

Authentic, ethnic fish restaurants are a relatively new phenomenon in Israel. Until quite recently, Israelis were anything but adventurous when it came to fish. For generations, Jewish holidays called for fish, but it was fish ground and molded into gefilte fish - the smell was there, there was a even a soupçon of taste, but mainly it was just another patty covered with sauce. The Jews of Poland used to cover their fish with a jellied sauce made of sugar and almonds. And when it was not ground and sauced out of

◆ *Back from an early morning excursion, Benny proudly displays a huge* palamida. *The large fish is cut into generous steaks.*

existence, fish was baked in the oven with vegetables and spices. When it finally arrived on the table, overcooked and falling off the bones, wives insisted that their husbands eat the heads. Since the most widely used fish in Jewish cooking was the impossible and dangerous carp, choking and coughing up bones was a customary part of all festival meals. Now we have discovered that carp is not the only fish worth eating, the excitement of the discovery is everywhere

evident. Diners are learning the names of local fish and pronouncing them with increasing confidence. They can tell a fresh fish from a tired one, a juicy one from an assemblage of skin and bones disguised as fish.

Trout are a new discovery. In northern Israel, in the Galilee region, there are numerous trout farms. The Dan and the Banias, which flow down from Mount Hermon into the Kinneret (Sea of Galilee), are two of the rivers whose cold choppy waters are used by trout farms. In spring, when the snow on Mount Hermon melts, the rivers are fierce. Now, in small pools and tanks strictly and scientifically supervised, Israeli trout grow to prize-winning proportions. They are sold locally or delivered weekly to the major cities.

Trout have caught on nicely. They are, in many ways, a fish for beginners - not too fishy, not too many bones, and easy to clean and cook. They are elegant, upmarket, easy to promote, and make a pleasant change from local gray mullet, red mullet and bream.

It is a geographical wonder that a country as small as Israel possesses four potentially fishy realms: the Eastern Mediterranean, the Red Sea, the Kinneret, and the Dead Sea. But ecological abuse and neglect have made the last two barren; the Dead Sea is culinarily useless, except for salt, and the Kinneret holds little or no fish, not even the famous St. Peter's fish, now transplanted to fish farms. At one time most fishing in the Red Sea was done along the shores of Sinai, but since this stretch of sea was returned to Egypt it

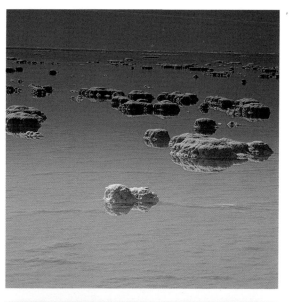

◆ *The Dead Sea.*

◆ *Eilat on the Red
Sea is Israel's
southernmost
region. Since the
return of the
Sinai Desert to
Egypt, Eilat has
enjoyed an influx
of tourists.*

◆ *Known for its
unique therapeu-
tic qualities, the
Dead Sea attracts
people from all
over the world.
A day covered in
mud does wonders
for the skin.*

◆ *Eli Avivi is self-
appointed head of
state of Achziv.
A stretch of white
sandy beach along
the Mediterranean,
Achziv is also the
site of a Club Med
village.*

◆ *Hammat Gader, a kibbutz on the Golan, raises crocodiles primarily for export. A restaurant specializing in croc meat is planned.*

◆ *Deep-sea fishing is forbidden in the Red Sea so divers use nets instead of air guns.*

has been out of bounds to Israeli fisherman. So Israel's need for fish is now supplied by fish farms and deep fishing in the Mediterranean.

The Mediterranean contains an extraordinary variety of fish waiting to be tasted by those tired of the ubiquitous frozen mullet. Around the coast of Israel there is a passion - which becomes an obsession in the summer - for catching and eating all forms of seafood. Benny Raba gets very cross about "all the silly fuss in summer." In summer, he says, the sea is too warm. The fish are already parboiled when you take them out. To get good fish in summer a fisherman must sail deep and far and only a few fishermen do that. Why on earth, he asks bitterly, do Israelis associate fish with summer?

To befriend a fisherman or the owner of a fish restaurant means accepting some strange delicacies, all with that unmistakable sea taste of iodine. For stronger stomachs, there are fan mussels and sinewy squid. For the conservative, there are bright red mullet, needing no scaling or gutting, grilled with fragrant herbs. The grouper, which can grow to a great size in the safety of deep rock holes, has a delicate flavor, and the *palamida*, or lesser tuna, has a more subtle taste than its larger relative, as well as being one of the most beautiful fish in the Mediterranean.

The factor that unites all the countries of the Mediterranean is a similarity of recipes for cooking seafood. The Greeks claim that *bouillabaisse* was originally a hearty fisherman's soup or stew. And so it is, and alive and cooking in Jaffa. In Israel fish are also eaten baked, with or without vegetables, or fried whole or in slices, or charcoal-grilled, with many different sauces. They are also braised in the style known as *hreimeh*, or minced and made into loaves and patties cooked in tasty courts-bouillons. All of these cooking methods can be applied to most locally caught fish.

F I S H

◆ Mousht,
St. Peter's
fish, is
Israel's
leading
fish.

Recipes

RED MULLET WITH ORANGE BUTTER

2 lbs/900g very fresh red mullet
rind and juice of 2 lbs/900g oranges
salt and pepper to taste
pinch of hot chili powder
1 clove garlic, minced
1 teaspoon sugar
2 tablespoons white wine
mixture of butter and oil for frying
1 cup/225g unsalted butter, melted

If the red mullet are small, simply wash them. If they weigh more than 3 oz/75g, scale and clean them. Cut the orange rind into very thin strips, blanch it in boiling water for 2 minutes, then drain. Put the orange juice into a saucepan and add the salt, chili powder, garlic, sugar, wine and the blanched rind, and simmer until half the liquid has evaporated.

In the meantime, pat-dry the fish, sprinkle them with salt and pepper, and dip them in flour, shaking off any excess. Heat the butter/oil in a skillet/frying pan until it begins to smoke, then slide the fish into the pan. For a crispy result, do not try to fry too many fish at once. Fry for 5 minutes on each side, depending on size, then drain quickly on paper towels/kitchen paper. Transfer the fish to 4 pre-heated main course/8 pre-heated starter plates.

Remove the orange juice/spice mixture from the heat and stir in the melted butter, or simply transfer both to a glass jar, screw the top on, and shake vigorously to a smooth, semi-transparent consistency. Pour the sauce over the fish and serve.

BAKED GRAY MULLET

3 or 4 cloves garlic
1 large green pepper, sliced very thin
4 tablespoons chopped fresh parsley
juice of 1 lemon
salt and freshly ground black pepper
3 tablespoons olive oil
1 onion, thinly sliced
1 gray mullet, about 3 lbs/1.4 kg, scaled and cleaned
lemon wedges, to garnish

Chop most of the garlic very fine and mix it with the green pepper, parsley, lemon juice, salt, pepper and oil. Pour this mixture over the sliced onion, reserving a little to flavor the inside of the fish.

Cut one or two shallow slits in each side of the fish and insert the rest of the garlic, cut into slivers. Spoon the reserved onion-herb-garlic mixture inside the fish. Lay the fish in a baking dish, surrounded by the rest of the onion-herb-garlic marinade, and leave in a cool place for at least 30 minutes. Turn once so that both sides of the fish have a chance to absorb the marinade.

Pre-heat the oven to 375°F/190°C and bake the fish for about 30 minutes, basting it once or twice and turning it once. When the flesh flakes easily, it is cooked. Serve garnished with lemon wedges, with the cooked marinade as a sauce. Serves 4 or 5.

◆ *Red mullet with orange butter.*

TWO SAUCES FOR GRILLED FISH

Grilling is by far the most popular method of cooking fish in Israel.

LEMON-GARLIC SAUCE

3 tablespoons olive oil
2 tablespoons lemon juice
3 cloves garlic, minced
1/2 teaspoon salt
1/4 cup/60ml water

Heat the oil in a small saucepan. Add the lemon juice, garlic and salt, and simmer for 3 minutes. Allow to cool. Serve cold.

ONION-LEMON SAUCE FOR FISH

4 tablespoons olive oil
2 scallions/spring onions, shredded very fine
1/2 teaspoon salt
1 tablespoon vinegar
1 1/2 teaspoons harissa *(see recipe p. 41)*
1/2 cup/100ml water

Lightly sauté the onion in the oil. Add salt, vinegar and *harissa*, and mix well. Add the water and simmer for 3 minutes. Allow to cool. Serve cold.

WHOLE FISH ON THE SPIT

1/2 teaspoon paprika
4 tablespoons coriander seeds
6 cardamom pods
1 tablespoon anise or dill seeds
2 onions, chopped
2 cloves garlic, crushed
2 tablespoons chopped fresh mint
4 tablespoons chopped fresh parsley
1 green pepper, cored and thinly sliced
2/3 cup/150ml plain yogurt, whipped
juice of 1 lemon or lime
3 lbs/1.4kg fish (sea bass, gray mullet),
cleaned, with heads and tails removed
salt and pepper
1/4 cup/60g clarified butter

Toast the paprika and coriander in a skillet/ frying pan, then grind them up with the other spices. Add them to the onions, garlic, herbs and green pepper, and mix to a smooth paste with the yogurt and lemon juice.

Prick the fish all over and rub in the spice and herb mixture. Season with salt and pepper and allow to marinate for 1 hour.

Thread the fish onto a barbecue spit, with a pan underneath to catch the juices. Grill for 15 minutes or until the herb paste is dry. Baste with the pan juices, then raise the spit and cook for a further 25 minutes over a gentle heat, turning once.

The fish are cooked when they flake easily. Lower the spit to raise the intensity of the heat, baste the fish with the clarified butter and continue cooking until the skins are crisp. Serve at once, with salad and potatoes. Serves 6.

Palamida
Marinated bonito/lesser tuna

Scale and clean the fish, slice them into 3/4-inch/2-cm pieces, and marinate overnight in the following mixture: 4 cups/1 liter water, 1/2 cup/100g salt, 1 teaspoon vinegar, 1 crushed clove garlic.

For an authentic Bulgarian Jewish breakfast, eat with onions, olives and thin slices of gray mullet roe, washed down with vodka.

◆ *Victor's is a delicatessen store deep in the heart of the Levinsky market in Tel Aviv. It is a typical deli specializing in smoked fish and herrings.*

◆ *Marinated palamida, stage two. The marinated fish is served with scallions, black olives and Turkish caviar (gray mullet roe sliced very thin).*

◆ *Marinated palamida, stage one. The fish is cut into chunks and covered with sea salt.*

TROUT BARBECUED IN GRAPE LEAVES

8 trout, 8-10 oz/225-275g each
1 cup/225ml olive oil
1/4 cup/60ml fresh lemon juice
scant tablespoon minced capers
2 tablespoons minced fresh parsley
1 tablespoon fresh chives, snipped small
1 teaspoon minced fresh basil
1/2 teaspoon minced fresh rosemary
8 sprigs fresh thyme
40 large grape/vine leaves, fresh or preserved
1 lemon, cut into wedges, to garnish
sprigs of fresh herbs, to garnish

Top, tail and bone the trout, leaving them otherwise whole. Then score them on both sides at 2 1/2 inch/6cm intervals, holding the knife at an angle of 30° and cutting a quarter of the way through the flesh.

Mix together the olive oil, lemon juice, capers and herbs and rub this mixture generously over the fish, inside and out. Put a sprig of thyme in each fish, then wrap each one in 5 grape leaves, overlapping them so that they entirely envelop the fish. Secure with string at 1-inch/2.5-cm intervals.

Prepare the barbecue. When the coals are ready, scatter soaked *mesquite* or fruitwood chips on top. When they begin to smolder, place the fish on the grill/rack and cover with foil. If the fish are about 1 inch/2.5-cm thick, they will take about 10 minutes to cook; if thicker, proportionately longer. Turn once during cooking.

To serve, remove the string but leave the grape leaves on, and garnish with lemon wedges and fresh herbs. Serves 8.

TROUT WITH POMEGRANATE

1 large pomegranate
4 fresh trout
salt and pepper to taste
pinch cardamom
1 onion, chopped
1/2 cup/100g butter
2 cloves garlic, minced
1 cup/100g pecans, coarsely chopped
2 tablespoons vinegar

Cut the pomegranate in half and tap rather than scoop out the seeds so that they remain intact. Wash and clean the fish. With trout, it is possible to break the backbone near the head and pull it out whole, leaving the fish intact but deboned.

Lightly fry the onions in a little of the butter. Season the inside of the fish with salt, pepper and cardamom to taste, then stuff them with the pomegranate seeds, fried onion, garlic and chopped pecans, and put a knob of butter in each. If necessary, close the openings with toothpicks/cocktail sticks.

Butter an ovenproof dish and lay the fish in it. Bake in an oven pre-heated to 400°F/200°C for 12 minutes. Serve on a bed of mustard and cress or watercress, garnished with the rest of the pomegranate seeds.

◆ *Trout with pomegranate on a bed of cress.*

GEFILTE FISH
Traditional poached fishballs

2 lbs/900g fresh carp
1 slice stale challah or 1/2 cup/60g matzo flour
1 hard-boiled egg
2 tablespoons oil
1 large onion
2 eggs
salt, black pepper and sugar to taste

BROTH/STOCK
4 carrots, sliced
2 onions, sliced
4 cups/1 liter water
salt, pepper and sugar to taste

Wash the fish and cut it into slices, reserving the roe for future use. Sprinkle the slices with salt and refrigerate for 1 hour. Soak the *challah* in water, and then drain.

Using a sharp knife, skin the fish, saving any unbroken rings of skin. Discard only the main bones. Ignoring all the other bones, grind/mince the fish twice with the hard-boiled egg and *challah* to achieve a smooth consistency. At this stage some cooks would add 8 oz/225g of pike fillet, a few almonds or a raw carrot, but these are optional.

Now blend in the 2 eggs, oil, salt and pepper, and sugar to taste - knowing the powerful emotions aroused by the subject of how much sugar gefilte fish should contain, we do not dare specify the amount of sugar to be added here - and refrigerate.

Put all the broth ingredients into a large saucepan, bring to a boil and cook for 30 minutes. Add the fish's head and continue to simmer. Meanwhile, form the chilled fish mixture into balls, wetting your hands to prevent the mixture sticking to them. If you managed to save any rings of skin, stuff them with the mixture too. Smooth them with your wet hands and slide them one by one, with the other balls, into the simmering broth. Cover the saucepan, leaving a small gap between the lid and the saucepan, and simmer for 2 hours. When cool, put in the refrigerator.

To serve, put 2 or 3 balls on each plate with a slice of carrot on top and some of the jellied broth. Serve the fish head to the head of the family. *Challah* and horseradish relish (see recipes p. 90 and 41) are an absolute must with gefilte fish. Makes enough for 8 starter portions.

HERRINGS IN SOUR CREAM

1 cup/225ml heavy/double cream
2 tablespoons sugar
2 tablespoons white wine vinegar
10 fat herrings
1 medium red onion, sliced very thin

Fillet the herrings and remove the skin, then cut each fillet into 5 or 6 pieces. Whip/whisk the sugar into the cream and stir in the vinegar. Put the fish into a glass jar, with layers of onion in between, and pour in the cream. Cover and refrigerate. Use within 10 days. Makes 20 servings.

◆ *Sunset over*

the Kinneret,

Israel's only

freshwater

lake.

POACHED SEA BASS
MARINATED IN LEMON & BASIL

rind of 1 lemon, pared off in strips
6 fillets sea bass, about 8 oz/225g each
1/2 cup/100ml fresh lemon juice
1/3 cup/80ml white wine vinegar
1 1/2 teaspoons salt
1/2 teaspoon sugar
1 1/2 cups/350ml extra-virgin olive oil
3 tablespoons finely choppped basil, plus sprigs
of basil to garnish
2 large cloves garlic, chopped
2 teaspoons dried hot red pepper flakes
1 cup/225ml dry white wine
2 bay leaves
2 sprigs parsley
4 cups/1 liter water
red bell pepper, finely chopped, to garnish

Put the lemon rind in the bottom of a shallow dish large enough hold all the bass fillets flat. Skin the fillets and cut them crosswise into strips about 1 1/4 inches/3cm wide.

Whip/whisk together the lemon juice, vinegar, 1/2 teaspoon salt, sugar and oil until the mixture emulsifies (thickens and goes cloudy), then whip in half the chopped basil, the garlic and the red pepper flakes.

In a large saucepan, combine the wine, bay leaves, parsley and the rest of the salt with the water, and bring to a boil. Turn down the heat so that the liquid is just simmering, then slide half a dozen strips of bass into the liquid and poach them for 1–1 1/2 minutes or until the flesh is just firm. Remove with a slotted spoon and transfer to the dish with the lemon rind. Poach the rest of the fish in the same way.

Pour the marinade over the fish, cover, and allow to marinate overnight in the refrigerator.

Let the fish stand at room temperature for 1 hour before serving. Transfer the fish slices to individual plates, strain the marinade through a fine sieve, whip it well to emulsify it, and drizzle it over the fish. Sprinkle with the red bell pepper and the rest of the basil, and garnish with basil sprigs. Serves 8 to 10.

MOUSHT WITH TAHINI
St. Peter's fish with sesame sauce

St. Peter's fish (*mousht* in Arabic) is a Sea of Galilee fish. It is a bony, tasty fish not unlike sea bream.

2 onions, sliced
1/4 cup/60ml vegetable oil
4 small mousht (or trout), cleaned
1/2 cup/100ml tahini/sesame seed paste
2 tablespoons lemon juice
1 clove garlic, crushed
salt and pepper
blanched vegetables
and sesame seeds, to garnish

Pre-heat the oven to 325°F/170°C. Using a large skillet/frying pan, sauté the onion in the oil until it is soft, then add the fish and cook them for 1 minute on each side so that they absorb some of the onion flavor.

Blend together the *tahini*, lemon juice and garlic. Transfer the fish and the onions to an ovenproof dish, sprinkle them with salt and pepper, and coat them with the *tahini* mixture. Bake, uncovered, for 30 minutes or until the fish flake easily. Garnish with blanched vegetables and sesame seeds.

Serves 4.

◆ Mousht

with tahini:

St. Peter's fish

with sesame

sauce.

B R E A D

◆ *Large, flat*

Iraqi pita are

baked in the

traditional

taboon, a

clay oven, in

Ashtanur

bakery,

Jerusalem.

The dough is

flattened

against the

interior of the

taboon and

falls off when

ready.

I f *falafel* were not such an in-

tegral part of Israeli folklore,

bread - any bread - would be the king of

Israeli food. But dethroning *falafel* would

be a political move requiring great bold-

ness and courage. Opposition would be

vocal and nasty. Yet we eat more bread than *falafel*, and how would *falafel* survive without *pita* bread? What other vehicle is there for those tasty little patties and handfuls of salad?

I am biased when it comes to bread. Bread is in my blood. I am a baker's son, and would have been a third-generation baker if I had not betrayed my heritage. My father sold the family's 50-year-old bakery when he became certain that I was a lost cause. He was as much to blame as I was, because this is what he told me about bread. People eat it all the time. It's so ordinary that they stop noticing it. It's invisible. When you bake an invisible staple, you too become invisible. People only notice you when your oven breaks down and your bread is ruined. Then they hate you. People who have never appreciated you resent you the first chance they get. Also, it's a hard, back-breaking job being a baker. Creativity does not come into it. Bread is not about creativity. It is about flour and water and yeast and the way they rise in the steam room and then brown in the oven.

We have always eaten bread in this country. When Jerusalem was under siege in the '48 war, everything stopped. No one came or went. The only convoys that got through were trucks bearing water and bread. When they didn't get through, people baked their own bread, if they had the flour and the yeast. Bread is what you eat when you have no other food.

Even in these affluent times, few Israelis dine without bread. Bread even enjoys a government subsidy - that is how important it is. Israelis have never

◆ *In Israel, the term "black bread" refers to the most common bread. This is subsidized by the goverment, so anyone can afford it.*

paid the full price of a loaf of bread. By subsidizing bread, the government shows a proper regard for one of the last tenets of socialism. Whatever happens, the government implies, we will always have bread. We will never starve.

If bread is the uncrowned king of Israel, then *challah* is the queen. *Challah* is the traditional Jewish egg-rich braided bread which is ritually blessed and served every Friday night when the members of observant families get together to re-establish the kinship and continuity of family life. On Friday nights one does not talk shop. Business matters are forbidden as a subject of conversation. The name *challah* actually means "the priest's share" and derives from the fact that a little piece of dough is symbolically removed from the main body of dough before it is shaped into loaves and put in the oven. The "priests's share" must rise on its own and be baked separately from the rest, and when it is baked it must be charred or burned beyond redemption - it is a sacrifice and not meant to be eaten. *Challah* is the bread we eat on festive occasions such as holidays and weddings. A special blessing involving a *challah*, usually quite a large one baked specially for the occasion, is part of Jewish weddings. Bread and salt are traditional gifts at a Jewish house-warming.

The heir-apparent is the *pita*, such an essential part of Israeli eating that it is hard to imagine life without it. Most starters or *mezze* dishes rely heavily on *pita*. Why use a fork to eat your *hummus* or *tahini* when you can use a hand-torn, edible scoop? *Hummus*-scooping is an art honed over many years. We expect *pita* to be there. We reach for it without even looking up from our newspapers.

◆ *Simcha Haddad of Netanya still uses the* taboon *to bake bread in her back yard.*

◆ *General view of the flat, fertile Jezreel Valley.*

A cultural war is now in progress between the followers of *pita* and the followers of bread. The two staples represent two cultures, Ashkenazi and Sephardic, in the process of become one nation. Jews who came to Israel from Arab countries, Sephardim, have always eaten *pita*. Ashkenazim, from Russia, Poland and Germany, are addicted to bread and have tried hard to preserve their heritage, but their efforts at baking the traditional breads of the old countries have seldom been successful. Over the years they have given up. Bread needs so much attention, with all the rising and kneading and rising again. Now they have to make do with local bread.

In other words, the bread versus *pita* war is not going bread's way at the moment, although the Tunisian open sandwich - a whole loaf of bread

cut in two, hollowed out and filled with salad, tuna, salami, and saturated with virgin olive oil - seems to be standing its ground, principally for heroic reasons. Gone are the days when traditional bakers scoffed at the quickly-made, non-rising Arab *pita*. Now there are specialized *pita* bakeries that do booming business day and night - long lines form in front of them in the dark hours - and the *pitas* they produce are not plain or ordinary. Adapting the principle of the pizza, Israeli *pita* makers have started to add different

◆ An old flour mill in the village of Shefar'am.

toppings. *Pita* with the salty herb mixture known as *za'atar* is a big hit. Then there are *pita*-pizza topped with egg, mushrooms, basil and tomato, and a dozen other flavors....This is the age of the *pita* and most Israelis eat *pita* in great quantities, whatever their country of origin.

$\mathcal{B}$ R E A D

◆ *The popular Abulafia bakery in Jaffa specializes in doughy pitas with assorted toppings. Abulafia also bakes bagels.*

$\mathcal{R}ecipes$

CHALLAH
Sweet braided bread eaten on the Sabbath

1 1/2 tablespoons dried yeast
1/2 cup/100ml lukewarm water, to activate yeast
1 teaspoon sugar
3 eggs
1/2 cup/100g sugar
1 1/2 cups/350ml lukewarm warm water, to mix with dough
1/2 cup/125ml vegetable oil
1 1/2 teaspoons salt
9 cups/1kg all-purpose/plain flour
2 eggs, beaten with 2 tablespoons water
sesame or poppy seeds, to garnish

Combine the yeast, the 1/2 cup/125ml luke-warm water and the sugar, and set aside. In a large mixing bowl, beat together the eggs and sugar, then add the 1 1/2 cups of luke-warm water, oil and salt. Stir in the frothing yeast mixture and beat well. Using a wooden spoon, beat in half the flour, adding a heaped tablespoonful at a time and beating well after each addition. At this stage, the dough will be sticky. Add half the remaining flour, beating in a tablespooonful at a time as before. The dough should now leave the sides of the bowl.

Dredge the rest of the flour onto a work surface, remove the dough from the bowl and knead it for 10 minutes until all the flour has been absorbed. Return the dough to the bowl, cover it with a damp towel, and let it rise in an unheated oven with the door closed for 1 hour or until it has more or less doubled in size.

Punch down the dough and divide it into three equal portions. Cut each portion into three and shape the thirds into long sau-sages. Braid/plait the sausages together to make three loaves.

Place the loaves on a greased and floured baking sheet, cover, and leave them to rise for about 1 1/2-2 hours, or until they have nearly doubled in volume. Pre-heat the oven to 400°F/210°C.

Brush each loaf with the egg and water mixture, sprinkle with poppy or sesame seeds, and bake for 15 minutes until golden. Tap the loaves on the bottom to see if they sound hollow - if they don't, give them an-other few minutes. When they do sound hollow, leave them in the oven for another 5 minutes. Cool on a wire rack. Makes 3 loaves.

◆ Challah *comes in many shapes and forms.* Round *challah with poppy seeds is hard to slice with a knife.* Kids *love to tear them to pieces.*

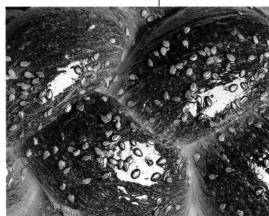

◆ *A slice of sweet* challah *with raisins.*

◆ *Abulafia's*

best, a tray of

pita, *bagels,*

ka'ahks

(bagels with

sesame

seeds), pita

with egg,

za'atar,

onion and

olives, and

Iraqi pita.

PITA
Middle Eastern flat bread/pocket bread

1 tablespoon dried yeast
1 tablespoon salt
2 tablespoons honey
2 1/3-3 cups/600-700ml lukewarm water
6-7 cups/700-800g all-purpose/plain flour

Mix together the yeast, honey and 1/2 cup/
125ml lukewarm water in a small bowl and
allow to stand for 10 minutes in a warm
place. Put 4 cups/450g of the flour into a
large mixing bowl, add the frothing yeast
mixture and 2 cups/500ml lukewarm water,
and beat vigorously for a minute or two.
Now add the salt and half the remaining
flour and beat again.

On a lightly floured board, knead the
dough for 10 minutes, adding more flour if
necessary to make a medium stiff dough.
Place the dough in a lightly greased bowl,
cover, and leave in a warm, draft-free place
to double in volume - this should take about
1 hour. Pre-heat the oven to 450°F/230°C.

Punch down the dough, knead it again,
then divide it into 12 equal portions, rolling
each one into a ball with your hands. Roll
the balls of dough into flat circles about 5
inches/13cm across and 1/4 inch/0.6cm
thick, place the circles on an ungreased
baking sheet, cover and allow to rise for 10
minutes. Cook on the bottom rack of the
oven for 8 minutes, or until the bottoms are
pale brown. If no pocket appears, raise the
oven temperature; if too brown, spray with
water. Allow to cool, then put into plastic
bags and refrigerate or freeze.

Pita bread should be served warm. Three
minutes in a pre-heated 350°F/180°C oven
should be enough to warm them through.
Any longer, and they become rock hard!
Makes 12.

SESAME PITA TOASTS

2 rounds pita *bread about*
6 inches/15cm across
3 oz/80g sesame seeds, lightly toasted
3 tablespoons unsalted butter, softened
salt

Pre-heat the oven to 375°/190°F. Cut each *pita* into quarters, then separate the quarters so that you have 8 more or less triangular pieces of bread. Dredge the sesame seeds onto a flat surface, spread the rough sides of the *pita* triangles with butter and press them, butter side down, onto the sesame seeds.

Arrange the triangles, sesame side up, on a baking sheet and bake in the oven for 8 - 10 minutes or until the toasts are crisp. Transfer the toasts to a cooling rack, sprinkle them with salt to taste, and serve warm or at room temperature.

CHILDREN'S PIZZA

1 pita
1/2 cup/100ml tomato sauce
1/2 cup/80g pitted olives
1 bell pepper, sliced
5 oz/150g canned tuna or sweetcorn, optional
7 oz/200g Gruyère cheese

Made by children, this can be a creative experience. First separate the *pita* into perfect round halves. Spread each half with tomato sauce, arrange the olives, pepper and canned tuna or sweetcorn on top, and cover with cheese, grated or thinly sliced. Put under the broiler/grill until the cheese is nicely melted. Chill and serve.

PITA WITH ONION & POPPY SEEDS

2 oz/60g fresh yeast
1 teaspoon sugar
salt
1/2 cup/100ml lukewarm water
8 1/4 cups/950g all-purpose/plain flour
3 tablespoons oil
3 eggs, lightly beaten
3 onions, finely chopped
1/2 cup/100g poppy seeds

Dissolve the yeast, sugar and a pinch of salt in the lukewarm water. Cover and leave in a warm place for 10 minutes until the mixture becomes frothy.

Put the flour into a large mixing bowl, make a well in the middle and pour in the yeast mixture, oil and 2 of the beaten eggs. Knead well. Cover with a towel, and put in a warm place for 30 minutes to allow the dough to rise.

Rub a little oil on your hands and roll the dough into about two dozen walnut-sized balls. Place the balls on a floured surface and roll them out into circles about 2 1/2 inches/7 cm across. Sprinkle each circle with onion, poppy seeds and a little salt, lightly pressing them into the dough with the rolling pin. Brush with the rest of the beaten egg. Cover and allow to rise for 30 minutes. Bake in a hot oven - 400°F/210°C - until golden brown.

Makes about 24.

BAGEL/KA'AHK
Pastry rings with cumin and coriander

4 cups/450g all-purpose/plain flour
1 teaspoon salt
1/2 oz/15g fresh yeast, or half this amount of
dried yeast
1 1/4 cups/300ml lukewarm water
pinch sugar
4 oz/100g unsalted butter or margarine, melted
1/2 teaspoon ground cumin
1/2 teaspoon ground coriander
1 egg, lightly beaten
sesame seeds

Dissolve the yeast in 2 tablespoons lukewarm water, add the sugar, and leave for 10-15 minutes.

Sift the salt, cumin and coriander into the flour, make a well in the middle and pour in the melted butter and frothing yeast mixture. Knead to a dough, adding the water a tablespoon at a time. Knead for 10 -15 minutes until the dough is smooth and comes away from the sides of the bowl. Cover the bowl with a damp cloth and leave in a warm place for 2 hours or until the dough has doubled in volume. Pre-heat the oven to 350°F/180°C.

Working on a floured surface, roll walnut-sized pieces of dough into thin 4 x 6 inch/10 x 15cm rectangles. Roll each rectangle into a cigar shape and bring the ends together to form a circle - press the ends firmly together with a little water. Arrange on a greased baking sheet, leaving 1 inch/ 2.5cm or so between each *ka'ahk*. Brush with the beaten egg and sprinkle with sesame seeds. Bake for 25-30 minutes until crisp and golden brown. Makes 20.

PRETZELS

1 oz/30 g active dry yeast
1 tablespoon sugar
1 cup/225ml lukewarm water
3 cups/350g sifted all-purpose/plain flour
2 tablespoons butter, softened
1/2 teaspoon salt
4 teaspoons baking soda
4 cups/1 liter water
coarse salt or sesame seeds, to garnish

Dissolve the yeast and a little of the sugar in the lukewarm water. When the mixture is frothing nicely, add it to the flour, butter and salt, and knead, knead, knead. Cover the dough with a cloth and allow it to rise to nearly double the volume. Punch it down, divide it into 12 equal portions and roll each one out into a ribbon 1/2 inch/1cm thick. Loop each ribbon into a figure of eight and leave in a warm place, covered with a cloth, to rise again. Pre-heat the oven to 450°F/ 230°C.

Dissolve the baking soda in the 4 cups/1 liter water and bring to a boil. Slide each pretzel into the boiling water and boil until it floats - about 1 minute. Remove with a fish slice and place on a baking sheet for 12 minutes. Before baking, sprinkle with coarse salt or sesame seeds. Bake until golden brown.

Although pretzels are delicious fresh, they will keep for up to 1 week. They are best eaten with butter.

◆ A "hero" sandwich, a favorite of Israeli construction workers. It has everything in it, on a 700g loaf of black bread.

MLAWAH
Flaky bread

3 cups/350g all-purpose/plain flour
1/4 teaspoon baking powder
1cup/225ml water
1cup/225ml butter, melted and clarified
1/2 teaspoon salt
1 teaspoon sugar
1 teaspoon vinegar, optional

Sift the baking powder into the flour, make a well in the center and add water, 1 table-spoon of the butter, salt, sugar and vinegar (if desired). Knead to a smooth elastic consistency. Cut into 6 equal portions, and allow to "rest" in a cool place for 20 minutes. Flatten each piece to a round the size of a *pita* - patience is a virtue here since the dough is springy and resists stretching and flattening! Liberally brush each round with the melted butter, then roll it into a tight sausage shape. Allow the rolls to rest for 20 minutes. Repeat the flattening, rolling and brushing procedure twice more, waiting 20 minutes between rolling and re-flattening. The final results should be flat and round like *pita*.

Using a non-stick skillet/frying pan, fry the *mlawah* on both sides until golden brown, flipping them over at half time. Serve with freshly puréed tomatoes and *zhoug*.

Mlawah freeze well. Just put waxed/greaseproof paper between them and seal them in a freezer bag.

LAHUHUA
Yemenite sponge bread

1 oz/25g yeast
3 cups/700ml lukewarm water
1 tablespoon sugar
3 1/2 cups/450g all-purpose/plain flour, sifted
1/2 teaspoon salt
5 tablespoons melted butter or shortening/lard

Dissolve the yeast in a little of the water. When it is frothing, combine it with the rest of the ingredients. Mix well, cover with a cloth and leave to rise in a warm place for 1 hour. Mix again, re-cover and leave for another hour.

Use a small non-stick skillet/frying pan to cook *lahuhua*. Start each pancake in a cold skillet, then cook for 2 minutes over a medium heat, then move the skillet to a very low heat and continue cooking for another 4 minutes. Cook on one side only.

Lahuhua are traditionally served with soups and stews. They are spongy and savoury, and not difficult to make.

◆ *Wheat harvest in the Jezreel Valley.*

◆ Lahuhua, *spongy Yemenite pancakes, with* zhoug *and soup.*

◆ *Fresh* pita *being baked in the ancient village of Pequi'in. The thin rounds of dough are placed on hot metal, flipped over and quickly removed.*

MEDITERRANEAN OLIVE ROLLS

1/2 oz/15g dried yeast
1 teaspoon sugar
1/2-1 teaspoon freshly ground black pepper
1 cup/225ml lukewarm water
3/4 cup/80g buckwheat flour
3 cups/350g all-purpose/plain flour
12 oz/350g brine-cured black olives, pitted and coarsely chopped
2 tablespoons extra-virgin olive oil

Mix the yeast, sugar and pepper with the water and allow to stand for 10 minutes.

Put the buckwheat flour and the all-purpose flour into a mixing bowl, make a well in the middle and add the frothing yeast mixture, the oil and the chopped olives. Mix to a soft, sticky dough. Transfer the dough to a floured surface and knead gently for 2 minutes. Dust with flour, return to the mixing bowl, cover with plastic wrap/cling film and leave in a warm place for at least 45 minutes or until the dough has nearly doubled in size.

Turn the dough out onto a floured surface, cut it into quarters, roll each quarter into a ball, and cut each ball into four - you should now have 16 pieces of dough of equal size. With floured hands, shape the pieces into balls and arrange on an oiled baking sheet. Put in a warm place for 30-40 minutes to nearly double in volume. Preheat the oven to 400°F/210°C.

Before you put the rolls in the oven, make a shallow slash in the top of each. Bake in the lower third of the oven for 20-25 minutes or until the bottoms sound hollow when you tap them. Cool on a rack.
Makes 16.

FATTOUSH
Vegetable and herb salad with toasted pieces of bread

1 large cucumber, chopped
5 tomatoes, chopped
10 scallions/spring onions, chopped
1 small green pepper, chopped
1 tablespoon chopped parsley
1 tablespoon chopped coriander leaves, optional
1/2 tablespoons chopped fresh mint
1 clove garlic, crushed
6 tablespoons olive oil
juice of 2 lemons
1/2 teaspoon salt
1/4 teaspoon black pepper
2 pita, toasted and broken into small pieces

Prepare all the vegetables and make sure the herbs are chopped very fine. Put them into a large salad bowl, add the oil, lemon juice, salt and pepper, and toss well. Chill until ready to serve, and at the last minute stir in the toasted pieces of bread.
Serves 5 or 6.

◆ Fattoush,
vegetable
and herb
salad with
pieces of
toasted
pita.

CHAPTER 5

TRADITIONAL DISHES

◆ *Go east young man and bring back a warm, fragrant pot of cholent. Weekends are made for take-aways and if you bring your own pot, there are many restaurants that will fill it for you.*

Israel's two most dominant culinary traditions, European and Sephardic/Arab, meet and blend in the casserole. The Jewish observance of the Sabbath, when cooking is forbidden, and the Arab penchant for

◆ *A view of*

Mea She'arim,

Jerusalem's

orthodox

Jewish

quarter.

slow cooking have led to a comfortable convergence. Casseroles are one of the pillars of Israeli cuisine. By casseroles I mean dishes which require a whole night of cooking in a very low oven, dishes of lamb and chicken which are the staples of North African cuisine, and Arab meat dishes brought to table in large bowls.

From nightfall on Friday, Jews are not allowed to use electricity or to light a fire, which means that all the Sabbath food has to be prepared in advance or put in a warm oven overnight. Food is the main attraction of the Sabbath. Israelis never work on Saturdays and, since orthodox Jews are forbidden to drive, most of the day is spent at home. Special Sabbath dishes have been devised over the centuries, dishes that do not compromise taste and appeal for the sake of observance, but by the very nature of the slow cooking process most of them are heavy and substantial.

Meat and potatoes in a special stew called *cholent* are the trademark of Eastern European Jews. Spicy chicken and lamb *tagines* are typical of Moroccan Jews. *Jihnoon* and *kubbaneh*, which are dough-based, are part of Yemenite Jewish cuisine. All of them go into the oven on Friday night, to be consumed during the Sabbath. The Yemenites start earlier than others; *kubbaneh*, a spongy, spicy bread, is eaten for breakfast, to be joined later by *jihnoon*.

As a rule of thumb, slow-cooked food is usually eaten slowly. There is nothing fresh or crisp or sparkling about it, and there is no point in eating it quickly. Strong Turkish coffee and tea with mint are served with it.

Arab and Jewish traditional cooking are alike in their refusal to allow any change in the role of women as cooks and servants. The Israeli who returns from temple expecting his food to be on the table has much in

◆ *Entrance*

to a public

bath house

in Mea

She'arim.

common with the Arab who never enters the kitchen and never offers to help. While orthodox Jews demand their food and do nothing except pray over it and eat it, Arab men are in charge once the food actually reaches the table. An Arab woman never leaves the kitchen during a meal, whether her husband is dining alone or with guests. Women and children invariably eat in the kitchen. Out front, in the dining room, the Arab man hovers around his guests. He fills their glasses. He fills their plates. He refills their plates at the slightest sign of a dent in the small mountains of rice and meat he has set before them. He urges them to eat whenever their attention wanders....

◆ *Bible class in Mea She'arim.*

Most of the recipes given in this chapter are made in pots of one kind or another. All of them are braised or stewed or baked very slowly, usually covered. They are, by their nature, food for winter. *Cholent* is a typical Eastern European dish, but it also has North African and Iraqi variants. The slow-cooking casserole has evolved wherever Jews have lived. The Morrocans eat *∂feena* and the Iraqis have *tabyeet* - both are versions of *cholent*.

Cholent and its relatives are served in large pots cosily placed in the center of the table so that the whole family can help themselves and come back for more. They are the focus of social occasions. A clear soup, vegetables, condiments and pickles are usually served with them.

A place of honor is reserved for *couscous*, the national dish of Morocco. *Couscous* is also popular in Algeria and Tunisia, and in Paris, where *couscous* joints have long provided bargain meals for students and tourists. *Couscous* and its accompanying condiments and salads were brought to Israel by North African Jews in the 1950s, and the genre continues to flourish.

◆ *A heder or classroom for little boys in Mea She'arim.*

The word *couscous*, as used above, describes a combination of steamed grain, stewed meat (usually lamb), poultry or fish, and vegetables, or sometimes only steamed grain and vegetables. The grain itself is also called *couscous*, and the hourglass-shaped vessel in which the dish is traditionally cooked is called a *couscousier*. When the *couscous* grain is taken from the steamer part of the *couscous-ier*, fluffed up, heaped on a platter and decorated with fragrant stew, the result is wonderfully satisfying, addictive even. Craig Claiborne has called *couscous* "one of the dozen greatest dishes in the world."

◆ *A couscousier,*

the authentic

vessel in which

to cook

couscous.

Couscous is usually served in a flat bowl or deep plate so that you can pour the stew broth over it. Flat *pita* bread is torn into pieces and used to scoop up the grain and stew, and then to mop up the juices in the bottom of the bowl. The condiment most frequently eaten with *couscous* is a paste based on red chili peppers called *harissa*. Moroccan cooks will diligently wash, drain and rake *couscous* with their bare hands for 20 to 30 minutes to add moisture and also get rid of any lumps. Then they steam it in a *couscousier*, toss it in cold salted water, and steam it again. There is a purpose to all this: the grains become remarkably fluffy and absorb the flavors from the vapors that rise from the stew bubbling beneath. But *couscous* does not have to be a career. You can buy quick cooking *couscous* from most specialty food stores and delicatessens.

Although most of the recipes in this chapter are not uniquely Israeli, they symbolize the way in which Jews from different cultures have assimilated here. It seems that food is the great glue that keeps us together.

TRADITIONAL DISHES

◆ *A crock of*

gold.

Cholent

is a meal in

itself.

Recipes

COUSCOUS WITH LAMB

3 lbs/1.5kg lamb, cut into chunks
1 tablespoon salt
1 teaspoon freshly ground black pepper
4 whole cloves, or 1/4 teaspoon ground cloves
1 teaspoon turmeric
2 bay leaves
4 large carrots (2 diced and 2 sliced)
4 onions (2 diced and 2 sliced)
2 sticks celery, chopped
12 pints/5.5 liters water
1 small cabbage, sliced
2 zucchini/courgettes, cut into bite-size pieces
2 turnips, cubed
10 oz/275g pumpkin, cut into large cubes
1/2 cup/75g raisins
2 lbs/900g quick-cooking couscous
1 lb/450g cooked chickpeas, drained

◆ *Moroccan carrot salad is a traditional complement to couscous. See recipe page 34.*

Put the lamb, salt, pepper, cloves, turmeric, bay leaves, diced carrots, diced onions and chopped celery into a *couscousier* or pan wide and deep enough to support a steamer or colander, and cover with water. Bring to a boil, lower the heat, and simmer for nearly 1 hour, or until the lamb is tender.

Pour the broth/stock through a strainer and reserve. Remove the meat from the strainer and reserve. Discard the vegetables.

Clean the *couscousier* or pan and return the reserved broth to it. Now add the sliced carrots, sliced onions, cabbage, zucchini, turnips, pumpkin and raisins. Partially cover the pan, and simmer for 5 minutes, or until the vegetables are tender. Meanwhile cook the *couscous* according to the directions on the packet. Add the reserved lamb and the drained chickpeas to the broth, then place the *couscous* container over the broth and turn up the heat so that the steam from the broth rises through the *couscous*. Steam for 20 minutes or according to directions, then heap the *couscous* onto a serving platter or onto individual plates and arrange the meat and vegetables on top. Spoon over a small amount of broth, and serve the rest in a jug. Serve with moroccan carrot salad (see recipe p. 34).

Serves 10 to 12.

◆ *Moroccan couscous with lamb. The golden semolina grains can be topped with all manner of broths and stews - lamb, chicken, fish and vegetables.*

ASHKENAZI CHOLENT

A layered hotpot of beans, chicken, marrow bones, dumpling and potatoes

12 medium potatoes
2 tablespoons salt
8oz/ 225g dry lima/butter beans
8oz/ 225g red kidney or adzuki beans
4 large onions, sliced
2 tablespoons vegetable oil
5 beef marrow bones
2 lbs/900g beef shoulder, cut into large cubes
1 cup/225g barley, washed
2 tablespoons sugar
2 tablespoons water
salt and pepper

CHOLENT KUGEL
1 onion, sliced
mixture of vegetable oil, margarine
& chicken fat
flour
slice of challah *bread (see recipe p. 90), soaked*
in water then squeezed dry
chicken soup powder
salt and pepper
1 egg, beaten
water

Peel the potatoes and soak them in water, with the 2 tablespoons salt, for 2 hours. Soak the beans in unsalted water for 2 hours, then drain them and season with salt and pepper. Season the marrow bones and beef with salt and pepper.

To make the kugel, sauté the onion in the oil/margarine/chicken fat, stir into the flour, add the *challah*, soup powder, salt and pepper, and knead to an elastic dough with the egg and water, adding more water if necessary. Roll the dough into a log shape, put it into a roasting bag, and prick a few holes in the bag.

In a large deep pan, sauté the 4 large onions in the oil. Remove from the heat and add, layered in the following order, the beans, the marrow bones and beef, the barley, the kugel in its roasting bag, and the potatoes.

Melt the sugar in a little water, turn up the heat and cook until the sugar turns dark brown. Stir in 2 tablespoons water, and immediately pour over the *cholent*. Add just enough water to cover all the ingredients, bring to a boil, and simmer briskly for 30 minutes. Cover the pan and transfer to a very low oven to cook overnight.

The *cholent* kugel is usually served separately from the *cholent*, cut into slices like a cake. The cholent kugel mixture can also be used to stuff calf's intestines, to create the famous *kishke*, or chicken necks.

Serves 6 to 8.

◆ *All the*

ingredients

for a fine

cholent.

SEPHARDIC CHOLENT

A layered hotpot of beans, meat, potatoes and eggs

12 medium potatoes
2 tablespoons salt
1 lb/450g dry lima/butter beans
salt and pepper
4 large onions, finely chopped
3 tablespoons vegetable oil
1 - 2 lbs/0.5-1.0kg beef, cut into slices
2 lbs/1kg calf's foot, cut into slices
3 small onions, unpeeled
10 hard-boiled eggs in their shells

Pare the potatoes and soak them in water, with the 2 tablespoons salt, for 2 hours. Soak the beans in unsalted water for 2 hours, then drain them and season with salt and pepper. In a large deep pan, sauté the onion in the oil. Remove from the heat and add, in layers, first the beans, then the sliced beef and calf's foot, then the unpeeled onions, then the whole, soaked potatoes, and lastly the hard-boiled eggs. Add just enough water to cover all the ingredients. Bring to a boil and simmer briskly, uncovered, for 30 minutes. Then cover the pan and transfer to a very low oven to cook overnight.

Serves 6 to 8.

DFEENA

Beef stew with calf's foot, hard-boiled eggs, potatoes and pulses. A Morrocan-Jewish version of *cholent*, eaten on festive occasions

1 calf's foot
2 large onions, finely chopped
vegetable oil
2 lbs/1kg stewing beef, cubed
6 small potatoes
6 eggs in their shells, well scrubbed
1 1/2-2lbs/350-450g chickpeas or
navy/harivot beans, soaked overnight
2 cloves garlic, crushed
1 teaspoon ground allspice
salt and freshly ground black pepper

Blanch the calf's foot in boiling water and drain. Fry the onions in oil until they are soft and golden.

Put these and the rest of the ingredients into a large ovenproof pot or casserole with a tight-fitting lid. Cover with water, put the lid on, and cook for 1 hour at 375°F/190°C. Then lower the oven temperature to the lowest setting and continue to cook for several hours, or overnight. Serves 6 to 8.

Note: If you are using beans rather than the more traditional chickpeas, do not add salt until the beans are tender - adding it before seems to prevent them softening.

CHICKEN SOUP WITH KNEIDLACH

Traditional Jewish chicken soup
with dumplings

3 lbs/1.5kg chicken, whole or in pieces, with feet
6 cups/1.5 liters water
2 medium onions, peeled
1 small head celery, chopped
4 carrots, scraped and chopped into thick pieces
pinch paprika
salt and pepper
bunch parsley

KNEIDLACH

1 1/2 cups/ 175g matzo flour
1 cup/ 225ml cold water
3 eggs
1 tablespoon oil
salt, black pepper

Immerse the chicken feet in boiling water for a few seconds and remove the outer skin. Then put the chicken or chicken pieces into a large saucepan, with the feet, and add the water and onions. Bring to a boil, then turn down the heat, cover, and simmer gently for 1 hour. Now add the onions, celery, carrots and other ingredients. Continue to simmer, with the lid on, for another 45 minutes or until the chicken is tender. Pour the broth through a strainer, skim off the fat, adjust the seasoning and return the vegetables to the soup. The chicken can be used for salad or served separately, cut up, with the soup.

To make the *kneidlach*, knead all the ingredients to a smooth dough, cover, and refrigerate overnight. Boil 1 gallon/3 liters water to which 2 tablespoons salt have been added. Roll the dough into balls the size of ping pong balls and cook in the boiling water for 30 minutes - use a slotted spoon to slide them in. Leave the *kneidlach* in the water, keeping hot, until you are ready to serve.

A bowl of grandma's chicken soup is always welcome, but instead of *kneidlach* you could add boiled rice, vermicelli, blanched vegetables or homemade soup checks (see recipe below).

SOUP CHECKS

pinch salt
1 tablespoon oil
4 eggs, well beaten
all-purpose/plain flour
oil for deep frying

Whip/whisk the salt and oil into the eggs, then add flour a tablespoon at a time until you have a soft, smooth dough - don't add too much flour or the dough will be too dry. Roll out the dough on a floured surface until it is pasta-thin. Cut into strips, then into squares of uniform size. Heat the oil. Fry a few squares at a time until they are crisp and golden. Drain on paper towels/kitchen paper. Allow to cool, then store in an airtight container until the grandchildren pay a visit.

◆ *Chicken soup with soup checks, a marriage between Jewish tradition and Israeli invention.*

KUBBANEH
Steamed sweet rolls

1 oz/25g yeast, fresh or dried
2 tablespoons sugar
1/4 cup/60ml lukewarm water
4 cups and 2 tablespoons/500g all-purpose/plain flour
3/4 tablespoon salt
1 cup/225ml water
2 tablespoons margarine

Combine the yeast, sugar, and water in a small bowl, cover with a clean towel and leave in a warm place for about 10 minutes for the yeast to work.

Sift the flour and the salt into a large mixing bowl, make a well in the middle and pour in the yeast mixture. Knead, gradually adding water, until the dough loses its stickiness. Cover with a towel, put in a warm place and allow to rise for about 15 minutes. Knead again.

Dissolve the margarine in a medium large saucepan which has a tightly fitting lid. Make sure the sides of the saucepan are coated with margarine.

Divide the dough into five portions. Wet your hands and roll each portion into a ball. Put the balls into the saucepan - the margarine will prevent them sticking together. Cover and cook over a very low heat until the balls of dough expand. Now slide an asbestos sheet under the saucepan and continue cooking over a medium low heat until they turn golden yellow and their tops are baked and not sticky. Turn off the heat.

Serve hot, turned upside down. Slice like cake. Serves 5. Serve on Sabbath mornings with *hilbeh* and *haminados* (see recipes pp. 119 and 154).

SENIYEH
A traditional Arab dish of ground meat and *tahini*

8oz/225g ground/minced beef, lamb or veal
2 tablespoons chopped parsley
2 tablespoons finely chopped onion
1 tablespoon flour
1 tablespoon vegetable oil
1/2 teaspoon zhoug (see recipe p. 39)
1/2 teaspoon salt
1/2 teaspoon pepper
2 tablepoons tahini paste
1 tablespoon lemon juice
2 tablespoons water
pine nuts, to garnish

Combine the meat with the vegetables, flour, oil, *zhoug*, salt and pepper, and press into a small, round ovenproof dish. Pre-heat the oven to 350°F/180°C.

With a fork, beat together the *tahini* paste, lemon juice and water, pour over the meat mixture and sprinkle with pine nuts. Bake for 30 minutes. Serve with salad and pickles. Serves 4.

◆ *Yemenite*

kubbaneh *with*

brown eggs

(haminados)

and hilbeh.

Kubbaneh *are*

eaten for

breakfast.

Hilbeh *is a*

relish made

from fenugreek

seeds.

MEJADARRA
Galilean Arab lentil and rice pilaf

1 lb/450g large brown lentils, soaked if
necessary
1 onion, finely chopped
3 tablespoons vegetable oil
salt and freshly ground black pepper
8 oz/225g long-grain rice, washed
1 cup/225ml water
2 onions, sliced into half-moon shapes

Generously cover the lentils with cold water and simmer until tender, removing any scum that rises and adding more water as necessary. Fry the chopped onion in half the oil until soft and golden, then add to the cooked lentils. Season with salt and pepper.

Add the rice and the extra cup of water to the lentils, cover, and simmer gently for about 20 minutes or until the rice is soft. If the rice absorbs the water too quickly, add a little more.

Fry the sliced onions in the rest of the oil until they are dark brown. Heap the rice and lentils onto a warm serving dish and garnish with the caramelized onions.

Mejadarra can be served hot or cold, with fresh yogurt. Serves 5 or 6.

◆ Mejadarra,

a classic

vegetarian

combination

of legumes

and rice,

served with

fresh yogurt.

NEW WAVE CHICKEN
Chef I. Nicolai was the father of professional cooking in Israel. This recipe, created in 1950, is typical of his work and of the style he founded.

1 chicken, weighing 3 lbs/1.5kg, cut into joints
1/2 cup/100g flour
5 tablespoons vegetable oil
1 cup/100g olives, pitted/stoned
12 cloves garlic, peeled
1 small head celery, diced
1/2 teaspoon black peppercorns
1 teaspoon dried tarragon
4 tomatoes, cut into quarters
salt
pinch ground ginger
3 tablespoons cognac
1/2 cup/100ml white wine
3 oranges, sliced fine

Dip the chicken joints in the flour and shake off the excess. In a large skillet/frying pan heat the oil and fry the joints, turning them occasionally so that they lightly brown on all sides.

Boil 2 cups/450ml water in a small saucepan and add the olives; bring to a boil, then drain and reserve the olives. Blanch 11 of the cloves of garlic in the same way, allowing them to boil for 3 minutes before draining them. Crush the other clove of garlic.

Add all the garlic, olives, celery, peppercorns, tarragon, tomatoes, salt and ginger to the skillet and continue frying for 30 minutes. Now add the sliced oranges. Heat the wine and cognac in a small saucepan, pour over the chicken and set a match to it. Serve immediately with fresh salad, brown bread and fruity white wine. Serves 4.

◆ *A version*

of chicken

with olives,

tarragon and

cognac.

KUGEL
Savoury noodle pudding traditional
among Eastern European Jews

8 oz/225g thin vermicelli
1/2 cup/100ml vegetable oil
1/2 cup/100g sugar
salt
1 1/2 teaspoons freshly ground black pepper
3 eggs, lightly beaten

Preheat the oven to 350°F/180°C. Cook the vermicelli in salted water until it is tender, then drain well and set aside. In a medium saucepan, heat the oil and add the sugar. Cook over a very low heat, stirring constantly, for about 10 minutes or until the mixture turns very dark, almost black. Immediately stir in the spaghetti, salt, pepper and beaten eggs. Taste to see if the mixture is peppery enough. If not, add more pepper. Place in a greased tube pan and bake, uncovered, for at least 1 1/2 hours, or until golden brown on top.

Remove the kugel from the oven and unmold it by turning it upside down on a plate. Serve slices with meat, salad or pickles. Other versions with raisins, onions or both are also popular, traditionally served after *cholent*.

◆ *Kugel*

in a pot,

waiting

its turn

after the

cholent.

HILBEH
Fenugreek relish, an exotic addition to
soups, excellent for health and stamina

2 tablespoons ground fenugreek seeds
1 fresh tomato, cut into quarters
1/2 teaspoon freshly ground black pepper
2 teaspoons zhoug (see recipe p. 39)

Soak the *zhoug* in cold water for 2 hours, then pour off excess water. Using a blender, mix all the other ingredients together, then whip/whisk until fluffy.

◆ *Kugel*

served with

pickles.

VEGETABLES

◆ *A colorful*

display of

summer

and winter

squash.

To city-dwelling Israelis, in Jerusalem, Tel Aviv and Haifa, working the land is a romantic, even noble occupation. They like to refer to Israel not as plain Israel but as "the land of Israel" as if annexing to

◆ *Corn*

stubble in

the fertile

Hulah Valley,

a mosquito-

infested

marsh before

it was

drained by

the early

settlers.

themselves the romance and nobility of the agricultural way of life. In truth, a very small proportion of Israelis lead this life today. Their lot is the city, an overwhelming density of traffic, and nowhere to park.

To Israel's early settlers agriculture was a necessity. Dreamers were not welcome; they were unproductive. And yet it was the dreamers who saw in an apple not a fruit but a laboratory, not the status quo but a point of departure for bigger, juicier, firmer apples and trees which yielded bigger crops at more convenient times. Advancing the cause of apples for the good of Israel was a long, tedious process, and the same can be said of many other fruits and vegetables. But the result has been that Israel is, and always has been, a driving force in advancing the principles of modern agriculture. Necessity has taught us to achieve better crops from given plots of land.

Many regional fruit and vegetable specialties have endured down to the present time, although few of our regions now enjoy the isolation which made them regions in the first place. Grapes and apples are grown on the Golan, cereals in the Jezreel Valley and the northern Negev, oranges in the Vale of Capernaum, winter vegetables and subtropical fruits in the Jordan Valley, tomatoes and other salad vegetables in the Judean desert. Today Israel is self-sufficient in vegetables and supplies planeloads of them, out of season, to Western Europe. Many of them are grown in miles and miles of plastic tunnels.

◆ *Most of the
country's
wheat is
grown in the
sandy soil of
the northern
Negev.*

◆ *Jacob Lichansky has played a part in creating the new Israeli cuisine. He has an unfailing sense of humor and a deep understanding of vegetables and fish.*

◆ *At the experimental farm of Neve Yaar, where new vegetables and fruits are coaxed from the soil - dwarf sweet corn of various colors and mini-watermelons without seeds.*

◆ *Kaspi is a*

local grower who

supplies the hotel

and restaurant

trade. He delivers

everything from

fresh quail eggs

to ripe pine-

apples.

◆ *Shimon Shalvi of*

Nahalal holds the

record for the

largest radish ever

grown in Israel.

He refuses to

reveal his secret.

His pickles are as

incredible as his

radishes.

Thrown in among local Arab communities, with few if any utensils brought from their countries of origin, the early settlers had no choice but to adapt to local conditions. They dug clay ovens in the ground, as the Arabs did. They churned their own butter, and drank the buttermilk. They discovered which vegetables grew and which did not. They made wine out of peaches, apricots and plums. It was a vast learning experience, but its aim was survival, not self-education. They ate what they raised, and they raised what they ate. If they discovered that you get a stronger, more durable orange tree by crossing it with a lemon, they went ahead and crossed it. Their victories were hard-fought and hard-won, and they resented citification and the different morality that it represented.

Longevity is one of the attributes of those who have devoted their lives to inventive farm work. We, or rather the kibbutzim or moshavim in which they live, do not generally allow such people to ease off until they reach their seventies or eighties. Our long-lived, patient, persevering agriculturalists have adapted papayas to regions they were not meant to grow in; perfected new shapes and sizes and flavors of apples (and often named them after their grand-

◆ *Freshly pressed olive oil is checked for color, aroma and consistency. The right blend of green and black olives yields the desired quality.*

◆ *During the olive harvest the entire village of Mrar is busy with olive oil production.*

daughters); introduced celery, broccoli, brussels sprouts and Chinese cabbage to a country that was perfectly happy with ordinary cabbages, potatoes and onions; pioneered the spaghetti squash, a peculiar melon-shaped fruit that disintegrates into noodles when you cook it; taken the thorns off prickly pears, and in the process rather modified our thorny image of ourselves; and done everything possible to ensure that seasonal produce matures on a precise day, at a precise hour, in order to hit the market at precisely the right moment.

It may sound surprising, but in a country known for the quantity and quality of its fruits and vegetables, the use of fresh herbs is only just beginning to catch on. Various ethnic groups have always used coriander and mint, but until recently neither of these herbs was grown commercially. Fresh herbs such as parsley, basil, oregano, tarragon, chives and sage are now available at most good produce stores, although they are still viewed with some suspicion. Nevertheless the appearance of a range of fresh herbs is a clear signal that a new culinary age has dawned. They suggest that hamburgers and processed foods may be in retreat.

◆ *Tomatoes are sorted according to size and quality before they are crated and shipped.*

$\mathscr{V}$ EGETABLES

◆ *Israeli*

salad is an

adaptation

of an earlier

Arab dish.

Recipes

AVOCADO WITH TAHINI YOGURT

1 cup/225ml plain yogurt
1/3 cup/80ml tahini paste
1/2 teaspoon ground cumin
pinch ground coriander
1/4 teaspoon finely chopped garlic
1 tablespoon lemon juice
1/4 teaspoon salt
1/4 teaspoon pepper
pinch cayenne pepper
3 ripe avocadoes
1/2 cup/100g flaked almonds, toasted

Beat the yogurt into the *tahini*, then add the spices, herbs, and seasonings. Blend well, cover and refrigerate. Peel the avocados a few minutes before serving, halving them lengthwise and removing the pits/stones. Thinly slice each half lengthwise and fan out the slices on individual plates. Spoon the yogurt dressing over them and sprinkle with toasted almonds. Serves 6.

Note: When preparing avocados, squeeze a little lemon juice into a bowl of water and dip the avocados into it as you peel or slice them. This will prevent the flesh turning an unappetizing grey-black.

◆ *Avocado and pomegranate salad. Israel and the avocado are almost synonymous. In fact avocados have now outstripped oranges as our top export.*

AVOCADO & POMEGRANATE SALAD

2 ripe avocados
1 pomegranate
4 oz/100g black grapes
lemon juice
water

DRESSING

1 teaspoon sugar
4 tablespoons white wine vinegar
2 tablespoons corn oil
1 tablespoon groundnut oil
4 tablespoons chopped mint
salt and pepper

Peel the avocados, remove the pits/stones, and slice into thick half rings. Drop the rings into a bowl containing water and lemon juice–this will prevent them turning black.

Cut the pomegranate in half and crush it over a bowl to remove and collect the seeds. Wash the grapes and mix them with the pomegranate seeds. Drain the avocado pieces and add them to the fruit.

To make the dressing, put all the ingredients into a glass jar, screw the lid on firmly and shake vigorously for 2 minutes. Pour over the avocado and fruit. Toss well before serving. Serves 4 to 6.

FRIED EGGPLANT SALAD

2 lbs/900g eggplants/aubergines
2 tablespoons coarse salt
1 cup/100g flour
oil for deep frying
1/2 cup/100ml white vinegar
4 oz/100g chili peppers, assorted colors, seeded
and finely sliced
6 cloves garlic, finely chopped
2 or 3 tablespoons water

Cut the eggplants, unpeeled, into slices 1/2 inch/1cm thick. Put them in a colander and sprinkle them with salt. Leave for 30 minutes to drain, then squeeze out excess moisture. Dust the pieces sparingly with flour and deep-fry in hot oil.

In a large bowl, mix the vinegar with the chili peppers and garlic, and add 2 or 3 tablespoons of water. Add the hot slices of eggplant and mix gently. Allow to cool, then pack into glass jars, seal and refrigerate. This salad can be eaten freshly made, but it improves with keeping.

SPAGETTI SQUASH WITH EGGPLANT & SESAME

1 large eggplant/aubergine
3 tablespoons olive oil
3 lbs/1.5kg cooked spaghetti squash
1/2 cup/100g sesame seeds
2 tablespoons butter
3 cloves garlic, minced
salt and pepper to taste
1 cup/100g grated Parmesan cheese

Pre-heat oven to 450°F/230°C. Top and tail the eggplant, cut it into 8 slices lengthwise and sprinkle with salt. Allow to drain for 20 minutes, then squeeze out excess moisture and pat dry. Brush with olive oil and place, in a single layer, on a baking sheet. Bake for 15-20 minutes or until the slices begin to soften.

To prepare the spaghetti squash, cut the squash in half, discard the seeds, and boil for about 20 minutes. Rinse under cold water to loosen the "spaghetti" and drain well. Lightly toast the sesame seeds, taking care not to let them singe. Dip the eggplant slices in the seeds, then roll them up with a spoonful of Parmesan inside. Heat the butter in a large skillet/frying pan and fry the garlic for 2 minutes. Carefully stir in the spaghetti squash, season with salt and pepper, and add the rest of the Parmesan.

Transfer to a warm serving dish, arrange the rolled eggplant slices on top and serve immediately.

◆ *Spaghetti squash undergoing further development at Neve Yaar.*

◆ *Spaghetti squash with eggplant & sesame.*

MEDITERRANEAN SALAD

6 tablespoons olive oil
1 large clove garlic, minced
1 teaspoon cumin seeds, crushed
1/4 cup/60ml fresh lemon juice
4 large tomatoes, cut into wedges, then halved
2 medium zucchini/courgettes, sliced into thin rounds
2 medium green bell peppers, cut into bite size squares
2 small onions, chopped
4 oz/100g black olives, pitted
4 tablespoons chopped parsley
salt and freshly ground black pepper

Heat the oil in a large, heavy skillet/frying pan, but do not allow it to smoke. Add the garlic and cumin and fry for 2 minutes until the cumin releases its fragrance. Remove from the heat and cool to room temperature. Stir in the lemon juice.

Combine the tomatoes, zucchini, peppers, onions, olives and parsley in a large bowl. Add the dressing and toss well. Season with salt and pepper. Cover and refrigerate. Serve chilled. Serves 12.

◆ *An old olive press in the Druze village of Mrar.*

ISRAELI SALAD

For this you need good vegetables, good olive oil and the ability to enjoy the simple things in life.

2 large tomatoes
2 cucumbers
1 large onion
4 tablespoons finely chopped parsley
1/2 lemon
1/4 cup/60 ml superb olive oil
salt and black pepper to taste
chopped fresh mint, optional

Dice the vegetables with a very sharp knife - they should be cut very small and evenly. Red cabbage, green bell pepper or garlic can be added to the standard recipe given above, but only one deviation is allowed at a time! Squeeze and strain the lemon juice over the vegetables, then add the other ingredients. Toss well before serving.

PICKLED CUCUMBERS

2-4 lbs/0.9-1.8kg baby cucumbers
fresh dill
10 cloves garlic
sea salt
water

Put a sprig or two of dill and 4 or 5 cloves of garlic in the bottom of a large glass jar, then pack the cucumbers on top. Cover with water, measuring it into the jar. For each cup/225ml of water added, add 1 tablespoon sea salt. Add more dill and cloves of garlic, then seal. Put the jar in the sun so that the cucumbers change color.

EGGPLANT STUFFED WITH MUSHROOMS & OLIVES

2 eggplants/aubergines
1 tablespoon salt
1 tablespoon vegetable oil
1 cup/150g olives, pitted/stoned
2 onions, sliced
1 bell pepper, cut into strips
12 oz/350g baby mushrooms
3 tablespoons fresh lemon juice
3 tablespoons olive oil
2 cloves garlic, crushed
2 tablespoon chopped dill
2 tablespoon wine vinegar

Pre-heat the oven to 375°F/190°C. Cut the eggplants in half lengthwise, sprinkle with salt, and leave to drain for 20 minutes. Squeeze out the excess moisture, then place on an oiled baking sheet. Bake until they are fairly soft, then scoop out some of the flesh and reserve.

Meanwhile, boil up a little water and blanch the olives in it - do this twice to remove their saltiness. Lightly fry the onions in the vegetable oil, remove the skillet/frying pan from the heat and add the pepper strips, mushrooms, lemon juice, olive oil, garlic and vinegar. Mix well together. Mash the scooped out eggplant and add to the mixture. Divide the mixture between the four eggplant halves and put them back in the oven for 10 minutes.

Serve sprinkled with dill, accompanied by a yogurt-based sauce.

PICKLED BELL PEPPERS

1 1/2 lbs/700g green bell peppers
1 1/2 lbs/700g red bell peppers
2 1/2 cups/600ml distilled white vinegar
1 1/4 cups/275g sugar
2 1/2 cups/600ml water
8 cloves garlic
4 teaspoons vegetable oil
2 teaspoons salt
4 sprigs dill

Remove the stems and seeds from the peppers and cut into 2-inch/5-cm wide strips. Put the strips into a large bowl, cover with boiling water and allow to stand for 5 minutes. Drain well, then pack the strips into 4 pint-sized (450ml) sterilized jars, adding 2 cloves of garlic, a teaspoon of oil, a sprig of dill and 1/2 teaspoon of salt to each jar.

In a stainless steel or enamel saucepan, combine the vinegar, sugar and water, and bring to a boil. Ladle this mixture into the jars, filling them to within 1/4 inch/0.5cm of the top. Wipe the tops of the jars with a damp cloth and put the lids on.

Place the jars in a deep saucepan with a rack in the bottom and add enough water to cover the jars by 2 inches/5 cms. Bring the water to a boil and boil for 5 minutes. Remove the jars from the saucepan with tongs and allow them to cool. Store in a cool, dark place.

◆ *Eggplant*

and garlic

could be the

cure to many

of the great

problems of

our time.

STUFFED VEGETABLES

Stuffed vegetables, as a starter or a main course, are the pride of everyone who serves them. They are very Mediterranean, whether baked, poached or gently stewed in a tomato sauce. The stuffing in the next recipe is a typical one, but it can be varied by adding liver or pine nuts, or by using lamb instead of beef. If you are stuffing eggplants, remember to salt and drain them first.

◆ *Assorted stuffed vegetables - onion, zucchini, eggplant, and red pepper.*

◆ *Eggplant stuffed with mushrooms, olives, red pepper and onion.*

STUFFED ONIONS

2 large onions
2 oz/60g butter
water
2 tablespoons lemon or lime juice

STUFFING
8 oz/225 lean beef, ground/minced
3 oz/80g rice, washed thoroughly and drained
2 tablespoons finely chopped parsley
1 teaspoon salt
1/2 teaspoon black pepper
1/2 teaspoon ground allspice

Peel the onions. With a sharp knife, make a cut in each one from top to bottom on one side, cutting toward the center. Cook the onions in boiling water for about 45 minutes or until the layers detach easily. Drain and leave until cool enough to handle.

Meanwhile, knead together all the stuffing ingredients to a smooth, well blended consistency.

Carefully separate the layers of onion. Into the hollow of each layer put 1 tablespoon of stuffing, more for the outer layers, less for the inner. Roll up each layer into a little parcel and tie with a piece of thread. Pre-heat the oven to 350°F/180°C.

Melt the butter in a skillet/frying pan and sauté the onion parcels, a few at a time, turning occasionally, until they are a light golden color. When all the parcels have been sautéed, pack them tightly into an shallow oiled ovenproof dish and pour in just enough boiling water to cover them by 1/2-inch/1cm or so. Sprinkle with the lemon or lime juice and cover.

Bake in the oven for about 1 hour or until the meat is cooked. Serve with fresh salad or boiled potatoes. Serves 4 to 6.

STREET FOOD

◆ Falafel

fried in the

traditional

manner.

The patties

are shaped

with a special

implement

which is also

used to slip

them into the

hot oil.

A lot of eating out in Israel is done standing up. The sit-down restaurant-type meal has only recently evolved, for in many ways we are still an eat-it-while-you-can society. We are obsessive, short-tempered, driven, on the move. We have a need to consume quickly, to eat and run. Leisure is not part of the Israeli lifestyle.

Nothing more clearly reveals this fact than the roaring trade done by restaurants and snack stands at gas stations. Most countries provide food and refreshment at gas stations, usually of the franchised, fast-food variety, but in Israel roadside culinary attractions are more ambitious. While the tank is being filled and the oil is being checked, you are invited to consume - quickly

of course - a sample of *mezze*, grilled meat or fish, or something in the dessert line. The quality is comparable to that of most average restaurants serving similar food. Do not expect gourmet. Do not expect fancy. When you stop in the middle of the desert on your way to Eilat, do not think *haute cuisine*. Think adequate. And you will be pleasantly surprised.

Gas station dining is now such an institution that we eat in gas stations even when we are not in the car. We walk there, treading gingerly around the oil slicks and gas puddles. We sit down. We order off a paper

◆ Mezze *are calculated to make gourmands of the most dedicated gourmets!*

napkin or off the wall. And the food arrives at a furious pace, whole trayfuls of it. Could we survive without *pita* bread? Probably not. Here it is, any way you want it - warmed over, grilled to a crispy cracker, cut open and toasted. Here comes the *mezze* selection - a dozen small plates of dips and salads and pickles. As the pumps ring, we scoop up their colorful contents with our *pita* bread. Knives and forks only slow you down. Sweet Turkish coffee to finish. With the last gulp, we move off. We do not linger. Traffic continues to pour in.

◆ *Turko is a*
borekas
vendor in
HaCarmel
market.
He fills his
borekas *with*
whatever his
customers
want.

◆ *A*
sunflower
seed
vendor on
his rounds
during a
soccer
game.

When leisure is not a part of life, food tends to be consumed rather than enjoyed, and Israel is not noted for its leisure time. So far, the need to eat and run has found many admirable solutions. Perhaps, when we slow down a bit, we will be less rough and ready, but never more colorful.

Pedestrians are exposed to other kinds of street food. The king - by popular consent - is *falafel*, fried patties made from chickpeas, herbs and spices crammed into *pita* bread with salads and relishes. Israel has contributed much to the course of *falafel*. It was here, ready and waiting, when we needed a national food. A newly created state, a toddler nation, what were we to eat that we could call our own? *Falafel*. It mattered little that *falafel* was an Arab invention, that it had existed longer than Israel and Israelis. We needed something, and *falafel* was it. Nutritious, tasty, spicy, quick and easy to prepare and plentiful at street corners. Colorful, photogenic *falafel* stands, manned by boisterous, aggressive vendors stuffing half or whole pockets of *pita* bread full to bursting with hot, round, fragrant patties, various salads and deep-fried potatoes dipped in batter - what could be better? The whole package was then handed to the customer, who proceeded to add the condiments of his choice from an array of large containers on a tray. All-round favorites were *harissa* (hot pepper paste) and *tahini* (savoury sesame seed paste), watery and diluted so that they trickled and flowed through the contents of the *pita* pocket, down your arm and into your sleeve...You ate leaning forward slightly, so that whatever dropped did not stain your shirt or land on your shoes.

That was then. In those days *falafel* was judged by its texture and taste, by the way the crushed chickpeas yielded to the teeth, by whether it was mild and restrained - the tamed Ashkenazi variety - or hot and spicy - the genuine Sephardic kind. The salads had to be fresh, the *pita* warm from the oven, the condiments fiery, aggressive and reeking of cumin.

◆ *Still life*
with
sunflower.
Sunflower
seeds are
high on
Israeli
shopping
lists.

That has all gone now. If you search hard, in Arab villages and along country roads, you may still stumble on an old-fashioned *falafel* stand. But you have to know where to look, and when you get there it may have disappeared. Today's *falafel* joints are huge hangars in which all the components are laid out like the ammunition of a fighter plane. Today *falafel* is about quantity, not

quality. Competition is fierce. Arab vendors, who prepare better *falafel* than anyone else, are confined to their own trading areas.

For the price of one *falafel*, you are allowed any number of refills, so really the *pita* pocket is all you pay for. We seem to have devised a way of having our *falafel* and eating it. But there is something demeaning about the free *falafel* economy. The sky-high piles of pickled cabbage and salad and assorted pickles, and the precariously balanced heaps of cold patties, are hardly inviting. Street food should be sensual, oily, noisy and satisfying. But by encouraging us to pig out on multiple, self-served refills, the *falafel* industry has set back the cause of street food. I want my *falafel* man to fill my *pita* himself. He knows his patties, his salads and his hot stuffs. As he assembles the package, he signs it with a seal of quality. He is a proud craftsman. He would not sell me cold patties or stale potatoes. By removing *falafel* from his supervision, we rob him of his art.

Which brings me to the lynchpin and sine qua non of the *falafel*, the *pita*. Whatever you do with a *pita*, it is always a meal. Even when we eat at a table, we Israelis would rather have our food in a *pita* than on a plate. The small *pita* is the most common, but a larger one, commonly called the Iraqi *pita* since

◆ *Jerusalem mixed grill is a whole meal in a* pita. *Chicken spleens, livers, hearts and spices are some of the ingredients.*

146

it was introduced by Iraqi Jews, is also popular. It does not have a pocket, so its role is limited to scooping up *hummus* and similar delicacies, and wrapping. There is a suburb of Tel Aviv, well known for its culinary offerings, which is big on Iraqi *pita*. When you order your favorite meal on a skewer, the grill man will place your skewer on a hot Iraqi *pita*, fold it once and pull the skewer expertly out, leaving the meat in place. He then opens the *pita*, adds *tahini* or *harissa*, a salad or french fries, and re-folds it in such a manner that it will not leak or break as you eat it. Folding an Iraqi *pita* is an art in itself.

The Tunisian answer to *falafel* is the *brik*, a crusty little triangle of *filo* dough filled with cheese or potato. In fact the *brik* is a cousin of the larger *boreka,* which plays a strong second to *falafel*. Today *borekas* are mass produced and franchised by a central bakery, but not so long ago vendors would fill a *boreka* in front of your very eyes and offer vegetables and a brown egg with it.

A lot of our street food moves. Since Israel is a small country and mostly flat, you can cover it quite easily with a pushcart. Fruit and vegetables, especially watermelons, are sold from the back of horse-drawn carts. Step out in your pajamas to meet the roving watermelon man! But gone are the days when small carts pushed by children brought prickly pears to the door. We used to buy them already peeled and almost thornless and eat them then and there.

Warm local bagels are still sold on street corners, but there are few vendors today who will freely and happily give you their home-mixed *za'atar*, a salty mixture of spices, hyssop and other herbs. They hide it and you have to ask for it. But once upon a time little cornets of *za'atar* done up in newspaper were openly displayed and you helped yourself. You dipped your chewy bagel into the *za'atar* between each bite.

A combination of the Israeli sweet tooth and the hot, humid climate is chiefly responsible for two other street food relics: the *tamarindi* seller and the *malabi* cart. *Tamarindi* is a sweet, syrupy beverage derived from the tamarind fruit and it is poured from a jar carried on the vendor's shoulder. *Malabi* is a dessert, a white, caramel-like custard sold in small tin cups. Since the mixture is practically tasteless, it is sold with a choice of syrups. You select a syrup flavor and the vendor splashes a generous amount of it into the little cup and hands it to you with a spoon. His little cart is totally self-contained catering unit. It has a bed of ice for the *malabi* to stand in, and a small water tank and faucet for washing out the empty cups. More than any other form of street food, the *malabi* cart is a magnet for a strange mixture of clients. Hurrying mechanics

and well-groomed businessmen flock around it, happily absorbing the contents of the little cups. *Malabi* is hardly food. It does not nourish or allay hunger. It is a dessert through and through. You only eat it because you are addicted to it.

◆ *A large*

Iraqi pita

used to

wrap a

kebab,

hummus,

mango

chutney

and

cabbage.

$\mathscr{S}$ TREET FOOD

$\mathscr{R}ecipes$

FALAFEL

1 cup/225g dried chickpeas
5 cups/1.2 liters water
1 teaspoon baking soda
1 teaspoon salt
1 teaspoon cumin seeds
1 teaspoon coriander
1 onion, quartered
2 tablespoons minced parsley
2 cloves garlic, mashed
freshly ground black pepper
1 tablespoon lemon juice
pinch chili pepper
vegetable oil for deep frying

Soak the chickpeas in the water for 24 hours, then drain them and put them and all the other ingredients, except the oil, through a meat grinder, twice. Mix together lightly with a fork. The mixture should be loose and crumbly.

Pour 2 inches/5cm of oil into a wok or other utensil for deep frying and set over a medium low heat; the oil should be 350-375°F/180 -190°C when you put the *falafel* in.

While the oil is heating, shape the first batch of patties. Use a generous spoonful of mixture for each patty and don't be too neat about the shaping. Because the mixture is crumbly, it will only just hold together. Each patty should be about 2 1/2 inches/6cm across and 3/4 inch/2cm thick in the middle. Slide the first batch of patties into the hot oil and fry for about 4 minutes, turning at least once. Remove with a slotted spoon and drain on paper towels/kitchen paper. Repeat until all the mixture is used up. Serve as a *mezze* dish, or in *pita* bread with salads, *zhoug, tahini* and more.

JERUSALEM MIXED GRILL

4 oz/100g chicken livers
4 oz/100g chicken hearts
2 oz/60g chicken spleens
2 oz/60g turkey fries, optional
2 tablespoons oil
1 onion, sliced
3 cloves garlic, chopped
1/2 teaspoon each of salt, ground cumin,
coriander and turmeric
2 pitas, halved and warmed

Jerusalem mixed grill is not grilled but fried! Cut the livers into small pieces, and halve the hearts and spleens. Using a heavy skillet/frying pan, heat the oil and sweat the slices of onion. Add the garlic, salt and spices, and fry gently until the meat is tender. Serve in *pitas*, perhaps with a lacing of *hummus* (see recipe p. 39). Real gourmets make their mixed grills with pigeon livers, hearts, etc.

◆ Falafel *stands*

are shrines of

creativity.

You pay for a

pita *and you*

assemble your

own filling.

Pickles, zhoug

and tahini *are a*

must.

CHEESE OR SPINACH BOREKAS

8 oz/225g filo *pastry*
2/3 cup/150g melted butter
1 egg yolk, beaten with 1 tablespoon water,
to glaze
sesame seeds, to garnish

CHEESE FILLING
1/2 cup/100g soft white cheese
1 cup/225g finely grated Gruyère
2 tablespoons cream cheese
1 large or 2 small eggs, lightly beaten
salt and pepper

SPINACH FILLING
1 lb/450g fresh spinach
1 egg, lightly beaten
1 cup/225g finely grated Gruyère
salt and pepper

Remove the *filo* leaves from the refrigerator 2 hours before you need them.

To make the cheese filling, simply mash all the ingredients together with a fork or combine them in a food processor.

To make the spinach filling, wash the spinach several times, put the wet leaves into a saucepan without any extra water, cover tightly and sweat over a medium heat for 4 or 5 minutes until tender. Drain in a sieve, pressing out any excess moisture. Chop fine and combine with the egg, cheese, salt and pepper.

Pre-heat the oven to 350°F/180°C.

Taking one leaf of *filo* at a time, cut it into a strip about 6 inches/15cm wide by 12 inches/30cm long and brush with melted butter. Now fold it in half so that it is the same length but half the width. Brush with

butter again. Place a heaped tablespoon of cheese or spinach filling at one end, and fold the end over to make a triangle. Butter the top of the triangle, then fold over again. Continue until the entire strip is folded into a triangle, brushing with butter between each folding. Put the completed triangles onto a greased baking sheet and brush the tops with egg yolk and water to glaze. Sprinkle with sesame seeds.

Bake for 25-30 minutes, until golden brown and puffy. Serve warm or cold, but not hot.

Borekas can also be made with puff pastry. Just fold the pastry over the fillings and proceed as above. Although baking is the traditional method of cooking borekas, many street vendors deep-fry them. The shape of a boreka usually tells you what the filling is - triangles for cheese, squares for potatoes, twists for spinach.

◆ *Assorted*

borekas with

brown eggs

(haminados).

The fillings vary

from cheese

through spinach

to potato.

GREEN OMELET

2 eggs per person
2 tablespoons water
1 tablespoon oil, or oil and butter together
2 tablespoons finely chopped parsley
1 tablespoon finely chopped coriander
1 tablespoon finely chopped dill
2 tablespoons finely chopped watercress,
optional
salt and black pepper
pinch cumin

This can be cooked with the greenery beaten into the eggs or spread on top of the finished article.

Beat the eggs and water together first. Heat the oil in a skillet/frying pan, make sure it is really hot, then swiftly cook two very thin omelets, turning them so that they cook on both sides. Serve in a brown bread roll with lettuce and a few slices of tomato.

HAMINADOS
Brown eggs

12 eggs
skins of 2 lbs/1kg onions
1 tablespoon flour

Put the eggs in a casserole of cold water, with the onion skins. Bring to a boil and cook for 30 minutes. Mix the flour with a little water, smear the mixture around the rim of the casserole, put the lid on, and put in a very low oven - 120°F/45°C - overnight. The flour makes a perfect seal. Serve with *borekas* and *hummus*.

◆ Borekas

served with

drinking

yogurt and

a brown

egg.

FRIED KIBBEH
Lamb and cracked wheat patties

1 1/2 cups/350g fine bulgur wheat/
cracked wheat
8 oz/225g lean lamb, minced three times
1 onion, minced
3/4 teaspoon curry powder
1/4 teaspoon ground allspice
1/4 teaspoon ground cinnamon
1/4 teaspoon paprika or cayenne
salt and pepper
1/4 cup/60ml olive oil

FILLING
8oz/225g ground/minced meat
3 tablespoons water
1 onion, chopped
2 tablespoons oil
1 teaspoon pine nuts, optional
black pepper and salt to taste
pinch allspice and cinnamon

Soak the bulgur in cold water for 10 minutes, then drain in a fine sieve and squeeze out the excess moisture.

Now combine the lamb, onion, curry powder, allspice, cinnamon, paprika or cayenne, salt and pepper with the soaked bulgur and knead to a smooth, even consistency (if you moisten your hands occasionally, the mixture will not stick to them).

To make the filling, knead the meat and water together, fry the onions in the oil until golden brown, then add the meat and the rest of the ingredients. Fry until fairly dry and crumbly. Chill.

Now form the bulgur mixture into sausages 4 inches/10cm long, and make a hollow in the middle with your finger - wet your finger so that the mixture does not stick. Fill the hollows with the crumbly meat mixture, and pinch the ends together.

(cont'd next page)

Heat the oil in a large, heavy skillet/frying pan until it is hot but not smoking, and fry the *kibbeh* for 3 or 4 minutes on each side or until they begin to color. Transfer them to a warm serving dish with a slotted spoon. Serves 6.

TUNISIAN SANDWICH

4 lemons
1 tablespoon coarse salt
1/2 teaspoon turmeric
2 potatoes
4 long brown loaves or 2 small baguettes
harissa (see recipe p. 41)
1 tomato, diced
1 cucumber, diced
1 onion, finely chopped
2 tablespoons capers
8 oz/225g canned tuna
4 oz/100g black olives

At the sandwich stand, they always seem to work very slowly, considering deeply such matters as proportion, tactics and the order of things. This is what sandwich selling is all about.

First you prepare 3 of the lemons, by slicing them, soaking them in cold water for 5 hours, boiling them, draining them, covering them with water again, adding salt and turmeric, and boiling again. Then you cut each slice into 4 triangles and add the juice of the fourth lemon. Then you boil the potatoes until they are soft, after which you drain and peel them, and cut them into 1/2-inch/1-cm cubes. Now you cut the loaves in half lengthwise, leaving a hinge of crust on one side, spread each half with *harissa* and pile in the lemons, potatoes, vegetables, capers, tuna, olives and lemons again.

◆ *Tunisian sandwich, a "hero sandwich" with an amazing filling.*

$\mathcal{B}$ ARBECUE

◆ *A leg of*

lamb

roasting

over an

open fire.

$\mathbb{I}$sraelis are prepared for two emergencies: army reserve duty and barbecues. The two are not necessarily separate. They may even be complementary. The gear in both cases is very basic. For the first one needs a pair of army boots, a backpack containing the bare necessities, and a licensed gun or pistol. The second requires a miniature hibachi forged from the cheapest tin, a pair of rusty tongs, and a bag of charcoal. Some reservists are more ready than others; some do not even bother to remove their equipment from the trunk of the car. Since emergencies always occur in the middle of the night, it is wiser to keep everything in the car rather than clang down the stairs at dawn.

Simple equipment has a lot to recommend it. It is the stripped down, modest approach which is chiefly responsible for the quality of grilled meat. Who needs fancy charcoal - *mesquite*, cherry wood, walnut wood, and so on? Honest charcoal has been made and used in Israel for ages - the largest Arab town, Um-el-Fahem, is named after the stuff. Most Israelis spend their lives within meat-turning distance of an open charcoal grill, but I do not remember a single conversation in which the nature of the charcoal was discussed. Nor do I remember any fancy fire starters. How do we start a grill? The most prevalent method involves heavy use of gasoline. You go into the woods, set up the hibachi, empty a bag of charcoal into it, then douse it liberally with gasoline from the car. You warn the children to stay away, then you throw in a match. The hibachi catches fire with a whoosh that endangers the whole forest, but the conflagration soon dies down and the coals reach the desired state of white glowing ashes. Generations of Israelis have grown up confusing the odour of gasoline with the taste and smell of grilled meat.

On calm windless days we resort to that indispensable tool of the dedicated griller, the fan. Any fan... the back of a broken chair, a piece of card, a magazine. Fanning is an art in itself. You hold your fan and wave, and the frequent gusts of air bring the coals to life. It is not a task to be taken lightly. It requires full attention, a flick of the wrist, a sense of rhythm and timing. Self-igniting charcoal, mostly French, was introduced here recently, but it takes

◆ *Our favorite pastime: cooking in the woods. Note the cardboard being used as a fan.*

forever to get going, and flickers and hisses gloomily when it does. There is no substitute for a good breeze or a talented fanner.

In Israel, barbecuing is part of the collective memory. It is a national pastime that spares no one, except members of the orthodox community. Twenty years ago, a barbecue was the highlight of a country outing.

Families drove into the hills, children picked wild flowers, mothers spread blankets and fathers got the fire started. Today it is customary to forego the beauty of the scenery and the fresh country air and make do with any grassy knoll. Some Israelis even grill their chops at the grassy intersections of busy streets.

The quality of Israeli meat is steadily improving. One can now ask for and get specific cuts of meat. There are butchers who really know their meat and hang it properly and recommend what cuts to buy. But even though the quality of our meat is better and we have learned to appreciate a good lamb chop, the grills we use allow minimal distance between the rack and the coals.

More than any other facet of Israeli cuisine, grilling meat over an open fire represents an assimilation of Arab tradition with that of Western and Eastern Europe. Most restaurants serving meat offer grilled skewers of meat. Arabs lean more heavily towards lamb, while Jews still prefer lean beef and ground meat. There are exceptions of course. South American Jews know a lot about *carne asado* and *chorizos*, and keep their meat away from open fire, and Jews from North Africa and the Yemen have a cuisine

◆ *Israelis*

raise geese

for their

livers.

◆ *Free-range*

chickens are

catching on.

which is all their own. But most of the grilled meat consumed in Israel is skewered in cubes on metal spits and quickly cooked over intense heat. Only fancy restaurants comply with requests for rare or medium rare. In most places you are not asked what degree of doneness you require. You get it well done.

"We stole this idea, like so much else, from the Indians," wrote one American food critic, referring to the barbecue. Late in the sixteenth century John White, who was with the settlement on Roanoke Island, Virginia, wrote about the Indians he saw "broyling their fishe over the flame", adding "they took great heed that they bee not burnt." In 1705 Robert Beverly, in *The History and Present State of Virginia*, described the "Indian thing" in a little more detail: "The meat was laid... upon sticks raised upon forks at some distance above the live coals, which heats more gently and dries up the gravy." Two centuries later the United States Department of Agriculture pronounced: "Barbecue is meat that shall be cooked by the direct action of heat resulting from the burning of hard wood or the hot coals therefrom for a sufficient period to assume the usual characteristics...which include the formation of a brown crust." All of these educated essays ignore the Middle East and its humble but considerable contribution to the history of the barbecue. It is difficult to say,

faced with so many conflicting stories, how or where the barbecue came into existence, but my opinion is that it did so 27,000 years ago, within hours of the discovery of fire. The first barbecue writer has to be Homer: "Automedon held the meats and brilliant Achilles carved them, and cut them well into pieces and spitted them."

◆ *Much of the beef raised in Israel ends up sizzling over a grill.*

◆ *Although*

they are no

longer

nomads,

Bedouins

still herd

sheep in the

Negev.

In 1960 James Beard, discussing the changing art of the American barbecue, wrote: "What a phenomenal change! Just twenty years ago when I first wrote about outdoor cooking, backyard chefs were few. And their usual fare was steak or hamburger, blackened in an inferno of smoke and flame." Without wishing to defame a whole nation, it is my sad duty to state that he must have had Israel in mind in that sentence. Unlike cooks in large parts of the rest of the world, Israeli cooks started with the barbecue and advanced backwards to sauces and soufflés.

I grew up knowing more about barbecuing than about any other method of cooking. For many years, going out meant eating grilled meat. Other people went out for hamburgers and pizzas, but we went out for kebabs. They were cheap and satisfying. A kebab is still the cheapest form of cooked meat one can buy. To the suspicious mind, the fact that it costs so little suggests meat of dubious origin. Once upon a time, when you asked for lamb, you got turkey laced with lamb fat, and when you asked for veal, you got chicken. If meat carved from a spit was mysterious, the ground meats used for skewered patties were even more so. But all this is changing. Steaks are usually beef, cut thin. When we come across genuine ground lamb, or cubes of lamb, we know what we are eating. Lamb is the king of kebabs - fragrant, spicy, sometimes spiked with cinnamon, and loaded with chopped parsley and pine nuts.

Considering the years of hostile criticism levelled at grilled meat, it took an amazingly long time for fish to make its way onto the barbecue rack. Mediterranean fish responds well to intense heat and a touch of smoke. Try it once, and you will be converted. The grill leaves gentle marks on the crisp skin and the sea taste is sealed inside. A good, lemony sauce is all the accompaniment it needs. We also have gentler methods of barbecuing fish, in wrappings of vine leaves for instance.

As all food and restaurant guides recommend on those rare occasions when they include Israel: when in Israel, barbecue.

BARBECUE

Recipes

◆ *Spitting*

images:

shish kebab,

skewered

beef marrow,

and lamb

shashlik.

SHASHLIK
Lamb on skewers

MARINADE
1/2 cup/100ml fresh lemon juice
1/2 cup/100ml dry red wine
3 tablespoons chopped fresh rosemary, or
1 tablespoon dried, and
rosemary sprigs to garnish
1 tablespoon finely chopped garlic
1 teaspoon dried hot red pepper flakes
1 1/2 teaspoons salt
3/4 teaspoon freshly ground black pepper
3/4 cup/175ml olive oil

MEAT AND VEGETABLES
leg of lamb weighing 4 lbs/1.8kg, boned and cut
into 2-inch/5-cm cubes
4 medium zucchini/courgettes
4 small onions
4 yellow bell peppers
1 lb/450g cherry tomatoes

Mix together the marinade ingredients, whipping/whisking in the oil in a steady stream so that the mixture emulsifies. Add the cubes of lamb and stir them around to coat them in the marinade. Cover, and put in the refrigerator for at least 6 hours or overnight.

If using wooden skewers, soak them in water for 1 hour before threading the meat and vegetables onto them; if using metal skewers, brush them with oil. Light the barbecue.

Cut the zucchini into quarters lengthwise, and then into 1 1/2-inch/4-cm pieces; cook them in boiling, salted water until just tender. The onions should be cut into 8 pieces, secured with toothpicks/cocktail sticks, and also blanched in boiling, salted water. Cut the bell peppers into bite size pieces.

Thread the meat, onions, zucchini, peppers and tomatoes onto the skewers (remove the toothpicks from the chunks of onion), and brush with a little of the marinade.

Grill on an oiled rack set 5-6 inches/15cm above glowing coals, basting frequently with the marinade and turning occasionally. The lamb will take 15 -18 minutes to cook, or less if you like your meat medium rare. Alternatively, put the skewers under a pre-heated broiler/grill; medium well done will take 12 - 15 minutes.

Discard the marinade when you have finished basting - it should not be served with the *shashlik*. Makes 16 skewers.

◆ *Romanian Jews*

like their kebabs

large and

liberally flavored

with garlic.

LEG OF LAMB MARINATED IN HERBS

MARINADE
1/2 cup/100ml white wine vinegar
1 cup/225ml olive oil
2 tablespoons fresh thyme,
2 tablespoons fresh rosemary, or
2 teaspoons dried
1 tablespoon fresh oregano, or 1 teaspoon dried
3 tablespoons fresh mint, or 1 tablespoon dried
2 large cloves garlic
1 teaspoon freshly ground black pepper

leg of lamb weighing 3 - 4 lbs/ 1.5-2 kg
12 cloves garlic, halved

Using a food processor, blend together all the marinade ingredients. Place the lamb in a large dish and pour the marinade over it; using a small knife, stab the leg randomly, and insert half a clove of garlic with each stab. Cover and refrigerate for 24 hours, turning occasionally so that the meat thoroughly absorbs the marinade flavors.

Remove from the refrigerator and allow to stand for 1 hour. Transfer the meat to the rack of a broiling pan/grill pan and sprinkle with salt. Pre-heat the broiler/grill and cook for 14 minutes on each side if you like your meat medium well. Alternatively, cook the meat on a rack set 6 inches/20 cm above glowing coals, allowing 12 minutes each side for medium rare.

Transfer the meat to a carving board and allow to stand for 10 minutes before carving. Holding the carving knife at an angle of 45°, slice the lamb thinly across the grain. Serve immediately with grilled vegetables.
Serves 8 to 10.

GRILLED LAMB CHOPS

1/4 teaspoon each of ground allspice,
black pepper, cardamom,
cinnamon and salt
8 lamb chops

Mix the spices and seasonings together and sprinkle over the chops. Put the chops on the barbecue or under a pre-heated broiler/grill and cook on both sides until brown and sizzling. Serve with rice.

◆ *Rosemary*

growing wild

in the grounds

of a monastery

near

Jerusalem.

RED CHICKEN À LA TOURAN

Many chefs and restaurateurs come from
this little village in the Upper Galilee

*4 poussins/spring chickens, weighing
1 lb/450g each
3 tablespoons coarse salt
3 onions, sliced
3 cloves garlic, crushed
1/2 teaspoon black pepper
1/2 teaspoon saffron
1/4 teaspoon ground cardamom
1/4 teaspoon ground cloves
2 tablespoons* somek *
1/2 cup/100ml olive oil
4 large* pitas

Clean the chickens, rub them with salt
inside and out, and refrigerate for 1 hour.
Put the onions and garlic into a shallow
casserole dish just big enough to hold all
four chickens. Mix all the spices together.
Take the chickens out of the refrigerator,
wash them, pat them dry and rub them with
the spice mixture inside and out. Put them
on top of the onions in the casserole dish,
breast up. Refrigerate for several hours.

Transfer the contents of the casserole
dish to a large shallow saucepan, add 2
cups/500ml water, bring to a boil, cover
and cook until the birds are very tender.
The water will evaporate, but if this happens too fast, add a little more. Remove
from the heat and add the olive oil. Transfer
to the casserole dish and broil/grill for 8
minutes. Spread the onions on the 4 *pitas*,
put the chickens on top and broil for another 5 minutes.

*Somek is a red, salty powder that gives a
pleasant flavor to almost any savoury dish. It is
an excellent addition to any spice shelf, but it can
be omitted here if difficult to obtain. Its chief
value in this recipe is its color.*

SHISH KEBABS

Ground meat on skewers

*12 oz/350g veal
1 1/4 lbs/550g lamb
small bunch parsley
1 onion
4 cloves garlic
1/2 teaspoon allspice
1/2 teaspoon cinnamon
salt and pepper to taste*

Grind/mince together the meat, parsley,
onions and garlic. Add the spices and mix
well. Take generous spoonfuls of the mixture and shape into thin sausages. Thread
onto flat metal skewers and broil/grill or put
on the barbecue until they sizzle and begin
to brown. Turn and cook the other side.

In Israel, grilled meat is usually served on
a plate by itself, *pita*, bread, *mezze* and Israeli
salad already being on the table. In the
street, grilled meat is put into *pitas* with
salad and *tahini*, or sold wrapped in the kind
of large *pita* shown on p. 148.

◆ *Red*

chicken

served on

pita

bread.

FISH GRILLED OVER CHARCOAL

2 lbs/900g fish (bass, grouper or red snapper),
or one small fish (bream, gray mullet)
per person
chopped parsley and lemon wedges,
to garnish

MARINADE 1
1/3 cup/80ml olive oil
1 tablespoon salt
1 teaspoon ground allspice
2 tablespoons fresh lemon juice

MARINADE 2
1 onion, cut into rings
2 tablespoons lemon juice
3 tablespoons olive oil
1 tablespoon salt
1/2 teaspoon black pepper
1 clove garlic, finely chopped
1 teaspoon ground cumin
4 bay leaves

Clean and wash the fish, and pat them dry. If you are using large fish, cut them into steaks. Mix the marinade of your choice and pour it into a shallow dish. Add the fish, turning them so that the marinade coats them all over. Allow to marinate for 2 hours.

Remove the fish from the marinade and put them on a lightly oiled grill/rack or onto skewers. Cook over charcoal, turning every 2 or 3 minutes and basting regularly with the marinade. Average cooking time is 15 - 20 minutes, depending on the size of the fish. The skin should be crisp and the flesh flake easily.

Transfer to a serving platter, garnish with parsley and lemon wedges and serve immediately.

SMOKE-GRILLED GROUPER

1 medium grouper
(or sea bass, red snapper, barracuda or bonito)

If you have the luck to meet and catch a grouper on a scuba fishing day, you can have yourself a real feast, and save yourself the hassle of getting the fish home and putting it into an already full refrigerator. You cook it right there on the beach.

Collect three big stones and arrange them in a triangle, with their tops level. Collect dry wood, put it between the stones and make a fire. Clean and scale the fish, rinsing it in sea water. Collect three sticks (or better still find three metal rods), wet them thoroughly, and place them on the stones so that they form a small triangle - this is your grill rack. When the fire starts to die down, place the fish on the rack. Cook for 20 minutes on each side - a fish weighing 4 lbs/2kg takes at least 45 minutes to cook. Now gather fresh herbs such as thyme, rosemary and marjoram (if you are not in Israel you may have to bring them with you!) and smother the fire with them. The aim is to work up a good smoke. Let the fish cure for 1 hour, and be ready to extinguish the herbs with sea water if they catch fire. Eat hot or cold.

◆ *A large grouper absorbing the flavor of fresh herbs over an open fire.*

CHAPTER 9

WINE & SPIRITS

◆ *Without quality grapes there can be no quality wines. Wine is now more widely appreciated in Israel.*

I sraelis are not drinkers. They may order a bottle of white wine with a meal, or nurse a bottle of beer for a whole evening, or even sit around a table covered with empty bottles, but they are not serious drinkers.

There are many reasons why Israel has never made it into the league table of drinking nations. History for one. Drinking was never a favorite pastime with Jews. They may have sneaked a schnapps in the long, cold winters of Russia or Poland, but most of their social drinking was done on Friday nights and on holidays. Their wine was blessed, but it was sacrificial and sweet, not the

◆ The trade-mark of Israel's largest wine maker shows the two biblical spies sent out by Joshua. They returned carrying grapes as proof that the land ahead was "flowing with milk and honey."

kind of wine that goes with dinner. Security is another reason. Despite the unaccountable state of readiness of the armies of various nations of heavy drinkers, we prefer to stay sober. Our unique security problems call for sobriety at all times. Weather is another reason. We have long, hot summers when it is just too hot to drink. When we do, we find that a cold beer, *arak* (an anise-based beverage not unlike ouzo or Pernod), or chilled white wine goes down best. Heavy, syrupy liquers are out and so are whiskies and cognacs.

The truth is that for many years we had no local wine industry to speak of. Even in ancient times, we were not great wine-makers. Wine culture and wine appreciation in Israel is really a phenomenon of the 1980s.

Most Israeli wineries date from the beginnning of this century. The two largest, in Rishon Lezion and Zichron Yaakov, were founded with the financial support and know-how of Baron de Rothschild. French wine-makers and local farmers planted vines. Two well-equipped wineries were built. But the wine they produced was too sweet to be true table wine. Yet when table wines were finally produced, the makers discovered that it was almost impossible to market them in Israel. The gourmet revolution that hit us in the eighties had not yet arrived. So although we had drinkable wine, we had no food to drink it with. In those days we had Sauvignon Blanc and Cabernet Sauvignon, and the

◆ Israel's first winery was founded by Baron de Rothschild in Rishon Lezion.

occasional bottle of Semillion or Colombard. These were distributed to small neighborhood stores where they were propped upright in direct sunlight. Of course they spoiled quickly. When the tentative gourmet tried his first bottle, it was sour, which naturally discouraged him.

So for the time being we stuck to beer. Our founding fathers realised that beer was the most fitting alcoholic beverage for a hot and busy country. Beer is a thirst quencher. It is filling, the liquid equivalent of bread. It is also a natural foil to the hot, peppery foods we are so fond of. We have three local brands of beer, more or less. All of them are adequate, but one of them - a clear and flavorsome European-style pilsner - is superb.

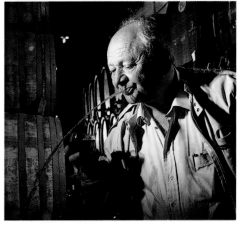

When the great food revolution finally came, Israel's wine producers were quick off the mark. To see how this happened, we must go back a decade or so. The first decent Israeli wine was fermented and bottled on the Golan Heights at the Golan Winery. Wine-growing on the Golan was the bright idea of a moshavnik who was very successful with apples. The soil of the Golan is unique, the result of volcanic eruptions that once shook the whole region. The cool upland climate - cold at night, pleasantly warm during the day, liberally sprinkled with rain, seldom touched by frosts - is also ideal for grape-growing.

◆ *The original site of the first winery in Rishon Lezion.*

◆ *The winemaster at work.*

In the early 1980s, after a few years of trial runs under the supervision of an American wine-maker from California, Golan produced its first commercial vintage, a very dry and distinctive Sauvignon Blanc. In the

◆ *A container of grapes harvested in the early morning is quickly sent to the winery.*

belief that it would be much easier to win honors abroad than sell their carefully perfected product at home, Golan sought and found an appreciative market in Europe and the United States. Their wine was a great success abroad. Not only was it good, it was also from Israel, where wine had been produced for centuries!

With chestfuls of medals and citations from international wine shows, Golan started to tackle the home market. Their timing was perfect. While their wines had been conquering the world, Israel had undergone its long-awaited gastronomic revolution. I do not use the word revolution lightly. The change was dramatic. Hundred of restaurants opened almost overnight, and the emphasis shifted away from Middle Eastern and Arab cuisine to International. For the first time we had an opportunity to find out what we really liked - French, Japanese, Italian, American....Acquiring a taste for good wine was a natural progression. When that happened, Golan was ready with new and exciting wines.

Today, instead of three home-grown wines to choose from, we have twenty-five. The old sweet wines were no longer commercially viable, and with Golan setting the pace, other wineries had no choice but to join the race. Wine began to be promoted and discussed. Wine societies and wine newsletters appeared. There were aggressive advertising campaigns, with each winery claiming supremacy. Consumers were faced with an array of labels and styles of wine. Prices were high to begin with, but increasing demand has brought them down.

We are still not a nation of wine-drinkers as the French or Italians are, but if we do decide to celebrate, we have good local wine to celebrate with.

$\mathscr{W}$ I N E & S P I R I T S

Recipes

GROUPER WITH FENNEL & ARAK

*1 large grouper (or sea bass, or red snapper),
scaled and cleaned
(allow 12 oz/350g per person)
4 bulbs fennel, thinly sliced
salt and freshly ground white pepper
2 onions, thinly sliced
3 cloves garlic, crushed
1/2 cup/100ml olive oil
1/2 cup/100ml arak (or ouzo, or any other
anise-flavored liqueur)*

Season the inside of the fish and the slices of fennel with salt and pepper. Mix the onions, garlic and olive oil with the fennel, and stuff the fish with half of this mixture. Cover the bottom of an earthenware baking dish with the rest, place the fish on top, cover the dish with foil, and bake in a moderate oven (350°F/180°C). A large fish will take about 1 hour to cook, a smaller one less than half that time. Warm the *arak*, pour it over the fish as it comes out of the oven, and set light to it. Serve as soon as the flames have died down.

◆ *Grouper*

with fennel

and arak.

BREAST OF MOULLARD IN WINE SAUCE

The moullard is a cross between a goose and a Berber duck.

2 moullard breasts (or duck, or goose),
weighing 12 oz/350g each
1 onion, finely diced
2 tablespoons dried cherries
1/4 teaspoon black pepper
pinch brown sugar
1 cup/225ml dry red wine
3 tablespoons rich brown sauce base/stock
4 tablespoons butter

Prick the breasts a few times with a fork, then lay them in a cold, heavy skillet/frying pan, fatty side down. Cook over a medium heat until the breasts color a deep brown, then add the onion, cherries, pepper and sugar. Turn the breasts, and add the wine and sauce base/stock. Remove the breasts, slice them, and transfer them to a warm serving dish. Reduce the contents of the skillet to a quarter, then remove from the heat and stir in the butter. Spoon over the slices of breast and serve straight away, with roast potatoes. Moullard should never be over-cooked. Serves 4.

◆ *Breast of*

moullard in

wine sauce.

GOOSE LIVER FLAMBÉ

4 oz/100g goose liver per person, well chilled
salt, white pepper
freshly grated orange rind
Halleluya liqueur (orange-based) or
Grand Marnier
rich brown sauce base/stock

Carefully cut the liver into slices 1/3 inch/0.8cm thick. Season with salt and pepper, and chill in the refrigerator.

Heat a heavy skillet/frying pan and sauté the slices for about 2 seconds on each side - no oil is needed since goose liver contains a lot of fat. Pour off excess fat for future use. Add a sprinkling of orange rind, 1 tablespoon of brown sauce base and 2 tablespoons of heated liqueur. Set alight with a match and serve immediately. This superb delicacy should be served by itself, accompanied by nothing but a good white wine.

SAUCE BASE

Most classic cookbooks contain a recipe for a rich brown sauce base made from beef, beef bones and vegetables. In Israel we make something very similar, often cooking it overnight and serving it as a soup.

◆ *Goose liver*

flambeéd

in orange

liqueur.

STUFFED PIGEONS

1 cup/225g rice
6 pigeons, plucked and cleaned, with livers
5 cloves garlic, crushed
1 cup/150g chopped walnuts or pistachios
4 tablespoons chopped parsley
salt and freshly ground black pepper
pinch ground cardamom
freshly grated nutmeg, to taste
vegetable oil
3 onions, sliced
1 carrot, sliced
1 teaspoon celery salt
4 cups/1 liter black non-alcoholic malt beer
1/2 cup/100ml brandy

Boil the rice in salted water for 12 minutes, then drain well. Cut the pigeon livers into cubes, then mix with the rice, 3 of the garlic cloves, the nuts, parsley and spices. Stuff the birds loosely with this mixture and close the openings with skewers. Fry the birds for 5 minutes on each side (a Dutch oven would give better results in this recipe), put them on their backs, then add the rest of the garlic, the onion, carrot and celery salt to the pan. Sauté for 10 minutes, then add the malt beer and brandy and transfer to an ovenproof dish.

Cover and bake for 2 hours in an oven pre-heated to 300°F/150°C. When the birds are cooked, the flesh should come easily off the bones. Uncover and continue cooking for another 15 minutes. Add a little more malt beer if the birds look dry. Put the birds on individual plates to serve. Strain the sauce, spoon a little over the birds and serve the rest in a jug. Serves 4 to 6, accompanied by pickles.

COMPOTE OF DRIED FRUIT IN RED WINE

equal quantities of dried apricots
prunes, raisins, dates and blanched almonds
2 cloves
2 cardamom pods
1 stick cinnamon
red wine
whipped cream, to serve

Soak the fruit in cold water for 10 minutes, then discard the water. Put all the fruit, the almonds and the spices in a heavy saucepan, and add enough red wine to cover them. Bring to a boil, then simmer for 12 minutes, stirring occasionally. Take out the cloves, cardamom and cinnamon, and allow to cool. Cover and refrigerate. Serve in individual glasses with whipped cream in a separate bowl.

ROSEHIP COCKTAIL

1 lb/450g rosehips, preferably from
damask roses
1 cup/225g sugar
1/2 cup/100ml lemon juice
2 cups/500ml rosé wine
1 cup/225ml white rum
juice of 1 pomegranate, optional

Wash the rosehips, cover in water and refrigerate for 4 hours. Boil the rosehips until they are soft, then strain the liquid into another saucepan and discard the rosehips. Add the sugar and boil for 5 minutes, then add the rest of the ingredients and chill. Serve with ice, with rose petals for decoration.

◆ *Stuffed pigeon with baby eggplants.*

◆ *Compote of dried fruit in red wine.*

FRUITS & DESSERTS

◆ *A feast of*

ripe figs

and peeled

prickly

pears.

The Hebrew word *sabra* means prickly, thorny, rough. A *sabra* (plural *sabres*) is a prickly pear, a regional and popular fruit, but it also describes an Israeli stereotype, an Israeli-born Israeli complete with all the traits typical of his or her fruity namesake. The epithet has been in use for so many years now that we have stopped being offended by it, and at times we even take a certain pride in it. How many other nations are named after a fruit?

For a time the name was appropriate. Prickly pears are thorny. They have a thick skin. They have a short season - less than two months in summer. They are extremely difficult to pick and they used not to be sold commercially, or at least not on a large scale. But when you do pick them, and remove the thorns, and peel them, and cut them open, they are sweet and unique in taste and texture. If a whole nation must be named after a fruit, perhaps *sabra* is not such a bad name.

◆ When you buy a watermelon the greengrocer willingly cuts out a little piece for you to try.

We used to buy prickly pears from the back of very small carts, most of them pushed along by kids who would clean the fruit and hand it to you on the street. You ate it straight away. It was rather special, something you could not buy by the kilo like other fruit. Then the plant breeders stepped in.

The prickly pear is now in decline, a victim of commercial sophistication. A new, improved,

◆ *Watermelon*

stands appear

in summer

and vanish

when the

season is over.

thornless, perennial *sabra* is now available. The moral of this story is that the *sabra* may no longer stand for what we are, unless of course we too have become new, improved, thornless and perennial.

◆ Rahat lokum, *Turkish delight, is still made by hand in an old factory in Jerusalem.*

The abundance of fruit in Israel is staggering. The fruit we grow today knows no season. Grapes start in spring and continue through to November. Watermelons and melons start in March and go on through September. Citrus fruit is available all year round. It is an amazing sight. The typical Israeli fruit stall is lush and heavy with fruit in all seasons, all ripe, all sweet, all ready to eat. And as if indigenous species were not enough, in the last few years we have also managed to grow tropical and exotic fruit - papaya/pawpaw and kiwi fruit, Sharon fruit/persimmons and carambolas, passionfruit and pineapples, lychees and kumquats, dates and figs, Chinese apples and feijoas. Every season brings a new arrival.

It has become almost a tradition that every year some far-seeing and resourceful moshav or kibbutz will introduce a new fruit that it has secretly nursed to perfection, forcing it to adapt to local conditions. Young botonists are busy changing the size and color of watermelons - they want the new generation of watermelons to be smaller, sweeter and seedless. They are also changing the shape and size of pickling vegetables. It is easier, they say, to pickle round cucumbers than long ones, so they are growing cucumbers that look like green tomatoes. Some of these exciting fruits survive for one season and never return. If they do not prove commercially attractive, why grow them? But there is alway as another designer fruit in the wings.

◆ *Assorted candies by Havillo of Jerusalem.*

We put our great variety of fruit to good use. For example, it almost compulsory for all house-

◆ *Fruit*
boulevard in
affluent
Ramat Hasharon,
a suburb of
Tel Aviv.
The simultaneous
display of
summer and
winter fruit is
an Israeli
phenomenon.

◆ *Some*

improvisation

is needed to

pick prickly

pears growing

by the

roadside.

holds to offer a large selection of fresh fruit, dried fruit and nuts to inmates and visitors. Fruit is not something we buy for special occasions. It is a staple. We eat it all the time. In fact it is a wonder that such a fruity nation ever bothers with cakes and pastries. Yet cakes and sweet desserts are an integral part of the culinary cultures of all the ethnic minorities living in Israel, and none of them has yet given up cakes in favor of fruit.

Baklava and *konafa* are the grandest of Arab pastries, although their origin is probably Turkish or Greek. They are made at home and commercially. Proud housewives may scorn store-bought pastries, but most are fresh and tasty and a good bet for those who do not want to bother. *Baklava* and *konafa* should be light, crisp and delicate, and the fillings should consist of pistachios and walnuts, and not peanuts. Although they look elaborate, *baklava* and *konafa* are easy to prepare, and they are dual-purpose, desserts as well pastries to be consumed with coffee or tea. No party or grand occasion is complete without them.

Another essential of Israeli dessert is Turkish coffee. A lot of myth and folklore is attached to the small demi-tasse cups of strong, fragrant liquid. The Bedouins brew their coffee in narrow-necked, long-handled pots called *finjans* or *tanakas*, which come in various sizes. Their coffee is made from very finely ground coffee beans to which a few cardamom seeds have been added, and it is drunk thick, strong, and usually very sweet. The coffee is boiled in the *finjan* seven times before it is served, the repeated boilings producing a froth which is very tasty and part of the enjoyment.

F RUITS & DESSERTS

◆ Old and new. Jaffa oranges have a world-wide reputation, but Israeli strawberries are less well known. Every year they get bigger and better.

Recipes

BAKLAVA
Layered pastry with nuts and syrup

1 lb/450g filo pastry (about 24 sheets)
1 cup/225g unsalted butter, melted
10 oz/275g pistachio nuts, walnuts or almonds,
coarsely chopped
2 tablespoons sugar

SYRUP
1 heaped cup/250g sugar
1/2 cup/100ml water
1 tablespoon lemon juice
1 tablespoon orange blossom water

To make the syrup, dissolve the sugar in the water and lemon juice, and simmer until it is thick enough to coat the back of a spoon. Add the orange blossom water and simmer for another 2 minutes. Allow to cool, then chill in the refrigerator.

To cook the *filo* pastry you will need a large round or square baking pan. Brush the bottom and sides of the pan with the melted butter, then lay half the *filo* sheets in the pan, brushing each sheet with melted butter as you lay it in and overlapping the sheets or folding the sides over as necessary. Pre-heat the oven to 350°-375°F/180°-190°C. Mix the chopped nuts with the sugar and sprinkle evenly over the top sheet of *filo*. Now lay the rest of the sheets of *filo* in the pan, brushing with butter as before. Brush the top sheet with melted butter. Using a very sharp knife, cut the pastry diagonally into diamond shapes.

Bake for 30 minutes at 350°-375°F/180°-190°C, then raise the oven temperature to 450°-475°F/230°-250°C and cook for another 15 minutes. The *baklava* should be very puffy and light gold in color. Remove from the oven and immediately pour the chilled syrup over the hot pastry. Leave in the dish to cool.

To serve, cut along the diagonal lines and arrange on a serving dish; alternatively, turn out upside down onto a large plate, put another plate on the bottom, turn the right way up, then cut along the original lines.

FROSTED ROSES
A very luxurious and special garnish for desserts

10 unblemished roses, half open,
with their stems
4 egg whites
4 or 5 tablespoons water
2 cups/450g sugar/castor sugar

Choose mostly red roses, and roses which have not been sprayed! Shop-bought roses have been sprayed, so pick roses from your own garden. Rose petals are edible and tasty.

Thoroughly stir (do not whip/whisk) the water into the egg whites and dip the heads of the roses into it, moving them about so that all the petals become coated with the mixture. Now stand the stems in a bowl and leave for 10 minutes. Using a sugar sifter, dust the flowers heavily with sugar. Do the same with any loose petals. Now hang the roses up by their stalks and let them dry for 2 days. Then put them on a tray and let them dry for another 3 days. Store carefully in an airtight container or in the freezer. Use for decorating custards and other desserts. Providing they are well coated with egg white and thoroughly dried, frosted roses should keep for up to 6 months.

◆ Layered pastries

with nuts and

syrup come in

different shapes

and flavors.

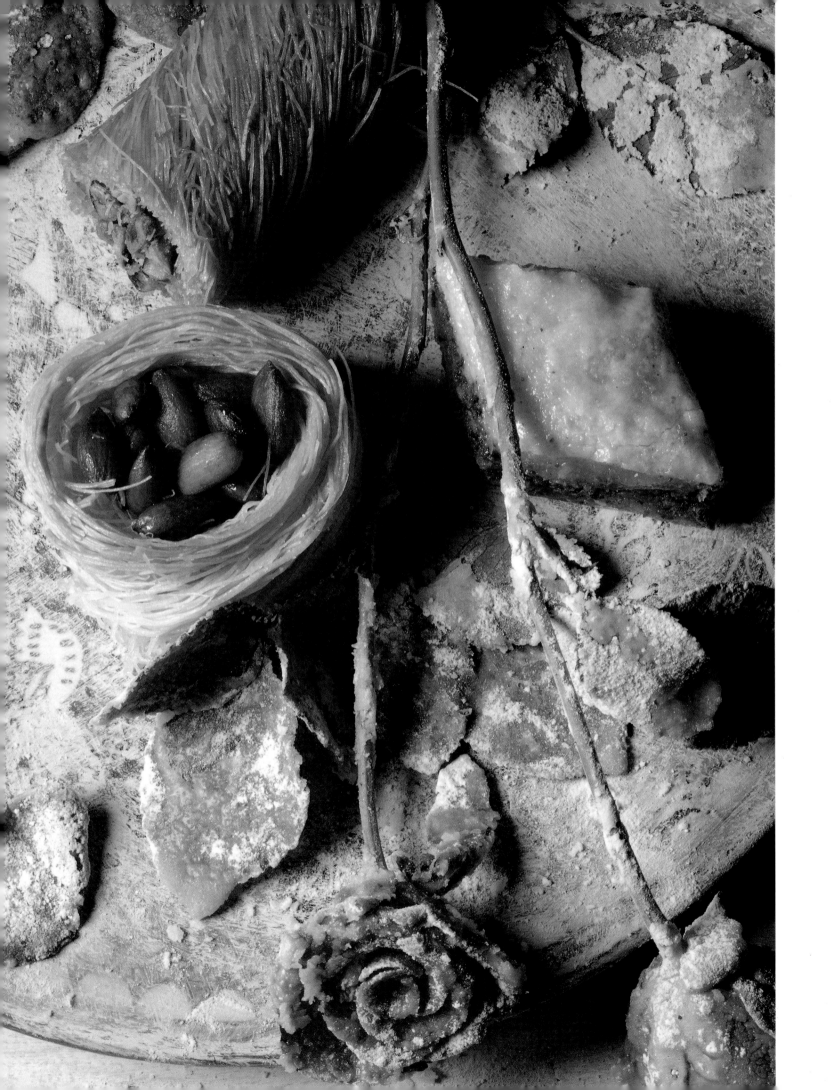

◆ *Sesame*

and

peanut

bars.

CONFIT OF FIGS

2 lbs/900g whole fresh figs
4 cups/900g sugar
1/2 cup/100 ml water
2oz/60g sesame seeds
2oz/60g blanched almonds
2 tablespoons fresh lemon juice

Wash the figs and prick them a few times with a fork. Dissolve the sugar in the water, add the figs, sesame seeds, almonds and lemon juice, and simmer over a very low heat for 2 hours. At the end of this time the figs should look almost transparent. Cool and serve at room temperature.

SESAME BARS

3oz/75g sesame seeds
1-1/2 cups/350g sugar
3/4 cup/175ml water
1 teaspoon cinnamon
pinch ground cloves
1/2 teaspoon lemon juice

Using a non-stick skillet/frying pan, fry the sesame seeds until they are golden (no fat is required because sesame seeds are rich in oil). Dissolve the sugar in the water, bring to a boil and continue boiling until the sugar begins to turn golden brown. At this point, add the sesame seeds, cinnamon, cloves and lemon juice, and continue to stir for 3 minutes. Remove from the heat, pour onto a wet marble slab and, using a wet rolling pin, roll the mixture to an even thickness of about 1/2 inch/1 cm. Using a fish slice or pallet knife, quickly lever the toffee off the marble slab and cut it into bars. Alternatively, leave it to harden and then snap it into chunks. Keep in an airtight container. Bars of almond or pine nut brittle can be made in the same way.

CANDIED ORANGE & GRAPEFRUIT PEEL

2 large oranges
2 thick-skinned grapefruit
4 1/2 cups/1kg sugar
2 cups/450ml water
juice of 1 lemon

◆ *Candied*

orange

and

grapefruit

peel.

Scrub the skins of the fruit with a hard brush, then cut them in half and scoop out the flesh. Put the half shells into a bowl of water, cover with a plate, and soak for 2 days, changing the water once during this time. Drain and cut into strips. Put the strips into a large saucepan, cover with water, bring to a boil and simmer for 15 minutes. Pour off the water. Cover with water again, bring to a boil, simmer for 15 minutes, and drain. Repeat the process once more.

Now add the sugar and 2 cups of water to the peel, bring to a boil and simmer very gently for 2 hours, with the lid of the saucepan off. When all the liquid has evaporated, stir in the lemon juice, making sure that it coats all the pieces of peel. Drain the peel and cut it into bite-sized pieces. Roll the pieces in sugar if you like but this is not absolutely necessary. Leave on a plate or on wax/greaseproof paper for several hours to harden. Store in an airtight container.

TANGERINE SORBET

1 cup/225g sugar
1 cup/225 ml water
2 lbs/900g tangerines
1/2 grapefruit
1 teaspoon Cointreau or orange liqueur

Dissolve the sugar in the water and bring to a boil. Cook for 5 minutes, remove from the heat and allow to cool. Pare the zest from 3 of the tangerines and reserve. Remove the segments from half the tangerines and carefully peel them. Squeeze the juice from the rest of the tangerines and from the grapefruit.

Blend together the syrup, zest, juice and liqueur, pour into a bowl and freeze and whip/whisk. Repeat the whipping every 20 minutes or so, two or three more times, so that the sorbet stays soft when frozen. Serve decorated with the tangerine segments.

◆ *Confit*

of figs.

BAKED APPLES

10 cooking apples
1 cup/225 ml red wine
2 tablespoons sugar
1 teaspoon powdered cinnamon
1 cup/150g raisins
1/4 cup/60g melted butter
Grand Marnier or orange liqueur, optional

Wash and core the apples, but do not cut right through to the base. Arrange the apples in a greased baking pan and pre-heat the oven to 350°F/180°C.

Mix together the wine, sugar, cinnamon and raisins and spoon a little of the mixture into each apple. Top with melted butter. Bake for about 1 hour. Serve hot or cold, with a teaspoon of Grand Marnier on top, if liked.

BAKED QUINCE OLYMPUS

5 quinces
2 pints/1 liter water
1 1/2 lbs/700g sugar
1 1/4 cups/300ml lemon juice
3 whole sticks cinnamon

Trim the quinces at both ends and cut them in half lengthwise. Peel them, then soak them in water with a little lemon juice added to it to prevent them from discoloring.

Dissolve two-thirds of the sugar in the water and bring to a boil. Add the lemon juice, cinnamon and quince halves and simmer for 15-25 minutes, or until the quinces are soft (prick them with a fork to see if they are tender). Place the quinces in a baking pan, cut side up, pour the syrup over them and sprinkle with the rest of the sugar. Bake in an oven pre-heated to 450°F/230°C until they are a dark golden color. Turn off the oven. Leave the quinces in the oven to cool. Serve at room temperature.

Serves 10.

◆ *Baked quince.*

◆ *Baked apple*

stuffed with

raisins.

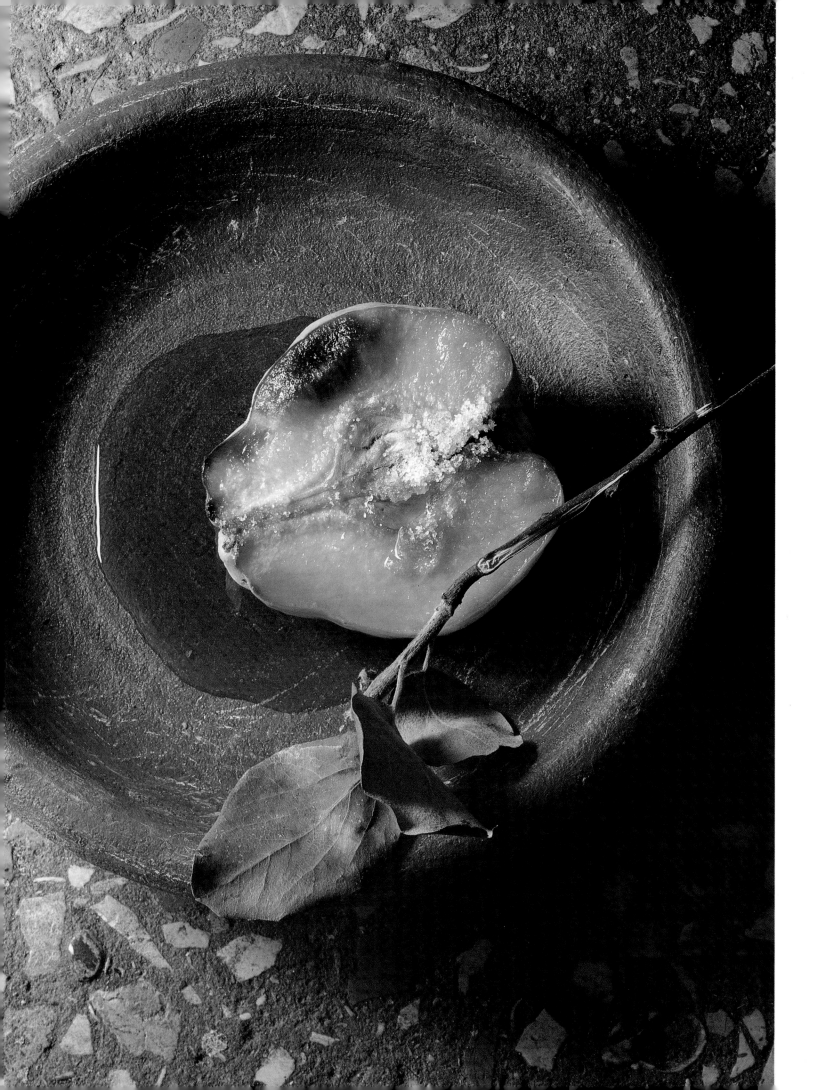

◆ *Prickly*

pear

salad.

PRICKLY PEAR SALAD

juice of 1 orange
juice of 1 lemon
1/2 teaspoon powdered cardamom
1 tablespoon nut oil
3 prickly pears
2 dessert apples, cut into small strips
1 red bell pepper, cut into small strips
pinch hot chili pepper

Combine the orange juice, lemon juice, cardamom and nut oil in a salad bowl. Carefully peel the prickly pears under running water, making shallow incisions in the flesh to remove the roots of the thorns. Slice and add to the bowl, together with the strips of apple, red pepper and cucumber. Sprinkle with a little chili powder, toss well and serve with other salads at the dinner table.

PRICKLY PEAR SAUCE

8 prickly pears
juice of 1/2 lemon
2 1/2 tablespoons Kirsch
2 level teaspoons arrowroot

Carefully peel the prickly pears. Chop them, then rub the flesh through a nylon sieve into a small saucepan. Add the lemon juice and Kirsch and warm through. Mix the arrowroot to a smooth paste with a little cold water, then stir it into the purée and Kirsch mixture. Bring to a boil and simmer gently for 2 or 3 minutes until the mixture turns syrupy. Serve hot or cold with fruit sorbets or brochettes of grilled fruit.

MA'AMOUL
Small pastries filled with dates & nuts

FILLING
4 oz/100g dried dates, pitted
4 oz/100g walnuts, coarsely chopped
4 oz/100g almonds or pistachio nuts, coarsely chopped
2/3 cup/150ml water
4 oz/100g sugar
1 heaped teaspoon ground cinnamon

DOUGH
4 cups/450g all-purpose/plain flour
1 cup/225g unsalted butter, melted
2 tablespoons rosewater
4 or 5 tablespoons milk
confectioner's/icing sugar

To prepare the filling, chop the dates, put them into a saucepan with the chopped nuts, water, sugar and cinnamon, and cook over a low heat until the dates are soft and the water has been absorbed.

To make the dough, sift the flour into a bowl, add the melted butter and lightly cut/rub it in. Add the rosewater and milk, and knead to a softish consistency. Divide the dough into walnut size pieces. Pre-heat the oven to 300°F/150°C.

Taking a piece of dough at a time, roll it into a ball between your palms, then hollow it out with your thumb, pinching the sides up to make a large thimble shape. Now fill the thimble with a little of the date mixture and press the dough back over the filling to make a ball. Slightly flatten the ball in the palm of your hand and use a fork to make an interesting pattern on top · straight lines are the traditional pattern.

When you have used up all the dough and filling, place the *ma'moul* on a greased baking sheet and bake for about 30 minutes. Do not allow them to brown or they will become hard. When they are cold, roll them in confectioner's sugar and store in an airtight tin.

HALVAH SOUFFLÉ

6 sponge fingers
6oz/175g halvah
2 level tablespoons/30g cornstarch/cornflour
2 tablespoons sugar
pinch salt
6 egg yolks and 4 egg whites
2 tablespoons brandy
1 cup/225 ml milk
2 level tablespoons/30g all-purpose/plain flour

For this you will need a 2 pint/l liter soufflé dish. Butter and flour the inside, and shake out any excess flour. Line the bottom with sponge fingers, trimming them to fit.

Crumble the halvah and mix to a smooth paste with a little water. Add the cornstarch, half the sugar, a pinch of salt, the 6 egg yolks and the brandy, and mix thoroughly. Heat the milk almost to boiling point, then pour it into the halvah mixture, beating non-stop with a fork as you do so. Now sift in the flour, give the mixture a brisk whip/whisk, and leave to cool. Pre-heat the oven to 400°F/210°C.

Whip/whisk the egg whites to stiff peaks with the rest of the sugar. Stir one third into the halvah mixture, and carefully fold in the rest. Pour into the prepared soufflé dish, put into the oven and bake for 25 minutes. Do not open the oven door while the soufflé is in – if there is a chance of the top burning, place a sheet of greased foil on top as you put the soufflé into the oven.

Serve immediately.

◆ Ma'amoul

are small

pastries

filled with

dates and

nuts

◆ *Halvah*

and thick

Turkish

coffee with

cardamom.

BISKOTCHOS
Crisp, salty tea-time cookies shaped like bagels

1oz/25g yeast
1/2 teaspoon sugar
1 cup/225g lukewarm water
3 cups/350g all purpose/plain flour, sifted
3/4 cup/200g margarine or shortening/lard, in small pieces
1 level teaspoon salt
1 tablespoon oil
powdered anise, cumin or coriander, optional
sesame seeds

Dissolve the yeast and the sugar in a little of the water and leave for 10 minutes. Make a well in the flour and add the margarine or shortening, the salt, the oil, the yeast mixture and the rest of the water. Add a little anise, cumin or coriander too, if liked. Knead to a smooth elastic dough. Cover and leave in a warm place for 1 hour. Pre-heat the oven to 350°F/190°C.

Divide the dough into 25-30 walnut-sized pieces. Sprinkle a board with sesame seeds and roll each piece into a pencil shape about 4 inches/10cm long, making sure it is well coated with sesame seeds. Pinch the ends together to form small rings. Arrange on an oiled baking sheet and bake for 45 minutes. Store in an airtight container.

◆ *Mint*

tea and

biskotchos.

◆ *A Jericho*

fruit and

vegetable

vendor takes

an afternoon

tea break.

EW ISRAELI CHEFS

Some of my best friends are cooks, and they are a strange lot. They stay up far into the night trying to remember the exact two weeks in spring when white Judean truffles bloom. If cornered, they will admit that the white Judean truffle, collected by Bedouins in the Judean desert, is not worth losing sleep over. It is a dry, powdery object, but it's the only truffle we've got, and we have to be patriotic. If we were not patriots, why on earth would we live in a country that does not have truffles, oysters, clams, lobsters and decent shrimps, which the laws of *kashrut* forbid us to cook in any case.

My friends also sit by their windows at night waiting for rain, for when it rains the fish are fresh and firm and the mushrooms grow. When I point out that the only mushroom that grows here is gooey and fleshy and requires

hours of cleaning, which spoils both the taste and the texture, they get furious.

Our gallant new chefs are first in the produce markets, poking the tomatoes, squeezing the lettuces, listening to the watermelons and angrily turning down fish with dull eyes. The merchants spot them a mile off. For you, they say, we have a catch of red mullet, just off the boat. See how bright and red their skin is. Come on, insist my friends, show us the good stuff. And the good stuff is always there, hidden at the back of large refrigerators, well away from Philistines. They squeeze the fish and purse their lips. It is not in the prime of youth and vigor, but it will have to do. Trout is delivered from the north once a week, and if they do not buy now they will be troutless for a whole week. It does not do to disappoint one's customers too often.

These, then, are the new Israeli chefs, although they have no use for the word "chef". They are cooks. They love good food. They adore new ideas. They attempt the impossible. They have a mission: to create an Israeli cuisine. There are food critics who believe it is a suicide mission. There are no more culinary frontiers, they say, no more gastronomic wildernesses to be discovered or created. Everyone has been everywhere and eaten everything. Israeli food is what it is and will always be, a lively hybrid, a medley of hits - a little Arab spice, a touch of the Orient, a dash of Eastern Europe, and the zest of fresh produce locally grown.

My friends beg to differ. Every once in a while they sit down and write new recipes, describing at length the new factor in the formula. For example, if you take avocados and make a soup out of them, omitting coriander and adding hyssop, the result is no longer Mexican but Israeli. Hyssop, an in-

digenous and biblical herb, has wrought a species change. If you leave out the pigeon in stuffed pigeon and use quail instead, the result is not French but Israeli. Our forefathers ate quail in the desert. Quail are our heritage. In fact it took us a long time to raise quail in captivity, but we managed it, so we must make the most of them. There is more. If you fry goat's cheese in batter and add mango sauce, and if both the cheese and the mangoes are locally produced, the result is 101 per cent Israeli. It cannot be anything else.

Israel's new cooks fortify themselves behind hot stoves, write books, and appear on television, but it is still too early to claim total victory over the critics. Their quest for a specifically Israeli culinary identity is sometimes spurious. Ever since Jordan severed its ties with the West Bank, Arab olive oil producers have been burdened with a glut of oil, of which only a portion can be consumed by Israelis, so now is not the time to be claiming olive oil as an Israeli invention. They also call Israeli an amazing carrot which grows only in Gaza; it is a vivid purple, crisp, tasty, and marvellous for garnishing. Their quest is also frustrated by the here-today, gone-tomorrow phenomenon. This was exactly the case with fresh ginger.

Ginger is widely used in Chinese and Japanese cooking of course, and was introduced here a few years ago. A few farmers began to grow it and there was a big publicity campaign, heartily endorsed by an Israeli cook who is an expert on Chinese cooking. Everywhere you went, people talked about ginger. A year later, the ginger was gone. The cook who had promoted it so hard called his supplier. Where is my ginger? he asked. Not profitable enough, replied the farmer. It never really caught on. What do you mean profitable? shouted the cook. Everyone's been talking about it. People bought bushels of the stuff. No, said the farmer, it was left to rot in the market. No one bought it.

And that was the end of the Israeli ginger dream. The Chinese-style cook still uses it, but he relies on friends and customers to bring it back from abroad.

Then there was the saga of the quail eggs. Where there is a female quail, there are eggs, and these eggs are ideal for pickling and cooking. Test kitchens around the country worked hard to come up with an original recipe. They were very close, so close they could almost taste it, but the closer they got the scarcer the tiny eggs became. What has happened to our eggs? they asked, and the hardy moshavnik who had promised them a lifetime's supply mumbled something about the productivity of quails going down in captivity. In captivity, it seemed, the quails were too crowded and too scared to lay eggs. We'll pay for larger cages, said the experimental cooks. We must have the eggs. Forget about the eggs, said the moshavnik. I have a new product: eels. How do you feel about eels?

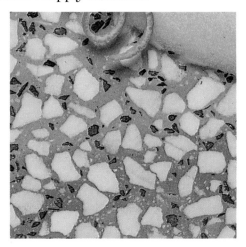

There was indeed something fishy about the farmer's story. Eventually the eggless cooks found out that quail eggs have strange healing properties, including the ability to cure asthma and allergies. The farmer who produced them had opened several fresh quail egg snack bars and was doing terrific business. People were driving in, quaffing the fresh eggs, and driving out feeling a lot better. No shipping, no packing, no mess.

A farmer from the southern part of Israel showed up recently with a sample of Japanese *shitake* mushrooms. He was sent packing.

New chefs also have to contend with a body of opinion which thinks it improper to promote good food and wine. These Jeremiahs see food as part of a long tradition of atonement and suffering. They like to believe that austerity is still with us, that none of our political problems have been solved, that we perch permanently on the brink of war, that the economy is on the skids. They eat to survive, not to celebrate life. To discuss the merits of beluga caviar or the bouquet of a new wine is decadent and irresponsible. There is nothing admirable or artistic about the preparation of food. They care about Israel, not about what Israelis eat.

Perhaps to escape the debilitating effects of such rhetoric our new cooks travel a lot. They must keep up. They go to food conventions, attend demonstrations and give lectures. Their peers judge them less harshly than their compatriots. They always have the avocado to fall back on, and the whole range of citrus fruits. They win medals, which give them great comfort, but they do not wear them at home. They make contacts, and if they are lucky they get invited to the great kitchens of Europe. Roger Verge might ask them to drop by and spend a few days nosing around the kitchen. Anton Mosimann at the Dorchester in London is known to be co-operative; he is a great host, free with advice, outgoing and friendly. Once a year they feel honor-bound to make it to Paris.

This is an expensive but priceless exercise, during which they visit lots of two-star restaurants and lay bets as to which will receive the coveted third star in the next Michelin. They go to Fouchon and spend silly amounts of money on canned truffles (of the Périgord variety), herb vinegars and extra-virgin olive oil. If the oysters at the fish market are fresh, they buy a cooler, fill it with crushed ice and cram it with a few dozen oysters. You can always recognize a new chef on the plane home. He's the one who sits upright for five hours clutching a giant ice box to his chest.

He and his peers belong to a culinary grapevine. He will be the first to know if an Iranian refugee escapes the ayatollahs with a cart of caviar. He is also a guru. Sheep farmers will carry whole sides of lamb up six flights of stairs to get his honest opinion. Deep-sea fishermen will seek him out if a stray lobster gets entangled in their nets.

What has emerged from all this is a young, bold and innovative cuisine. It has been worth waiting for. Cooking is one of those rare professions where the process is as rewarding as the end result.

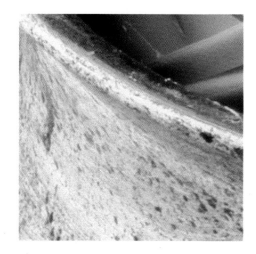

N E W I S R A E L I C H E F S

Recipes

HAIM COHEN

LAMB CUTLETS WITH BAKED TOMATOES

MARINADE
1 cup/225ml dry red wine
1/4 cup/60ml olive oil
3 cloves garlic, unpeeled and crushed
1 bay leaf
fresh thyme and rosemary
1 onion, sliced
1 carrot, sliced
salt and freshly ground black pepper

rack of lamb containing 12 cutlets
4 or 5 large tomatoes

◆ Haim Cohen.

is the young

chef of Keren

à la Carte,

a French

restaurant.

Cohen

frequently

visits France

to study under

a master chef.

Mix together the marinade ingredients and marinate the lamb for 24 hours. Remove the lamb from the marinade, and trim the flesh and fat from the ends of the bones so that the cutlets are easy to pick up. Pre-heat the oven to 425°F/220°C.

Drain the lamb and thoroughly rub the strained marinade liquor into it before placing in a baking tray and roasting in the oven for 10 minutes. Turn down the heat to 350°F/180°C and cook for another 15 minutes, basting with the cooking juices.

Remove the rack of lamb from the oven, and allow it to rest for 5 minutes before separating the cutlets. Meanwhile add some of the marinade to the cooking juices and reduce over a high heat. Spoon this over the cutlets as you serve them.

The tomatoes, sliced in half, sprinkled with sea salt and fresh thyme and placed on an oiled baking tray, can be baked with the lamb; in a moderate oven, they take about 15 minutes. Serves 4 or 5.

MINTED MELON WITH DATES AND ARAK

16 dried dates, pitted and finely chopped
12 leaves fresh mint, finely chopped
1/2 cup/100ml arak (or ouzo)
3 small melons

Marinate the chopped dates and mint in the arak for 3 hours. Cut the melons in half, remove the seeds, and fill with the date and mint mixture. Chill before serving.
Serves 6.

SALAD ROCKET WITH PINE NUTS

2 lbs/900g salad rocket
16 spinach leaves
1 romaine/cos lettuce
3 tomatoes
olive oil
salt and pepper
3/4 cup/175g toasted pine nuts

Wash and pat dry all the greens, and remove the stems of the rocket. Cut the tomatoes into thin slices and shred the lettuce.

Spread the rocket and pine nuts on a bed of lettuce and arrange a circle of tomato slices on top. Add another layer of rocket and pine nuts and a layer of spinach, and season with the olive oil, salt and pepper. Serves 6 to 8.

◆ Lamb cutlets

with baked

tomatoes.

AVOCADO SOUP

1/2 onion, finely chopped
1/4 cup/60g margarine
3 tablespoons all-purpose/plain flour
2 pints/1 liter milk
2 ripe avocados
2 cloves garlic, crushed
3 tablespoons lemon juice
1 tablespoon chopped fresh dill
1/2 cup/100ml heavy/double cream
2 egg yolks
salt and freshly ground black pepper

Fry the onion in the margarine until golden brown. Reduce the heat and sift in the flour. Add the milk, stirring all the time, then bring to the boil and simmer gently until the mixture thickens.

Peel and mash one of the avocados with the garlic and 2 tablespoons of the lemon juice. Peel and cube the other avocado and sprinkle with the remaining lemon juice so that it does not turn black. Over a low heat, stir the mashed avocado into the thickened milk, then add the avocado cubes and dill. Blend the cream and egg yolks together and add them to the soup, with salt and pepper to taste. Serve warm. Serves 6.

Note: Do not allow this soup to boil or the avocado will taste bitter.

MOUSHT IN MANGO SAUCE
St. Peter's fish with puréed mango

juice of 1 lemon
2 tablespoons Worcestershire sauce
salt and freshly ground black pepper
2 fresh mousht (or trout), about 1 1/4 lb/600g
each, cut into fillets
2 tablespoons all-purpose/plain flour
vegetable oil
1/4 cup/60g butter
1/2 cup/100ml dry white wine
1 mango

Mix together the lemon juice, Worcestershire sauce, salt and pepper, and pour it over the fish. Allow the fish to marinate for at least 30 minutes. Pour off the marinade and reserve it.

Flour the fish, then pan-fry them in hot oil on both sides. Remove the fish from the pan, discard the oil, and add the butter, white wine, and the reserved marinade juices.

Peel the mango and cut away the flesh. Purée half and thinly slice the rest. Add the slices to the pan. Return the fish to the pan and continue cooking until it flakes easily. Lay the fish on a hot dish. Stir the puréed mango into the pan juices and spoon over the fish. Serves 4.

URI GUTTMANN

◆ *Avocado*

soup.

223

URI GUTTMANN

◆ *Uri Guttmann is a*

well established

chef who represents

Israel at

congresses and

international

food shows.

He is the owner

of the Panorama

Restaurant in

Tel Aviv.

BANANAS TEL-KATZIR

FILLING
1 cup/225ml milk
1 tablespoon sugar
2 tablespoons butter
vanilla extract/essence
1 tablespoon cornstarch/cornflour
1 egg yolk
salt
3/4 cup/150g shelled pecans
8 fresh dates, pitted and whole
4 dried dates, finely chopped
grated rind of 1 orange

4 bananas, peeled and whole
4 crêpes (thin pancakes)

SAUCE
1/4 cup/60g butter
1 cup/225g sugar
1/2 cup/100ml fresh orange juice

Boil the milk with the sugar, butter and vanilla. Mix the cornstarch with the egg yolk, add a pinch of salt, and add to the boiling milk, stirring well as the mixture thickens. Allow to cool, then cover and chill.

Grind the pecans in a food processor, then add them, with the fresh dates and the finely chopped dried dates, to the chilled custard. Stir in the grated orange rind. Preheat the oven to 425°F/220°C.

Put a spoonful of filling and a banana onto each crêpe and roll up. Place in a lightly oiled baking dish, and cook in the oven for about 20 minutes, or until the bananas are soft. Transfer the filled crêpes to a warm serving dish.

To make the sauce, melt the butter in a small saucepan over a very low heat and add the sugar. When the sugar has dissolved, add the orange juice. When the mixture is thoroughly hot, pour it over the crêpes. Serves 4.

BREAST OF MOULLARD WITH HYSSOP

1 teaspoon honey
2 cloves garlic, finely chopped
2 teaspoons hyssop
salt and freshly ground black pepper
4 tablespoons brandy
1 cup/225ml water
2 tablespoons butter
2 moullard (or duck) breasts,
about 12 oz/350g each
fresh melissa/lemon balm leaves,
to garnish

Mix together the honey, garlic, hyssop, salt and pepper, brandy, and water to make a marinade. Add the moullard breasts and marinate for 2 hours.

Having removed the breasts from the marinade, fry them quickly in butter on both sides, transfer them to a baking dish, add half the marinade, and cook for 5 minutes on each side in a hot oven. Slice the breasts, and serve sprinkled with hyssop, with the marinade as a sauce. Garnish with melissa leaves. Serves 4.

EREZ KOMAROVSKY

LAMB CUTLETS WITH WATERMELON

12 lamb cutlets
1/2 cup/100ml red wine
1/4 cup/60ml extra-virgin olive oil
1 clove garlic, thinly sliced
4 tablespoons finely chopped fresh coriander
sprig lemon grass (Cymbopogon citratus),
minced very fine
sprig fresh sorrel
sprig salad rocket
1 lb/450g watermelon, without skin or seeds
8 oz/225g goat's cheese

Marinate the lamb cutlets in the wine, olive oil, garlic, coriander and lemon grass for 1 hour. Wash the sorrel and salad rocket and pat dry. Cut the watermelon into small regular-sized strips.

Put the cutlets in the broiler/grill pan with a little of the marinade, and cook under a hot broiler/grill for a few minutes. Turn the cutlets and put a slice of goat's cheese on each. Cook for another 5 minutes or so until the cutlets are done, but don't overcook them. Serve the cutlets on a bed of sorrel, salad rocket and watermelon strips, with some of the grilling juices poured over them.
Serves 6.

FIGS AND PRICKLY PEARS WITH ROSE & VANILLA YOGURT

1/2 cup/100g sugar
1/2 cup/100ml water
1/2 vanilla pod
handful of rose petals
1 cup/225ml plain fresh yogurt
butter
1 lb/450g ripe figs
1 lb/450g prickly pears

Dissolve the sugar in the water, then add the vanilla pod and most of the rose petals. Bring to a boil and simmer for 5 minutes. Pour the liquid through a nylon sieve and let it cool. Now stir the yogurt into it and put the mixture in the refrigerator for at least 1 hour. Pre-heat the oven to 390°F/ 200°C.

Wash and dry the figs. Carefully peel the prickly pears, under running water, preferably with gloves on, and place them on a buttered baking sheet. Bake for 10 minutes. Serve hot with the cold sauce, decorated with the rest of the rose petals.
Serves 6 to 8.

◆ *Erez Komarovsky offers Japanese delicacies with an Israeli flavor.*

EREZ
KOMAROVSKY

RED SNAPPER WITH MYRTLE

1 extremely fresh red snapper,
weighing 2lbs/900g
6 cups/1.2 liters water
1 tablespoon sea salt
fresh myrtle leaves
1/2 cup/100 ml extra-virgin olive oil
1 chili pepper, very finely chopped
4 cloves garlic, crushed
4 baby eggplants/aubergines
2 or 3 lemons

Fillet the fish and make several diagonal incisions in the skin. Bring the water and salt to a boil. Plunge the fillets into the boiling water for 30 seconds, then transfer them immediately to a bowl of ice-cold water. When cold, drain and pat dry with paper towels/kitchen paper.

Rub the myrtle leaves between your hands to release their fragrance and put them in a shallow dish with the chili (wear gloves while you are chopping it!) and garlic. Lay the fillets in the dish. Steam the eggplants until soft, remove the skins and put them in the dish as well.

Allow the fillets to marinate for at least 3 hours, turning once so that they absorb the other flavors.

When ready to serve, remove the fillets from the marinade, drain them and garnish with one of the eggplants cut into quarters.

Serves 4 as a main course or 8 as a starter.

◆*A*

version

of red

snapper

with

myrtle.

RED MULLET IN GRAPE LEAVES

8 large fresh grape/vine leaves
4 tablespoons olive oil
juice of 1 lemon
1 tablespoon chopped fresh parsley
20 coriander seeds
1 tablespoon fresh chopped basil
salt and freshly ground black pepper
8 red mullet, about 8oz/225g each,
cleaned and patted dry

Blanch the grape leaves in hot water for 20 seconds, then drain on paper towels/kitchen paper (if you are using grape leaves preserved in brine, see instructions given for stuffed grape leaves, p. 28). Mix together the olive oil, lemon juice, parsley, coriander seeds, basil, salt and pepper. Prick the fish all over with a needle, spread the oil and herb mixture over them and leave them to marinate for 1 hour.

Fold a grape leaf around each fish, leaving the head sticking out. Brush the leaves with olive oil. Pre-heat the broiler or grill and cook for 2 minutes on each side. Serve with other *mezze*. Serves 8.

BOTTLED KUMQUATS

2 lb/450g fresh kumquats
1 1/2 cups/350ml water
4 cups/450g sugar
1 tablespoon rose water, if liked

Wash the kumquats thoroughly, then slice them lengthwise. In a large saucepan, dissolve the sugar in the water, add the kumquats, bring to a boil, and simmer gently for 1 hour. Remove from the heat, stir in the rosewater, and allow to cool. Store in a jar with a tightly fitting lid.

MEDITERRANEAN TART

PASTRY
2 cups/225g all-purpose/plain flour
1 cup/225ml olive oil
1/3 cup/80ml water
1 egg
salt and freshly ground black pepper

FILLING
1 small eggplant/aubergine
2 cloves garlic, finely chopped
2 onions, thinly sliced
1/4 cup/60ml olive oil
6 small tomatoes, thinly sliced
4 small zucchini/courgettes, thinly sliced
1 teaspoon fresh thyme
2/3 cup/150g black olives, pitted and halved
salt and freshly ground black pepper

Put all the pastry ingredients in a food processor and mix for 2 minutes with a plastic blade. Roll the dough into a ball, wrap it in plastic wrap/cling film, and chill in the refrigerator for 1 hour.

Cut the eggplant/aubergine in half lengthwise and slice each half very thinly. Using a moderate heat, fry the garlic, onions and eggplant in the olive oil for about 15 minutes, or until the eggplant softens. Stir in the salt, pepper and most of the thyme, and set aside. Pre-heat the oven to 425°F/220°C.

Roll out the pastry and line a tart pan (the type with a removable base). Cut off any excess pastry around the edges, and prick the base with a fork. Spread the eggplant and onion mixture over the pastry, and arrange the tomatoes and zucchini decoratively on top. Top with the olives, add a sprinkling of thyme, and brush with olive oil. Bake for 45 minutes. Serve hot or cold.

Serves 5 or 6.

◆ *Mediterrenean*

tart.

ISRAEL AHARONI

◆ *Israel Aharoni,*

owner and chef

of one of

Israel's leading

Chinese

restaurants,

Yin-Yang.

Aharoni's other

passion is

French food.

ZACHI BUKSHESTER

◆ *Zachi*

Bukshester

is the owner

and chef of

The Pink

Ladle. He

serves Israeli

nouvelle

cuisine with

great

attention to

presentation.

HORN OF PLENTY

4 leaves filo *pastry*
1 tablespoon flour
vegetable oil

MARINADE
1 tablespoon olive oil
1/2 tablespoon brown sugar
1 tablespoon white wine vinegar
1 clove garlic

BEAN SAUCE
1 lb/450g fresh fava/broad beans
1/4 cup/60ml cream
1 cup/225ml chicken broth/stock
dill, nutmeg, salt and pepper to taste

FILLING
1/2 lb/225g fillet steak, cubed
1/2 lb/225g fillet of sea bass
1 tablespoon pistachio nuts, shelled
1 small onion, chopped
2 oz/60g carrots, diced small
2 oz/60g leeks, chopped
6 oz/180g asparagus, chopped
2 oz/60g turnips, diced small
1/2 cup/100ml dry red wine

Roll each leaf of *filo* into a cone shape, sticking the pastry to itself with a dab of flour and water. Allow the cones to dry.

Mix the marinade ingredients together, add the beef, fish, pistachios and onion, and allow to marinate for 1 hour.

Boil or steam the beans until just tender, then drain. Purée them with the cream, chicken broth and spices in the food processor, and keep warm.

Simmer or steam the carrots, leeks, asparagus and turnips until they are *al dente*.

Drain the beef, fish, pistachios and onion, sauté them in butter in a hot skillet/frying pan, and add the cooked vegetables and red wine.

Deep fry the *filo* cones until they are crisp and golden, then fill them with the meat and vegetable mixture. Make sure the bean purée is nice and hot, then spoon it onto individual plates and place a filled *filo* cone on top.
Serves 4.

PRICKLY PEARS FLAMBÉES

1/2 tablespoon butter
1 teaspoon brown sugar
powdered cardamom
2 prickly pears per person, peeled and sliced
2 tablespooons Sabra or Grand Marnier liqueur
whipped cream, to serve

Melt half the butter, add the sugar and cardamom powder, and sauté the prickly pear slices in this mixture for 1/2 minute. Add the liqueur and set light to it. When the flames die down, add the remaining butter and allow it to melt. Serve with whipped cream.

FRIED GOAT'S CHEESE WITH MINT SALAD
See p. 56

◆ *Horn of*

plenty

ITAMAR DAVIDOV

◆ *Itamar*

Davidov is

chef and owner

of the Pitango

restaurant.

He blends

local produce

with French

tradition and

is renowned

for his food

combinations.

JERUSALEM ARTICHOKE CREAM SOUP

1 lb/450g Jerusalem artichokes, peeled
2 pints/1 liter chicken broth/stock
juice of 1 lemon
4 oz/100g chicken breast, skinned and cubed
1/4 cup/60g butter
3 tablespoons all-purpose/plain flour
salt and freshly ground white pepper
4 strands saffron
1 cup/225ml heavy/double cream
freshly ground black pepper

Cook the artichokes in the chicken broth and lemon juice until they begin to soften. Strain off the broth and reserve it, then purée the artichokes, adding just enough broth to make blending easy.

Stir-fry the chicken cubes in half the butter - 2 minutes is enough, or until the pink turns white. Drain on paper towels/kitchen paper.

Melt the remaining butter, add the flour and cook for 3 or 4 minutes, stirring constantly. Stir in the reserved chicken broth, artichoke purée, salt, white pepper and saffron. Bring slowly to a boil, stirring all the time, and allow to simmer for 5 minutes.

Add the chicken cubes and adjust the seasoning if necessary. At the last minute, stir in the cream. Serve sprinkled with black pepper. Serves 5 or 6.

DATES & POPPY SEEDS IN HOT TOFFEE

1/2 cup/100ml heavy/double cream
1/2 cup/100g sugar
2 tablespoons water
20 fresh dates, pitted and whole
3 teaspoons fried poppy seeds
1 1/2 cups/350ml heavy/double cream, whipped

Heat the 1/2 cup/100ml cream in a bain-marie. In a small saucepan, dissolve the sugar in the water, turn up the heat and boil until the mixture turns golden. Remove from the heat and stir in the hot cream. Bring the mixture to the boil and cook for 5 minutes, stirring all the time. The mixture should now be toffee, thick and smooth. Stir in the dates and poppy seeds and cook for another minute or two. Serve warm, topped with the whipped cream.

Serves 4.

◆ *Dates*

and

poppy

seeds in

hot toffee.

CELIA REGEV & REVIVA APPEL

◆ *Celia and*

Reviva are

restaurateurs

who have

introduced

new tastes in

pastries and

desserts.

JAFFAS BAVAROISE

6 oranges
fresh mint or citrus leaves, to garnish

BAVARIAN CREAM FILLING
1/2 cup/100g sugar
8 egg yolks
1 cup/225ml orange juice
2 level teaspoons/10ml gelatin
1 cup/225g heavy/double cream, whipped

SAUCE
1/2 cup/100g sugar
1 cup/225ml orange juice
4 tablespoons lemon juice

Peel the oranges and remove the segments. Grease 6 individual molds with butter and line the bottom of each with a circle of wax/greaseproof paper cut to size. Sprinkle the sides of the molds with sugar and tap out the excess. Line the sides of the molds with orange segments, trimming them to fit snugly.

To make the Bavarian cream filling, whip/whisk the egg yolks and sugar together until pale and fluffy, then bring the orange juice to a boil and add it to the egg yolks. Dissolve the gelatin according to the instructions on the packet. Cook the egg yolks and orange juice over a low heat until the mixture is thick enough to coat the back of a wooden spoon, then add the dissolved gelatin. Stir well and pass through a sieve. Allow the mixture to cool, then put it in the refrigerator until it is on the point of setting.

Remove from the refrigerator and fold in the whipped cream. Pour the cream into the molds and leave to set for 3 or 4 hours.

To make the sauce, dissolve the sugar in the orange and lemon juice, bring to a boil, and simmer for a few minutes to thicken. When cool, spoon onto individual plates and turn out the molds. Decorate with a mint or citrus leaf. Serves 6.

SORBET OGEN

1 1/4 cups/300g sugar
1 1/4 cups/300ml water
11 oz/300g puréed Ogen melon, chilled
juice of 1 lemon

Dissolve the sugar in the water and bring to a boil. As soon as the mixture begins to bubble, remove from the heat, cool, then refrigerate.

Mix the puréed melon with the lemon juice and the chilled syrup, pour into a shallow container and put in the icebox/freezer until barely firm. Remove from the freezer and blend to a smooth consistency, then re-freeze. Serve in chilled glasses with sugar-frosted rims. Serves 4.

◆ *Jaffa*

bavaroise.

DALIA PENN-LERNER

SALAD OF FOIE GRAS & POMEGRANATE

8 oz/225g fresh foie gras (or chicken livers)
various salad leaves (romaine/cos, radiccio,
endive, spinach)
1 tablespoon white wine vinegar
2 or 3 tablespoons pomegranate seeds
salt and freshly ground black pepper

DRESSING
1 tablespoon white wine vinegar
1 tablespoon lemon juice
4 tablespoons olive oil
salt and pepper

Cut the liver into 1/2-inch/1-cm cubes. Cover and refrigerate until firm. Put the salad leaves in a bowl, beat together the dressing ingredients, pour over the salad and toss well.

Pre-heat a non-stick skillet/frying pan (only add oil if you are using chicken livers, which have very little fat compared to goose liver). Quickly stir-fry the liver - the cubes should remain pink inside - and transfer to a warm plate.

Pour off any fat that has accumulated in the skillet, and add the vinegar. Remove from the heat, return the liver cubes to the skillet and season with salt and pepper. Spoon the warm liver and the pomegranate seeds over the salad and serve immediately. Serves 4.

CHEESE PARCELS

full fat feta or goat's cheese
fresh savory or thyme, finely chopped
filo *pastry*
melted butter
fruit (watermelon, ripe figs, grapes)

Mash the cheese with a fork and season with savory or thyme. Cut the sheets of *filo* into 4-inch/10-cm squares. Place a teaspoon of the cheese mixture in the center of each and draw the sides up to form a little pouch. Press the edges together with water to seal them. Pre-heat the oven to 375°F/190°C.

Brush the pouches with melted butter and bake for 10-15 minutes until crisp and golden. Serve with cubes of watermelon, figs, grapes, etc.

If making pouches sounds too fiddly, you could make triangular or square parcels instead. Deep-frying would also be an alternative to baking.

◆ *Dalia Penn-Lerner, a former actress, is a chef, food writer and editor who has travelled widely.*

◆ *Cheese parcels.*